ESSAYS

IN

OTTOMAN HISTORY

Publisher
Muhittin Salih Eren

İstanbul 1998
34-98-Y-70-080

ISBN 975-7622-58-3

First published 1998

EREN Yayıncılık
Kitap-Dağıtım Tic. ve San. Ltd. Şti.
Tünel, İstiklâl Cad. Sofyalı Sokak No: 34
80050 BEYOĞLU - İSTANBUL
Tel: *+90* (212) 251 28 58 - (212) 252 05 60
Fax: (212) 243 30 16
E-mail: eren@turk.net

Published in İstanbul

Essays
in
Ottoman History

Halil İnalcık

Professor, Bilkent University

EREN

Contents

Preface

In this volume are collected papers published between 1960 and 1994, dealing with early Ottoman history and historiography, and Ottoman urban and legal history.

In Article I-1 an attempt is made to ascertain periods in Ottoman history. After a brief review of the ideas of Ottoman historians themselves on this theme, the article proposes a division on the basis of an analytical approach. This takes account of the state of equilibrium established between the Ottoman Empire and foreign powers, the changes in the ruler's authority within the empire, and the functioning of the system of land-tenure upon which the military, financial and social institutions of the empire relied. Written thirty years ago this paper has to be modified or totally replaced by a new essay in the light of investigations made since then.

Article I-2 is an essay examining the life and work of the most important Ottoman chronicler of the first two centuries of Ottoman history. When critically used the work provides authentic and substantial information, even for the early years of the Ottoman state. It is a mistake to dismiss altogether these traditions on the assumption that everything in them is pure legend, as has been believed by some recent authors (see Article II-1 in this volume). On the other hand, 'Āshiḳ Pashazāde's interpretation of the events of his own age is strongly colored or distorted by his prejudices and interests. In this essay I tried to show some of the personal interests and biases which affected his history.

In Article II-1 the Greek and Ottoman accounts of 'O̱smān's siege of Nicaea and the ensuing battle of Bapheus are analyzed comparatively. Although totally ignored or misinterpreted by historians this event is the most important in early Ottoman history, clearly responsible for Osman's appearance as a charismatic leader in the Bithynia frontier region and for the foundation of the Ottoman dynasty.

In Article II-2 a detailed critical review is made of Franz Babinger's book, *Mehmed der Eroberer und seine Zeit, Weltenstürmer einer Zeitenwende*, considered as the definitive account of the Conqueror's history. In this review the important sources neglected by the author are noted, his interpretations discussed and mistakes in chronology shown, (in the English version of this work references are made to this article by the translator).

In Article II-3 the decision-making process in Ottoman government meetings as well as the ruler's actual position in the process are discussed. The important question as to what extent the consolidation of independently organized groups of bureaucrats, ulema or soldiery as well as established customs or law-codes provided a check on the independent or arbitrary orders of the Sultan is examined.

In Article II-4 kadi-ship, the paramount institution in the Ottoman administration system, is examined in its various aspects including ranks and the procedure of assignments as well as conflicts within the group. All this in done on the basis of the original appointment lists of the kadıaskers preserved in the archives of the shaykhulislamate, Istanbul Müftülüğü.

Article II-5 asks the question why, during Suleyman I's reign, an attempt was made to reinterpret and adjust Ottoman laws on landholding and taxation to the shar'ī principles established by the authoritative jurists of the second century of Islam. Ebûssu'ûd argues that the appropriation by individuals of the state-owned (*mîrî*) lands is illegal, and the attempt to create new sources of revenue for the state treasury by raising the rate of tithes from 8 percent to 5 percent was made because of the kharādjī nature of the mîrî lands. Thus, the reasons for the islamization of Ottoman state laws under Suleyman the Lawgiver are examined.

Article II-6 is an inquiry on the basis of an official report of the malpractices committed by the defterdār of Syria. Employing a set of documents we attempted also to explain the struggle between the Ottoman administration and the Druze chieftains for control of the fiscal and economic resources of the Mountain of Lebanon.

Article II-7 reexamines the theory that under the Ottomans the Greek Orthodox Patriarch enjoyed an autonomous position, representing the Greek nation with full religious, judicial and administrative powers. With a revision of this theory our study attempts to correct this highly exaggerated theory, showing that the Patriarch was closely dependent on the Sultan for his acts outside religious affairs, and that the Christians, having the status of dhimmī, were the direct subjects of the sultan.

Article III-1 is a brief essay on the islamization of the Turks in general, and on Islam in Asia Minor in particular. A bibliographical essay is added to this new edition covering the period from the early Turkish conversion to Islam in East Europe and Central Asia.

Article III-2 is an attempt to show what measures Mehmed the Conqueror took to rebuild the conquered city of Constantinople and whether or not the typical Islamic city had a ground plan with well-defined urban sections determined by Islamic concepts and traditions.

In Article III-3, first with an analysis of the ahdnāme, the document of the surrender of Genoese Galata to the Ottoman state, misinterpretations made on the nature of this act by western historians are corrected. In the second part of the paper the process by which the Genoese city was transformed into an Ottoman one is discussed, mainly on the basis of the original Ottoman documents.

Article III/4 describes, on the basis of the archival documentation, the important roles the Greek subjects of the Sultan played in the economy and finances of the empire. An interesting observation is that during the Ottoman period members of the Byzantine aristocracy continued their pre-Ottoman activities as tax-farmers.

In Article III-5 a detailed investigation is made of the origin and organization of a group called “Arab boghurdjular”, Arab camel drivers, (read as *Azebs* in Barkan) in western Anatolia. Ottoman archival evidence and anthropological data suggest that these "Arabs" might originally have been a mixed population of Arabs, Turcomans and other ethnic groups, rearing camels and employed by the Ottoman government under a special organization in the transport service of heavy goods, principally salt, in the region.

Article III-6 examines, again in light of the Ottoman archival materials, how and exactly when the Ottomans established complete control of the Straits and the Black Sea traffic.

In Collecting these articles here in one volume, no attempt has been made to revise them except to add a few necetlary footnotes. While in the original of some of the articles terms and personal names are rendered in transliteration alphabets in others modern Turkish spelling is followed.

Here is a list of the original editions.

I-1: "Periods in Ottoman History”, Published for the first time in this volume.

I-2: “How to Read ‘Ashıḳ Paşa-zāde’s History” *Studies in Ottoman History in Honour of Professor V.L. Ménage*, edited by Colin Heywood and Colin Imber, Istanbul: Isis Press, 1994, 139-156.

II-1: “O̱smān Ghāzī’s *Siege of Nicaea and the* Battle of Bapheus”, *The Ottoman Emirate (1300-1389)*, ed. Elizabeth Zachariadou, Rethymnon: Crete University Press, 1993, 77-98.

II-2: "Mehmed the Conqueror (1432-1481) and His time", *Speculum*, XXXV (1960), 408-427.

II-3: "Decision Making in the Ottoman State", *Decision Making and Change in the Ottoman Empire*, ed. Caesar E. Farah, Kirksville: The Thomas Tefferson University Press, 1993, 9-18.

II-4: "The Rūznāmçe Registers of the Kadıasker of Rumeli as Preserved in the Istanbul Müftülük Archives", *Turcica*, XX (1988), 251-275.

II-5: "Islamization of Ottoman Laws on Land and Land Taxation", *Festgabe an Josef Matuz: Osmanistik -Turkologie- Diplomatik*, eds. C. Fragner and K. Schwarz, Berlin: Klaus Schwarz Verlag, 1992, 100-116.

II-6: "Tax Collection, Embezzlement and Bribery in Ottoman Finances", *The Turkish Studies Association Bulletin*, 16. (1992).

II-7: "The Status of the Greek Orthodox Patriarch under the Ottomans", *Turcica*, XXI-XXIII (1991), 407-436.

III-1: "Islam in the Ottoman Empire", *Cultura Turcica*, 5-7 (1968-1970), 19-29.

III-2: "Istanbul: an Islamic City", *Journal of Islamic Studies*, I (1990), 1-23.

III-3: "Ottoman Galata, 1453-1553", *Première Rencontre Internationale sur l'Empire Ottoman et la Turquie Moderne*, ed. Edhem Eldem, Istanbul-Paris: (1991), 17-105.

III-4: "Greeks in Ottoman Economy and Finances, 1453-1500", *TO ΕΛΛΗΝΙΚΟΝ: Studies in Honor of Speros Vryonis, Jr.*, Vol. II. Byzantinoslavica, Armenica, Islamica, the Balkans and Modern Greece, J.S. Allen *et alia*, New Rochelle- New York: A.D. Caratzas 1993, 307-319.

III-5: "Arab Camel Drivers in Western Anatolia in the Fifteenth Century", *Revue de Histoire Maghrebine*, X/31-32 (Tunis, 1983), 247-270.

III-6: "The Ouestion of the Closing of the Black Sea under the Ottomans", *Arkheion Pontou*, 35 (Athens, 1979), 74-110.

Part I

Historiography

1

Periods in Ottoman History

Periods in Ottoman History

I believe we have to consider first whether the Ottomans themselves divided their history into periods, whether they were conscious of a distinction between the age in which they lived and earlier ages, and what ideas they had about periods in history.

In the prologue to the elaborate history which he wrote at the command of Bayezid II, Kemāl Pashazāde compares the Ottoman history with earlier Moslem dynasties and sums up under three heads, *vücūh-i rüchān,* 'the reasons for their superiority'.[1] First, he says, the Ottomans unlike other Moslem dynasties, came to power not through the violent overthrow of older Moslem states within the Islamic community, but through the conquest of territories pertaining to the infidel world, the *Dār ul-Harb.* Secondly, in the Ottoman state the authority of the sovereign and the validity of the laws are complete and absolute. Thirdly, the Ottoman state is richer, more populous and more extensive than all others. No other state possesses the military power of the Ottomans; the Ottomans have powerful artillery and a great maritime power; the aims of the Ottoman Sultan are *'tedbīr-i 'imāret-i rūy-i zemīn'* to make the face of the world to flourish', to destroy the foes of the true Faith, and to uphold the Holy Law.

In popular works such as 'Āshiḳ Pashazāde's history and the anonymous *Tewārīkh-i āl-i 'Os̱mān,* we find the ideas of a distinction between different periods expressed in a more subjective fashion. In the Anonymous Chronicles[2], for example, we find in the reign of Bayezid I (1389-1402) quite a violent expression of the reaction of the classes upholding the traditions of the *Ucbeyligi,* —the Principality of the Marches— against the imperial centralist policies of the Sultan.

These chronicles contan bitter criticisms of the elaboration of the court ceremonial and the development of a centralized administration, and of the adoption of various "Frankish" customs which occurred during Bayezid's reign. These criticisms contrast sharply the 'new' period with the period that

---

[1] Kemāl Pashazāde, *Tevārīh-i Āl-i Os̱mān, Defter I,* ed. Şerafettin Turan, Ankara 1970; similar points are made by pseudo- Rūhī, Oxford Bodleian Library, Marsh 313.

[2] *Tawarīkh-i Āl-i 'Os̱mān* (*Die alt osmanischen amonymen Chroniken*), ed. F. Giese, Breslau 1922, 30; a more complete text: Topkapı Sarayı Müzesi Kütüphanesi, M.R. 700.

preceded it. In the works written during the reign of Bayezid II, we find similar criticisms of developments which had taken place under Mehmed II.

Mehmed III (1595-1603) toward the end of the 16th century when recounting the abuses in the administration in the famous *'Adāletnāme,* 'Declaration of Justice' which he promulgated upon his accession to the throne, points to the reign of Süleyman as an ideal period and demands a return to the laws and principles of that time.[3] Nevertheless, in his own reign the crisis grew still more serious and plunged the empire into half-a-century of complete disorder and degeneration. It is in this period that Ottoman statesmen and writers became sharply aware of a distinction between the former Golden Age[4] and the age of decline in which they live, and in works written in the style of the old *naṣīḥatnāmes*, "Mirrors-for-Princes', there began to appear various realistic observations and criticisms concerning the defects in Ottoman administration. Though Koçi Beg is the best known writer in thes genre, he had several predecessors at the end of the 16th and the beginning of the 17th centuries.[5] Toward the end of the 16th century, 'Ālī, in his *Nushat al-Salātīn*[6] and finally at the beginning of the 17th century 'Ayn-i 'Alī, and the author of Kitāb-i Mustaṭāb,[7] puts forward general views on the breakdown of law and order and insist that in the earlier times things were well and properly ordered. They trace the origin of the breakdown to the reigns of Murad III (1574-1595) and Mehmed III in the last quarter of the 16th century, and in general regard the reign of Suleyman as the model to be followed. From this time until the 20th century, there appears among the Ottomans a fairly extensive literature on the laws of historical development and the concept of periods in history reflecting the successive ideas on the decline of the empire and the reforms which were needed to arrest it. In general the Ottoman writers follow the political theories of Ġazālī, Fārābī,

[3] H. İnalcık, "Adâletnâmeler, "*Belgeler* (Turkish Historical Society), II/3-4, 105.

[4] On Suleyman's reign considered as *Golden Age*, see H. Inalcik, "Suleyman: The Man and the Statesman," ed. G. Veinstein. Paris.

[5] For Ottoman memorialists see H. Inalcik, "Military and Fiscal Transformation in the Ottoman Empire, 1600-1700", *Archivum Ottomanicum*, VI (1980), note 1; "The Rūznāmče Registers", *Turcica*, XX (1988), 256 note 10.

[6] See A. Tietze's edition and translation: *Mustafa 'Ālī's Counsel for Sultans of 1581,* I: Text, II: Translation, Vienna 1979-1982.

[7] 'Aynī 'Alī's *Kawānīn-i Āl-i 'Os̱mân der khulāṣa-i Mez̤amīn-i Defter-i Dīvān*, İstanbul 1280 H.; this edition is a popular one, a new edition with critical apparatus is prepared by Douglas Howard; for Kitâb-i Musṭatâb see Y. Yücel's edition: *Osmanlı Devlet Teşkilâtına Dair Kaynaklar:* Kitāb-i Müstetāb, Kitābu Meṣāliḥu'l- Müslimīn ve Menāfi'l-Mu'minīn, Ḫirzü'l-Mulûk, Ankara, 1988.

Nasīr al-dīn Tūsī, Dawānī, and especially Ibn Khaldūn.[8] Among them Kātib Çelebi and Na'īmā deserve particular consideration. The first, in his treatise *Dustūr'ul-'amal,*[9] postulated a complete parallelism between the character and development of societies and the nature and development of Man. Societies, like human beings, pass through three periods, the first that of growth, the second the stable period of maturity, and the third that of decline. But, in societies with a strong constitution, decline sets in late, and it is possible by taking due precautions to postpone the decline. Nevertheless, it is impossible to escape altogether the inevitable end. Kātib Çelebi, considering in turn peasantry, that is, the basic producers, the military classes, and financial administration of the state, tries to establish when the weaknesses and decline in each began to appear. His starting-point is that of the old *Naṣīḥatnāme*s, namely that the ruler is dependent on the army, the army on wealth, wealth on the well-being of the subject-peasantry, and their well-being on justice. It is interesting that he should attempt to diagnose the causes of the decline by examining these special classes. He regards the period of maturity as extending to the time when the Celālīs appeared in 1593. He also maintains that by about 1610 the villages in the Ottoman realm had been ruined by heavy taxation, abuses of administration, and the farming out of taxes. He, too, regards the age of Suleyman as a period when the various elements which made up the state were in balance.

In the prologue to his history, Na'īmā[10] summarizes the ideas on society and history expressed by 'Ālī, Kātib Çelebi, Kınalızāde and especially Ibn Khaldūn, whom he regards as the greatest historian. Na'īmā following Ibn Khaldūn, after enunciating the various principles and factors which govern the development of states and civilizations, summarises Ibn Khaldūn's theory of five periods. In his endeavour to reconcile the phases of Ottoman history to this scheme, Na'īmā interprets the series of defeats following the second Vienna campaign of 1683, and the pacific policy that ensued as being the symptoms of the fourth period — that is, the period of resignation and tranquility, when the principles and laws of the preceding age are followed and in which the older generation is limited and the state tries as far as possible to live in peace with its neighbors.

---

[8] Now see C. Fleischer, "Royal authority, Dynastic Cyclism, and Ibn Khaldûnism in Sixteenth-Century Ottoman Letters," *Journal of Asian and African Studies*, XVIII (1983), 198-220; Farābī, Tūsī, and Dawânî's influence, see Kınalızâde 'Alā al- Din 'Alī, *Akhlāk-i 'Alā'ī*, Bulak 1248 H.; II, 5, 105-112.

[9] Mustafā b. Abdullāh known Haji Khalife or Kātib Çelebi, *Dustûr al 'amal li-Iṣlâḥ al-khalel*, İstanbul 1280 H.; translation into German W.F. A. Behrnauer, *ZDMG*, XI (1857), III-132.

[10] Mustafā Naīmā, *Târîkh-i Na'îmâ* I-VI, İstanbul 1280 H.; Introduction in vol. I.

The ideas of Ibn Khaldūn were adopted increasingly by the historians of the period of decline after the time of Na'īmā, who saw in them a theory which clearly explained the course which Ottoman history was following. Indeed we are justified in seeing the effect of Ibn Khaldūn's ideas in the rigid adherance after 1700 by 'Amcazāde Hüseyin Pasha and later still, Rāghib Pasha to a policy of peace in the hope of saving the empire from a fatal convulsion. Let us recall too that Na'īmā wrote his history for 'Amcazāde Hüseyin Pasha and that at the same period the *Mukaddima* of Ibn Khaldūn was translated into Turkish.[11]

The first Ottoman historians to endeavour to systematically divide Ottoman history into periods according to the ideas of Moslem political philosophy were Cevdet Pasha[12] and Muṣṭafā Nūrī Pasha[13] in the middle of the 19th century. They, like Kātib Çelebi, divide Ottoman history primarily into three main periods—youth, that is growthi middle-age, that is of stable maturity; and old-age, that is, decline. They then sub-divide each period into stages.

The important characteristic of Muṣṭafā Nūrī Pasha is that in his endeavour to identify the periods of Ottoman history he used the criterion not only of political history but also of the history of institutions and cultural developments. In his view, during the third stage (that is, broadly speaking, the 16th century), the love of luxury increased, moral qualities were lost, and the first signs of decline appeared. But if the real decline set in only after the repulse before Vienna in 1683, the stage from 1595 to 1683 must be counted as belonging to the period of maturity. This anthropomorphic division of Ottoman history into three periods of growth, maturity and decline has been transmitted through 'Abdurrahmān Sheref and Yūsuf Akçora to our own day, to become and has become the classic division on which our Turkish school textbooks are based.

In endeavouring to divide history into periods we have no need for a rigid framework based upon a pre-conceived theory of history. I propose now to examine from the viewpoint of the successive stages of firstly, the state of equilibrium established between the Ottoman Empire and foreign powers, then the development within the empire of the ruler's authority and the state of equilibrium which it established vis-a-vis the other forces within the empire, and finally the functioning of the system of landtenure upon which the military, financial and social institutions of the state relied.

---

[11] Translated by Pīrīzāde Mehmed Sā'ib, *Mukaddime-i Ibn Hhaldūn*, I-II, İstanbul 1275 H.; Completed by A. Cevdet Paşa, İstanbul 1277 H.

[12] A. Cevdet (Paşa), *Vekāyi'-i Devlet-i 'Aliyye* (Târih-i Cevdet), İstanbul 1271-1301.

[13] *Netā'ic'ul-vuḳū'āt,* I-IV, İstanbul 1294-1327 H.

Jihād, or ghazā, the Holy War, remained the dynamic principle of the Ottoman state until the end of the 17th century. By 1354, the Moslems of Iznik (Nicaea) in discussions with thir prisoner Gregory Palamas, Archbishop of Salonika, already spoke of the occupation of the Christian West as inevitable,[14] and as early as 1333 the Byzantine emperor had begun to turn to the pope for help against the Ottoman menace, and to offer the Union of the Churches in return for assistance. Nevertheless, it was not until the time of Bayezid I (1389-1402) that the *Jihād* had ceased to concern only the Byzantine Empire and the Balkan countries, and had become a European question. It was only after the Ottomans had, in the years between 1393 and 1396, reached in one direction the Adriatic and the Morea, and, in the other the banks of the Danube, that Hungary and Venice undertook definite action and were able to rouse the Western Christian world to undertake a crusade.[15] The real question at issue was the dispute for the possession of Constantinople and Balkans between Venice and Hungary on the one hand and the Ottomans on the other. Mehmed II, who represented the culmination of the policy of the *Jihād,* solved the problem in favor of the Ottomans. He was halted, however, before Rhodes and Belgrade, the gates of the Mediterranean and of Central Europe.

With the fall of Belgrade in 1521 and of Rhodes in 1522 a new stage in East-West relations begins. In this period an important change takes place in the Ottoman attitude to the *Jihād*, or rather in the structure of the state. The Ottoman state was is no longer a border-state of *ghāzī*s on the bounds of the Islamic world: It now embraced the most important countries of the Moslem world and had in fact become the Caliphate itself. Even the powerful Mehmed the Conqueror (1451-1481) in the letter sent to the Mamluk Sultan after the Conquest of Constantinople (1453) had to recognize the position of the Mamluk Sultan as protector of Mecca, to 'facilitate the fulfillment of the pilgrimage', and claimed for himself only the duty of supporting the *ghāzī*s.[16] Selim I (1512-1520) and Suleyman the Great (1520-1566), however, claimed both obligations. Suleyman sent military help to the Sultan of Açe in Sumatra against the Portuguese and to the king of Gujerat in India[17], while continuing

---

[14] G.G. Arnakis, "Gregory Palamas among the Turks and Documents of His Captivity as Historical Sources, "*Speculum*, XXVI (1951) 104-118.

[15] For a new interpretatim, see H. Inalcik, "The Ottoman Turks and the Crusades, 1329-1522, "*A History of the Crusades*, general ed. K.M. Setton, vol. VI: The Impact of the Crusades on Europe eds. H.W. Hazard and N.P. Zacour, Madison 1993, 221-353.

[16] See A. Ferīdūn, *Munsha'āt al-Salāṭīn,* I, İstanbul 1275 H.; 236.

[17] See H. Inalcik, "The Rise of the Ottoman Empire,"*Cambridge History of Islam*, eds. Holt, Lambton and Lewis, Cambridge 1970, 320-323; —, ed., *An Economic and Social History of the Ottoman Empire*, Cambridge, 1994, 327-331.

the bitter struggle against the Hapsburgs in the Mediterranean and in Central Europe. We see that by the mid-sixteenth century now the *Jihād* has become world-wide and that the Ottoman state was active on every front as the protector of the Moslem world.

At this point we must emphasize that the guiding principle of Ottoman policy was always to keep the Christian world divided. In the 16th century the Ottomans accepted, both the Hapsburgs and the Papacy who were endeavouring to unit Europe, as their two irreconcilable enemies, and supported every action against them in Europe. The Ottoman alliance with France is well known. Ferīdūn's collection of state papers contains a letter of Suleyman to the Lutheran princes of Germany, written in 1552[18] where he bound himself by oath never to attack them as long as they made common cause with his ally, France. The Ottomans supported the activities of the reformers all over Europe. The letter of encouragement which was sent to the Dutch in their rebellion against Philip II is also in Ferīdūn Beg's collection. The Ottomans attached importance to establishing friendly relations with Queen Elizabeth I who was in pursuit of the same aim and supported the English in the Levant trade instead of France which had conformed to catholic policy[19]. In addition they always strongly supported the Calvinists in Hungary.

But in 1683 the overconfident Ḳara Muṣṭafā provoked a united attack of the European powers. The Holy League was established in 1684 with the Pope at its head. It was joined by Russia in 1686. After fighting on all fronts for sixteen years, the Ottomans finally had to accept defeat (The treaty of Carlowitz, 1699). The *Jihād* was now abandoned. We have seen Na'īmā's frank expression of this pacific attitude. In the 18th century Austria and Russia continued the attack. In that period France supported the Ottoman empire because half of her commerce depended on the Levant markets and also because of the alliance against the Hapsburgs. We have before us the beginning of that Eastern Question which was continually governed the pattern of relationships between of the Ottoman empire and Europe in the period 1700-1914.

From the time of Mehmed the Conqueror (1451-1481) the Ottoman sultans used the title of 'Ruler of the Two Continents and Two Seas'. By expanding westwards into the Balkans and eastwards into Asia Minor Ottoman empire formed these two areas into what they had been in the days of Eastern Rome — a united empire centered upon the Straits. Just as the Ottomans were obliged to wage a long struggle in the Balkans, in Asia Minor

---

[18] A. Ferīdūn, *op.cit.*, II, 542-544.

[19] H. Inalcik, ed. *An Economic and Social History* mentioned in note 17, 367-372.

they also had to contend with a traditional political situation which had persisted for centuries. The Seljuk Sultanate of *Rūm,* had in the 12th century, been regarded as a frontier province of the Great Seljuk empire which ruled in Iran. The Ottoman principality is recorded in the Ilkhanid financial registers as one of the frontier provinces of that empire as late as the time of Orhan Ghāzī. Only in the reign of Bāyezīd I (1389-1402) did the Ottomans attempt to make themselves masters of the old Seljuk territories of Anatolia. Bāyezīd applied to the Caliph that he be granted the title of 'Sulṭān'ur-Rūm'[20] which the Seljuk Sultans of Asia Minor had borne, but at that time Timur was emerging from the East with the ambition of reviving the old Mongol empire in an Islamic garb. Timur laid claim to sovereignty over Anatolia and demanded of Bāyezīd that he should be recognized as overlord. He defeated Bāyezīd near Ankara in 1402, and revived the Anatolian principalitis as vassal states, thereby making the Ottoman realm a vassal state like the other principalities. At this point I should like to emphasize that Mehmed I (1413-1421) and Murad II (1421-1451) throughout their reigns, that is to say, for a period of about half a century, recognized the Timurids as their overlords. Timur's son, Shāhrūkh, sought to preserve the settlement which his father had established in Asia Minor. In a letter which he sent to Mehmed I in 1416, Shāhrūkh warned that he did not approve of the action expelling his brothers and uniting the territories which Timur had granted to them. In the letter which he wrote to Shāhrūkh in 1441, Murad II, while addressing him in the terms appropriate for a vassal sovereign to his overlord, claimed that the territory which the Ottomans recently seized from the Karamanids were not lands granted to his brothers by Timur.[21] In one word, then, the Timurids were still upholding Timur's settlement in Anatolia as late as 1441. It is precisely in this period that the tradition of their descent from *Ḳayı* and *Oghuz Khan* was adopted by the Ottomans. Uzun Hasan himself, master of Eastern Asia Minor and Iran, was claiming sovereingty over the whole Asia Minor when Mehmed II began to absorb the Anatolian principalities from 1461 onward. This Türkmen sovereign took the expelled princes under his protection and challenged the Ottoman Sultan. The troops which he sent to support the prince of Karaman in 1472 penetrated into the heart of the Ottoman realm. On this occasion the Ottoman Sultan was strong enough to defeat his rival in the East (1473), and Anatolia fell decisively under the sway of the master of Constantinople.[22] Thus, a political situation which had endured for four centuries in Asia Minor, namely the dependence of Anatolia

---

[20] See "Bāyāzīd I, "*Encyclopaedia of Islam*, 2nd ed. (*EI*²).

[21] For the correspondance of Mehmed I and Murad II see Ferīdūn, I, 150-152, 177-178.

[22] See "Mehmed II, "*İslâm Ansiklopedisi* (İA), 523-527.

on one of its great neighbors in the East, came to an end. Nevertheless, when the Safavids rose to power in Iran at the beginning of the 16th century, Ottoman sovereignty in Anatolia was again seriously threatened; but in 1514, thanks to the skilful use of firearms, Selim I was able to inflict a decisive blow on the enemy. By occupying the highlands of Eastern Anatolia he pushed back the danger. The struggle with Iran in the 16th and 17th centuries was played on in Transcaucasia, Azerbeijan and Irak[23].

We must point out here that the Western and Eastern enemies of the Ottomans tried to establish contacts with one another. In pursuance of their designs upon the Ottomans, Timur sent letters to the French court, Uzun Hasan made an alliance with Venice, and the Safavids sent embassies to the Hapsburgs of Germany and Spain. The Ottomans took great care to follow a policy of alternate war and peace in order to avoid having to fight simultaneous wars on two fronts. But during the long war aganist the Hapsburgs in the years of 1593-1606 Shah 'Abbās' attack in Azerbaidjan fozced the Ottomans to fight on two fronts at the same time with disastrous consequences.

Let us now glance at the changes in the internal structure of the Ottoman state.

The Ottomans, in order to cary on a world-wide struggle in both the East and West, were obliged to maintain all their resources in a state of permanent readiness and at the disposal of a single will. Thus, the Ottoman state brought into existence an absolute and centralizing authority, to successful a degree such that theoreticians of absolute government in Europe, hastened to present it as a model.

In the early period, the greatest threat to the central authority of the Ottoman Beg came from the frontiers.[24] The policy of the Ottoman rulers was consciously aimed at preserving control by the center: Thus, the *Uc-begis*, leaders of the frontier forces were prevented from establishing independent principalities in the newly-conquered territoires as, for example, had happened in the principality of Germiyan. The *beg* who controlled the border region of Izmid was Osman Ghāzī's comrade-in-arms, Akça-Koca. Orhan appointed his own son Suleyman to govern that region, upon the death of Akça-Koca. Suleyman was later sent to govern Karesi, the most important march area conquered around 1340.

---

[23] Now see "Selim I ", *EI*^{2},

[24] On the crucial role the *Uc-begis* played until Mehmed the Conqueror's time, see *Gazavât-i Sultan Murad Han*, eds. H. İnalcık and M. Oğuz; and "Mehmed I", *EI*^{2}, "Murad II," *İA*.

He then crossed the Dardanelles to create the march of Gallipoli on European soil in 1352. Prince Suleyman became the most powerful *uc-begi* of the period and he would have become the natural heir to the Ottoman throne if he had not died before his father in 1357. When Murad I (1362-1389) ascended the throne he placed his most reliable officer, his tutor Lala Shahin, at the head of the border-forces of Rumelia as *Beglerbegi* or commander-in-chief of the Ottoman forces in Europe. But, even at that time the rivalry between the *Beglerbegi* and the *Uc-begi*s was evident. The *Uc-begi*s seemed to have played an important part in prince Savcı's rebellion in Rumelia in 1373. In the period of civil war following the fall of Bāyezīd I in 1402 the *Uc-begi*s gained comparative independence. The Evrenuz-oghulları in the border region of Serres, Pasha-Yigit at Usküp and the Mihal- and Kümülü-oghulları in the Danubian Bulgaria, supported, as they were, by *akıncıs, yürük*s and *sipāhī*s, who were directly bound to them personally, formed in effect "feudal" families. It was they who played the predominant role in the civil war between 1403-1413. During the reign of Murad II, of 189 timariots in the region controlled by Isa Beg, the Uc-begi of Üsküp, about 160 were his own *kul*s, slaves, and retainers.[25] The *Uc-begis* made private agreements with the neighboring foreign states and levied *kharāc* (tribute). But they were unable, however, to preserve their former position in the face of Mehmed II's (1451-1481) vigorous *ghāẓī* personality and strong policy of centralization. Mehmed II managed to bring the *Mihal-oghulları,* in particular, under his control.

During the reign of Mehmed II, the strongest power in the state resided not on the frontiers but in the center — in the forces of *Ḳapı-ḳulları.* More than any other factor, the *ḳul* (slave) system[26] ensured the maintenance of the central and absolute authority of the Sultan. This system had existed at the court of Orhan. When, in the years following 1361, a number of central institutions were set up to meet the demands of the greatly-expanded state, recourse was made to the *kul* system; And the Janissary-force, a paid standing army of *ḳul*s personally bound to the Sultan, was establied. This force numbered 1,000 when it was founded, 6-7,000 under Bāyezīd I (1389-1402), 4-5,000 under Murda II (1421-1451) but in the reign of Mehmed II (1451-1481) it increased to 8-10,000. Thanks to this force the Ottoman Sultan was always stronger than the *Uc-begi*s. Moreover, whenever the border regions were exposed to powerful enemy attacks, the Sultan could use this central force to intervene and strike the decisive blow, as for example, in the battles of Kossova (1389) and Nicopolis (1396). Also these *Ḳapı-ḳulları*

---

[25] H. İnalcık, *Fatih Devri Üzerinde Tetkikler ve Vesikalar*, Ankara 1954, 149-150.
[26] See "Ghulām, "*EI*[2].

literally the slaves of the Porte, were under the name of *yasaḳ-ḳulu* to enforce the Sultan's commands and ordinances in the provinces.[27]

The Janissaries formed only a part of the *Ḳapı-ḳulları.* As early as 14th century the *ḳuls* of the Sultan included not only the military force at the center but also an important proportion of the *tīmār* ḥolding *sipāhī*s in the provinces. After progressing through a definite series of posts within and without the palace service, *ḳul*s who had been trained in the palace were sent to every corner of the empire as timariots, *su-bashıs, sanjaḳ-begi*s and *begler-begi*s, that is to say, soldier-administrators who embodied the political and executive authority of the Sultan[28]. The extensive use of *ḳul*s in the imperial administration began under Bayezid I. The process was completed when Mehmed II granted the highest post of all, the grand vizirate, to *ḳul*s. In short, the increase of the central and absolute authority went hand in hand with the development of the *ḳul*-system. In enumerating the reasons for the Ottoman Sultan's superiority over other Moslem rulers Kemāl Pashazāde emphasizes that, thanks to their *ḳuls,* the Ottoman Sultan were able to enforce their commands everywhere, absolutely, but that they did not allow any *ḳul* to achieve a privileged position.

The Ottoman Sultans, particularly Bāyezīd I and Mehmed II were careful to remove local dynasties and feodal lords in all regions, and to abolish all local privileges.[29] In the Balkans, the peasant classes, no longer cooperating with the petty princes and lords who had proved unable to protect them, became the subjects of the Ottomans with the status of dẕimmī. Former local military classes and monasteries also found it safer to attach themselves to the new centralized system, which guaranteed their rights over the *pronoa*s and *charistia*s which they held. In short, the central Ottoman government acted as a focus of power in the Balkans where they revived the old imperial traditions. From Anatolia too, ghazīs, *ulema,* and land-hungry peasants migrated in every-increasing numbers to enter the service of this reliable and ever-expanding power. Moreover, the incorporation of the Ottoman custom of fratricide by Mehmed II as a clause in his *ḳanūnnāme,* and the abolition by the end of the 16th century of the custom of sending the princes out to govern sancaks are landmarks on the way to the establishment of an absolute central authority. The Ottoman house had thus moved from the old Turkish tradition

---

27 See *Ḳānūnnnāme-i Sulṭānī ber Mūceb-i 'Örf-i 'Oṣmānī,* Ankara 1956, nos. 2-5, 8-12, 20-24, 30, 32, 36, 39, 40, 45.

28 See H. Inalcik, *The Ottoman Empire: The Classical Age 1300-1600,* second reprint: London: Phoenix, 1995, 76-118.

29 H. Inalcik, "L'Empire Ottoman," *Studies in Ottoman Social and Economic History,* London: Variorum II, 1985, 85-87; —, "The Rise of the Ottoman Empire," *Cambridge History of Islam,* I, 295-303.

of sovereignty, by which the suzerainty belonged jointly to all the members of the ruling family, to the old oriental idea of indivisible and sacred authority centered in the person of one ruler.[30]

But from the end of the 16th century onwards, the power upon which this absolute authority rested, namely the palace household and the *Ḳapı-ḳulları* grew so much in influence as to bring the state under their own control. Towards 1018/1600 the Janissaries numbered some 35-50 thousand, and in 1622 they even murdered the Sultan Osman II. As the *Kapı-kulları* gained complete power in the state and appropriated the sources of revenue in the provinces to their own use, the provincial troops began to resist them by force, and for a time in 1625, under the command of Abaza Mehmed Pasha,[31] seized control over Anatolia. This crisis of authority lasted until Köprülü Mehmed brought the situation under control in 1656. In the 17th century the Janissaries, whose numbers had increased enormously in the capital and in the provinces, and who now formed a kind of militia, deposed Mehmed IV and Ahmed III. Only after the destruction of the Janissaries in 1826 were the Padishah and the palace able to re-establish an independent authority over the state affairs. Not only the Janissary force but the other bodies making up the *ḳul* establishment changed their original character in the 17th century.[32] In investigating the reasons for the decline of the state and the general chaos that prevailed, Koçi Beg puts at the head of the list the breakdown of this slave system.

Finally we have to consider the system of land-tenure. It is true to say that the social and economic foundation of the centralized regime of the Ottoman Empire was, as it had been in other empires of the Near-East, a special system of land-tenure which ensured close control of all land holdings by the state.[33]

State-ownership of land made it possible for the central government to control social order in accordance with the aims of state policy and to apportion revenues according to these aims and the needs of the moment. In pre-Ottoman times, too, under the Seljukids and in the Byzantine empire, the state's control over land had determined the social and political structure of the empire. During the period of the decline of these empires both the land and the peasant had fallen under the control of local officers or notables. During the days of its expansion as a conquering power, the Ottoman empire

---

[30] H. Inalcik, "The Ottoman Succession and its Relation to the Turkish Concept of State", *The Middle East and the Balkans under the Ottoman Empire: Essays on Economy and Society*, Bloomington 1993, 60-61.

[31] See "Mehmed Paşa, Abaza" *İA*.

[32] See H. Inalcik, "Military an Fiscal Transformation "mentioned in note 5.

[33] See *An Economic and Social History* mentioned in note 17, 103-154.

had been able to universally reenforce the principle of state-ownership of agricultural land. As a rule, it abolished the rights of the former landlords, both secular and religious, and newly conquered regions as well as lands which were later brought under cultivation were placed under state control.

In fact, this was a three-tier system of land-tenure: the right of ownership of the land was reserved for the state; the peasant had the right to use the land as permanent tenant; between the two was the *sipāhī* who, as timar-holder and representative of the state, was empowered to see that state's rights were not infringed. It was he who collected principal land-taxes and enforced the laws that were passed to prevent the land being left uncultivated. The *sipāhī* owed certain military duties to the state, and used certain taxes he collected as his pay. In states in which a money economy had not developed fully, taxes in kind, which formed the state's main source of revenue, could be collected by tax-farming: It was the system of tax-farming that enabled taxes in kind to be converted into cash for the central treasury. But in the Ottoman empire, which, as a *ghīzī* state, needed great numbers of soldiers, these taxes in kind were not made over to tax-farmers but left as timars to support the *sipāhī*s placed in the villages. Thus, under the Ottomans the system of land tenure, the tax system and the military organizations formed an integrated whole.

It was not difficult for the Ottomans to impose this system in regions of the *Dār ul-ḥarb* which they had conquered, that is, from the Byzantine empire and the Balkan states. But, in the territories of the former Seljukid state in Anatolia, where land had been made over as *mülk*, freehold, and *wakf,* pious foundation, before the Ottoman occupation, and where these transactions had been confirmed by deeds drawn up in accordance with the *Shar'ī'a,* various compromises had to be reached[34]. The land- owners were obliged to supply troops to the state by what was called the *eshkinci* system. During the reign of Bāyezīd I (1389-1402) state control over such land was extended: This is probably one of the main reasons for Bāyezīd's unpopularity in Anatolia. The period from his reign to the reign of Mehmed II was one of tolerance in this respect: The internal crises of this period compelled the central government to grant large areas of *mülk* to influential leaders in Rumelia as well as in Anatolia. These *mülk*s, private estates, were usually converted by the owner into family-wakfs as a precaution against confiscation. But, impelled by his need for more troops, Mehmed the Conqueror, in the years around 1476, brought most of these lands back under state-ownership. He abrogated *wakf*s which evaded their purpose and which had not been confirmed by the Ottoman rulers. He confiscated them for the state and redistributed them as *timar*s. As a result of this reform, some 20 thousand (?) villages and estates

---

[34] *Ibid.*, 126-131.

were taken over.[35] This action caused the religious classes in particular to turn against the Sultan. Upon his death, there was a violent reaction and a large proportion of the land that had been seized was returned to its former owners and *wakf*s. But it was not long before the old course was resumed: During the reign of Suleyman the need for troops, the increase in population, and the bringing of extensive areas of new land under cultivation led to a great increase in the area of the state domains. Records of these additional lands, referred to as *ifrāẓāt,* fill the registers of this period.

From the end of the 16th century an acute and extensive crisis developed in the country districts, in both agriculture and the system of land-tenure. The main reasons for this were firstly, the flood of cheaper silver from Western Europe from about 1580 onwards and the ensuing inflation which threw the Ottoman finances, the economy of the empire and administrative machine into confusion.[36] When the timars suddenly fell in value, the sipahis tried by various illegal means to extort more revenue from the peasants. Secondly, the halting —indeed the receding— of the tide of conquest which took place in this period led to an incease in the number of candidates for the available timars and to bitter competition to acquire them. Thirdly, the *Ḳapı-ḳulları* were managing to appropriate timar-lands everywhere as private estates, thus making the shortage of timars still more acute. As a result, many landless soldiers and unemployed mercenary companies *sekban*s and *sarudja*s, began to ravage the villages and twons as bandit gangs; later they gathered around leaders in still greater force and even began to defat government troops sent against them. These rebels are known under the general name of *Jelālī*s.[37] The *Ḳapī ḳullarī* too who were sent to deal with them were no better than another marauding force who afflicted and plundered the peasantry. In the end, the continuing war and inflation compelled the state to impose *'awāriẓ* -exactions as a regular and heavy money-tax. All these circumstances induced the peasants, especially in Anatolia, to abandon their lands in droves and flee to the towns or join bandit-gangs. This movement, which was particularly strong in the years from 1595 to 1610 is known to Ottoman historians as the Great Flight. In the same years the first serious attempts at revolt occured among the Christian peasantry in Rumelia.[38]

---

35 "Mehmed II" *İA*, 75, Cüz, 53.

36 H. İnalcık.

37 For *djelālī*s see M. Akdağ, *Celâlî İsyanları*, Ankara 1963; cf. H. Inalcik, "Military and Fiscal Transformation..." mentioned in note 5.

38 See I. Khassiotis, "Sull' organisazione, incorporazione Sociale e ideologia politica dei Greci a Napoli, dal XV alla metà del XIX sec., " Epistimoniki Epetiris is Philosofikis scholis tou Aristoteliou Pamepistimiou, Thessalonikis 20 (1981); "The European

During this great crisis, the foundations on which the successes of the earlier period had been built —that is to say the timar system and the system of land-tenure— crumbled away. Koçi Beg who lived through these years, says 'the timar holding soldiery ceased to exist and the *Ḳapı-ḳulları* [were] all powerful'. The state lost its control over the land in the provinces, which subsequently passed largely into the hands of the *Ḳapı-ḳulları* and of influential local people connected with the military class.

The *khass* lands of the Padishah more exactly of the central treasury, which formed half the territories of the empire, were generally farmed out as *muḳaṭa'a* leases. A large proportion of these *muḳaṭa'a* were taken up by members of the military class. In following years this class, which had gained control over the state domains in addition to *muḳaṭa'a* gave rise to the *a'yāns* , provincial notables, who lorded over the peasantry[39]. The state was no longer able to carry out the regular land-surveys necessary to re-assert its control over the land. These influential *a'yāns,* who were now in fact masters of the land, began to maintain military forces who were bound to them personally. As the regular timar-holding troops were non-existent for the most part, the state encouraged these local leaders with strong military forces to join the imperial army, and gave many of them the rank of pasha. In the 18th century, in every part of the empire there grew up local dynasties who controlled large tracts of *muḳaṭa'a*-land and powerful private armies. In this period we can speak of a feodalisation of the empire similar to that seen in Europe. At the end of the 18th century the centralized empire had ceased to exist. Not until Mahmud II founded a new army and put down the local *a'yāns* one by one was it possible to re-establish in some degree, at least in Anatolia and Rumelia, an empire that recognized the authority of the central government.

Thus far we have tried to describe the developments that we consider the most fundamental aspects of the Ottoman history, namely ghazā, power relationship with the outside world, central authorty and finally, land-tenure, as the basis of social structure of the empire.

Powers and the Problem of Greek Independence from the Mid-fifteenth through the Early Nineteenth Century", *Ellada: Istoria kai politismos*, Salonica 1981.

39 See H. Inalcik, "Centralization and Decentralization in Ottoman Administration," *Studies in Eighteenth Century Islamic History*, eds. T. Naff and R. Owen, London 1977, 27-52.

2

How to Read 'Āshıḳ Pasha-zāde's History

How to Read ʻĀshıķ Pasha-zāde's History

I. Notes on ʻĀshıķ Pasha-zāde's Life and Work

In his chronicle ʻĀshıķ Pasha-zāde (hereafter Aşpz.) gives his genealogy as "Dervīsh Aḥmed ʻĀshıķī, son of Yaḥyā, son of Selmān, son of Bali, son of ʻĀshıķ Pasha, son of Mukhliṣ Pasha, son of Bābā Ilyās, who was one of the *khalīfa*s of Abū'l-Wafā'".[1]

We have Aşpz.'s signature at the bottom of the *mülknāme* of Hādjī Beg dated 1 Rabīʻ I, 891/12 January 1491[2] as "Fakhr al-Mashāyikh Aḥmed b. ʻĀshıķ Pasha". In the document, before his name, we find the name of Seyyid Welāyet rendered as "ʻUmdat al-Awlād al-Rasūl Mawlāna Seyyid Welāyet bn Al-Seyyid Aḥmad bn Al-Seyyid Abū 'l-Wafā'al-Baghdādī". The name of the ķādīʻasker Mawlānā Wildān Efendi precedes their names. This document is a definitive proof that Aşpz. was still alive on that date. Aşpz. says that members of his family are all called ʻĀshıķī, and were all born and lived in the territory under the Ottoman sultans, and the Ottoman dynasty always extended their favors to them.

The *zāviye* of Elvān Çelebi[3] at Mecidözü near Çorum, where Aşpz. was born and lived in his youth, was located in the area of Meḥmed Çelebi's

---

[1] I am using Çiftçioğlu N. Atsız' edition in his collection of early Ottoman chronicles, *Osmanlı Tarihleri,* Istanbul: Türkiye Yayınevi 1949, 91 ff; in his edition Atsız combined earlier editions by ʻĀlī, *ʻĀşıķ Paşa-zāde Tarihi,* Istanbul 1332 H., and F. Giese, *Die altosmanische Chronik des ʻĀšiq pašazāde,* Leipzig 1929; cf. *idem,* "Die verschiedenen Textrezensionen des Āšiq pašazāde bei seinen Nachfolgern und Ausschreibern", *Abh. der Preuss. Ak. der Wiss., Phil.-Hist. Klasse, Nr. 4;* since none of the editions are satisfactory a new critical edition with appropriate emendations is absolutely necessary (here are some examples of misreadings: "Makam oldu *dene* Allahu Ekber" (Atsız, 96) (*dene* > *dīne*); "Gerekdür yâr u hemdem ü *münasib"* (p. 98) (*münasib* > *muṣāḥib*); "Bunun üstadını buldumdu hakdan" *(buldımdı* > *bildimdi);* "Osman Gazi yerlü yerinde kondı" (p. 105) (*kondı* > *kodı*); "Bu Tatār'a gerçe and verdük" (p. 108), editions skipped over the phrase "ammā Tatār and bekler ṭā'ife olmaz" (cf. Neshrī, Unat-Köymen ed. 124). M. F. Köprülü, "Âşık Paşa-zâde", *İslâm Ansiklopedisi,* I, summarized what was known by his time about Aşpz.'s life.

[2] The fine original roll with Bāyazīd II's gold *tughra* is now in my possession. I purchased it from Cahit Öztelli about twenty five years ago. I am preparing it for publication; see the photos of the beginning and the end of the document in the *Appendix.*

[3] On Elvān Çelebi and his *zāviye* see *İslâm Ansiklopedisi* (thereafter *İA),* 701-708; Semavi Eyice, "Çorum'un Mecidözü'nde Âşık Paşa-oğlu Elvan Çelebi Zâviyesi", *Türkiyat*

headquarters in his struggle against his brothers for the Ottoman throne in the years 1402-1413. Meḥmed I's success in gaining the support of the local Turcoman begs and dervishes in the area seems to have been a key factor for his final victory over his brothers in the sultanate. In this region, densely populated by Turcomans since the Danishmendids, *bābāī* dervishes including Elvān Çelebi must have had a particularly strong influence. When, in his final confrontation with his brother Mūsā, Meḥmed I left Bursa in 1413 Aşpz. was not able to accompany him because of his illness. On his way from the Elvān Çelebi convent to Bursa Aşpz. fell ill at Geyve and stayed in the house of Yakhshi Faḳı (Faḳīh) son of Isḥāḳ Faḳı, the imām of Sultan Orkhan. There, Yakhshi Faḳīh gave Aşpz. his *Menāḳib-i Āl-i 'Osmān,* an Ottoman history down to Bāyazīd I (1389-1402). Aşpz. states that "he transmitted *(naḳl)"* the Ottoman history down to the reign of Bāyazīd I from this source.[4] After his victory, Meḥmed I put Mikhal-oghlu Meḥmed in prison at Tokat. Mikhal-oghlu had supported Mūsā as the leader of the *udj* forces in Rumili against Meḥmed Çelebi. When in 1422, in his crucial struggle for the Ottoman throne against his uncle Muṣṭafā, Murād II sought the support of the well known spiritual leaders of the time, he obtained the support of Emīr Sulṭān in Bursa. Also he released Mikhal-oghlu Meḥmed from his prison in Tokat. On his way to Murad II's camp on the Ulubad river Mikhal-oghlu visited the convent of Elvān Çelebi at Mecidözü köyü (also known as Elvān Çelebi köyü) near Çorum and took Aşpz. with him. Elvān was then venerated as one of the leading *walīs* in Anatolia.[5] Evidently, Aşpz.'s presence in the young Sultan's army was believed to be a support

---

Mecmuası, XV (1969), 219-226; for Mehmed I see "Meḥmed I", (H. Inalcik), *Encyclopaedia of Islam,* second edition (thereafter *EI²*).

4 See Aşpz. Atsız ed., 91; on Yakhshi Faḳı (Faḳīh)'s family see H. N. Orkun, "Yahşi Fakih..." *Dergâh,* VII, 107, and *MOG,* II, 320; V. Ménage, "Yakhshi Fakīh", *BSOAS* XXVI (1963); Yakhshi's family were favored by Ottoman Sultans since Orkhan's time: an official record published by Barkan, *İstanbul. Üniv. İktisat Fakültesi Mecmuası,* II-2, 243, shows that Yakhshi Faḳīh inherited from his grandfather a *waḳf* land originally granted by Sultan Orkhan, at Geyve; approved by Bāyazīd I and Meḥmed I the *waḳf* is confirmed later on Yakhshi Faḳīh's son Meḥmed by the diplomas of Meḥmed II and Bāyazīd II. Yakhshi Faḳīh's *menāḳibnāme* as transmitted by Aşpz has the characteristics of the popular epic style, which combined genuine historical information with folk stories from various origins, Turcoman or Greek. Instead of dismissing *menāḳibnāmes* as pure legends efforts should be made to sift the historical message and information from them. Shikārī's dynastic history of the Karamanids is another example of the genre; there is a striking difference between the rather archaic, epic style of the passages in the section on the first three sultans in Aşpz. and the style coming directly from Aşpz.'s pen in the last section on Bāyazīd II.

5 Eyice, *art. cit.,* 212; now see A. Y. Ocak's introduction to Elvān's *Menāḳib* mentioned in note 39 below.

for his cause. This may indicate the special favor Aşpz. was going to enjoy with the dynasty from that time on.

Aşpz. was born in 795/1392-1393, apparently at Elvān Çelebi village, and lived there among the dervishes until in 1422 Mikhal-oghlu took him to join Sulṭān Murād II. Aşpz.'s detailed reports on the events which occurred in the zone of Amasya and Çorum and on Yörgüc Pasha's activities in the area as governor of Amasya in the period 825-828/1422-1424 suggest[6] that Aşpz. returned and lived in the convent of Elvān Çelebi in this period. Aşpz. states that he participated in all of Murād II's campaigns and whatever he writes about the Sultan comes from his personal observations. He went to Mecca to fulfill his religious duty as a pilgrim in 840/1436 and on his return home next year we find him in Üsküp with the famous *udj* beyi Isḥāḳ, participating in *ghazā* raids. Apparently he was present at the siege of Constantinople, although there is no evidence about being settled there afterwards. After the conquest of Istanbul Sultan Meḥmed must have been particularly content to host the son of 'Āshıḳ Pasha in his capital since the bitter rival of his house, the Karamanids, were associated with Bābā Ilyās' descendants from the beginning.[7]

In 861/1457, according to the *waḳfiyya* of the Conqueror's mosque[8] Aşpz.'s home was located at the Unkapanı Çarşısı, adjacent to the house of the famous scholar and first cadi of Istanbul, Khodja-zāde. He is referred to in this document as 'Āshıḳ Pasha-oghlu al-Ḥādj Aḥmed. The evidently large house of his in the quarter of Unkapanı passed later in the possession of the Kürkdjü-Bashı, who used to pay a rent *(muḳāṭā'a)* to the treasury at an annual rate of 48 akça. This detail can be taken as a proof that the house was originally a Byzantine structure. Aşpz. had another house in the quarter of the *Üskübī Mescidi* near Unkapanı. He owned another house in the quarter of *Saru-Demirci,* which by 926/1519-20 came into the possession of the Grand Vizir Pīrī Pasha, and was endowed as a *waḳf* by him.[9]

---

[6] Aşpz. Atsız ed. 166-171; cf. H. Hüsameddin, *Amasya Tarihi,* III (1927), 198-201.

[7] See Ocak, *Menāḳib;* Aşpz. visited shaykh 'Abd al-Laṭīf-i Muḳaddasī in Konya on his way back from Mecca in 841/1437.

[8] On this *waḳfiyye*'s various versions see, "Istanbul" (H. Inalcik), *EI*², IV, 244; for references to Aşpz. in a sixteenth century Turkish version of the *waḳfiyye* see, *Fatih Mehmed Vakfiyeleri,* Ankara: Vakıflar Genel Müd. 1938, 79-81, 127, 232.

[9] See *Ayasofya Evḳāfı Defteri,* dated 926 H., Belediye Library, İstanbul, Muallim Cevdet Kitapları, no. 64, 227; for the quarters of Unkapanı, Üskübī (Üsküplü), Mimar Sinan and Sarı Demirci (Saru Timurcu) around 1480 see the map in E. H. Ayverdi, *İstanbul Mahalleleri, Şehrin İskânı ve Nüfusu,* Istanbul 1958.

According to another *waḳf* record dated 1473,[10] Aşpz. owned depots and shops in the business district of Galata. He had to pay, for example, a rent *(muḳāṭā'a)* to the Sultan's treasury for a shop in the Al-Ḥādj Ḥamza quarter in Galata, which was one of the state's properties from Genoese times. What is clear from these documents is that Aşpz. possessed several properties in Istanbul and Galata and paid *muḳāṭā'a* (rent) for them to the treasury.

According to an official register of the waḳfs of Istanbul,[11] a mosque and a convent called *'Āshıḳ Pasha Mesdjidi ve Zāviyesi* were built by the eunuch Hüseyin Agha of the Old Palace (Sarāy-i 'Atīḳ) in the quarter of Mi'mār Sinān (Old) already under Meḥmed II.

In the year 908/1502 Hüseyin Agha added new endowments, consisting of houses and shops in Istanbul and Galata. The supervision of all of these *awḳāf* was given to the Shaykh of the convent.

In view of the last event in the Aşpz. chronicle occuring in the year 908/1502, and of the new endowements made in November in the same year, it may be supposed that Aşpz. died in 1502.

The author of an anonymous chronicle, when speaking about its source on Ede-Bali says:[12] "The source of this information is a very old dervish by the name of Aḥmed 'Āshıḳī, a hundred years old. He survived down to the time of our Sultan (Bāyezīd II). His family line included such illustrious figures as Bābā Ilyās, Mukhliṣ Pasha, 'Āshıḳ Pasha and Elvān Çelebi". Aşpz. was the shaykh of the *'Āshıḳ Pasha Zāviyesi* in the quarter of Mi'mār Sinān. By 876/1471, however, *'Āshıḳ Pasha Zāviyesi* was called *Bābā Ṣaltuḳ Zāviyesi* (or *Mescidi)* bearing the name of the famous Turcoman Bābā Ṣaltuḳ who had migrated with a group of Turcoman clans to Dobruja in the 1260's. It is interesting that Aşpz. chose this place to settle with his dervishes who occupied the rooms around the convent.[13] The Shaykh of the *zāviye* received a daily stipend of five *akça* by 963/1555.

The large convent *(k͟hāniḳāh)* belonging to Seyyid Welāyet, the son-in-law of Aşpz., was located in the same quarter. A register of Istanbul *awḳāf*[14]

---

[10] For this particular *waḳfiyye* see note 8.

[11] *İstanbul Vakıfları Tahrir Defteri, 953/1546 Tarihli,* eds. Ö. L. Barkan and E. H. Ayverdi, İstanbul 1920, nos. 1434, 1480, 1626-1645, 1713, 2510.

[12] MS, Bibliothèque Nationale, Paris, Supplément turc 1047, 6b-7a.

[13] For an official reference to the *'Āshıḳ Pasha Zāviyesi* in 1012/1603, see Barkan and Ayverdi, 176; for a description of the zāviye see R. E. Koçu, *İstanbul Ansiklopedisi;* for the relation of Bābā Ṣaltuḳ to Kalenderī/Abdāl shaykhs and Bābāīs, see A, Y. Ocak, *Marjinal Bir Sufilik: Kalenderîler, XIV-XVII. Yüzyıllar,* Ankara: TTK 1992, 69-74.

[14] *İstanbul Vakıfları Tahrir Defteri,* mentioned at note 11, p. 278, no. 1644, the editors' reading *müstefidīn* should be corrected as *musta'idīn,* "those showing ability".

contains a *waḳf* made by the daughter of Aşpz. and wife of Seyyid Welāyet, dated Djumāda II, 934/March 1528. She built ten rooms in the inner court of the convent of 'Āshıḳ Pasha for the use of "able" madrasa students in need. Rich endowments were made to it by several people including Faṭma Sultan, also known as Sūfī Sultan Khātūn.[15] In her *waḳfiyya,* dated Djumāda I, 907/November 1501, she stipulated that on Friday nights the readers of the Qur'an and dervishes *(zākir)* assemble in the presence of Seyyid Welāyet and pray. The supervision *(nežāret)* of the mosque is given to the Shaykh himself. In 1501 this function belonged to Muṣṭafā Çelebi son of Seyyid Welāyet.[16]

Seyyid Welāyet is known in the sultan's court as "dāmād-i veled-i 'Āshıḳ Pasha".[17] Seyyid Welāyet was buried in a mausoleum in the same quarter, which existed down to our time.

From the references to Aşpz. in the archival documents[18] we also learn that "Veled-i 'Āshıḳ Pasha" was a member of the *djamā'at* of *müteferriḳa* and *zawāyid-khōrān* of the *awḳāf* of the Conqueror's *'imāret.* He had a daily stipend of seven akça in 6 Rabī' II, 897/6 February 1492 (in other words, in his own time Aşpz. was known as either Aḥmed 'Āshıḳī, used rather as pen-name, or *Veled-i 'Āshıḳ Pasha).* The group known as *müteferriḳa* in the Palace included the "distinguished", accompanying the Sultan at the ceremonies, such as the sons of vassal princes, pashas and famous ulemā'. In 909/1503-1504 Sultan Bāyazīd II gave a *ṣadaḳa* (alms and gifts) to Dervsīh Ilyās son of 'Āshıḳ Pasha [-zāde] among the venerable religious people of Istanbul and to "Seyyid son-in-law of Veled-i 'Āshıḳ Pasha".[19]

Aşpz.'s *Menāḳib-i Āl-i 'Osmān*

Aşpz. is the author of a *Menāḳib-i Āl-i 'Osmān.* Such *menāḳibnāme*s were designed to be read and listened by groups during the military campaigns, in *boza*-houses or in other meeting places.[20] In one place Aşpz. addresses

---

15 *Ibid.,* p. 275, no. 1631.

16 *Ibid.,* p. 275, no. 1631, on Seyyid Welāyet see note 62 below.

17 *Defter-i Müsevvedāt-i In'ām,* ed. Ö. L. Barkan, *Belgeler,* IX-13 (1979), 329-350.

18 "Fâtih Cami ve İmareti Tesislerinin 1489-1490 Yıllarına âit Muhasebe Bilançoları", Ö. L. Barkan, *İktisat Fakültesi Mecmuası* (Istanbul), XXIII, 319; for the date see the facsimile.

19 Barkan "İstanbul Saraylarına dair Muhasebe Defterleri", *Belgeler,* X, 329, 350.

20 O. Köprülü, *Tarihî Kaynak olarak XIV.ve XV. yüzyıllarda Anadolu'da Bazı Türkçe Menâkıbnâmeler,* unpublished doctorate thesis, İstanbul Üniversitesi, Edebiyat Fakültesi 1953.

The word *menḳiba* in the Turkish of the fifteenth century stands for "deeds" both in religious and lay meanings.

himself to the ghāzīs, saying:[21] "O ghāzīs, all *these menāḳib*s which I composed are based, I swear on God, on the knowledge and sources which I personally reached; do not think that I have written from nothing". On several occasions he asserts that he examined and "summarized" books of *menāḳib* or reported events which he personally observed or heard. "When people", he says, "read or listen to the deeds of the Ottoman sultans, they make their prayers on their souls".[22] Begun in the year of 881/1476 when Mehmed II left Istanbul for his campaign against Bogdan (Moldavia),[23] Aşpz. wrote Ottoman history down to the accession of Bāyazīd II in the year of 886/1481.[24] His history is continued with the events of Bāyazīd II's reign down to the month of Safar in the year 908/August 1502.[25]

As noted above, Aşpz. tells us that his source on early Ottoman history was a chronicle written by Yakhshi Faḳı son of Isḥāḳ Faḳı. Isḥāḳ Faḳı was an imam to Sultan Orkhan. Yakhshi Faḳı's lost work on Ottoman history, Aşpz. tells us, comprises events down to the reign of Bāyazīd I (1389-1402). But, Aşpz. says, he added the things which came to his knowledge through personal experience in seeing and hearing (bilüp işitdügümden, bazı ḥallerinden maḳallerinden).

Those who asked Aşpz. to write the history of the Ottoman dynasty were a group of *'azīz*. The word *'azīz* is used in the Turkish of that time as a term for dervishes. Thus, the audience which he had in mind in writing his book was in the first place the dervishes, primarily those belonging to the *Wafā'iyya* order.

He says, his purpose was to tell about Ottoman family's origins *(nasab wa nesl, aṣl),* their original country, migration and conquest. But also, one of his main purposes, we shall see later, was to demonstrate how the *Wafā'ī khalīfa* Ede-Bali and his own family played a crucial role in the establishment and rise of the Ottoman dynasty.

Aşpz.'s work is deeply influenced by and reflect the vibrant conflicts between the elite and the state, which arose as a result of the Conqueror's radical measures in taxation and landholding during his reign. It can be said that these disputes, in which Aşpz. himself was personally involved, lend his

---

21 'Ālī ed. 35.

22 Atsız ed. 136.

23 *Ibid.,* 114; writing under Meḥmed II (1451-1481) Aşpz. repeated in his work stories against Çandarlı Khalīl whereas Neshrī, writing under Bāyazīd II (1481-1512), when the Çandarlı family was rehabilitated, omitted them, see V. L. Ménage, *Neshrī's History of the Ottomans, The Sources and Development of the Text,* London: OUP, 1964.

24 Aşpz. Atsız ed., 249.

25 *Ibid.,* 252.

history a strong polemical character. When disputing he did not hesitate to present the facts in the direction of his arguments, and in order to criticize the Conqueror's policies he chose the Sultan's forefathers as examples, praising emphatically "their good acts and policies". To be able to sift historical facts and original statements from his sources we have to ascertain clearly these controversial issues in his book.

The background to these issues is the radical changes in state policy under The Conqueror.[26] For his imperial policy, The Conqueror wanted to increase his military forces and expand his revenues, while in order to create his centralist autocracy, he attempted to reduce the power of those groups capable of offering resistance, principally the ulema and the old "aristocratic" families. Trusting in his great charisma as *Abū'l-Fath,* or The Conqueror of *Kosṭanṭiniyya al-Kubrā,* Mehmed could eliminate first the powerful Çandarlı family from the government. Also, he succeeded in reducing to a closer dependence the old frontier *beg* families of Rumili. In order to establish his full control in state affairs, The Conqueror brought now to the most important positions his palace *ḳul*s, and favored the members of the old Byzantine aristocratic families in state finances. As tax farmers of the principal sṭate revenues[27] the latter were to become the target of bitter attacks by Aşpz.

One of the delicate issues in connection of The Conqueror's efforts to find new sources of revenue was the *muḳāṭa'a,* or rent imposed upon the Byzantine houses and plots acquired by the treasury after the conquest of Istanbul.[28] The contemporary historian Ṭursun Beg informs us how the conflicting decisions of the Sultan on the matter caused widespread discontent and confusion among the elite and people at large.[29] We have seen earlier that Aşpz. owned such properties, for which he had to pay rent to the treasury. Aşpz. accused Rūm Mehmed Pasha of the re-introduction of the rent on such properties,[30] and said:

---

26 In general, see "Meḥmed II", (H. İnalcık), *İA,* Fasc. 75 (1969), 531-535.

27 H. İnalcık, "Notes on N. Beldiceanu's Translation of the Ḳānūnnāme, fonds turc ancien 39, Bibliothèque Nationale, Paris", *Der Islam,* vol. 43/1-2 (1967), 154-157; *Idem,* "The Greek Merchants, 1453-1500", *To ΕΛΛΗΝΙΚΟΝ, Studies in Honor of Speros Vryonis, Jr.*, II, eds. J. Stanojevich Allen *et al.*, New Rochelle 1993., 307-319.

28 H. Inalcik, "The Policy of Meḥmed II Toward the Greek Population of Istanbul and the Byzantine Buildings of the City", *Dumbarton Oaks Papers,* 23-25 (1969-1970), 231-240.

29 Tursun Beg, *The History of Mehmed The Conqueror,* eds. H. Inalcik and R. Murphey, Minneapolis: Bibliotheca Islamica I, 1978, 53b-54b.

30 Aşpz., Atsız, ed. 196.

> He was the son of an infidel an became very intimate with the Sultan, and one of his viziers. The infidels from the old [Byzantine] families were his father's friends. They warned him saying that look: these Turks have succeeded in reconstructing this city [of ours] and settling; you have to do something. They took our country and possess it in front of us. Since you are now a favourite of the sultan, you can do something which would prevent this people from the reconstruction and settlement so that the city will remain in our hands as before. The Vezir replied: Let us bring back the *muḳāṭa'a* which was imposed previously, so that this people would give up building their *mulk* properties and the city would remain in ruins and eventually in our hands. One day, on an occasion, the vizir was able to put this idea in the Sultan's head and made him to bring back the *muḳāṭa'a* [on the plots and old houses]. They sent one of the deceiving infidels [as surveyor] together with a deceiving *ḳul* whose name was a Muslim name. Whatever the non-Muslim said the *ḳul* followed it and registered it [in the *muḳāṭa'a* register]. Now, tell us who was this vizir. It was *Rūm* Meḥmed who was responsible for the re-imposition of the *muḳāṭa'a* which is still in force. Because of this *muḳāṭā'a* people gave up the reconstruction and began to leave the city.

In his history, on every occasion, Aşpz. displays his hostility to Rūm Meḥmed Pasha,[31] who actually did good services for the Sultan, particularly in the conquest of Agriboz (Euboea), and also built a beautiful mosque at Üsküdar. Rūm Meḥmed, Aşpz. claims, was also responsible for the discontinuation of the Sultan's gifts to the state notables, ulemā' and shaykhs. Aşpz. ends his remarks about him in the most revengeful words, saying: "In the end they strangled him as a dog".

In the last years of his sultanate, especially following his great victory over Uzun Hasan in 1473, the Conqueror did not hesitate to carry out radical reforms in landholding by subjecting to a revision throughout his empire all the *mulk* and *waḳf* lands in the hands of the old Turkish families and religious groups, including hundreds of the *zāviye waḳf*s belonging to the old shaykhly families. Ṭursun Beg, who was personally involved in the revision and abrogation *(nasḫ)* operation as a director in the finance department, testifies that over twenty thousand villages,[32] *mezra'a*s and *çiftlik*s were confiscated for the state treasury and distributed as *timar*s to the

---

[31] Aşpz., Atsız, ed., 216-218, 243.

[32] The History mentioned in note 29, 18a; but in another place, p. 169a, the number of the abrogated *mulk* and *waḳf*s was given as only one thousand, the second figure may stand for only villages.

military. Given the size of the operation this was a revolutionary measure and shook the Ottoman society as a whole. Affecting Ottoman politics deeply, it became the principal issue for the following decades. One can see the significance of the operation in the Ottoman society through the *tahrīr* registers of Bāyazīd II where hundreds of *waḳf* and *mulk* lands were returned to their former owners. In fact, Bāyazīd's reign constituted a total reaction to The Conqueror's policies in all state affairs, in particular in landholding. In contemporary works Bāyazīd was greeted as "the restorer of the Sharī'a", or actually as one who restored the means of support of the ulema and shaykhs. People made him a *walī.* Aşpz. underlines Bāyazīd II's act of justice in returning the *waḳf* and *mulk* villages to their former possessors.[33] By this act, he points out, Bāyazīd put an end to the old innovations and illegal *(bāṭil)* dispositions.

The discontent and protest was particularly strong among the shaykhs and dervishes who had lost their means of subsistence and *waḳfs* for their convents. The following story in Aşpz. should be interpreted in this context. Aşpz. describes 'O̱smān Beg as a simple man comparable to a shepherd or dervish, telling us that at his death 'O̱smān Ghāzī left no silver or gold, but only a caftan *(tekele),* a shouldersack *(yancuk),* containers of salt and spoons and a pair of boots, several horses and herds of sheep.[34] Meḥmed The Conqueror's harsh financial measures to fill up his treasury for the continuous campaigns and reconstruction of his new capital had put the country under such a strain (and affected Aşpz.'s life) that it is easy to see why our dervish historian gives such a description of 'O̱smān Beg. What is surprising is that modern historians took it at its face value and built up theories on the beginnings of the Ottoman state.

II. Ede-Bali and 'O̱smān ghāzī

Another story which has confused modern historian concerns the relationship between 'O̱smān and shaykh Ede-Bali. In a special chapter (*Bab* 4) Aşpz. relates 'O̱smān Ghāzī's dream in Shaykh Ede-Bali's home and the Shaykh's interpretation that 'O̱smān's offspring is destined to rule over the world. This is a topos of medieval literature for the legitimation of the origin of dynasties. But what is historically true and important is that Aşpz. gives this role to a well-known *khalīfa* of his own *Wafā'iyya* order, who lived actually in 'O̱smān's time. Revealing God's favor for 'O̱smān Ede-Bali said "my son 'O̱smān, be it good news that God granted you and your descendance the pādishāhlıḳ. Congratulations, now my daughter Mālkhatūn has become a

---

[33] See "Meḥmed II", (H. İnalcık), *İA,* VII, 53.

[34] Atsız ed., 115.

lawful wife for you". Actually, the belief that God favors a man for sovereignty and reveals it through a holy man, a shaman or saint, goes back to a Central Asiatic Turco-Mongol tradition. The Ottoman Sultans, challenged by rival dynasties —the Timurids, Ḳāḍī Burhān al-Dīn and the Karamanids in particular— felt compelled to assert the divine origin of their authority as the tradition required. Aşpz. endeavours to demonstrate that such a function was fulfilled by Ede-Bali. But, who was Ede-Bali? Here is a full translation of the biographical note about Ede-Bali by Aşpz.[35]

> Ede-Bali lived for one hundred and twenty five years. He married two women, one in his youth, the other in his old age. He gave his daughter from his first wife to 'Os̱mān. His second wife, whom he married in his old age, was the daughter of Tādj al-Dīn Kurdī. Since the other daughter of Tādj al-Dīn was given in marriage to [Çandarlı] Khalīl, Ede-Bali and [Çandarlı] Khayr al-Dīn became *bacanaḳs*. I heard this news from Maḥmūd Pasha, son of Ede-Bali, who lived under Sultan Meḥmed son of Sultan Murād. This Maḥmūd Pasha lived for over one hundred years. Later, when 'Os̱mān captured Bilecik, he bestowed on his father-in-law the revenue of the town as tīmār.

According to the Ottoman archival records[36] there was indeed a Shaykh named 'Ede' in 'Os̱mān's time who received favors from him.

Here are translations of the records of the *awḳāf* of the *zāviye* (convent) of 'Ede' in Bilecik.

> ***The record, dated 892/1487*:**
>
> The village Koz-Agacı is a *waḳf* given by 'Os̱mān Beg; previously in the possession of *Maḥmūd Paşa* son of Ede, it is now in the possession of Shaykh Meḥmed: Households 17 (8 çifts). Also [among the *waḳfs*] there are three unbelievers (slaves) living at Söğüd, again given by 'Os̱mān Beg: 4 households (3 çifts).

---

[35] Atsız ed., 96, 105; cf. Tashköprülü-zāde, *Shaḳā'iḳ*, see note 61 below.

[36] *Hüdavendigâr Livası Tahrir Defterleri*, I, eds. Ö. L. Barkan and E. Meriçli, Ankara: TTK 1988, 282.

Revenues are as follows:

	Mud	Value (in akça)
Wheat	20	1,000
Barley	15	450
Chick-peas	1	30
Çift-tax and sheep tax		60
Tithes from cotton		100
Poll-tax		40
Total		**1680**

(One *mud* equals 512 kg)

***The record in the survey of 1521*:**

The village of Koz-Agaç is a *waḳf* given by Orkhan beg to the convent of Ede Shaykh; in the record taken from the survey book prepared by Kirmastī it was found in the possession of Meḥmed son of Ede Shaykh. It is stated in the early survey book that he is holding the confirmation diploma from the Sultan. It states that the aforesaid Meḥmed be the shaykh of the aforesaid convent, hold the aforesaid village as a *waḳf* and fulfill the provisions of the *waḳf* deed, serving the travellers coming to and going from the convent. The offspring of the endowed unbeliever slaves were found still keeping their Christian faith in the *waḳf* village, paying 200 akça for poll-tax.

The *mezra'a* of Kozca was also a *waḳf* property of the convent of Ede from 'O͟smān Beg with a revenue, toward the end of the fifteenth century, of 298 (akça). It was transformed into a village when the villagers of Koz-agaç came and settled there.

We learn from the above records that Shaykh Mehmed, grandson of Ede was alive under Mehmed II, and that the trust of the *waḳf* then passed to a certain Mu'min Dede (or Faḳīh); apparently Ede's descendants had expired by 1521. By 1573 the village population abandoned the village to settle in a *mezra'a.* The deserted land of Koz-Agaç is then cultivated by a group of *piyāde (yaya)* militia.

In the official records we have only the name of 'Ede', not *Ede-Bali.* That *Ede* and *Ede-Bali*[37] are the same person is clear from the fact that Shaykh Maḥmūd is mentioned by Aşpz. as the son of Ede-Bali who, he said, lived in the reign of Meḥmed I (1402-1421). In his youth Aşpz. met Maḥmūd and collected information about Ede-Bali and his relatives.

---

[37] *Ece,* from Mongol, means an *elderly person, chief, master, notable.* In the fifteenth century Ottoman Turkish it is rendered in the forms of *ece* and *ede* with the same connotations. Bali is a personal name widely used in the Ottoman Turkish of the period.

Thus, the family tree of Ede-Bali can be established as follows.

Shaykh Ede-Bali or Ede Shaykh (living under 'Os̱mān and Orkhan)
Shaykh Maḥmūd Pasha (living under Orkhan through Meḥmed I's time)
Shaykh Meḥmed (living under Meḥmed II and Bāyazīd II)

In brief, the official records confirm that Ede-Bali, also known as Ede Shaykh, had a *zāviye* in Bilecik, for which he received as *wakf* from 'Os̱mān Beg the village of Koz-agacı (or Koz-agaç) and the *mezra'a* of Kozca in the *kaḍā* of Söğüd. In these records, however, there is nothing particular which confirms his being father-in-law of 'Os̱mān Beg, and the *wakf* revenues are quite modest, altogether only 1680 akça in the early records.[38]

Completed in 700/1300, Elvān Çelebi's *Menākibnāme,*[39] telling us the deeds and *silsile* of the Bābāī Shaykhs, mentions Shaykh 'Bali' or 'Ede-Bali' as one of the well known *khalīfa*s of Bābā Ilyās, the founder of the Bābāī order.

Elvān mentions him as leading the atheist and unbelievers to salvation by his penitence. Elvān adds that Ede-Bali and Ḥādjī Bektash were both the followers of Bābā Resūl, and that Ede-Bali learned from Ḥādjī Bektash *not to covet worldly power.* Until then, Bābāī shaykhs, Bābā Ilyās, and Mukhliṣ Pasha had openly claimed to control both the spiritual and material worlds, as the ṣūfī doctrine of *kutbi-i 'ālem* in *bābāiyye* and *Kalandariyye* preaches.[40] This note on Ede-Bali fits well Aşpz.'s description of him as a holy man *supporting* 'Os̱mān's sovereign power. The *Wafā'ī* shaykh Seyyid Welāyet under Meḥmed II embodied this close cooperation between shaykh and sultan with growing *sunnī* accent while in the same period an authentic *abdāl/kalandarī* shaykh, Otman Baba, openly claimed dominion of both the material and spiritual worlds. The change can perhaps be explained by the fact that by the time of Meḥmed the Conqueror the Ottoman sultans were coming increasingly under the influence of urban *sunnī* ulemā' and were no more like those Turcoman Begs who had venerated the *abdāl*-type dervishes

---

[38] On the historical authenticity of 'Os̱mān Beg's relationship with Ede-Bali see I. Mélikoff, *Sur les traces du soufism turc. Recherches sur l'Islam populaire en Anatolie,* Istanbul 1992, 134.

[39] *Menâkibu'l-Kudsiyye fi Menâsıb'l Ünsiyye,* eds. İ. E. Erünsal and A. Y. Ocak, İstanbul 1984, 168-169.

[40] H. Inalcik, "Dervish and Sultan: An Analysis of the Otman Baba Vilāyetnāmesi" *The Middle East and the Balkans under the Ottoman Empire,* Bloomington 1993; A. Y. Ocak, who devotes a whole chapter (Ch. 2, 141-174) to the doctrine of *kalanderī*s in his *Kalenderiler* (see note 42 below) does not deal with this central doctrine of *kuṭbiyya* in their belief system.

and were little differentiated from their Turcoman frontier *ghāzīs*. However, from the beginning, unlike the shaman-like abdāls, the Wafāī dervishes were known as faithful observers of the *Sharī'a*. This can clearly by seen in 'Āshıḳ Pasha's *Gharībnāme.*[41] Also speaking of the *khalīfas* of the *Bābāī* Shaykhs, Elvān underlines that they were both "knowledgeable in and observers of the *Sharī'a* and gnostic in mystical perception and practice".

Ahmed Y. Ocak has shown that the militant shaykh Bābā Ilyās, also known as Bābā Resūl, was one of the shaykhs in Anatolia of the *Wafā'iyya* order founded by Seyyid Abu'l-Wafā' of Baghdad (died in 1107).[42] Although after Bābā Ilyās a *bābāī ṭarīḳa* appears to have been in the way of formation the family down to Aşpz. was known as belonging, primarily, to *wafā'iyya* order.

By contrast, combining Central Asiatic shamanistic beliefs with popularized pantheistic formulas, originally expounded by such great Sūfīs as Muhyī al-dīn ibn al-Arabī, Djemāl al-Dīn Sāwī and Djalāl al-Dīn Rūmī, Turcoman *abdāl bābās* believed that "the Pole of the Age" *(Ḳutb-i Zamān)* possessed an absolute control over the things and events in this world and in the heavens.[43] They claimed to embody *Wilāyat wa nubuwwat,* sainthood and prophethood, in their person. It is believed that in a continuous state of ecstasy *(djazba)* they were in constant communication with God. To use Max Weber's term, the "mystagogue", challenging temporal authority, became the refuge and hope of the unprivileged and oppressed members of society. They professed that the time would come when "The Pole of the Age" would decide to take direct control of the worldly sultanate, as attempted in the uprisings of Bābā Ilyās, Mukhliṣ Pasha, Shaykh Badr al-Dīn and Shāh Ismā'īl.[44] It was only through Shāh Ismā'īl that the ambition was finally accomplished in Iran, with the support of the heterodox Turcomans.

The Sultans became permanently suspicious of the popular shaykhs, who gathered large groups of followers around them. The Ottoman sultans tried either to eliminate, or to attract and make dependent, through grants of *waḳfs*,

---

41 See M. F. Köprülü, "Âşık Paşa", *İA,* 704-706.

42 *La revolte de Baba Resul ou La formation de l'hétérodxie musulmane en Anatolie au XIII siècle,* Ankara 1989, see in particular, 53-57, 75-131; also Erünsal and Ocak, *Menâkib,* LXXIV; on Kalandariyya in Anatolia now see A. Y. Ocak, *Kalenderîler,* 61-137; Ilyās could not be a khlalīfa of Abū'l-Wafā' as Aşpz. claimed, see Krupp, *op. cit.*, 8-10. M.F. Köprülü "Abdal", *Türk Halk Edebiyatı Ansiklopedisi,* I, Istanbul 1935, 23-56.

43 See H. Inalcik "Dervish and Sultan" mentioned in note 40.

44 Shāh Ismā'īl (Khaṭāyī) wrote: "İki 'ālemde sultandır ḳalender", cited by Ocak, *Kalenderîler,* 158.

such popular shaykhs.[45] In 1492 a dervish of the *ıshıḳ* type attempted to kill Bāyazīd II during his campaign in Albania, which precipitated a mass execution and deportation of this type of dervish in Rumili, who found refuge and support with the frontier *(udj)* begs. Conversely, conformist dervishes gave their full support to the Ottoman dynasty by claiming sainthood for the sultan himself. Aşpz. presents Murād I as a true *walī* favored by God and adds saying "this Ottoman dynasty is such a family that their miraculous deeds are apparent".[46] It was not just a literary expression that Ottoman Sultans Murād I, Bāyazīd II, Süleymān I and Murād III were elevated to the stature of a *walī.* The poet Taşlıcalı Yahyā , following the tradition, wrote these verses for Süleymān the Magnificent: "He is the *ṣāḥib-ḳirān* of this world; he is exalted with miracles; he is the ruler over people and the shadow of God; in fact he is the absolute *walī.*.[47]

In other sections of his history Aşpz. further tries to demonstrate that Ede-Bali played a key role in the establishment of the Ottoman dynasty and state. He notes that under 'Os̱mān Beg he was consulted on various crucial matters concerning Islamic law.[48] For example, upon the conquest of Karaca-Hisar Ṭursun Faḳīh consulted Ede-Bali whether it was necessary to obtain the Seljukid Sultan's approval to read the *khuṭba* in the name of 'Os̱ mān and appoint a cadi, since in Islamic tradition it was the exclusive right of the Imām-Sultan to appoint a *khaṭīb* and a cadi as his representative over the community. Thereupon, 'Os̱mān, Aşpz. adds, interfered arguing that he alone had the right to make the appointments himself since, he said, he conquered the town with his own sword and that God who gave the Seljukid ruler the sultanate granted 'Os̱-mān *khanship* through leadership in *ghazā (ghazāyile khanlık).* If, he said, the Sultan claims that he made 'Os̱mān a *beg* by conferring him a *sancaḳ* (the symbol of political authority), 'Os̱mān says: "I carried myself the *sancaḳ* of *ghāzā* and fought against the unbelievers. And, if the sultan says that he is of (the imperial) house of the Seljukids I say I am a descendent of Gök Alp. If the sultan says that they came into this country before them, I say that my great grandfather Süleymānshāh arrived before them". Imperial ancestry and the *ghazā* were the two principal claims to dynastic legitimation and recognition for the Ottomans. But, obviously, all

---

45 See "Murad II" (H. İnalcık), *İA,* fasc. 86, 611.

46 Atsız ed., 194.

47 Olki ṣāhib-ḳirān-i 'ālemdir
Her kerāmāt ile mükerremdir
Vālī-yi ḥalḳ ü sāye-yi Ḥaḳdır
Fi'l-ḥaḳīḳa velī-yi mutlaḳdır

48 Atsız ed., 103.

these claims were not voiced in the time of 'Os̱mān, as Aşpz. writes, but later, when the dynasty grew in power through conquests in the Balkans, when they asserted the dynasty's primacy in the Islamic world, particularly in the face of the ruling houses in Iran. Bāyazīd I wanted to assert his claim to the *Sultanate of Rūm* in succession to the Seljukid sultans in Asia Minor in the face of Timūr's challenge, and asked the Abbasid Caliph in Cairo to send a formal *manshūr* affirming the title.[49]

Evidently, all these ideas were circulating among the Ottoman elite when Aşpz. was writing his history. In fact, in his letter to the Mamluk Sultan after the Conquest of Istanbul the Conqueror claimed that he was chosen by God to be the leader of Muslims in *ghazā*. Then, Selīm I and Suleymān I employed the same argument of being the sole leader of *ghazā* and protector of Muslims in the world to legitimize their claim to "the Caliphate over all Muslims in the world".[50]

In the elaboration of the early Ottoman traditions by such authors as Rūhī, Ibn Kemāl and Idrīs, all writing under Bāyazīd II,[51] it was claimed that Ottoman Sultans superseded all Muslim rulers except the first righteous Caliphs.[52]

Ede-Bali's advice on crucial state affairs with legal consequences, Aşpz. claims, was sought under Orkhan, too. When Orkhan decided to increase and re-organize his soldiery, his brother 'Alā' al-Dīn said he had to consult the cadis on the issue. Orkhan asked the opinion of Çandarlu (or Djenderelü) Karadja Khalīl, then the cadi of Bilecik, and Ede-Bali on the matter.[53]

Also it should be remembered that Aşpz.'s attempt at magnifying Ede-Bali's place in 'Os̱mān's time is seen in his statement that 'Os̱mān bestowed the whole revenue of Bilecik by way of *tīmār* on his father-in-law.[54] This is obviously a distortion of the fact that 'Os̱mān granted Ede-Bali as *waḳf* the village of Koz-Agacı and *mezra'a* of Kozca for his *zāviye* in Bilecik. Aşpz. also emphasizes that the Ottoman sultans descended from the marriage of 'Os̱mān with Ede-Bali's daughter. "The mother of Orkhan Ghāzī", he says, "passed away and one or two months later his *grand-father* Edebali, too,

---

49 See "Bāyazīd I" (H. Inalcik), *EI*².

50 See "Pâdişâh", (H. Inalcik), *İA*.

51 The changing image over time of the Ottoman Sultans about themselves as their power grew is reflected in their titles and in the new versions of their history; this point is dealt with in my article "Pâdişâh" mentioned in note 50; C. Imber, "The Ottoman Dynastic Myth", *Turcica*, XIX, 7-28, actually follows what is said in that essay.

52 In pseudo-Rūhī, Bodleian.

53 Atsız ed., 117-118.

54 *Ibid.*, 105.

found God's mercy".[55] He adds that this occurred in the year of the conquest of Bursa in 1326. 'Os̱mān buried them in the fort of Bilecik.[56] Three month later 'Os̱mān himself died in Sögüd.[57] The *waḳfiyya* of Orkhan Beg, dated March 1324, testifies that Māl-Khātūn was actually the daughter of Ömer Beg.[58] Thus the Ottoman sultans may not have descended from Ede-Bali's daughter Māl-Khātūn as Aşpz. claims.

In view of Ede-Bali's association with his family and the *Wafā'iyya* order Aşpz.'s concern in inserting in the traditions the stories about Ede-Bali's crucial role in the foundation of the dynasty is understandable.

The archival evidence proves that in fact Ede-Bali actually received favors from 'Os̱mān Beg as the *khalīfa* of the *wafā'iyya* order and had a *ẓāviye* in Bilecik. As Aflākī's authentic stories show, the leaders or *khalīfa*s of the religious orders from Konya and Karaman used to visit the flourishing *udj* emirates and were warmly welcomed.[59] It is apparent that Ede-Bali, a *khalīfa* of the *Wafā'iyya* shaykhs arrived and settled in the *udj* area, definitely before 1300, perhaps already under Ertughrul, 'Os̱mān's father.

In addition to the Ede-Bali story, Aşpz. makes another reference to the role of the *Wafā'ī bābā*s in connection with the rise of the Ottoman dynasty. Aşpz. describes Geyikli Bābā as the disciple *(murīd)* of Bābā Ilyās and of the ṭarīḳa of Abū'l Wafā'.[60] This statement provides another evidence that Bābā Ilyās belonged to the *wafā'iyya* order and his *murīd*s included the heterodox *abdāl bābā*s. A group of them, Aşpz. said, had come and settled in the appanage of Ṭurgud (or Durgut) Alp in the Inegöl district. Orkhan Beg showed interest in obtaining the blessing of Geyikli Bābā. The Bābā planted a "sacred" poplar tree in Orkhan's palace, a vestige of the shamanistic tree

---

[55] *Ibid.,* 114.

[56] *Ibid.,* 122.

[57] 'Os̱mān was alive in September 1323 as the *waḳfiyya* of Asporça Khātūn corroborates, see, I. Beldiceanu, *Recherches sur les actes des premiers Sultans,* Munich 1967, 78-82; Orkhan Beg must have been on the Ottoman throne in 1324; he minted a silver coin dated 727/1326-1327, see İ. H. Uzunçarşılı, "Orhan Beg'in Hükümdar olduğu Tarih ve İlk sikkesi" *Belleten,* 207-211; in fact, by 727/1327 the Ilkhanids of Iran had lost control in Anatolia as a result of Timurtash's rebellion.

[58] The text of the *waḳfiyya* is published by İ. H. Uzunçarşılı: "Gazi Orhan Bey Vakfiyyesi", *Belleten,* V (1941); Ede-Bali's daughter is given in Aşpz. as *Mālhūn, Māl-Khātūn or Bala-Khātūn;* I. H. Uzunçarşılı *(Osmanlı Tarihi,* 2 d ed., Ankara 1961, 105, note 3) suggests that Māl-Khātūn was the mother of 'Alā' al-Dīn, brother of Orkhan; in some Anonymous chronicles, for example MS Bibliothèque Nationale, Paris, supplément turc 1047, 6b, Ede-Bali's daughter is named *Rābi'a.*

[59] Shams al-Dīn Aḥmed al-Aflākī, *Manāḳib al-'Ārifīn,* II, Text, 2d ed. Ankara (1962), 924, 947, 950.

[60] Atsız, ed. 122; on Geyikli Bābā, see A. Y. Ocak, *Kalenderîler,* 90-91, 195.

cult among the Turcoman bābās. Official records testify that there was indeed a village called *Geyiklü Bābā* or *Bābāiler* in the *Ḳaḍā* of Inegöl.[61] Evidently, the village was settled by the bābāī dervishes as mentioned by Aşpz.

The translation of the *Menāḳib-i Tādj'ul-'Ārifīn Abū'l Wafā'* contains interesting details on Aşpz.'s association with the *Wafā'iyya* order. The translation was made on the suggestion of Seyyid Welāyet himself, the *Wafā'ī* shaykh and son-in-law of Aşpz. Seyyid Welāyet was alive in the time the translation was completed, but Aşpz. was already dead. The author gives interesting details on Seyyid Welāyet's life noting that he was born in Bursa in 855/1451 and married Aḥmed 'Āshıḳī's daughter in 874/1469.[62]

In the introduction added to the translation of Seyyid Welāyet, 'Os̱mān Beg's relation with "the Shaykh's noble *silsile*" is told. Reproducing Aşpz.'s

---

61 *Hüdavendigâr,* mentioned in the note 36, p. 110, no. 178; Aşpz., Atsız ed. 105, tells us that 'Os̱mān had bestowed Inegöl district to Durkut Alp, later called Durkut (or Turgut)-İli; here once again the authentic character of Aşpz.'s source is confirmed by archival record.

62 In Tashköprülü-zâde, Medjdī's trans. *Ḥadā'iḳ al-Shaḳa'iḳ,* Istanbul, 1269 H., 251, Seyyid Welāyet's full name is given as Muṣṭafā son of Aḥmed al-Ṣadrī al-Ḳonevī; he is better known as *Ibn Wafā;* Tashköprülü-zāde, obviously using the translation of the *Manāḳib* of Abū'l Wafā'-i Baghdādī, expanded with additions on Seyyid Welāyet. We learn from the additions that S. W.'s shaykhs were Muṣliḥ al-Dīn and then 'Abd al-Laṭīf-i Mukaddasī; in the *silsile* the latter was shown also among the shaykhs of 'Āshıḳ Pasha-zāde; Ottoman Sultans Mehmed II and Bāyazīd II showed a profound veneration for Seyyid Welāyet, granting him special favors. His expert knowledge in Islamic law, referred to by Tashköprülü-zāde, must have particularly been appreciated by Mehmed the Conqueror. Bāyazīd II personally attended S. W.'s funerals. This special interest in Seyyid and Aşpz. himself evidently originated from the close connection of the dynasty with the *wafā'iyya* order, starting from 'Os̱mān Beg's time; on S. W. also see M. Lāmi'ī Çelebi, *Terdjüme-i Nafaḥāt al-Uns,* Istanbul 1270 H., 559-60; also see H. J. Kissling, "Scchejch Sejjid Vilayet (1451-1522) und sein angebliches Menāqybnāme," *ZDMG* 113 (1963), 62-68; A. Krupp, *Studien zum Menāqybnāme des Abu'l-Wafā' Tāğ al-'Ārifin,* Münich: R. Trofenik, 1976. The son-in-law of Aşpz., Seyyid Welāyet asserted his descent from the Prophet and parentage to the founder of the wafā'iyya order, thereby receiving an unusual veneration and support from Ottoman sultans throughout his life. Seyyid Velāyet must have had a special interest and the motivation in disseminating in Ottoman Society a Turkish translation of the *Menākibnāme of Abu'l-wafā al Baghdādī* (for the original Arabic Ms. see, Krupp, 19-25). In the section added to the original *Menākibnāme,* the translator who was a disciple of Seyyid Welāyet and made the translation on his directive, claimed, albeit in equivocal terms, Seyyid Welāyet's parentage to Muhammed Abu'l-Wafā' Tādj al-'Ārifīn (for the latter's origin and *siyāda* see Krupp, 28). In the Ottoman soicety the radical *bābās* of the Abdāl-Kalenderī sect, for example Otman Bābā, vehemently denounced and accused with hypocrisy those shaykhs who sought, for wordly ends, the favors of the ruler. The *Vilāyetnāme* of Otman Bābā, written in the same period, describes his attacks against the Seyyid Velāyet or Aşpz. type of dervishes and the popular response they received (see H. İnalcik, "Dervish and Sultan" mentioned in note 40 above. For Aşpz. criticism of such dervishes see Atsız, ed., p. 153-154: "Kimi der şeyhimiz sultan olısar").

story of Ede-Bali, the author says: "'Oṣmān Khan reached the throne of sultanate and the *crown of sainthood* through the divine favor at the (Shaykh's) sublime *dergāh*", thus underlining the role of the *Wafā'iyya* in the rise of the Ottoman dynasty. Confirming Elvān Çelebi our author identified Ede-Bali as one of the *khalīfa*s of Shaykh Seyyid Muḥammed Abū'l Wafā' of Baghdad. In this version of the story on Ede-Bali's spiritual guidance to 'Oṣmān Ghāzī he asserted that 'Oṣmān's first *ghazā* success, the capture of a fort near Inegöl in 684/1295, was due to Ede-Bali's spiritual support. All the subsequent *ghazā* successes were accomplished "with the help of the *awliyā*". Basically the story is based on Aşpz. but it stresses that the rise of the dynasty was due to the *Wafā'iyya* shaykh.

Aşpz. confirms the continuation of the Wafā'ī shaykhs' influence with 'Oṣmān's successors. It attributes an outstanding influence with Orkhan to Akhī Ḥasan, Ede-Bali's nephew. He tells us (Atsız ed. 110, 115) that in 1326, in a campaign against Atranos (Adranoz) and Bursa, Orkhan wanted to have Ede-Bali's son shaykh Maḥmūd and Akhī Ḥasan with him. In general, Ottoman army commanders believed that the presence of such popular dervishes in the army heightened the ghazā zeal among their men.[63] Aşpz. tells us that when the *Tekvur* of Bursa surrendered the city, Akhī Ḥasan was the first to climb on top of the main tower on the walls. Upon 'Oṣmān Beg's death Akhī Ḥasan is shown to have played a crucial role at the succession.[64] Oṣmān's two sons, Orkhan and his brother 'Alā' al-Dīn, coming together in Ḥasan's convent, deliberated, in the presence of the dervishes *('azīzler)*, on the matter. Orkhan had the advantage of having led the ghāzīs in various campaigns under 'Oṣmān and of being the patron of the Wafā'ī dervishes. Later, upon the surrender of Nicaea "Ḥādjī (Akhī?) Ḥasan "whose grandfather was a disciple of Ede-Bali" was appointed as the shaykh of the first *'imāret* founded in the city by Orkhan. Aşpz. testifies[65] that down to his time Ḥasan's descendants kept the trust of this hospice in their possession. In all this, Aşpz. takes pains to underline that after Ede-Bali it was Akhī Ḥasan, his nephew and disciple, who possessed an outstanding position vis-à-vis the Ottoman ruler. The 'Āshıḳ Pasha tradition remained paramount with the Ottoman Sultans in the following centuries. According to Topçular Kātibi,[66] during the campaign of 1630 the standard of 'Āshıḳ Pasha was taken along with that of Ayyūb Anṣārī to the field of action.

---

[63] See H. Inalcik, "Istanbul: An Islamic City", *Journal of Islamic Studies,* I (1990), 1-4.

[64] Atsız ed. 115.

[65] *Ibid.,* 119, 120.

[66] MS, Staatsbibliothek, Vienna, 338b.

The wakfiyya of Hādjī Beg, dated 1 Rabī' I, 891 H.

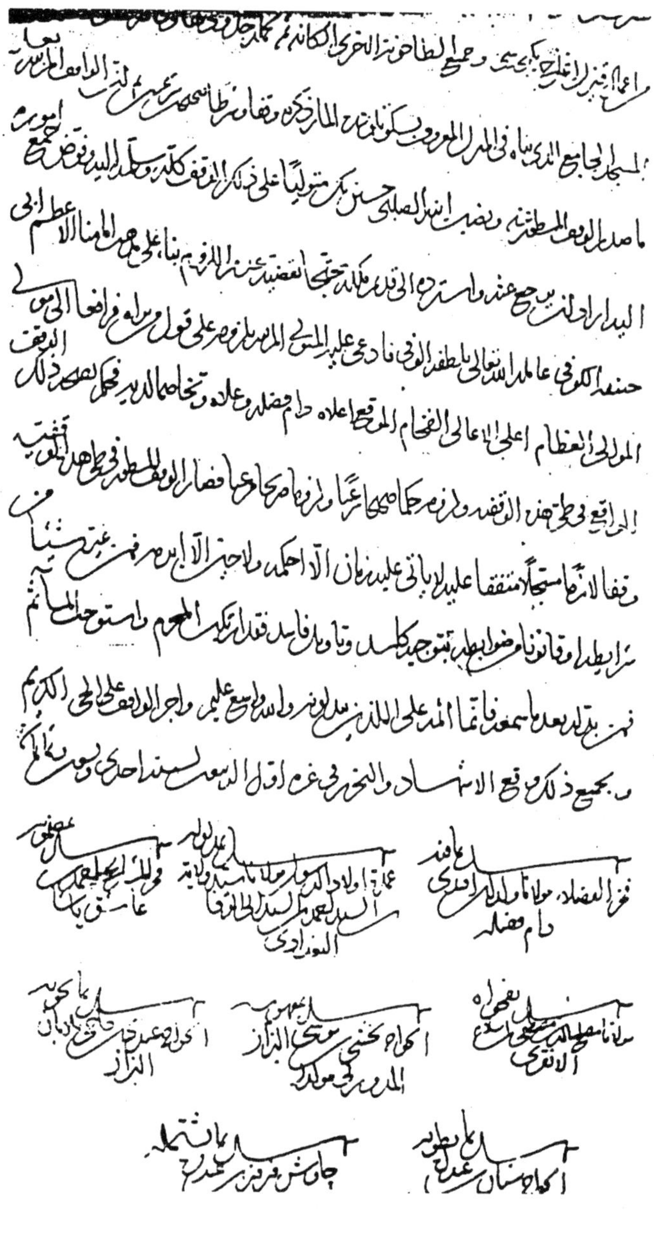

The upper and lower parts of document

Part II

Sultans and Policies

1

‘Oṣmān Ghāzī's Siege of Nicaea and The Battle of Bapheus

‘Osmān Ghāzī's Siege of Nicaea and The Battle of Bapheus

During the period 1075-1086 Nicaea became the capital city of the Seldjukid ruler Süleymānshāh I, founder of the Seldjukid Sultanate of Anatolia.[1] Lost to the Byzantines as a result of the siege by the crusaders from the west in 1097 its re-conquest remained a constant concern for the Seldjukids. Seldjukid rule was restored in Nicaea in 1105, but the city was lost again in ca. 1147 to the Byzantines.

The dry Eskişehir plain where Turcomans were pushed back now became a frontier between Byzantines and Seldjukids. Pastoralist Turcomans needed the hilly country with good mountain pasturelands beyond the borderline and quite often penetrated with their herds into the Byzantine territory. Against them Emperor Manuel I Comnenus (1143-1180) built or reinforced fortresses on the border including Karaca-Hisar on a mound just three kilometer from Eskişehir. However, the crushing Seldjukid victory at

[1] See "Süleyman-Şah I", (O. Turan) *İslâm Ansiklopedisi* (thereafter *İA*) fasc. III (1967), 210-219; S. Vryonis, *The Decline of Medieval Hellenism in Asia Minor and the Process of Islamization from the Eleventh through the Fifteenth Century,* Berkeley: UCP 1971, 96-142; C. Cahen, *La Turquie pré-Ottomane,* Istanbul: Institut Français des Etudes Anatoliens, 1988, 13-15; Ali Sevim, *Anadolu Fatihi Kutalmışoğlu Süleymanşah,* Ankara: TTK, 1990; Süleymānşāh I conquered Nicaea in 1075 and made it the capital city of the Seldjukid Sultanate in Anatolia. Emperor Alexios Comnenus recognized his possession of Nicaea with the treaty of Dragos-Creek (near Maltepe) in 1081. Upon Süleymānşāh's death in June 1086 (See Ali Sevim, 37-39) the Seldjukid Sultan Melikshāh sent his general Porsuk, and then Bozan to take possession of the city. Abū'l Ḳasim, lieutenant of Süleymānşāh at Iznik, approached the emperor to be able to resist the Seljukid emirs until he was put to death by Bozan in 1087. It is to be noted that Abū'l Ḳasim is credited with the conquest of Nicomedia (Izmit) before his death. Osman Turan, 217-218, asserted that the state Süleymānşāh founded gave rise among the Turcomans in this part of Anatolia to a tradition of "the frontier state of the ghāzīs". The claim in the early Ottoman traditions that Süleymānşāh was the ancestor of ‘Osmān Ghāzī may be taken as an evidence of such an enduring tradition over centuries. However, Enverī, *Düstūrnāme* (ed. M. H. Yinanç, Istanbul 1928, 18) correcting the error on the basis of the better sources, recognizes Süleymānşāh as the son of Ḳutalmış and gives a different genealogy for ‘Osmān's ancestors. What is important here is that the re-conquest of Nicaea and revival of the Turkish-Muslim state of Iznik must become the ultimate ambition among the Turcomans settled in this area. On the Seldjukid presence in Nicaea in general, see S. Vryonis, *op. cit.,* 31-36, 52-58, 112-116, 146-155.

Myriokephalon in 1176 totally changed the conditions on this frontier, encouraging the westward expansion of the Turcomans; for Sultan's first condition for peace was the demolition of the recently built fortresses in the region.

Apparently the Seldjukids, in particular their frontier *ghāzīs,* never gave up the idea of the re-conquest of Nicaea for Islam. For Muslims, a land once being made part of the *Dār al-Islām,* is considered always an Islamic territory and its loss was believed to be only temporary. At any rate, after Süleymānshāh the Seldjukids seem to have always regard Nicaea a city just at the border of their territory. In fact, when Ghiyāṯ al-Dīn Mes'ūd II (1283-ca. 1301 and 1303-1308) was bestowed by the Mongol Khan the Seldjukid Sultanate in Anatolia his territory was supposed to encompass all the lands "up to the border of Nicaea".[2]

Also, about 1261 when the Turcoman clans dependent on Sultan 'Izz al-Dīn Keykāvūs migrated to join him in Byzantium, "they went to Iznik pretending that they were going to their own winter pastures, and in a short period of time from there many Turkish nomad families (Türkevi) passed over to Europe".[3] As will be seen below, Oṯmān Ghāzī's strategy makes us believe that his ultimate goal was to reconquer Nicaea. In effect, comparative examination of the Byzantine and Ottoman sources show that the battle of Bapheus itself was an episode resulted from 'Oṯmān's attempt to capture Nicaea.

As a contemporary observer Pachymeres is, in general, our most reliable source for 'Oṯmān's activities, in particular for the battle of Bapheus.[4] In the introduction to his history Pachymeres makes it clear that his account is based either on his own observations or the statements of those who were the eye-witness of the events. Nevertheless, Pachymeres should be used critically, comparing his information with Ottoman traditions. For example, Pachymeres as well as modern authors following him seem to be mistaken

---

[2] Yazıdjızāde 'Alī, *Tārīkh-i Āl-i Selçuk,* Topkapı Palace Library, Revan Köşkü K. No. 130, 517; on this source see "Ibn Bîbî" (A. S. Erzi), *İA,* V-2, 715-718.

[3] Yazıdjızāde, *op, cit.,* 462-464.

[4] George Pachymeres' account on 'Oṯmān Ghāzī's activities has been examined by various specialists including G. Caro, "Zür Chronologie der drei Letzten Bücher des Pachymeres", *BZ* 6 (1897) 116 ff., G. G. Arnakis, *Early Ottomans,* Athens 1947, 71 ff, in particular note 153; Tinnefeld, "Pachymeres und Philes als Zeugen für ein frühes Unternehmen gegen die Osmanen", *BZ.* 64 (1971), 46-54; E. Zachariadou, "Pachymeres on the 'Amourioi' of Kastamonu", *Byzantine and Modern Greek studies,* (1971), 57-70; Professor Zachariadou most kindly clarified for me several points in the Greek text. I am also indebted to Timothy O. Baldwin for his translation for me of the whole section on 'Oṯmān into English.

by showing 'Osmān active in lower Sangarus prior to 1300. Confusion seems to originate from the fact that Pachymeres in his story, leaving 'Osmān for a moment aside, goes back to an earlier period when the Paphlogonian Çobanid emirs were involved in the activities in the area.[5] In the Ottoman traditions it was Akça-Koca who was active in the lower Sangarius (Sakarya) area around Düz-Pazarı (Ada-Pazarı, today) down to Orkhan's time. Akça-Koca was an ally, and then a vassal, of 'Osmān Beg.

Actually, Pschymeres going back to earlier times describes the stituation in Bithynia prior to the major confrontation at Bapheus in 1301. He tries first to explain how the defense of the region was weakened as a result of the ill-measures taken by the usurper emperor Michael VIII Palaeologus in the 1260s. Greeks living in the district of Nicaea, Pachymeres tells us, rose up against the usurper, and harsh treatment of the rebels totally alienated the population in the region from him. When the Emperor abolished tax exemptions of the native soldiers in the fortresses they did not hesitate, Pachymeres adds, to join the Turks. "Some of them even served them as guides", a fact confirmed by the Ottoman sources. The Greek historian denounces the governor of Nicaeae who was acting toward the population "as a bandit rather than a soldier". The monks living in the monasteries in the area were severely persecuted as heretics.[6]

And then, narrating co-empreror Michael's campaign in western Anatolia in 1302, Pachymeres starts to tell us how 'Osmān became a pressing threat to the provinces close to Constantinople, Nicaea in particular. Summarizing first in a digression, the events preceding 'Osmān's raids "on the Sangarius river" he then tells us how 'Osmān crossed over the mountain (obviously the *Avdan* range in the Ottoman sources) and began to forage and pillage the land of "Halizonoi" in coastal plain, on the peninsula of Nicomedia/Izmit.

---

[5] Zachariadou, *art. cit.*, argues that the digression dates back to the events in the years 1290-1293 when Çobanid 'Alī, the chief of the Turcoman ghāzīs in the lower Sangarius made peace with Byzantium and gave up raiding into the Byzantine territory. Then, 'Osmān assumed the leadership of the ghāzīs, and vigorously continued the raids, which resulted in the siege of Nicaea. The passage is discussed by H. Inalcik, *Cambridge History of Islam,* I, eds. P. M. Holt, A. K. S. Lambton and B. Lewis, Cambridge 1970, 267; and Y. Yücel, "Çoban-Oğulları Beyliği", in *Anadolu Beylikleri Hakkında Araştırmalar,* I, 2. ed. 1991, 33-51; It is a Seldjukid source, *Musāmarat al-Akhbār* by Aksarāyī (ed. O. Turan, 1944) that brought clarification to Pachymeres' account.

[6] See A. E. Laiou, *Constantinople and the Latins,* Cambridge 1972, 86-93; on the conditions of life of the Greeks on the frontier zone and the attitude toward the Ottomans early Ottoman traditions contain information confirming the Greek sources; on Ottoman conciliatory policy of *istimālet,* see H. Inalcik, "Ottoman Methods of Conquest", *Studia Islamica,* II (1954), 103-129.

Pachymeres gives details on the state of the blockade to which Nicaea was subjected following the Ottoman invasion of the surrounding areas. Its communication with Constantinople, he said, was cut off except through the road from Cio (Cius, Turkish *Gemilik* or *Gemlik*).[7] Travellers stayed at Cio and crossed the land in the night to reach the lake and enter the city at the only gate which was left open. All the other gates, Pachymeres continues, were closed because the enemy forces had surrounded the city on all other sides. We shall return to this point of detail when we discuss the authenticity of the Ottoman tradition.

Like the Ottoman tradition, Pachymeres too, describes the battle of Bapheus as resulted from 'Osmān's blockade of Nicaea.

Here are the main points in Pachymeres' account of the events leading to the battle of Bapheus.

1 On the 27th of July 'Atman' ('Osmān) appeared suddenly in the vicinity of Bapheus, a place near Nicomedia together with his followers numbering many thousands.

2 Pachymeres then tells us how the raiders of 'Osmān attacked Mouzalon at *Telemaia* prior to the battle of Bapheus. The success encouraged him to cross the mountain passes and come to raid the "Halizonoi".

Comment: This first success apparently was a surprise attack of a vanguard of "about one hundred men". Arnakis believs that it happened one year before the battle of Bapheus,[8] which is plausible (see infra, Chronology).

3 Other Turcomans from near the "*Meander*" river joined 'Osmān's troops when he decided to confront the Byzantine army. Many Turcoman allies, he says, joined him in this campaign.

Comment: Who were these allies?

It is not plausible that Turcomans from such a far away region as the Meander came to join 'Osmān Ottoman tradition (see infra), however, states that when Osman learned that Emperor was preparing an army against him he asked aid from the Sultan of Konya who sent orders to the Turcomans of Sahibin-Karahisar (Afyon) for his support. In fact, Karahisar was the principal Seldjukid frontier center in this section under the direct dependence

---

[7] Already Abu'l Kasim built, obviously with the cooperation of the indigenous Greek craftsmen, a fleet at Cios/Gemilik around 1086, see Anna Comnena, II, 110-114, cited by Vryonis, *op, cit.* 481.

[8] *Op. cit.*, p. 129-131.

of the Sultan.[9] Turcomans of Aydın and Menteshe advancing on the Meander valley were better known in Constantinople at this time while Karahisar had become a back country in the wake of the conquests by the Turcomans over the Byzantines in western anatolia in the period 1290-1304. This may be another confusion in Pachymeres' account.

General Situation in the years 1298-1301

Ottoman chronicles[10] make sufficiently clear that at this point 'Osmān had not yet become a leader among the chiefs in the area, each of whom acted independently. Prior to the battle of Bapheus, during the raid against Göynük-Taraklı on the main road from Kastamonu to Nicaea, 'Osmān had to rely on the cooperation of the local Turcoman and Greek lords in the area between the Sakarya and Göynük rivers. Köse Mihal, one of these lords, appears to have been not his vassal but his ally at this time. Apparently, 'Osmān's allies in the area joined him to confront the major Byzantine reaction threatening all of them. Pachymeres adds that at this particular time Emīr 'Alī (son of the Çobanid Emīr Yavlak Arslan), seeing the general onslaught against the Byzantines, resumed his offensive policy against the Byzantines on the lower Sakarya valley in the Adapazarı area. This explains Pachymeres' digression on the Çobanids of Kastamonu. No connection, however, between 'Osmān and 'Alī is alluded to. 'Alī's action, Pachymeres notes, had no significant consequence. 'Osmān emerged as the leader confronting the imperial army. In any case, while 'Osmān moved to Yalak-Ova against Mouzalon with his troops the Byzantine frontiers from the lower Sakarya river all the way down to the river portages at Geyve and Lefke, which controlled the roads from the east to Nicaea, were under attack.

In general, the Turcoman frontier lords intensified their raids into the Byzantine territories at times when they felt secure from a Mongol threat in their rear.

The years 1298-1301 were particularly favorable for Turcomans to resume their hostile activities against Byzantium all over the western frontiers.[11] In 1298, in Anatolia Mongol general Sülemish had risen up

---

9 40 On the powerful Seldjukid emīr Sāḥib Fakhr al Dīn 'Alī and his sons who with their stronghold Karahisar had a dominant position in western frontier lands, see Aksarāyī, *op. cit.*, Index: Fakhr al Dīn 'Alī, in particular 145-153.

10 For these chronicles see H. Inalcik, "The Rise of Ottoman Historioghaphy", *Historians of the Middle East,* eds. B. Lewis and P. M. Holt (London 1962), 152-167; for a detailed examination of the early traditions on 'Osmān see second part of this paper.

11 On the decisive events in western Anatolia during this period, see P. Wittek, *Das Fürstentum Mentesche, Studie zur Geschichte Westkleinasiens im 13.-15. Jh.* Istanbul:

against the Khan while Bayıncar, or Bayancar, the new commander-in-chief of the Mongol regiments in Anatolia, put 'Alā' al-Dīn Keyḳubād III on the Seldjukid throne in Konya.[12] In the winter of 1299, Sülemish killed Bayancar. The important event is referred to in the early Ottoman traditions. In the years 1299-1300 Mongol troops under Emīr Kutlushāh and Emīr Çoban were kept busy quelling the Sülemish rebellion. Sülemish was popular among the frontier Turcomans. When he was eliminated Mongol forces under him moved to the west and took refuge in the Eskishehir-Bithynia area, becoming neighbors to 'Os̱mān. All these events have a confused reflection in the Ottoman popular chronicles. However, it must be pointed out that Sülemish's scene of activity was in the distant area of Amasya-Tokat where the Turcomans became his main supporters.

Our contemporary principal source on the Ilkhanids of Iran, Rashīd al-Dīn observes that "Sülemish gained the support of the Mongol troops in the province of Danishmend (the Tokat-Amasya region) and took conrol of the *Udj,* or frontier areas, granting the symbols of *beg*ship, the flag and the military band, to many lords (in the Danishmend province)". Z. V. Togan[13] speculated that the Ottoman tradition about Sultan 'Alā'al-Dīn granting the symbols of *beg*ship to 'Os̱mān may actually be related to Sülemish. In any event, it is a fact that in the period 1299-1302 the Turcomans on the western frontiers rose up in a general offensive against the Byzantine territories form the lower Sakarya valley down to Ephesus.[14]

Istanbuler Mitteilungen 2, 1934; reprint Amsterdam: Oriental Press 1967, 15-24; Zachariadou, 'Pachymeres', 57-70; Laiou, *op. cit.,* 85-126.

12 See *'Āshiḳ Pasha-zāde Tārīkhi,* ed. Atsız, Istanbul 1949, 97; according to Ottoman traditions Bayancar's arrival is coincided with the siege of Karaca-Hisar and the date given is 687 of Hejira, which begins on February 6, 1288; details of this episode are well known through the Seldjukid and Ilkhanid sources: see Z. V. Togan, *Umumî Türk Tarihine Giriş,* 2nd., ed., Istanbul 1970, 243, 328-331, 468-488; Bayancar's arrival in Anatolia as governer general actually occured toward the end of the year 1298. By 1299 Sülemish, supported by the anti-Ilkhanid Turcomans, took under his control the entire central and western lands of the Seldjukid Sultanate (Togan, 330). According to Togan (331) 'Os̱mān must have been involved in this struggle on the side of Sülemish. Sülemish is captured, and executed in Tabriz in 1301. In brief, Sülemish rebellion coincides with 'Os̱mān's activities against Nicaea; thus in the years 1298-1301 the Mongol Khans lost control over the Turcomans in the western frontier zone. The Byzantines believed that the Turcomans were effectively under the Khan's control and could be checked by him in their anti-Byzantine raids, hence, the marriage arrangement of a Byzantine princess, Maria, the sister of Andronicus II to Ghazan Khan (died, 1304); "Maryam" was married to Ghazan's successor Öldjeytü in 1306, see B. Spuler, *Die Mongolen in Iran,* Berlin 1955.

13 *Op. cit.,* 331.

14 Wittek, *op. cit.,* 15-23.

Evidently, 'Osmān profited from the massive advance of the Turcomans in western Anatolia in the years 1296-1301, which prevented the Byzantines to maintain their position against 'Osmān in Bithynia. In any case, 'Osmān's move against Nicaea must be considered within this general picture. Now let us turn to the Ottoman traditions on the battle of Bapheus.

Since the original text for the early traditions compiled by Yakhshi Faḳīh, son of Ishaḳ Faḳīh, the imam of Orkhan Ghāzi is lost we have to reconstruct them by comparing various Ottoman sources which have made use of this source. The most complete among them on the events we are concerned about here is Anonymous Tewārīkh-i Āl-i 'Osmān.[15]

The Early Ottoman traditions on the Battle of Koyun-Hisar (Bapheus)

I. The passage on the siege of Nicaea and the battle of Bapheus in the Anonymous Tewārīkh-i Āl-i 'Osmān.

The anonymous account is the most detailed version available in the Ottoman traditions dealing with the siege of Nicaea. We followed basically the critical text established by F. Giese.[16] Other copies, not utilized by him, namely those of İzzet Koyunoğlu, Ayasofya, and Beshīr Çelebi do not contain important variants concerning the above-noted events. The Giese's text and Koyunoğlu MS retains the stories of the Tekvur's daughter and of the dervish while other copies lack one or both of these stories.

Among the later varsions of the same tradition, Lûtfi Pasha writing his History of the Ottoman House on the basis of an anonymous chronicle provided the most detailed version.[17] He omits, however, the legend of the daughter of the Tekvur but retains the story of the dervish. Here is a translation of the text:

> Another son was born to 'Osmān. He gave to him the name of 'Alī Pasha. He stayed with his father while Orkhan Ghāzī was active in conquering lands. He captured Köprü-Hisar by assault and let his ghāzīs pillage it. Then, he came and lay siege to Iznik. In those days Iznik was a city extremely well fortified, of good repute and populous.

[15] F. Giese, *Die altosmanischen anonymen Chroniken,* vol. I, Breslau 1922; the following manuscripts are also been utilized: The İzzet Koyunoğlu MS, *Milli Kütüphane,* Ankara, Microfilm archive no. A. 1465, 10-16; the Ayasofya MS, no. A. 233, fol. 6-10; Türk Tarih Kurumu MS, no. A. 1701, 8-17; Beşir Çelebi, *Tevārīkh-i Āl-i 'Osmān,* ed. İ. H. Ertaylan, Istanbul 1946, 11-18; Orudj's chronicle: F. Babinger, *Die frühosmanischen Jahrbücher des Urudsch,* Hannover 1925, generally following the anonymous, skips over the siege of Nicaea.

[16] Giese, *Chroniken,* vol. I, p. 7-9.

[17] *Lûtfi Pasha Tarihi,* ed. 'Ālī, İstanbul 1341 H., 23-25.

It was surrounded on its four sides by swamps so no force could approach it. In addition, it had a very large population. It is related that from each of its four gates one thousand men mounted on piebald horses could ride out at a moment's notice. You may estimate, by comparison, how many men mounted on one-colored horses there were and how populous the city was. But in those days ghāzīs were well trained and each of them was like a dragon and did not turn his back even if attacked by a thousand infidels. They had an unshaken faith in God and God granted them his favor. So, blessed in their faith they came and pillaged the land around Iznik. When each time the infidels came out to attack, ghāzīs, with God's favor, defeated and drove them back into the city, but, in the end the ghāzīs saw that this city could not be taken by assault because it was protected by water on all four sides, and by no means wolud it be possible to approach it [so that they changed their tactics]. They went and built a watch-tower *(havāle)* on the slope of the hill on the side of Yenişehir and garrisoned it with troops.

A strong man, reputed for his valor in those days, known as Ṭāz ʻAlī, was stationed there with forty men under his command to watch and intercept the city's traffic with the outside world. At the present time that small fort is called Ṭāz-ʻAlī Ḥiṣārı. There is a high rock above the fort at the foot of which a spring gave forth cool water. This spring now also bears the name of Ṭāz-ʻAlī-Pınarı.

Thereafter, the infidels, being thus closely controlled, remained confined to their city because the ghāzīs with their raiding did not let them exit from the city gates. No one from the outside was able to enter Iznik. Besieged in the city, the infields finally were able one day to dispatch a man to the Tekvur of Istanbul to report their condition, saying: The Turk attacked and overwhelmed us and cut off contact with the outside world; we can not do anything to change the situation. If you can help us do it as soon as possible, otherwise we are not in a position to resist. They will [take the city and] enslave our sons and daughters. If you do not help us, we shall perish from starvation.

[They asked help from him] since in those days Iznik was under the rule of the Tekvur of Istanbul. When the Tekvur learned the situation he prepared a number of ships filling with soldiers and sent them out to drive away the ghāzīs from the district of Iznik. The troops in the ships, put under the command of a trusted man of the Tekvur, were supposed to land on the coast at Yalak-ovası and thence go over to Iznik to make a surprise attack on ghāzīs. While they made this plan among themselves, a spy, working for the ghāzīs, came among the enemy troops and learned where they were coming to land. At the risk of his life, the spy hastened to come and inform the ghāzīs.

Thereafter the ghāzīs came to Yalak-Ova and hid themselves in an ambush, waiting on the beach where the infidels were supposed to land. For their part, the infidels sailing in their ships arrived and started to land in the night on the beach at the Yalak-Ovası and to scatter around while each of them was busy in guiding out his horse and assembling his weapons the ghāzīs, shouting the name of Allāh and trusting themselves to Him, made a surprise attack by dashing their horses headlong into the infidel ranks. By putting many to the sword they stirred up such a panic among the enemy troops and created such a massacre that only God knows the number who died. The rest rushed into the sea and drowned. Only those who were fortunate enough were able to return to the ships. In short, the greater part of the infidels perished and only a small number of them could save their lives. Once they were in the ship they thought of nothing but to get away. They arrived in Istanbul and told the Tekvur what had happened. Hearing the news the Tekvur became very sad and moaned. But what else could he do except to sit in patience, feeling completely helpless.

When the news of the Tekvur's failure reached the infidels in Iznik, they lamented and mourned. Finally they discussed the situation among themselves and reached a decision. They agreed that those who had chosen to flee had run away already; now, for those who stayed, there is no alternative but to surrender and submit. So they did and surrendered the city-fortress to the ghāzīs. By gaining the city the ghāzīs gathered in much booty.

After they conquered Iznik, the ghāzīs turned in the direction of Yalak-Ovası. At that time, this area was defended by strong forts in the mountains at locations difficult to reach, and there were also countless prosperous settlements around. On the hills all the way to Iznikmid (Nicomedia) there was not a single tree, but many forts, prosperous towns and villages. The forest, they say, later covered these hills when the area became uninhabited [after the attacks of the ghāzīs]. This is related by those who lived in those days and it is true. They state that there were several reasons for the well-being of the area. One of them was that the area was hilly and rugged [difficult to penetrate]. Another was that many people who ran away out of fear of ghāzīs came and settled in this area. One other reason was that the Tekvur of Istanbul had a beautiful daughter....

Here, Greek and Turkish folk stories, obviously picked up in our popular histories, came into the historical narrative. Here is told the legend of how the princess was afflicted by leprosy and recovered in the Yalak-Ovası thermal sources. Thus the Tekvur was moved to build bath houses on the site. Also here is added the legend concerning a dervish with a wooden sword who showed miracles and caused the Greeks of this area to convert to Islam. Immediately following the legends came the coalition among the tekvurs of Bursa, Adranos, Batnos, Kestel and Kite who united against 'Os̱ mān and confronted him at Dimboz. Then, the story of the siege of Bursa with the construction of the two *havāle,* forts for the blockading of the city followed.

II. *Neshrī's Version*

Neshrī's history, completed somewhere between 1486 and 1493, is the earliest compilation to elaborate the original tradition for dynastic claims.[18] The following translation of Neshrī follows the critical text established by Unat and Köymen, comparing the Menzel codex published by Franz Taeschner.[19]

The independence of 'Os̱mān Ghāzī and Sultan 'Alā' al-Dīn's sending of a sword of honor to him.

Following his conquests of Bilecik, Yar-Hisar, İnegöl and Yenişehir with all their dependencies, 'Os̱mān Ghāzī showing zeal [for further ghazā] proceeded to make a raid against Iznik. He came and cut off the roads coming to the city so that all supplies from outside stopped. Since famine broke out and the population became greatly distressed they secretly sent a courier across the lake to ask for help from Istanbul. [An army] was about to be sent from Istanbul. Thereupon 'Os̱mān addressed the ghāzīs saying "now a rather large army is coming form Istanbul". If we leave this place [and retreat] the infidels around us will become as bold as lions and attack us; we must find a way to repulse them. The ghāzīs responded saying: Since our forces are small in number, we must seek aid from Sultan 'Alā' al-Dīn and so they sent immediately a courier to Konya and reported their recent conquests and what was happening. The Sultan, hearing all this, became extremely content and decided that a drum and flag be bestowed [upon 'Os̱mān] and

[18] On Neshrī's history and its editions see V. L. Ménage, *Neshrī's History of the Ottomans, The sources and Development of the Text,* London: OUP, 1964; H. Inalcik, "The Rise", 152-167.

[19] *Ğihānnümā: Die altosmanischen Chronik des Mevlānā Meḥemmed Neschrī,* ed. Franz Taeschner, Band I: Einleitung und Text des cod. Menzel, Leipzig 1951.

ordered that several thousand men from Ṣahibin-Karahisarı (Afyon Kara-Hisar) go to their aid. But before the courier returned, the infidel troops coming from Istanbul started marching over the pass at the Dil.

> The infidels, believing that the Turks had run away encamped without taking precautions. 'Osmān meanwhile captured a man from the fortress of Yalaḳ-Ḥiṣarı and being informed of the infidels' carelessness suddenly fell in the darkness of the night upon those who already had come over the pass and put them to the sword. Those who ran away were drowned in the sea. Those who had not proceeded over the pass returned to Istanbul. The ghāzīs took much booty. 'Osmān then did not concern himself further with Iznik, and sending the good news of the victory to his people and with the intention to reach his capital, he set out. His mother and other relatives came out to meet him at one or two days' distance. By coincidence on the same afternoon, the drum, flag, diploma and robe of honor arrived [form the Seldjukid Sultan].

III. *Ahmedī's Version*

The earliest reference to the siege of Iznik comes from the poet Aḥmedī, writing in his *Iskendernāme* the section dealing with the Ottomans around the year 1410.[20]

Here is the full translation of his verses on the events leading to the siege of Iznik:

> That champion ('Osmān) conquered Bilecük, Inegöl and Köprü-Hisar and never stopped; sending out troops in every direction he took many lands in a short time. Burning and destroying the infidels' land he laid siege to Bursa and Iznik.

Aḥmedī provides a clear testimony that the source used by Anon., Aşpz. and Neshrī is a common one prior to their histories, most plausibly Yakhshi Faḳīh's lost *Manāḳibnāme* written ca. 1405.[21] In Aḥmedī the sequence of 'Osmān's conquests prior to his blockades of Iznik and Bursa is closely reminiscent of the later compilations (Yenişehir and Yar-Hisar are omitted by our poet Ahmedī, but the conquest of Köprü-Hisar, preceeding the blockades

---

20 Now a critical text of this section of *Iskendernāme,* established by Kemal Sılay is available: "Ahmedī's Ottoman History", MA Thesis, Department of Uralic and Altaic Studies, Indiana University, 1990.

21 On Yakhshi Faḳīh's *Menāḳibnāme* now see V. L. Ménage, "The Menāqib of Yakhshi Faqīh", BSOAS, XXVI (1963), 50-54.

is added). 'Osmān's blockades, not the capture, of Iznik and Bursa follow these conquests mentioned in Aḥmedī, and in later compilations. Obviously Aḥmedī, writing a short epic, skipped over the details. In essence, the main events are told *in the same sequence.* Aḥmedī also shows that Anonymous' statement of the Ottoman conquest of Nicaea at this date is a distortion of the original source.

IV. *Compilations made upon Sultan Bāyazīd's order: The Histories of Idrīs-i Bidlīsī and Kemāl Paşa-zāde.*

The Idrīs' writing between 1502 and 1506, and Kemāl Pasha-zāde about the same time represent later compilations made for the Sultan Bāyazīd II, using chiefly copies of the Anonymous chronicles, which obviously differ from our copies and Neshrī.

In Idrīs' arrangement the sequence of events is as follows: 'Osmān married his eldest son Orkhan to Nilüfer, to whom he granted the province of Kara-Hisar "Otherwise known as Sultan-önü"; he granted Eskişehir to his own brother Gündüz Alp, and the fortress of In-önü and Yund-Hisar to Aygud Alp, the province and fortress of Yar-Hisar to Hasan Alp, that of Inegöl to Turgut Alp, and finally, he bestowed the entire revenue of the province of Bilecük to Shaykh Ede-Bali.[22] Then, 'Osmān chose Yenişehir as his capital city. His younger son, 'Alā' al-Dīn Paşa remained in Bilecük beside his mother. He himself stayed most of the time in Yenişehir. Then "in the year 701 which is the third year in his accession to the sultanate" he marched for the conquest of Köprü-Hisar.

After the fall of Köprü-Hisar, the fortress of Marmara near Köprü-Hisar and Dimboz surrendered. 'Osmān then returned to his capital city and planned to conquer Iznik.

> 'Osmān Bey considered its coquest one of the most important undertakings and without warning he marched toward that land". 'Os mān found a strong resistance but his men overran and laid waste the countryside outside the fortress, pillaging and killing as they moved. Before leaving the place, they built in the vicinity of Iznik a strong watch-tower and placed a garrison of a hundred men there, who kept provisions from reaching this large populous city. "The tower built by

[22] This addition to the Yakhshi Faḳīh's original history belongs to 'Āshıḳ Pşz., who tried to show that Shaykh Edebali of the *Wafāiyya* order was the spiritual mentor of the Ottoman dynasty; 'Āshıḳ Pşz. himself was of the same *ṭarīḳa* as his ancestors 'Āshiḳ Pasha and Elvān Chelebi were, see H. Inalcik, "How to Read 'Āshiḳ Paşa-zāde's History" see no.II in this volume.

'Osmān became known as Targay-Hisarı[23] after one of his brave and trusted men. The ruins of this tower are still visible.

Idrīs finds the rationale for this great plan in ‘Osmān's beilef in his mission revealed in an extraordinary dream ‘Osmān experienced while sleeping in Shaykh Ede-Bali's convent: "The divine promise will become in the end a reality through such exploits for Islam".

Kemāl Pasha-zāde[24] puts the battle of Yalak-Ovası before the conquest of Köprü-Hisar and the siege of Iznik, and "‘Osmān's succession to the sultanate of the Seldjuks" after the battle. While Kemāl Pşz. evidently follows Neshrī ("the messenger via the lake" in both) in the description of the events preceding the battle and of the battle itself, he diverges from it on "‘Os mān's succession to Sultanate" and follows Rūhī or the Bodleian Anonymous chronicle.[25]

The story of the battle is missing in ‘Āşıḳ Pşz. He merely makes a very brief reference to the raid and siege of Iznik and the blockade.[26]

I Siege of Nicaea

In the following, versions of the original tradition of Yakhshi Faḳīh as we find in later compilations will be compared and discussed.

1 *A son was born to ‘Osmān; he named him ‘Alā’ al-Dīn and kept him at his side.*

Anon. and Aşpz. appear to be the most faithful to the original text.

Actually this statement is designed to tell us that the elder son, Orkhan, was given the command of the raids. Orkhan was the elder son of ‘Osmān beg. It was a Turco-Mongol steppe tradition to keep the youngest son at the hearth and to send the eldest to the most advanced frontier for raids.[27] This

---

23 A close examination of his text shows that he misread Ṭāz-‘Alī as Ṭargay; the correct form is Dirāz-‘Alī which is shortened to Ṭāz-‘Alī in the chronicles, see below.

24 *Tevârikh-i Âl-i 'Osmān,* II. Defter, ed. Ş. Turan, Ankara: Türk Tarih Kurumu 1983, 130-146.

25 On Rūhī and The Bodleian MS, see Ménage, Neshrī , 12-14, 26.

26 Atsız ed. 105: "Iznig'ün vilâyetine segirtdiler. Şehrün kapusını yapdurdılar. Bir nice gün ceng etdiler. Dört yanı vilâyet dapdılar. Kal’a üzerine er kodılar. Dapan vilâyeti timar erlerine verdiler; kendiler gene Yenişehir'e çıkdılar".

27 See H. Inalcik, "Ottoman succession and its Relation to the Turkish Concept of Sovereignty", in *The Middle East and the Balkans under the Ottoman Empire,* Bloomington, 1992, 37-69.

custom survived with all of the Turcoman emirates and continued with the Ottomans for a long time. Being in command of the frontier forces gave to the eldest son a greater chance of succeeding his father as ruler.

2 *Osman completed the conquest of Bilecük, Yar-Hisar, Inegöl and Yenişehir, and then he began to make raids into the province of Iznik.*

Neshrī here elaborates his source, telling us first 'Os̱mān's four earlier conquests and his following major feat of the siege of Iznik and adds that this led to his rise to the status of an "independent" *beg* (ruler) whereas in the original tradition (cf. Anon.) it was actually Orkhan that made the raid and captured Köprü-Hisar.

It is interesting to note that the same four places, Bilecük, Yar-Hisar, Inegöl and Yenişehir with the same sequence is to be found in the *Taḳvīms* which are Neshrī's source. One particular *Taḳvīm* dated ca. 1446, presents the conquest of Bilecik (or Bilecük) with the other three forts a turning point in Osman's creer.[28]

Actually these conquests in the years 699-702 H. appear to have constituted part of his plan to capture the two most important cities in Bithynia, Iznik and Bursa. Then, he moved his headquarters to Yenişehir situated in the middle of these two cities. There, he settled his ghāzīs and made it a new *udj* leading into Bursa plain in the west and that of Nicaea in the north. The latter city was only about 25 km. from Yenişehir. 'Os̱mān's ghāzīs in the new *udj,* the tradition says, "wanted to continue the raids all the time".

Before he attacked Nicaea 'Os̱mān organized raids in the valley of Göynük river and the Sakarya valley to take control of the main highway coming through Göynük-Taraklı-Lefke or Mekece to Iznik from the east. The highway Göynük-Taraklı to Lefke in the south or Geyve to the north remains still today the main thoroughfare from the inner Anatolian plateau to Iznik and Izmit.

3 *The raid against Iznik.*

In the Anon. Orkhan alone is responsible for the raid. It is to be remembered that the original tradition comes from Yakhshi Faḳīh , son of Orkhan's imam.

---

[28] *Tarihî Takvimler,* ed. O. Turan, Ankara, 1954, 16, 52.

4 *The conquest of Köprü-Hisar.*

Anon.: Orkhan conquered Köprü-Hisar by force and plundered.

Aşpz.: Orkhan and 'Osmān together conquered Köprü-Hisar and plundered.

Neshrī here omits the conquest of Köprü-Hisar. In a previous chapter he says (Menzel 32; Unat. 92) 'Osmān had aided the *Tekvur* of Bilecük in his capture of Köprü-Hisar. Perhaps Neshrī thought that when 'Osmān conquered Bilecük Köprü-Hisar, too, came into 'Osmān possession among the lands conquered. However, the original source asserts that Köprü-Hisar was conquered later in connection with the raids against Iznik.

Between Yenişehir and Iznik rose the Avdan mountain range and the passes over it was defended by Kızıl-Hisar and Köprü-Hisar fortresses. The Ottoman surveys, or *taḥrīr defteris* of Hüdāvendigār supply interesting details on them.

The passage concerning Köprü-Hisar in the survey of 1571 says: "Since the mountain pass called Dirāz-'Alī, situated on the public road coming from Iznik to the village named Köprü-Hisar is frightful, dangerous and uninhabited a report is formerly sent to the Porte asking to station there guards. "The aforesaid pass", the record continues, "is one *menzil,* or a day's march away from Iznik to Köprü-Hisar and it is extremely difficult to guard it if the guards are placed in the middle of the pass". It is proposed that half of the guards, thirty people, should be stationed in the Kızıl-Hisar fort in the middle of the pass to watch the road coming from the side of Iznik and the other half of the guards at Çamlıca to watch the road coming from Köprü-Hisar. The area was covered with forests. In 1571 sixty *yaya* militia were appointed guards with exemption from ordinary and customary taxes.[29]

It is of crucial importance for us to note that this document confirms the fact that the place-names and topography given in the narrative traditions such as the Anonymous chronicles can not be inventions or contrived legends but well-informed authentic sources. No contrived story could give such precise topographical details.

The note from the surveys establish the fact that in order to descend to the plain of Nicaea, 'Osmān's forces had first to get control of the Dirāz-'Alī mountain pass. Also known as Ṭirāz 'Alī or Dirāz-'Alī, a hero in our narrative sources, the man is obviously an historical figure who left his name in various place-names along the strategic road from Yenişehir to Iznik. The

[29] *Hüdâvendigâr Livası Tahrir Defterleri,* eds. Ö. L. Barkan and Enver Meriçli, Ankara: 1988, pp. 219-220; no. 366 and p. 225, no. 378/2, p. 274; today Dıraz Ali Köyü.

same survey (p. 225, no. 378/4) tells us that a winter pasture, or *kıshlak,* in the Kara-Dere village on the Avdan mountain is called Uzun-Oghlu (son of the tall one), most probably the son of our *Dirāz (tall* in Persian) 'Alī. The name of *Avdan* is found among Turcomans as that of a nomadic clan.

Later on, in the fifteenth century the *ketkhudā* of Isḥaḳ Pasha built a dervish convent at Köprü-Hisar to give shelter to the travelers, and he made *waḳf* of his freehold village called 'Isā-Vīrānı in the Inegöl district. According to a record in the same survey book, there was another mountain pass called *Katranlu-Derbendi* between the sea-landing *(iskele)* of Samanlu and Yenişehir, frequented by merchants. The villagers from Çardak, Sartı-Oğlu, Makri, Dimboz, and Menteşe were appointed guards at this pass. While Dirāz-'Alī-Derbendi led 'Os̱mān to the plain of Iznik the Dimboz-Koyun-Hisar mountain pass led 'Os̱mān into the Bursa plain. Following the battle of Bapheus a major confrontation would take place at this pass between 'Os̱mān and a coalition of the Tekvurs of the Bursa plain, namely, those of Bursa, Adranos, Batanos, Kestel and Kite and the victory would open to 'Os̱mān the entire plain of Bursa.

5 *The surrender of the "district of Marmara".*

Aşpz. refers to it.

In the Anon. and Neshrī missing.

The "Marmara vilāyeti" is the area between Yenişehir and Bursa just before the strategic pass of Dimboz, leading to the Bursa plain. There is a swamp called Marmaracık-Gölü there today. The Greeks of this area surrendered to 'Os̱mān to avoid the ghāzī attacks. As the Ottoman tradition puts it "they came and submitted, and 'Os̱mān Ghāzī left everyone on his land *(yerlü yerinde)".* This piece of information is omitted in Anon. and Neshrī perhaps because they believed it was not important. Among later compilers, Kemāl Pşz. (I, 143-144) and Idrīs (p. 66) mention the surrender of the population of Marmara. Idrīs provides further details referring to a "fortress of Marmara" and its surrender when its inhabitants saw the fate of Köprü-Hisar.

In any case, 'Os̱mān must have deemed it necessary to make a raid into the Marmara district obviously to safeguard his capital of Yenişehir before he set out for the siege of Iznik.

6 *The siege of Iznik, the construction of a watch-tower (havāle) to intercept the city's traffic with the outside world. The ghāzīs made raids and subdued the countryside around the fortress of Iznik.*

Anon., Aşpz. and Neshrī all have this information. While Aşpz. and Neshrī are laconic on the siege of Iznik and the subsequent raids in the plain, the Anon. gives deatils coupled with folk stories of Greek and Turkish origin about the ancient city of Iznik and the conversion to Islam of the population in the area. However, in essence, the three sources, using evidently the same source, agree with each other. Anon. and Aşpz. make clear that 'Osmān's forces laid siege to the city and fighting lasted quite some time. Our three chroniclers agree that by making a blockade and organizing raids in the countryside, the ghāzīs subdued the entire population outside the city walls.

The details which the Anon. transmitted are interesting. Firstly, Iznik is described as a populous and strongly-garrisoned city which was not true in that time period. As a result of the recovery of Constantinople from the Latins in 1261 and the subsequent increasing Turcoman raids, part of the Nicaea's inhabitants had already left for Nicomedia or Constantinople, and Michael VIII. Palaeologus reportedly neglected its defense. Ibn Baṭṭūṭa's eyewitness report (1332?) of the city as a ruined one belongs to a period when the Ottomans had taken control of the city (March 1331) and had permitted the inhabitants to leave. Anon.'s exaggerated statement evidently must be a reminiscence of the situation under the Lascarids. In any case, 'Osmān's failure at the siege needed explanation in the Ottoman account. Emphasis is also put on how the city's defense was enhanced by the surrounding waters and swamps.

In the first part of the tradition, the Anon. admitted that the city could not be taken by storm ("Gördüler kim cenk ile alınmaz.") so that 'Osmān built the Ṭāz-'Alī, rather Dirāz-'Alī, fort to keep the place under siege. But in the paragraph concerning the aftermath of the victory over the emperor's troops at Yalak-Ovası (Bapheus) the Anon. claims that the Nicaeans surrendered the city to the Ottomans. The author of the Anon. might have thought that the logical outcome of the victory should be the fall of the city so that he changed the original source at this point. In any case, Aşpz. and Neshrī, following the original text literally stated that 'Osmān's men gave up the fight against the fortress of Nicaea and concerned themselves with subjecting the population in the open country around the fortress.

The story about the erection of the *havāle,* or the fort for the blockade, is related only in Anon. Aşpz. does not mention it; Neshrī refers to the blockade without mentioning the fort. Later compilers, Idrīs (67) and Kemāl Pşz. (145), obviously following Anon., mention it.

Always by following the Anon., which appear to have reproduced the original source in a most detailed fashion, we find that under Ṭāz-ʿAlī the men in the fort, numbered one hundered but in some copies of the Anon. it is changed to forty, a sacred figure. The watch-tower intercepted the traffic to the city coming from the outside so that famine resulted. The Anon. asserts that this situation lasted for quite sometime ("bir nice zaman"). Thus, the date of the actual siege might have taken place one or two years before the battle of Bapheus, between 1299-1301. The main cause leading to the battle of Yalak-Ovası is attributed, in the original tradition, to the fact that Iznik, under blockade, distressed by famine, finally succeeded to send a messenger to the Emperor in Istanbul stating that if the relief forces do not arrive in time they have no choice but surrender.

Neshrī adds that the messenger was sent *over the lake* (compare Pachymeres). In order to explain why the people of Iznik asked for help from Istanbul, the Anon. adds that "at that time the Tekvur of Istanbul ruled over Iznik, too."

II The Battle of Bapheus

Now, the question remains to determine whether or not the Ottoman account of the battle of Yalak-ovası and Pachymeres' account of the battle of Bapheus refer to the same event. Let us review comparatively the main points in the two sources.

1 *The circumstances and causes leading to the battle*

According to Pachymeres ʿO̱smān's threat to the land of "Halizonoi" made the Emperor decide to send an army under Heteriarch Mouzalon. As seen earlier Pachymeres stops at this point and goes back to earlier events connected with ʿO̱smān. He then tells us how "a group of 'O̱smān's men numbering about one hundred made a surprise attack on Mouzalon and almost captured him". This emboldened ʿO̱smān, Pachymeres adds, to cross "Siphonas Mountains" and to descend on the "Lând of Halizonoi".

The Ottoman account of the battle does not speak of this vanguard activity but concentrates on the battle of the Yalak-ovası on the shore. However, both Pachymeres and the Ottoman chronicles refer to ʿO̱smān's earlier activities around Nicaea, the latter source giving full details about the siege of the city and the urgent appeal of the besieged to the Emperor. It becoms clear that Emperor sent Mouzalon to relieve Nicaea from the blockade. The "Land of Halizonoi" is obviously the Ottoman Yalak-ovası, the flat coastal plain between Yalova and Kara-Mürsel.

Pachymeres clearly said that 'Osmān sent his vanguard before he set out to pass through the valley leading to the coast (for the valley and the highway *infra).* In the valley there is a fort called today Çaban-Kale (Shepherd's Fort) (see Photo 3 and 4), a few kilometers from the coast, controlling the highway Dil-Hersek-Iznik.

'Osmān sent the vanguard to make sure that the garrison in the fort, apparently reinforced by Mouzalon's men, would be neutralized to open his way to the plain on the Gulf of Izmit. The surprise attack by his vanguard must have taken place near the fort surrounded by hills. In fact, Pachymeres talks about the hills where 'Osmān's men, at first repelled by Mouzalon's soldiery, retreated and then made a successful counter-attack. The success made 'Osmān decide to pass through the valley to reach the Yalak-Ovası on the coast.

Çoban-Kale is situated between the village of Karadere and that of *Ayazma* where there is a Greek *Hagïasma.* Local people say the fort was built by the Genoese. Çaban-Kale is in ruins today, shepherds come there with their herds to rest, thence its name Çoban-Kale. Koyun-Hisarı, as referred to in the Ottoman tradition in this connection must have been our Çoban-Kale (see infra).

It is suggested that the skirmish must have occured one year prior to the battle of Bapheus.[30] If this is correct Muzalon must have been at the fort prior to his coming back with a sizeable army to confront Osman's invasion, the following year. In fact, subsequent to the vanguard's success 'Osmān's mustering a large army by calling on his allies, to which Pachymeres refers, would take some time.

In any case these are the principal antecedents and causes which appear to have led to the major confrontation on the plain of Yalak-Ovası in 1301 (for the date *infra).* On the whole, both the Byzantine and Ottoman accounts agree and complement each other on the background of the battle of Bapheus.

2 *The location of the Battle-Field*

Pachymeres tells us that 'Osmān, crossing the mountain pass with "allies and partners for his raids" entered the "Land of Halizonoi". He adds that Bapheus is in "the area around the wonderful city of Nicomedia" and Byzantine troops when defeated "swarmed ignobly into the nearby city of Nicomedia". The Ottoman tradition identifies the battle-field as Yalak-Ovası or Yalak-Plain on the sea coast. Thus, both of our sources agree that the

---

30 Arnakis, *op. cit.* p. 129-131.

battle took place on the coastal plain on the south shores of the Gulf of Izmit (Nicomedia) in a place where the highway coming from Nicaea reached the coastal plain.

During the Byzantine times the imperial "Military Road" passing through Dakibyza (Gebze), reached Aigialoi "where they crossed the narrow entrance of the gulf of Astakos to Kibotos and continued their journey by land to Nikaia".[31] The ferry from Aigialoi to Kibotos was in use under the Byzantines as well as under the Ottomans. Aigialoi must be the *Dil* (the *tongue* or promontory) of the Ottomans, and Kibotos, the Hersek Town (see Photo 2). During the Ottoman times this main highway between Istanbul and Asia Minor was known as the "Baghdad Caddesi" through which passed caravans and armies (see Photo 5 and 6). At the Hersek Town, under Bāyezīd II, grand vizier Hersek Ahmed Pasha built a *waḳf* complex with a caravanserai, mosque, fountains and other facilities for the confort of the travellers before they started their long trip through the Yalak-Dere valley and Nicaea into Asia Minor. About twenty five km. to the west of the Hersek Town lies Helenopolis (the vulgar pronounciation Eleinopolis) or Turkish Yalova. Yalak-Hisar mentioned in the Ottoman tradition must be Helenopolis. Turkish name of Yalova must rather derive from Yalak-Ova(sı).

Farther west between Helenopolis and the promontory Poseidion lies Pylai which was also used as a landing place by the Byzantine emperors on their way to Asia Minor. The city of Pylai was still an important commercial center in the thirteenth century. In order to protect the city Manuel I Comnenus (1143-1180) built the fortress of Pylai and forts.[32] Our Çoban-Kale or Koyun-Hisarı in the valley leading to the coastal plain must have been one of these newly built or repaired forts.

When Orkhan resumed his father's plans of expansion on the Yalak-Ova coast following the conquest of Nicaea (1331) the fortress of Yalak-Ova (Yalova) and Koyun-Hisar in the area put up resistance until Nicomedia surrendered (1337).

According to the Ottoman tradition, by 1337 fortresses of Yalak-Ova and Koyun-Hisarı formed the appanage of a Byzantine princess. The fortresses are described exactly as follows: "the fortress in the valley *(deredeki)* in the

---

[31] W. Ramsay, *The Historical Geography of Asia Minor,* London 1890, reprint 1962, 200-201; cf. Evliya Çelebi, *Seyāhatnāme,* II, 60-61; F. Taeschner, *Das Anatolische Wegenetz nach Osmanischen Quellen,* Leipzig: Mayer and Müller 1924, 66-67, 99-100.

[32] H. Glykatzi-Ahrweiler, "Les fortresses construites en Asia Mineure face à l'invasion seldjoucide", *Akten des XI. Internationalen Byzantinisten Kongresses,* München 1958, eds. F. Dölger and H. -G. Beck, Munich 1960, 186-189; Vryonis, *op. cit.,* 116.

Yalak-Ova belonged to an infidel by the name of Yalknya (or Balknya), and on the hill there was another fort which they call Koyun-Hisarı at the present time". Yalak-Ova was the name given to the area between Yalova and Hersek or Kara-Mürsel. Ottoman tradition adds that Koyun-Hisarı was put under the command of Kaloyan, brother of the "master" *(sāḥib)* of Yalak-Ova, Yalknya.

Joseph von Hammer correctly identifies Bapheus with Koyun-Hisarı[33] but confuses it with another Koyun-Hisarı ner Dimboz where 'Osmān confronted the coalition of the tekvurs of the Bursa plain. Just before the battle of Bapheus 'Osmān had captured a man from Yalak-Hisarı and learned from him that his ambush at the Yalak-Ova was not known to the enemy.

The Koyun-Hisarı village in the Kite cadiship had its *karye* (village) status in the 16th century and then mentioned in the following survey registers as a simple *mezra'a,* or an abandoned village. Apparently, it was a gathering point of the sheep herds the tax revenue of which was levied by the *Koyun-emini.* In this period the yürüks, mostly Akça-Koyunlu, are mentioned in the area.

3 *The Armies and the Battle*

Let us first attempt to analyze Pachymeres' account of the battle.

Mouzalon's army consisted of the Byzantine soldiery, the Alan mercenaries and the local militia, altogether about two thousand men. But this army lacked unity because, Pachymeres tells us, just before the battle the money and horses belonging to the militia were given to the Alan mercenaries, which made them jealous and reluctant to cooperate.

As regards 'Osmān's troops they, Pachymeres says, largely outnumbered the Greeks because he attracted allies, and even men from Paphlagonia who, for booty, joined him enthusiasticaly. Pachymeres tells us they included footmen as well as horsemen.

Because of the non-cooperation, Pachymeres asserts, of the local militia and of the troops' carelessness, the Greek army's attack collapsed and they began to run away. Many fell, but most fled. They swarmed into the nearby city of Nicomedia. At this critical point, the Alans courageously counter-attacked giving the great mass of infantry the chance to retreat. Encircling the Ottoman troops, the Alans attacked soldiers on foot and wounded the horses of the cavalry by sending salves of arrows crosswise. Thus, in order to secure, Pachymeres adds, the retreat of the Greeks, the Alans sacrificed themselves and fell one after another.

---

33 Joseph von Hammer, *Geschichte des Osmanischen Reiches,* Pest 1935, I. 67, 85.

In brief, in his attempt to explain the Greek failure, Pachymeres underlines the superiority of 'Os̱mān's troops in number, the non-cooperation of the local militia on the battlefield and the lack of discipline among the Byzantine soldiery. The Alan mercenaries coming from the northern Black Sea area where they had served under Emir Nogay (d. 1299 or 1300) and trained in the Turco-Mongol steppe tactics proved that they were a match for the Turcoman fighters.

The victory at Bapheus signalled the approaching uninterrupted Ottoman successes against the Byzantium or the Balkan states in the following decades. The explantion of it is that in addition to the superiority in tactics the Ottoman rulers received from Anatolia innumerable ghāzīs, or professional Turcoman soldiers who later on under Orkhan would be organazed as Yaya troops. Turcoman ghāzīs rushed to fight under Ottoman flag just for the anticipated booty, while the Byzantine and Balkan rulers had to enroll and maintain professional soldiery including *Turcopouloi* by paying huge sums from their dilapidated treasuries. The advantageous position of the Turcoman begs was obvious, and from the beginning Byzantium was doomed to loose its desperate struggle. Andronicus II's dismantling the expensive and ineffecient Byzantine navy in 1284 made perfect sense because what was then desperately needed was the mercenary troops in order to stop the Turcoman onslaught in Anatolia.

In 1354, in his speech of abdication John VI Cantacuzenus confessed the invincibility of Turkish soldiery. Believing in the professional military superiority of the Turcoman, he himself stuck during all his career to his alliance with Umur Ghāzī of Aydın, and then Orkhan since they brought to his aid Turcoman troops against his rivals while his enemies in Constantinople failed to attract this decisive element to their own side.[34]

Ottoman chronicles give a different version on the course of the combat. According to this source the Emperor sent a relief army by sea for Nicaea which arrived at Yalak-ovası and began to land to make a surprise attack on 'Os̱mān's troops. But informed through a Greek spy of the enemy's plan, 'Os̱mān laid in ambush. Neshrī's verison includes the interesting detail that the Byzantine army began to pass from Dil[35] to Yalak-ovası during the night. The Ottoman forces made a surprise attack as the Byzantine troops began to

[34] See H. Inalcik, "The Rise of the Turcoman Maritime Principalities, Byzantium and Crusades", *Byzantinische Forschungen,* IX.

[35] The streams from the Iznik-Hersek valley in the south and the Dil-Ovası valley from the north of the Izmit bay made tonguelike deltas on both sides, narrowing the sea passage at this point; both deltas are called *Dil;* the southern *Dil* is also called Hersek-Dili (see Photo 1 and 2).

take their horses out of the ships, and thus being scattered around and caught by surprise many Byzantines were massacred and of those attempting to reach their ships were drowned. Those who could escape to the ships sailed back to Constantinople.

In this story what is definite is that 'Osmān fought against an army "sent by the Tekvur of Istanbul"; so there is no doubt that both Greek and Ottoman sources speak of the same event. But how to explain or combine the divergent descriptions of the battle in the Byzantine and Ottoman accounts.

Pachymeres contains no details on how the army under Mouzalon arrived at Bapheus/Yalak-Ovası whether directly by sea or by the land route Gebze-Dil-Bapheus. In his entire account there is no reference to ships. However, according to him prior to confrontation Mouzalon had been long enough in the area to organize his troops (taking the horses of the local militia and giving to the Alan mercenaries, etc.).

For a surprise attack, the Emperor must have sent the main troops by sea rather than the long land route. But, even if the land route was used, the troops had to pass over the narrow sea passage from Aigialoi (Dil) to Kibotos (Hersek) on ships as Neshrī's version confirms. An Ottoman surprise attack near Kibotos is in order in either case or, the Byzantine troops from Constantinople arrived partly by land and partly by sea. As for the course of the battle the only theory to reconcile the two divergent reports is that each deals with a different stage of the confrontation. Apparently, first the Ottomans attacked the Byzantine soldiery arriving on ships from Constantinople, and when the Byzantine local militia took in panic the route to Nicomedia, the Byzantine regular troops rushed under the cover of Alans back to their ships waiting on the shore. The Ottoman tradition possibly preferred to concentrate on this dramatic flight to the ships of the main Byzantine soldiery and made it the main theme of the battle.

4 *The Date of the Battle of Bapheus*

Since Muralt's "Essai" Byzantinists have discussed the date of the battle. Most of them agree on 27 July 1301 and thus have rejected the date 27 June 1302 accepted by Muralt.[36]

Pachymeres mentions 'Osmān and the battle of Bapheus in the context of the retreat of the Co-emperor Michael IX from Magnesia to Kyzikos and finally to Pegai (Kara-Biga on the Marmara shore) in the year 1302. On the

---

36 Muralt, *Essai,* 479, No. 12; cf. Hasluck, "Bytinica", *Ann. Br. School at Athens,* XIII (1906-1907).

other hand, the Catalan expedition to western Anatolia, which took place in 1303-1304, is related in Pachymeres to the account on 'Os̱mān's attack.

By discussing, on the basis of the contemporary sources Pachymeres and Philes, Andronikos II's military and diplomatic activities in the period 1296-1299, F. Tinnefeld suggests that in 1298 Emperor sent a military expedition against "the barbarians in Bithynia" (referred to by Philes).[37] The Byzantine failure at this expedition marked the beginning of the successful expansion of Ottomans in the region. Lastly, P. Schreiner discusses the dates 1301 and 1302, comparing Pachymeres with the notices in the Byzantine short chronicles.[38] He suggests that the year 1304 may also be considered for the battle of Bapheus since in that particular year our sources speak of a general assault of the Turks in western Anatolia and of the flight in mass of the Greek population toward fortified places including Constantinople.

As for the Ottoman tradition on the date of the Yalak-ovası battle this is placed immediately before the battle of Dimboz against the *Tekvurs'* coalition in the Bursa region on the Hegira year of 702 which starts on 26 August 1302. So, the battle of Bapheus must have taken place in the previous year, in the summer of 1301.

In conclusion, with the siege of Nicaea and his victory over the emperor's relief army 'Os̱mān won an incomparable fame and charisma among the frontier Turcomans and leaders, securing him and his offspring an enduring legitimation for primacy and sovereignty. Neshrī and other compilers around 1500 were right in associating his beg-ship or "independence" to the event. The contemporary Byzantine historian Pachymeres mentioned 'Os̱mān after his victory as one of the most energetic Turcoman emirs, threatening Byzantium.

The compilations arranged at Bāyazīd II's request by Idrīs and Kemāl Pşz. after his accession to the throne put 'Os̱mān's rise to sultanate or to empire as the successor to "the Seldjukid Sultan of Konya" or "the *Ḳayṣer* (Ceasar) of Constantinople" upon his victory over the Byzantine Emperor's army. Thus, at a time when Mehmed the Conqueror's claim to universal empire had become a dynastic assertion to primacy among the states to the East and to the west, the Ottomans used 'Os̱mān's victory at Bapheus as the dynasty's legitimation to imperial sovereignty already in the time of the dynasty's founder.

---

[37] F. Tinnefeld, "Pachymeres und Philes als Zeugen für ein frühes unternehmen gegen die Osmanen", *BZ*, 6 (1971), 51.

[38] Peter Schreiner, *Die byzantinischen Kleinchroniken,* 3. Teil: *Teilübersetzungen, Addenda et Corrigenda, Indices,* Wien: Akademie der Wissenschaften, 1979, 217-219.

The eleborate formula and apparatus added by the later compilers to the original candid story of the humble origin of the dynasty should not be an excuse for the historian to dismiss both the early folk traditions and the later elite elaborations. Such later additions as the divine revelation of the imperial power through the dream and its interpretation by a shaman-like holy man, or the Seldjukid sultan's recognition of the exalted lineage of 'Oṣmān are, in fact, extremely interesting and meaningful for the historian. Also it is equally misleading to dismiss as pure myth and legend the early Ottoman traditions altogether because of these later elaborations.

For legitimation to the empire some of the compilers did not find strong enough even the Seldjukid Sultan's recognition of 'Oṣmān as his successor, and had recourse to the "right of sword", or victory, as a sign of divine *ta'yīd* (support) and consider him 'mu'ayyad min 'indillāh', 'sovereign by God's support'.

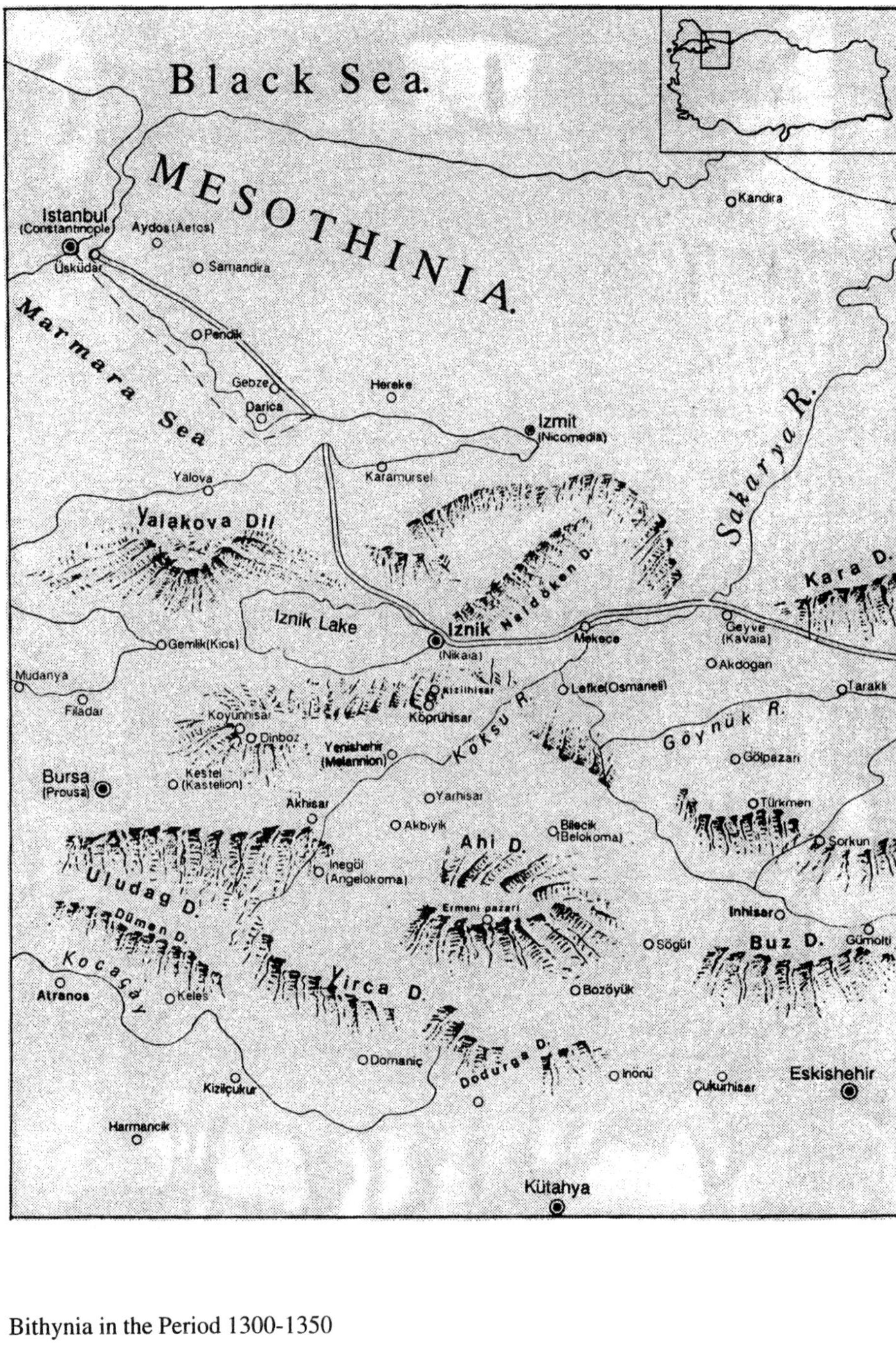

Bithynia in the Period 1300-1350

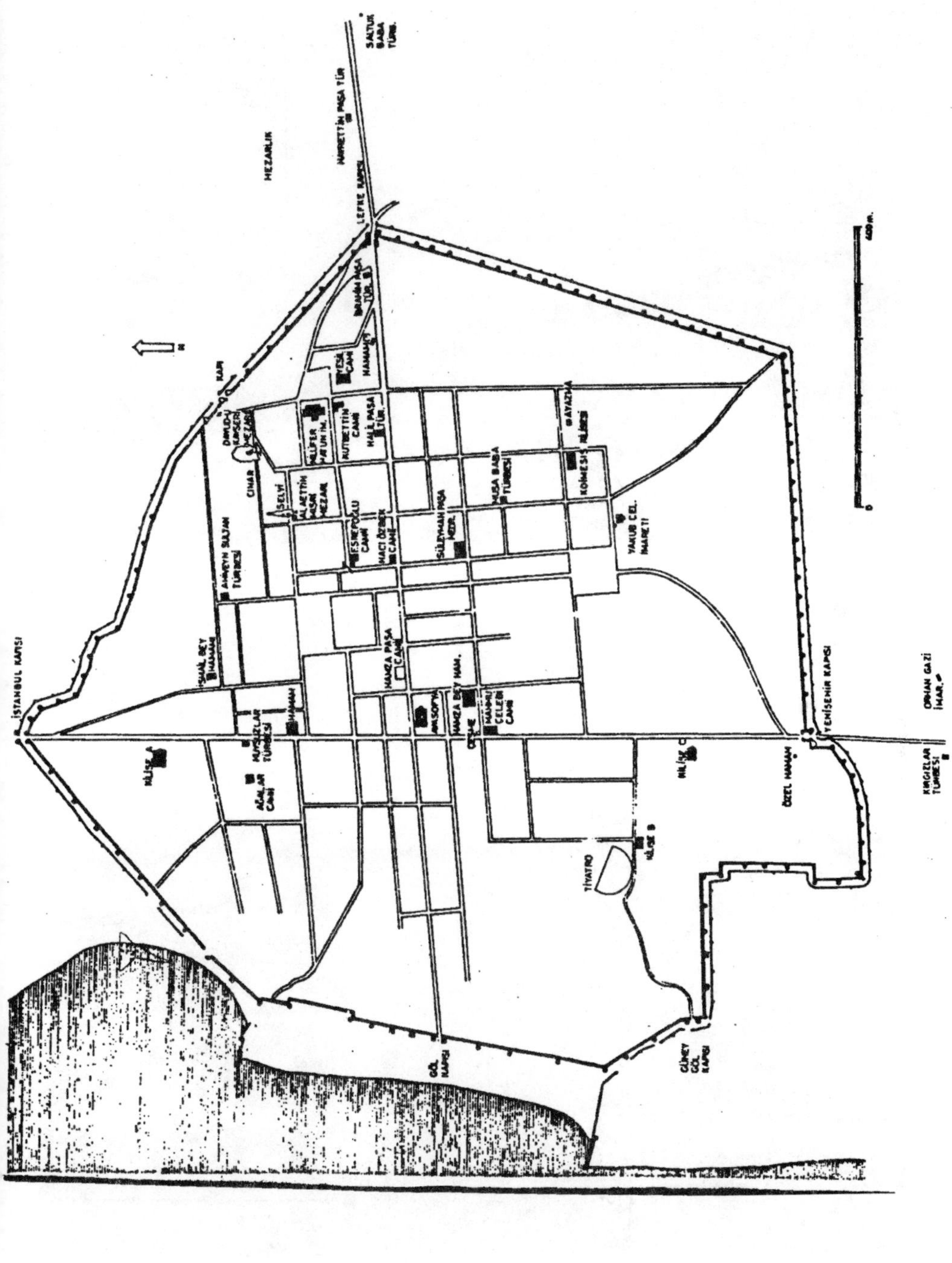

City of Iznik plan. (Professor Semavi Eyice).

Photo 1. The Dil (Tongue) of Hersek.

Photo 2. The Plain of Hersek (Yalak-Ova).

Photo 3. The Fortress of Bapheus (Koyun-Hisarı).

Photo 4. The Fortress of Bapheus from Distance.

Photo 5. The Imperial Highway (Baghdad Caddesi) from Yalak-Ovası to Nicaea.

Photo 6. The Ottoman Bridge on the Yalak River.

2

Mehmed The Conqueror (1432-1481) and His Time

Mehmed The Conqueror (1432-1481) and His Time

On the occasion of the five-hundredth anniversary of the conquest of Constantinople by the Ottoman Turks there appeared a number of publications on the last days of Byzantium and on the rising empire of the Ottomans (A bibliography of the publications in western languages can be found in the 1950-1956 issues of *Byzantinische Zeitschrift;* Turkish publications are listed in *İstanbul Enstitüsü Dergisi,* 1955-1956). Foremost among all these new publications is the work of Professor Fr. Babinger, the well-known German orientalist.[1] His work deserves special attention because of its scope and the great variety of sources and studies utilized. One reason we have not had a detailed review of the book until now is probably that the author promised in his prefce to publish a second volume with the source material and bibliography on the subject. But I believe it is not too difficult for a student of the period to find out which sources are used in it and which are not.

Professor Babinger has clearly used the best known sources, such as Ducas, Sphrantzes, Chalcocondyles, Critovoulos, G.-M. Angielello, and the collections of documents from the archives in Ragusa, Venice and the Vatican, as well as the classic works by Jireček, Kretschmayr, Von Pastor, Zinkeisen, and Jorga. But it is not easy to explain why he completely overlooked some of the most essential contemporary Ottoman sources of the period, available in printed form for a long time, which he himself described in his book on the Ottoman soruces, *Geschichtsschreiber der Osmanen und ihre Werke* (Leipzig, 1927). These particular sources could have saved him from various mistakes. I shall try to review the book with the help of these sources and also add some new data from the archive material to support them.

---

[1] Franz Babinger, *Mehmed der Eroberer und seine Zeit, Weltenstürmer einer Zeitenwende,* Munich: F. Bruckmann, 1958, xiv, 592; — *Mahomet II le Conquérant et son temps (1432-1481), La Grande Peur du Monde au tournant de l'histoire;* trad. H. E. del Medico, revue par l'auteur, Paris: Payot, 1954, 636 pp; — *Maometto il Conquistatore e il suo tempo,* Turin, Italy, 1957.

Let us first examine the Ottoman sources which were available but insufficiently or not at all used by the author. The most important ones are Tursun Beg's *Târîkh-i Abû'l-Fath* (published in *TOEM* in 1921), Enverî's *Düstûrnâme* (ed. M. Halil Yinanc, Istanbul, 1928); and Kemâl Pasha-zâde's (hereafter Kemâl Pşz.) *Tawârîkh-i Âl-i 'Os̱mān* (facsimile edition of the manuscript in *Fâtih Kütüphanesi,* No. 4205, by Dr. Ş. Turan, Ankara, 1954).[2] Tursun's work has a particular interest. A member of a very influential family (his uncle was governor of Bursa) and an expert in state finances, Tursun served first as government surveyor in Constantinople, and then as a secretary in the office of the grand vizier Mahmud. Later he was a commissioner of land and population surveys in Anatolia and finally he was made a *defterdâr.* Based exclusively on his personal experience, his work is a first hand source for Mehmed's reign. His position gave him access to valuable information about military as well as financial matters. His story of the siege of Constantinople is the most detailed Turkish account by a contemporary Ottoman. Tursun says explicitly that he accompanied the grand vizier Mahmud on his expeditions in Serbia (1458), Trebizond (1461), and Bosnia (1463 and 1464). As a secretary in Mahmud's service he wrote the surrender ultimatum to the ruler of Kastamonu in 1461, and he was sent by Mahmud to inform the Sultan of the success against the Venetians in the Morea in 1463. He also accompanied Mahmud Pasha in his expedition against the Venetians in Midilli (Mitylene) in 1462. Tursun's account especially of the military operations in Serbia and Bosnia in 1458-1464 includes many interesting details not found in other sources. Being in the service of this statesman for years, Tursun is the only source giving interesting information about rivalries among the high dignitaries. Writing his history after the death of Mehmed II, whose policies were sharply rejected by his successor, Tursun could feel free to be critical when dealing with Mehmed's measures. Tursun's important book was not used widely by later Ottoman historians. Kemâl Pşz. skilfully combined Tursun's account with Neshrî's well-known work and with anonymous chronicles as well as with oral traditions from reliable persons. The latter included his own father, a vizier of Mehmed II, and the officials and soldiers who took part in the Sultan's expeditions (e.g., he records an interesting narrative of the conquest of Otranto in Italy by a soldier who took part in the operation). Kemâl Pşz.'s work, recently published and known to Babinger by title (see *GOW,* 61-63),

2 Hereafter abbreviated as Tursun, Enveri, and Kemâl Pşz., respectively. Due to the different forms in the old and new script Turkish forms of names have not been reproduced here consistently. Modern Turkish undotted *ı* is reproduced here as i. The specialist in the field should have no difficulty in recognizing the proper nouns.

is undoubtedly the most important Ottoman history written on the reign of Mehmed II.

Another great compilation is Idrîs-i Bidlîsî's *Hasht Bihisht,* written on Bayezid's order. Although mostly dependent on Neshrî, the anonymous chronicles, and Rûhî (or, more probably, a source Rûhî used), it gives some original accounts, especially of events in Anatolia. *Hasht Bihisht* gives a detailed description of Mehmed's army and administration in a long separate chapter unique among the contemporary sources. Sa'deddîn utilized Idrîs, Neshrî, and the anonymous chronicles as his main sources in his *Tâj at-Tawârîkh.* This was translated into Italian by V. Bratutti and has been considered a standard Ottoman source in the West, but –apart from the fact that he did not use Tursun, Kemâl Pşz. and Enverî– his compilation must always be checked with his original sources.

Enverî's *Düstûrnâme* (see I. Mélikoff-Sayar, *Le destān d'Umur Pacha* [Paris, 1954], pp. 23-42) is also dedicated to Mahmud Pasha and in its last chapters, dealing with the reign of Mehmed II, Enverî records information of certain events to which he was an eye-witness and which are to be found in no other source.

Rûhî's work (see J. H. Mordtmann, *MOG,* II, 129) is also of great importance for the reign of Mehmed II because it reproduces an unknown independent source with chronological data which are often accurate. It is utilized by Neshrî, Idrîs, and Kemâl Pşz. We have also the official calendars called *Taḳvîm-i Hümâyûn* of the middle of the fifteenth century, arranged for the Sultan's use, which contain chronologies of the important bygone events (see my *Fâtih Devri* [Ankara, 1954], p. 23).

Taking as a basis 'Āshıḳ Pşz.'s fundamental compilation of Ottoman history in the first two centruries Neshrî interpolated into it Rûhî's chronicle and the data from the *Taḳvîms*. His interpolations made 'Āshıḳ's already confused chronology even more confused. Kemâl Pşz.seems to know Rûhî only through Neshrî's compilation (cf. volume I of Fr. Taeschner's edition, Leipzig, 1951).

My intention here is not to describe all the Ottoman sources of this period[3] but to show the relative importance of the basic ones which were overlooked by Babinger in his book.

---

[3] For example, the works composed in verse and dedicated to the Sultan by Kâshifî and Mu'âlî may be mentioned here in addition to the works which Babinger included in his *GOW.* These sources occasionally give quite important information missing in other sources (see *Fâtih Devri,* p. 107), but they have never been systematically utilized. Ḳıvâmî's work, discovered and edited by Babinger (Istanbul, 1955) can be classified among such works.

Babinger's chief Ottoman sources are Neshrî, Sa'deddîn, Uruj, and the anonymous chronicles. He has not utilized, as it appears, Tursun, Enverî, Kemâl Pşz. Rûhî and Idrîs. The first two were completely unknown to the chronicles which Babinger used.

The works of Ashık, Neshrî, Rûhî, Idrîs, and Kemâl Pşz. are all general histories of the Ottoman house written in the reign of the Bayezid II. When Bayezid came to the throne, after a widespread social and political reaction, he wanted to present himself as a promoter of a new era and ordered the scholars of his time to make a general account of the Ottoman dynasty before his accession. This comes out clearly from the prefaces which Rûhî, Kemâl Pşz., and Idrîs put in their works. In them the reaction to Mehmed's policies can be seen in many details, especially in financial matters and in the rehabilitation of the Chandarlı family.

A determining factor in all the major political developments of Ottoman history between 1444 and 1453 was the struggle for supreme power between Chandarlı Khalîl Pasha, the all powerful grand vizier since 1436 or 1437, and a group of ambitious military leaders including Shihâbeddîn Shâhin, Zaganos, and Turakhan, who were seeking to seize the control of the government by claiming to be protectors of the young Sultan's rights (he was only twelve in 1444). By repudiating Chandarlı's peace policy they became responsible for Mehmed's aggressive expansionist policy from the outset and revived the idea of the conquest of Constantinople. By this policy they hoped to secure their own authority as well as the young Sultan's. Having failed in 1446, when Chandarlı managed to bring back Murad II to the throne, they finally gained the upper hand after Mehmed's restoration in 1451, and caused Chandarlı's dismissal and execution immediately after the conquest of Constantinople in 1453. Babinger relates the popular stories about Chandarlı's so-called cooperation with the enemy but does not look for the real source and meaning of it. Such rumors were obviously serving the purpose of his opponents. In the formtion of Mehmed's personality and imperialistic policy the influence of Shâhin and especially of Zaganos can not be overestimated.

Babinger is justified in giving considerable space to the struggle between Hungary and the Ottomans for control of the lower Danube from Belgrade to Chilia. This actually appears to have determined not only the future of this region but also that of Byzantium. Wallachia's position in this rivalry is not clearly depicted by Babinger. Culminating in the years 1443-1448, the Ottoman-Hungarian struggle involved Wallachia vitally during this entire period. We know that Chandarlı's diplomacy and the victory at Varna in 1444 had secured at least the neutrality of the Serbian Despot; but Wallachia, always under Hungarian influence, continued to be a constant threat to the

Ottomans. In the spring of 1446 the defeat of Dâvûd Beg by Vlad I, who had seized Giurgiu from the Ottomans the preceding winter, appears to have been considered as a most serious event in Adrianople. It was after the Ottoman victory over the Hungarians at Kossova in 1448 that the Ottomans recaptured Giurgiu (Yerkögü) on the left side of the Danube and put Vlad II on the throne as a loyal vassal (see *Fâtih Devri,* p. 98). This meant for the Ottomans a further step for the control of the lower Danube.

Mehmed's wedding with Sitt-Khâtûn was the subject of considerable research by Babinger; (see his long article, "Mehmed's II. Heirat mit Sitt-Chatun, 1449", *Der Islam,* XXIX, 2, 1949). The exact date of this wedding ceremony is given by Enverî *(Düstûrnâme,* p. 93) as Shawwâl-Dhulka'de, 854 of the Hijra (the winter of 1450-1451), which is in agreement with Ducas, Chalcocondyles, and the Ottoman Anonymous Chronicles. Also overlooked by Babinger was Tursun's account of the conquest of Constantinople.

Tursun is in complete agreement with Western and Greek sources when he describes the reaction of the Ottoman army to the naval failure on 20 April 1453, the effect of the division between the Greek and Latin defenders during the siege, the panic resulting from the retreat of the wounded Giustiniani, and the decisive role of the Ottoman artillery in the conquest. The conflicting views of Chandarlı and his opponents resulted in dramatic collisions twice during the siege, once after the naval failure on 20 April 1453 and then on 26 May when the rumors of a Western military intervention spread amognst the army. The second crisis made the Sultan decide on a general attack, which resulted in the conquest. Here is a partial translation of a letter of Shaykh Aḳ-Shemseddîn to the Sultan (the original is in the Topkapı-Sarayı Museum, No. 5584; see also my *Fâtih Devri,* p. 217), testifying to the difficult situation in the Ottoman camp after 20 April: "This failure on the part of the navy caused a lot of disappointment and sorrow; there seemed to have been an opportunity the loss of which created a new activity. In the first place the religious one: the Christians rejoiced and made fuss; in the second place people in our camp ascribed this to your misjudgment and lack of authority... Under these circumstances you have to make proper inquiris on this dissension and neglect, and punish severely those who were responsible for it, lest, they commit the same neglect when the time comes to attack the walls and to fill the trenches". Even before the discovery of this document, this critical moment was emphasized by Tursun: "This event [naval failure] caused despair and disorder in the ranks of the Muslims... the army was split into groups" (see *Fâtih Devri,* p. 127).

From Babinger's book one gets a confused picture of Mehmed II's activities between the conquest of Constantinople and his expedition into

Serbia in the spring of 1454. To discuss these chronological problems let me start by what Babinger says about Chandarlı's execution: "The third day after the conquest Chandarlı was imprisoned and the fortieth day after his arrest, that is, 10 July 1453, he was executed in Adrianople, where he had been transferred" (German edition, p. 108; but the French edition, p. 128, has 10 June). We read in Uruj's chronicle: "Khalîl Pasha was executed forty days after the conquest of Enos" (Babinger's edition [Hanover, 1925], pp. 66-67). From various sources (Ducas and Critovoulos) we know that Enos was conquered toward the end of January 1456. Now was the execution of Chanderlı so long delayad, or do we have to put the name of Constantinople instead of Enos (Enez) in Uruj's sentence, as Babinger seems to do? The apparent contradiction comes from the confusion in Uruj of the actual conquest of Enos in 1456 with its earlier submission in the summer of 1453. More explicit on this point, an anonymous Ottoman chronicle (Manuscript in Topkapı Sarayı, Revan Köşk., No. 1099) reads: "After the conquest of Constantinople Sultan Mehmed was about to send forces against İnez. When the *tekvour* (lord) of the fortress learned this he immediately sent to the threshold of the Sultan the keys, thus surrendering it and submitting to the Sultan". Critovoulos, who was directly concerned in the affair, informs us that when, after the conquest of Constantinople in 1453, the Sultan returned to Adrianople in "the harvest time" he received there a delegation from the islands under the Gattilusi and entrusted Imbros to Palamedes, lord of Enos. Critovoulos begins the next chapter: "During the same period the Sultan arrested Khalîl, one of his first rank men and very powerful and put him in prison. And after torturing him in many ways he put him to death" (trans. Ch. T. Riggs [Princeton, 1954], p. 87). Now, according to Ducas (Bonn edition, pp. 313-314), Mehmed II left Istanbul for Adrianople on 18 June 1453 and entered the city on the night of 21 June. This date agrees not only with "the harvest time" of Critovoulos but also with the date given in the contemporary Ottoman registers of *tîmâr*s which show Ḳaraja Beg, the governor-general of Rumeli, in Injigiz, a small town on Istanbul-Adrianople route on 18 June. Submission of Enos obviously took place after that date in the midsummer of 1453, and, if we follow Uruj's statement, the execution of Chandarlı Khalîl in August or even later in September.

Once asserting the Sultan's arrival in Adrianople to have taken place on 21 June 1453 (German edition, p. 107; French edition, p. 127)[4] Babinger contradicts himself when he says that Mehmed II spent 35 days in Anatolia during the summer of 1453 and returned to Adrianople in August (p. 112; p.

---

[4] Hereafter page references will be first to the German edition and second to the French edition, with a semi-colon separating the two numbers.

132). Before leaving Constantinople, after the conquest in 1453, Mehmed had sent orders to every part of his realm "... that as many inhabitants as possible be transferred to the City" (Critovoulos, p. 93; according to Ducas, p. 313, he had asked 5,000 settlers to be sent by September 1453; cf. Iorga, *Notes et extraits,* IV, 67). According to Critovoulos (p. 89), the Sultan returned from Adrianople to Constantinople in the autumn of 1453. His main concern at this time seems to have been the repopulation and defense of Constantinople before embarking on a new expedition in the West. In the autumn of 1453 his purpose seems to have been to inspect the repair work and the progress in repopulation. He acted so as to attract the Greeks for his purpose of resettlement of the city and on 6 January 1454 appointed Gennadius patriarch (Critovoulos, pp. 93-95). "Having thus settled affairs in the city (Constantinople) the Sultan crossed over into Asia". He arrived in Bursa, put in good order all the affairs in Asia and appointed new governors "and all in the space of thirty-five days" (Critovoulos, p. 95). This trip was not for rest, after the hardships of the siege of 1453; the severe measures taken were probably motivated by the failure of the officials there to send the ordered number of settlers. The resistence of the well-to-do to emigration for the settlement of Istanbul is testified to by Tursun (p. 60). The record books of the *kâdîs* of Bursa of Mehmed's time prove that the emigration from this city to Istanbul actually took place. At any rate, Mehmed II returned from Bursa to Istanbul, where he remained only a short time, and set out for Adrianople in the winter of 1454 (Critovoulos, p. 95). There he could make his preparations for the expedition against Serbia in the spring of 1454 without worrying much about Istanbul.

The succession in the vizierate after the downfall of Chandarlı has always been a problem for historians, and here Babinger adds nothing new. He first maintains that "... after the execution of Grand Vizier Chandarlı-oghlu Khalîl Pasha the highest post in the government remained vacant for one year" (p. 117; p. 138). But in another place he adds: "Critovoulos is the only source to say that the vacant post of grand vizier was occupied by Ishak Pasha for a short time. In the summer of 1453 Mehmed II entrusted this office to one of the most remarkable figures in Ottoman history, Mahmud Pasha" (p. 118; p. 139). Now let me at once say that before Mahmud's appointment, Zaganos Pasha was grand vizier, and only in 1456 was Mahmud promoted to the grand vizierate. This date is well established by Ottoman sources. As to the theory that the grand vizierate was vacant for one year, there is nothing in the basic sources to support it. Then, who was the immediate successor of Chandarlı in the grand vizierate, Ishak or Zaganos? Ishaḳ, who had collaborated with Chandarlı in deposing Mehmed II in 1446, was dismissed from the vizierate (he was then third vizier; see *Fâtih Devri,* pp. 102-103) and sent to Anatolia as its *Beglerbegi* immediately after the second accession of Mehmed II in 1451 (see Ducas, p. 22). Ishak was mentioned as Beglerbegi of Anatolia during the siege of Constantinople in 1453 (see Critovoulos, p. 41; Kemâl Pşz., p. 46) in 1454 and in 1456 (see Kemâl Pşz., pp. 112-122; Uruj, p. 72). All this does not support the theory that he succeeded Chandarlı as grand vizier in 1453. As for Critovoulos' statement, let me quote it in full: "In the place of his man [Chandarli] the Sultan substituted Ishak, a man of the wisest sort, experienced in many spheres but especially a military leader and a man of courage. After a few days he *also dismissed Zaganos",* and Mahmud was appointed grand vizier (Riggs trans., p. 88). Here the person whose appointment, dismissal, and replacement by Mahmud is mentioned in sequence must be logically one and the same person, Ishak or Zaganos (Whether the names of Ishak and Zaganos in Greek were mixed up or this was merely the editor's mistake can be determined only by examining the original manuscript in Topkapi Sarayı Museum, Istanbul).

Kemâl Pşz. asserts (pp. 114, 122, 146) that in 1456 Zaganos was grand vizier and Ahmed Pasha (Veliyüddîn-oghlu) second vizier. According to the same source, Mahmud replaced Zaganos as grand vizier only after the Belgrade expedition in 1456 (cf. Uruj, p. 72). That Zaganos was grand vizier from Chadarlı's execution in 1453 up to 1456 can be further recalled from these facts: Zaganos was the second vizier toward 1453 (Sphrantzes, p. 286; *Fâtih Devri,* p. 134), and it was a rule generally applied in the Ottoman government to promote viziers one rank higher when the first vizierate became vacant. Thus, when Chandarlı was eliminated it was natural for the second vizier, Zaganos, to become first vizier, i.e., grand vizier. On the other hand, as the chief opponent of Chandarlı, Zaganos was responsible more than anyone else for the conquest of Constantinople (see *Fâtih Devri,* pp. 128-133), which made him a natural successor to Chandarlı. It is also significant to find Zaganos' signature at the bottom of the imperial decree *('ahd-nâme)* given to the Genoese of Pera on 1 June 1453. (This document is now in the British Museum; see *Echos d'Orient,* XXXIX [1942], 161-175, and T. C. Skeat, in *The British Museum Quarterly,* XVIII [1952], 71-73; it must be noted that this is not a *treaty).*

Using Neshrî and Sa'deddîn always as his chief sources, Babinger suggests (p. 291; p. 327) that upon Mahmud's dismissal (1468) Rum Mehmed Pasha was appointed grand vizier and then dismissed and executed about 1470, when he was succeeded by Ishak (p. 306; p. 343).

In 1468 the successor of Mahmud in the grand vizierate was not Rum Mehmed but Ishaḳ, whom we find as second vizier in 1461 and 1464 (Tursun, p. 125, and *Fâtih Mehmed II Vakfiyeleri,* II [Ankara, 1938], p. 339). During and after the Euboea (Agriboz) expedition in 1470 he was mentioned by Rûhî and Kemâl Pşz. (p. 325; also see H. Hüsâmeddin, *Amasya Tarihi,* III, 227) as grand vizier. When the Ottoman army was in action in Euboea Ḳâsim Beg, the Karamanid prince took the offensive and advanced as far as Ankara. In the summer of 1471 Ishaḳ, *Düstûr-i a'zam* (grand vizier) was sent against him (Kemâl Pşz. p. 307). Failing to suppress him, he was dismissed (Kemâl Pşz. p. 332) and his place given to Rum Mehmed (1471), already a vizier in the Dîvân. Rum Mehmed had distinguished himself during the expedition of Euboea in 1470 *("Fetihnâme" Fatih ve İstanbul Dergisi,* I, 281). But according to Babinger he was not even alive at that time. The inscriptions on the buildings he ereceted with endowments bear the date 876 of the Hijra, 1471-1472 A. D. (E. H. Ayverdi, *Fatih Devri Mimarisi,* p. 210). Rum Mehmed Pşz. was dismissed at the alarming news from the East that the Akkoyunlu forces had captured and sacked Tokat in the summer of 1472 (Kemâl Pasha, p. 350). Babinger's confusion seems to stem from the fact that he relied on the Ashık and Neshrî narratives, the chronologies of which are often misleading, especially on the events about Karaman. According to the *Hasht Bihisht,* a well informed source on the events in Karaman, Rum Mehmed appears to have been active as *Atabeg* to young Jem Sultan in his governorship in Karaman as late as 1474. In Babinger's source, Neshrî (p. 205), this campaign is mixed up with Rum Mehmed's earlier activities there. Rum Mehmed's disastrous campaign against Varsaks in the Taurus mountains had taken place in 1474 *(Hasht Bihisht)* and this caused his final dismissal and execution. Babinger (p. 273; p. 307) adopts also the judgments of 'Āshıḳ against Rum Mehmed, judgments which seem to me completely biased.

Upon the Akkoyunlu-Karamanid invasion in 1472 Mehmed II decided that he should entrust the government again to the able Mahmud Pasha. But at the end of the campaign against the Akkoyunlus Mahmud was arrested and his office was given to Gedik Ahmed Paha, who finally crushed the Karamanid resistance and thus ensured Ottoman rule in central and southern Anatolia (1474). In one passage Babinger doubts whether Gedik Ahmed had ever been grand vizier (p. 361; p. 403), but in another (p. 397; p. 442) definitely states that he was. At the same time he suggests that Khoja Sinân might have been grand vizier between 1474-1476 or in the winter of 1476-1477. That toward 1471 Sinân may have been one of the viziers in the Dîvân can be established by various sources (see *Shakâyiḳ-i Nu'mâniyye,* p. 165; Neshrî, p. 231; T. Gökbilgin, *Paşa Livası* p. 75), but for his grand vizierate we have no evidence whatsoever. The Sinân Beg who is mentioned as "Commander over the other commanders" in May 1476 (p. 397; p. 442) must be another Sinân, most probably the Sinân Beg who was the Beglerbegi of Anatolia toward the end of Mehmed's reign, whereas Khoja Sinân, a noted scholar, had no record of military leadership. As for Gedik Ahmed, he was the beglerbegi of Anatolia in 1461, a vizier in 1470, and second vizier in 1472, and, so, appears to have been promoted to first vizierate after Mahmud's fall (November 1473). Gedik Ahmed is mentioned in *Hasht Bihisht* as grand vizier *(Vezîr-i a'zam).* Mehmed's last grand vizier was Ḳaramânî Mehmed, who held this office for five years.

The grand viziers of Mehmed II were: Chandarlı Khalîl, February 1451-30 May 1453; Zaganos, 1453-August or September 1456; Mahmud, 1456-July 1468; Ishaḳ, 1468-1471; Rum Mehmed, 1471-Summer, 1472; Mahmud, second time, 1472-November 1473; Gedik Ahmed between winter 1473-1474 and winter 1476-1477; Ḳaramânî Mehmed between winter 1476-1477 and May 1481.

Babinger could not find in his sources much about the keen competition between Mehmed's viziers —especially between Rum Mehmed, Gedik Ahmed, and Ishaḳ on the one hand, and Ḳaramânî Mehmed on the other— which affected the whole administration and internal policy of the Sultan (see my "Mehmed II" in *Islâm Ansiklopedisi* [Istanbul], VII, p. 533).

One looks in vain for an answer in Babinger's book to the question why for over five years after the conquest of Constantinople Mehmed II had to concentrate his efforts on the Serbian question. Babinger follows chiefly C. Jireček's account on the subject *(Geschichte der Serben,* II [Gotha, 1918], 201-216) with some additional details from Neshrî. But he has left out significant points, such as the agreements between George Branković and Mehmed II in 1455 and the King of Bosnia and Mehmed II in 1459.

From Babinger's disconnected story of the Ottoman campaigns in Serbia in 1454-1459 one may get the impression that they all originated as a mere whim of Mehmed II. But it appears that events dictated his course of action, as I shall try to show.

First, it must be remembered that ever since 1427, when the Hungarians seized Belgrade from the Serbians, the most important question for the Ottomans was how to ensure control of the Danube. This was essential for protection of their position in Rumeli (the Balkans). During the first difficult months after Mehmed's accession to the throne in 1451, when Anatolia was in turmoil, the young Sultan had to yield to the demands of the Byzantine Emperor and the Serbian Despot and return to the latter some territory in the upper Morava valley (Krushevać or Alaja-hisar and its dependencies, in Kemâl Pşz., p. 110; Toplića and Glubočića around Leskovać, according to Jireček, p. 194). The Sultan had also to guarantee the Despot's rights in the armistice with John Hunyadi, concluded some months later, which meant a further increase of the Hungrian influence in thes region (see Jireček, p.

194). Upon the fall of Constantinople conditions changed radically and the time for the restoration of Ottoman control of the Danube against Hungray had come. It is significant that the Despot immediately surrendered what he had taken from Mehmed II in 1451 (Kemâl Pşz., p. 110; Rûhî; Neshrî, p. 183). The *Düstûrnâme* reads: "With the instruction of the Hungarian King, Vılk-oghlu [George Branković] returned the country which he had taken [from the Ottomans]".

The *Hasht Behisht* says that the Despot had not then surrendered all the places claimed by the Sultan. According to one Dalmatian document (see Jireček, p. 201), these places might be Smederevo (Semendere) and Golubać (Gügercinlik) on the Danube. Now the so-called ultimatum cited by Ducas has a special meaning which clarifies the course of events in 1454-1455. In it Mehmed II claimed his priority of rights against George Branković to the heritage of Stephan Lazarević (1389-1427), which included Smederevo, Golubać and Belgrade. He would agree only to leave to George a part of the country of his father Vuk (Vılk). Incidentally, "Sofia" mentioned as part of the lands of Vılk in Ducas (p. 315) must certainly be a city other than Sofia in Bulgaria, most probably "Scopia" (Skoplje), which was indeed a part of Vılk's country (see Jireček, p. 127).

In short, Mehmed's campaign into Serbia in 1454 should be discussed in the context of these facts. During this expedition he did not make a serious effort to capture Smederevo. According to Rûhî, he did not even pitch his pavilion before it. Ducas himself does not speak of any serious fighting there. Mehmed's main military achievement was the capture of "Omol". When Ducas gives details of Mehmed's siege of a "castle" on his way back from Smederevo, the author must have meant Omol (Ostrovića then was under siege by Ishaḳ Pasha, see Rûhî and Kemâl Pşz,. p. 112). Babinger makes no mention of Omol (and neitler does Jireček) but he mistakenly takes all the details of the siege of the "castle" mentioned in Ducas and shifts them to the so-called siege of Smederevo. The conquest of Omol, along with that of Ostrovića, is termed the most important result of this expedition by all the Ottoman sources (according to Ducas, p. 317, the "castle" did not surrender; *Düstûrnâme,* p. 97, which gives an original account of the siege of Omol from apparently an eye-witness, says that, absorbed in looting, the Ottoman soldiers left the Sultan alone to fight in person and finally force the enemy back into their castle). Sphrantzes (p. 384) mentions as the principal conquest in this expedition a city named "Homobrydum" (Omolridon?). Later on Omol remained an important Ottoman fortress with its Serbian *voinik*s in the Ottoman *vilâyet* (county) of Braničeva southeast of Smederevo *(Başvekâlet Archives,* İstanbul, Tapu No. 16).

Babinger asserts (p. 113; p. 134) that the Sultan was back in Istanbul after this expedition on 18 April 1454. In fact, he started the expedition in this month right after making the treaty with the Venetians. He spent the summer of 1454 in Serbia to consolidate his new conquests (Neshrî, p. 183; Kemâl Pşz., p. 114, and chronological data from a contemporary register). The military governor appointed by the Sultan there was not "Fîruz beg" as stated by Jireček (p. 202) and Babinger (p. 114; p. 134) but his son *(Hasht Bihisht).*

It should be empasized that Mehmed II shifted the military operations to Vılk-eli (the land of Vılk) in the following summer. He conquered and organized it as a new province. The first official survey *(taḥrîr)* of this province, made immediately after the conquest in 1455, and preserved in Başvekâlet Archives, Istanbul (Tapu Defteri, No. 2 M.), gives a good idea of the conditions at that time (see *Fâtih Devri,* pp. 151-152). Its rich silver mines were vitally important for the expanding economy and finances of the Ottoman empire, and Mehmed II tried to secure this important source of silver supply for the empire by special regulations (see my "Türkiye'nin İktisadi Vaziyeti..." *Belleten,* No. 60 [1951] pp. 651-660). Strategically this region was most important for the control of Kossovopolje, connecting Macedonia with Serbia. In view of this last point, disturbances by the Serbians of the communications between Prishtina and Skoplje (Üsküb), given by Rûhî and Neshrî (p. 183) as the main cause of the campaign, must be noted. In fact, the Serbians had made counter-attacks in this region in the fall of 1454 (see Jireček, p. 202; mention of it is also made in *Hasht Bihisht).* The most important sources for the 1455 expedition are Kemâl Pşz. (pp. 114-120) and a letter to the Sultan of Egypt from Mehmed II which tells of his conquests. The letter, dated 13 November 1455, has been published in *İstanbul Enstitüsü Dergisi,* II (1956), 170-173.

Just after taking possession of Vılk-eli, Mehmed II made a peace treaty with George Branković in the summer of 1455. Babinger not only seems to be unaware of the information in the Ottoman sources of this agreement (Rûhî, Neshrî, Idrîs and Kemâl Pşz.) but ignores Jireček's good account of it (p. 205). Jireček cites a Venetian document of 20 February 1456 which leaves no doubt about such an agreement. The Despot, now in conflict with the Hungarians too (see Jireček, pp. 204-205), had no choice but to accept Mehmed's terms. Here is the Ottoman version of the agreement by Kemâl Pşz. (pp. 115): "Vılk-oghlu [George Branković] will possess his old territory and obey the Sultan's orders; he will also get possession of the castles and cities which he had before, but he is to pay to the imperial treasury a yearly tribute at the amount of three million *dirhem-i 'Osmânî (akča)".* Kemâl Pşz. also notes that the conclusion of this agreement was chiefly due to the insistance of Mahmud Pasha. The amount of the tribute is thirty thousand *floris* (Venetian gold ducats) in Rûhî (Neshrî, p. 183, says thirty thousand *akča* which is obviously a mistake); in a Christian source, dated February 1457, it is given as 40,000 gold ducats (see Jireček, p. 208, n. 3). One Venetian ducat was 36 *akča* (Ottoman silver coin) in 1436, and 45 in 1477 (see *İktisat Fakültesi Mecmuası,* XI [1954], 63). Critovoulos' statement (pp. 102-103) about the treaty is consistent with Kemâl Pşz. Thus, by the agreement George had obtained the recognition of his rights on Stephen's heritage which were challenged by the Sultan in 1453; moreover, Omol and Ostrovića in this region seem to have been returned to him, as the Ottomans had to conquer them again in 1458 (see Kemâl Pşz,, pp. 149, 154). In return George had to give up all Vılk-eli, his patrimony, to Mehmed II. Finally, the Despot's ties to the Ottoman Sultan were greatly strengthened at the expense of the Hungarians. Thus Mehmed II appeared to have achieved the objectives which he had been aiming at ever since 1453. With Serbian neutrality as secure as it had been in 1444 he could now attempt to drive the Hungarians from Belgrade.

It is true that during the campaign of 1456 against Belgrade the Serbians, still suspicious, took strong defense measures against the Ottomans and the Sultan sent a division to watch Lazar, the Despot's son, in Rudnik (Kemâl Pşz., pp. 124-126). But the passage of the Ottoman army through Serbian territory caused no serious fighting except some inevitable skirmishes before Smederevo. Mehmed stayed there only one day. Jireček's statement about the Ottoman defeat "mit grossen Verlusten" (p. 206) before the city is apparently an exaggeration. To keep the Serbs neutral it was in Mehmed's own interest to stand by the agreement of 1455. It is significant that after the Ottoman retreat from Belgrade the Despot himself twice sent George Golemović to Adrianople to "renew" (Jireček, p. 207) the agreement.

On the siege of Belgrade two important German reports are utilized by Babinger (cf. Jorga, *Notes et Extraits,* IV, 145-147). Let me add this detail from Kemâl Pşz. (p. 128): To complete the encirclement of Belgrade Mehmed II had transported overland a small fleet from the Danube to the Sava. Among the causes of the Ottoman failure in this siege are disagreement in the Ottoman army and discontent among the Janissaries because of the hardships experienced in the expedition against Enos in the winter of 1456. Furthermore, Mehmed had declined the advice of the more experienced military chiefs (see Tursun, p. 74). During the fierce fighting against Hundayi's counterattack the Sultan received a wound on his forehead according to Kemâl Pşz. (p. 138). Three weeks after George Branković's death, on 15 January 1456, his son Lazar succeeded in renewing the agreement with the Sultan. Two years later, on 20 January 1458, when Lazar died without a male descendant, the question of the Serbian succession put Hungary and the Ottomans in conflict again. This new crisis did not allow the Despotate to continue its role of buffer state between the two powers. There was a strong pro-Ottoman group in the country which appeared to include many of the nobility and a great number of military men. They had reason to hope that their status would be maintained under the Ottoman regime (cf. *Fâtih Devri,* p. 144). The Serbs in general feared Catholic domination. Thus the Ottomans were able to establish their rule without serious resistance by the Serbs. It is safe to say that in 1458 and 1459 the Ottomans had to face Hungarian rather than Serbian resistance (cf. Jireček, pp. 210-216, and L. von Thallóczy, *Studien,* pp. 95-100).

Let me give some further evidence from Ottoman sources which were not utilized. Tursun, who because of his personal contact with the grand vizier is our best informant, says that toward the spring of 1458 the Serbs "sent their envoys with letters inviting the Sultan to come and take possession of the country. As their desire to submit to the Sultan was so obvious, it was decided that he need not go personally; instead he set out for Morea, the conquest of which had also become necessary". Apparently the person who sent this delegation to the Sultan was Michael Angelović, brother of the grand vizier Mahmud. Michael was one of the three members of the regency and the leader of the pro-Ottoman faction in Serbia (See Thallóczy, pp. 96-99; Jireček, pp. 210-211). In March 1458 Mahmud Pasha left Adrianople for Smederovo with a relatively small army accompanied by blind Gregory, now a pretender to the Serbian throne. After a short time the Sultan started for Morea. Mahmud had fixed his headquarters in Sofia. There he received a new delegation from the Serbs informing him that they had changed their minds about surrender of the cities because the Sultan did not come himself and that they had accepted the more favorable terms offered by the Hungarians. Tursun adds that: "the Hungarians had offered several hundred thousand gold coins as well as the castles on the other side of the Danube". This is consistent with what we learn from Christian sources (Thallóczy, p. 98). This sudden change in the attitude of the Serbs is a direct result of the revolution in Smederevo, which had taken place at the end of March. The Hungarian faction revolted and imprisoned Michael and then sent him to Hungary about the middle of April (Thallóczy, p. 104). Now the grand vizier was in a dilemma. Tursun (p. 85) testifies:

> In Sofia the commanders argued: 'The Sultan is far away in another campaign and the Serbian castles do not surrender to us easily. Furthermore, the army does not have the means for a siege ready. Under these circumstances all that we should do is to go only as far as

> Sofia. Besides it is, as well, a great service to protect the Ottoman territory. The enemy with whom we contend [for Serbia] is powerful and bars the way. If they ever attack to prevent our advance we may not be able to withstand them, which can cause the failure of the Sultan's purposes.

Mahmud Pasha, however, decided to take quick action and invaded Serbia. Taking Omol and Resava, he quickly reached Smederovo and fought his way into the outer part of the city but could not take the castle. The besieged threatened him by saying that the Hungarian army would come in three days. Mahmud gave up the siege and entered Mačva, south of Shabać on the Sava, took *Ḥavâle* (Avala) or Güzelje-Hisar overlooking Belgrade, as well as Sifrice-Hisar (Ostrovića) and Rudnik. He returned to Yelli-Yurd, a summer headquarters near Nish, where he passed the sacred month of Ramadân (it started on 13 July 1458). He was in contact with a pro-Ottoman group in Golubać, who surrendered the city to him, but he had to use force to reduce the inner castle. The operation of an Ottoman fleet on the Danube at that time is witnessed by the Western (see N. Jorga, *GOR,* II, 106) as well as the Ottoman sources. The terms of the surrender of Golubać are preserved in an official Ottoman record-book of Mehmed II's chancery (today in Başvekâlet Archives, Istanbul, Tapu No. 16). It reads:

> The city of Gügercinlik (Golubać) has an imperial charter to the effect that people shall have full possession of their vineyards and gardens as well as fields and be exempted from the taxation of kharâj, ispenje and 'ushr [the basic Ottoman taxes] and also from military services and charges; nobody shall interfere with their sons and daughters and cattle, or attempt to take anything by force; prisoners taken by the [Serbian] Martolos shall not be detained unduly, but these in return shall fulfill devotedly the services required for the fortresses and the boats [on the Danube].

The native Christian soldiers such as pronija-holders, Martolos, Voiniks, Eflaks (Vlachs), musketeers (Turkish *Tüfekji)* were incorporated in the local Ottoman forces (see *Fâtih Devri,* pp. 144-148). It is to be recalled that they had already experienced Ottoman administration between 1427-1444.

The second invasion of Serbia by Mahmud Pasha is not mentioned by Babinger. He thought that Golubać was surrendered before Mahmud's siege of Smederevo. Babinger writes (p. 165; p. 190) "Wann Mahmûd-Pascha wieder nach Osten abzog und warum er von der Einnahme Semendrias Abstant nahm oder nehmen musste, bedürfte der Klärung". He could have found the answers to his questions in Tursun's account of this expedition.

The threat of the Hungarian army under Matthias Corvinus on the Sava river (see L. von Thallóczy, *Studien zur Geschichte Bosniens und Serbiens im Mittelalter* [Munich-Leipzig, 1914], p. 99) made Mahmud decide to retrat again to Nish and he sent word to the Sultan, who was returning from his successful campaign in Morea. Mehmed II then appeared in the city of Üsküb (Skoplje) in upper Macedonia. Mahmud joined him there. Babinger thinks (p. 171; p. 196) "Üsküb, worunter indessen sicher nicht die Stadt in Mazedonien (Skoplje), sondern wohl der gleichnamige Ort im Istrandscha-Gebirge (ö. von Qyrq Kilise, heute Kırklareli) zu verstehen ist. Um diese Jahreszeit pflegte Mehmed II. mit Vorliebe die frische Höhenluft balkanischer Landschaften zu geniessen". Now let us see what Neshrî (p. 187) says" "In Üsküb the Sultan was planning to dismiss the army, but Mahmud Pasha warned him saying that the Hungarians had mustered an army. And then it was learned that he Hungarians were crossing the Danube at Belgrade. So Sultan Mehmed distributed salaries in advance to the provincial cavalry of Anatolia [to keep them in field]". The same source, giving details about how the forces sent by the Sultan checked the advance of the Hungarians, further adds that after that the Sultan came to Adrianople. These military operations are confirmed through the Christian sources also (see Jireček, p. 212). Now "the city of Üsküb" mentioned in the Ottoman sources as the meeting place of Mehmed and the grand vizier must be Üsküb (Skoplje) in upper Macedonia. It is definitely not the Üsküb in the Istranja mountains. What misled Babinger is apparently the statement by Critovoulos (p. 137) that after some days of rest in "Pherae in Macedonia" the Sultan arrived in Adrianople about the middle of the autumn. It is hard to imagine why Mehmed II and his grand vizier would go to the Istranja mountains, to the east of Adrianople, for fresh air while the Hungarian army was threatening to invade Serbia.

On the expedition of 1459 Babinger (following Jireček, Jorga, and Zinkeisen) writes (p. 174; p. 199) "Inzwischen machte Mehmed II. ungehindert mit seinem Heerbann den Mauern und Türmen von Semendria..." In fact, he came only to Shehirköy (Pirot), and the keys of Smederevo were handed to him by the Serbian envoys in Sofia (cf. *Düstûrnâme,* p. 98; Tursun, p. 96; Kemâl Pşz., p. 181; also *Mon. Hung. Hist., Acta Exetera,* IV, 46, No. 32). Then the Sultan sent an imperial order to the Sanjakbegi of that region to take over Smederevo (see Tursun, p. 96). This Sanjakbegi was probably Ali Beg, who had been blockading the city before the Sultan's expedition (see Critovoulos, pp. 118, 126).

Thallóczy (p. 102) points out that the ease with which Smederevo was taken by the Ottomans remains unexplained. It is true that the Hungarian King was then too busy in the west with the German emperor. A great number of people in Smederevo were on the side of Turks (letter of Barbuci, who had visited Smederevo on 27 May 1459: Thallóczy, p. 107). Stephan Tomašević was urgently asking military aid from his father, the king of Bosnia, so that he could hold out there (Stephan had married, under Hungarian auspices, the daughter of Lazar and had himself settled in Smederevo in the spring of 1459). The position of the King of Bosnia was thus of primary importance in the whole matter and the Sultan made an agreement directly with the king. The importance of this agreement for Smederevo has never been stressed enough. Rûhî says: "When the Sultan started out for Sofia the envoys of Bosnia found him on the way and proposed the exchange of Smederevo for Srebrnića. The Sultan agreed to it and took possession of Smederevo" (see also Neshrî, p. 189; the Anonymous Chronicle says: "The King of Bosnia gave up Smederevo of his own will"). When the Ottomans took possession of Smederevo they let Stephan Tomašević go home unmolested. Srebrnića and its district on the Serbo-Bosnian border had long been an object of dispute between the two countries (see Jireček, pp. 184-211; Thallóczy, p. 91).

It must be emphasized that the Ottoman rule did not cause an upheaval in Serbia, as is often said. Despite its incorporation (as the *sanjaḳ* of Semendere) into the empire, Serbia maintained its own legal and financial system to a considerable degree, as well as its basic social structure, with its nobility possessing lands as *pronija* (now *tîmâr)* or *bashtina* (see *Fâtih Devri,* pp. 144-184, for the record books and documents of this period in the Turkish Archives).

An eye-witness, Tursun, says that the Sultan came back to Istanbul after the surrender of Smederevo; "but, encouraged by his good fortune and the long time available (for a new expedition), he wished to add a new conquest". So he started out against Amastris (Amasra), a Genoese castle on the Black Sea coast. The date in Rûhî and Neshrî (p. 190) is given correctly, as 863 of the Hijra (XI. 1458-IX. 1459 A. D.). But Babinger thinks: "Mehmed II., dessen Aufenthalte nach dem Sturze von Semendria sich schwer verfolgen lassen, dürfte gegen Sommerende wieder in Stambul eingetroffen sein". He then says (p. 203; p. 231) that Amastris was taken by the Ottomans "im September, jedenfalls aber in Spätherbst 1460". Finally he seems to admit that Amastris was taken during the campaign of 1461 against Kastamonu, Sinop and Trebizond (p. 209; p. 236). Tursun, whom we know to have been present in this campaign, does not mention the name of Amastris in 1461. And all the principal sources (Rûhî, Idrîs, Tursun, pp. 97-98, Neshrî, p. 191) unanimously assert that in 1461 the Sultan came to Bursa, and then moved to Ankara, whence he started his expedition against Kastamonu and Sinop and took Trebizond.

In May 1461 Mehmed II was in Ankara. There the auxiliary forces of Kastamonu under Hasan Chelebi, son of Ismail Beg, and the Karamanid forces under Ḳasim, son of Ibrahim Beg, joined the Ottoman army (Babinger does not mention Ḳasim). They were sent by their fathers, who had pledged to do so by the treaties of vassality (see the text of the treaty with Ibrahim Beg in *Belleten,* I, 120). Mehmed II actually wanted these princes with him as hostages to safeguard his rear while he was in remote Trebizond. These points are missing from Babinger's account, which seems here to depend entirely on Ducas (pp. 241-242).

When speaking of the motives of the expedition against Trebizond, Kemâl Pasha (p. 186) makes a remark worth quoting here:

> The Greeks used to live on the coasts of the Black and the Mediterranean Seas in the good habitable areas which were protected by the surrounding natural obstacles. In each area they were ruled by a *tekvour,* a kind of independent ruler, and they gave him regular taxes and military dues. Sultan Mehmed defeated and expelled some of these tekvours and wanted to do the same with the rest. The goal was to take away from these people all sovereignty. Thus he first destroyed the tekvour of Constantinople; he was considered as the principal tekvour and head of this people. Later on he had subdued successively the tekvours of Enos, Morea, Amasra (Amastris) and annexed their territories to the empire. Finally the Sultan's attention was drawn to the tekvour of Trebizond.

This view of the famous Ottoman scholar who lived his early life in the Conqueror's time is surely more than his own interpretation and seems to reflect one significant aspect in Mehmed's conquests: reunification around Istanbul of the old Byzantine territories which were portioned under the local dynasties.

During Mehmed's long absence in 1461 Ishak Pasha, then second vizier, who was left in Adrianople, tried to safeguard Rumeli with a small force stationed there, but he could not cope with the situation *(Düstûrnâme,* p. 99; Neshrî, p. 195), since Wallachia and Mitylene, with the support of the West, were in rebellion. Vlad Drakul, Voivod of Wallachia, had taken the offensive already in the summer of 1461 when the Sultan was in Anatolia (Tursun, p. 103; *Düstûrnâme,* p. 99). In Mitylene Niccolò Gattilusio had eliminated his brother with the accusation of being friendly toward the Ottomans (Critovoulos, p. 180) and opened his ports to the Catalan corsairs who infested the Ottoman coasts. It was this situation that in 1462 induced Mehmed to undertake his twin expeditions against Wallachia and Mitylene.

Emphasis should be put on the interrelation of all these events in 1461-1462. Enverî *(Düstûrnâme,* pp. 99-100), who took part in the expeditions of 1462, must be considered as an important source on them.

As to the expeditions of Mehmed II to Bosnia in 1463 and 1464, Tursun is again most important as an eye-witness source (other important Ottoman sources on this event are ʻĀshıḳ Pşz., Neshrî, and Rûhî). Many details in Babinger could be modified or supplemented by a comparative use of these sources. Let me only point out that immediately after the occupation of Bosnia 'Īsā, son of Ishaḳ Beg of Üsküb, was appointed first governor. However, blamed for the flight of Hersek Stephan, 'Īsā was soon replaced by Mehmed, son of Minnet Beg (in Babinger, p. 240; p. 271: Minnet Beg, the first governor of Bosnia).

The Venetian defeat in Corinth in the fall of 1463 appears to be the result of the concerted operation of Ömer Beg, governor of Thessaly, and Sinân Beg (son of Elvân) governor of Morea, who, besieged in Corinth, had suddenly fallen on the Venetians. No mention is made of Sinân Beg by Babinger, who seems to follow only Chalcocondyles' partial story (pp. 545-551). Babinger also does not mention the Sultan's presence in Thessaly, where he recieved from Tursun news of victory from Mahmud Pasha, which caused Mehmed II to return to his capital.

It should be stressed that during the period of 1464-1473 the developments in Anatolia preoccupied Mehmed II increasingly more than the events of the west. Babinger's treatment of these developments in the east is unsatisfactory. He claims (pp. 261; p. 294) that "... wie auch über die Beziehungen Mehmeds II. zum Sultanshof in Kairo bisher so gut wie alle Angaben fehlen". However, one cannot quite agree with him when one discovers that he did not utilize such contemporary Arabic sources giving important information on the Ottoman-Mamluk relations as *Havâdith ad-Duhûr* by Ibn Tagribirdi, edited by W. Popper (Berkeley, California, 1930-42) and *Badâiʻal-ẓuhûr* by Ibn Iyâs (ed. Bulak, 1311-1312). The Persian chronicles concerning this period, particularly *Ahsan at-Tawârîkh* by Hassan Beg Rûmlû, are essential to understand Mehmed's oriental policy. A good bibliography of the subject can be found in M. Halil Yinanç, "Akkoyunlular" in *İslâm Ansiklopedisi* (Istanbul, 1941), cüz 4, 268-269; also C. A. Storey, *Persian Literature* (London, 1927-1939). We must also mention here numerous state papers and diplomatic correspondance on oriental affairs in Topkapı Sarayı Archives, Istanbul; see *Arşiv Kılavuzu,* 1-2 (Istanbul, 1938) and in the *münşeât*s (for these collections of state papers see M. H. Yinanc, "Akkoyunlular", and A. Erzi, "Akkoyunlu ve Karakoyunlu..." *Belleten,* No. 70).

Pressed by Mehmed II, Ishak Beg, the Karamanid prince, agreed in 1464 to give the Ottoman Sultan the Akshehir-Beyshehir region, but he was asked to surrender also the territory west of the Charshamba river. There is no explanation of this in Babinger (see pp. 289-291; p. 324). Actually, the Ottomans had had to abandon the Akshehir-Beyshehir region to Ibrahim Beg in 1444 and Mehmed II had been forced to confirm this in 1451. On the other hand the Charshamba river was fixed as the Ottoman-Karaman border in 1391 and was changed to the advantage of the Karamanids in 1402.

Ibrahim Beg, the Karamanid, and Uzun Hasan, the ruler of the Akkoyunlus, had made an alliance against the house of Dulgadır (Zulkâdir) which in turn had been an Ottoman ally since the end of the fourteenth century. When in 1464 the question of the Karamanid succession tended to upset the balance in central Anatolia, Uzun Hasan took action against Arslan Beg of Dulgadır and then entered Karaman to install Ishak Beg on the throne. When Ishaḳ was expelled from Karaman in 1465 he took refuge in Uzun Hasan's court; and as before he also sought the protection of the Mamluk Sultan of Egypt. Ishaḳ died in the summer of 1466 in exile (Ibn Tagribirdi, *Hawâdith,* III, 631). This is the most reliable source as Ibn Tagribirdi was able to see personally the reports coming to the Mamluk Sultan on Anatolian affairs. When Babinger shows Ishak still active in 1468 and even later (pp. 289, 290, 324, 325, 327, 363) it is obvious that he has confused Ishak with his brother Pîr Ahmed, who also ended by opposing Mehmed II, his suzerain, in 1468. It is not correct that in 1468 the Ottomans occupied the whole territory of the Karamanids (pp. 290-291; p. 327). The mountainous part of Karaman on the Taurus range and the Mediterranean coast was then out of Ottoman control. Only in 1471, and then for the second time in 1474, did the Ottomans succeed in bringing this part of the country into submission. After the Conqueror's occupation of the Konya plain in 1468 Pîr Ahmed attacked and routed the rear of the departing Ottoman army under Mahmud Pasha and captured large quantities of supply. Pîr Ahmed wrote of his success to the Mamluk Sultan and asked his protection *(Hawâdith,* III, 631, 651, 684). The failure of Grand Vizier Mahmud in the Karaman affair seems to be the real cause of his dismissal in July 1468 (Tursun, p. 139). What we find in Babinger on that is a simple repetition of 'Āshıḳ Pşz's story that Mahmud Pasha was dismissed because he had spared the rich in Karaman from being deported to Istanbul. The Ottoman sources conceal or misplace the Karamanid success. Mehmed II was back in Istanbul already in August 1468 (in Babinger, German ed., p. 291: November 1468).

Since at that time the Sultan of Egypt considered Pîr Ahmed and Uzun Hasan as his protégés and Dulgadır as his vassal, Ottoman intervention in Karaman and in Dulgadır affairs caused tension between Cairo and Istanbul.

That is why not only Venetian sources but also Tursun (p. 138) assert that the campaign of 1468 was originally planned against the Mamluks. But when later Uzun Hasan attempted to occupy the territory of Dulgadır and thus threatened the Mamluk dominions on the upper Euphrates, friendly relations between the Mamluks and the Ottomans were rapidly restored. In late 1472, when Uzun Hasan laid siege to Bîra, a Mameluk crossroad town (see Ibn Iyâs, II, 144-145), the two states even made an alliance against him. Mehmed's peace negociations with the Venetians in 1470-1471 were also, to a great extent, determined by the growing danger in Anatolia.

In 1473, when Mehmed II was away in Eastern Anatolia, his son Jem Sultan was left not in Istanbul (p. 330; p. 369) but in Adrianople (see Tursun, p. 150; *Magyar Diplomacziài Emlékek,* II, 246-248; Thuasne, *Djem Sultan,* [Paris, 1892], p. 6). The battle against Uzun Hasan in 1473 was the most critical one Mehmed ever waged. Victory not only solved the Anatolian question but also deprived the Christian West of its most effficient ally. Babinger does not mention the peace treaty between Mehmed II and Uzun Hasan, who had sent his envoy Ahmed Bekridjî first to Karahisar in September and then to Istanbul in November in 1473 *(Hasht Bihisht;* Rûhî; Kemâl Pşz., p. 404, and especially Uzun Hasan's letter to Mehmed II, in Topkapı Archives, No. 4476). Seeing Uzun Hasan still in close relationship with the Venetians, who were pressing him for a new war against the Ottomns, Mehmed II proposed to the Timurids in Central Asia that they take a common action against Uzun Hasan (see the letter in Ferîdûn Beg, *Munsheât-i Salâṭîn* I [Istanbul, 1274], 284). Mahmud's failure in handling the Uzun Hasan affair appears to be the essential cause of his second fall from the grand vizierate (for other reasons such as the intrigue of his personal enemies, see Kemâl Pşz., pp. 411-412).

The military operations in the eastern Black Sea in 1479 are left in complete obscurity by Babinger (pp. 441-442; pp. 489-490). He does not localize the places mentioned in these expeditions and gives the wrong date of 1480 for them. The lord of "Torul" as well as the Georgian princes were protected and even incited by Uzun Hasan against the Ottomans. On Uzun Hasan's death in 1478 it seems that Mehmed II thought it was time for him to complete his unfinished work on the eastern boundaries of the empire. He sent orders to his son, Bayezid (in Amasia), who had under his control all the territories as far as the Georgian border, to invade Torul and Georgia. The former was a tiny principality with a castle called Torul (today a *nâhiye* with the same name) on the strategical mountain pass between Gümüshhâne and Trebizond. Under the protection of Uzun Hasan a local Greek lord maintained possession (details are provided in a survey of the province of Trebizond made in 1487, Başvek. Archives, Maliyeden Müd. def., 828).

Bayezid's vizier, Mehmed Pasha, son of Hızır Pasha, and Raḳḳâs Sinân Beg annexed it and a strip of land in western Georgia called "mathahalyet", most probably *Mathakhal'et* ("The land of Mathakhel"). It seems that the name has survived in the village name of *Machakhel* in the county of Borchka near the Turkish-Georgian border.

Babinger also doubts that any expedition to Kopa and Anapa in Circassia took place, considering the great distance between Amasia (Amasya) and Anapa (p. 441; p. 490). In fact this was an independent maritime expedition made in the same year. The *Hasht Bihisht* is clear enough: "After the conquest of Caffa, Kopa was still in the hands of the remaining Franks, because of some natural obstacles (that prevented its conquest). Now the Sultan sent there thirty ships under the governor of Koca-eli (Izmit, Nicomedia)" (we use the manuscript in Nuriosmaniye K. Istanbul, No. 3209, 485 b; cf. Kemâl Pşz., pp. 520-522).

On Mehmed's relations with the Khans of the Crimea and the Genoese the interesting correspondence between Mehmed II and Mengli Girei (Giray, Kirey) and Eminek Mirza should have been consulted (for a bibliography and corrections see *Belleten,* VIII, 30 [1944], 205-229). Mehmed's relations with the Golden Horde are not touched upon by Babinger. It must also be emphasized that Crimean affairs involved Mehmed in the significant developments in eastern Europe, inasmuch as he supported the Crimean-Russian bloc against the Golden Horde-Jagellonian alliance. Even Moldavia had direct interests in the Crimea; toward 1475 its Voivod had sent a small force to Crimea to capture the principality of Mangup for his brother-in-law (A. A. Vasiliev, *The Goths in the Crimea* [Cambridge, Massachusetts, 1936], pp. 244-252). Briefly speaking, Mehmed's activities in the Crimea and Moldavia must be studied in the broader context of his northern policy.

The treatment of Mehmed's internal policy is probably the most superficial part of the book. Generally speaking, Mehmed's tremendous efforts to build up a unified and centralized empire strained the country to the utmost. He needed increasingly large resources, especially to make his unending military expeditions and to increase his army and naval forces. The unusually radical financial measures which he had to introduce created a very tense atmosphere in the country in his later years. These measures were: 1. The issue of new silver coin, forcing people to exchange the old coin at its metal value with the new one at its face value. The difference at the rate of one sixth meant a heavy tax on the possessors of cash in silver. He used this hated device three times after 1471 (see further details, *Belleten,* No. 60 [1951], pp. 676-679). 2. The extension of state proprietorship over most of the agricultural lands in the possession of the old families in the forms of *mülk* or *vaḳf.* Thus, according to Tursun, who was a high official in the finance department, over twenty thousand villages or estates came under direct state control, which meant a new heavy taxation. Applied in the same period after 1471, this reform alienated the old land-owning classe, especially in central and northern Anatolia, as well as many large religious groups. 3. The extension of the monopolistic tax-farming system to many necessities of life and the implementation with an unusual strictness of the laws governing these monopolies (a collection of such laws has been published by R. Anhegger-H. Inalcik, *Kânûnnâme-i Sultânî ber Mûceb-i 'örf-i 'Osmânî* [Ankara, 1956], also see H. Inalcik, "F. S. Mehmed'in Fermanları" *Belleten*, No. 44).

Toward 1481 the state treasury had in its chests about three and a half million ducats worth of ready money (Topkapı Sarayı Archives, No. E. 9713).

On Mehmed's unusual centralizing policy and its far-reaching social and political consequences, which surely prepared the way for the recationary policy introduced under Bayezid II upon his accession, Babinger presents little save a translation of some biased hints in 'Āshıḳ Pşz.'s chronicle.

In this connection it should be added that the Janissaries *(Yeni-cheri)* always disliked Mehmed II and showed their discontent on several occasions. Their number was increased from four or five thousand to ten or twelve thousand by Mehmed II. On his death they burst into a fearful revolt and were instrumental in bringing to power a reactionary administration.

That the Ottoman expansion in the Levant caused the Westerners discover the new maritime routes across the Atlantic Ocean (p. 377; p. 421) is a theory subject to much controversy today. I hope to supplement Lybyer's critical views of this theory *(American Historical Review,* XIX, 141) in a separate paper on the basis of new data provided by the Ottoman archives.

In the last chapters of the book are some mistakes in names. The commander who laid siege to Croïa (Akchahisar) in 1476 and was ordered to blockade Scutari in 1478 was not Gedik Ahmed Pasha (pp. 390; 401; pp. 435; 446) but Sarı Ahmed Beg, son of Evrenos, governor of Albania in this period (see Kemâl Pşz., pp. 509, 607; cf. Donado da Lezze [G.-M. Angiolello], *Historia Turchesca,* published by I. Ursu at Bucarest in 1909). During the incursion of 1479 into Transylvania it was 'Īsā Beg son of Hasan, who was the *sanjak-beg* of Silistre (Silistria) and not (p. 411; p. 458) "Hassan Beg and 'Īsā Beg" (cf. Kamâl Pşz., p. 466). The invasion of Carniol in 1479 was commanded by Dâvûd, then governor of Bosnia. For the large-scale incursions into Styria and Hungary in the years of 1477-1479 Kemâl Pşz., (pp. 477-481 and 527-562) gives detailed accounts which are completely overlooked in Babinger's book.

Mehmed died at Hunkiar-chayırı, which is between Pendik and Maltepe (see Ferîdûn Beg, I, 297).

In general it can be said that information drawn from the sources on individual events is usually summarized by Professor Babinger in a simple chronological order without much critical analysis and without seeking to establish the real relationship and sequence of the actual historical developments. On the other hand, Babinger sometimes uncritically accepts the biased statements of his sources as truth. One of the main concerns of Babinger appears to be to establish a correct chronology of the events, which is certainly the first important thing to do. He has been successful in clarifying many chronological data, but as we have seen, there remains some confusion[*].

---

[*] I am indebted to Mr. S. Vryonis for checking some Greek texts.

3

Decision making in the Ottoman State

Decision making in the Ottoman State

In his analysis of the patrimonial state, Max Weber often refers to the special patrimonial character of the Ottoman State. In general, he states that the patrimonial state "makes administrative and military organization a purely personal instrument of the master to broaden his arbitrary power".[1] Patrimonial authority "where it indeed operates primarily on the basis of discretion...will be called sultanism which is distinct from every from of rational authority". It is also totally different from estate-type domination as existed in the medieval west. Sultanism is characterized by a complete reliance on military force and arbit nary power or despotism. There occur a complete "differentiation between military and civil subjects and an increasing professionalization of the army. The Janissary and Mamluk armies, Weber observes, consisting of slaves, were typical examples of such professional armies. They were fully integrated into the ruler's household and served the ruler with absolute loyalty.

As Weber rightly notes, the ruler's exercise of power in the interest of maintaining a balance between rival status grops was a fundamental principle of the Ottoman political system. The Sultan's *kuls* versus the *reaya,* ulema versus bureaucrats, janissaries versus sipahis, or salaried army versus timariot army, and low ranking cadis against high ranking ulema were all status groups traditionally in conflict. However, "Sultanism" is also modified by tradition. According to Weber, tradition is primarily the origin and validation principle of patrimonial domination. "What is customary and has always been so" had a sacred character and demanded obedience to the particular person who represented it. The "ruler's powers are legitimate insofar as they are traditional".[2] Tradition thus defined by Weber functioned as a factor modifying the personal discretionary power of the ruler.

In general, patrimonial domination according to Weber "establishes itself through an administrative apparatus. Either by virtue of a constellation of interests or by virtue of authority, domination expresses itself and functions

---

[1] Max Weber, *Economy and Society: An Outline of Interpretive sociology*, trans. G. Roth and C. Wittich (Berkeley: CUP.1978), I, 231-232, II, 1031

[2] *Max Weber on Law in Economy and Society*, trans. E. Shils and M. Rheinstein, ed. M. Rheinstein (New York: Clarion 1954), 330.

through law and administration". Under a patrimonial ruler, the army and the bureaucrats are selected and organized as in a patrimonial household and respond exclusively to the ruler's demands. Government offices are organized and maintained along purely personal lines. In the selection of officials, loyalty to the ruler supersedes all other concerns. Officials are selected from among the ruler's personal attendants. Professional training and specialization are not considered necessary prerequisites. Promotions depend not on objective criteria but on the ruler's favor.

The ruler makes his official's economic compensation completely subject to his descretion with no provision for hereditary service. Officials never constitute a corporate group or a monopolistic, legally autonomous, sodality. In brief, the basic features of the patrimonial bureaucracy stem from its personal-patrimonial character. According to Weber[3] the household characteristics of the patrimonial state were maintained "to a grotesque degree ... at the Turkish court" up to the nineteenth century. Weber also observes that in the course of financial rationalization the patrimonial state in general moves imperceptibly toward a rational bureaucratic administration.[4]

In their conceptual approach, recent studies on Ottomn bureaucracy rely to a great extent on Weber's typification. Even when these studies tend to define Ottoman "sultanism" as being modified by an autonomos bureaucracy and objective laws, *kanuns*, they follow essentially Weber's theory.

Most recently Cornell Fleisher, in his book on Mustafa ʻĀlī,[5] suggested that in its most developed form in the late 16th century, Ottoman government was heavily bureaucratized. Before the 16th century "the position of the bureaucracy", Fleischer states, "the initially undifferentiated chancery and financial organization of the men of the pen fell somewhere between the sword and learning and shared characteristics (administrative responsibilities and literacy - respectively) with both". In the 16th century, "the need to regularize the Empire-wide administrative practice and to cope with growing financial problems led to the formation of an increasingly professionalized bureaucratic establishment...". In conclusion, Fleischer speaks of "an independent bureaucratic career track" and the growth of *kanun* consciousness in the late 16th century Ottoman Empire.

---

3 *Op. cit.*, II, 1031.

4 .Op. cit., II, 1025, on Max Weber's notion of "Sultanism" also see H. Inalcik, "Comments on *Sultanism*, Max Weber's Typification of Ottoman Polity," *Princeton Papers*, I.

5 C. Fleischer, *Bureaucrat and Intellectual in the Ottoman Empire: The Historian Muṣṭafā 'Ālī (1541-1600)*, Princeton: PUP, 1986.

The question is, taking into account this bureaucratic development, are we justified in rejecting Weber's initial characterization of the Ottoman state as a "sultanism" based on arbitrary patrimonialism. This development can never be interpreted as a typical bureaucracy as existed in Europeam states, and Ottoman *kalemiyye* always remained a complete tool of sultanism. It may be argued that the Ottoman political system could never allow the emergence of a corporate bureaucratic establishment in Weber's sense. Therefore, it is of key importance whether the bureaucratic group really attempted to assert itself as an autonomous body with well-defined responsibilities and immunities guaranteed under the *kanun* and attempted to carry out government activities within the pre-established rules and regulations. The argument is that their attacks against clientship, favoritism and bribery-institutions which were inseparable from a patrimonial system of government apparently, all aimed to establish such a bureaucratic system. *Kanun,* as an objective rule in the conduct of governmental affairs could bring a certain rationality and objectivity and ensure a controlling position to the bureaucrats in government.

I believe this is what Fleischer examined in the biography of Mustafa ʻĀlī. It is true that throughout Ottoman history there were periods when members of the *kalemiyye* became more influential with the sultan and thus participated more directly in the decision making process than other times. This, however, was possible only through a typical patrimonial institution, *musahiblik.* One can argue that as a rule kuttab were regarded as simple employees or tools providing technical expertise to the responsible men representing sultanic authority. Mention of the *kalemiyye* or *ahl al-kalam* side by side with the *seyfiyye* and *ilmiyye* occurred only in a later period. In the earlier works on government and politics the hierarchy ranks first *seyfiyye,* men of the sword, followed by *ilmiyye,* men of learning, without any mention of *kalemiyye.*

Let us first examine the question of how absolute the power of the sultan really was. The Ottoman, or I would say, Middle Eastern, concept of *Padishah* implied an autocrat concentrating all power and means of power in his own hands. He was considered to be chosen and supported by God and God alone. This concept manifested itself in practice in every facet of governmental dispositions. All governmental decisions, appointments, and title deeds are issued in the sultan's name. When his officials had to make reports or take decisions the documents always end with the phrase *baki emr Sultanımındır,* ultimate command belongs to the sultan. His will and authorization expressed in *berat*s, *menshur*s, *mulkname*s, etc. is the only means of legitimation of the exercise of power.

From Grand Vizir or Patriarch of the Greek orthodox church to the simple district *imam* or guild master every person exercising authority had to obtain the sultan's *berat* and exercise authority in the name of the sultan. "Land and raiyyet belong to the sultan" is the fundamental principle of Sultanism as expressed in the Ottoman Law codes. This constitutional principle aimed at abolishing all hereditary rights with political or so-called feudal implications gave the sultan absolute control over the land and the peasants so that he would be able to create and maintain a unified empire under his absolute imperial power. His power was so perfectly absolute because his accession to the throne was believed to be determined by God, and the Sultan, God's shadow on earth, was the only legitimate source of power. But the actual situation was not so simple. Every new succession in the Ottoman history proves to be a revolution. With the death of a sultan not legitimate authority exists. All his legal dispositions, apointments, and titles to possessions become null and void. In order to prevent anarchy the grand vizir tries to conceal the Sultan's death although his own authority and actions are no longer legal or legitimate. Only when the new Sultan renews and confirms, *tedjdid* and *takrir,* everything under his own seal then does the legal, normal course of the affairs resume. At no other time than the accession and death of a sultan does the nature of the sultanic power become explicit. Now the theory or fiction is superseded by reality. The new Sultan comes from his provincial seat to the capital of the Empire with his household which is a miniature of the central government with his lala, or tutor, secretaries as well as his councillor companions, *musahib*s. They expect to assume the government positions from the men of the dead sultan. There are usually fierce rivalries and eventually compromises between the two groups.

It was of key importance for a sultan to know how to use his limitless authority to attain the goals implied in the imperial system. The success of a sultan depended on the ways in which he used his authority to control and to maintain balance and harmony between the bearers of the delegated power. There was indeed a kind of checks and balances system in the Ottoman administration which was designed to prevent any member of the government from acquiring complete control. The unique source and possessor of power was the sultan himself. Decision making processes at various levels is illustrative of the actual exercise of power in the Ottoman administration. In ordinary governmental affairs as well as in emergencies, *meshveret,* consultation was considered a duty in the decision making process. As recommended by Islamic sources, the Qur'an and Prophetic traditions, *meshveret* was an obligation even for the sultan. The defeat at the battle of Raab in 1664 is attributed to the commander-in-chief's neglect of the *meshveret* system before the battle. The Ottoman *diwan,* imperial council, meeting at the Porte of the sultan was a permanent place to discuss and take decisions on the most important affairs of the state as well as the high court.

The sultan had to preside at it in principle. Extraordinary or emergency meetings in which vizirs, dignitaries, commanders, ulema and even dismissed dignitaries took part were intended to share responsibility in taking important decisions. It reminded the Mongol *kuriltay* and *kengeş*.

The general procedure in a *meshveret* was as follows. The experts spoke first. Then the officials of lesser rank were invited to express their opinions. The sultan or grand vizir or commander-in-chief, or whoever represented the highest authority announced his own opinion and his decision last. From this moment on, no one had the right to speak. There was no putting the matter to a vote or balloting. Balloting was a nineteenth century innovation borrowed from the West. In the elections of the guild officers or on other such occasions the leader is the eldest or the wealthiest or most influential man known to everybody and no balloting or voting method is used. However, there were cases in which we are told the minority had to follow the decision of the majority. Decisions made at a *meshveret* may be interpreted as a kind of check on the arbitrary power of the sultan. However, such decisions did not have any legal or binding effect. On the other hand, none of the *meshveret* councils assumed the nature of a permanent establishment before a state consultative council under the typical name of the *Meclis-i Vala-yi Ahkam-i Adliyye* and later *Shura-yi Devlet* was set up in the 19th century. This was a compromise of the Ottoman *meshveret* tradition with the western type legislatures. In Ottoman history only under quite exceptional circumstances did the sultan agree to a typical covenant called *shar'î sened* containing defined provisions and privileges. In the *Sened-i ittifak* of 1808 the parties were the sultan and the body of the provincial notables, *a'yan*, for whom the sultan confirmed certain permanent statutory privileges in return for certain obligations. But this unusual document which may have opened a new era for the Ottoman sultanate became a dead letter.[6]

While as a rule imperial commands are issued directly from the *diwan* in the name of the sultan, in some cases the sultan gives a direct order in a written note on top of a report, *'arz* or *telkhis,* and then the formal decree is prepared at the chancery. Such a firman is distinguished from others by the note *ba khatt-i humayun* which makes it irreversible and absolute being a direct order of the sultan. The furmala often used in the *khatt-i humayun* "let it be done as required" is too general in meaning and shows the sultan's respect for the established rules or the requirements of the circumstances.

One of the key factors in the Ottoman system of government is the personal companion, *nedim, musahib* or *mukarrib* of the ruler. From among

---

[6] H. Inalcik, "The Nature of Traditional Society: Turkey", *Political Modernization in Japan and Turkey.* R.E. Ward and D.A. Rustow, Princeton 1968, 42-63.

his favorite attendants or secrataries the ruler chooses one who helps him as his closest, most intimate advisor. A *musahib* is expected also to serve the ruler as an agent in his secret contacts and to enlighten him about events outside the seraglio and to advise him as to whom he can entrust with the supreme power. A pre-Islamic Iranian institution, *nedim*-ship always existed in Islamic states as one of the key institutions of palace government. At the same time, it is an institution which underlines the patrimonial, personal character of the sultanic government. Since the *musahib* was seen as the man who could influence the ruler's decisions and thus interfered with the government's independence, he became the main target of the bureaucratic critics and was seen as one of the causes of irresponsible and arbitrary rule.[7] In essence, these critics believed that the ruler should have a loyal, wise and experienced advisor whose concern would be to serve the ruler as well as *Din u Devlet.* Submitting reports to advise how the ills of government could be corrected, the bureaucrat-critics anticipated such a role for themselves. In *Nushat al Salatin* 'Ālī presents himself as an experinced, learned and loyal *musahib* to advise the sultan.

Thus far, we have tried to show the personal, patrimonial character of the Ottoman system of government in its most developed form in the 16th century. Now we shall turn to the arguments in favor of the theory of the formation of an autonomous bureaucratic body in the course of the 16th century.

All appointments and promotions start with the *'arz*, report of the immediate superior of the candidate a military assignment with the commander usually alay-begis in the sancak, a palace service with the kapıagası, a vizirate with the grand vizir. This initial *'arz* is of crucial importance in the appointment process and tends to become a personal favor of the superior. The favor involves personal attachment, protection and clientship or bribery. Of course, in the report of service, *ehliyyet,* ability, valor and *eskilik,* precedence and experience is always mentioned in support of the candidate. However, in practice, bribery and favoritism were intrinsic elements in the system. The Topkapı Palace archeves are full of documents demonstrating how the reporter's personal retainer *kapı* or *tevabi'i* was favored at the expense of more qualified candidates in military or *ilmiyye* appointments and only occasionally the injured party had courage enough to bring the case to the sultan's attention which is the last resort in redressing the injustices. It should be emphasized that in the Ottoman system the regulations, *kanun*s governing career lines and promotions were designed to eliminate favoritism and bribery. But it is equally true that these *kanuns*

---

7 See "Süleyman: the Man and the Statesman," in this volume.

themselves were the product of certain circumstances. A recent study of a register of cadi appointments brought to light the fact that new rules governing cadis' careers were added under the pressure of an ever growing number of jobless candidates. Since the number of judgeships was limited and could not be increased at will a new regulation introducing *dawr* and *mulazemet* or *nevbet* was declared in the mid-sixteenth century, and later in 1597 the regulation was refined with new provisions designed to prevent malpractices, nepotism and favoritism and congestion in the cadre. Now while outsiders were denied cadiships, the active service was subjected to a rotation system. The tenure period of a cadiship was limited to three years by the end of the sixteenth century then to two years and later to twenty months in the first half of the seventeenth century. For higher positions the tenure was only one year in the late seventeenth century. Complaints against favoritism and bribery were so common that it became the main theme of the bureaucratic critics in the memoranda presented to the sultan.[8] The *mulazemet* system was also followed in *timar* appointments because of the same problem of the ever growing number available in the provinces. In both careers, cadiship and timar, thousands desperately struggling to obtain a post were ready to use the most common and efficient means, bribery, if they did not already have an influential protector Lord. In brief, this pressure which led to political action was at the source of Otoman *kanun*-making and bureaucratization in the 16th century.

In appointments and promotions personal supervision of the sultan as was the case in the beylik period was not possible as the state grew into an empire. The proliferation of regulations in the new period, which was mostly the work of the great bureaucrats, is indicative. When the malpractices, favoritism and bribery became widespread and complaints from below threatened the entire political structure reforming bureaucrats attempted to control the situation and cure the ills by imtroducing new regulations. Actually this was an attempt to appease the ever-growing mass of protesters. I believe this was the mechanism of bureaucratic development in the 16th century. Growth and complexity leading to specialization, professionalization and bureauratization have to be explained by concrete historical conditions and by the circumstances necissating the formulation of new *kanun*s.

Now despite the pragmatic nature of the kanuns are we justified in assuming that a quasi-corporate body of bureaucrats was in the process of formation during the 16th century. Unlike Weber, modern political sociologists, among them Eisenstadt, include the Ottoman Empire as a centralist bureaucratic empire and place emphasis more on its bureaucratic-

---

[8] See "The Rūznāme Register..." in this volume.

managerial nature than on its system of patrimonial-personal rule. The bureaucratic system with the autonomous action of a body of professionals under objective rules was indispensable for the survival of these wast and complex empires which had to implement control over labor and all sorts of sources of revenue.

Now what will be our conclusion. In actuality it appears that two opposing principles are in struggle in the Ottoman system. One is the patrimonial principle that in its pure application requires the absolute independence of the supreme authority. In reference to its typical characteristic, that is arbitrariness, sociologists sometimes call it despotism. In Ottoman history Mehmed the Conqueror, Selim I, Murad IV, Mahmud II and Abdulhamid II are viewed as despotic rulers who attempted to make their personal authority supreme in every way and they are sometimes called *müstebid,* despot, by their opponents. *Istibdad,* arbitrary power of the sultan, or Weber's "sultanism" is actually a logical or "typical" expression of the patrimonial principle. The second principle is supremacy of the objective rules which place limits and guide the ruler in making decisions and determining policies. It is advocated by *ulema* and *küttab,* bureaucrats. As we discussed earlier, they appear to be an outcome of the clash and compromise of political forces. Those who feel themselves underprivileged and those who aspire to monopolize decision making power among the ruling elite advocate respecting the rules, that is the *shari'a, kanun* or *âdet,* thus restraining the arbitrariness of decision making. In practice, *kanuns* or regulations were always prepared by the bureaucrats and enforced by the decrees formulated in the name of the sultan. *Adaletnames*, justice-rescripts, were the general reform declarations forcing the sultan's agents in executive positions to respect the *kanun.* Interestingly enough the goals and principles which the justice-rescripts upheld in general are those which are formulated in the advice-books for a good and just government. Basically justice was the respect of the *kanuns* which protected the *reaya,* tax paying subjects, against exactions, forced-labor and oppression.

At this point I would like to raise the question of whether the reaya, populace itself made any influence in policies and decision making. Yes, and to quite an important degree. As noted above, the justice-rescripts were intended to eliminate the exactions committed against the peasants, because this was the main cause of the peasant's flight and abandonment of the land which meant the loss of tax revenues for the public treasury. Dispersal of the reaya and desertion was considered a serious matter and the peasantry were well aware of this concern on the part of the government. In the petitions, *arz-i mahzar*, sent to the central government for the prevention of exactions or reduction of taxes the peasantry always warned that they might abandon their land and disperse, *perakende ve perişan olmak.*

Because of their importance in the period of disorders in the 17th century such petitions were then classified in special registers called *şikayat defter*s. The increase of *hâlî, harab,* that is deserted villages in the time immediately after the conquest and at times of disorders and wars constitute one of the fundamental, yet little studied, questions of Ottoman social history.

In conclusion, we can say that the arbitrary power of the sultan was modified by the *kanun,* and the concern for the preservation of *Din u Devlet,* which were espoused and maintained by the traditional institutions represented by both the küttâb and ulema.

4

The Rūznāmçe Registers of The Kadıasker of Rumeli as preserved in the Istanbul Müftülük Archives

The Rūznāmçe Registers of The Kadıasker of Rumeli as preserved in the Istanbul Müftülük Archives

I The Archives

It is with a deep sense of relief that we have learned of the baselessness of the rumours that the entire archives of the Shaykh al-*Islām* in Istanbul had perished in a fire at the beginning of this century. These archives, consisting of over ten thousand volumes, are in fact presently housed in a building at the entrance of the Office of the *Müftü* of Istanbul (the *Istanbul Müftülüğü* located behind the Süleymaniye Mosque). These archives are definitely the most important source on the history of the Ottoman *'ilmiyye* establishment, Islamic jurisprudence, the history of Istanbul, and the social and economic history of the Ottoman empire in general.

It was under Abdülhamid II (1876-1909) that, as a reaction to the *Tanzīmāt* policy of adopting western institutions and laws, emphasis was placed on the sources of Islamic law, and measures were taken to improve religious education and the administration of religious law. In 1894 the two buildings on either side of the gate of the *Müftülük* (then officially called *Bāb-i Wālā-yi Fatwā, or Dā'ire-i Djalīl-i Meshīhatpenāhī*) were built to house the archives and the library. The building on the right side of the gate houses the archives of the *Shaykh al-Islām* and those of the law courts of Istanbul, Galata, Üsküdar, Eyüp and their dependencies. By making the basic literature on Islamic law and the Ottoman court documents available, the library and the archives provided the sources necessary for the functioning of the *Bāb-i Fatwā* up to the last days of the empire. According to the State Annuaries (*the sālnāmes*),[1] the archives then formed a directorate under the responsibility of the *Ṣadrayn Evrāḳ Me'mūru* and the *Sidjillāt-i Shar'iyye Müdürü*. These ten thousand volumes, containing at a rough estimate over five million documents, consist of four collections divided as follows:[2]

---

[1] For example, *Sālnāme-i Devlet-i 'Aliyye-i 'Oṣmāniyye* of the year 1321/1902-1903, Istanbul, 1904, 200-213.

[2] I am indebted to the *Müftü* of Istanbul, S. Kaya and his staff for their help while I was working at the archives. My special thanks go to Dr. Abdülaziz Bayındır who let me use his unpublished doctorate thesis: *Teorik ve Pratik Osmanlı Muhakeme Hukuku*, Atatürk

Collection I. The *Rūznāmçe* registers of the two *kadiasker*s of Rumeli and Anatolia: 257 registers of the *kadiasker* of Rumeli covering the period 952/1545-1312/1894; and, 120 registers of the *kadiasker* of Anatolia for the period 1076/1665-1310/1892.

Collection II. The registers of *Naḳīb al as͟hrāf* : 33 *defters* altogether, covering the period 943/1536-1116/1704.

Collection III. The registers of seals (*mohr ṭaṭbīḳ defterleri*) containing the stamped seals of the cadis to verify the documents sent by them: 16 registers altogether.

Collection IV. The S͟har'ī court registers: 9,870 registers of the 27 courts of Istanbul and its dependencies, covering the period 919/1513-1343/1924. The S͟har'iyye courts were abolished in 1924.

The court registers constitute by far the most important collection comprising the *i'lām*s (court decisions), *hud͟jd͟jat*s (certifying documents), and *ma'rūḍ*s (cases submitted to the Sublime Porte).[3] Estate lists of the deceased, *waḳf* deeds, and all kinds of notarial documents are included in these registers. Below is a list of these 9,870 registers as divided by the courts to which they belonged and the periods they covered.

At the present time these archives and the library are under the authority of the *Müftü* of Istanbul who is appointed by the *Diyanet İşleri Başkanı* in Ankara (requests for scholarly research and applications are to be submitted to the *Başkan*).

The series called *ḳāḍī'asker rūznāmçesi* (daybooks kept under the *ḳāḍī'asker*) constitute a particularly important source for the study of the Ottoman *'ilmiyye* career, as they contain the appointments made by the *ḳāḍī'asker*s.(hereafter kadîasker) The earliest defter available in the series covers the period 952/1545-958/1551. It starts with a list of candidates (*mulāzim*), introduced by Mawlānā Pīr Aḥmed, known as *Leys-zāde,*[4] which

---

Üniversitesi, İlâhiyat Fakültesi, Erzurum, 1984, now published under the title, *Muhakeme Hukuku* (*Osmanlı Devri Uygulaması*), Istanbul, 1986, 273-281.

[3] For the court registern in Turkey see Mücteba İlgürel, "Şer'iyye Sicillerinin Toplu Kataloğuna Doğru", *Tarih Dergisi,* 28 (İstanbul Ü. Edebiyat Fakültesi, 1975), 123-166.

[4] For Leys Çelebi and his son Pīr Aḥmed, see M. 'Ārif's introduction to his edition of Ḳānūnnāme-i Āl-i 'Os͟mān, supplement to *Ta'rīkh-i 'Os͟mānī End͟jumeni Med͟jmū'ası* İstanbul, 1330, 6-7: Pīr Ahmed died in 952/1545 (Mad͟jdī, *Tard͟juma-i S͟haḳā'iḳ-i Nu'māniyye*, İstanbul 1269/1852, 405). His father Nūr al Dīn Ḥamza, also known as Leys Çelebī, played major political role during the reigns of Bāyezīd II and Selīm I. He was known as Nūr al-Dīn Sarıgürez (in modern literature mistakenly mentioned as Sarıgürz, see İ. H. Uzunçarşılı, *Osmanlı Tarihi,* II (Ankara: Türk Tarih Kurumu, 2nd edition 1964), pp. 239, 240; *gürez* means handsome). For *rūznāmçe* see M. İpşirli,

was made at the beginning of his tenure (*nawba*). The following record is about the candidacy of Mawlānā Dja'fer,[5] the *tezkiredji* of Mawlānā Abū's-Su'ūd who was previously *kadiasker*, now appointed Shaykh al-Islām. The candidacy (*mulāzemet*) was submitted to the Sultan and approved.

From the middle of the sixteenth century on, the appointment of the *mawālī,* i. e., professors of higher *madrasas*, and judges with a daily income of more than 300 *akça,* was under the responsibility of the *Shaykh al-Islām*. The appointment of minor judgeships, with a daily income of 300 *akça* and below, was the responsibility of the kadiaskers of Rumeli and Anatolia. In this paper, by examining the *rūznāmçe* of the *kāḍī'asker* of Rumeli between November 1647 and March 1648, we shall discuss the regulations and the patterns of appointment of the town cadis (*ḳaṣabāt ḳāḍıları*), and attempt to provide definitions for the terminology used.

Each register is introduced by a note specifying the date of the posts submitted to the Sultan for approval (*al-manāṣib al-ma'rūḍa*). Each separate item in the register consists of two parts.[6] In the first part, the identity of the previous office-holder is given with the exact period of his tenure as well as the reason why the office became vacant. In the second part, beginning with the identity of the candidate and a description of his career, the appointment is recorded after being submitted to the Sultan. The *Kadiasker* 's note contains the exact date of the appointment and its duration. As will be seen later, all these specifications are of key importance for the smooth functioning of the system. Each record is coupled on the margin with a note showing at first glance the place and the nature of the appointment.

"İlmiye Teşkilâtında... Mülāzemet Kayıtları", *Güney-Doğu Avrupa Araştırmaları Dergisi*, 10-11 (1983), 221-23.

[5] For Dja'fer efendi see M. İpşirli, "Şeyhülislâm Sun'ullah Efendi", *Tarih Enstitüsü Dergisi,* XIII (İstanbul, 1987), 209; Sun'ullāh was his son. Dja'fer himself was a son of'Abd al-Nabī, uncle of Abū's Su'ūd.

[6] See the text given in facsimile in *Appendix:* No. II.

Court or *office*	*Number of Registers*	*Period covered*
1. Istanbul	334	1021-1342
2. Istanbul Bāb	544	1076-1327
3. Kasımpaşa	179	1004-1342
4. Ewḳāf-i Hümāyūn Müfettis͟hliği	801	888-1342
5. Kısmet-i 'Askeriyye	2142	1000-1342
6. Üsküdar	802	919-1342
7. Ahiçelebi	664	1063-1327
8. Davudpaşa	192	1196-1342
9. Bakırköy (Makriköy)	16	1302-1342
10. Kartal	40	1129-1342
11. Adalar	8	1178-1262
12. Beykoz	3	1328-1342
13. Bilād-i Metrūke	36	1247-1296
14. Galata	1040	948-1343
15. Hawāṣṣ-i Refī'a	629	978-1342
16. Beledī Ḳassāmlıg͟hı	155	1066-1303
17. Balat	155	964-1254
18. Yeniköy	174	959-1333
19. Hasköy	40	955-1254
20. Rumeli Ṣadāreti	644	955-1343
21. Maḥfel-i S͟her'iyyāt	108	1271-1327
22. Anadolu Ṣadāreti	177	1247-1341
23. Beşiktaş	231	960-1327
24. Tophane	275	960-1327
25. Mahmudpaşa	246	1042-1341
26. Ewḳāf Muhāsebed͟jiliği	129	1043-1255
27. Māliye Beytülmāl Ḳassāmlıg͟hı	106	1254-1327
TOTAL	9,870	

II. The *'İlmiyye*

Before we begin analyzing the data from the *rūznāmçe* register, let us have a bird's eye view of the *'ilmiyye* organization and its relationship to other groups.[7]

The *'ilmiyye* class as a whole was a privileged group whose status and hierarchy was based on the level of certified knowledge in the Islamic sciences. Its members represented the spiritual authority side by side with the military-political authority (*beylik* or *seyfiyye*) whose status and privileges were based on professional skill and experience in military arts and government. The ruler, as the *imām* and the *pādishāh*, united in his person these two authorities (or *Dīn u Dawla*). The bureaucracy (*ḳalamiyye*) constituted an instrument to functionalize the ruler's authority in the political domain. In the Ottoman Empire, the *'ilmiyye* had its own autonomous bureaucratic machine, but in the last analysis, it was dependent on the ruler's authority. As the one and only deputy of the ruler, the grand vizier supervised both the *seyfiyye* and the *'ilmiyye*.

Within the *'ilmiyye*, the *tadrīs* (teaching) and the ḳaḍā' (administration of the law) were two branches closely interrelated in their function. The second Ottoman Sultan Orhan (1326-1362) had founded the first *madrasa* chiefly for the purpose of training the cadis to be employed in his realm. The cadis were also authorized to execute the Sultan's orders concerning public administration. Professorships and judgeships were classified according to the fixed daily revenue for each rank. Judges' revenues were calculated as ten *akça* for each one thousand houses in the area of jurisdiction. As early as the reign of Mehmed II (1451-1481), judgeships were divided into two main categories, those with a daily revenue of 300 *akça* and below, and those above 300 *akça*.[8] The latter, distinguished by the title of *mawlā* or *molla* (plural *mawālī*), or by the rank of *mawlawiyyet*, made up a "noble" group (*a<u>sh</u>rāf*) among the other status groups with privileges. However *'ilm* had to be within every Muslim's reach, and a with privileges. However, *'ilm* had to be within every Muslim's reach, and a student of any background had the

---

[7] For a general outline see İ. H. Uzunçarşılı, *Osmanlı Devletinin İlmiye Teşkilâtı*, Ankara: Türk Tarih Kurumu, 1965 (poorly edited); most recently R. C. Repp, *The Mufti of Istanbul*, London; Ithaca Press for the Board of the Faculty of Oriental Studies, Oxford University, 1986; also H. Inalcik, *The Ottoman Empire, the Classical Age 1300-1600*, London: Weidenfeld and Nicolson, 1973, 165-178; C. Baltacı, *XV-XVI. Asırlarda Osmanlı Medreseleri*, Istanbul: İrfan Matbaası, 1976.

[8] On these rates see K. Dilger, *Untersuchungen zur Geschichte des osmanishen Hofzeremoniels*, Munich, 1967; and Repp, *op. cit.*, 32-36.

opportunity to move up the ladder to the highest rank in the *'ilmiyye* pyramid. Below is a chart of the *'ilmiyye* ranks and career lines.

Tadrīs			Ḳaḍā'	
Student	Professor	Tenure	Ḳaḍā'	Tenure
Sūhte (softa)	Dismissed prof. from 40 *madrasas*	—	Judgeship of 150 and below (small town judgeships)	Two years[9] (1006/1597)
Dānishmend	*Madrasas* of 20 and 25 (*Tadjrīd* m.) *Madrasas* of 30 and 40 (*Miftāh* m.)	Two years (1006/1597)	Judgeship of 300 and below (small town judgeships)	
Dānishmend	*Madrasas* of 50 (mawlawiyyet) *Ḫāridj* and *Dākhil*		Judgeships above 300 (*mawlawiyyet*)	
Dānishmend	*Madrasas* of *Ṣaḥn-i ṣamān* and *Ayasofya Madrasas* of 60: *Suleymāniye*		Judgeships of 500 (*mawlawiyyet*)	One year (17th century)

At each stage of his studies, a student had to obtain a certificate (*tazkira* or *tamassuk*) from the professor under whom he studied. Later regulations required that the certificate specify the texts studied and the duration, as well as a detailed description of the student's identity to prevent its fraudulent use by others.

It was the *mulāzemet* (*mulāzama*),"attendance" of the *mawālī*, which was considered a prerequisite for one's candidacy to the *manāṣib* ; and candidates were carefully listed chronologically with their qualifications in the registers kept at the *Shaykh al-Islām*'s or the *kadiasker*s' offices. Qualification was also determined by official tests when necessary. A third method for the selection of candidates was a direct recommendation by the *mawālī* who chose a certain number of candidates from among his students, assistants (*mu'īd*), or his own sons who were supposed to have had their education from their father.

It is to be remembered that those members of the *'ilmiyye* who sought a *manṣib* (plural *manāṣib*) at a *madrasa* or a *ḳaḍā'* had to complete strictly

[9] According to the rescript introducing reforms into the 'ilmiyye dated 1006/1597, facsimile copy at the *Appendix* , No. I.

defined degrees at the *madrasas* or to be in the attendance of the *mawālī*, the authorities in Islamic sciences. Those who preformed minor religious services for the people at mosques or similar institutions received only the *d̲jihet* (plural *d̲jihāt*), not the *manṣib.* The former were called *ahl-i manāṣib* and the latter *ahl-i d̲jihāt.* But in reality, and particularly through patrimonial relationships, these rules and regulations were frequently overlooked, as contemporary critics have disclosed.[10] While the *mawālī* formed quite a small, and in later periods practically a closed group (they numbered 296 individuals in 1883),[11] small town cadis were quite numerous. At the bottom of the pyramid, the *imāms*, *mu'azzins* and *k̲h̲atīb*s serving in the mosque as well as the *dānishmend*s and *sūhte*s constituted in fact large social groups.

The members of the *'ilmiyye* and of the *d̲jihāt* were all exempted from taxation, as were the members of the *sayfiyye* and the *ḳalamiyye* status groups.

III. The Systems of Rotation (Dawr or Nawba) and Mulāzemet

Pressure from the candidates waiting for a position must have imposed a rotation system (*dawr* or *nawba*, *nöbet*), to provide employment to as many candidates as possible, since the number of judgeships was limited and could not be increased at will. For example, a change in the regulation in 1127/1715[12] would have deprived of candidacy more than a thousand *madrasa dānishmend*s who had been waiting for more than five years. On the other hand, since an *'ilmiyye* career ensured social prestige and exemption

---

[10] During the general dissolution of the classical imperial system between 1590-1650, critics who almost entirely were of the bureaucratic group sought to advise the sultans about the causes of Ottoman reverses and criticized the disregard for the established regulations in the *'ilmiyye* career line. Of this group, see Muṣṭafā 'Ālī (now see C. H. Fleischer, *Bureaucrat and Intellectual in the Ottoman Empire*: *The Historian Muṣṭafā 'Ālī ,1541-1600*, Princeton: P.U.P. 1986, Index: views, p. 347), and Koçi Beg (*Koçi Bey Risālesi*, ed. A. K. Aksüt, İstanbul, 1939; R. Murphey, "The Veliyüddin Telhīs: Notes on the sources and interralations between Koçi Beg and contemporary writers of Advice to Kings", *Belleten* 43 (1979), 547-571; a scholarly edition of the *Risāle* is still needed); these are the best known, used by Uzunçarşılı and others for the *'ilmiyye*; also see, *Ḳānūnnāme-i Sulṭānī li'Azīz Efendi,* ed. and trns. R. Murphey, Cambridge: Harvard University, 1985, 20, and *Kitâb-i Müstetab*, ed., Y. Yücel, Ankara: Üniversite Basımevi, 1974, 39-40); all of them emphasize on the abandonment of the established order; a systematic and critical study of the Ottoman advice to kings literature is needed for its use in historical research: see C. H. Fleischer, "Royal Authority, Dynastic Cyclism, and Ibn Khaldûnism in Sixteenth-Century Ottoman Letters", *Journal of Asian and African Studies*, XVIII (1983), 198-220 and "Süleyman ..." in this volume.

[11] For *mawālī* see M. C. Zilfi, "The Ottoman 'Ulemā', 1703-1839 and the Route to Great Mollaship" (Ph. D. dissertation, University of Chicago, 1976).

[12] Mehmed Rashid, *Tā'rīkh*, IV, Istanbul, 1282/1865, 50-51.

from taxes,[13] thousands of young men, particularly of peasant origin, flocked to the small town *madrasas*, or even created their own *madrasa,* in the Anatolian provinces during the sixteenth century. Appalling *sūhte* (softa) disorders of that period[14] forced the government to shut down most of the provincial *madrasas*, and the reform rescript of 1006/1597 stipulated (see Appendix no. 1, line 48) that "from now on, no candidate shall be admitted from provincial *madrasas (kenār madrasa)* unless that was a rule from a long time ago". Thus, cadi appointments and tenure periods concerned a large social group in Ottoman society,[15] and the so-called *sūhte* uprisings during the second half of the sixteenth century should be studied within this context.

The reform rescript of 1006/1597[16] described those groups which were responsible for further swelling the waiting list. The first group includes those employees of minor religious services who , by becoming clients of an influential person in the *'ilmiyye*, or through other loopholes, find access to candidacy. Thus, Muṣṭafā 'Ālī observes[17] that "so many Turks of condemnable character of the *randjbar* class have been honored by the posts of *ḳaḍā'* ". An 'ilmiyye career was the only way left for a Turk of *re'āyā* origin to climb on the social ladder and thus share the privileges of the military class in the Ottoman empire, when in the sixteenth century, the ruling group's monopoly over the positions of power became more rigid than ever, as a logical evolution of the political system. The graduates of the provincial madrasas flocked into *Iç-il* (the imperial core region composed of the

---

13 *Dānishmends* do not pay the *rusūm-i ra'iyyet*, but "those who claim to study but go around idly pay all *rusūm-i ra'iyyet*; this is an ancient rule" (Kānūnnāme, DTCF, University of Ankara, İsmail Saip Collection, p. 24).

14 See M. Akdağ, "Medreseli İsyanı", *İstanbul Üniversitesi İktisat Fakültesi Mecmuası*, XI, 361-387.

15 "Those who carry turban" (arbāb-i 'amā'im), i. e., *ahl-i manāṣib* and *ahl-i djihāt* together numbered about forty thousand toward the end of the fifteenth century (pseudo-Rūḥī, Oxford University, Bodleian Lib. Marsh MS: no.313, fol. 8).

16 Süleymaniye Library: Âşir ef. collection, *Ḳānūnnāme*, no. 1004, 69b-71a; the document is abridged by Uzunçarşılı, *op. cit.*, 244-246, in Latin characters; and again by C. Baltacı, *op. cit.*, 630-632, with a facsimile copy, see Appendix No. I.

17 Andreas Tietze, *Muṣṭafā 'Ālī's Counsel for Sultans of 1581*, Part I, Vienna: Akademie, 1979, Text: 174-180, English trans. 75-79. Tietze (p. 78) translates *randj-bar* as merchant; in fact it includes all "those people who earn their livelihood by work and pay taxes", as differentiated from the military class. 'Ālī certainly does not confine the meaning to *merchant.* In the previous paragraph the author speaks of peasants. Also in the page (H 65 r) only one village, not two villges, are in question. *"Fallāḥīn-i ḍiyā'"* translated as "*the fallāḥīn* of the villages" (trans. p. 78) are obviously not correct, *ḍiyā'*meaning fields. In this section dealing with the *'ilmiyye*, 'Ālī played with words which were particular to the profession, such as *mulāzemet (mulāzama), taḳṣīr, sharkh, matn-i matīn, ṭawāli'*, etc. (see text 62 v margin). Text is given in facsimile and transliteration in Tietze's work.

Istanbul, Edirne and Bursa districts) from the provinces, accepting any religious position they could find, to later seek a *mulāzemet* (candidacy for judgeship). The second group of outsiders consisted of soldiers of the Porte, including the janissaries, *sipāhīs*, cannoneers, etc. Since the study of religious sciences was encouraged for every Muslim, a soldier, too, could attend free public courses at a mosque, and obtain some kind of certificate. We are informed that college professors without students admitted anybody regardless of his vocation and ability.[18]

Thus, these outsiders were to be denied the way to cadiship partly because they caused congestion in the cadre, and thus upset the established order, and partly because they belonged to separate status groups and had different loyalties. Since the *'ilmiyye* career brought social prestige and many advantages, including exemption from taxes, even the high echelons of the military class sought the *'ilmiyye* career for their sons.[19]

When such pressures from outside became too strong, as it occurred from the mid-sixteenth century on, the ulema class became more status-minded, and, increasingly monopolistic regulations were promulgated in order to consolidate its ranks. This led to a growing authority and control of the high ulema as well as the bureaucratization of the *'ılmiyye*. It may not be a coincidence that growing control of the spiritual authority over state affairs paralleled this development. Both trends had already appeared under Süleyman (1520-1566) with the rise of Abū's-Su'ūd's (*Shaykh al-Islām*:1545-1574) influence. Several collections of registers similar to the one analyzed here bear witness to this growing process of bureaucratization.

Trying to restrict the qualifications through Sultanic rescripts the reformists set up a bureaucratic tradition to prevent the inroads of patrimonialism. Complaints and pressure from the lower ranks[20] as well as their occasional revolts often forced the Sultan to replace the *ulema* in power[21] with those favored by the reformist ones supported by the lower rank 'ilmiyye people, including the dānishmends and the small town cadis

---

[18] Rescript of 1006 mentioned in note 9, above, see Appendix no. I. lines 105-110.

[19] The *'ulemā* considered themselves higher than tha *umerā'* in terms of dignity and rank (cf. Madjdī, *Ḥadā'iḳ*, *op. cit.* 381 (for this translation of Tashkoprī-zāde's *al-Shaḳā'iḳ*, see Repp, 3-5).

[20] The *ulema* submitted in a *riḳ'a* their complaints against the *kadiasker* directly to the Sultan (Uzunçarşılı, 105) in the same manner as the *ra'āyā* , who appeared in the presence of the Sultan with *riḳ'a* , asking justice against the authorities (see H. Inalcik, *The Ottoman Empire, the Classical Age*, London: Weidenfeld and Nicolson, 1973, 88-93). The cadis' complaints caused the dismissal from office of Bāḳī, the *kadiasker* of Anatolia (*Selānīkī, Tā'rīkh*, MS: İsmail Saip collection 80 a).

[21] See Uzunçarşılı; *op. cit.*, 105.

(*ḳaṣabāt ḳādīları*). Thus, the reformist ulema, acting in the name of the *Dīn u Dawla* (Islam and Islamic State), attempted to suppress patrimonial and personal interventions in the *ṭarīḳ* (the hierarchical line defined by the regulations), i.e., the *shafā'at* (intercession) and the *'āṭifet* (favor). It should be remembered that, in order to prevent the swelling of the number of the cadi candidates, the reformers[22] insisted that the number of candidates to be admitted upon the *mawālī's* recommendation be restricted. However, the *mawālī*, as the recognized authorities in the Islamic sciences, had always the prerogative of entering in the list of mulāzims, one, two or more advanced students (*dānishmends*). In fact, it was a rule that to be a mulāzim a student had to have an assistant-ship under a molla for a certain period of time. This was believed to be a guarantee for knowledge and experience in the *'ilmiyye*, thence a guarantee for the authority and privilege of the high ulema class. Their sons, as they were considered to have access to a good education, were recognized for candidacy without the formalities to which others were subjected. However, the regulation provided that the prerogative not be abused.[23]

The *Molla*s were warned not to admit too many *dānishmend*s and not to attempt to enter in the list more than the number of *mulāzim*s as determined by law according to their rank. All *mulāzim*s had to wait for the beginning of the new shift (*nawba, nöbet*), and none could be registered in the interim, even if a special favor was extended by the Sultan himself. Only two of the *dānishmend*s of a deceased *molla* were to be admitted to *mulāzemet*. Such *mulāzim*s were called *mawtā mulāzimi* (*mulāzim*s of the dead). The historian 'Ālī[24] tells us how the list of the *dānishmend*s of a deceased *molla* might be a source of revenue for the heirs who sold candidacy regardless of qualification. The rescript of 1006[25] ruled that from the list of a deceased molla, *dānishmend*s should be admitted in specified number according to their rank only for "two shifts" (*iki nöbetlik*) and the remaining *dānishmend*s in his list should be placed to serve under other *molla*s.

At any rate, the mollas' prerogative seems to have been the source of widespread rumours of bribery and favoritism, whether true or unfounded. The regulation, once made, was considered a fixed line (*ṭarīḳ*) and the candidates or *dānishmends* insisted that the *ṭarīḳ* rules be strictly applied, that the prerogatives not be abused, and that qualification be established on the basis of proficiency. But the latter could be established only by the

---

22 The Rescript of 1006, lines 40-60; also see Uzunçarşılı, *op. cit.*, 46.

23 *Ibid.*, lines 100-115.

24 *Op. cit.*, H 64 r, trans. 78.

25 Lines 40-45.

recognized authorities, i. e., the *mawālī*s who issued a written certificate and recommendation, or by a formal examination at the *kadiasker's* office. The *ṭarīḳ* 's authority was based on tradition established by the founding Sultans, Mehmed the Conqueror, and Suleyman the Lawgiver. In the later reform rescripts, reference was always made for validity to the *ṭarīḳ* established by them.

Shaykh al-Islām Abū's-Su'ūd is credited with introducing fundamental bureaucratic reforms including the *mulāzemet*, the *'ilmiyye* system,[26] and for assuming responsibility for the appointments of the *molla* judgeships.[27] However, a report[28] to the Sultan, apparently of an earlier date, provides evidence that basic features of the organization, including the *mulāzemet*, were established before him. The principle that cadi appointments should be made from among the *madrasa* professors (*mudarris*) was in force at the time the report was written. The reporter tells us that contrary to this rule, *nā'ib*s with no regular *madrasa* education, or other inferior religious functionaries, had gained access to judgeships thanks to their bribed intercessors. It points out that in the appointment of judges, the most important criterion should be the mastery of the religious sciences, which could be acquired only through a regular *madrasa* education and by attendance (*mulāzemet*) on the authorities (*mawālī*). He complains about the malpractice that "any candidate, whether qualified or not, enjoys the Sultan's favor if supported by an intercessor". Such intruders, he says, enjoy promotion without waiting for the *mulāzemet*. Thus, *mulāzemet* was considered to provide additional training under the *mawālī* and enabled one to obtain a higher assignment. It is interesting to note that even in this early period, bribery and favoritism were indicated to be widespread malpractices resorted to, with the aim of obtaining and keeping judgeships.[29] Anticipating all the later critics, the reporter notes that under the

---

26 New'ī-zāde 'Aṭā'ī, *Ḥadā'iḳ al-Ḥaḳā'iḳ fī Takmilat al-Shaḳā'iḳ*, İstanbul, 1268 H., 184; Repp, *op. cit.*, 272-296.

27 Uzunçarşılı, *op. cit.*, 155-156, 179-181; this information from 'Ālī, *Kunh al-Akhbār*, needs further investigation, cf. C. Baltacı, 51-53; Repp, 293.

28 See the important document published by M. Cezar, *Osmanlı Tarihinde Levendler*, İstanbul: Güzel Sanatlar Akademesi, 1965, 469-470, undated; internal evidence (accession to the throne of Pādishāh-i Suleymān-i Zaman) suggests early reign of Suleyman I (1520-1566).

29 Anonymous *Tawārīkh-i Āl-i 'Osmān* which was originally compiled under Bāyezīd II (1481-1512) gives interesting details on the appointment of cadis. It states (Giese edition, 30; a more complete text TKP Library, M R. 700) that before Bāyezīd I's time (1389-1402) whenever there was a vacant cadiship no appointment was made until the time when an able dānishmend from madrasas was found. Also, considering great responsibility, candidates were not eager to become a cadi. But now, people, Anonymous says, "kill each other to seize a cadi office. In our days merit is not

circumstances those who were studying the religious sciences were no longer held in esteem, and adds that "no more serious failure can be imagined for a Sultan who is tolerant on the matters concerning the Sharī'a, and does not bother to see whether his commands are executed."

IV. Data from The Rūznāmçe Register

Let us now examine a routine appointment case from the register. The record we have chosen for our purpose (11, Siroz or Serres)[30] says: "It was submitted to the Sultan (*ba'd al-'arḍ*): this *ḳaḍā'* of Siroz is granted (*buyruldu*) to Mawlānā Khalīl, who has left the *ḳaḍā'* of Ahyolu with three hundred akça and has completed his time of two years out of office (*infiṣāl*) and the time of presence in Istanbul (*Āsitāne*), on condition that Mawlānā Meḥmed, son of Bahā' al-Dīn who is at present the cadi of Siroz, holding it for a limited time (*muwaḳḳatan*), completed his tenure period (*tekmîl-i müddet ettikden sonra*)".

The terms *takmīl-i müddet (mudda), muwaḳḳatan* , *infiṣāl* and *Āsitāne* are all connected with a quite complex procedure of appointment.

A judgeship was limited to a tenure period. The famous rescript of 1006/1597 stipulates (lines 74-77): "a new candidate (*mulāzim*) shall not be appointed before he completes three years (of waiting).... The cadis of small towns shall be in possession of their post for two full years".

The *müddet* or *müddet-i 'urfiyya* determined the duration of judgeship at a post. Before 1006/1597, it was three years,[32] and was shortened later on to two years, and then to twenty months, as attested to in our register (13, Kirebene). It was again further reduced to eighteen months during the second half of the eighteenth century. As a rule tenure started on the first day of the month of Muharram. Establishing the period of tenure was called *'urfī* because it was based on the Sultan's order and could be changed at any time

---

considered important for the appointment. An ignorant person who happens to have been in the service of an influential man for some time obtains cadiship through his mediation.... In those days, candidates used not to come in crowd to the kadiasker's service and to be in attandance (mulāzemet), humiliating themselves». This abridged text clearly shows that clientship, mulāzemet, and keen competition among the candidates were already burning issues toward the end of the fifteenth century. Evidently, things had not necessarily been better in earlier times as our source shows.

30 *The Rūznāmçe of the kadiasker of Rumeli*, p. 11, reproduced in Appendix No. II.

32 Selānīkī, 223b, MS mentioned in at note 3, p. 9; around 1006/1597, tenure period was reduced to two years. However, those cadis who were active in the service of the collection of provisions for the army (*nüzül*) could stay for three years. Extension of the tenure for those who were performing such services was in force as late as the eighteenth century.

as he saw fit. The tenure period of the *mawlawiyyets*, i. e., the high *ulema* ranks, was one year in the seventeenth century.[33]

Earlier, we pointed out that as a rule, the number of *ḳaḍā's* (*ḳāḍā'* meant the authority and area of jurisdiction of a cadi)[34] could not be increased at will. However, economic conditions as well as administrative expediency could bring about changes. In fact, towards the year 1057/1647, an order of the Sultan restored all the *ḳāḍā's* which had previously been abolished and annexed to others. This meant an increase in the number of posts available to candidates, a measure which evidently made the incumbent *kadiasker* who initiated the change, popular with the entire *'ilmiyye* group because the move (*hareket*) involved promotions at every level down to the *dānishmends*. On the other hand, partitioning signified smaller jurisdictions with reduced revenues. Sometimes a *ḳaḍā'* was united with the *arpalıḳ* (pension) of a *molla*, which caused the incumbent cadi to lose his source of income (114, Izdin). This was another reason why lower level ulema were resentful of the *mollas*' privileged status.

In 1078/1667, *Shaykh al-Islām* Minkārī-zāde Yaḥyā Efendi ordered the *kadiasker* of Rumeli 'Abd al-Ḳādir Sinānī Efendi to revise all the *ḳaḍā'* posts in Rumeli and make a new list.[35] Accordingly, Sinānī Efendi convoked in his *dīvān* the high ranking cadis (*eshrāf-i ḳuḍāt*), revised the existing *ḳaḍā's*, and made a new list by unifying the *ḳaḍā's* of insufficient revenue. The new listing contained 361 cadiships (kadılık), divided into twelve categories. Later on, however, the number was increased to 477.

We can establish the actual tenure periods from the *kadiasker's* *rūznāmçes* (cf. Table I). In general, the shortening of the tenure period must have been determined primarily by the growing number of the candidates waiting for their appointment. The pressure becomes apparent by the fact that complaints were constantly expressed about appointments made against the *'ilmiyye* regulations through bribery or nepotism. Such malpractices, which caused longer waiting periods for the candidates, sometimes gave rise to serious political crises which ended with the change of the *kadiasker* or the *shaykh al-Islām* in office. Thus, having serious political implications, each new regulation was promulgated with the Sultan's strict order prohibiting

---

33 *Millī Tetebbu'lar Medjmū'ası*, I (Istanbul, 1331/1915), 541.

34 Cadis are the agents of the Sultan, "their ruling power (*wilāya*) is derived from the Caliph's autorization": Abū's Su'ūd, "Ma'rūḍāt",. *Millī Tetebbu'lar Medjmū'ası*, I, 339-340.

35 M. Kemal Özergin, "Rumeli Kadılıkları'nda 1078 Düzenlemesi," *İsmail Hakkı Uzunçarşılı'ya Armağan*, Ankara : Türk Tarih Kurumu, 1976, 251, 259.

such malpractices. This was issued in the form of a *khaṭṭ-i hümāyūn*, i. e., an order written personally by the Sultan himself.

Our register demonstrates (see table I) that even before large-scale revisions, new *ḳaḍā's* were formed or abolished when a particular area experienced a considerable growth or decline in population and/or prosperity.[36] However, it appears that a merely administrative motive —to create new cadiships to alleviate the congestion at the lower levels, or to meet a high revenue jurisdiction for a particular candidate— was responsible for most of the changes (as mentioned earlier, a cadi's revenue was calculated on the basis of ten ten *akça* for every one thousand houses). The partition of a *ḳaḍā'* is called *ifrāz*, and its unification is called *ilḥaḳ* Both the *ifrāz* and *ilḥāḳ* created problems as far as the rotation period of the actual office holder was concerned. When a judge lost his *ḳaḍā* because of its annexation to another jurisdiction, the cadi was usually transferred to a vacant *ḳaḍā'* to complete his tenure. But then, the remaining months out of the twenty months of *müddet-i 'urfiyya* had to be filled with a shorter appointment. There are many such arrangements to fit actual cases in our register.

When a cadi completed his tenure period (*takmīl-i müddet*) in a *ḳaḍā'*, he spent a certain period of time in "separation" (*infiṣāl*) before he came to Istanbul (*Āsitane*), and stayed there for a certain period of time in *mulāzemet* under the *kadiasker* he served. This *mulāzemet* period was three years in the rescript of 1006/1597. In our register (1647), the shortest infisal *infiṣāl* (out of office) period was one year, and the *mulāzemet* in Istanbul also was one year. The duration of the "complete period" (*kāmil*) for both infisal and *āsitāne* cannot be determined from our source . The *mulāzemet* is considered to be a period during which the cadi could increase his knowledge and experience to qualify for a higher position.

When a cadi completed his tenure period (*takmīl-i müddet*) in a *ḳaḍā'*, he sepent a certain period of time in "separation" (*infiṣāl*) before he came to Istanbul (*Āsitane*), and stayed there for a certain period of time in *mulāzemet* under the *kadiasker* he served. This *mulāzemet* period was three years in the rescript of 1006/1597. In our register (1647), the shotest *infiṣāl* (out of office) period was one year, and the *mulāzemet* in Istanbul also was one year. The duration of the "complete period" (*kāmil*) for both *infiṣāl* and *Āsitāne* cannot be determined from our source. The *mulāzemet* is considered to be a

36 For an actual case of creating a new *kaḍā'*, see the document published by Ö. L. Barkan, in *İstanbul Üniversitesi İktisat Fakültesi Mecmuası*, II-2, p. 235, document no. XXI (41 villages were separated from the kada's of Vize, Hayrabolu, Baba-Eskisi, Çorlu and Pınar-Hisar and a new *kadılık* was established at the *nāhiye* of Burgoz), A *kadā'* may encompass from 50 villages to 300 or more.

period during which the cadi could increase his knowledge and experience to qualify for a higher position.

If the cadi was dismissed for any reason from office before his *müddet* was completed, this was called the *'azl* or *raf'*, and he himself was included among the dismissed (*ma'zūl*). The reasons for dismissal varied: it might result from popular complaint, usually in written form, signed by the local notables ('arḍ-i maḥḍar),[37] or, from the cadi's failure to fulfill an important public assignment, such as collecting tax, or gathering men for some public service. For example, in our register, the cadi of Alasonya failed to gather oarsmen (*kürekçi*) in due time, so he was replaced by another who pledged to complete the service in time. The loss of one's office before the expiration of the tenure period was considered unjust (*maghdūran*) when it occurred as a result of a bureaucratic mistake, or in violation of the regulations. In such cases compensations were arranged such as deducting the remaining time of the *müddet* from the waiting period at the *mulāzemet*. In general, the *kadiasker* was sympathetic to a judge who lost his tenure, and who thus remained without income (*ṣifr al-yad*). The tenure period could be extended (*madd* or *ḍamm*), or shortened (*ḳaṣr* or *taḳṣīr*) under special conditions. When travelling became hazardous due to adverse weather conditions or other factors, the central government would agree to grant an extension of several months. Sometimes an incumbent judge agreed by his own free will to an extension in favor of the departing judge, and both judges would then, by mutual consent, submit for the government's approval. However, an early arrival of the new cadi often caused friction so that a general order[38] was issued so as not to offend the new comer. In addition to dismissal (*raf'*), death or resignation (*farāgh*) also entailed shorter terms.

The extension of a tenure for an incumbent cadi, usually of a few months, was not infrequent, and was made on the testimony that he conducted himself well (*husn-i sulūk*), successfully fulfilled a special order of the Sultan, or helped the tax farmer in his job (13, Platamona). In the special case referred to, the testimony came from the cadi who came to replace him.

In addition to the bureaucratic concern of finding employment for as many candidates as possible, considerations of a political nature also affected the government's decision to grant a shorter period of tenure (*taṣarruf*). In any case, it was a kind of "constitutional" precept in the Ottoman patrimonial

---

[37] For *'arḍ-i maḥḍar* see H. Inalcik, "Şikâyet Hakkı: *'Arz-i Ḥâl ve 'Arz-i Mahzar'lar*", *Journal of Ottoman Studies*, vol. VII-VIII dedicated to Professor John Walsh (Istanbul, 1987).

[38] Kānūnnāme, I. Saip, Col. no. 5120, 147v.

system not to allow government agents to hold a provincial position for too long, lest he establish local connections and be integrated into the community. In fact, having a key position, and thus secure economic advantages some of the dismissed cadis, taking advantage of the special conditions which arose in the eighteenth century, actually settled in the towns, and they, or their offspring became local notables. Many of the *a'yān*s then were former *ḳāḍī*s or *ḳāḍī-zāde*s.

During the *mulāzemet* period in Istanbul, on Wednesdays when the *kadiasker*'s council (*dīwān*) was convoked, all the cadis who were out of office attended the meeting in their ceremonial attire.[39] Those who had completed the mulāzemet period applied for a post with promotion.

Verifying his qualifications, i. e., his former service with income, his time in "separation" (*infiṣāl*) out of office, and *mulāzemet* (*Āsitane*), with the register called *ṭarīḳ defteri* or *aḳḍiye defteri,* the office of the *kadiasker* would prepare a register called *maṭlab* (register of requests), to be submitted for the Sultan's approval.

Then, the *kadiasker* would issue a signed order (*buyruldu*)[40] notifying the candidate of the Sultan's approval, specifying the *ḳaḍā'* jurisdiction, the daily revenue, the starting date and the duration of his tenure.

The *buyruldu*s were copied chronologically in the *ṭarīḳ defteri*, also known as the *rūznāmçe* (daybook), like our register. The appointment (*tawdjīh*) brought about the *ittiṣāl* (joining the office). A diploma of the Sultan (*berāt* or *nishān*)[41] established the possession of his *ḳaḍā'* jurisdiction and his authority over the community in the *ḳaḍā'*. Each *ḳaḍā'* had its definite boundaries where the cadi's jurisdiction, exercised in the name of the Sultan, was absolute. Another cadi could ask him to see to a matter by sending him a letter called *murāsala.*

There were two *kadiasker*s; the *kadiasker* of Anatolia was responsible for the cadis of Anatolia and Arabia, and the *kadiasker* of Rumeli, for those of the cadis of the Balkans and the northern Black Sea. As a rule, a judge had to stay throughout his career under either of them. The cadiships of Rumeli were considered of higher status.

It was possible for a cadi to be transferred from Anatolia to Rumeli after submitting for the Sultan's approval. For example, in our regīster, Ḥalīl who was appointed to the *ḳaḍā'* of Ladik in Anatolia, was transferred to Izdin in

---

[39] Uzunçarşılı, *op. cit.*, 104, but the day of *mulāzemet* was Thursday in the nineteenth century: see A. Cevdet, Tā'rīkh, I, 111.

[40] A specimen is to be found in Uzunçarşılı, *op. cit.*, 90.

[41] A specimen in Uzunçarşılı, *op. cit.*, Levha XVIII, (for a molla), 112.

Rumeli, a *ḳaḍā'* of corresponding revenue and rank (*bedel*), upon the Sultan's approval (14, Izdin).

As explained earlier, the *mulāzemet* period was considered to provide additional training. Besides, the patrimonial character of the Ottoman administration required that a report (*'arḍ*) by the immediate supervisor testify to the ability and qualifications of the candidate for any appointment. Similarly, a dismissed *sipāhī* who did not participate (*mulāzemet*) under a sandjak bey in the campaigns for seven years, would lose his qualification for military service, and be reduced to the status of *re'āyā* (tax-paying subject). However, it should also be noted that in all appointments Ottoman bureaucratic rule stipulated that the candidate should qualify not only by keeping the company (*mulāzemet*) of his supervisor, but should also prove his ability and knowledge (*ehliyyet*) for the job. In other words, *istiḥḳāḳ* (right acquired by precedence) and *ehliyyet* were two basic qualifications which were required, as a rule, for office.

In our register, the previous service and the *mulāzemet* at the *kadiasker*'s office were mentioned in the document submitting (*'arḍ*) the case to the approval of the Sultan. By submitting it, the *kadiasker* assumed the responsibility that the candidate had fulfilled the required conditions. The Sultan's approval was a formality.

Overriding the *istiḥḳāḳ* and the *ehliyyet*, the Sultan could, without formalities, order the integration of a member of the *'ilmiyye* community into the candidacy list by special favor (*'āṭifet* or *'ināyet*). But even then, the rules of appointment were not overlooked, because no one, not even the Sultan, could act arbitrarily in matters concerning the application of the *Sharī'a*..

During the infiṣāl (separation) and mulāzemet (Āsitane) period the conditions in the capital of the empire actually imposed a costly lifestyle, with mounts, frequent visits of high dignitaries, etc., due to the patrimonial relationships which were necessary for future appointments and promotion.

The author of *Kitāb-i Musṭaṭāb,*[42] exaggerating of course, wrote: "Those cadis who are present in Istanbul after their dismissal from office, live lavishly, having houses and country homes with gardens, servants and retainers all acquired by borrowed money. When he is finally appointed to a judgeship, this is obtained by bribery. He can hold this position for one and a half years, or at most two years if he has a supporter. Now to make money, enough to meet all these debts, including the bribe money given to the state dignitaries, and to save up for the years of dismissal ahead, he robs the *re'āyā*. If he does his job within the bounds of the *Sharī'a* and in justice, it is

[42] *Kitâb-i Müstetâb*, ed. Y. Yücel, Ankara, 1974, 39-40.

obvious that his revenues can never go beyond four thousand gold pieces a year." On the other hand, a short tenure period, leading to the plundering taxpayers, was a major problem not only in the *'ilmiyye*, but also in governorship and in tax farming. Then, the bureaucrats, changing the system under pressure from those with vested interests, would introduce life tenure (*mālikāne*) in tax farming and landholding, especially during the eighteenth century. However, the tenure period for judges and governors did not change under the new regime. The cadis' rapaciousness became proverbial. Evliyā 'Çelebi, with candor or sarcasm, mentions that such and such a cadiship brought an annual revenue so much 'in justice' but twice as much 'in injustice' as if this were quite a routine case. Ottoman bureaucratic concern led to a strict definition in the regulations and laws of all kinds of service fees and other dues which the cadis were to collect for themselves and their assistants.[43] On the other hand, a cadi's position was quite precarious in the Ottoman patrimonial system. He could be deprived of his office at any time, despite the stipulation that the appointment had been made for a definite period of time. The diary of a relatively successful *mudarris-ḳāḍī*, Ṣidḳī Muṣṭafā,[44] reveals anxieties due to such uncertainties. The revenue of the post might be too little. And, as Koçi Beg[45] puts it, "cadis have become extremely despicable and contemptible. Upon a complaint of a *subashı* ar *ḫarādj* collector, they are dismissed from their office. So many of them are discharged without justification."

The *kadiaskers*, too, were accused of bribery, nepotism and favoritism. It was the Sultan's highest responsibility to see that "those who are his deputies in the administration of the *Sharī'a* did not abuse the power entrusted to them". Just as provincial cadis were inspected by secret agents assigned directly by the Sultan, the Sultan tested his *kadiaskers* by sending secret agents who would attempt to bribe them. The author of such an inspection reports[46] those cadis who obtained an office by being an assistant (*nā'ib*) at a cadi court, or through a minor religious appointment. He discloses those cadis who were known to be drinking wine, taking bribes, or simply, to be ignorant.

Similar criticisms of ignorance, of appointments outside the line and the regular promotion system, of bribery and favoritism were to be levelled later on by bureaucrats (Selānīkī, Muṣṭafā 'Ālī, Akhiṣārī, the author of *Kitāb-i*

---

[43] See H. İ., "Adâletnâmeler", *Belgeler*, II (Ankara, 1967), 78.

[44] See M. Zilfi, "The Diary of a Muderris", *Journal of Turkish Studies*, I (1977), 157-174; for the executed cadis see, Uzunçarşılı, *op. cit.*, 106-107; on cadis' malpratices and abuses see H. İ., "Adâletnâmeler", 75-79.

[45] Uzunçarşılı, *op. cit.*, 252.

[46] See above note 28; a similar report in Uzunçarşılı, *op. cit.*, Levha XVII.

Musṭaṭāb, Koçi Beg and others).[47] They all stress that two basic principles of *istiḥḳāḳ* and *ehliyyet* should be followed in the appointment of judges, and that all cadis should be appointed from among the madrasa professors, and they serve under the *mawālī* in the *mulāzemet* period. In other words, the bureaucratic tradition believed it was imperative that the rules and regulations be followed against personal and patrimonial favors, including those coming from the Sultan, to ensure that such a fundamentally important sector of the administration function properly.

Ferīdūn Beg's collection of state papers[48] includes an important document on the issues which the cadis were concerned about at the turn of the sixteenth century. The document is the Sultan's order to the *kadiasker* of Rumeli about a joint petition of the cadis in which they complained about the difficult times they were facing, particularly with regard to mistreatment by agents of the Sultan.

In this document they acknowledge the relief they had as a result of the careful observation of the tenure periods (*tavḳīt*) which secured an increase in the number of cadiships available. Prior to that time, those cadis who were in Istanbul to complete their candidacy (*mulāzemet*) period were stricken by poverty and hardships as a result of the *Djelālī*s looting their homes and properties in the provinces. At present, they said, when the collection of extraordinary impositions (*'awāriḍ*) such as wheat, barley, or flour from the *re'āyā* was ordered, they made every effort to collect and deliver the goods at the place ordered despite many difficulties. But the army agents to whom they made the deliveries were unwilling to issue the consignment documents unless the cadis agreed to pay an excessive fee. Some of the agents, claiming that an excessive amount was collected from the *re'āyā*, pressured the cadis for money and even caused the Sultan to order an investigation against the cadis, and without a court decision they broke into their homes and seized their properties. When a consignment document was obtained after the payment of a large amount of money, it was not accepted when they arrived in Istanbul; what is more, those agents in charge of collecting the arrears there imprisoned them and pressured them for extra payments.

Secondly, the cadis complained that the number of small cadiships had recently decreased because they had been combined with the cadiships of the ranks higher than 150 *aḳça* despite the Sultan's order. According to this order, these small cadiships should have been separated and assigned to those cadis who were entitled to them.

---

47 For these see note 10 above.

48 *Munsha'āt al-Salāṭīn*, (Istanbul, 1275/1858), 225

Thirdly, they requested the Sultan's specific order that only the *kadiasker* should be responsible for the appointment of the cadis, and that the vizirs, *defterdārs* or anyone else shall not interfere. The *kadiasker* should hear the case if a cadi is liable for punishment or prosecution for appropriating public revenue; and the judges and other officials in charge of the collection of taxes in the provinces should not interfere. The case should be examined in the presence of the *kadiasker* in the imperial council and the cadi should be punished when the charge is decided in due process of law. But, they said, what actually happened, was that those officials who were empowered to protect the public interests in the provinces either initiated a public investigation and arrested the cadis and confiscated their properties, or inflicted severe punishments and even found a pretext to hang them, against the established rule that no cadi or ulema is subject to execution. So the cadis lost all respect and dignity and they became powerless in administering the commands of the *Sharī'a*.

Fourthly, they said there were cadis who obtained their posts on a permanent basis (*ta'bīd*), or by bribery, or being present in Istanbul less than the legal candidacy period, or without any service in the provinces they were appointed. Such cadis should be removed and their posts assigned to those who were entitled to them.

When all these illegal practices were submitted to his attention, the Sultan ordered that no shortening of the tenure period was to be allowed without a just reason and, when the tenure period (*tawḳīt*) was to be shorttened under certain circumstances, this should be restricted at most to a couple of months. Also he ordered that as far as the collection of *'awāriḍ* taxes was concerned, the cadis should not be pressured when they held a delivery document, and that of those posts added to higher ranking cadi benefices, those which were created lately should be separated, because permanent appointment (*ta'bīd*) is not permissible in the cadiship. This is permissible only for *madrasa* professors who hold tenure long enough and merit such a favor.

In the same edict the Sultan also ordered that those cadis whose unlawful acts may entail severe punishment or execution shall be heard by the kadiasker in the imperial council; but in cases in which investigations involved the rights of common people, and decisions were already given by the trustworthy judges, it was an old established rule that a general inspection was to be ordered against the cadis. The Sultan promised that in such cases inspection was to be entrusted to the persons whose reliability was commonly attested. The Sultan also ordered that a cadiship assigned by the commanders in chief during a campaign should not be actually occupied by the appointee unless he is added to the kadiasker's appointment list (ruznamçe).

This firman illustrates the widespread discontent among the lesser cadis who called for reform in the last years of Mehmed III's reign. The fact that it was included among the important state papers shows the significance attributed to it in the period.

This imperial order was promulgated during the kadiasker-ship of Rumeli of Akhī-zāde 'Abd al-Ḥalīm (his appointment was in 1010 Safer/August 1601).'Abd al-Ḥalīm was a scholar highly acclaimed by his contemporaries.[49] He was known to be responsible for establishing a new list of candidates for the cadiship (nöbet) and for obtaining the Sultan's approval in Receb 1011/January 1602. He became very popular among the cadis and the ulema, and one of his contemporaries addressed him saying: "You are the shah on the throne of justice with perfect religious zeal and virtue, and every order of the Sultan relies on your rolls and council." Actually, to make the Sultan approve a new list of candidates for cadiships meant that the kadiasker had to create a new group of clients for himself.

---

[49] N. 'Aṭāī, *Ḥadā'iḳ al-ḥaḳā'iḳ fi takmilat al-shaḳā'iḳ*, ed. M. Re<u>dj</u>ā'ī (Istanbul, 1268), 496.

Table 1
The Ḳaḍā' appointments made upon the Sultan's approval, by the Kadiasker of Rumeli according to the Rūznāmçe Register of 1057/1647

					Yawmiyye	
Ḳaḍā'	Müddet	Infiṣāl years	Asitâne years	Bâ-berât	Previous ak'ca	New ak'ca
Alasonya	after completion	2	complete	no	150	200
Livadye	after completion	4		yes	40	100
Livadye	after completion	ca.1	1	no	150	200
Siroz (Serez)	after completion	over 2	complete (kāmil)	no	300	300
Vodena	after completion	2	complete	no	100	150
Istifa	after completion	ca. 2	complete	no	80	130
Köstendil	because of his good conduct two months extension (*ḍamm*)					
Mundeniça	after completion	4	complete	no	40	130
Bosna Brodu	after completion	2	complete	yes	130	150
Balya-Badra	after completion	complete	complete	no (*ifrāz*)	40 (*madrasa*)	130
Sarta	annexed to the ḳaḍa' of Akkerman					
Egri	after completion	3	complete	yes	40 (*madrasa*)	130
Akçahisar	after completion	complete	complete	no	80	100
Kızılcahisar	unjustly dismissed				150	?
Ilbasan	because of his good conduct two months extension					
Lipva	after completion	complete	complete	no	100	130
Karinabad	mudarris prepared for outside service			no	40	150
Delvine	after completion		complete	yes	40	100
Seksar	after completion	17 months	complete	yes	70	80
Pilevne	after Mas'ud completed his time to be assigned to Mahmud and then to Ahmed					
Platamona	since the holder resigned the normal time shortened					
Izladi	annexed to the *nāhiye* of Etrepoli					
Kirebene (Grebene)	because of the good conduct of the cadi in office two months extension of his tenure					
Iskaradin	shortening because of death					

Ḳaḍā'	Müddet	Infiṣāl years	Āsitāne years	Bā-berāt	Yevmiyye Previous akça	New akça
Maçin	after completion	3	2	no	50 (madarasa)	100
Arnavaud Belgradı	after completion	2	complete	no	200	300
Üsküp	extension because of previous shortening					
Pojega	after completion	—	complete	no	40 (madarasa)	150
Segedin	shortening of the tenure because of death, then, it was learned that the news was not true, it was confirmed (*ibḳā'*)					
Preveze	four months extension because of good conduct					
Hezargrad	after completion	?	complete	yes	300	300
Kefe	no one was willing to assume, so it was annexed to the ḳaḍā of Alushta					
Akhisar	after completion	complete	complete	no	130	150
Inebahtı	after completion	complete	complete		150	150
Izdin	fallen vacant, it is assigned to Khalil who had the *ḳaḍā'* of Ladik of 130 akça in Anatolia					
Bereketli	fallen vacant, assigned to *mudarris* Mawlānā 'Alī				40	150
Başagaç	after completion	complete	complete	no	40 (madrasa)	150
Beckerek	after completion	4	complete	no	40 (madrasa)	130
Ürgüp	after completion	complete	complete	no	40 (madrasa)	150

TABLE II
PROMOTIONS TO JUDGESHIP ACCORDING TO THE REGISTER OF 1057/1647*

Ḳaḍā' (Judgeship)		*Mudarrislik* (Professorship)	
Previous grade	Promoted to	Grade at madrasa	Pramoted to *ḳaḍā'*
50	100	40	100
70	80	40	130
100	150	40	150
120	150	50	100
150	200		
200	300		

* It is obvious that a factor other than previous grade can always be valid. However, promotion from 200 leads regularly to a 300 *akça* judgeship. On the other hand, a *mudarris* of 40 *akça* could have a *ḳaḍā'* of 100, 130 or 150 *akça*. A *mudarris* of 50 *akça* did have a ḳaḍā" of 100. Most of the new appointments occurred with a promotion (*taraḳḳī*). If the appointment was made without a promotion, this was called *mişliyle*, i.e., with the same (compensation). In this category were included the judges who wanted to be appointed a specific *ḳaḍā'*, or who asked for some other kinds of favor.

Appendix I

Source: Süleymaniye Library. İstanbul, Âşir Efendi K. No. 1004, 69 b-71 a: see Baltacı, *op.cit.*, 630-634.

Appendix II

Rumeli kadiaskeri Rūznamçe Defteri, 1057/1647.

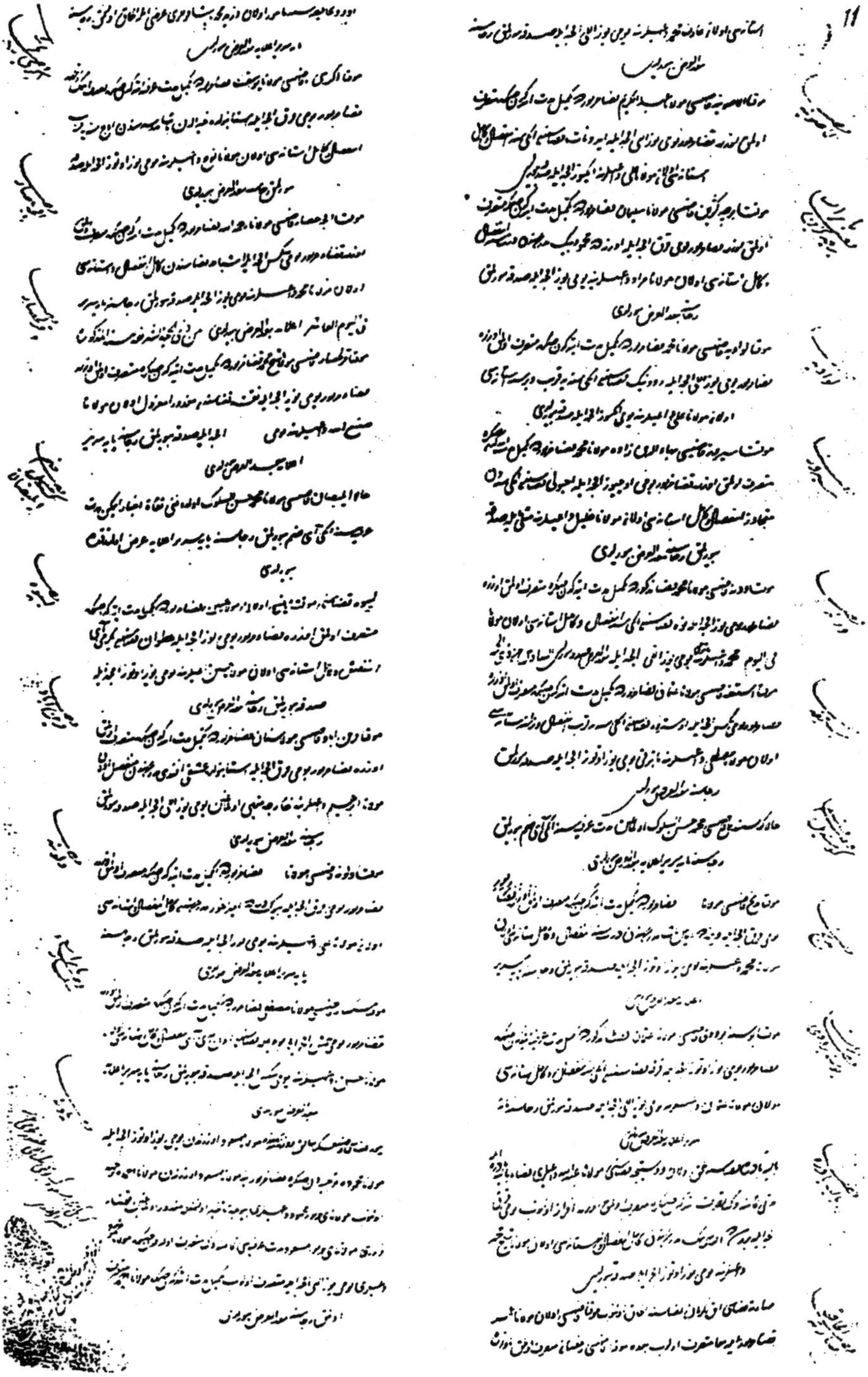

13

5

Islamization of Ottoman laws on land and land tax

Islamization of Ottoman laws on land and land tax

Following the Ottoman occupation of Hungray in 1541, the practical question arose as to how Islamic-Ottoman land law was to be applied in this newly-conquered Christian country. Out of concern for acting in strict conformity with the precepts of Islamic Law, Sultan Süleyman apparently asked the Ottoman jurist Ebū's-Su'ūd Meḥmed (who was the Rumeli ḳaḍī-'askeri in 1537 and Şeyḫülislām in the period 1548-75) to give an authoritative opinion on this matter based on the Sharī'a.

In the introduction to the survey registers of Budin (Hungary),[1] Ebū's-Su'ūd first summarizes the Sultan's order[2] to the effect that in this newly conquered land the population is not to be relocated, and full security is to be guaranteed for the people and their offspring. The decree continues:

"They are to keep their movable properties as well as their houses and shops and other buildings in the towns and villages, and their vineyards and orchards in the countryside, as their freehold property (*mülk*) to dispose of as they wish, by sale, donation, etc. When they die these properties are to pass to their heirs in full ownership, and no one shall interfere with them on condition that they pay legal taxes (*ḥuḳūḳ*) on their vineyards and orchards. Also, the fields (*tarla*) which they have cultivated are to be left in their possession, and [their rights of possession] confirmed (*muḳarrer*).

The fields, however, are not considered as freehold property in the manner of their other possessions. As elsewhere in the well-protected territories [of the Ottoman Sultans] they are rather considered as *memleke* lands, also known as *mīrī*.[3] On these lands the *dominium eminens* (*raḳaba*)

---

[1] The first survey of the Budin province, now preserved at the Başbakanlık Ottoman Archives, Istanbul, is drawn up in 1546. See G. Káldy-Nagy: *Kanuni Devri Budin Tahrir Defteri.* Ankara: DTC Fakültesi, Pub. no. 177, 5. This defter does not have the text of the *ḳanūnnāme*. A later survey (BOA, no. 987), also made under Suleyman I, has it. Apparently it is originally written by Ebū's-Su'ūd as a *fetvā* and it appears to have been re-formulated later on as the Sultan's order.

[2] See Barkan: *XV. ve XVI'ıncı Asırlarda Osmanlı İmparatorluğunda Ziraî Ekonominin Hukukî ve Malî Esasları.* İstanbul 1943, 296-297; cf. "Osmanlı Kânunnâmeleri". *Millî Tetebbu'lar Mecmuası* (hereafter MTM) I (1331 H.), 49-50.

[3] According to Ebū's-Su'ūd the *mīrī*, or, *memleke* (mamlaka) land as found in the Ottoman practice, means the land under the state *raḳaba* or ownership; the term *arḍ al-mamlaka*

belongs to the public treasury (*beytü'l-māl*) of the Islamic community. The fields are considered to be in possession of the *re'āyā* on a lease (*'āriye, 'āriyet*); the *re'āyā* may sow grain or other crops as they choose, and must render the *ḫarāc-i muḳāseme* under the name of tithe (*'öşr*) and other taxes. Thus, they may cultivate these lands as they wish. No one shall interfere and transgress [their possession of their lands] as long as they continue to cultivate and improve them appropriately and to render taxes in their entire amount. They possess the land during their lifetime and at their death their sons inherit and hold possession in the same manner as described above. If no son survives, the land is to be given on a lease to a person outside the family who is capable of cultivating it in return for the payment of a rent paid in advance (*ücret-i mu'accele*). Thereupon he too holds the land in his possession under the aforementioned conditions. The plots of their vineyards and orchards are also included in the category of state lands (*mīrī*) when the vines and trees are depleted. Then the plots are to be possessed in the same manner as fields. Thus, the plots should not be assumed to be their private property in the same manner as their vineyards and orchards".

In this document Ebū's-Su'ūd, following Şeyḫülislām Ibn Kemāl[4] and other Ottoman şeyḫülislāms before him, attemps to interpret the nature of state ownership of the land and peasants' possession rights in terms of the notions of Islamic jurisprudence. The point he emphasizes is that *mīrī* land, as a specific category, comprises only the fields reserved for the cultivation of grain, and excludes vineyards and orchards. The entire land, however, including vineyards and orchards, as well as the building lots in the towns, is considered under the *raḳaba* (*dominium eminens*) of the Sultan. When the land was no longer used as a vineyard or an orchard it was again included in the category of *mīrī*.[5] Ebū's-Su'ūd, always following the classic interpretation of the ninth century Muslim jurists,[6] interprets the *ḫarāc* tax as

---

instead of *mīrī* with the same meaning is in common use in the works of Islamic jurisprudence (*Tātārhāniyye,* for example).

4 In: "Osmanlı Kânûnnâmeleri". *MTM*, I, 54-55, 62.

5 Since the land of a vineyard is considered *mīrī* it is subject to rent for the state treasury. Bursa court records witness to the application of this principle. Likewise a rent, *muḳāṭa'a,* is to be paid for building plots in the conquered cities. See H. Inalcik: *The Policy of Mehmed II Toward the Greek Population of Istanbul and the Byzantine Buildings of the City.* In: Dumbardon Oaks Papers 23-25 (1969-1970), 242-249.

6 Abū Yūsuf Ya'kūb b. Ibrāhīm: *Kitāb al-Ḫarāc.* Bulak 1302, second edition Cairo 1352 H. Chapter on Sawād: 47-62; H. M. Tabātabā'ī: *Kharāj in Islamic Law.* London: Anchor 1983, 88-89; Ziaul Haque: *Landlord and Peasant in Early Islam.* Research Institute, Islamabad 1977, 164-171, 328.

a rent (*ücre* or *kirā'*) on the land, which is leased (*icāre* or *'āriye*) by the state. In 1568, when he was asked to make the surveys of Üsküp (Skopje) and Salonica, Ebu's-Su'ūd, in the introduction of the register he drew up,[7] summarized in a more systematic manner his interpretation of the existing Ottoman land law in accordance with Islamic Law. Here is a translation of this important text in its entirety:

"In the former registers no attempt was made to determine the true nature of various forms of landholding in the well-protected territories of the Ottoman state. Since it was not scrutinized and clearly stated whether the lands are *'öşrī* or *ḫarācī,* and whether they are the freehold property (*mülk*) of their possessors, the peasant *re'āyā,* considering the lands in their possession as *'öşrī* (private property subject to tithe), dispute paying as much as one-eighth of their produce, and also buy and sell land among themselves like the rest of their property; some even think they can make *evḳāf.* And the judges, being unaware of the true *mīrī* status of the land, deliver certifying documents for their buying and selling, and draw up *vaḳf* deeds contrary to the sacred Sharī'a. Since this situation has caused a substantial deterioration in the orderly functioning of state affairs, and confusion in the transactions made among the people, the present Sultan [on his accession to the throne] ordered that, in the introductions to the imperial survey registers, the true nature of land and the possession rights of their owners in the well-protected territories be thoroughly investigated with the task of making a survey of the provinces of Üsküp (Skopje) and Selânik (Salonica), he set about drawing up the survey, placing his trust in God.

At the outset it is to be explicity stated that, in accordance with the sacred Sharī'a, there are three categories of land in the Islamic territories. The first is tithe land (*öşrī*) which are granted to the Muslims as their private property (*mülk*). It is legally their freehold property, to dispose of as they wish in the same manner as the rest of their properties. Because it is against Islamic Law to subject the Muslims to *ḫarāc* at the beginning [i. e., at the time of the conquest], only the tithe is imposed [as the land tax]. They cultivate the land and pay tithes out of the grain which they harvest, and nothing else; and the tithes are distributed to the poor and the disabled. The religion forbids that the tithe be taken by the military or others. Lands in the Hejaz and Basra are of this category.

---

[7] Barkan: *op. cit.*, 297-299; the regulation is drawn up on the accession of Selim II in 976 of the hijra year beginning on June 26, 1568; here, apparently Ebū's-Su'ūd expanded one of his early fetvās compare fetvā no. II and III in the facsimile.

The second category is *ḫarācī* lands, those which were left in the hands of the unbelievers at the time of the conquest. They are recognized as their freehold property (*temlīk*). Tithe is imposed on these lands at the rate of one-tenth, one-eighth, one-seventh or one-sixth, up to one-half, depending on the fertility of the soil. This is called *ḫarāc-ı muḳāseme.* In addition, they are subject to pay annually a fixed amount of money which is called *ḫarāc-i muvaḍḍaf.* This category of lands, too, is considered the legal freehold property (*mülk*) of their possessors, which they may sell and purchase, or dispose of in any kind of transaction. Likewise, those who purchase such lands may cultivate them and must pay the *ḫarāc* due in both its forms of *muḳāseme* and *muvaḍḍaf.* If the purchasers are Muslims, the two kinds of *ḫarāc* which were paid by the unbelievers do not lapse; the new owners, too, must render them in full. Although it is not legal according to the Sharī'a to impose *ḫarāc* on Muslims at the beginning, it is lawful to exact it as transferred from an initial status of the land. Those who are in possession of such land, whether *Dhimmī* or Muslim, dispose of it as they wish without any interference from outside as long as they keep it under cultivation. When its owner dies, the land is inherited by his heirs in the same manner as the rest of his property, whether movable or immovable. The land of the Sawād in Iraq is of this category. The categories of land which are known and are dealt with in Islamic legal treatises consist of these two.

There is a third category of land which is neither *'öşrī* nor *ḫarācī* of the type explained above. This is called *arḍ-i memleke.* Originally it, too, was *ḫarācī,* but its *dominium eminens* (*raḳaba*) is retained for the public treasury (*beytü'l-māl-i müslimīn*) because, were it to be granted as private property to its possessors, it would be divided among his heirs, and since a small part would devolve on each one, it would be extremely difficult, perhaps impossible, to determine the share of *ḫarāc* tax to be paid by each in proportion to the land in his possession. Therefore, such lands are given to the peasants on a lease (*'āriye*). It is ordered that they cultivate them as fields, or make them into vineyards, orchards or vegetable gardens, and render *ḫarāc-i muḳāseme* and *ḫarāc-i muvaḍḍaf* out of the harvest.

According to some of the legal schools established by the great imams, the land of the Sawād in Iraq are of this category. Lands in this fertile country also belong to the *memleke* category and are known as *mīrī.* They are not the private property of the peasant *re'āyā,* who hold it in their possession on a lease (*'āriye*), farm it or otherwise cultivate it and, render *ḫarāc-i muḳāseme* under the name of tithe (*'öşr*) and *ḫarāc-i muvaḍḍaf* under the name of *çift akçası*. So long as they continue to cultivate it and maintain it in the proper condition in the manner described above, and pay the taxes (*ḥuḳūḳ*), no one is allowed to interfere in their possession. They may dispose of it as they wish until their death; when they die their sons shall take their place and possess the land in the same manner as described above. If no son survives, the land is given in *tapu* to a person other than a family member who is capable of cultivating it in return for a rent paid in advance (*ücret-i mu'accele*). Thereupon he too holds it in his possession under the aforesaid conditions. If the possessor of the land ceases to cultivate it for three [consecutive] years it is taken from him with the legal decision of the cadi (*şar'ile*) and given to another peasant's possession under the *tapu* regulations. No one is permitted to hold the land in his possession in contravention of the conditions specified above. All transactions relating to selling, buying, donating, endowing, or otherwise disposing it as freehold property, in any way whatsoever, are entirely null and void. Also the certifying documents and endowment deeds which judges may issue on such transactions are all null and void. However, when a peasant wishes to cede the land in his possession to someone else, he may do so under the supervision of his *sipāhī* who takes a certain amount of money for fee paid (*ḥaḳḳ-i ḳarār*); then it is lawful and acceptable if the *sipāhī* gives the land under *tapu* to the party [for whom the cession is made]. By God, the Omniscient and Wise."

In this document, Ebū's-Su'ūd's insistence on the *ḫarācī* character of *mīrī* land is the key to his argument, reconciling the Ottoman and Islamic traditions. Some of the early authorities held that the religious status of the landholder determined the nature of land possession. Abū Ḥanīfa maintained that land held originally by a non-Muslim remainded *ḫarācī* even if acquired later by a Muslim.[8] In general, the Ottoman jurists followed this opinion; but some jurists held that the status of the land was ultimately decided by the Imām or Caliph. The identification of *ḫarācī* lands with "those lands belonging to all Muslims or to the Imām" best fits the Ottoman definition of *mīrī*. The *ḫarāc* tax is interpreted as a rent, whether the land was acquired by force or by agreement, or belongs to the category of ownerless lands (the so called *enfāl*, comprising wasteland, forests, meadows, abandoned lands, or

[8] Tabātabā'ī: *op. cit.*, 109; Z. Haque: *op. cit.*, 198, 207-210, 216-218.

lands belonging to the pre-conquest rulers).[9] It appears that in Iran as well as in the Ottoman Empire this broad interpretation became prevalent.

As Ebū's-Su'ūd indicated, and as court records attest, *mīrī* lands became the subject of sales among the people. Although it was extremely difficult to sell a piece of *mīrī* land —since the local sipāhīs or other agenst had a vested interest in keeping the *mīrī* status of the land intact, and when sold it was supposed to revert to its original *mīrī* status, the buyer losing its sale price— there were loopholes and legal devices by which the law, however, could be circumvented.

Once sold with a court document, land could not revert *mīrī* to status because it became the subject of a sale contract which, under the Sharī'a, established absolute ownership.[10] It required the Sultan's radical decision to recover such lands for the state. The Sharī'a, of course, was supreme, and it was a sin to act contrary to its prescriptions. It is for this reason that, in the survey books and cadis' registers, in records concerning private estates and *vaḳf* land, we frequently find a note emphatically stating that the land in question was acquired through a Shar'ī sale. Sometimes the transaction even gives the impression of a collusion. The same device was widely employed by private interests to convert *ḫarācī/fey'* lands into private estates in the early centuries of the caliphate.[11] It was obviously to serve the state that some jurists introduced the rule that any sale of *ḫarācī* lands was contrary to the law and consequently null and void.

Ebū's-Su'ūd's[12] words give the impression that by the middle of the sixteenth century the illegal sale of *mīrī* lands had become widespread enough to cause alarm in government circles. Since the religious courts were instrumental in these sales, the opinion of the şeyḫülislām, the leading

---

9 Tabātabā'ī: *op. cit.,* 112, 122; it appears that the greater part of the arable land in the Abbasid empire belonged to the category of the *ḫarācī* lands.

10 The *farāġ,* transfer or sale of the possession rights, was widely practiced as the law court documents show. Another way was the "sale" by a peasant of fields from his farm for debt. Both kinds of "sale", and the difficulty to pursue such "sales", were responsible for the loss of the *mīrī* character of the land.

11 Ziyaul Haque: *op. cit.,* 216-219, 313-314; on *fay'* see F. Løkkegaard: *Islamic Taxation in the Classic Period.* Copenhagen 1950, 38-72.

12 On Ebū's-su'ūd, 1490-1573, see "Ebüssu'ûd efendi", *İslâm Ansiklopedisi,* IV-2, 62-69 (Cavid Baysun); after the routine service as *müderris* and *cadi* in Ottoman *ilmiyye* career line he was appointed *ḳāḍī'asker* of Rumeli in August 1537, *şeyḫülislām* in 1545, keeping this post until his death in 1573. Süleyman had a complete confidence and affection for him, calling him brother.

religious authority in the realm, was needed to stop the practice. Ebū's-Su'ūd ruled that "the delivery by the cadis of such documents of sale is absolutely null and void". In various fetvās[13] he declared such sale documents to be absolutely against Islamic Law and *ḥarām*, i. e., forbidden by Islam. The question was even raised whether a cadi who issued such a document was liable for punishment. It appears that in most cases a sale of *mīrī* land was made because the situation was ambiguous, or it was impossible for the cadi to investigate and establish the true nature of the possession. Of course, bribery or favoritism also played a role. Successive sales of such lands further consolidated the proprietary rights of their owners.

Ambiguity stemmed mainly from the fact that the transfer (*farāġ*) of state land in return for monetary compensation, which was a lawful transaction, was also called a sale. To reduce this ambiguity, the fetvā required that in such transfers the cadi in question should specifically state that "the possessor of the land transferred its full possession (*taṣarruf*) to so-and-so with the sipāhī's permission in return for such-and-such a payment of money; thereupon the sipāhī confirmed it by giving it in *tapu* for such-and-such an amount paid as *ḥaḳḳ-i ḳarār* (payment for the establishment of possession rights)". Such a formula made it definite that the object of the transaction was not a regular sale with *raḳaba* but a simple transfer of possession or tenure.

When an influential member of the ruling (*'askerī*) class entered into possession of land by sale, he usually went to the Sultan to obtain a *temlīk* document at the same time in order to consolidate his property rights.

Since they were given by the most authoritative religious scholar of the time, Ebū's-Su'ūd's fetvās had a decisive effect on the way in which the Ottomans subsequently interpreted landholding and taxation practices in the empire. His formulation on *mīrī* land was to be included in the new law codes and survey registers as the ultimate and definitive commentary on the

---

[13] Ertuğrul Düzdağ: *Şeyḫülislām Ebus-Suud Efendi Fetvaları...*, İstanbul 1972, indentified 37 copies of *Fatāwā-yi Ebū'ssu'ūd* in Istanbul libraries. They vary in length from 30 to 517 folios. Scattered in various collections a complete list of fetvās of Ebū's-Su'ūd has still to be made. Düzdağ's selection based on the copies of Fatih Ali Emiri, no. 80, and Bayezid Umumi Kütüphanesi, no. 2757, consists of 29 fetvās directly concerning the land and land taxes (*op. cit.*, nos. 824-852). The fetvās we are publishing here are not included in Düzdağ's selection. They come from a Münşe'āt collection preserved at the Âtif Efendi Library, no. 1734.

Ottoman land law.[14] Obviously, Ebū's-Su'ūd's main concern was to give an authoritative definition of the Ottoman *mīrī* regime and land taxation in accordance with Islamic Law, in order to stop practices which threatened to undermine the Ottoman landholding system. Of particular interest is his statement that some judges who were unaware of the *mīrī* status of certain types of land were issuing documents legalizing the freehold rights on such lands, and that this malpractice had become so widespread that it threatened the entire traditional order in the public as well as the private sectors.

In effect, Süleyman the Lawgiver's şeyḫülislam tried to explain the Ottoman *mīrī* regime according to principles formulated by the great jurists of the ninth century, in particular Abū Yūsuf, the most liberal exponent of the Hanefī school.[15] Ebū's-Su'ūd stressed that all lands in the Ottoman empire were acquired by military force, and were therefore all *ḫarācī* lands, subject to land tax at the rate of *ḫarāc*. This interpretation was bound to have drastic effects on the Ottoman peasantry because, prior to this ruling, the Ottoman imperial laws had fixed the tithe at only one-eighth on lands reserved for the cultivation of grain. And the survey registers show that this law was actually applied in the conquered lands in the fourteenth (Bythinia, Thrace, Bulgaria, and western Anatolia), fifteenth (Albania, Serbia, and Bosnia) and sixteenth centuries. Only in lands conquered after Ebū's-Su'ūd issued his religious commentary –i. e., Cyprus (1570-71), Georgia (1578), Egri (1596), Crete (1669), and Kameniça (1672)– was the rate of one fifth applied. In general, tithes at the rate of one-eighth were maintained in the lands conquered earlier, while the *'avāriḍ* or extraordinary taxes were now more frequently imposed. It appears that in one way or another the state revenues had to be increased in order to meet the needs of a rapidly expanding budget. But, as Ebū's-Su'ūd informs us, in his time the peasants wished to take "tithe" (*'öşr*) in its literal

---

[14] Ebu's-Su'ūd's text is reproduced in the *ḳānūnnāme* of Mora dated 1716 (Barkan: *op. cit.*, 326); redactor of the *ḳānūnnāme* of Koceli followed Ebu's-Su'ūd in his identification of *čift-resmi* as *ḫarāci muvaḍḍafa* (Barkan: *op. cit.*, 33), etc. His fetvā is interpolated in the introduction of the imperial survey register of Manastir: Başbakanlık Arşivi, Tapu defteri, no. 182. The principles he formulated became the basis of the later interpretations and legal provisions: see Ömer Hilmi: *Ahkām al-Arāḍī*. Istanbul n. d., 48-62, reference to Ebu's-Su'ūd, 67; also see *Arāḍī ḳānūnnāme-i Hümāyūnu*, 2nd edition, Istanbul 1330 H., 15-32.

[15] Abū Yūsuf: *op. cit.*, Chapter 3; Turkish translation by Ali Özek: *Kitabü'l-Haraç*. İstanbul Üniversitesi publ. no. 1548; for his discussion of the *'öşrī* ('uşrī) and *ḫarācī* lands, see Chapter XI; on Abū Yūsuf see "Ebü Yûsuf", *İslâm Ansiklopedisi*, IV, 59-60 (Kufralı), and J. Schacht: *EI*², I, 164-165.

meaning of one-tenth, and so disputed their requirement to pay one-eighth.[16] This must have been another reason why the government asked him to issue his opinion on the Islamic basis of the current taxation system.

On the other hand, Ebū's-Su'ūd justified, on the basis of practical necessity, the rule that a peasant's standard farm (*çift*) cannot be divided. For if that land were distributed among the heirs in the same manner as ordinary property it would be impossible to determine the share each heir was to pay for *ḫarāc*. State control, he concluded, was imperative; a regime of private ownership and freedom of disposition would lead to the collapse of "the order of public affairs", since the fiscal, economic and military –even political– structure of the empire depended on the state's control of the land and the peasantry.[17]

In the final analysis, the question of the nature of land ownership was closely bound up with the more practical issue of taxation. In his effort to bring Ottoman taxation practices in conformity with the Sharī'a, Ebū's-Su'ūd, following the early jurists, focussed on the methods of assessment of the land tax. Considering all lands as acquired by force (*'anwā*) or *ḫarācī,*[18] he interpreted the tithes (*'öşr*) and the *çift resmi* –the two basic Ottoman rural taxes– as two different methods of assessing *ḫarāc*. He argued that in the Ottoman empire the *'öşr* had been mistakenly used for *ḫarāc-i muḳāseme,* while *çift resmi* was identified as *ḫarāc-i muvaḍḍaf.*

---

[16] See Barkan: *op. cit.,* Index: *a'şâr, 'öşr.*

[17] That the state ownership principle is primarily determined by the special conditions vital for the peasant subsistence becomes clear by the fact that only the fields reserved for growing grain were made subject to the *mīrī* regime. This is stressed in the regulations and fetvās repeatedly. Ebū's-Su'ūd affirms: "The lands within towns are freehold property; the *mīrī* lands are those cultivated lands that lay around the villages". Conversion of such fields into pastures, vineyards or orchards is prohibited because the latter category of lands can be disposed as private property; they can be sold, donated or given as surety. It is to be noted that under the Abbasid Caliphate "only arable, not residential, land was subject to kharadj" (Tabātabā'ī: *op. cit.,* 35). In the Ottoman empire it is made clear that "sapan girüp zirā'at olunan yerler arḍ-i mīrīdir, tapu ile verilir". "Osmanlı Kanunnâmeleri", *MTM,* I, 87). Diminshing of the grain production may result in famine, deficit in the public revenue and drop in the income of the provincial timariot cavalry.

[18] When a region is aquired through fighting the land in its entirety is considered as taken in *'anwa* even when certain groups within its boundaries submitted without fihting or accepted Islam (Tabātabā'ī: *op. cit.,* 107). During the Ottoman expansion there were towns and regions which submitted by agreement but the land was still put under the *mīrī* regime.

In this interpretation, *ḫarāc-i muḳāseme* was the land tax levied on the basis of a fixed percentage of the produce, while *ḫarāc-i muvaḍḍaf* was a lump sum paid annually per unit of land. Originally, both types were associated in Islamic tradition with the Roman and Sassanian forms of land tax assessment.[19] In Islamic terminology, the first was known as taxation by *muḳāseme* (percentage of the produce), the second as taxation by *muvaḍḍaf* (or *misāḥa,* measurement of the land).[20]

In practice, both methods of assessment were controversial as they entailed important consequences for the peasantry. In general, assessment by measurement was advantageous for the treasury as it secured a guaranteed amount of revenue from land. As early as the Sassanian period, however, objection was raised about the unjust effects of this method, since the peasant had to pay the tax even if he sufferd losses from natural disasters or the breakdown of the irrigation system.[21] In general, the peasantry preferred the percentage method.[22] Taxation based on measurement was also discouraged on religious grounds since Islamic Law did not accept speculative obligation in contract (*selem*). By the percentage method, in fact, the peasantry gained when prices were low, while the government gained when prices increased. On the other hand, the percentage method was only suitable for crops which could be stored for a sufficient period. Consequently, it was predominantly used in taxing grain, while the measurement method was used in taxing fruit.[23]

Although Ebū's-Su'ūd assumed that the percentage method (*muḳāseme*) was used in the assessment of tithes in the Ottoman lands, in actual Ottoman practice the measurement method (*misāḥa*) was used, because tithes were fixed not at every harvest year but for quite a long period of time, from ten to

---

19 For Iran see Tabarī: *op. cit.,* Turkish transl. Z. K. Oğan and A. Temir, 2nd edition, III, İstanbul 1965, 1136. In Egypt there were two types of assessment of the agricultural land, a fixed money rent or payment in kind and rent as a certain portion of the corps. A. H. M. Jones: *Later Roman Empire.* Oxford 1964, II, 803; Kosei Morimoto: *The Fiscal Administration in the Early Islamic Period.* Dohosho: Asian Monographs I, 1981; Gladys Frantz-Murphy: *The Agrarian Administration of Egypt from the Arabs to the Ottomans,* Institut Française d'Archéologie Orientale, Cairo 1986, 65-79.

20 See Løkkegaard: *op. cit.,* 108-125; Morimoto: *op. cit.,* 48-51; Frantz-Murphy: *op. cit.,* 65-79.

21 Tabarī: Turkish trans., III, 1135.

22 Løkegaard: *op. cit.,* 113; Abū Yūsuf: *op. cit.,* 28, discusses the advantages of the *muḳāsame* method.

23 Løkegaard: *op. cit.,* 109.

thirty years and even longer. They were recorded in the registers in terms of a fixed amount of produce, and calculated with a price fixed by the government for the entire period. It is true that the amount to be rendered as tax was computed on an average of three years, and thus whether harvest years were good or bad was taken into consideration. But, aside from the shortcomings of this computation method, climatic conditions and prices were also factors that could fluctuate drastically within a period of thirty years. In this system the tax payer had to deliver a fixed amount, in kind or cash, for a certain amount of land in his possession, without any adjustment over a long period. The percentage method was actually applied only in sharecropping (*ortakcılık*), but in this case the landowner's share was very high, usually no less than half the produce.[24]

The Ottoman government fixed grain prices for each region; but here too, the actual measurement in use should be taken into account. The grain measure –whether *mud, kile,* or *yük*– varied widely from region to region, and this variation must have some connection with the fixed price factor.[25] We should remember that tithes were assessed according to the local measure, and the totals were given in this unit in the survey registers. In fertile regions, where the average harvest was usually high and prices low, the measure was generally larger than in the less fertile regions. Thus the sipahi, or the government, which received larger amounts of grain in a fertile area per unit of measurement, realized approximately the same amount of cash per unit as in the less fertile areas.[26] Thus, the effects of price discrepancy were evened out. This situation must be one reason why the government did not insist on the standardization of grain measures throughout the empire. We should also bear in mind that trade in grain between different regions –except in coastal areas– was impractical under normal conditions because of prohibitive transportation cost. In order to protect the peasants, the central government spent much effort to enforce the law requiring the delivery of tithes always to be made in kind, since the timariots or other government agents preferred payment in cash when grain

---

24 Ziaul Haque: *op. cit.*, 310-346, considers *muzāra'a,* sharecropping, as the prevalent method on the *ḫarācī* lands. But, in general, this method is the one which was prevalent on the lands of the grandees reclaimed from the wasteland where agricultural labor lacked; Morimoto interprets *muzāri'ūn* simply as cultivators. *Muzāra'a,* metayage, is rejected by Abū Ḥanīfa.

25 See H. Inalcik: "Yük (Himl) in Ottoman Silk Trade, Mining and Agriculture", in: *Turcica,* XV, (1984), 131-156.

26 *Ibid.*

prices were low and in kind when prices were high. In any event, the Ḥanafī jurists, Abū Yūsuf in particular, had been against the fixing of prices by the government since, they argued, prices were determined by circumstances known only to God.[27]

Ebū's-Su'ūd's identification of the Ottoman *çift resmi,* paid annually as a fixed sum per land/household combination, with *ḫarāc* assessed by measurement of the land, should be considered with reference to its pre-Ottoman origins. *Çift resmi* was actually a combination of land and hearth tax that had been generally applied in the Middle East and the Mediterranean world since ancient times to the dependent registered or attached-to-land peasants.[28]

The points made in the lawcodes are actually formulated in Ebū's-Su'ūd's various fetvās which were compiled later on in the collection known as *Fetāwā-yi Ebū's-Su'ūd al-'Imādī.* His fetvās on landholding and land tax are partly published by Ertuğrul Düzdağ. In these fetvās the specific points Ebū's-Su'ūd ephasizes are the same as in the lawcodes, namely the state's absolute dominium eminens (*raḳaba*) on all arable lands, and the illegality of practices attempting to convert such lands into freehold estates. At the same time, he endeavors to interpret various taxes imposed upon arable lands and peasants in terms of traditional Islamic rules and notions. While the land in the towns, he asserts, are freehold (*mülk*), the cultivated fields surrounding the villages are *mīrī* lands which cannot be sold, donated, or endowed as *vaḳf* (Düzdağ: no. 825). The *mīrī* or *memleke* nature of arable lands is most emphatically declared (Düzdağ: nos. 825, 826, 836) and their conversion to freehold or *vaḳf* is absolutely frobidden by the Sharī'a. Incidentally, the term *memleke* for such lands is preferred to *mīrī* since it is a legal term meaning "land under the absolute authority of the Imām (Caliph or Sultan)".

Ebū's-Su'ūd's commentaries on the taxes connected with timar revenue of the sipāhīs also demonstrate his efforts to islamicize age-old state taxes or to reject them as incompatible with Shar'ī principles. He states, for instance, that sheep tax is to be interpreted as the *zekāt* on sheep (nos. 835, 842) and *çift resmi* and *ekinlü bennak* tax as *ḫarāc-i muvaḍḍaf* (no. 848), while there

---

[27] H. Inalcik: *op. cit.,* 76; Løkkegaard: *op. cit.,* 114.

[28] H. İnalcık: "Osmanlılar'da Raiyyet Rüsûmu", in: *Belleten* XXIII, (1959); it is due to the misunderstanding of the dual nature of this tax that scholars cannot decide whether *ḫarāc* is a poll tax or land tax, for a most recent discussion see Morimoto: *op. cit.,* 53-59; for *ḫarāc* as a land tax see Frantz-Murphy: *op. cit.,* 87-100; and C. Cahen: "Kharādj", in: *EI*², IV, 1031-1034.

is no Shar'ī basis to legitimize personal taxes imposed upon unmarried (*mücerred*) and married (*müte'ehhil, müzevvec*) peasants without land (no. 838). The swine tax is not religiously lawful, but "it has been collected for a long time, so it would be inappropriate to change it" (no. 844). Here, a new principle of legitimation is introduced, viz. the commonly established tradition, or in Shar'ī terminology "consensus of the Muslims" (*icmā'-ı ümme;* nos. 844, 847). Making a general rule he asserts that "all *mīrī* lands are *ḫarācī*" (no. 839), so that tithes (*a'şār*) are in fact *ḫarāc-ı muḳāseme* (no. 845).

The *fetvās* I am publishing here are in their formulation closer to the lawcodes drawn up by Ebū's-Su'ūd himself. Evidently, he took them from his fetvās and adapted them to the language of the state regulations.

Ebū's-Su'ūd is responsible for interpreting and adjusting the existing Ottoman state laws (*ḳawānīn-i örfiyye)* to the prescriptions of the Sharī'a and the commentaries of the great jurists of the ninth century, in particular to the writings of the most liberal of the Ḥanafī jurists, Abū Yūsuf. In the introduction added to the selection of his fetvās, he reportedly said to Sultan Süleyman that "for the order of the religion and the state, and the affairs of the realm, it is appropriate to act in accordance with the commentaries of certain religious authorities on certain problems in the empire". Upon the accession of Selim II, successor to Süleyman, some of the fetvās of Ebū's-Su'ūd on certain controversial issues were compiled under the title of *Ma'rūḍāt.*, introduced with the same arguments.[29]

While in the sixteenth century *nişancıs*, like Hamza Paşa (died about 1605), continued the old Ottoman tradition of *'urfī*-state rulings on landholding problems now şeyḫulislams' fetvās became prevalent on such problems in the "new and valid" lawcodes of the sultans.[30] The curious thing is, however, that şeyḫulislams followed, though using Islamic terminology, the well-established Ottoman notions in landholding, so that no basic changes occured in the Ottoman *mīrī* system until 1700 when a new notion with the *mālikāne* and *icāreteyn* systems revolutionized the whole possession-ownership system of the empire.

---

29 H. Inalcik: "Suleiman the Lawgiver and Ottoman Law", in: *Archivum Ottomanicum*, I, 1960, 132.

30 For the "Ḳānūnnāme-i Cedīd ve Mu'teber", see *MTM,* I, 49-112, 305-337; "Ḳānūnnāme", *EI²*, IV, 566.

I.

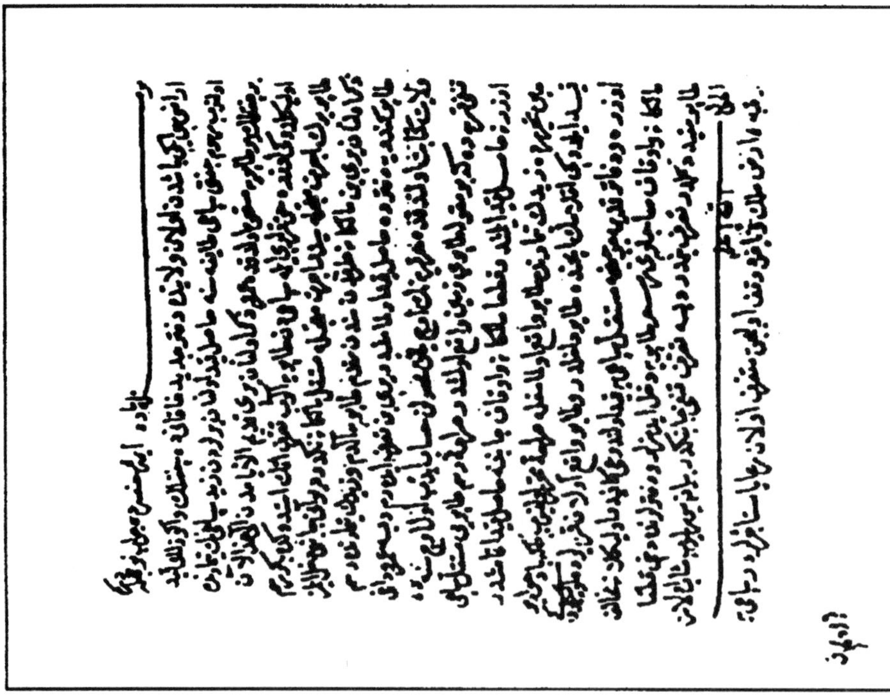

Ebū's-Su'ūd's *Fetvas* on Land (ca. 1540-1550). Münşe'at, Atıf Efendi Library, no. 1734.

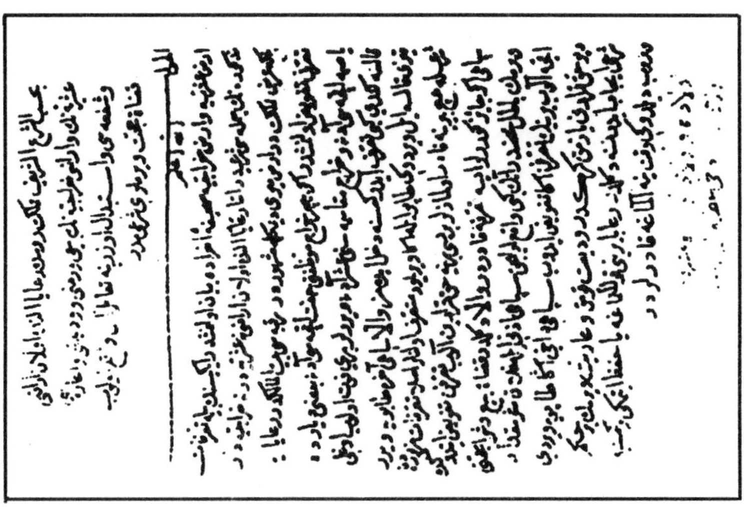

Ebū's-Su'ūd's *Fetvas* on Land (ca. 1540-1550). Münşe'at, Atıf Efendi Library, no. 1734.

6

Tax collection, embezzlement and bribery in Ottoman finances

Tax collection, embezzlement and bribery in Ottoman finances

The three Ottoman documents discussed and published here concern the embezzlements and malpractices of Ottoman finance officials in Syrian Tripoli, and the procedures the government followed to recover the treasury's loss. The first document is a secret report to the Porte on the embezzlements for which the *defterdār* Ali Beg was responsible. The second deals with the actual procedure of inspection and investigation used to uncover the embezzlements and recover the stolen funds. The third considers tax farms in the late-seventeenth century. An analysis of these documents, which confirm contemporary observations about the widespread practices of bribery and embezzlements in Ottoman administration,[1] first demands a discussion of Ottoman Tripoli.

Tripoli, the Main Port City of Syria-Lebanon

Under the Ottomans, Syrian Tripoli became the principal port for imports and exports to and from Aleppo and Damascus. In the second half of the sixteenth century European trade shifted there initially because the ship tax for foreign vessels was lower at Tripoli than at other ports.[2] Then, a new regulation was issued in 1571 (see Tables I and II) which ordered large European ships departing from this port to pay 614, middlesized ones to pay 200, and small

---

[1] Ottoman memorialists, including Koçi Bey *(Risale,* A. K. Aksüt [ed.], 1939, 21, 31, 46, 49, 60 and 73-74), find bribery the main cause of the troubles in Ottoman administration. In his *relazione* dated 1596, Venetian Bailo Malipiero says that the grand vezirate is obtained through eighty-thousand gold pieces, and the finance ministry through forty-or fifty-thousand. Once in the office they redeemed the bribe money by taking bribes for other major appointments so that all officials were involved in bribery (cited by N. Jorga, *Geschichte des Osmanischen Reiches,* vol. 2, Gotha 1908, 268). In a letter to the king, dated 13 March 1607, French ambassador De Salignac wrote: "Voila, Sire, ce qu'll y a icy de nouveau qui fera juger à Vostre Majesté l'estat de ce grand Empire où toutes choses defaillent; mais surtout les hommes de commandement et l'argent qui fait qu'il faut qu'ils se servent de personnes très incapables, et qui, pour recouvrer de l'argent ils facent mille injustices et ruinent tout le pays" (cited by Adel Ismail, *Histoire du Liban du XVIIe siècle à nos jours,* vol. 1, *Le Liban au temps de Fakhr-ed-din II (1590-1633),* Paris, 1955, 51-52. On bribery in the Ottoman empire see Ahmed Mumcu, *Osmanlı Devletinde Rüşvet,* Ankara 1969.

[2] Ömer Lûtfi Barkan, *XV ve XVI ıncı Asırlarda Osmanlı İmparatorluğunda Ziraî Ekonominin Hukukî ve Malî Esasları,* İstanbul 1943, 211.

ones to pay 25 *akçes*. Interestingly, this regulation was agreed to, after long negotiation, by the Ottoman customs agents and European merchants. Only then did the sultan approve it and make it law. By 1571 the ports of Lazikiye (Latakia), Cebele (Djbail), Banyas (Banias), and Antartus were dependencies of Tripoli, making a customs zone of that part of the Syrian coast.[3] Tripoli became a principal port for the import of European textiles, woolens and silks, minerals, tin and steel, and the export of spices, raw silk and cotton. As the sixteenth-century Ottoman regulations make clear, ships visited Tripoli from Venice, France, Chios, or Cyprus, the latter two of which were important transit centers for European merchants who did not have capitulatory guarantees for trade within Ottoman dominions. Indeed, most European states used these islands to import their goods and obtain oriental goods. The French in 1517 and the English in 1580 obtained capitulations from the sultan and began to frequent the port. The Tripoli regulation even makes special reference to the corals of Tunisia. In fact, when the merchants of Marseilles had obtained the rights to coral fishing off Tunis, they took most of the coral to Alexandria and Tripoli to exchange for Indian spices.

Spices from Tripoli competed with those imported from Lisbon on the French market. Some of these spices, landed at Marseilles, found their way as far as Rouen and England.[4] Even at Antwerp, the European emporium for spices under Spanish control, the Levant spices arriving regularly competed with those coming from Lisbon. After the English were granted capitulations, they also imported large quantities of oriental goods, mainly from Tripoli. In May 1609 an English ship from Syria had a cargo worth about 150.000 crowns in silk, indigo, gall-nuts and cotton goods.[5] The Ottomans permitted the English at Tripoli to buy even cotton and cotton yarn, which were, as a rule, among the goods prohibited for export.[6]

Goods caravaned from Iran and Syria arriving at the Tripoli market were subject to the scales tax (see Table III): valuable goods such as silk were weighed at small precision scales (mīzān) and bulky goods such as cotton or leather at big scales (ḳanṭār). The scales tax, which was much lighter than customs duties, corresponded to marketplace dues. In addition to the scales tax which seller and buyer usually shared equally, a dragoman fee

---

[3] For a comparable zone in western Anatolia, see Daniel Goffman, *Izmir and the Levantine World (1550-1650)*, Seattle 1990.

[4] Fernand Braudel, *The Mediterranean and the Mediterranean World in the Age of Philip II*, vol. 1, Harper & Row, 1966, 547-48.

[5] *Calendar of State Papers, Venice*, vol. 12, London 1880, doc. 497.

[6] Mübahat S. Kütükoğlu, *Osmanlı-İngiliz İktisadi Münasebetleri (1553-1610)*, Ankara 1974, 17, n. 43.

(tercümāniyye) at the rate of 0.75 or 1.5 percent *ad valorem* was to be paid for every transaction between a European merchant and a Muslim or a Jew. Many Europeans, however, seem to have concluded their transactions in Damascus or Aleppo and thus did not pay the taxes in Tripoli.

Tripoli's trade with other parts of the empire was also important. Goods from Egypt including rice, henna, dates and all kinds of cloth imported by sea paid a customs duty of 2 percent. When weighed at the government scales, they paid in addition one *akça* scales tax and one *akça* pen-fee.

Goods loaded on ships at Tripoli destined for Ottoman and other Muslim countries also paid this 2 percent customs duty. Abundant supplies of olive oil and alkali ashes in Syria supplied an active soap industry in Tripoli and other Syrian towns. The region exported large quantities of soap to Istanbul and other parts of the empire. The customs duty was two gold pieces for each box of soap or ten *akça*s per *ḳanṭar* of soap. Four state-owned soap factories that existed in Tripoli before 1571 subsequently shut down, apparently as a result of competition from private soap factories. One-thousand *ḳanṭar*s (about fifty-six tons) of soap were sent to the imperial palace in Istanbul annually.[7]

In addition to wool, Tripoli imported from Anatolia comestible goods such as dried fruit, cheese and honey for consumption in Syrian cities. These goods were subject to a high rate of customs duty (5.5 percent *ad valorem* in 1571).

The spice trade remained the most important branch of international trade throughout the sixteenth century. Along with precious textiles, raw silk and precious stones, trade in spices was big business in terms of capital investment and profit margin. "Capitalist spirit", Hermann Kellenbenz pointed out in a European context,[8] "found in the commerce of pepper one of its most important fields of activities". To a great extent this statement also applies to the Ottoman world. According to the Bursa court records of 1480-1550, the wealthiest merchants were those involved in the spice trade and, next to silk, the largest capital investments were in spices.[9] In 1479, for

---

[7] Archives, Istanbul, Osmanlı Arşivleri, Fekete Tasnifi, no. 165. On soap manufacture and trade see E. Ashtor, "The Economic Decline of the Middle East During the Later Middle Ages", *Asian and African Studies* 15 (1981): 253-86. Soap making flourished in Tripoli and other Syrian towns under the Mamluks. Venetians and other Italians learned how to make it in the mid-fourteenth century and became exporters to Egypt and other parts of the Levant in the fifteenth century. Gaeta was the center of soap industries in Italy.

[8] H. Kellenbenz, "Les frères Fugger et le marché international du poivre autour de 1600" *Annales,* E. S. C. 22 (1968).

[9] Halil Inalcik, "Bursa and the Commerce of the Levant", *Journal of the Economic and Social History of the Orient, III* (1960): 133-35.

example, Khodja Surūr of Aleppo brought to Bursa the equivalent of 33,242 *akças* (665 gold coins) in pepper and the cloth of Yemen; and another Aleppan merchant, Hajji Abū Bakr, in 1500 imported spices valued at 200,000 *akças* (4,000 gold coins).

As we have seen, the Ottomans acquired revenue from this rich commerce through a series of regulations. Our three documents help us gauge their success.

Document I: *A Report on the Embezzlements of the Defterdār Ali Bey*

Document I (see facsimile 1) comes from the Topkapı Palace Archives. It bears no date. To date our document we have to identify the *defterdār* Ali Bey and İbrahim Pasha, the governor.[10] Defterdār Ali Bey appears to have been at the same time a *nāẓir al-amwāl,* a high official supervising the financial affairs in a large area. The one who may be our İbrahim is Mısırlı-zāde İbrahim, the governor of Tripoli in the years 1083-87/1671-76, who had to flee to Egypt upon the uprising of the population of Tripoli.[11] In the eighteenth century, there were three İbrahims who were governor of Tripoli (in the years 1119/1707, 1139/1727, and 1147/1734 respectively).[12] However, the low rate of the "registration fee" (four *akças)* cited in the document and its reference to the spice trade in Egypt and Syria may indicate an earlier date. Also, the state owned soop factories must have been shut down in late sixteenth century as stated above. In short, our document cannot be conclusively dated. It may have been drawn up most probably in late sixteenth century.

Translation of and Commentary on "A Report on the Embezzlements of the *Defterdār* Ali Bey".

1. *He had two-hundred* fusha *of soap made in the name of the fisc and sold them at 9,500* akças *per* fusha, *the total sale price amounting to 1,900,000 akçes.*

Comment: As noted above, Tripoli was perhaps the most important center of soap manufacture in the empire. There were state-owned soap factories in Tripoli.

---

[10] Mehmed Süreyya, *Sidjill-i 'Osmānī,* İstanbul 1308 H., 91-165. The author lists a number of İbrahim Pashas who became governor of Damscus or Tripoli. On the *defterdār,* see M. A. Bakhit, *The Ottoman Province of Damascus in the Sixteenth Century,* Beirut 1982, 143-63.

[11] Süreyya, *Sidjill,* 112.

[12] Süreyya, *Sidjill,* 18, 127, and 136.

2. *He levied two* kharādj *in one year in the "Arab Land". In addition he levied four* akças *from [each person subject to]* kharādj *for his own pocket.*

Comment: It is unclear how he could collect *kharādj* or *djizya*[13] twice in a single year. Apparently, the *defterdār,* as *nāẓir al-amwāl,* must have had an extensive jurisdiction over the entire non-Muslim population in the Arab provinces. The next paragraph confirms that, as far as customs was concerned, he had such a jurisdiction over Damascus, Aleppo, Egypt, Hama and Beirut.

Since 1521 there actually existed an office of *defterdār* of the Arab provinces—the *'Arab Deftırdārı.*[14] As for the four-*akças* fee for the *defterdār,* we assume that a four -*akça kātibiyye* or registration fee went to the *defterdār* in this period. *Udjret-i kitābet* was one *para* in 1691.[15]

3. *He sent me a memo* (tezkire) *asking to levy customs duty on all kinds of spices sold in Damascus, Aleppo, Egypt, Hama and at the port of Beirut. Complying with it, ḳāḍis and emīns began to levy the tax. [Ali Bey] delivered another memo to the merchants, who paid bribes to him, authorizing them not to pay customs duty* (gümrük).

Comment: This may be a clue for the document's early date. The places mentioned were active in spice trade only until the 1630s, when the Dutch and English totally diverted it to the Atlantic. Nevertheless, prior to the seventeenth century the regional *defterdārs* enjoyed wide responsibility in matters of customs in the places under their jurisdiction. There was no tariff in that period.

4. *Accepting in bribe an orchard worth two-hundred-thousand* akças, *he bestowed the office of* emānet to the Emīn Ahmed, *nicknamed Bitlü, who actually owes the treasury a debt of five- or six-hundred-thousand* akças.

Comment: Emānet or the office of *emīn* (commissioner) implies a financial ability and responsibility to perform, temporarily or permanently, a government job with complete trust and control. As a rule, an *emīn* is a public agent with salary. Procurement of materials for the Palace or army, or supervision of a construction work, was entrusted, with sufficient funds, to an *emīn*, who had full responsibility and authority to complete the work. He then presented a detailed account or *muhāsebe* to the finance minister. An *emīn* was expected to have the expertise and experience necessary to accomplish the job entrusted.

---

[13] See Halil Inalcik, "Djizya", *Encyclopaedia of Islam,* 2d ed.; see also Daniel Goffman, "The Jews of Safed and the Maktu' System in the Sixteenth Century: A Study of Two Documents from the Ottoman Archives", *Journal of Ottoman Studies III* (1982): 81-90.

[14] See Bakhit, *Ottoman Province of Damascus,* 144.

[15] Inalcik, "Djizya".

An alternative to *emānet* was *iltizam,* in which a private person undertook governmental work under contract. A third possibility was that an *emīn* assumed a job in accordance with conditions negotiated with the government. This arrangement is called *emanet bā iltizam.* As a director of finance, the provincial *defterdār* carried out his various responsibilities through the services of *emīns* or *mültezims.*

5. *The [illegal profits] he has made on the raw silk produced on the mountains of Beirut is so considerable that no estimate can be made. He cannot deny it since it is known to everybody.*

Comment: Lebanese silk became an increasingly important export after the mid-sixteenth century, when European countries (France and England) established their own silk industries and began to consume more and more silk cloth. Although most silk supplies arrived by caravan from Iran to Aleppo, Bursa and Izmir, where European merchants purchased them, warfare between the Iranians and the Ottamans sometimes severed the routes. The resultant high prices stimulated and considerably expanded Lebanese silk production (see below).

6. *He also amassed a fortune through gifts* (pīsh-kesh).

Comment: Offering a gift, *pīsh-kesh,* to a superior was a Middle-Eastern tradition dating back to ancient Iran. It signified the allegiance and renewal of loyalty between patron and client or ruler and vassal.[16] Anyone coming into the presence of the sultan or of a state dignitary had to present a *pīsh-kesh.* The custom was often abused in order to extort substantial gifts from anyone who had dealings with the government. In this case, it degenerated into a mere bribe.

7. *Taking a bribe, he assigned an infidel by the name of Luvizo a public office in the city of Tripoli with a daily salary of fifteen* akças *despite the fact that he was in debt in the amount of 2,800,000* akças *to the sultan's [treasury].*

Comment: From the establishment of the Ottoman Empire anyone, even a non-Muslim foreigner, who was financially secure could be entrusted an *emānet* or *iltizām.* In the fifteenth century many Genoese and Venetians served the Ottoman government as *emīns* and *mültezims.* So, the appointment of Luvizo was not exceptional. What the informer found suspicious was that Ali Bey appointed Luvizo *emīn* without financial security.

---

[16] On *pīsh-kesh* see Halil Inalcik, "Ottoman Archival Materials on Millets", in Benjamin Braude and Bernard Lewis (eds.), *Christians and Jews in the Ottoman Empire,* New York 1982, 447-48.

8. *Also, taking a bribe, he appointed another* frenk *by the name of Anton Griman as* simsār, *or the head of bazaar brokers, with a salary of ten* akças [a day], *despite the fact that he was in debt in the amount of 1,200,000* akças *[to the sultan's treasury].*

Comment: A simsar (from Latin censarii) supervised the *dellāls,* or brokers, in the bazaar who were responsible for selling the merchants' commodities at a just price for the seller and buyer. While brokers went around the bazaar area, *simsārs* remained at a fixed location to be available and hear compliants. Thus, *a simār* occupied a strategic position in the exchange of imports and exports in the bazaar. The appointment of an Italian, possibly a Venetian, might have been a wise choice in this case.

9. *During his office as neẓāret, extraordinary levies* (avāriẓ) *have been collected three times. If an investigation is made, an immense amount of money [acquired by illegal means] will come out of him.*

Comment: In Ottoman finances, the *neẓāret,* or office of nāzir, represented the highest authority supervising all kinds of fiscal matters in an area. The intent was to guarantee the fairness of operation, and particularly to protect the interests of the sultan's treasury. The collection of *avāriẓ* was a complicated operation, which lent itself to bribe taking and extortions.

10. *Winning the favor of İbrahim Pasha for the warden of the garrison at the fortress of Tripoli (a certain Haydar Agha) whose annual salary was only six-thousand* akças, *[Ali Bey] secured his appointment to a* subaşılık *of twenty-five-thousand* akças *a year.*

Comment: Since those entitled to receive timar or *zi'āmet* slots were always much greater than those available in the provinces, there was always a fierce competition for such prebends. Consequently, bribery and favoritism flourished here perhaps more than in any other branch of Ottoman administration.[17]

Document II: *The Procedure to recover An Embezzled Revenue*[18]

This is a summarized version (see facsimile 2).

Order to the cadi of İzdin (Zituni) in Greece: Since it became necessary to examine the accounts of the *khāṣṣ* revenues of the Badradjık (Muslihiddin) by the names of Mustafa and Ali Bey from their books of daily records *(müfredāt defterleri),* I order that at the arrival of my servitor *(ḳul)* so and so you should call to the court the aforesaid *emīns* and other persons who

---

[17] See *Belgeler,* 2/3-4 (1965): 118, doc. 7.

[18] State Archives, İstanbul, Osmanlı Arşivleri, Maliye Ahkâm Register I.

worked with them and examine their books of daily records and make further investigation on the spot whenever it is possible.

You will recover the sums which will be found owed by them to the treasury from their accounts and embezzlements upon the legal investigations at the court and send them by my servitor to the Porte. You will see whether the tithes were levied and stored in the storehouses or are still on the taxpayers. If they say that they are not yet levied, you shall call to the court the persons in debt and investigate and determine how much they owe in tithes and whether the amounts declared correspond to the records in the survey books. If any embezzlement becomes evident you will ask my servitor to levy it in full. If they say the tithes are in the storehouses, you will ask the peasants to carry them to the port of İzdin and see that they are sold to the ships coming to purchase grain. There you will see that no one from outside offers to exchange his grain until all government grain has been completely sold.

A copy signed and sealed by my treasury *defterdār*s of the latest survey book of Tırhala (Triccala) which the *emīn* surveyors had brought to my Porte is sent to you. If the new estimates of the revenues for the aforesaid district show an increse you will take proper care to offer the *muḳaṭa'a* to the auction and find a reliable contractor to undertake it. You shall make a contract for one year and will notify the treasury in Istanbul of the names of the contractor and his sureties with the full amount of the sum agreed upon. Formerly when the aforesaid *zi'āmet* (of Badradjık) and other sources of revenue in the *ḳaḍā* of Tırhala as well as the village of [blank] in the district of Dömeke were included in the imperial *khāṣṣ* they were given under contract to the aforesaid Muslihiddin (Mustafa), but at the present time they are separated from the imperial *khāṣṣ* and their bestowal to the *sipāhi*s is ordered. If any revenue accrues in the intervening period until they are given to the *sipāhi*s you shall levy and send it by my servitor to my Porte.

This document was written on 20 Rabī' II 927/1 April 1521.

* * *

The Porte appointed Fakhr al-Dīn Ma'n to the *sandjaḳ* of Sayda in 1618 because he was considered an efficient tax-farmer, and thus legitimized his power and control over the entire area.[19] In fact, his success in increasing the *muḳaṭa'a* revenues explains his appointment. Fakhr al-Dīn's wise policy helped expand production of cotton and raw silk, the district's main export staples.

The *muḳaṭa'a* system appears to have constituted the foundation of the administrative and financial organization in the region. As the principal tax-farmer, the *emīr* obtained complete control over land and peasant labor, the sources of revenue. As long as he met his obligations determined in the *muḳaṭa'a* contract, the sultan continued to support his authority and legitimacy. Mount Lebanon was usually inaccessible and refractory to Ottoman tax collections, and government was content to find there an efficient and reliable collector. Leaving to the community or tribal chief the task of tax collection and delivery of the revenue as a lump sum to the treasury was a well established Ottoman practice followed in regions where local "feudal" families had control over land and population. The Mountain enjoyed this privilege at all times, due to its geographic situation and intractable population. The *muḳaṭa'a* or *maḳṭū'* system furnished a legal basis and legitimation for such an autonomous status. Attempts to centralize these lands always proved futile, caused long resistance, and cost the government immense military expenditure. Also, whenever a corrupt Ottoman governor or fiscal agent attempted by his illegal demands to upset the rules, open resistance followed. Thus, the central government was particularly concerned with the unjust and illegal acts of its agents in sensitive districts such as Mount Lebanon. These conditions determined its history, which was punctuated by chronic rebellions and repressions, or peaceful, prosperous periods under autonomous *emīrs* acting as Ottoman *multazim* (mültezim). Writing in 1670, Evliya Çelebi candidly admits that if the government attempted to extend its centralist tax system to the Mountain, it could assemble "an army of a hundred-thousand men, all equipped with muskets", and rebel, as had happened in the time of Ma'n.[20] Our document is evidence of the despoilage to which Ottoman agents like Defterdar Ali Bey subjected the area. Evliya Çelebi adds that the Mountain Druzes never let the Ottoman

---

[19] On Fakhr al-Dīn Ma'n see K. Salibi, "Ma'n", *EI²*; idem, *A House of Many Mansions: The History of Lebanon Reconsidered,* Berkeley 1988, index: Maan. For a detailed account of his career, see Ismail, *Liban*, in particular pp. 11-15, 45-70, and 119-65, and for the production and trade of silk, pp. 132-36. See also A. Abu-Husayn, *Provincial Leaderships in Syria, 1575-1650,* Beirut 1985, and Bakhit, *Ottoman Province of Damascus,* 168-70.

[20] Evliya Çelebi, *Seyāhatnāme,* vol. 9, İstanbul 1935, 404-5.

government register them in the tax surveys.[21] Since Selim's conquest, their own *shaykhs* collected taxes and delivered them to the governor. The whole province of Tripoli, he remarks, enjoyed fiscal autonomy under the Ottoman system of *serbestiyyet* with privileges of *mafrūz al-ḳalam* and *maktū'al-ḳadem* (exclusion from the tax registers in the government's bureaus and exemption from the interference of local Ottoman authorities). As a rule, the government accorded the same kind of autonomy to freehold land grants *(tamlīks)* and *wakfs*. Such enclaves in Ottoman territories were spared the enactments and malpractices of the governors, agents of the fisc, or tax collectors. They flourished and attracted peasants from the surrounding areas throughout the seventeenth century.

Fakhr al-Dīn and his successors, who kept the *muḳaṭa'a* of the Mountain in the family,[22] enacted the life-long tenure or hereditary *muḳaṭa'a* before this type of tax-farm —called *mālikāne* and enjoying the serbestiyyet privileges— became the norm in the eighteenth century, thereby contributing to Ottoman decentralization and the rise of *a'yāns*. It should be remembered that a concern to protect the producer and the sources of revenue formed the rationale for such a policy. Under Fakhr al-Dīn Lebanon flourished, and the Porte could not ignore it. In a sense, the Ma'n family constituted the prototype for the *a'yān* families or powerful "hānedāns" who dominated the Ottoman Empire in the eighteenth century. It is misleading, however, to see in such *a'yān* families the conscious forerunners of the Arab nation-states of the twentieth century.

It must be added that the extensive power and autonomy which Fakhr al-Dīn enjoyed was due primarily to the Jelālī upheaval in Asia Minor and Syria in the period 1596-1610. Like Jānbulāt and other Jelālī leaders, Fakhr al-Dīn's main troops consisted of *sekbans* (sokman) (mercenaries equipped with

---

[21] *Ibid.*, 404-5. As an eyewitness Evliya (MS, Topkapı Palace, Bagdad, vol. 3, no. 305, fol. 34a) tells us how in 1649 a large army under the governor of Damascus, Murtaza Paşa, set out against the Druzes to collect the tax arrears of the previous years. The Druze leaders, Shaykh Sirhan, the sons of Shihab and the sons of Tarabay, who were denying any such arrears to the treasury, finally came down with gifts to the Pasha and delivered 170 *kīse* or 85,000 *guruş* to the *defterdār* of Damascus. In 1695 the Ottoman government sent twenty-thousand men against the sons of Sirhan who, in alliance with the sons of Ma'n, supplanted the tax farmers appointed by the government. They "assumed the *muḳaṭa'āt* by force, but did not make complete payment due to the government at the end of the year", see Rāshid, *Ta'rīkh,* II, Istanbul 1282/1865, 194 and 255.

[22] Ahmed Ma'n became a *multazim,* or tax-farmer, for the long period 1667-97. Later, other members of the Ma'n family assumed the same responsibility (see Salibi, "Ma'n"). For a Druze family involved in tax farming in 1530, see Bakhit, *Ottoman Province of Damascus,* 169-75.

muskets). It is said that he once had an army of twelve-thousand *sokmans,*[23] a number typical for the bodyguard of oriental rulers, including Ottoman sultans. Maintaining this relatively large army demanded his full control of the sources of revenue of the Mountain, which he secured when the Porte gave him its *muḳaṭa'a.* Cut off from this remote province by the Jelālī rebels who controlled Asia Minor and northern Syria, only thus could the Porte pry any revenue from the area. Fakhr al-Dīn was particularly successful in increasing the Mountain's economic resources, and thereby *muḳaṭa'a* revenues.

Describing the wealth of the province of Tripoli, Evliya Çelebi notes that every six months English, Dutch and French ships loaded raw silk, olive oil and supplies of the alkali ashes, which "thousands of camels" had transported to Tripoli from the interior.[24] Together with cotton, these three staples constituted the region's main export items and source of wealth and prosperity. Besides his revenue from customs and other commercial dues, the *emīr* must have collected, as tithes or from sharecroppers, and marketed a considerable amount of cotton, silk, wheat and olive oil. From sharecroppers in his family territory of Shūf, for example, he took as much as one-third of the produce.[25] As with the eighteenth-century *a'yān*, he had a stake in expanding production, and in 1627 planted thousands of mulberry trees on the coasts of Tripoli and Beirut. Silk production depended on mulberry plantations, which flourished on the coasts near Tripoli as well as on the high plateaus of Shūf and Bsharri under the enlightened administration of the *emīr* Fakhr al-Dīn (1590-1633). The high-quality silk of Lebanon competed with that of Iran and India in the European markets. The port city of Saida, the *emīr* Fakhr al-Dīn II's capital and the center of French trade in Syria, annually exported to Marseilles four-thousand quintals of raw silk and generated for the *emīr* an annual revenue of eighty-thousand piastres, one-fourth of his total revenue. In the mid-seventeenth century, however, the Lebanese silk trade declined due to the extension of French home production of raw silk and Armenian competition which channeled the Irnian and Syrian silk to Europe.

In this emīr's time, annual cotton exports to France reached 58,450 quintals, raw silk 4,000 quintals, and alkali ashes 142,000 quintals.[26] Venetians took quantities of alkali ashes for their glass factories of Murano. The French also bought it for soap production (96,000 quintals per year). Fakhr al-Dīn's well-known alliance and cooperation with the Duke of

[23] Ismail, *Liban,* 68.

[24] Ismail, *Liban,* 131-32.

[25] Ismail, *Liban,* 59.

[26] Ismail, *Liban,* 131-37.

Tuscany obviously had an economic basis. His endeavors to develop the region's economy coincided with the aggressive mercantilist policy of the Duke of Tuscany Ferdinand I who strove to make Livorno (Leghorn) a rival of Venice. Already in 1593, Livorno became a free port, and in the following decades it grew into the center of silk trade between east and west. Fakhr al-Dīn found there a profitable market for his growing silk production. Although in the 1600s Florence apparently did not renew the capitulations granted by Mehmed the Conqueror,[27] Fakhr al-Dīn extenden free trade privileges to his friend, the Duke of Tuscany.[28] Under Fakhr al-Dīn Saida's trade even overshadowed Tripoli and Beirut, and between 1610 and 1630, merchants (particularly French and Venetian) moved there from Tripoli.[29] This move has been attributed to Fakhr al-Dīn's better treatment and protection of merchants than the Pasha of Tripoli, who, the French claimed, oppressed them with arbitrary acts and extortions.[30] Fakhr al-Dīn's economic interests called for and explain his tolerance toward Christian subjects as well as his close cooperation with Europeans, the French in particular. One can argue that the commercial decline of Lebanon (or more exactly Saida) began in 1633, with replacement of Fakhr al-Dīn by Ottoman governors.[31] It seems that the latter's main concern was to amass wealth as quickly as possible by wresting funds from foreign merchants. Our third document, from the court records of Tripoli, may coincide with this new period.

The court records of Tripoli, of which only the series starting from the year 1666 still exists, constitute the major source for the history of both Tripoli and Lebanon in general.[32] Here we shall concentrate on those records concerning *muḳaṭa'a* in the year 1666-67.

In this period, Ahmed Pasha served both as governor of the province of Tripoli[33] and as a *mutaṣarrif.* As *mutaṣarrif,* he acted as a *mültezim* (tax-farmer), and consequently was responsible for the collection of both public

---

[27] Halil Inalcik, "Imtiyāzāt", *EI*[2]. IV.

[28] Ismail, *Liban,* 127-29.

[29] Ismail, *Liban,* 125 and 138.

[30] Ismail, *Liban,* 125-31.

[31] Ismail, *Liban,* 155-65.

[32] The first register is published under the title *Documents du Tribunal Şar'î de Tripoli,* Intro. O. Tadmuri, F. Maatoux and Kh. Ziade (Tripoli: Université Libanaise, 1982).

[33] According to 'Aynī 'Alī, *Risāle* (İstanbul, H. 1280), p. 54, by 1609 the province of Tripoli was made up of the *livā*s of Tripoli, Hama, Hims, Salamiyya and Jhabaliyya. The total revenue of the 63 *ziamet*s and 571 *timar*s amounted to 5,608,400 *akçes,* and the *timariot* army was suposed to reach 1,400 men (including *djebelüs*). A record in the *sidjill* of Tripoli indicates that around 1078/1667, the *livā* of Hama was removed from the province and made an independen *livā* under the *iltizām* of Mustafa Pasha.

revenues and his own yearly salary (800,000 *akçes*). Other than the *timar*, revenue sources, or *mukaṭa'as*, in the province included—in addition to the governor's *khāṣṣ* revenue—*kharādj* on trees, a tax on raw silk, and the *djizya* of the non-Muslims. Minor sources of revenue included the *khardj-i dīwān* (fee for registration) and the tax on churches. Most revenue, however, derived from silk production, and the three-fourths of it under contracts had to be delivered at the "time of silk", that is, "when it was ready for processing". In order to collect taxes, however, the governor was utterly dependent upon the local Arab *shaykhs* who actually controlled the process of tax collection.

In 1078/1667 the *mukaṭa'a* of the *nāhiyes* of Akkar, Zanniya, Jebbe, Bsharri, Cubayl, Batrun, Sur —including the revenue belonging to the pasha of the province— was farmed out to *Shaykh* Ahmed Ma'n in the amount of 121,000 *esedī guruş* (One *esedī,* or Dutch silver coin, was about two-thirds of one regular gold ducat). Shaykh Sirhan, son of Hamada, and other relatives became surety for Shaykh Ahmed. The tax farmer for the previous year was Shaykh Zaydan, and his sons Djānbulād and Bashīr. At the same time, the contractor's family was placed in the Pasha's custody *(rahn).* None of them could leave the city until the entire revenue was paid. Finally, in their capacities as *mutawallīs* —trustee-administrators— local Arab *shaykhs* had gained control of the main religious endowments *(awḳāf)* in the province.

Our third document is concerned with the sale of the *mukaṭa'a* of the nāhiye of Safita. It is a diploma testifying that Shaykh Mehmed and his brother Shaykh Zaydan farmed out the revenue for fifteen-thousand *esedī guruş* for one fiscal year. In addition to pledging all their possessions, they placed their sons and wives in the Pasha's custody and pledged to collect and deliver two-thirds of it at "the time of silk" and the rest three months prior to the end of the year. The diploma empowering them to collect the enumerated taxes asked them to refrain from committing injustice and illegal acts against the taxpayers. The diploma bears the seal *(pençe)* of the governor, and is dated 1 March 1667.

Table 1
Western Goods Imported at the Port of Tripoli, Syria, 1571
(in *akçes*)

	Customs Duty percent ad valorem	"Pen-fee" (resm-i ḳalem)	Scales Tax (kantar)
Woolen cloth	2	1 per bolt	30 *akças* per 100 *zira* of kersey
Satin *(atlas)*	2		6 per 100 zira
Brocade *(kemkhā)*	2		6 per 100 zira
Velvet, plain or with gold thread and other varieties	2		8 per 100 zira
Coral of Tunis	3	1 per kantar	1 per kantar
Amber	3		
Copper	3	8+8	8
Iron	3		
Lead	3		
Chemicals	3		1 per *kantar*
Paper	7		or 7 pieces
Knives	7		or 7 pieces
Objects of crystal	7		or 7 pieces
Steel	4 per batman	10 per kantar	10 per kantar

Source: Ömer Lûtfi Barkan, *XV. ve XVI inci Asırlarda Osmanlı İmparatorluğunda Ziraî Ekonominin Hukukî ve Malî Esasları, I: Kanunlar,* İstanbul 1943, pp. 211-16.

Table II
Customs Duties on Spices, Silk, Cotton and Other Goods Exported to Europe from Tripoli, 1571
(in *akças*)

1 kantar = 56.5 kg

	Custom Duty percent ad valorem	Pen Fee	Scales Tax *(kapan)*	
Spices including pepper, cinnamon, cloves, ginger, indigo, coconut	10+11		1	Customs duty is shared equally by seller and buyer
Iranian raw silk	110 per kantar		1	4 for weighing tax
Syrian raw silk	110 per kantar		1	4 for weighing tax
Rhubarb	110 per kantar		1	
Cotton	4	1	1	
Cotton yarn	4	1	1	
Raw silk	110 per kantar		1	
Mohair	60 per load			each load (*denk*) contains 50 pieces
Tafetta	60 per load			each load (*denk*) contains 50 pieces
Cowhides	3			
Leather	44 per load of 75 pieces	2		
Henna	110 per each 100 batman		1	
Gallnut	3		1	1 per kantar of gallnut value: 700 *akças*
Beeswax	3	1	1	
Carpets	11 per load			

Source: Ömer Lûtfi Barkan, *op. cit.*, pp. 211-16.

Table III

Tax on Transit Goods Arriving at the Tripoli Market from Iran and other places, 1571

(in *akçes)*

1 batman = 7.69 kg; 1 kantar = 56.5 kg

	Scales tax (mizan or kantar)
Iranian raw silk	2+2 per *batman*
Rhubarb	4+4 per *batman*
Leather	8+8 per *kantar*
Cotton	4+4 per *kantar*
Yarn	5+5 per *kantar*
Gallnut	4+4 per *kantar*

The tax is equally shared by the seller and the buyer

Source: Ömer Lûtfi Barkan, *op. cit.,* pp. 211-16.

Document 1.

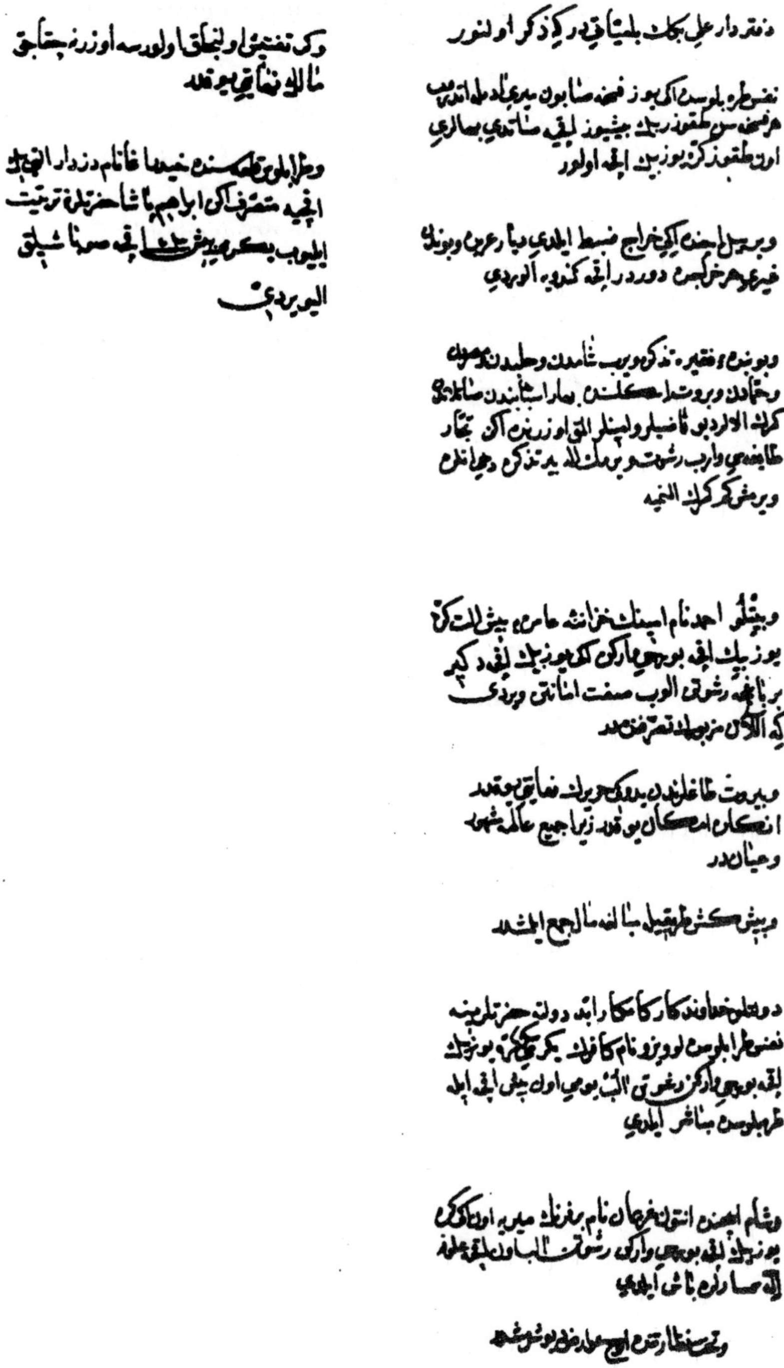

Document 2

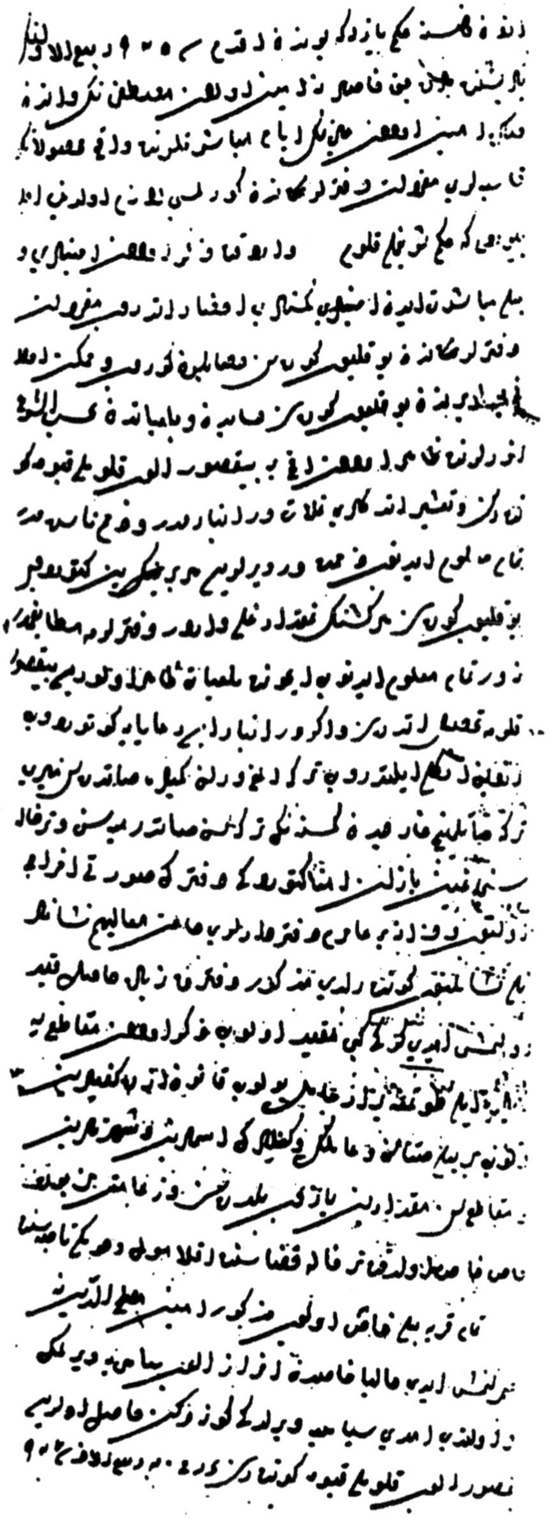

Document 3

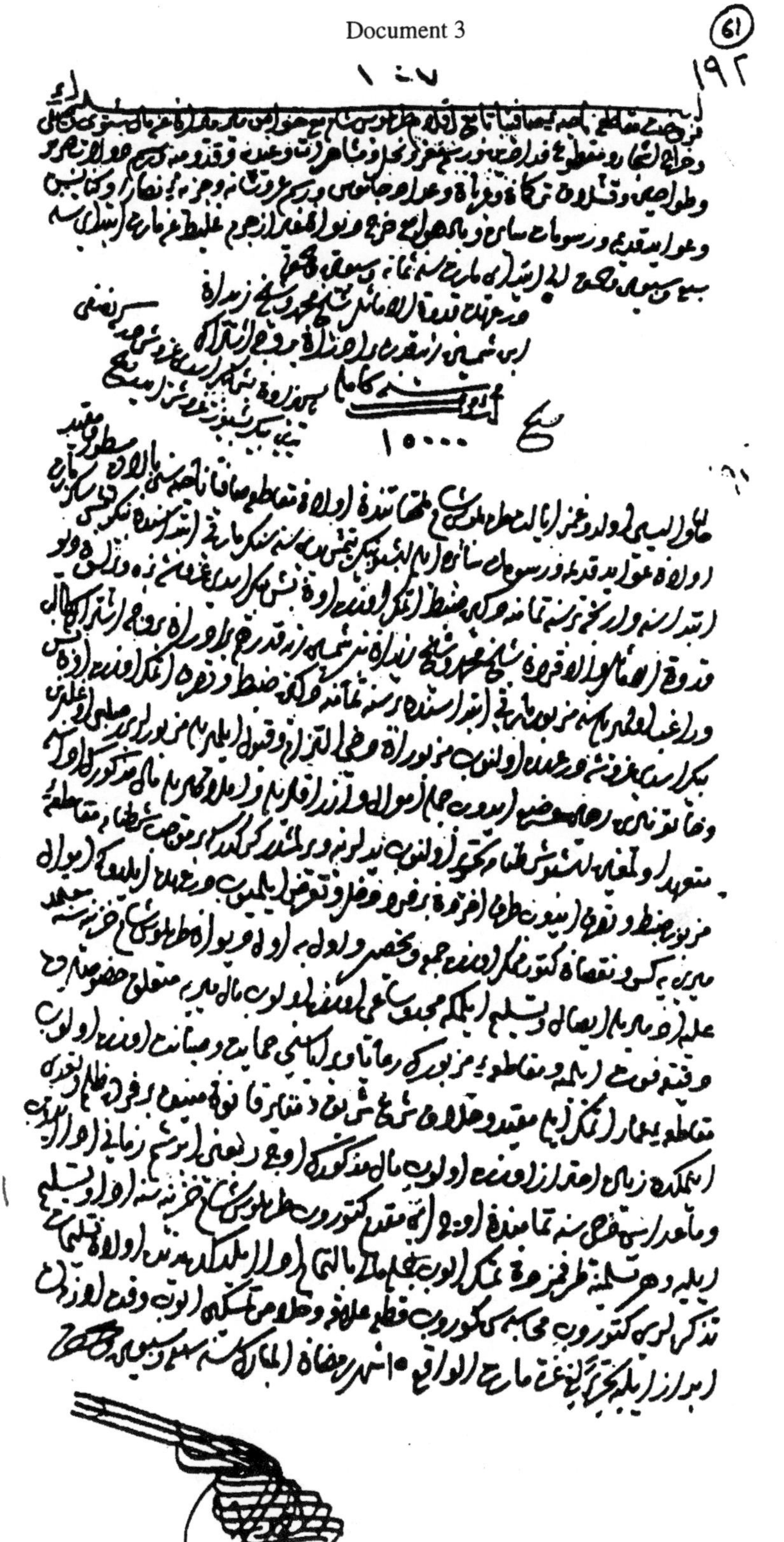

7

The Status of The Greek Orthodox Patriarch under The Ottomans

The Status of The Greek Orthodox Patriarch under The Ottomans

It has been assumed that the document issued originally for Gennadius in 1454 was a kind of pact, similar to capitulations given to non-Muslim foreigners in Islamic territory, granting to them certain privileges and guarantees under oath. The same document was also interpreted as a charter, organizing the Orthodox Christian community under Ottoman rule into an autonomous body under the Patriarch.[1]

N. J. Pentazopoulos, the distinguished Greek legal historian,[2] said that Mehmed II "recognized not only the ancient religious privileges of the Patriarch, but, beyond these, he granted them considerable political authority as well". The grant of such privileges, he added, carried with it *jus singolare* and *extraterritoriality*, as had existed in all the empires founded in the Mediterranean world since ancient times. Under the Ottomans, Pentazopoulos continued, the Patriarch's authority "was not only extended over all the Orthodox Christians of the empire, but this authority was further expanded by newly acquired '*politico-religious jurisdiction*' over all the arthodox reaya. Pentazopoulos agreed, however, that such power and "status of authority" was achieved only over time by the "tolerance or concession of the Turkish

---

[1] For S. Sidarouss, *Les patriarchats dans L'Empire Ottoman et spécialement en Egypte,* Paris, 1906, p. 5, *berāts* given to the patriarchs were simply "bilateral contracts concluded between Christian nations and Islamic governments". According to Theodore H. Papadopoullos, *Studies and Documents Relating to the History of the Greek Church and People under Turkish Domination,* Bibliotheca Graeca Aevi Posterioris-1, Brussels, 1952, pp. 7-10, the berāt given to Gennadius was a "constitutive chart and made the Patriarch millet-bashı or 'national chief'". It invested in him, Papadopoullos adds, "beside his spiritual jurisdiction with a civil jurisdiction extended over the whole nation of the Christians". This interpretation is basically shared by Byzantinists, most recently by G. Hering, "Das islamische recht und die Investitur des Gennadios Scholarios (1454)", *Balkan Studies* (Salonica) II, 1961, pp. 249-251; also see S. Runciman, *The Great Church in Captivity*, Cambridge, 1968. pp. 167, 170, 181. J. Kabrda, *Le Sytème Fiscal de l'Église Orthodoxe dans l'Empire Ottoman,* Brno, 1969, pp. 14-15, notes "la position prééminente des métropolites dans les éparchies au point de vue politique" which resulted from extensive jurisdiction of the ecclesiastical courts over civil matters as well as spiritual.

[2] *Church and Law in the Balkan Peninsula during the Ottoman Rule,* Thessaloniki: Institute for Balkan Studies, 1967, pp. 7-10, 19, 23, 86.

authorities",[3] or by encroachment upon the privileges granted them. Pentazopoulos emphasized the point that, by styling himself in the ecclesiastical documents as "the leader of the eminent race of the Romans" with the titles of the Byzantine rulers, *Afentis,* and *Despotis*, and by using the imperial emblem of the two-headed eagle, the Patriarch appeared as the embodiment of the "Byzantine political ideal" under the Ottomans.

It should be made clear at the outset that the Ottoman system by which the state's relations with the religious communities were governed followed closely the pertinent stipulations of Islamic law and tradition, both in its basic structure and in its details. As for as the *ahl al dhimma* is concerned, in dealing with organization and practical matters, one has first to look at the authorities of the Hanafi school of law, a method which M. d'Ohsson wisely pursued in his *Tableau Général de l'Empire Ottoman.* On the other hand, during the formative period of the empire, the Ottomans introduced an independent body of practical rules and regulations based on the ruler's judgement of what the situation actually required. These were usually interpreted as temporary measures, based on sharī'a principles as applied to particular situations. Sometimes, it is true, these practical regulations were hard to accomodate with the principles of the sharī'a; for example, the maintenance of an organized christian community in Istanbul was against tha sharī'a in principle since the city had been taken by force *(ḳahran)* as was the taking of *pīshkesh,* actually a disguised tax upon the clergy. On dealing with the so-called *millet* system in tho Ottoman Empire, a primary task is to uncover and to find a historical explanation for those Ottoman practices and institutions which were actual innovations vis-àvis the sharī'a.[4] Furthermore, those institutions introduced by the Ottomans changed, even though their original names were retained, through the transformation of the empire itself and its policies.

Four principal periods are to be distinguished in the study of the conditions under which the non-Muslim communities and their institutions survived in the Ottoman empire.

It is now a commonplace that in the early period of their expansion, the Ottomans pursued, primarily in order to facilitate conquest, or to make the indigenous population favorably disposed, a policy called *istimālet.* It was intended to win over the population, peasants and townspeople, as well as military and clerics, by generous promises and concessions, sometimes going beyond the limits of the well-known, tolerant stipulations of Islamic Law

---

[3] *Ibid.* p. 10.

[4] See "Kānūn" *Encyclopaedia of Islam,* second edition, IV, pp. 558-562.

concerning non-Muslims who had submitted without resistance. Within this policy of *istimālet,* the Ottomans, especially during the first transition period, maintained intact the laws and customs, the status and privileges, that had existed in the preconquest times, and what is more unusual, they incorporated the existing military and clerical groups into their own administrative system without discrimination, so that in many cases former *pronoïa* holders and seigneurs in the Balkans were left on their fiefs as Ottoman *tīmār*-holders.[5] But the most fundamental and perhaps the most effective component of the *istimālet* policy was, from the beginning, the recognition of the Orthodox Church as part of the Ottoman state. The Ottomans did not merely extend the protection stipulated by Islamic Law and practice to the Church, but they integrated it into their administrative system. The leaders of the Orthodox Church, the Metropolitans, were assigned *tīmārs* in the frontier provinces, a practice which meant their inclusion in the ruling class. We have records of this from as early as the *tīmārs* register of Albania dated 1432,[6] well before the conquest of Istanbul, the seat of the Patriarchate. There is every reason to believe that through such a policy towards the Orthodox clergy and monasteries the Ottomans established close ties with the Patriarchate in Istanbul before 1453. The fact that the Ottomans favored openly the Orthodox Church, restoring it everywhere they went to its former position of superiority vis-à-vis the Latin Church, is a clear indication of the political intent of their of attitude.

In a recent article, Nicolas Oikonomides has shown,[7] on the basis of Byzantine sources, that, upon the Ottoman conquest in 1383, the monasteries of Mount Athos were left in possession of their properties, to which were even added new ones. What is more interesting, a tradition survived on the Mountain claiming that the monasteries had recognized the suzerainty of the Ottoman Sultans even before the conquest of the area.[8] A similar situation for the monastery of Saint John Prodrome near Serres is attested to by a document dated somewhere between 27 December, 1372 and 5 January, 1373, when the city was still under Byzantine rule.[9] Before the Sultan's

---

[5] See H. Inalcik, "Ottoman Methods of Conquest", *Studia Islamica,* IV (1954), pp.103-129.

[6] H. Inalcik (ed.), *Sûret-i Defter-i Sancak-i Arvanid,* Ankara: T.T.K. 1954.

[7] "Monastères et moines lors de la conquête ottomane", *Südost-Forschungen*, XXXV (1976), pp. 1-10.

[8] *Ibid.*, p. 5.

[9] The controversy about whether or not the document or its date is authentic and correct (see P. Lemerle, *Philippe et la Macédoine Orientale,* Paris, 1945, pp. 215-217; G. Ostrogorskij, "La Prise de Serres par les Turcs", *Byzantion*, XXXV (1965), pp. 302-319; I. Beldiceanu-Steinherr, "La prise de Serres et le firman de 1372 en faveur du

conquest, asserts Oikonomides (p. 6), "ils lui offraient une grande victoire morale et s'assuraient en échange la sécurité de leurs monastères et l'inviolabilité de leurs privilèges". Evidently, the Ottoman government was taking advantage of the presence of Greek metropolitans already within their domain to establish relations, within the policy of istimālet, with churches and monasteries beyond Ottoman state boundaries.

The second period for the so-called *millet* system began with the conquest of Istanbul in 1453. In accordance with his concept of an universal empire, the Conqueror re-organized the Ottoman state, published Sultanic codes of laws, and made his capital the seat of the heads of the three recognized non-Muslim communities, Orthodox Greek, Armenian and Jewish, who represented a large number of his dhimmī subjects. Considering the fact that no other Muslim state had had non-Muslim subjects in so large number, and that the Conqueror's concept of Sultanic law and authority was so comprehensive, it may be appropriate to regard his reign as ushering in a new age for the non-Muslim communities in Ottoman history, perhaps even for the whole of Islamic history. The imperial structure as established by the Conqueror, and the historical position of the non-Muslim communities within it, developed in what we call the classical age of the Ottoman empire, until the seveneenth century when the first signs of decentralization appeared. When, with the rise o the a'yāns in the eighteenth century, decentralization[10] became a general feature of the Ottoman administration, the church organizations also partook in this trend. The Greek Orthodox Church in particular, consciously taking advantage of the new conditions moved toward autonomous organizations in the capital and in the Metropolitanates in the provinces. In fact, the movement in the non-Muslim communities during this century was the rise of a new bourgeois class, which tried to dominate the Church and which led to, alongside the Church, the development of certain civil

---

monastère de Saint-Jean-Prodrome", *Acta Historica,* Societas Academica Dacoromana: IV, Munich, 1965, pp. 15-24; E.A. Zachariadou, "Early Ottoman Documents of the Prodromos Monastery (Serres)", *Südost-Forschungen,* XXVII Munich, 1969, pp. 1-12) stems from a misunderstanding. After the Ottoman victory at Chermanon in 1371, the frontier *ghāzī*s under Evrenos (Evrenuz) Beg invaded the Serres plain, but the city itself continued to resist. Evrenos placed there for the continuous blockade of the city, Delü Balaban (Idrīs Bidlīsī, *Heşht Bihişht*, MS Topkapı Sarayı Museum, Section Murad I.) The monastery, apparently in the area fallen under Ottoman control already in 1372, obtained from the Sultan Murad I the document granting tax exemption and protection. E. Zachariadou (*ibid.*, p. 9) showed that the document is authentic and I. Beldiceanu-Steinherr's arguments are not acceptable.

[10] H. Inalcik, "Military and Fiscal Transformation in the Ottoman Administration", *Archivum Ottomanicum,* VI, pp. 311-337.

organizations with a certain degree of actual autonomy.[11] While these develcpments prepared the way for the emergence of the Christian states in the Balkans in the nineteenth century, within the Empire the Tanzimat and especially the Khatt-i Humāyūn of 1856 brought in absolutely new legal concepts for the re-organization of the non-Muslim communities. Special *niżāmnāmes*, regulations, were drawn up for the non-Muslim communities during this period, which came to a close with the treaty of Lausanne in 1923.[12]

Periodization of this type are not only convenient for the study of the non-Muslim communities in the Ottoman empire but are also historically necessary in order to avoid controversy about generalizations made through the studies of conditions in a particular period. In each of the periods defined above, the circumstances of the individual member of the non-Muslim communities differed, in actuality and sometimes also *in jure.*

In arranging their relations with non-Muslims who had submitted without resistance the Ottomans were careful to follow the prescriptions of Islamic Law, in which these matters were governed by long tradition and precise rules going back to the time of the Prophet. The earliest contracts of this type were of such a nature as could only be classified as *'uhūd,* compacts, concluded between the non-Muslim communities and the Prophet or the first Caliphs.[13] During the Prophet's time the term *amān*, amnesty was used as a synonym of *'ahd*, *dhimma* and the pre-Islamic term *djiwār.*[14] In the early period security pacts were generally called *'ahd*, agreement under oath. Later, when large numbers of non-Muslims came under Islamic rule, a special status as *ahl al-dhimma* was recognized for them and the concept of *amān* was differenciated from that of *dhimma.* Eventually, it was established in Islamic Law that amān was the temporary pledge of security and safeconduct to non-Muslims of the *Dār al-Ḥarb*, Abode of War, the conditions of which were usually defined in an *'ahd*, while *dhimma* was a permanent pledge of security

---

[11] N. Iorga, *Byzance après Byzance,* ed. Association Internationale des Études du Sud-Est Européen, Comité National Roumain, Bucarest, 1971, pp. 226-247; Th. Papadopoullos, *op. cit.,* pp. 122-158; Runciman, *iop. cit.,* pp. 306-406; for changes in a provincial context see J. Hackett, *A History of the Orthodox Church in Cyprus,* London, 1901.

[12] For the *niżāmnāme* (constitutive regulation) of 1862 see R. Davison, *Reform in the Ottoman Empire,* Princeton, 1963; the Turkish text in Düstūr, II, 902-938; cf. also Vartan H. Artinian, *A study of Historical Development of the Armenian Constitutional System in the Ottoman Empire,* Ph. D. Dissertation, Brandeis University, 1968.

[13] M. Hamidullah, *Documents sur la Diplomatie Musulmane à l'époque du Prophète et des Khalifes orthodoxes,* Paris, 1935; idem, *Medjmu'a al-Wasā'iḳ al Siyāsiyya*, Beyrouth, 1969; N. Khadduri, *War and Peace in the Law of Islam,* 2nd edition, 1969; A. Fattal, *Le statut légal des non-musulmans en pays d'Islam*, Beyrouth, 1958.

[14] J. Schacht, "Amān", *EI*[2] pp. 429-430.

to non-Muslims who had submitted and become the subjects of Islamic state. The conditions of this pledge were pre-determined by Islamic Law. Some Muslim jurists also accepted an intermediate territory between the *Dār al-Islām* and the *Dār al-Ḥarb*. This was called the *Dār al-'Ahd* and included those non-Muslim states which had submitted by treaty to an Islamic state but had not been incorporated into it.[15] Upon submission and pledge of a yearly tribute, such countries were granted *'ahd wa amān*, under which the Caliph or Sultan pledged peace, protection from internal and external enemies, no colonization by Muslim peoples, and no interference by Muslim officials in internal affairs. Thus, both the earliest Muslim pacts concluded with the non-Muslim communities as well as the *amān* documents given to people from the *Dār al-Islām* are called *'ahd*, *'uhūd* or sometimes, *shurūt*, or in Ottoman usage *'ahdnāme*. The distinctive character of an 'ahdnāme is that it is guaranteed by oath, *'ahd*, which binds the Muslims before God to respect the provisions specified in the document. Observance of such a covenant is ordered by God as revealed in the Koran (XVI, 93 and 94).

An 'ahd is out of question for the ahl al-dhimma, subjects of an Islamic state. When certain special privileges were to be granted to the ahl al-dhimma, individually or collectively, the document by which this was done was called an *amr* or *hukm*, an imperial order from the ruler to the ruled. Special terms for such an order establishing privileges were *manshūr*, *mithāl* and *berāt*. Ottoman usage also included *nishān* and *biti*.[16]

The document given by the Abbassid Caliph Muktafī II (1136-1160) to the Nestorian Patriarch, Abdīsho III (1138-1147), in 1138,[17] is worthy of note for purposes of comparison with the Ottoman diplomas to the Patriarchs. It is called a *mithāl*, or diploma. It first ratifies the election of the Catholicos by the community, and establishes his position as head (*za'īm*) of the *ṭawā'if*, communities of Greeks, Jacobites and Melchites living in the land of the Caliphate. It then enumerates the rights granted (*en'ām*) to him and to the members of his *milla*, promising protection of their lives and property, of their churches and monasteries, all in conformity with the conduct of the orthodox Caliphs and their successors. The Caliph also guarantees to ensure by threat of punishment respect for the authority of the Catholicos on the part

---

[15] See "Imtiyāzāt", "Dhimma", and "Dār al-'Ahd", *Encylopaedia of Islam*. 2nd ed.

[16] See below note 44.

[17] A. Mingana, "A charter of Protection granted to the Nestorian Church in A.H. 113 by Muktafī II, Caliph of Baghdad", *Bulletin of John Rylands Library*, Manchester, X (1926), 126-133; E. Tisserant, "Nestorienne (Église)", *Dictionnaire de théologie catholique*, XII; also see E. Khedoori, "Charters of Privileges granted by the Fatimids and Mamluks to St Catherine's Monastery of Tur Sinai (ca. 500 to 900)" Dissertation, University of Manchester, 1958.

of his subordinate clerics, and promises to intervene for the enforcement of judicial decisions. In return the Caliph demands obeisance and full payment of the djizya, and, again at the end, compliance with what had been ordered therein. This document and the ones given by the Muslim rulers in Egypt to the heads of the religious communities before the arrival of the Ottomans can be classified simply as diplomas granted by the sovereign.

The diplomas given to the monks of Sinai by Al-Malik al-ʻĀdil, the Ayyubid ruler of Egypt, in 1195,[18] and by Selim I in 1517 hold of special interest for us. In Al-ʻĀdil's diploma, which in the document itself is entitled a *man<u>sh</u>ūr*, *mi<u>th</u>āl*, and *amr*, the monks are considered to be among the Sultan's reʻāyā. It is stated that "the Sultan appointed as their superior those whom they (the monks) preferred". It is further ordered that the monks continue to live in their monastery according to their old established customs and rules, and, that they be protected against all harm and damage, all changes in their dues and taxation, all interference by the Bedouines, and finally, that free passage be granted their visitors from Syria. As is the case with all such diplomas, here too the privileges being established were specified and third parties were ordered to respect them. The ruler's will alone was the source of and the support for the privileges granted.

In the *hukm,* or ni<u>sh</u>ān, given to the monks of the Monastery of Sinai in 1517 by Selim I,[19] reference is made to the ʻahdnāme (compact) of the Prophet, to the *marsūms* and *murabbaʻāts* (diplomas) and *tamassukāt* (certificates) of the Orthodox Caliphs; in contrast Sultanic documents are simply called amr, ni<u>sh</u>ān, or berāt.[20] Selim's ni<u>sh</u>ān is more detailed than that of Al-ʻĀdil. It specified what kinds of damages were wrought by the Bedouins and what tax exemptions the monastery was to enjoy. More details on these matters were to be included in subsequent diplomas. As also occurred with the capitulations granted to the musta'min, when specific points became the subject of controversy, new Sultanic orders were issued and their contens were finally introduced formally into new diplomas.[21]

To conclude, the documents given to the heads of the non-Muslim communities following the formative period of early Islam cannot be

---

[18] S.M. Stern, "Two Ayyubid Decrees from Sinai", *Documents from Islamic Chanceries,* ed. S.M. Stern, Cambridge, Mass., 1965, pp. 10-25.

[19] Klaus Schwarz, *Osmanische Sultansurkunden des Sinai-Klosters in türkische Sprache*, Freiburg-im-Breisgau, 1970, pp. 24-30, no. 45.

[20] Schwaz, *ibid.*; in later times distinction between ʻahdnāme, nishān or berāt for such privileges was not made clear cut, see. ibid., p. 63, no 125; pp.78-79, no 138.

[21] See Schwarz, pp. 74-75, no. 131; pp. 78-80, no. 138; pp. 89-92, no. 211; pp. 97-100, no. 138.

classified as compacts or covenants.[22] They were simply diplomas, granted by the ruler to his subjects, dhimmī re'āyā. The Seldjukid state of Anatolia (1071-1308) maintained these institutions at the fullest stage of development. Metropolitans had existed in the large cities and most of the time normal relations had been maintained with the Patriarchate of Constantinople. In Konya, the capital city of the Sultanate, for example, the Metropolitan heard disputes among the members of the Greek community. The early thirteenth century, on the other hand, saw an Armenian bishop, Ananias of Sivas, supported by Sultan Kaykhusraw, raise his bishopric into a rival Catholicate.[23]

Mehmed the Conqueror did not have to innovate in establishing a system to handle relations with his non-Muslim subjects. There is documentary evidence from the Ottoman archives of the appointment of Metropolitans in Ottoman territories before 1453. The earliest known reference to the appointment of a Metropolitan is one concerning Antalya (Satalia) in the time of Bāyezīd I. This international trade center, which had a sizeable Greek population, was seized by Bāyezīd from the Teke Beg in 1399.[24] After the conquest, apparently, the Sultan appointed a Metropolitan, or perhaps re-affirmed the previous one, to head the Greek community.[25] In an Ottoman official register[26] we find records concerning the Metropolitans of the city in the times of Mehmed I and Murad II. There remained a sizeable Greek community in the area of Antalya down through at least the middle of the seventeenth century, as is attested to by the relatively large pīskhesh, 20 gold ducats, paid by the Metropolitan at that time.[27] Also, an Ottoman register of

---

[22] C. Cahen, *Pre-Ottoman Turkey,* 1071-1330, Londan, 1968, pp. 206-215. Cahen, p. 191, asserts that Muslim law does not recognize corporate bodies, collective organizations intermediate between the individual and state.

[23] Cahen *op. cit.,* p. 212. For the attitude of the Seljukid Sultans towards non-Muslims in general, see O. Turan, "Les souverains seldjoukides et leurs sujets non-muslumans", *Studia Islamica,* X (1953), pp. 65-100.

[24] Ibn Baṭṭuṭa, *The Travels*, trans. H.A.R. Gibb, vol. II, Cambridge, 1962, pp. 417-424; S. Vryonis, *The Decline of Medieval Hellenism in Asia Minor and the Process of Islamization from the Eleventh through the Fifteenth Century*, Berkeley, Los Angeles and London, 1971, pp. 294-296, 316; W. Heyd, *Histoire du Commerce du Levant*, ed. F. Raynaud, vol. II, Leipzig, 1936, p. 355; B. Flemming, *Landschftsgeschichte von Pamphylien, Pisidien und Lykien im Spätmitte alter*, Wiesbaden, 1964, p. 105.

[25] Vryonis, *op. cit.,* pp. 295-296.

[26] Flemming, *op. cit.,* pp. 107-108; the register is published by A. Refik, "Fatih Zamanında Teke-Eli", *Türk Tarihi Tedkik Encümeni Mecmu'ası,* XIV-2 (fasc. 79), 66-72.

[27] B. Braude and B. Lewis (ed.), *Christians and Jews in the Ottoman Empire,* I, New York, 1982, p. 442.

tīmārs dated 1432[28] contains documents concerning the appointment of a Metropolitan at Berat (Belgrad), Albania, under Mehmed I (1413-1421) and by his successor. It is evident from the records that a Sultanic berāt was necessary for such an appointment.

These historical facts, corroborating contemporary observations by Critovoulos demonstrate that Mehmed the Conqueror did indeed give a berāt to Gennadius at the time of his appointment. It is inconceivable that while the Sultans had appointed Metropolitans by berāt before 1453, the Conqueror should abstain from doing so when appointing the Patriarch. Gennadius himself said that he was elevated to the Patriarchate following election by the Synod,[29] and we know that the Sultans always ratified the electians of the Synod with a berāt. True, the details about the "ceremony of investiture" and the allusions to the privileges granted are all contained only in a late sixteenth century text written by Macarius Melissenus. It has been observed, however, that Macarius used reliable sources for his history, long attributed to Sphrantzes.[30] In the original "diary" of Sphrantzes, there is not even a word about the appointment of Gennadius. [31] It must be true, as had already been claimed early in the sixteenth century, that the original berāt of Mehmed the Conqueror was lost, perhaps in one of Istanbul's frequent fires. [32]

Historians of the Greek patriarchate are unanimous in asserting that not only the Patriarch but also the Greek Orthodox population were given extensive "privileges" under this "charter". Recently, Gunner Hering[33] claimed to have come up with an explanation for why Mehmed the Conqueror had revived the Greek patriarchate as an autonomous institution with

[28] *Sûret-i Defter-i Sancak-i Arvanid,* ed. H. Inalcik, Ankara, 1954, see Index: Medrepolid and Peskopos (*Peskopoz*).

[29] See G. Hering, "Das islamische Recht und die Investitur des Genadios Scholarios" *Balkan Studies*, II-2 (Thessalonoki, 1961), p. 248. The thesis that there is no positive historical evidence supporting the appointment of Gennadius by Mehmed II with a special diploma is discussed in B. Braude's paper, B. Braude and B. Lewis (eds.), *op. cit.*, pp. 69-88.

[30] See V. Grecu, "Georgios Sphrantzes, Leben und Werk, die Ausgabe" *Byzantino-Slavica,* XXXVI (1965), pp. 62-73.

[31] Cf. Hierax, *Threnos ou histoire de l'empire des turcs,* composé vers 1597, trans. A. dethier, *Mon. Hungarica Hist.* vol. XXI-2, p. 420; the latter asserts that Mehmed II's motivation for the appointment of a Patriarch was his concern to repopulate his new capital, for the same see especially Critovoulos, *History of Mehmed the Conqueror,* trans. C.T. Riggs, Princeton, 1954, pp. 93-95; H. Inalcik, "The Policy of Mehmed II toward the Greek Population of Istanbul and the Byzantine Buildings of the City", *Dumbarton Oaks papers,* XXIII-XXIV, pp. 231-249.

[32] See H. Mordtmann, "Die Kapitulation von Konstantinopel im Jahre 1453" *Byzantinische Zeitschrift,* XXI, (1912), pp. 129-135.

[33] Hering, *art. cit.,* p. 249.

extensive powers going well beyond the limits set by Islamic Law for dhimmī subjects. Mehmed the Conqueror, he argued, acted under special historical circumstances. In particular, when his attempt to repopulate the ruined city with Turkish deportees failed, in urgent need he turned to the Greeks for resettlement. I agree with Hering that the re-population of Istanbul was indeed among the major motivations of the Conqueror's revival of the patriarchate, as in fact all the contemporary Byzantine and Turkish sources confirm,[34] but this situation would not necessarily have led to the creation of an organization with such extensive powers and to the renunciation by the Conqueror of his rights over his dhimmī subjects, all in defiance of the explicit provisions of Islamic Law as well as the Conqueror's well known concern about his own absolute sovereing rights.[35] The whole argument is without foundation since it is based upon the supposition that the Conqueror's "charter", which is lost, just might have contained extensive concessions. None of the documents given to the Patriarchs before or after the Conqueror's time which are available for examination, excepting perhaps the 'ahds of the Prophet and the first Caliphs, contain anything like the concessions mentioned above. Some writers, rationalizing the situation of the ahl al-dhimma under the law of Islam or under the later Ottoman system of communal autonomy, have even gone so far as to say that "the right to life, property, religion and extraterritoriality were granted in exchange of economic returns".[36] Extraterritoriality could never have been considered for the *dhimmī* subjects of an Islamic state. It is a right recognized only for people from Dār al-Ḥarb, foreign non-Muslims, who were settled temporarily in Islamic territory under guarantees of amān.[36] Perhaps the expression in the berāts which allowed such a loose interpretation was that "the Patriarch elect was to hold the office in complete freedom the way his predecessors had". In similar Ottoman diplomas this expression meant that the recipient

---

[34] See Inalcik, *art. cit.*, pp. 238-249, where Critovoulos' observation is compared with the evidence from Turkish sources.

[35] See "Pâdişâh", *İslâm Ansiklopedisi*, IX-2, p.493.

[36] Pentazopoulos, *op. cit.*, p. 19; for a more cautious interpretation see Papadopoullos, *op. cit.*, 24. Against persistent misinterpretation, a German Orientalist, Fr. Giese, "Die geschichtlichen Grundlagen für die Stellung der christlichen Untertanen im osmanischen Reich", *Der Islam*, XIX (1930), p. 276, said: "Jedenfalls ist die Behauptung bei Sidarouss, S. 273, S.v. u. von einem 'contrat bilatéral des peuples chrétiens avec le gouvernement musulman' eine Verdrehung schlimmster Art".

36 See "Imtiyāzāt", *EI²*. Pentazopoulos, *op. cit.*, pp. 13-15, is in a totally wrong direction when he compares the privileges in *berāts* for Patriarchs with those given by non-Muslim rulers with extraterritorial rights.

shall be free from the interference of local authorities.[37] Critovoulos,[38] a contemporary and reliable source, informs us that Mehmed the Conqueror, in appointing Gennadius to the Patriarchate, had made it clear that he was to enjoy "all its power and authority, no less than that enjoyed previously under the Emperors". [39] The question remains to what extent the Patriarchs were able to take advantage of this license for their continued existence and to expand in later periods their authority within or beyond the limits of Islamic tradition. What is certain is that Greek influence with the Conqueror and his successors had its ups and downs, and, that the strength of the position of the Patriarchate depended on the situation at a given time.[40] In the sixteenth century, when under the pressure of an increasing Muslim population, a need was felt for mosques in districts of Istanbul that had previously had a Greek majority, the question was raised of the legality of the Greeks' keeping their churches in a city which had been captured by force. The question was resolved legally in favor of the Greeks, and the whole affair recorded for reference in the Turkish documents.[41]

Below is the translation of a berāt of appointment given to a metropolitan written under Mehmed II or Bāyezīd II which can give[42] an impression of the berāt of Gennadius:

> The order of the imperial diploma (*ni<u>sh</u>ān*), may God keep it in force until the final day, is this: Since the holder of this imperial diploma

---

[37] See Papadopoullos' interpretation, *op cit.*, p. 6 ("absolute freedom"), and p. 32 ("exercise of authority").

[38] Critovoulos, *op. cit.*, p. 94.

[39] For politico-religious jurisdiction of the Orthodox Church under the Byzantine emperors see Pentazopoulos, *op. cit.*, pp. 8-19; *The Cambridge Medieval History,* IV, The Byzantine Empire, Part II: Government, Church and Civilization, pp. 105-133 (E. Herman).

[40] From 1456 to 1473, The Conqueror appears to have been particularly favorable to Greeks. Mehmed II favored and brought to important positions Palaeologi and Greeks during this period; see F. Babinger, *Mehmed the Conqueror and His Time,* trans. R. Manheim, ed. W. Hickman, Princeton, 1978. Index: *Khass Murad, Mesih, Critoboulos.* See also my "Mehmed's Policy"; Gennadius lost the favor of the Conqueror and was replaced by Patriarchs more submissive to the Sultan's government: see S. Runciman, *The Great Church...*, pp. 194-196.

[41] J.H. Mordtmann, *art. cit.*; F. Giese, *art. cit.*, pp. 273-276; Ahmet Refik, *On Altıncı Asırda İstanbul Hayatı,* İstanbul, 1935, p. 45, document no. 4.

[42] *Ḳānūnnāme-i Sulṭānī ber Mūceb-i ʻÖrf-i ʻOsmānī*, eds. R. Anhegger and H. Inalcik, Ankara, 1956, pp. 65-66, no. 46; its translation into French by N. Beldiceanu, *Les actes des premiers Sultans conservés dans les manuscrits turcs de la Bibliothèque Nationale à Paris*, I, Paris and The Hague, 1960; for corrections of his translation see H. Inalcik, "Notes on Beldiceanu's Translation....", *Der Islam*, XLIII/1-2 (1967), p. 151.

> (*mithāl*), the monk by the name of (name not copied), delivered to my imperial treasury the pīshkesh in the amount of (blank) in florin, I have conferred upon him the Metropolitan See (*midrepolidlik*) of (name not copied). My order is that from now on he be Metropolitan there, and, as God ordered: 'Leave them in what they profess', he perform their rites as they have been performed, and that he exercise as a Metropolitan over the priests, monks (*kalyoros*), and other Orthodox Christians of that district and place as his predecessors did, and that he enter into possession of the churches, vineyards, orchards and plots of land which were in the possession of his predecessors, and that he be exempt from the *djizya* and all extraordinary impositions such as the *ulaḳ* and the *djere-hōr* as his predecessors were, and that the priests, monks and Orthodox Christians of that place acknowledge him as their Metropolitan and bring to him all the litigations under the jurisdiction of the metropolitanate.

This berāt, is the same as the earlier Caliphal or later Ottoman diplomas in its basic structure.

Diplomas from Islamic chanceries were of various types with respect to the authority or privileges they conferred.[43] In the Ottoman Empire, a berāt[44] given to a *serdār-i ekrem*, a commander-in-chief, was different in scope from that given to a simpe tīmār holder. Furthermore, such berāts appointing officials differed in substance from those granting tax exemptions to individuals or groups of *re'āyā* status and from those establishing particular social privileges or functions. *Berāt*s of the last category, which includes those given to the heads of the guilds, are of special interest for the topic under examination. The Sultan, as the highest and the sole source of authority in the Empire, issued such a *berāt* to the *ketkhudā* upon his election by the members of his particular guild, to ratify that election and to empower him with authority over the members of the guild. The Sultan ordered third parties, guild members and local authorities to recognize the *ketkhudā* as the head of that guild and to recognize his authority in matters governed by internal guild regulations or customs, and he promised to use the coercive

---

43 For berāt or diplomas of investiture and appointment in pre-Ottoman Islamic states, see H. R. Roemer, *Staatsschreiben der Timuridenzeit,* Wiesbaden, 1952, Einleitung, pp. 1-20; S. M. Stern, *Fatimid Decrees,* London, 1964.

44 For Ottoman berāt, see L. Fekete, *Einführung in die osmanisch-türkische Diplomatik der Türkischen Botmässigkeit in Ungarn,* Budapest, 1926; P. Wittek, "Zu einigen frühosmanischen Urkunden", *WZKM*, XLII (1957), pp. 300-313; XLIV (1957), pp. 240-256; LV (1959), pp. 124-141; LVI (1960), pp. 267-284; H. Inalcik, "Notes on Beldiceanu's Translation", pp. 140-141; *"Berāt", EI²*, I, pp. 1170-1171; but there is no detailed study on berāt with definitions of each type.

powers of the state to enforce the orders of the *ketkhudā* if necessary. In light of this we can examine the situation in 1695 when the Patriarch of Peč complained of not being able to collect alms from the *re'āyā* because his *berāt* had not been renewed by the new Sultan. From the point of view of public law, there is a great deal of validity to the comparison, as suggested by Pentazopoulos, of the organization of the Patriarchate with that of a guild.[45]

The question of why the Ottoman Empire maintained the Churches, each to represent its own community, in a manner similar to that of other organized bodies, must be examined within the context of the peculiar social system of the Islamic empires, in which socio-economic and religious organizations were the units through which the authority of the state was often mediated to the individual. The use by some scholars of the word "corporate" to describe this system has led to sharp controversy among Islamicists. But it is an undeniable fact that in these vast empires the central government had to operate, for practical reasons, through such already established social organizations, religious or professional, in which communal identity was essential. That is, in these medieval empires, individuals were not considered citizens in the modern sense of the word; rather they were perceived as members of a community, which was the only type of entity officially recognized within the larger political framework of the Empire. This system was based on the Sultan's recognition, through a diploma, of the existence and limited authority of such communities. The organization of such communities, at least officially, followed a given pattern. The *re'āyā*, however, always remained as dhimmīs, subjects of the Islamic state, enjoying the privilege of looking after their communal affairs in certain defined spheres of activity, in this case within the Church organization. Such a diploma did not confer total autonomy to a community. An autonomy established by diploma was to be found in the real sense of the word only in the *Dar al-'Ahd,* the Abode of the Covenant.[46] On the other hand, it is also an exaggeration to say that the Ottomans regarded the Patriarch as a "state official" during the classical period, that is, up until the turn of the sixteenth century.[47] The Patriarch was elected by a Synod as a representative of the Church, and as such his position was legally very similar to that of a ketkhudā in a craft guild. The state always exhibited a concern to prevent

---

45 H. Inalcik, "The Appointment Procedure of a Guild Warden Ketkhuda", *Wiener Zeitschrift für die Kunde des Morgenlandes,* Vol. 76, *Festschrift Andreas Tietze*, Vienna 1986, pp. 135-142.

46 See *EI*², II, p. 116.

47 State officials held authority and title through a sultanic *berāt,* but unlike the Patriarch, they received a salary (*'ulūfe*) or a benefice (*tīmār*) for services to the state. All of the state officials belonged to the so-called "military" (*'askerī*) class.

local authorities from interfering in the elections for ketkhudā or for Patriarch and Metropolitans.

It must be emphasized that the basic legal status of the Patriarch and the Church did not change in the Ottoman state, not even in the eighteenth century when the decentralization policies of the government furnished them with new responsibilities towards their flocks in certain civil matters and especially in taxation. As, upon the request of the central government, the Muslim communities, under *a'yān* councils, headed by cadis, undertook this type of responsibilities,[48] so too did the Christian communities under their religious leadership. In the *berāt*s granted in this period, for example, it was indicated that the newly nominated Patriarch, for whom the Sultan's approval had been sought, was not only favored by the community but had also been proven "fully able to collect the taxes due to the Imperial Treasury (māl-i mīrī)".[49] The term dhimmī, used for the Greeks in all berāts, clearly define their status under Ottoman rule. Emphasis upon the autonomy of the Greek "nation" under the Ottoman Sultans or upon the sovereign rights of the Partriarchs, allegedly agreed to by Mehmed II, merely shows a distorted interpretation of Islamic and Ottoman legal concepts as well as of historical reality.

Notes on the fiscal Status of The Greek Orthodox Church

In principle, men of religion—whether Muslim, Christian or Jew—who were not engaged in profit-making activities, were exempt from taxation including dyizya. However, with time non-Muslim clergy were required to pay various kinds of "gifts" and taxes to the Ottoman treasury, the earliest being *pīshkesh* (in vernacular *peshkesh*).

The imperial bureau created under the name *Peskopos Muḳāṭa'ası* in the finance department dealt with such revenues. According to the register covering the years 1641-1651, the Greek Orthodox Patriarch paid as *pīshkesh* 20,000 groush and provided 105 okka of meat per day or its equivalent for the imperial gardeners (*bostāndjıs*).[50]

Originally, pīshkesh was not a tax but simply "an offering" or a "gift".[51] Since the time of the ancient Iranian empires, such customary offerings

---

[48] See H. Inalcik, "Centralization and Decentralization in Ottoman Administration", *Studies in Eighteenth Century Islamic History,* eds. T. Naff and R. Owen, London 1977, pp. 27-52.

[49] See for instance the *berāts* published by Kabrda, *op. cit.*, pp. 36-58.

[50] See H. Inalcik, "Ottoman Archival Materials on Millets", in B. Lewis and B. Braude, eds., *op. cit.,* p. 441.

[51] *Ibid.*, pp. 447-448.

symbolized an expression of allegiance and dependence by a vassal or inferior to the ruler.The ruler responded by granting symbols of authority such as an imperial diploma or caftans bearing the ruler's emblem. All state dignitaries customarily offered a *pīshkesh* to the ruler. *Pīshkesh* was established over time as a cash payment to be delivered in a fixed amount upon reveiving the diploma of appointment. The governor generals, for instance, paid the treasury 10,000 aḳcha on the occasion. The *pīshkesh* paid by the high clergy was called *pīshkesh* of diploma (*berāt*). Over time, the rates of such *pīshkesh* were elaborately fixed in a regulation for the Patriarch, Metropolitans, Archbishops and Bishops.[52] In order to pay the *pīshkesh* these church dignitaries had to impose taxes on the faithful and the subaltern priests in the provinces (see infra: *mīrī rusūm*).

As enumerated in the berāts,[53] the principal ecclesiastical taxes paid by the Orthodox clergy or by the re'āyā in the seventeenth century were as follows:

Mīrī rusūm or māl-i mīrī
Patriḳliḳ and Metrepolidlik tax
Zitiye
Żarar-i ḳaṣṣābiye
Taṣadduḳ (alms)
Ayazma and Ayasmoz
Manastır resmi
Panayır
Marriage taxe

The origin and coverage of the mīrī rusūm, literally "taxes belonging to the fisc", is controversial. Joseph Kabrda[54] argues that it means the total of the ecclesiastical taxes and dues which the metropolitans levied in their dioceses to meet the annual payment to the patriarchate and for their own expenditures.

We know that the Patriarch was required to pay a certain amount of money to the fisc annually in addition to the *pīshkesh* paid at the time of investiture. When and how *pīshkesh* was converted to an annual payment is not known. But it is well known Ottoman practice to convert the customary payments and fees into regular taxes.[54] It was also an Ottoman practice to incorporate pre-Ottoman taxes into their own tax system as long as they did not conflict with the Ottoman principles of taxation. On the other hand, at

---

[52] *Ibid.*, pp. 440-444.

[53] *Berāt*s quoted by Kabrda, *op. cit.*, pp. 36-58, pl., XXVIII, XXXIII, XXXIV, XXXVII.

[54] Kabrda, *op. cit.*, p. 62.

[54] H. Inalcik, "Military and Fiscal Transformation...", pp. 317-322.

every accession to the throne, all berāts throughout the empire had to be renewed in the name of the new Sultan. So, the Patriarch had to pay *pīshkesh* for the renewel of his berāt. In any case, each Patriarch had to pay *pīshkesh* at the time of his investiture as well as an annual mīrī tax. The annual mīrī tax existed already by the mid-sixteenth century. On the other hand, the Ottoman government demanded contributions from the members of the tax exempt "military" class in times of financial crisis as an "emergency tax".[55] The 105 okka of meat contribution required from the Patriarch was that kind of contribution used to satisfy the "military" divisions attached to the palace. There were various ways in the Ottoman system to introduce new regular taxes. Most probably the occasional *pīshkesh* was the origin of the annual regular "state taxes" (*mīrī rusūm*).

The Sultanic berāt was the official document authorizing Metropolitans to collect the state tax (*māl-i mīrī*) as well as the canonical dues from their respective sees.[56] It was also through a berāt that the possession rights of the church properties and administration of the Metropolitan or Patriarch were legally established.[57] The taxes and the income from such properties provided the Metropolitans the means to meet their financial obligations to the state, personal and ecclesiastical expenditures. Thus, from a legal standpoint, the Ottoman government considered all of the taxes collected by the clergy as belonging to the state (mīrī) and the clergy as tax-farmers. The word *iltizām*, tax farm, was used for the Metropolitan's authority over his diocese. Actually, the Patriarch depended for his revenue on the Metropolitans. Through their agents the latter collected taxes owed by the subaltern priestes and the faithful. Thus, in the last analysis it was the village or neighborhood priest who actually levied taxes or fees from the faithful.

Delays and arrears in payments to the Patriarch resulted in the government action including sending the Patriarch every four of five years to recover the arrears and punishing the recalcitrants (see Appendix I).

While Kabrda asserts[58] that all taxes and dues levied in a diocese, even such purely canonical taxes as the marriage tax, were included in the *rusūm* or *māl-i mīrī*, we believe that the *Patriḳliḳ* tax, also called *mīrī Patriḳliḳ*, was a specific tax to cover the contribution to the Patriarch's annual payment to the fisc. Each *re'āyā* household had to pay 12 aḳcha and subaltern priests one gold piece annually to the Patriarch. *Metrepolidlik* tax, again 12 aḳcha for

---

55 *Ibid.*

56 Kabrda, *op. cit.*, p. 61.

57 See also Kabrda, *op. cit.*, pp. 36-37; cf. below, Appendix I.

58 *Ibid.* pp., 62-63.

each *re'āyā* household and one gold piece for the priests must have been designed to make up the personal income of the Metropolitan.[59]

Żarar-i ḳaṣṣābiye or *Ż. lahm* constituted part of the mīrī taxes for the Ottoman fisc. It was a tax introduced in the late sixteenth century to meet the enormous state expenditures covering the difference of the fixed state and market prices of meat supplied for the divisions of the standing army in the capital. The Patriarch alone had to contribute 105 okka of meat per day for the impreial gardeners (*bostandji*).[60] Mīrī and Ż. ḳaṣṣābiye were the main taxes reserved for the imperial treasury.

One of the principal ecclesiastical taxes was the *zitiye*. It was a contribution in cash or in kind paid by the faithful to the Patriarch and local Metropolitan to meet the expenditures of the church. It is identified as the Byzantine *kanonikon.*[61] An important source of revenue for the church *taṣadduḳ* (alms), in slavic *milostinja,* consisted of voluntary contributions in cash or in kind. But expressions in the Ottoman documents give the impression that it was converted, like *pīshkesh,* into a regular annual tax. Mīrī rusūm, zitiye and żarar-i ḳaṣṣābiye were considered the most important taxes by the Ottoman government.

Apparently, being a local tax the *manastır resmi* was occasionally included among the mīrī taxes in the *berāt* of the Metropolitans. It was an annual tax paid to the metropolitan. The Metropolitan also took possession of the property left by deceased monks and nuns. Ayazma (*hagiasma*) appears to be another important source of revenue for the church. When the faithful visited a sacred spring (*hagiasma*) near a church or monastery looking for a cure, they gave alms or paid a fixed fee from which the Metropolitan claimed a share.[62] Panayır or "fair" tax was also considered a religious tax since fairs were usually held near a place of pilgrimage or a *hagiasma* on the occasion of a religious festivity. An important part of the revenue realized at such fairs went to the Metropolitan who maintained his agent at the church or monastery in order to collect the revenue. It was a privilege granted by the Sultan through a special berāt that a rural market or fair was organized. The tax revenue which accrued belonged to the holder of the privilege, which was not infrequently a church or monastery. The latter was considered a kind of tax farmer who paid the government a lump sum for the privilege of collecting the tax and a portion of the tax went to Metropolitan who had the church or

---

59 *Ibid.* pp., 39-40, facsimile 34, pl. 45.

60 A. Greenwood, "Istanbul's Meat Provisioning", Ph. D. Dissertation, University of Chicago, NELC, 1988, pp. 8-61.

61 Kabrda, *op. cit.,* p. 68.

62 *Ibid.*, p. 78.

monastery within his diocese. In general, the revenue connected with a certain monastery or church was farmed out at a sum agreed upon by the clergy associated with the place. Thus, religious function and tax collection for the government were intimately associated under the Ottomans.

Established during the Byzantine time, the marriage tax, *nikāh resmi* in Turkish, was fixed at 80 *akcha* at the first marriage, 160 at the second and 240 at the third in the seventeenth century Ottoman documents. It was paid by the faithful and priests to the Metropolitan. Its rate increased as Ottoman silver coin, *akcha,* underwent a sharp inflation, reaching 400, 800 and 1,200 *akcha* respectively by 1776.[63]

Another source of revenue enumerated among those belonging to the Metropolitan was *bankā*, the sale of candles in the churches on a bank called *pangar* in Greek, *bankā* or *panka* in Turkish documents. The Metropolitan took a share from this revenue realized in the churches within his diocese.[64]

Other kinds of revenues exclusively reserved for the church included the taxes called *parasiye,* from Greek *parrésiai* and *portesi/protesi,* from Greek *prothésis*, alms for the dead or testamentary donations or fees taken at the ceremonies for the dead.[65] In the Sultan's berāts or orders the local Muslim judge is required to secure such alms and donations for the church from the inheritance of the dead.

In addition to the taxes reserved for the Church mentioned in the Ottoman documents, there were others which were referred to exclusively in the ecclesiastical sources, namely *filótima, embatikia* and *cheirotoniai.*[66]

Briefly speaking, various taxes paid by the re'āyā as well as by the local priests and monks can be classified into three categories: Taxes going directly into the Ottoman treasury, those reserved for the Patriarch and Metropolitans, and those which were exclusively levied for the local clergy and never mentioned in the Ottoman documents.

The taxes and *pīshkesh,* which the Patriarch and Metropolitans had to pay to the Ottoman fisc, constituted for the re'āyā a heavy addition to their tax burden as a whole since all of the payments had to be eventually met by the faithful. Annual mīrī tax increased by such additional Ottoman taxes as ḳaṣṣābiye in the late sixteenth century. It appears that the Orthodox Church became another instrument for the Ottoman fisc to expand its tax basis to meet the rapidly increasing state expenditures.

---

63 *Ibid.*, p. 76.

64 *Ibid.*, p. 38.

65 *Ibid.*, p. 88-84.

66 *Ibid.*, p. 89, pl. LII, dated 1755.

In general, the Patriarch used to send an agent (*vekīl*) to the provinces to collect taxes from the Metropolitans.[67] The agent had the power to punish or dismiss from his post the priests or monks who refused to meet their tax obligations. When the Metropolitan of Salonica did not pay the *māl-i mīrī* to the Patriarch for two years the Sultan, upon his request, sent a *chawush* to force his compliance.

The Sultan provided protection and immunities for the agents of the Patriarch and Metropolitans in their tours; there was to be no harrassment and no imposition of commercial dues on the taxes in kind collected for the Church.

Metropolitans were fully empowered by the Sultan's *berāt* to deal independently with the clergy in the churches and monasteries under their jurisdiction. They were also authorized to dismiss and punish the priests and monks, to place the Patriarch's agents at the churches and monasteries to levy taxes due and to see to it that marriages, divorces or inheritances were executed in accordance with the canonical laws. Since many Greeks preferred the cadi's court to evade ecclesiastical taxes or enjoy extra security.[68] Sultan gave orders in favor of the Metropolitans to prevent such interferences. The Metropolitan's *berāt* also promised that he would receive aid from the local cadi against the recalcitrant Greek *re'āyā*. A Metropolitan had the authority to punish the priests and monks who did not fulfill their tax obligations. Canonical penalties included shaving the head or being dismissed from the post.[69] When necessary, he was given a specific sultanic order to this effect.[70]

The cadi could also bar, upon the Sultan's order, a Metropolitan from taking possession of his office.[71]

The will of a Greek subject in favor of the Orthodox Church or clergy was executed by the local cadi under the testimony of the Greek witneses.[72]

In general, the Ottoman government considered it to be a public duty to protect the churches and monasteries against the abuses of local authorities. One frequent subject of complaint was that governor's men, equipped with a special order to investigate crimes and recover runaway slaves, exacted food and money in the course of their tour.[73] Another abuse often mentioned in the

---

[67] *Ibid.*, pl. 32.

[68] Pentazopoulos, *op. cit.*, p. 80.

[69] Kabrda, *op. cit.*, pl. XLVI.

[70] *Ibid.*, pl. XXXI, dated 1715.

[71] *Ibid.*, pl. XXXVI, dated 1715.

[72] *Ibid.*, pl. LII, dated 1755.

[73] *Ibid.*, pl. 43; F. Bayraktarević, *Turski Dokumenti,* Sarajevo, 1935, doc. 24.

documents was that *tīmār*-holders or *wakf* trustees did not permit the agents of the Metropolitans to levy taxes on the Christian peasants and workers in their territory.

It was not easy for the poor to find money enough to pay ecclesiastical taxes which were added to *djizya* and other governmental taxes. As Ottoman documents[74] make clear, not infrequently the *dhimmī* re'āyā rendered their tax obligations in grain or fabrics. Alms in particular were given in goods—wine, butter, olive oil or honey.

Under the high dignitaries of the Church, the village and parochial priests appear to have shared the hardships of the poor in meeting the ecclesiastical taxation. As explained earlier the priests were obliged to pay one gold piece to the Patriarch and one gold for the Metropolitan each year.

Interestingly enough, it was the Ottoman government that came forward to protect the re'āyā against the illegal and excessive demands of the high clergy. The Ottoman government pursued those metropolitans who overtaxed the faithful and took action when a complaint was received.[75]

Examining ecclesiastical taxes and fiscal administration of the Greek Orthodox Church, Josef Kabrda concluded[76] that the Church came actually to cooperate with the Ottoman government in consolidating Ottoman rule over the Christian masses while at the same time the Church succeeded in preserving and developing the national cultural traditions and Christian spiritual values.

---

[74] Kabrda, *op. cit.*, p. 38, and facsimile XXXIV; pl. XLIV, dated 1755.

[75] *Ibid.*, pl. XXXVI, dated 1715.

[76] *Ibid.*, pp. 101-103. It is argued that in Bosnia the Church dues imposed by the Greek Orthodox Church might be one of the causes of the conversion to Islam of the followers of the "Bosnian Church"; "Bosna", *EI*², I, p. 1265.

APPENDIX I

Sultan Suleyman's Order to Governors and Cadis of Rumeli about the Patriarch Joasaph II's Inspection Tour[77]

To the sandjaḳ-begis and cadis of the province of Rumeli: when the imperial order arrives may it be known that the Patriarch over the infidels of Istanbul by the name of Yuvasif has sent to my exalted Porte a letter which says that it has been a requirement for the Patriarchs of a long standing practice to make an inspection (*yoḳlama*) every four or five years of all the metropolitans, bishops, 'goumenos' and other priests of the aforementioned province, and accordingly asked for permission to carry it out. In the letter he also said that he is owed back payments from these priests out of the dues of the past years including the present year which were to be collected in accordance with their religious law by the Patriarch as laid down in his diploma of appointment (*berāt*) and he requested permission to go and to collect them in person. Upon the receipt of this letter I order that you, the *cadis,* will summon in your presence the metropolitans, Bishops, priests, 'goumenos' and monks within your jurisdiction when the Patriarch arrives with my imperial order and bring them to face with him and make your investigations in accordance with the sharī'a. You will let him collect in full the back payments from the past years and the present year in the amounts which will be established by your examination.

On his way back to Istanbul with the *mīrī aḳcha* which he has collected, the Patriarch shall not be forced on the routes and stopping places to surrender either his own mules and pack horses or those belonging to his retinue. You will help him through the mountain passes and dangerous places under the best conditions so that no harm will come to the public revenues (*māl-i mīrī*). He reported that some metropolitans and bishops make excuses for not paying the tax due by saying that we still have fifteen or twenty days until we are liable to pay. You will not listen to their excuses and will make them pay their debts in their entirety to the Patriarch. When metropolitans, bishops, monks and priests die without any apparent heirs those estates of 5,000 or more *aḳcha* are to be claimed for the state treasury and those less than 5,000 are to be taken by the Patriarch. The *beyt'ül-māldji*s used to interfere and claim both the estates belonging to the Patriarch and black robe of the priests, scepter, silver cup, cap and mule which belog to the church. You will see to it that when one of the above mentionned priests dies without

[77] This document comes from a collection of state papers in a manuscript preserved in the Âtıf Efendi Library, no. 1734, ff. 121-123, see Facsimile I.

apparent heir and his estate belonged to the state treasury the estates of 5,000 *aḳcha* or more shall be handed over to the *mevḳufdjus*. As to those estates of less than 5,000 *aḳcha*, you will let the Patriarch take them in accordance with the established practice.

As for the belongings, clothes, and other things which the priests carry, the old regulations followed until now will be applied as before. You will see that those priests who acted against their canonical law and custom (*āyīn*) are dismissed and replaced by another priest through the action of the said Patriarch and you will submit your report on the proceedings to my Porte. While the said Patriarch is on his way to and from Istanbul you shall prevent *yava kharādjdjı*s or collectors of fugitives *kharādj* from taking this tax from him and the men in his company. The Patriarch complained that local *sandjaḳ-begi*s, *su-bashi*s, *sipāhı*s, janissaries and others prevent him from collecting the arrears which (the priest) owed him. You shall forbid those who want to interfere with his collection of the arrears, and report to my Porte a list by name in writing of those who do not obey the prohibition. Each of you *sandjaḳ-begi*s and *cadi*s should be properly concerned with this matter. And if the said Patriarch, during his inspection tries to take from the metropolitans and bishops money in addition to the dues which they had to pay according to their religious law and custom (āyīn-i bāṭila), you shall forbid him to inflict such an injustice. If he does not hear your warning you will immediately report to my Porte. You shall help the said Patriarch with the purchase by his own money of the things which are necessary for his sustenance and fodder for his horses during his travelling and lodging. You shall see that he shall not unlawfully demand things from the *re'āyā* and that he thus shall not oppress them. You shall be the one to answer if later *re'āyā* come and complain that the said Patriarch extorted from them. You will be properly concerned with it. I will not condone the extortion of any of the *re'āyā*. I want you to always show proper concern. You should be forewarned and trust in my imperial seal put above.

Comment

Under Suleyman I (1520-1566) patriarchs, equipped with authority through the Sultan's diploma, traveled widely and made their presence felt in their sees all over the empire. By his travels "Jeremia I", N. Iorga (Jorga) notes,[78] "appears to have the intention to review the Orthodox world and to have his supreme authority recognized as an ecumenical one. He visited Cyprus, then

---

[78] Iorga, *op. cit.*, p. 93.

still under Venetian rule, and Jerusalem, recently annexed to the Ottoman empire. Since Mehmed II's time, the Ottomen sultans recognized the Greek Church as the highest among the Christian churches and supported re-establishment of the unity of the Orthodox Church under their protection. For the Ottoman sultans who considered themselves as the heir to the Eastern Roman Emperors and assumed the title "ḳayṣar" (Ceasar), such a policy appeared quite normal, and obviously aimed at exploiting the title for their political goals. For exemple, Suleyman's Grand Vizir Ibrahim (1523-1536) extended a special favor toward Jeremia.[79] Taking advantage of this favor, Jeremia fought against the attempts of the Patriarchate of Ochrida which was seeking to extend its jurisdiction over all Slavic speaking subjects of the Sultan in Rumili. In 1545 we find him trying to consolidate his authority over the clergy in Wallachia and Moldavia.

Joasaph II (1555-1565), our Patriarch in the document, continued the same policy as his predecessors. The Ottoman sultans, then at the zenith of their power, and confident that their Greek subjects would never think of an alliance with the enemies of the Empire, looked rather benevolently at the extention and consolidation of the Patriarch's authority.[80]

At his accession to the Patriarchate, Joasaph II was able to persuade the Porte to reduce the *pīshkesh*[81] from 3,000 gold ducats to 2,000, but, after he left office it would be raised again to 3,000.[82] The reduction might be connected with a financial difficulty as our document suggests.

Iorga[83] suggests that the patriarchal tours of the provinces were primarily motivated by a need to fill the treasury of the Patriarchate. By 1580, the Patriarch needed an annual revenue of 20,000 "thaler" or 13,300 gold pieces to supply the Patriarchate with a staff of about twenty persons.

Joasaph was involved in the negociations with the Lutheran Church to reach an agreement.[84] At that time the Ottoman government was encouraging the Protestants all over Europe in their opposition to the Papacy and the Habsburgs.[85]

---

[79] *Ibid.*, p. 94.

[80] *Ibid.*, p. 98.

[81] For *pīshkesh* see H. Inalcik, "Ottoman Archival Materials on Millets", in Lewis and Braude, *op. cit.*, pp. 447-448.

[82] Runciman, *op. cit.*, 202; it was raised in 1526 to 5,600 and in 1730 to 15,000 gold pieces; in the mid-seventeenth century, it was 20,000 *groush* or about 12,500 gold pieces (see H. Inalcik, "Ottoman Archival" p. 44)

[83] op.cit. *Ibid*, p. 96.

[84] Runciman, *op. cit.*, pp. 245-247.

[85] H. Inalcik, *The Ottoman Empire: The Classical Age,* 1300-1600, London, 1973, pp. 37-38.

An interesting episode during Joasaph's Patriarchate is Ivan IV of Muscovy's attempt to obtain the Patriarch's confirmation of his title of *Tsar* (Ceasar).[86]

Michael Cantacuzenus, the Sultan's powerful khāṣṣa merchant with the monopoly of fur imports from Russia, caused Joasaph's dismissal from the Patriarchate in 1565. Joasaph's contemporaries describe him as "one of the most distinguished and learned of Patriarchs, personally popular among all the Orthodox and fully supported by the monks of Mount Athos". After a successful reign of ten years, he was deposed because he would not further one of Michael's ambitious family-marriage schemes, on the ground that it infringed canon law.[87]

APPENDIX II

Ottoman Official Translation of the Patriarch Gabriel IV's Petition*

In this petition submitted to the Sultan the Patriarch says: A number of metropolitans had left their sees and taken refuge in Istanbul because of the oppressive acts. Thereupon, the Sultan had sent orders to all the provinces to stop such acts an asked eight metropolitans to stay in Istanbul to hold Holy Synod in accordance with the tradition of the Orhodox Church and the rest to go to their respective sees. So, they all immediately left Istanbul except the eight metropolitans. Since it is not possible to hold the Holy Synod with eight metropolitans, the Patriarch is requesting that two more metropolitans be allowed to stay on. (If this is approved) the Sultan's order to this effect might be added in the form of a comment on the decree already issued and its copy be rendered to the Patriarch in the way of certification.

[The Patriarch's Signature]: Your Servitor,
The Patriarch of Istanbul and the Corps of
the Metropolitans, resident in Istanbul,
(no date)

---

[86] Runciman, *op. cit.*, p. 330; H. Inalcik, "Power relationships between Russia, the Crimean Khanate and the Ottoman Empire, as Reflected in the Titulature", in Ch. Lemercier-Quelquejay, G. Veinstein and S. E. Wimbush (eds.), *Passé turco-tatar, présent soviétique,* Etudes offertes à Alexandre Bennigsen, Louvain-Paris, 1986, pp. 175-186.

[87] Runciman, *op. cit.*, p. 98.

* See Facsimile II and III; Gabriel IV was the Patriarch of the Greek Orthodox Church in the years 1780-1785. I am indebted to Professor Speros Vryonis for this information.

Comment

The oppression referred to in the document is explained in a petition** submitted by the Metropolitan of Yanya (Ioannina), Inebahtı (Naupactus) and Narda (Arta) and over seventy citizens, dated 20 *Djumāda* I 1195/13 May 1781. According to the petition the flight of Metropolitans was the result of attacks and plundering by Albanian "outlaws" under the command of Ali Bey of Depedelen.

** See Facsimile IV.

Facsimile I: Suleyman I's Order for the Patriarch's Inspection Tour in Rumeli.
Source. Âtıf Efendi Library, no. 1734, 121ᵛ-123ᵛ.

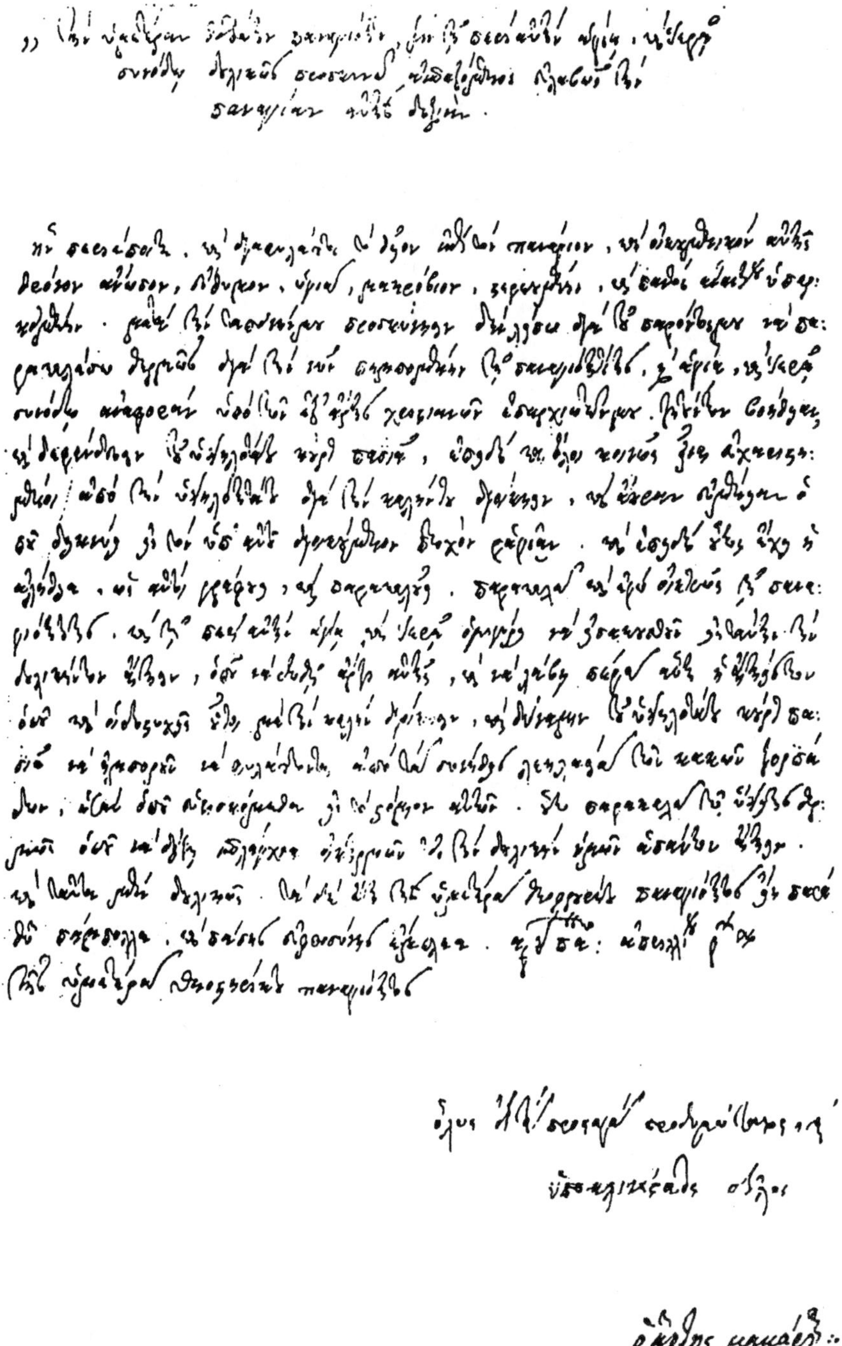

Facsimile II: A Petition by the Patriarch.
Source. The Topkapı Palace Archives, no. 1519.

Facsimile III: Offical translation of the Patriarch's Petition.

Source. The Topkapı Palace Archives, no. 1519.

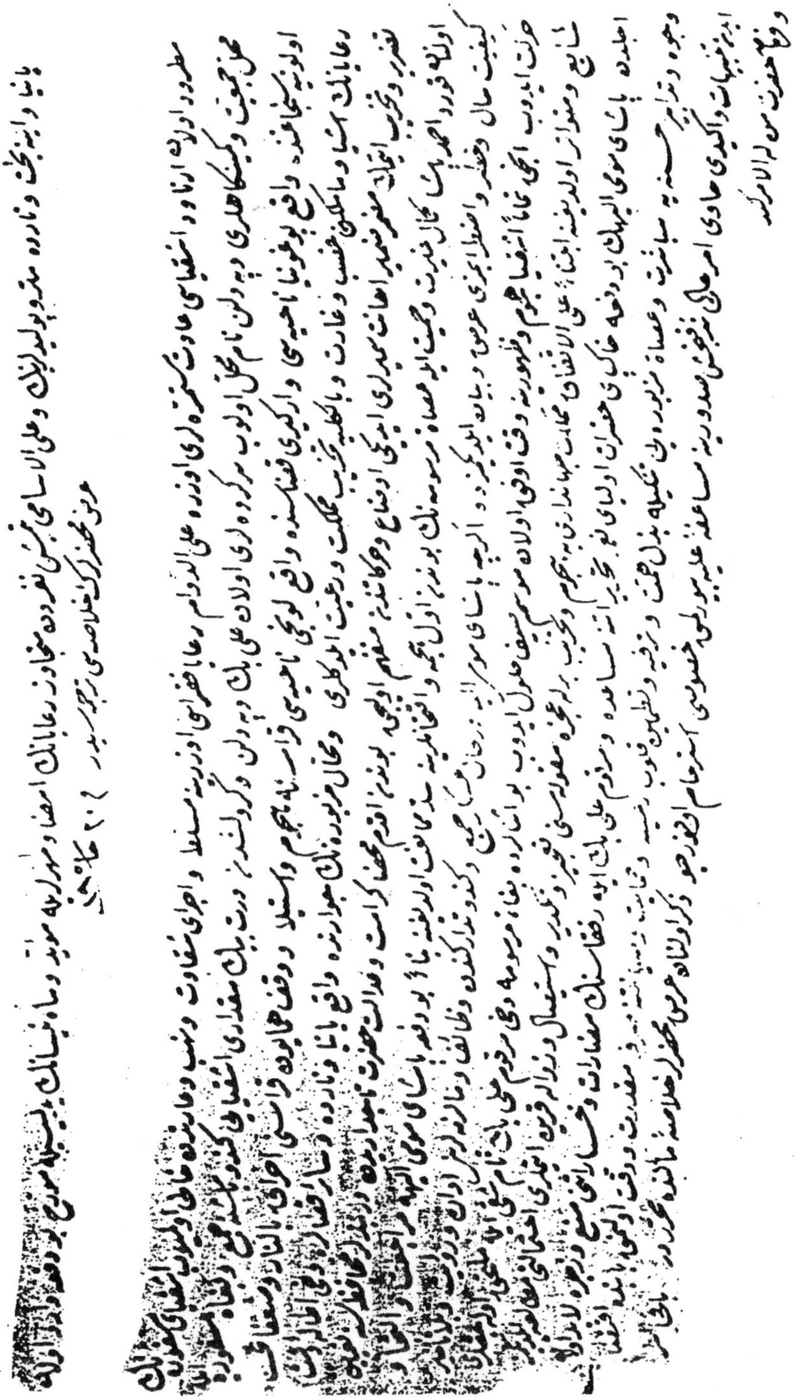

Facsimile IV: Petition of the Metropolitans of Yanya, İnebahtı and Narda.
Source. The Topkapı Palace Archives, no. 1519.

Part III

Society and Economy

1

Islam in the Ottoman Empire

Islam in the Ottoman Empire

The first Turkish peoples to convert en masse to Islam were the Bulghar Turks of the middle Volga region and the Turks under the Karakhanid dynasty in the area between Kashgar and Lake Balkash in Central Asia, in 921 and around 960 A. D. respectively. It was not a coincidence that these were the regions in the Turkish world where commerce was most developed, and Muslim caravan trade and merchant colonies had long flourished. As representatives of the then most civilized part of the world, these Muslim traders must have impressed the Turkish rulling class as conveyors not only of luxury goods but also of refined manners and high cultural values. What I am trying to say is that Turkish conversion to Islam was the result of a long process of acculturation before it took a definite and massive form with the formal decision of a ruler. In 921 the ruler of the Bulghars asked the Caliph Muqtadir for ulema to teach the Bulghars Islam and for experts to build fortresses against the powerful Khazars. The conversion decision of the Karakhanid ruler seems also have had political implications since it entailed the conquest of Transoxiana from the Samanids who were known for their zeal in defending and expanding Islam among the steppe peoples beyond the Syr Darya river. The Karakhanid and Bulghar kingdoms were to become the centers of the most sophisticated and orthodox forms of Islamic culture. As early as the eleventh century, important religious works in Arabic and literary works in Turkish were composed under the Karakhanids.

It was not, however, these Turks, Muslim Bulghars and Karakhanids who were destined to play a major role in the history of Islam, but the Oghuz-Türkmen tribes of the steppes beyond the Syr Darya and Khwarizm. These tribes were mostly Islamicized through the *ghazā* activities of the Samanids and through religious propaganda from disciples of the Sufi orders. Like the Abbasid Caliphs before them the Samanids employed large numbers of Turks as mercenaries in their armies, and this practice became a most effective means of islamization. Thus, from the beginning, *ghazā*, Holy War, and popular mysticism gave Turkish Islam its original and permanent features. The employment of steppe Turks as slave warriors or mercenaries by the Caliphs and the Sultans from the ninth century accelerated with the changing historical circumstances of the eleventh century. The growing demand for their services gave rise to a mass migration of the Oghuz tribes into Eastern

Iran. Now, organized under their own chiefs as mercenary or raiding units, many of these Oghuz groups began to pursue their own interests and at the same time to identify themselves increasingly with Islam. Eventually, one of them, Toghril Beg, son of Seljuk, was able to unite under his leadership large bodies of Oghuz and to supplant the Ghaznevid Sultanate of Eastern Iran, a state founded by a Turkish slave-mercenary group dedicated to *ghazā* expeditions into the Indian sub-continent.

By bringing under his control the easternmost provinces of the Caliphate and delivering the Caliph of Baghdad from the domination of the heterodox Buyids, Toghril could lay claim to being the temporal power of the Caliphate and the protector of the "true" Islam. Indeed, under the Seljukids, the independent nature of the Sultanate, the formal embodiment of temporal power became a fact of political life, thus inaugurating Turkish political supremacy that was to endure in the Islamic heartlands down to the twentieth century. The initial Turkish role in Islamic history continued to aim at unifying and protecting Islam through continuous *ghazā*, Holy War, against the initially successful counter-offensives of Christendom, both Byzantine and European, and at combating schismatic and heretical movements by organizing Islamic teaching in the madrasas and upholding universally adopted religious and cultural precepts. Most of the Turkish Muslim dynasties realized the neccessity of achieving these policies in order to maintain their own rule in the Islamic world. That is, they sought legitimization through the espousal of the "right" cause. It has also been suggested that with the reestablishment of stable political power and military vigor, the Islamic society under Turkish rule was enabled not only to survive but even to experience a regeneration.

What is historically ascertained is that the Turks introduced and superimposed a new concept of state and law based on the twin elements of strong, independent state-power and political action for the public good. The traditions and beliefs current in the Turkish Empires of Central Aisa supported the view that the state subsisted through the maintenance of the *törü* or *yasa,* a code of law laid down directly by the founding Qaghan. They thus identified political with legislative power. In Islam the Turkish dynasties endeavored to create an independent public law in support of their absolute political power. To this end they received the cooperation of Muslim legists who reconciled the new concept of state according to such Islamic principles as *maslaha,* public good, or *'urf,* custom. Under the Caliphate the same principles were invoked to accomodate the Caliph's administrative regulations within Islamic Law. Al-Māwardī, the famous Muslim jurist (died 1052) justified the necessity of secular power, *kuwwa al-saltana,* and the Sultan's authority to make *qanun*s, as a means of ensuring the public good and of implementing the *Sharī'a,* the Islamic religious law itself. Now, with the Turkish dynasties, the concept of independent state law was greatly strengthened. In the states founded by the Turks in Central Asia, Iran, Anatolia and India, decrees issued by the rulers on matters of state organization, military affairs, taxes, land tenure, and penal law created a rich corpus of state law entirely independent of the *Sharī'a.* In the same period, the revival of the Iranian political traditions strengthened this trend. Since the first Turkish states in Islamic territory were founded in Iran, the native Iranian bureaucracy in Turkish service became instrumental in this. In fact, this bureaucracy strove to revive the old Iranian traditions vis-a-vis the Caliphate and the *Sharī'a.* Subsequently in the states founded by the Turks in the Islamic world, the conflict between state law and the *Sharī'a* overlaid a politico-social struggle among the bureaucracy, the ulema and the ruling military class.

The Ottoman state, an offspring of the Seljukid empire, appears to have gone farther than any previous Islamic state in asserting the independence of state affairs and public law vis-a-vis the religious law. Mehmed the Conqueror (1444-1446, 1451-1481), the true founder of the Ottoman empire and promoter of a centralized and absolutist imperial system, further strengthened the principle of the ruler's legislative authority. Apparently he was the first ruler in Islamic history to promulgate codes of law based exclusively on sultanic authority. A contemporary Ottoman historian, Tursun Beg, interpreted the "good order", *nizām,* of this world as necessarily requiring the absolute coercive authority of the sultan and particularly the sultan's right to promulgate decrees of his own single will. But the early years of his successor Bayezid II (1481-1512) saw a strong reaction by the upholders of the *Sharī'a* against the Conqueror's untrammeled legislative activity. Although Suleyman the Lawgiver was inclined to assert the *Sharī'a's* control over state law, it preserved its independence under him, too.

The Sultan's independent legislative power affected even the field of religious law. It was a long established practice in Islam that in case of a serious dissention among the religious authorities on certain legal points the ruler might, in public interest, in order to avoid rifts within the community, decree that the precepts of one specific *madhhab* (school of Islamic Law) be followed. Thus, under the Seljukids and the Ottomans it was made obligatory for the judges to follow the rules of the Hanafī school in their courts. Such a decision greatly affected the direction taken by later legal development and practice since the Hanafī school was characterized by its broader principles to allow the state to introduce measures to cope with newly arising problems. Let me give you an example. Abū-s Su'ūd, *Shaykh ul-Islām* of Suleyman the Lawgiver (1520-1566), regarded the use of money to establish a religious endowement entirely acceptable to the *Sharī'a,* whereas Mehmed Birgivī, his opponent, regarded it as utterly illegal on the basis of the opinions of another school of law. Since the economic conditions encouraged money endowments and their abolition would destroy many already established charitable institutions, the state supported the Shaykh ul-Islām on his stand. Also it should be pointed out that reforms which proved to be of vital necessity for the existence of the Ottoman empire, and, by interpretation, for the good order of the Islamic community, were to be introduced only under broad principles of the Hanafī school by the decision of the ruler. Thus, it was no wonder that major modernization reform in modern Islam started and found its most radical implementation in the Ottoman empire. Before taking up this point in more details I would like to broach briefly on the rise of the *ghazā* movement and regeneration of the Caliphate with the foundation of the Ottoman empire.

With the rise of the Seljukid Empire in the Middle East, comprising Iran, Irak, Syria, and Palestine, a mass migration of the Oghuz tribes from Central Asia into the Middle East started, an historic phenomenon of great importance entailing structural changes in the ethnic, social and political setup of the region for subsequent centuries. Hastening to get rid of these nomads, the Seljukid central administration drove them out to the borderland against the Byzantine Empire. As *ghāzīs,* warriors for Islam, on these frontiers they first penetrated inland as small raiding parties and then under able leaders, they were organized and conquered the whole of Asia Minor down to the Aegean Sea when in 1071 the Seljukid Sultan Alp Arslan (1064-1072) defeated a Byzantine imperial army at Mantzikert. Highly mobile, the Oghuz now poured in growing numbers into Asia Minor from the East, occupying pasture lands in the central plateau and mountain ranges, and providing a high military potential for further expansion and conquest. The Crusaders starting in 1095 found Turkish Asia Minor difficult to pass through because of the fierce resistance of these Oghuz tribes.

First, principalities had emerged under the leaders of the conquests and finally an ousted branch of the Seljukid dynasty Suleyman shah, son of Kutalmısh (1075-1086) had been able to create there a Sultanate on the model of the Great Seljukid Empire in Iran. During the first decades of the 13th century, Seljukid Anatolia became a promised land in the Islamic world with its developing international trade, thriving cities and highly sophisticated social and intellectual life. The great mystics of the Islamic world, Muhyī al-Dīn al-'Arabī and Djalāl al-Dīn Rūmī found refuge in the Seljukid capital Konya. Now, the warlike Oghuz Türkmen tribes were concentrated on the mountains of the frontier zone against surrounding Christian lands. When the Seljukid state in Anatolia was subdued by the Mongols in the middle of the thirteenth century these frontier Türkmens resisted them. Repressed in their struggle again and again by the Mongol forces they finally turned their efforts to conquer the Byzantine provinces in Western Anatolia. They eventually established with the aid of the miltary leaders and, ulema who joined them from flourishing small states in the frontier zone, and dedicated themselves to continous ghazā activity in the Aegean and the Balkans. At the beginning the Ottoman state was simply one of these ghāazī principalities. From the middle of the thirteenth century, the frontier Türkmens collaborated with the Mamluks of Egypt in a common effort to save Islam from the domination of the heathen Mongols. In actual fact, it was the Mamluks and Türkmens of Anatolia which were to be considered in the Islamic world as representing the only military power capable to face the Mongol armies. Thus, it was the Mongol threat, then definitely more dangerous than the Crusaders, that prepared the rise of the typically military states of the Mamluks and the Ottomans, dominant powers in the subsequent period of Islamic history later on. The Ottomans annexed the Muslim states in the region, including the Mamluks to form a common front now in the face of the growing challenge of Christian Europe. It was mainly their ability to adopt modern war technology and to become a sea power that enabled the Ottomans to assume this tremendous task. This new Muslim empire was, in the last analysis, an achievemnt which Islamic culture, in its creativeness and adaptability made possible. On the other hand, the Ottoman supremacy in the Islamic world sought its legitimization in the revival of the idea of a universal caliphate under a new form.

Now let me give some details on the controversial subject of the Ottoman Caliphate. According to one tradition, at a ceremony held in the Ayasofya Mosque in Istanbul, the Abbasid Caliph al-Mutawakkil officially transferred to Sultan Selim I, upon Selim's conquest of Egypt in 1517, all rights to the Great Caliphate. In fact, however, there is no contemporary record of Selim's receving or claiming to receive the Caliphate from al-Mutawakkil. It seems that in order to support certain political goals, the tradion originated much later in the 18th century. In reality, Selim or his son Suleyman must not have felt that his claim to supremacy in the Islamic world required such a transfer of rights. However, what is historically established is that Selim then took the title of "Servitor of the Two Holy Sanctuaries", Mecca and Medina, the most exalted title at that time for a sultan claiming preeminence in the Islamic world. In any case, the concept of the Caliphate at that time was different from what it was in classical Islam under the Abbasids.

In their studies on the Caliphate, Barthold and Arnold showed that the classical concept the of Caliphate as formulated under the Abbasids of Baghdad, namely one *umma* (community) and the Caliph as commander of the faithful and as successor to the Prophet, radically changed in the 13th century, especially when the Mongol invasions left the Muslim world without a Caliph and partitioned, with an important part of area ruled by Mongol rulers. Subsequently, some Sunni legists revised the theory of the Caliphate to say that the Caliphate had really only lasted for thirty years after the death of Muhammed and that the Caliph need not be of the Quraysh, the Prophet's tribe. By the turn of the 14th century, Ibn Khaldun recognized that the function of Caliph could be assumed by the sultans of countries widely separeted from one another. Thus, the practice became widespread that any independent Muslim sovereign could assume the title *Khalīfa* (Caliph). From the 14th century on the Ottoman Sultans, too, used the title *Khalīfa* to signify an independent Muslim ruler. In the reign of Suleyman the Lawgiver, however, the question was posed as to whether it was licit for the Ottoman Sultans to use the titles of *imām* and Caliph of all the Muslims, in the absence of any lineal descent from the Prophet's tribe. According to Lutfī Pasha, Suleyman, as the effective ruler, with God's help of all Muslim lands from Central Europe to the Yemen, "is the Imām of the Age in fulfilment of the relevant stipulation relating to the maintenance of the Faith and guardianship of the homeland of Islam". This is reminiscent of Selim's previous invitiation to the Shirvan-Shah to accept Selim's "Supreme Caliphate", *Khilāfat-i 'Ulyā* and to cite his name in the Friday prayer in the Shirvan-Shah's land on the grounds that Selim was the supreme Sultan who protected the pilgrimage routes and the Holy Places, Mecca and Medina. In other words, as the Ottoman Sultans considered it their task to defend the world of Islam and to protect the holy sanctuaries, both of which were matters of common Muslim concern, they claimed to hold the predominant position in Islam. Although they did not descend from the Prophet's tribe, they maintained that God had chosen them for this task. In this fashion the new concep of the Caliphate came to be based on actual power and influence with God's support, and eventually served as a policy aimed at establishing Ottoman mastery over the world of Islam. The idea was obviously derived from the idea of Holly War, the cornerstone of the Ottoman state itself. In the decline period, when the Empire lost its actual power and ability to protect other Muslim lands, the Sultans relied more on the theoretical conception of the Caliphate stressing their rights over all Muslims as universal Caliphs. The idea of universal Caliphate was employed for the last time during the First World War when the Ottoman Sultan and Caliph called all the Muslims to *djihād,* Holy War, against the Allied powers.

A few words should be added here about Islam in the Ottoman Empire, particular Ottoman religious policy, and the spread of Islam. As a ghāzī state owing its success mainly to its espousal of the role of guardian of Islam, the

Ottoman state paid special attention to abiding by the stipulations of the religious law in all aspects of life. The state law, too, was considerd as based on Islamic principles, and in complete conformity with the religious law. Thus, in the first one and a half centuries of its history the vizirs, in charge of state affairs and the organization of the newly conquered lands, were mostly of ulema origin. *Ḳādī*s, Muslim judges, could be promoted to become governors and vizirs during this period. The Sultans always showed great concern for justifying their conduct in terms of the *Sharī'a.* For example, in order to justify war against their Muslim rivals the Ottoman Sultans often demanded that *muftī*s give *fetwā*s (written opinions based on the religious authorities). The question was asked as to whether or not it was legal to fight Muslims who attacked the Ottomans and thereby prevented the ghāzīs from fulfilling their duty of Holy War. In addition, war against heretics was justified by religious authority. After the foundation of the Ottoman state with all the trappings of a typical Middle East state, the *Kïzïlbash,* Oghuz-Türkmen nomads or peasants who retained their own special organization and adhered to an extremist heteredox order, remained on the Anatolian plateau and mountains as a large group alienated from the Ottoman state and society. When, in the 16th century, they gave their allegiance to the Safavid Shahs of Iran of the shiite secte, they were held to be the most dangerous enemies of the Ottoman state and were mercilessly persecuted. On the basis of the religious law the Ottoman ulema approved their suppression and even enslavement although according to Islamic law no muslim can be enslaved. It was, indeed, the dangerous struggle against the *Kïzïlbash* sect on the one hand and the Ottomans' Caliphate' policies on the other that made the Ottoman Sultans, from Suleyman the Lawgiver onwards, increasingly concerned with the more stringent application of the religious law.

Parallel to these phenomena, popular fanaticism was heightened by a group of preachers, so called *faqīh*s following teachings of Mehmed Birgivī, who employed the teachings of the Hanbalī school of Muslim jurisprudence to attack the various innovations introduced into Islam since the death of the Prophet. The *faqīh* regarded such practices as holding ceremonies to commemorate the dead oı visiting tombs, to seek aid from the deceased as contrary to authentic Islam. In their belief, mysticism, all non-Islamic sciences, and even Islamic theology were forms of blasphemy. At the same time in thier sermons as *wā'iz*, preachers in the principal mosques of Istanbul they attacked the luxury and extravagance of the ruling classes and railed against the injustices and lax morals of the age. In 1656, in a scheme to suppress all dervish convents in Istanbul their efforts to strike religious heresy at its roots found considerable support among poor *medrese* students and humble tradesmen. At this point the high ulema and the bureaucratic class in general opposed them and claimed that they undermined state and society and sowed dissent among the people. Finally, grand vizier Köprülü Mehmed (1656-1661) was able to quiet them and prevent civil war only by exiling the *faqīhs* from Istanbul. The theoretical basis of the dissent was the question of "innovation", *bid'a* in Islam. Later on the contention would re-emerge first as a militant religious movement of the Wahhabis of Arabia in the 18th century, and as an intellectual-religious movement called *Salafiyya* against the innovations which were invading the Islamic society in the 19th century as a result of the accelerated of westernization.

The Ottomans not only considerably extended the realm of Islam into the Balkans and East-Central Europe while maintaining their position in the Mediterranean, they also caused the spread of the Muslim religion in the Balkans. According to the estimates made in the middle of the nineteenth century the population of European Turkey, then including Serbia, Bulgaria, Bosnia and Herzegovina, Macedonia, Thessaly, Thrace, and the Islands was about 12 millions. One fourth of it, that is a population of three millions were Muslims, Anatolian Turks being 800,000 in this total. In 1878 when Turkey in Europe was reduced to Albania, Thessaly, Macedonia and Thrace there were 5 million and 335,000 inhabitants. Two millions and 601,000 or hardly more than half were Muslims and in this total Muslim Turks were 834,500.

Population of Rumeli, Ottoman census of 1894

Province	Muslim	Greek	Armenian	Bulgarian	Jewish	
Edirne	434,366	267,220	16,642	102,245	13,721	
Manastir	630,000	228,121	29	-	5,072	
Yanya	235,948	286,294	-	-	3,677	
Ishkodra	330,728	5,913	-	-	2,797	Catholic
Girit	74,150	175,000	500	-	200	
Adalar	30,809	226,590	83	2	2,956	
Čataldja	18,701	35,848	585	5,586	966	
Selānik	463,000	277,000	1,257	223,000	37,206 (2,311 Catholic)	
Ḳosova	419,390	29,393	-	274,826	1,706 (5,588 Latin)	

Source: K. Karpat, *Ottoman population*, Madison 1985, 155.

In fact, the Ottoman state followed an Islamization policy no more than any other Muslim state, always remaining scrupulously within the bounds of the Islamic *Shari'ā.* In their policy of rapid expansion, they readily granted the Islamic *amān,* amnesty to the submitted Christian population, which guaranteed them, under the status of *dhimmīs*, the protection of the Islamic state for their lives, property and freedom of cult. Only in case of open rebellion they exposed themselves once again to the harsh conditions which the *Shari'ā* stipulated for the enemies of Islam. Furthermore, desiring to make his capital the center of a universal empire, Mehmed the Conqueror officially recognized the autonomous religious administration of the non-Muslim communities by establishing the Greek Partiarchate, and Armenian Patriarchate, in Istanbul. No mass Islamization by force is recorded in Ottoman history since the religious law does not approve of it. Indeed, according to the *Shari'ā* even a slave cannot be forced to convert to Islam. However, as a socio-cultural process Islamization was a continuous phenomenon in the Ottoman society. First of all it should be remembered that the non-Muslim *re'āyā* always remained *socially* second class citizens in the Islamic society in spite of the guarantees of *dhimma* status. Thus, in spite of the restrictions on dressing, riding etc. the non-Muslims sought to identify themselves with Muslims in their life style, in order to escape social discrimination. Of course, Muslim-Ottoman culture also had an immense attraction and prestige among the subject nations, and even among Europeans who lived long enough amidst the Ottomans conversions were not rare.

The Ottomans, of course, encouraged conversions. For example, money was granted to help the converts dress as Muslims from a special fund called *nev-Muslim akchası,* the fund for new Muslims, at the imperial council. The new convert was led in ceremony on a horse along the streets of the city to receive the joyous congratulations of his fellow Muslims. The most widespread social factor leading to conversion was the marriage of Muslim men to non-Muslim women. In Islamic law there was no stipulation against marrying a non-Muslim female who, in fact, was permitted to continue the practice of her faith even though married to a Muslim. Murad II's wife, Mara Sultan, daughter of Serbian despot, had her special place of worship in the Place and remained a Christian until her death. The custom had found particular favor among the Ottomans since the time of the frontier ghāzīs. The cadi records of the newly conquered lands bear testimony of its widespread practice frequently followed by the woman's conversion.

Enrollment in the military organizations and Palace services of Christian boys of the so-called *devshirme,* levy boys, was the principal state institution in which one can detect "forced" Islamization. It was argued that Christians converted after the descent of the Qor'an were not entitled to the status of *dhimmīs,* and that most of the *dhimmīs* in the Balkans had been conquered by force, thus the levy of the Christian boys was held to be in conformity with Islamic Law. An Ottoman historian, Sa'deddīn, denied the allegation of forced Islamization on the grounds that children were born with no religion, and levy boys became Muslim as a result of their contact with Muslims and not through force. At any rate, the scrupulous Ottomans sought to justify the levy on the basis of the religious law. But we can assert that the *devshirme* was not, as H. A. Gibbons puts it a device to convert Christian subjects. This does not, however, prevent, Sa'deddīn from stating that in 200 years over 200,000 Christians were converted to Islam merely through the *devshirme* process.

It has frequently been suggested that the strongest pressure leading to mass conversions to Islam was the aggravated tax burden on non-Muslims in the form of the *djizya,* Islamic capitation tax and dues imposed by the Orthodax church. The *djizya* was imposed upon non-Muslims at the rate of one gold ducat generally throughout the Ottoman Empire, but it was considerably increased from the end of the sixteenth century. The Christian peasantry living in poverty stricken areas found it especially difficult to pay this cash tax, and it has been argued that mass conversions took place precisely in such mountainous, unprivileged regions as Albania, Bosnia, Rhodopes, and Crete, the four principal regions where converted Muslims speaking their native tongues formed the majority or a substantial part of the population by the first decades of the 19th century. If we take into consideration only the historical, social and cultural factors, the following observations can be made about the Islamization of native populations in the Balkans. First, conversions occured among members of the native military class, who were incorporated into the Ottoman provincial cavalry army as *sipahis* in possession of their lands as *timar* and of their privileges. Documentary evidence from the Ottoman state papers shows that Islamization among this group was rather a socio-cultural process, in some cases involving three or four generations. Individual converts among the *re'āyā,* ordinary tax-paying subjects, are occasionally recorded in the Ottoman survey books particularly among townsfolk or groups performing some service for the state. Here, too, frequent social contact with Muslims apparently played a major part in these sporadic individiual conversions. They are registered in the survey books as New Muslims. Also, groups of converts known as *Akhariyān,* from Greek word *Agarene*, most probably converted under the pressure of the frontier ghāzīs were to be found on the frontier zones in the early centuries of Ottoman expansion. They do not seem to have enjoyed, among the Muslims, the same esteem and privileges of true believers.

In the period of the Ottoman decline employment of Christian mercenary troops from Albania and Bosnia in the Ottoman army apparently became one of the main factors in the spread of Islam in these two areas. In Bosnia, Islam became the dominant religion of the native Slav population with Sarajevo as its cultural and commercial center by the 18th century. For the Islamization of Bosnia it has been suggested that the Bogumils persecuted by the Catholic Church under the Bosnian kings, adopted Islam en masse upon the Ottoman conquest. On the evidence of the Ottoman survey books it is now demonstrable that Islam spread here gradually by several stages over a long time, as occured in Albania. In the early period of the conquest, many members of the lesser military class of the Bosnian kingdom and some aristocratic families were incorporated, under the Ottoman reconciliatory expansionist policy, into the Ottoman *tīmār* system. In 1489 there were, in the *sandjak* of Bosnia alone, about 4,500 Muslim households as against 25,000 Christian households. In the sixteenth century, as cities and towns expanded they became centers of Islamic culture and further Islamization. According to the survey of 1953 the population of the People's Republic of Bosnia and Herzegovina in Yugoslavia was 2,847,790 out of which 911,191 were Muslims, that is over 32% of the whole population.

From the first decades of the 17th century on, the harmony and mutual trust that had existed between the Muslims and non-Muslims was upset partly because of heavier taxation and the widespread abuses of the local authorities, and partly because of the growing tendency among the Christian *re'āyā* to cooperate with the crusading plans of Christendom. It is interesting to observe that while Muslims and non-Muslims used to belong to and work together in the same crafts in the earlier period, they now tended to have their own separate craft guilds. This is also the period in which the Catholic missions settled and extended their activities in the Ottoman Empire. In the 18th century growing commercial and cultural ties between Europe and the Christians of the Ottoman Empire and the rise of national movements in the Balkans in the following century, threw the Islamic set-up of the Empire info disorder. Ottoman efforts to create a new kind of loyalty among the non-Muslim populations by furthering the idea of Ottomanism, that is equality before the law of all Ottoman subjects, as a kind of secularized state, eventualty failed. These developments, however, made a strong impact on the Muslim-Turkish society itself and prepared the way for the rise of the secular national state of Turkey in the twentieth century.

Addendum

This addendum is rather a bibliographical essay to the general survey above

A. On the Religion of the Turkic Peoples before Islamization

M. Eliade, *Shamanism*, Princeton 1972; U. Harva, *Die religiösen Vorstellungen der Altaischen Völker*, Helsinki 1938; A. İnan, *Tarihte ve Bugün Şamanizm,* Ankara 1954; R. Giruad, *l'Empire des Turcs celestes*, Paris 1960; B. Ögel, *İslâmiyetten Önce Türk Kültür Tarihi,* Ankara 1962; B. Ögel, *Türk Mitolojisi,* Ankara 1971; J. P.Roux, *La religion des Turcs et des Mongols*, Paris 1984; N. A. Alekseev, *Šamanizm tjurkojazyčnyx narodov Sibiri*, Novosibirsk 1984; İ. Kafesoğlu, *Eski Türk Dini*, Ankara 1982; P.B. Golden, *An Introduction to the History of the Turkic Peoples*, Wiesbaden 1992, 211-230; Shamanism, practiced as a religio-cultural lore, perpetuates among the Ṣaha (Yakut) Turks today.

B. On the Islamization of the Turkic Peoples in East Europe

The Khazars, Bulghars, Kıpçaks and Tatars of the Golden Horde

First Muslim armies reached the Khazar frontier at the *Darband-i Khazaran* in the year 30/650. War and commercial relations with the Arabs in the Caucasus exposed the Khazars to Islam. Already in the year 737 their Kaghan was forced to convert to Islam (see P. Golden, *The Introduction*, 236-244). Al-Istahrī, writing about 951, said about the Khazars: "The smallest group (of them) are the Jews, most of them are *Muslims* and Christians, except the king and his people of distinction. (Translation of P. Golden, "Khazaria and Judaism," *Archivum Eurasiae Medii Aevi*, III, 1983, 141). In the tenth century Muslim sources the Khazars are mentioned as "Muslims and Christians" while Judaism was professed by the ruling elite (Ibid, 141-143). The Kabars of the north Caucasus under the Khazars converted in majority to Islam. As the Khazar-Arab conflict worsened the Qagan destroyed the Friday Mosque of Atıl/Itil and killed the müezzins in 310/922 (*Ibid.* 153). Ibn Miskawaih (II, 209) claims that the Khazar ruler converted to Islam in the mid-tenth century, (P. Golden, *An Introduction*, 243). Golden (*Ibid.*) suggests that "Khazar Muslims contributed to the Turkic-speaking and Turco-Muslim communities of the Volga basin and North Caucasus" (On the Khazars see, K. Czegledy, "Khazar Raids in

Transcaucasia in A.D. 762-764." *Acta Orientalia Academiae Scientiarum Hungaricae,* XIII, 243-251; E. Esin, "Conversion of the Turks to Islem," (unpublished paper; P.B. Golden, *Khazar Studies*, Bibliotheca Orientalis Hungarica, XXV/1-2 Budapest, 1980); T.S. Noonan, "Why Dirhams Reached Russia: The Role of Arab-Khazar Relations in the Development of the Earliest Islamic Trade with Eastern Europe," *Archivum Eurasiae Medii Aevi*, IV, 151-282; M. Kmosko, "Araber und Chazaren," *Körösi Csoma Archivum*, I (1922), 280-292, 356-368, Turkish version: *Türkiyat Mecmuası*, III (1930), 132-155. It appears that the Danubian Bulghars showed some interest in Islam even earlier than the Itil Bulghars. According to al-Nadīm (*The Fihrist of al-Nadīm*, ed. and trans. B. Dodge, New York 1970, 254, 400) the king of the Danubian Bulgars asked the Caliph al-Ma'mūn (813-833) to send him answers to his questions about Islam. P.Golden thinks (*The Introduction*, 250-251) "this is hardly surprising" when we consider the international conditions at that time, the struggle between Bulghars, Byzantium and the Caliphate. As for the Itil (Volga) Bulghars' conversion the main source is A. Z. V. Togan, *Ibn Fadlāns Reisebericht, Abhandlungen für die Kunde des Morgelandes* XXIV, III, Leipzig 1939; Rihla's Turkish translation with annotations R. Şeşen, Istanbul 1975; H.A. al-Dākūkī, *Dawlat al-Bulghār al-Muslimān fī Hawz al-Wolga*, Baghdad 1982; P. B. Golden, *An Introduction* 270-282, 291-293, 297-301.

Ibn Fadlān's observation clearly indicates that the decision to adopt Islam by the ruler of the Volga Bulghars was prompted by political considerations-deliverance from the Khazar domination. At any rate, his people were in commercial relations (for trade) from very early times with Muslims some having settled in their cities (Golden, *The Introduction* 256-257) A late tradition says that a Muslim merchant who cared the king and his wife of an illness was responsible for the conversion (Ibid, 258). In brief, politics, continuing trade and cultural relations appear to be responsible for the conversion of the Bulghars to Islam. Upon the visit in 921-922 of a Caliphal mission to Bulghar the Bulgarian ruler, the Yil-Tawar/Ilteber Almosh converted to Islam taking the name Ja'far b.Abdallah. Then, the Baranjar in the King's retinue, numbering five thousand men and women all embraced Islam (Golden, *The introduction*, 255-256; Ibn Fadlan, *Rihla*, trans. R. Şeşen). The Kıpçaks who succeeded the Khazars as the dominant power in East Europe remained basically shamanists (Golden, *"Imperial Ideology"*, 70). Linguistic evidence in the Codex Cumanicus, however, proves beyond any doubt that Kıpçaks were in close commercial and cultural relations with Muslim countries, the Mamluks of Egypt, Iran and Khwarazm in particular (see D. Drüll, *Der Codex Cumanicus. Entstehung und Bedeutung*, Stuttgart, 1980). For recent inquiries on the Kıpçaks see B. Kumekov, (ed.), Kypčaki central'noj Azii v srednie veka, Alma Ata 1993. The Golden Hord Khan Berke adopted Islam under the influence of merchants or Shaykh Sayf al-Dīn Bakharzī of Buhara (P. Golden, The Introduction, 290). His conversion, perhaps politically motivated, strengthened his ties with the Mamluks of Egypt, who were originally of the Kıpçak Turks, against his rival in the Caucasus Hülegü, Ilkhan of Iran see, I. Vásáry, "History and Legend in Berke Khan's Conversion to Islam," in D. Sinor, *Aspects of Altaic Civilization*, III, Bloomington 1990, 230-252; now Deven DeWeese, *Islamization and Native Religion in the Golden Hord: Baba Tükles and Conversion to Islam in Historical and Epic Tradition*, Philadelphia: Pennsylvania State University Press, 1994.

C. First Contact with Islam and Islamization of the Central Asiatic Turks

In Central Asia, the first contact of the Turks with the conquering Muslim armies occurred in 18/639. The prince of the Sul (Çöl?) Turks in Dihistān and Djurdjdān recognized the Caliph as his suzerain. Later on Kül-Tegin converted to Islam around 98/719 in whose territory *ribāts* were erected. The Oghuz Turks were then living across the border at Manghıshlak. A grotto mosque dating back to the same period is discovered at Manghıshlak (Emel Esin, *Ibid.* citing M.M. Mendikulev, Pamyatniki arxitektura poluostrova Mangıshlaka, Alma-Ata 1956). Further to the east Turgish rulers (658-766), vassals of the Kök-Türk Kagans, put a staunch resistance to Muslim armies, which nevertheless could not prevent them finally to invade western Turkestan. Local dynasties, Iranian-Soghdian or Turkish in western Turkestan, recognized Caliphal authority, some of them converting to Islam (see W.Barthold, *Turkestan Down to the Mongol Invasion*, Third edition with addenda and corrigenda by C.E. Bosworth, London 1968, 180-220).

However, in Khorassan and Transxiana where the resistance and intermittent rebellions of the local dihkans and dynasties were supported by the Turkish states beyond Syr-Darya, first by the Kök-Türks (the first empire 552-585, the second empire 682-744), and then by their successor Turgish Kaghans (716-766), Arab rule and Islamization proved to be precarious. The Abū Muslim uprising which secured the Caliphate to the Abbasids was, in fact, the outcome of this situation, complicated with the question of *djizya* whether or not new Muslims should be subjected to it. His execution in Baghdad (755) caused further alienation of the local population, and of the shiite Arabs in the region. It is no coincidence that in later centuries Abū Muslim was to become a most venerated folk hero with the Islamized (heterodox) Turks in Iran and Asia Minor. Abū Muslim's follower Ishak was known as Turk who declared himself the successor of Zardusht (Barthold, *Turkestan*, 190-198; I. Mélikoff,) *Abū Muslim, le "port-hache" du*

Khorassan dansla tradition epique tureo iranienne, Paris 1962. The local resistance and heterodox movements continued with the support of the Tokuz-Oghuz, the Karluk Turks, and Tibetans (Rāfi' son of Layth's rebellion toward 809). "Thus, the Turks" Barthold points out (*Ibid*, 201-202)," intervened in the disorders occurring in Transoxiana, the rebels themselves appealing to them for help".

Eventually the Abbasid Caliphs, understanding the necessity of a compromise, left the rule of the region to the local dynasties, first the Tahirids and then the Samanids (872-999) in Transoxiana and Farghana. The final subjugation of Transoxiana to Muslim rule occurred under the Samanids although the resistance against the Arab dominion never ceased (Barthold, *Ibid*, 210). Now espousing the Islamic ghazā ideology zealously the Samanids became responsible for the spread of Islam among the Turks beyond the Syr-Darya. Also employing large groups of Turkish mercenaries and war captives in their armies they opened the era of the use of the Turkish soldiery in the Caliphate (for the Turkish soldiery in the capital of the Caliphate see Abū 'Os̱mān ‘amr b. Bahr al-Djāhiz, *Hilâfet Ordularının Menkibeleri ve Türklerin Faziletleri*, çeviri R. Şeşen, Ankara 1967; H. D. Yıldız, *İslamiyet ve Türkler*, İstanbul 1980). Turkish mercenaries or slaves trained as part of the royal households in the Islamic world formed Muslim military elites in the Abbasid Caliphate and later on in the states rising in Egypt (the Mamluks of the Bahrī period, 1260-1382), in Afghanistan (the Ghaznavids 977-1040) and in India (the Delhi Sultanate 1206-1413). These military elites and dynasties played a major role in the spread of Islam (see. C. E. Bosworth, *The Ghaznevids; Their Empire in Afghanistan and Eastern Iran,* 944-1217, Edinburg 1963; *The Later Ghaznevids, Splendour and Decay*, Edinburgh 1977; and in the defense of Islam a role eventually leading to the complete dominion on Islamic countries under the Seljukids and the Ottomans. Under the Abbasid Caliphs, illustrious generals and governors of Turkish origin were distinguished such as Tolunids (868-896) and Ikhshids (937-969) who ruled in Egypt. Samarra near Baghdad, built for the Turkish soldiery, became a center of Turkish culture from central Asia. For the studies on the role and contributions of these Turks in the Abbasid politics and administration as well as in Islamic sciences and arts see, Emel Esin, *op. cit.*, and R. N. Frye and A. Sayılı, "Selçuklulardan evvel Orta-Şark'da Türkler", *Belleten* 37 (1996). Ribāṭs, fortified religio-military centers, built along the borders of the Turkish zone in Central Asia, played a decisive role in the spread of Islam among the Turks (for ribāṭs, see, Barthold, *Turkestan*, index and M. F. Köprülü, "Ribat" *Vakıflar Dergisi*). The murābiṭs, fighters for the spread of Islam, stationed in the *ribāṭs*, were particularly active under the Samanids (see, R. N. Frye "The Samanids" *Cambridge History of Iran*,

IV, 1-2, 1980). It is not a coincidence that under the Samanids systematic study and teaching of Islamic sciences flourished in the cities of eastern Iran and Central Asia, which had a mixture of Iranian and Turkis inhabitants. First Marv, then Bukhara under of Samanids became the capitals of Central Asian Islam where various high cultures of Central Asia had converged before the advent of Islam (E. Esin, *Ibid.*, stresses the influence of Buddhism). The great representatives of the Islamic sciences Muhammed Bukhārī (810-870), Muhammed Māturīdī (öl. 944) of Samarkand, Abū Bakr Abdullah b. Tarkhan, Muhammad b.Tarkhan b. Uzlugh al-Fārābī al-Turkī (ca. 870-950) originated in the central Asiatic cities of this period prior to the mass conversion of the Turks, in the east under the Karakhanids occured.

Although initially it is a simple act to convert to Islam just by declaring the *shahadeh*, the testimony of faith the educational institutions whether *ribāt*, mosque or madrasa, played a decisive role in the consolidation of the proper systematic Islam. Where such institutions did not come into existence a popular Islam, a commixture of Islam with the native religious beliefs and practices, prevailed. In the eight and ninth centuries first the madhhab of Shāfi'ī, and then, that of Hanafī were reported to be dominant in Central Asiatic Islam. Emel Esin points out that along with this, Islamic mysticism, too, appeared in Central Asia. First as a result of the activities of the Muslim sufi Shaḳīḳ of Balkh (died 790), and under the influence of Buddhism and the Iranian dualism such beliefs as *tenāsukh,* transmigration of souls, *hulūl,* epiphany and *fakr* powerty as well as the veneration of 'Alī on the one hand and Turkish shamanistic practices on the other formed the main features of Islamic sufism with various Turkish heterodox sects. While Hanefism, became the state policy of the Turkish states (the Karakhanids were sunni) popular sufism was prevalent among the Oghuz tribes. These two dominant features of the Turkish Islam appearing already in this early period would determine the evolution of Islam among the Turks in Central Asia and Asia Minor in later centuries.

To explain why the Hanafī school of law became prevalent in the Turkish states scholarship pointed out that favoring *idjmā*, consensus and *ḳıyās,* syllogism, in Islamic jurisprudence the Hanafī school was liberal enough to allow the Turkish rulers to keep their independent authority. In fact, in Central Asia, India and Turkey Turkish rulers declared their own state laws, *törü, yasa* or *kanun* which were based on customs or requirements of the conditions of the time (see "Ḳānūn" and "Ḳānūnnāme" (H. Inalcik) *Encyclopaedia of Islam,* second edition; O. Turan, "Türkler ve İslâmiyet", *DTCFD*, 1946; —, *Selçuklular ve İslâmiyet*, İstanbul 1971; İ. Kafesoğlu, *Türk Milli Kültürü*, İstanbul 1983, H. D. Yıldız, *İslâmiyet ve Türkler*, İstanbul, 1976).

2

Istanbul: an Islamic City

Istanbul: an Islamic City

Conquest as an act of Faith

The prophet himself is said to have ordered the first military action of Muslims against the Byzantines, namely in Palestine in the year 624.[1] A mere twenty-six years after that, a Muslim army approached the gates of Constantinople. In some sense, from a Western viewpoint, the forces of Islam may be regarded as having espoused the ancient struggle of Sasanid Persia against the Greek empire. However, among Muslims it was a conviction, from the time of the Prophet onward, that the conquest of Constantinople was predestined for them by God. The Ottomans adopted that conviction as their own. Altogether the Muslims had organised twelve separate expeditions against the Byzantine capital before Mehmed II eventually took it in 1453.[2]

Constantinople was so powerful a symbol of resistance to the expansion of Islam that a whole series of *aḥādīth*, some authentic and some not, as well as legendary and folk-epic material, spread about the future Muslim conquest of the city.

The Ottomans would recall, and cite on every appropriate occasion, one of these *aḥādīth* which said: 'One day Constantinople will definitely be conquered. What a good amir and what a good army is the one that will accomplish this'.[3] They claimed to have found the tombs of many Companions of the Prophet who had taken part and fallen in the sieges of Constantinople under the Umayyads. Following the conquest, they constructed mausolea for them which became the most venerated places in and around the city.[4] In the Ottoman tradition, the number of Companions who had actually fallen came to be multiplied by as many as seventy (a sacred figure).

---

[1] See Abū Bakr Muḥammed b. Aḥmad al-Wāsiṭī, *Faḍā'il al-Bayt al-Maqdis̱* (ed. Isaac Wasson, The Magnes Press, Jerusalem, 1979), 52-3; E. Sivan, 'Le caractère sacré de Jerusalem dans l'Islam aux XII-XIII siècles', *Studia Islamica,* xvii (1967), 149-82.

[2] M. Canard, 'Les Expéditions des Arabes contre Constantinople dans l'histoire et dans les légendes', *Journal Asiatique,* (1926), 61 - 121.

[3] Evliyā Çelebi, *Seyāhatnāme*, (İstanbul 1314/1896), vol. I.

[4] See Süheyl Ünver, *İlim ve Sanat Bakımından Fatih Devri* (Belediye Press, Istanbul, 1948), i, 108 - 11, *İstanbul'da Sahabe Kabirleri*, İstanbul 1953; *Necdet İşli, İstanbul'da Sahabe Kabir ve Mezarları,* Ankara, n.d.

The most venerated of these Companions, the Prophet's standard-bearer, Abū Ayyūb al-Anṣārī,[5] became the patron saint of Ottoman 'Islambol'. That Abū Ayyūb was indeed one of the Prophet's companions and did take part in and die during the siege of Constantinople in 668 is historically attested.[6] Mehmet II chose Abū Ayyūb as the patron saint of the conquered city, perhaps because he had declared himself the standard-bearer of the ghazā' in the whole Islamic world.[7]

Mehmed the Conqueror believed that the conquest would be the work of Allah, a miracle of His providence. The sufi Şeyh Aq-Şemseddīn, a follower of the famous mystic philosopher of light, 'Umar al-Suhrawardī, became *murşīd* (spiritual guide) to the Sulṭān and his army during the siege. The young Sulṭān asked the *murşīd* to go into religious retreat in order to know the divine decision of the exact date of the conquest. The conquest did not occur on the date the *murşīd* gave, rather the Christians recorded a naval success on that day. The letter written by the şheyh to the Sulṭān after this event has been discovered in the Palace archives.[8] In it the Şeyh acknowledges that rumours about the failure of his prayers and the Sulṭān's lack of wisdom and authority had spread to the army. He attributes the failure to the fact that many soldiers in the Ottoman army were not true Muslims, having converted to Islam under pressure. But, being a practical man, he at the same time advises the Sulṭān to severely punish the commanders responsible for this disgraceful situation. He adds that when he went back to sleep after reading the Qur'ān, God revealed to him the good news of ultimate success. From the *gesta et vita* of the Şeyh[9] we learn that, during the final attack, the saints (all clad in white robes and led by the Prophet of miracles, Khiḍr) guided the Sulṭān's army to victory. Aq Şeyh claimed that the

---

5 Paul Wittek, 'Ayvansaray, Un sanctuaire privé de son héros', *Annuaire de l'Institut de Philologie et d'Histoire Orientales et Slaves* (Brussels, 1951), 505-26.

6 'Abū Ayyūb Khālid b.Zayd b. Kulayb al-Naḏjdjārī al-Anṣārī, (E. Levi-Provençal), *EI*², i, 108-9.

7 Ferīdūn Aḥmed, *Munsha'āt al-Salāṭin* (Istanbul 1274/1858), i, 236, cf. A. Ateş, 'Fatih Sultan Mehmed Tarafından Gönderilen Mektublar ve Bunlara Dair Gelen Cevablar', *Tarih Dergisi,* (İstanbul, 1952), iv-7, 16.

8 See H. İnalcık, *Fatih Devri Üzerinde Tetkikler ve Vesikalar* (Türk Tarih Kurumu: Ankara 1954), 217-18. on Şihāb al-Dīn Abū Hafṣ 'Umar al-Suhrawardī and Anatolian sufism see A. Y. Ocak, *Osmanlı İmparatorluğu'nda Marjinal Sûfilik: Kalenderîler, (XVI.-XVII) Yüzyıllar,* Ankara 1992, XXV, 61.

9 Manāḳib-i Aq Şemseddīn [shams al-Dīn] by Seyyid Husayn Enīsī; many copies in the MS collections in Turkey and Europe, see Mustafa Faya, 'Aq Şemseddin', Ph. D. thesis, Faculty of Theology, University of Ankara. I used here the MS in the Nuruosmaniye Library, Istanbul, no. 2175.

conquest was the work of providence through the prophet Khiḍr and Faqīh Aḥmed whom he called Quṭb-i 'ālem, the pole of the universe.[10]

The role and influence of Aq Şeyh in the events leading up to the conquest were further amplified in folk imagination. According to popular traditions related by Evliyā Çelebi, Aq Şeyh had revealed the impending conquest in 1444, long before the siege itself, when Mehmed was not yet the Sulṭān.[11] Placing his dervish cap on Mehmed's head, the Şeyh foretold that, according to God's favour, the conquest of Constantinople would be Mehmed's doing. Aq Şeyh is portrayed in all of these traditions as more powerful than the Sulṭān. Evliyā claimed that during the siege three thousand men of religion, including şeyhs and 'ulemā, exhorted the soldiers to fight and that the well-known şeyhs participated actively in attacking the city's main gates.

According to some folk traditions[12] even the great şeyhs of the Islamic world came and fought alongside the Muslim army on this great day for Islam. The Sulṭān had promised the şeyhs that, after the conquest, he would allocate half the booty to them, build for each of them a convent, and do other charitable works besides. Evliyā[13] also tells us that a group of Greek priests, spiritually overwhelmed, came out of the fortress to join the Muslim army. This is a general theme in the folk epics of this period: that God eventually guided Christian priests towards the 'ultimate truth'—Islam. The significance of all of these stories is that the Muslim populace in those days believed that the city had been conquered through the spiritual power of the Muslim saints. It remains uncertain whether the Sulṭān shared in these beliefs. But there is every reason to affirm his belief in the necessity of having and keeping the blessings of these charismatic holy men on his side.[14]

The Sulṭān's decisions for the reconstruction of the conquered city fell in with the overwhelming religious zeal among the Muslim masses. Indeed, in that Islamic reconstruction of the city, the religious orders assumed a key role.[15]

---

[10] Cf. H. Inalcik, Dervish and Sultan:'An Analysis of the Otman Baba Vilāyetnāmesi', paper read at the Colloquium on Saints and Sainthood in Islam, held at the University of California, Berkeley, 1986, April 3-5, *The Middle East and the Balkans under the Ottoman Empire* (Bloomington 1993), 19-36

[11] Evliyā Çelebi, *Seyāhātnāme*, 94, 97, 105; also the Conqueror's waqfiyya 29/32, mentioned in n. 16, where the conquest is attributed to the spiritual power of Aq Şeyh.

[12] Evliyā Çelebi, *Seyāhātnāme*, 97.

[13] *Ibid.*, 111.

[14] H. Inalcik, 'Analysis ...' (n. 10 above).

[15] *Ibid.* Mehmed II apparently did not like the popular *ḳalenderī* dervishes, but recognized their immense popularity with the populace and army.

Şeyh Aq Şemseddīn was also charged, upon the Sulṭān's order, with locating the tomb of Ayyūb al-Anṣārī. Its discovery by the Şeyh was no less miraculous and significant than the conquest. It assured the Muslim that providence was still on their side. Later, Mehmed built a mausoleum at the site, a mosque and a dervish convent.[16]

Ayyūb's tomb, which rapidly grew into a town outside the walls of the city on the Golden Horn, became the most sacred place in Istanbul. Each day hundreds of believers would visit with offerings and seek the saint's help. The most famous of the dervish convents as well as a huge cemetery clustered around the tomb. It is also significant that each Sulṭān upon his accession to the throne visited the tomb following the same route as the legend described for Ayyūb.[17] At the site, the most venerated Şeyh of the day girded the Sulṭān with the sacred sword of *ghazā'*. Thus, the saint's presence not only made the whole area of Istanbul a consecrated place for Muslims, but also gave the Sulṭān's rule over the Muslims a religious sanction.

It should be noted that every Ottoman city had its own *wālī* or saint whose tomb, usually located on a hill-top outside the city, combined Islamic mystic tradition with a pre-Islamic mountain cult.[18] Cities were regarded as persons and a prayer formula recited each time the name of the city was mentioned.

Constantinople becomes 'Islambol'

After the conquest, Mehmed's first act was to convert Constantinople into an Islamic city. The preamble of his *waqf* deed for his mosque reads:[19] 'Sulṭān Mehmed conquered *Kostantiniyye* with the help of God. It was an abode of idols ... He converted its churches of beautiful decoration into Islamic colleges and mosques.' There were six churches converted into mosques and one into a college. Interestingly enough, the monastery of Aya-Marina was

---

[16] Wittek, 'Ayvansaray ...' (n. 5 above), 523-4. For the waḳfiyya of the complex see *Fatih Mehmed II Vakfiyeleri* (Vakıflar Umum Müdürlüğü, Ankara, 1938), 285-327.

[17] On the ceremony of swordgirding see İ. H. Uzunçarşılı, *Osmanlı Devletinin Saray Teşkilâtı* (Türk Tarih Kurumu, Ankara 1945), 189-200. On the town of Eyüp now see *Eyüp: Dün/Bugün, 11-12 Aralık 1993*, İstanbul: Tarih Vakfı, 1993, 1-23.

[18] On the dervish convents built on a hill outside the Ottoman towns see Semavi Eyice, 'Zaviyeler ve Zaviyeli Camiler', *İstanbul Üniversitesi İktisat Fakültesi Mecmuası*, xxiii (1962-3), 23, 29; F. Hasluck, *Christianity and Islam under the Sultans* (ed. Margaret M. Hasluck, Oxford, 1929), i, 324-5; G. E. von Grunebaum, 'The Sacred Character of Islamic Cities', A. Badawi, ed., *Mélanges Taha Husain* (Cairo, 1962) 25-37.

[19] The Conqueror's waqfiyya in Evliyā Çelebi, *Seyāhatnāme*, (see n. 11), 30-31.

given to Baba Ḥaydarī dervishes.[20] In general the best sites were assigned either to members of the military or to the men of religion including the Sūfī orders.

On the day following the conquest the Sulṭān went straight to St Sophia church and converted it into a mosque, saying there his first prayers, an act that symbolized the dedication of the city as an Islamic one. He also solemnly gave it the name 'Islam-bol' (Islam abounds),[21] which actually reflects the centuries-long aspiration of Muslims to convert the great city of Constantine ('Qosṭanṭiniyya al-Kubrā') into a city of Islam. The new name was hereafter strictly maintained by the ulema, though the people at large continued to use the pre-Ottoman Turkish name Istanbul. Folk memory of the congregational prayers after the conquest, as described by Evliyā Çelebi,[22] records: 'When the muezzins began to recite the verse inn' Allāha wa mala'ikatahu'[23] in a touching tone, Aq-Şemseddīn, taking Sulṭān's Mehmed by his arm in great respect led him to the pulpit. Then he called out in a strong deep voice, "Praise to God, Lord of all creatures," and the ghāzīs present in the mosque, deeply touched, broke into tears of joy.'

Islamic faith and the popular imagination combined to convert Constantinople into *Islambol.* For the Ottomans it was a Muslim city from the time it held the sacred remains of the Prophet's companions. In Islamic tradition, a place where Muslims had built a mosque and prayed was considered Islamic territory. The churches, Hagia Sophia in particular, were admired as works of God which the Muslims believed He would ultimately grant to the true religion. Legend tells us[24] that Abū Ayyūb al-Anṣārī performed his prayers there before his martyrdom. Also, while an area or a city of non-Muslims who had submitted to a Muslim state was accepted as, administratively, a part of Islamic territory, its ultimate islamization remained a constant hope. Tolerant enough to resettle the city with Greeks, Armenians, and Jews, Mehmed the Conqueror nevertheless took measures to ensure that 'Islambol' had a Muslim majority - a policy systematically applied to the major cities conquered for Islam.[25]

---

20 Mentioned in the Ottoman survey of Istanbul made in 1455. The survey, preserved at the *Topkapı Palace Archives*, Istanbul, is being prepared for publication.

21 See H. Inalcik, 'Istanbul', *EI*[2], iv, 224.

22 Evliyā Çelebi, *Seyāhatnāme*, 111.

23 The Qur'ān, 2: 30-34.

24 Evliyā Çelebi, *Seyāhatnāme*, i, 76.

25 H. Inalcik, 'Istanbul', (n. 21), 238. H. Inalcik, 'Ottoman Methods of Conquest', *Studia Islamica,* II, (1954), 122-9. For the Balkans see *Structure sociale et développement culturel des villes sud-est européennes et adriatiques* (Bucharest, 1975); N. Todorov, *La ville balkanique aux XV-XIX siècles, développement socioéconomique et démographique*

For the Ottomans, the most celebrated symbolic action, after conquest of a Christian city, was to convert the churches into mosques. The minaret for the call to prayer (*adhān*) became the visible symbol, and most striking feature, of the Islamic city. In their descriptions of conquests, the Ottomans always referred to this as the symbol of Islam's victory.

Every city or town with a Muslim population had to have a Friday Mosque or *masjid* (smaller mosque) and it was a religious duty to assemble there on Fridays. Suleyman the Magnificent, in order to extirpate the Kızılbash heresy, extended this obligation to villages.[26]

The great mosque in the centre of each nāḥiye (see infra) was the centre not only of religion but also of various other aspects of urban life. Aside from the *madrasa* built within the mosque complex, regular courses were held in the mosque for the general public (ders-i 'ām):the teaching of Islam was considered one of the greatest pious acts in the Islamic tradition. It was a religious duty for the Sulṭān (as well as the ordinary Muslim citizen) to go to prayers in the great mosque of the capital city, especially on Friday (*Jum'a*). It was there that Sulṭān had direct contact with ordinary people and received oral and written grievances (*riq'a*) on abuses of power they had suffered. The ceremony was symbolic of the Sulṭān's concern for his people's suffering, a concern regarded, in the Islamic state tradition, as the ruler's most important function. In miniature paintings of the Sulṭān receiving a *riq'a* from the hands of an old woman, symbolically the most helpless of the subjects, an image of the Sulṭān as the ideal ruler is created. The sermon (*khuṭba*) following Friday prayer, delivered by the most venerated Şeyh of the time, had more than a religious function. The congregation (*jamā'a*) would respond to the praises of the Sulṭān offered in the *khuṭba*—a ceremony interpreted in Islamic society as recognition of the Sulṭān's sovereignty by the public. Indeed, this Friday mention and the minting of coins were always regarded as the two necessary symbols for the independence of any ruler in Islamic lands.

Furthermore, the law courts were customarily located at the mosques. The busiest of them was in the courtyard of the Grand Vizier Mahmud Pasha Mosque, situated on the main street of the city in the vicinity of the Great Bazaar.

(Bucharest, 1980); and *Istanbul à la jonction des cultures balkaniques, méditerranéennes, slaves et orientales:* Actes du colloque organisé par AIESEE, Bucharest, 1977

26 'Osmanlı Kanunnameleri' (Ḳānūnnāme-ı Djedīd ve Mu'teber), *Millî Tetebbu'lar Mecmu'ası*, I, 338.

The Organization of space in 'Islambol'

The world view of Islam determined the physical and social landscape of the city which was prepared as a space where the prescriptions of the Islamic religion could be observed properly and in their entirety.[27]

The basic objective in the expansion of Islam was to acquire political control over an area and establish the symbols of Islamic sovereignty. An area inhabited by non-Muslims which had submitted to the power of Islam was considered to be within the *Dār al-Islām*, that is, part of the Islamic territory, whether or not the people living there had converted to Islam. If the city had to be taken by force, Islamic Law allowed that the inhabitants could be removed as captives, the buildings becoming the property of the Islamic state. This happened in Constantinople on 29 May, 1453 over thirty thousand were enslaved and removed from the city.[28] Under Ottoman rule, anyone who wanted to build a house had to pay rent to the state treasury for the plot used. The principle of state ownership of land had the most significant consequences for the reconstruction of the city under the Ottomans. The Sulṭān was free to carry out his own plans for the location of the palace, bazaars, military barracks, and storehouses: he had a free hand in organizing the space and creating a typical Islamic-Ottoman city.

It is often argued that the Islamic city came into being spontaneously without any sort of planning and that its population was only 'an amorphous crowd.'[29] The Ottoman practice, which we know basically followed Islamic

---

[27] Cf. G. E. von Grunebaum. *Islam*: *Essays in the Nature and Growth of a Cultural Tradition* (London: Routledge and Kegan Paul, 1955), 142; Al Māwardī, *Tashīl al-Naẓar...*, ed. Riḍwān al Sayyid (Beirut, 1987), 209-13.

[28] H. Inalcik, 'Istanbul', (n. 21), 224-5.

[29] M. E. Bonine, 'The morphogenesis of Iranian Cities', *Annals of the Association of American Geographers* ix/2 (1979), 208-24; Ira Lapidus, *Muslim Cities in the Later Middle Ages* (Harvard University Press, 1967), in particular ch. 3, 'The Urban Society' and 185-91; M. E. Bonine, 'From Uruk to Casablanca, Perspectives in the Urban Experience of the Middle East', *Journal of Urban History,* III/2, 141-80. Comparing always with the chartered cities and communes of medieval Europe, urban historians stress that in Islamic history there was no urban organization that can properly be called Islamic, that Muslim cities had no independent or autonomous guilds or workmen associations; see A. H. Hourani and S. M. Stern, eds., *The Islamic City* (Oxford, 1970); C. Brown, ed., *From Madina to Metropolis* (Princeton: Darwin, 1973); R. B. Serjeant, ed., *The Islamic City,* (Paris, 1980); H. A. Miskimin and A. L. Udovitch, 'A Tale of Two Cities', in *The Medieval City,* eds. D. Herlihy and A. L. Udovitch, (New Haven, London: Yale University Press, 1977), say (144): 'the Muslim conquerors... founded many more towns themselves, which provides at least a partial justification for using the epithet "Islamic" to designate the cities and towns of the medieval Near East.' Now see in particular, *Urbanism in Islam* (Tokyo, 1989, 5 vols.). Also see Excursus I and II

tradition, challenges this view. The urban space of Istanbul, as with other cities before it that had been founded or reorganized by the Ottomans, followed a traditional pattern of organization laid down under the direction and supervision of the Sulṭān.[30]

The view that an Islamic city lacked any planning really does need to be modified. The founders of pious endowments followed a traditional plan in establishing the main complexes of the religious and commercial centres of the city. The complexes themselves had a distinct arrangement of buildings within their boundaries. Of whatever origin—Hellenistic, Sasanian or Central Asiatic—a certain type of planning was followed in creating such centres. On the other hand, the lack of planning in the residential sections of the city is a fact and can be explained by certain Islamic concepts to be discussed later.

As early as 1453 the Sulṭān had issued orders for the construction of certain buildings without which the Ottomans would not consider a city as

---

at the end of this paper. On space organization see P. Wheatley, 'Levels of Space Awareness in the Traditional Islamic City', *Existics*, XLIV (1976), 354-66.

30 See H. Inalcik 'Istanbul' (n. 21), 226-48. A pioneer on Ottoman urbanism is Osman Nuri Ergin, *Medjelle-i Umūr-i Belediyye* (İstanbul, 1922), vol. i; idem, *Türkiye'de Şehirciliğin Tarihi İnkişafı* (İstanbul, 1936). On Turkish urbanism in Asia Minor see Faruk Sümer, *Eski Türklerde Şehircilik* (İstanbul, 1984); Uğur Tanyeli, *Anadolu Türk Kentinde Fiziksel Yapının Evrim Süreci (11-15 yy),* (İstanbul, 1987); Tuncer Baykara, *Konya* (Ankara, 1985); *Tarih Içinde Ankara* (Seminar Papers, Ankara, 1984); Emel Esin, 'The Genesis of the Turkish Mosque and Madrasa Complex', *Proceedings of the Twenty Seventh International Congress of Orientalists* (Napoli, 1967): (Annali dell'Istituto orientale di Napoli, 1972), n. s. xxii, 115-23. For Ottoman urbanism, publications of the qāḍī records are essential: for titles see *Türkologischer Anzeigner,* ed. A. Tietze; Cengiz Orhonlu, *Osmanlı İmparatorluğunda Şehircilik ve Ulaşım,* ed. S. Özbaran, *Türk Tarihinde ve Kültüründe Tokat,* Symposium, 2-6 July 1986 (Ankara, 1987). An important sixteenth century source for the Ottoman idea of city with plans showing the basic buildings and complexes is Nasühu's-Silāḥī (Matraḳçı), *Beyān-i Menāzil-i Sefer-i Iraḳeyn-i Sulṭān Süleymān Ḥān,* ed. H. G. Yurdaydın, (Ankara, Türk Tarih Kurumu, 1976); İlhan Tekeli, 'On institutionalized External Relations of Cities in the Ottoman Empire: A Settlement Models's Approach', *Études Balkaniques* (Sofia, 1972), ii, 49-72; Z. Vesela-Prenosilová, 'Quelques remarques sur l'évolution de l'organisation urbaine en Empire ottoman', *Archiv Orientalni* (Prague, 1974), 200-224; Ö. L. Barkan, "Türkiye Şehirlerinin Teşekkül ve Inkişaf Tarihi Bakımından İmaret Sistemlerinin Kuruluş ve İşleyiş Tarzına ait Araştırmalar", *İktisat Fakültesi Mecmuası,* XXIII, (İstanbul, 1963), 239-398. For examples of the cities 'created' by the Ottomans' *waqfs* see Ö. L. Barkan, "Vakıflar ve Temlikler: I. İstilâ Devirlerinin Kolonizatör Türk Dervişleri", *Vakıflar Dergisi* (Ankara, ii, 355); cf. E. Pauty, 'Villes spontanées et villes créés en Islam', *Annales de l'Institut d'Etudes Orientales,* IX, (1951); K. Liebe-Harkort, Beiträge zur sosizalen und wirtschaftlichen Lage Bursas am Anfang des 16. Jahrhunderts (Hamburg, 1970); S. Faroqhi, *Towns and Townsmen of Ottoman Anatolia: trade, crafts and food production in an urban setting,* 1520-1650 (Cambridge: CUP, 1984); idem, *Men of Modest Substance, House Owners and House Property in Seventeenth-century Ankara and Kayseri,* (Cambridge: C.U.P. 1987).

complete.[31] Important among these were a citadel within the walls surrounding the Golden Gate of the Roman city, a royal palace on the hill of Forum Tauri, in the centre of the city, and a huge bazaar with a central bedestān (compact hall) for valuable commodity imports.[32]

The citadel, symbol for the Sulṭān's power, and housing the state treasury, was the main stronghold in the city, its garrison the ultimate force for city-defence in the event of invasion or popular uprising.

The royal palace (later abandoned for another on the Topkapı site) was also surrounded by walls making it a fortified city within the city. The Sulṭān's palace was revered as a quasi-sacred place where God's disposition for His creatures manifested itself in the Imām, the Sulṭān. As the Prophet's saying reads: 'The Imām is the trusted agent of Allah amongst his people and the proof of His care over His creatures and His representative over the country.'

On the day of conquest, Mehmed announced that Istanbul was his capital city in these words: 'From now on Istanbul is my taht (throne)'.[33] The capital is called *tahtgāh* or dār *al-Salṭana,* literally 'the abode of the throne' or of the salṭana (political sovereignty, distinct from khilāfa, the supreme spiritual-political authority of the successor of the Prophet). The capital was thus conceived as the place of residence of the holder of the salṭana.

Beyond the main gate of the palace or Bāb al-Sa'āda is where the subjects live, the palace gate therefore manifests the ruler's authority.[34] It is an elaborate structure topped with a golden dome, symbolic of the heavens or the universe, under which the ruler sat enthroned to receive people in a most elaborate court ceremony. The spot where the throne was placed was the quasi-sacred centre of the realm, around which the whole Empire revolved.

All Ottoman terminology connected with the Sulṭān's authority was based on this concept. The government was the *Sublime Porte,* the city itself *Der-i Sa'ādet,* the 'Gate of the Good Fortune'. Proximity to the Sulṭān's person determined the degree of authority and fortune enjoyed —for example, the pages of the privy chamber were candidates for the highest positions in the Empire.[35] The state officials in the capital represented the highest ranks in

---

[31] See H. Inalcik, 'Istanbul' (n. 21), 226-9.

[32] See H. Inalcik, 'The Hub of the City: The Bedestān of Istanbul', *Inernational Journal of Turkish Studies* (Madison, 1980), 311-58; and Excursus II at the end of this paper.

[33] Tursun Beg, *The History of Mehmed the Conqueror*, eds. H. Inalcik and R. Murphey (Minneapolis and Chicago Bibliotheca: Islamica, 1978), Text: 52b.

[34] H. Inalcik, *The Ottoman Empire: the Classical Age 1300-1600*, trans. N. Itzkowitz and C. Imber (A. D. Caratzas: New Rochelle, repr. 1989), 76 and 89-100.

[35] *Ibid.,* 76-88.

each class— the qāḍī of Istanbul, for example, was the supreme qāḍī in the Empire. In sum, the world-view, with its basic notion of a divinely sanctioned and supported centre of power, gave rise to the hierarchical and centralized structure of the Ottoman Empire. It was no mere mystical theory. In the mid-seventeenth century, Evliyā Çelebi observed that security and wealth diminished in the provinces in proportion to the distance from the 'Gate of Good Fortune'.

Apart from these 'political' formative elements of the Ottoman-Islamic city, the main urban zones, including the *bedestān -çarşı* or central market place, were brought into existence under the *waqf-'imāret* system.

The Waqf-'imāret system

In large metropolises such as Bursa and Istanbul the city developed not around a single nucleus but around several, variously located, each constructed as a well-planned complex of religious buildings (mosque, *madrasa,* hospice, etc.), and supported by a waqf. In Istanbul, around such nuclei built by the Sulṭān or viziers, developed new divisions (nāḥīye), each under the jurisdiction of a surrogate judge appointed by the cadi of Istanbul. Each complex, as it answered the basic spiritual and material needs of a Muslim community in religion and education, as well as in water supply and even (through the hospice, 'imāret or soup kitchen) in food, became the centre of a settlement which grew over time into a full-fledged nāḥīye. Through such a system Muslim Istanbul developed in the 16th century into Europe's largest city.

Through the waqfs, with sources of revenue such as shops rented to the merchants, traders, and artisans in the city, or villages and farms in rural areas, an immense amount of wealth constantly flowed into the city for the maintenance of such complexes. For example, the Fatih complex built by Mehmed the Conqueror had an annual revenue of 1.5 million akça or thirty thousand gold ducats which was spent as follows:[36]

	akça
Stipends for personnel and others	869,280
Food for the Hospice	461,417
Expenses of the Hospital	72,000
Repairs	18,522

[36] H. Inalcik, 'Istanbul' (n. 21), 229.

The total number of the personnel in various units was 383. At least 1,117 persons received two meals each day.

In the location and construction of the mosque, hierarchical considerations were given priority. It was forbidden to build a mosque larger or more stately than the Sulṭān's, a rule respected by all. The second largest mosque was built by the Grand Vizir or other vizirs. In the provinces, the governor-general or frontier beg was entitled to build a large mosque in the provincial centre. The founder was required to seek the written permission of the Sulṭān, while for the small district mosque *(mesjid)* the local qāḍī was able to grant permission for construction and to approve location.

For the location of a mosque a prominent site in the city's landscape or a crowded centre such as the bazaar area were preferred—that is, the criterion was either aesthetic or functional. The actual construction had to be in durable materials, mostly stone and such metals as iron and bronze. A larger mosque was the central building among a complex of buildings including the *madrasa* (college), the library, hospital, hospice, convent for dervishes, school for children, and fountain for ablution. A *türbe* (mausoleum) was also usually added for the founder. It was only the Sulṭāns and the vizirs who built such *'imāret*s or large complexes. They served as a kind of infrastructure for the creation of new districts in the reconstruction process in Istanbul. In 1459, Mehmed the Conqueror gave orders to his vizirs to build such complexes on various sites within the walls.[37] These complexes became the nuclei for subsequent districts.

It can safely be said that the reconstruction process of Ottoman Istanbul depended essentially on the Islamic institutions of *waqf* and *'imāret.* The construction of such complexes would sometimes follow the rapidly expanding settlement of a particular district. A number of districts came into existence spontaneously as a result of economic conditions. Smaller district mosques or *masjid*s were built by leading figures of the local community, mostly merchants and craftsmen. A district was named after the founder of the local mosque.

The list below shows a breakdown of the districts of Istanbul according to the founders of mosques by mid-seventeenth century[38] it will be seen that 65 per cent of the founders of mosques belonged to the 'ruling class':

---

37 *Ibid.*

38 *Ibid.*, 231.

Ulema	46
Merchants and bankers	32
Trades people	28
Aghas of the Palace	18
Begs	16
Pashas	14
Officers of the Kapı-Kulu	12
'Bureaucrats'	8
Architects	6
Others	39
Total	**219**

Large-scale urban utilities, such as the water system, store-houses for provisions, slaughterhouses, etc., were all built by the Sulṭān as part of the pious foundation of the mosque. The construction of the city's water system —aqueducts, water conduits in the city, and public fountains— was likewise a part of the *waqf*s of the mosques. In the sixteenth century, when the population in *intra muros* Istanbul alone surpassed 250,000, the Ottomans renovated the entire water system with new aqueducts and a distribution system in the city. A permanent organization called *su-yolcuları* had already been created to supervise and carry out the repair work. Suleyman the Magnificent, who considered improvements in the water supply for the urban population to be one of the most meritorious religious acts, was responsible for extending the system to all the big cities in the Empire, including Mecca, Medina, and Jerusalem. These cities relied, until very recently, on the water system introduced by the Ottomans.

The mosque, or rather the complex of religious and charitable buildings affiliated with it, was the meeting place of the urban community. It was not only the forum for their major religious, political and judicial affairs, but also for trading, socializing and entertainment. For example, the large square outside Bayezid II's mosque was surrounded by shops and 'thousands of people', Evliyā notes,[39] who 'enjoy the shady places under the trees and do shopping for their needs, buying all sorts of goods.'

The *bedestān* and the Great Çarşı were built as part of the *waqf*s for the Aya-Sofya (Hagia Sophia) mosque.[40] The rents were to be spent for the upkeep of the mosque and other charitable foundations. Thus, through the *waqf*

---

39 *Seyāhatnāme*, 144.

40 H. Inalcik, 'The Hub of the City: The Bedestān of Istanbul', *Studies in Ottoman Social and Economic History* (London: Variorum Reprints 1985).

system, all the works designed to enhance the city were interpreted as works of charity for the good of the Muslim community.

The Great Bazaar with bedestāns, khans for merchants and çarşıs (sūq) for handicrafts, was built according to a Turco-Islamic plan on the former Byzantine site of crafts and guilds.[41] The high street called Divan-Yolu from Edirne-Kapı to Aya-Sofya (Hagia Sophia) was, as under the Byzantines, the main imperial road with all the important public buildings, including the Great Bazaar and the customs house for the caravans entering the city through Edirne-Kapı. This thoroughfare ran parallel to the port area on the Golden Horn, and the streets connected the business centre of the caravans with the port. In fact, the triangle between port area, Galata, and Üsküdar (the terminus for the caravans from Asia) became and still is the hub of the city's economic life. The streets extending from it to the Bazaar channelled goods arriving by sea to the great marketplace of the city. The entire system with its infrastructure of bazaars, market halls, storehouses, and groups of shops was established by the Sulṭān or high dignitaries as a source of revenue for the pious foundations, as though ultimately intended for the purpose of serving the religion. This world is, in Muslim beliefs, only a temporary station en route to the eternal life hereafter.

The main urban functions were viewed as being complementary to or extensions of the religious establishment or the imperial palace. The crafts were housed in the bazaars constructed by the founders of the pious endowments, *waqfs*. Each was put under the control of the respective craftsman appointed to the Sulṭān's palace. All of the jewellers were put under the *kuyumcubaşı* or chief imperial jeweller, all of the physicians under the *hekimbaşı* or chief imperial physician, all the tailors under the *terzibaşı* or chief imperial tailor, all of the architects under the chief imperial architect, and so on. Each examined and issued licenses and promulgated regulations for people in their respective professions. Their services, however, were intended not only for the benefit of the palace but also for the Muslim community at large. Head of the officers responsible for the needs of the palace and the city was the *şehir-emīni* or city 'prefect'. His primary duty was to oversee everything the Sulṭān's palaces needed, from provisions of the bazaar to repair work, etc.

The Residential section of the city

It was noted above that the residential areas of the city lacked any kind of planned arrangement. This can be explained in relation to certain fundamental beliefs and concepts of the Islamic religion and culture.

---

[41] See H. Inalcik, 'Istanbul', 227.

The sacred principles of the Sharī'a, *ḥalāl* (lawful) and *ḥarām* (unlawful, prohibited) govern all human activities in society, the more so in an urban environment. Islamic Law embraces not only matters related to ritual, social relationships and conduct, but also food, habitation and environment.

Due to the prohibition of intoxicating beverages and pork, the non-Muslim citizens were strictly forbidden to sell these items to Muslims and were required to keep their shops outside of the Muslim districts. Drinking houses were restricted mostly to Galata on the other side of the Golden Horn, an area regarded by Muslims as a place of sin.

The right of privacy is a religious principle in Islam that helps explain many features of a Muslim city. While the decisive sources of Islam, i.e., the Qur'ān and Ḥadīth, gave rise to a detailed legal theory on the matter, the Ottoman court records provide abundant evidence of how that theory was actually implemented in the Islamic city.

The right of privacy encompassed family as well as religious life, which is the principal explanation of the division of the Ottoman —or, more widely, the Islamic— city into two main zones, residential and commercial. In the commercial zone, religious identity did not interfere with the daily routine, and Muslims and non-Muslims intermingled—only shops selling comestibles were segregated. In the residential zone people operated under the rules, and performed the rituals, of their own religions, within their own communities, in separate or 'private' districts. As a rule, each religious community occupied a specific area in the residential section and had its own cemetery. The quarters (*maḥalle*) grew up around a masjid, church, or synagogue. Greeks, Armenians, Jews or Karaites had each their own separate areas. Segregation of the Muslim districts from the non-Muslim ones was particularly stressed. The Sharī'a demanded that the nona-Muslims not perform their ceremonies or rituals within sight or hearing of the Muslims. However, the Muslims went to great lengths to make their own ceremonies visible, which was thought to be the most efficient way to propagate Islam.

Islam makes a number of stipulations concerning private life and privacy. The family and the home are sacred, a transgression of which, though sometimes committed by the state authorities, is a major sin and may result in legal action against the transgressor. In particular, the part of the house where one's family lives is called ḥarīm and considered inviolable, and the Law prohibits entry to it by outsiders.[42] Without considering the Islamic rules on the sanctity of privacy, we cannot explain the particular forms which

42 A Ḥadīth says: 'every land has its appurtenance forbidden [to other than the proprietor].' See M. Hamidullah, *Muslim Conduct of State* (Kashmir Bazar, 4th ed., 1961), 92.

domestic architecture and the streets took in the Ottoman or Islamic city. The Ottoman buildings and street patterns adhered closely to the rules and regulations of Islamic Law.[43] They were controlled by such public authorities as the chief architect *(ser-mi'mār)*,the prefect *(şehir-emīni)* and the superintendent of the water conduits *(su-yolu nazırı)* in cooperation with the city's qāḍī. Disputes were settled by the qāḍī in accordance with the regulations and, in the final analysis, by the rules of the Sharī'a. Under the regulations, non-Muslim could not build near a Muslim place of worship and their houses were not to be more than nine *dhirā'* (6.82 metres) high or higher than a Muslim house. This regulation, however, was responsible for the construction of all sorts of 'extensions' on the tops of the buildings. The Istanbul court records contain frequent cases filed when a neighbour built a higher building to protect the interior of his house from being overlooked.

The residential section of *maḥalle*s was the area in which the Muslim community and the other religious communities lived, in their separate districts, their private lives. Government officers rarely showed themselves in these areas. The ketkhudā and imām, elected by the *maḥalle* and approved by the qāḍī, were responsible for the public affairs of the community. They mediated between government and community in such matters as tax collection and security. The city's population consisted of groups classed religiously and socially autonomous. The government did not think it appropriate to impose regulations on the residential areas except in matters affecting the entire city, such as a fire.

Non-intervention in social and economic life was vigorously defended by a group of Muslim jurists, among them Imām Abū Yūsuf (d. 798). In the sixth chapter of his *Kitāb al-Kharāj,* Abū Yūsuf, quoting several aḥādīth, ruled that the prices of the market are determined by God, not by human wisdom.[44] The Prophet himself declined to intervene when people complained about rising prices at the market. Abū Yūsuf argued that abundance or scarcity are not the only reasons for the rise or fall of prices. Here again we see the key attitude of Islam as far as social arrangements are concerned. It was believed that in such cases human intervention is an act against the divine purpose.

---

43 On the Ottoman regulations on the construction of houses in the city of Istanbul, see Osman Nuri Ergin, *Mecelle-i Umūr-i Belediyye* (İstanbul 1922), 1059-72; A. Marcus, 'Privacy in Eighteenth-Century Aleppo', *IJMES*, 18 (1986), 165-83.

44 See M. N. Siddiqi, 'Muslim Economic Thinking: A Survey of Contemporary Literature', *Studies in Islamic Economics*, ed. Khurshid Ahmed (Glasgow, 1981), 249, 263, cf. D. Gimaret, 'Les théologiens musulmans devant la hausse des prix', *JESHO* , xxii/3 (1979), 330-7.

The striking difference between the unplanned Muslim cemetery and the usually neatly planned Christian cemetery may also be explained in the same way. To the Muslim the tombs scattered on the cemetery grounds were a passage to the other world where the dead are visited and questioned by the angels (malā'ika) within forty days of burial. Even when the mausolea were erected for members of the ruling élite, the most pious among them asked in their wills that the dome of the tomb be left open to the sky. At the cemetery, things had to be left to the will of God.

The Qāḍī as an independent representative of the urban community

Every city and town was placed under the jurisdiction of a qāḍī who represented Islam and Sharī'a. Istanbul intra muros was under a qāḍī who held the highest rank among the qāḍīs, while the three towns which were separated from Istanbul by water or by city walls, namely Galata, Üsküdar and Haslar (also called Eyüp) had their own separate jurisdictions under independent qāḍīs. As a general rule, a qāḍī's jurisdiction (qāḍā') included nāḥīyes or district as well as suburbs and villages around the urban centre. The central *(merkez)* nāḥīye included those nearby summer pastures *(yayla),* villages and other lands economically an integral part of the town and vital for the supply of provisions and raw materials (cotton, wool, and hides in particular).

Here I shall focus on the role of the qāḍī and 'the council of the court' *(Majlis-i shar')* from the point of view of the Muslim city as an urban community. Although the qāḍī , as with any other executive officer, was appointed by the Sulṭān this appointment was made in the Sulṭān's capacity as imām (religious head) of the Islamic community. The qāḍī, therefore, had all the delegated powers as head of the urban community under his particular jurisdiction. The qāḍī.as autonomous with respect to the military and administrative authorities of the area and had direct access to the Sulṭān. He even had a kind of autonomy over the Sulṭān whenever the Sharī'a made him virtually autonomous, since no one could interfere in his decisions and actions in this field. Occasionally the opinion of the religious authorities was sought, but the qāḍī was not bound by it in his decisions. If his decision was challenged, the Porte could only ask him to hear the case again, or to transfer it to another qāḍī , or the case could be heard by the imperial council which then acted as a supreme court with higher judges (i. e. *qāḍī'asker*). The qāḍī's independent status as an administrator of the Sharī'a made it possible for the Islamic community to survive under foreign domination (of the Mongols in 13th century Iran, of Europeans in 19th century North Africa). In such circumstances the qāḍī assumed even greater authority and autonomy as the true and sole representative of the Sharī'a and thence of the Islamic community.

It should be remembered that in Muslim society, the Sharī'a was the final and absolute authority in governing Muslim life not only with regard to private matters but also in many areas of public life. That is why the Islamic communities energetically denounced the efforts of the colonial powers to secularize the law in administrative matters, which often led to prolonged resistance movements as seen in the nineteenth century North African Muslim countries. We cannot exaggerate the role of the qāḍī 's leadership in the local urban community and in political life, even in the highly centralized Ottoman empire. The notables of the urban community led by the local ulema assembled in the qāḍī's court and conveyed their demands to the Sulṭān on such matters as lowering taxes or expelling an oppressive officer. The qāḍī usually presented and signed the document called the *maḥẓar*.[45] Indeed, at such meetings the qāḍī's council swelled to include the leaders of the urban community. This was true even when the local notables were the real power behind him, as during the *a'yān* regime which prevailed in the eighteenth century Ottoman cities.

It was a part of a qāḍī's religious duties, included in the ḥisba jurisdiction,[46] to make sure that goods were manufactured according to set standards, and that any violations or profiteering were prevented in the market place.

An officer, the *muḥtesib*, in charge of ḥisba services, was on duty all the time at the market under the supervision of the city's qāḍī. The muḥtesib's function of insuring the welfare of the urban community was inferred by the ulema from the Qur'ānic verse[47] which commands believers 'to follow good known and recognized as such by everybody (*al ma'rūf*)' and 'to abstain from evil known and recognized as such by everybody.' All ethical-social action with the purpose of establishing good and preventing evil in the society was based by the Muslim jurists on this Qur'ānic principle. Thus, the *muḥtesib*'s duty transcended that of a simple market inspector such as the Greco-Roman agoranomos.[48] Whatever its institutional origin, it is in fact an Islamic religious office. Under the Ottomans the *muḥtesib* was nominated by

---

45 See H. Inalcik, 'Şikâyet Hakkı: 'Arẓ-i Ḥāl ve'Arẓ-i Maḥẓarlar', *The Journal of Ottoman* Studies, vii-viii (1988), 33-54.

46 On the application of ḥisba rules in the Ottoman empire, see Osman Nuri Ergin, *Mecelle-i Umūr-i Belediyye*, 302-470; 'Ḥisba' EI^2, iii, 485-90.

47 The Qur'ān, 3: 104, 110, 114.

48 B. R. Foster, 'Agoranomos and Muhtesib', *JESHO,* XIII/2 (1970), 128-14, in particular 141.

the qāḍī and appointed by the Sulṭān's diploma, which defined his authority and responsibilities.

In principle, he was responsible for seeing to it that Muslims in the city followed the precepts of the Sharī'a and lived a thoroughly Muslim life. In cooperation with the qāḍī, he was responsible for affairs bearing on public morality as the Sharī'a defines it. Because *ḥisba* was a religious office, its incumbent had to be a religious man with knowledge of Islamic jurisprudence. The Ottoman Sultans appointed a *muḥtesib* in each major city and promulgated *ḥisba* regulations. However, the *muḥtesib* under Ottoman rule, as in earlier times, under the 'Abbasids for example, was active only in the commercial zone and not in the residential zone. His main concerns were to prevent fraud in the marketplace, to apply the *ḥisba* (*iḥtisāb*) regulations, and to uphold the declared price lists. One of his most important duties was to check the accuracy of weights and measures at the market. This restriction of his jurisdiction to the marketplace can be explained by the fact that inviolability of an individual's privacy was the most important rule, and moral supervision was left to the *maḥalle* community and its leader, the imām.

Together with the qāḍī, who had the power to pronounce decisions on everything connected with the Sharī'a and the Sulṭānic law, the *muḥtesib* without doubt performed a major role in controlling urban life, its economic activities in particular.

In Ottoman Istanbul as well as in other big cities, two other office holders, *şehir-ketkhudāsı* and *şeh-bender,* exercised some degree of supervision over city life as a whole. They are enumerated, though after the military and the ulema, among the *a'yān* and *ashrāf* (notables) of the city. Unlike other office holders they belonged to the re'āyā' class. The former represented the craft guilds and the latter the merchants, and both assumed responsibilities after nomination by their respective groups and registration by the qāḍī. They played an important part in matters directly concerning the city. They represented the city population in the qāḍī's council on various occasions, particularly as spokesmen of their respective groups whenever a dispute involving the whole group called for their mediation or arbitration. Whenever the interests of the government were not involved, neither the government authorities nor the qāḍī interfered in their election, and registration by the qāḍī was simply a formality. On such occasions the qāḍī served as a notary public to register the election. The same was true for the election of guilds in the city. This state of affairs, known only through recent research on court documents,[49] allows us to speak of a certain kind of urban autonomy in the Ottoman or Islamic city.

In looking at the various 'spaces' in the city, one can speak of a spiritual-Islamic dimension or 'space', which was dominant in the Ottoman city. We have discussed this aspect above. There was also an 'existential space' whose definition varies depending on whether we talk about the imperial institution with the palace and the standing army in the capital, or the pious endowments with *waqfs*, or the merchants and ordinary townsmen.

Conclusion

To sum up, the Ottoman city had a definite physical and social organization which was based on and reflected the ideal of the Islamic Sharī'a for Muslim life. The division of the city into two main sections, a commercial-industrial zone on the one hand with the *bedestān,* the central bazaar, crafts and caravansaries, and on the other hand, a residential section with *maḥalle* communities organized around the local temple,[50] definitely originated from Islamic concepts.

It was the Sulṭān or members of the élite who were responsible for the planned construction of building complexes in the commercial section. They were conceived and built to serve religious foundations. As for the residential section, it was composed of *maḥalle* or quarters, each of which was organized as an autonomous community under an *imām* or *kethudā* elected from among the members of the *maḥalle* community. Religion, not lineage, played the central role in the formation of the *maḥalle* when necessary, the qāḍī called the *imāms* of the *mahalle* or *kethudās* of the city to his court to reach a decision concerning the interests of the community.

Although the city seemed to be an assemblage of such autonomous units, the unity of the city itself was secured by its commercial-industrial centre shared by all citizens, and by its political and Islamic-judicial institutions. Representing the latter, the qāḍī played a crucial role, not only as mediator between the urban community and the government, but also as an authority supervising all urban matters.

In practice, the qāḍī acted in many instances as representative of the local Muslim community and assumed the responsibility of defending its common interests. Under a qāḍī, the Ottoman or Islamic urban population acquired a communal identity and unity.

---

49 See my publication of documents from the Bursa qāḍī court in *Belgeler* (Ankara: Turkish Historical Society, vol. x, 1981; vol. xi, 1987).

50 See E. Wirth, 'Die orientalische Stadt', *Saeculum,* 26 (1975), 75-94.

Comprising religious, charitable institutions with the revenue-producing commercial installations, the *waqf* system was the key institution in creating a typical Ottoman-Islamic urban structure.

The *waqf-'imāret* system, which gave the city its basic physical-topographic features, was originally an act of Islamic piety, designed to organize urban space to enable one to live a complete Muslim life. Chosen and located on commercially or visibly prominent areas, such religious complexes determined and gave impetus to the development of the main districts (*nāḥiye*) of the city. The formation and growth of the districts, however, was left to chance.

Excursus I: 'Islamic City'

In this paper, on the basis of original sources, we have argued the significance of the Islamic faith and culture for the characteristics of the topography and social structure of the Ottoman city of Istanbul. Obviously this does not exclude other determining factors —geographic setting, Roman-Byzantine heritage and, most particularly, historical circumstances.

The marked physical divide in the layout of the Islamic City, between a business centre and a residential section, has deeper social-political origins. There was a latent conflict between the all-powerful ruler who organized the city and sought to control the whole society in the name of a divine purpose and the re'āyā', the subject population, confined to economic activities. The tension is seen in affairs to do with price structure and settlement, in fact all social and economic activities governed by factors other than explicitly politico-religious ones. Indeed, there was an unending struggle on the part of the ruler's bureaucracy to maintain the ruler's order against the encroachments resulting form inevitable demographic and economic changes in the city. The Ottoman state's overriding preoccupation with, and efforts to resolve the problems are vividly recorded in the Ottoman archival collections.

Equally, however, it should not be forgotten that Islamic Law recognized the rules governing religious and private life of Muslims as distinct from those governing economic relations which were applicable to the non-Muslims, dhimmīs, as well as Muslims. The first category of rules demanded a religiously segregated residential area and the second a commercial-industrial section where peoples of various faiths mingled and worked together.

In recent publications, anthropologists and historians have continued to stress the unorganized features of the 'Islamic City'. Clifford Geertz argues that 'the (Islamic) urban landscape is not merely various, as are all such landscapes, it is disjunct'.[51] Ira Lapidus remarks that 'Muslim Cities are cities by virtue of social processes which are not peculiar to any given culture.[52] Recently, to be sure, some anthropologists and geographers have changed their two-dimensional view of urban landscape with the discovery of a third dimension, namely the evolutionary past, and realized the dangers of generalized verdicts on the basis of fieldwork focused on a town or city of their choosing: for an example, see D. F. Eickelman's generalizations on the basis of an anthropological study of one Moroccan town.[53]

It is still argued that in general the Islamic City was not a planned construction.[54] The fact is that the strict grid pattern of streets was not something unknown in the commercial part of the typical cities founded by Muslim rulers. Only the residential part grew haphazardly, over time, through the private initiative of Muslim settlers. But then, in most European medieval cities we find the same pattern—a planned city core for commerce and administration, and an unplanned agglomeration of residential quarters which grew up over time around that core.[55]

It is time to find a middle way between an over-idealized interpretation of Islamic social institutions—the most recent such approach may be found in *Studies in Islamic Economics* (1980)[56] —and totally ignoring the determining role of Islamic norms— for an example, see C. Geertz, *Islam Observed* (1968).[57] It would save much misunderstanding if we still held to the theory of the congregational-mosque and bazaar or the palace core theories instead of seeing in the historical cities of Islam nothing but chaos.

M. Bonine rightly complains that there are 'great gaps in our understanding of the structure of the city in Middle Eastern society. Lack of

---

51 *IJMES*, vol. 21, iii, 292.

52 'The Evolution of Muslim Urban Society' *Comparative Studies in Sociology and History,* xv (1973), 48.

53 'Is there an Islamic City?', *IJMES* v (1974), 274-94. Following the rather discredited orientalist tradition André Raymond now brings up the third dimension explaining the creation and evolution of the Islamic cities in *Artisans et Commerçants au Caire au XVIII éme siècle,* (Institut Français de Damas, 1973-74, 2 vols); and *The Great Arab Cities in the 16th-18th Century: An Introduction*, (New York: CUP, 1984).

54 Most recently, M. E. Bonine, 'The Sacred Direction and City Structure: A Preliminary Analysis of Islamic Cities of Morocco', a discussion paper presented to the Geography and Environment Workshop, the Univesity of Chicago, 26 April 1988.

55 See for instance, towns founded by the Genoese in the Levant, M. Balard, *La Romanie Génoise* (Genoa, 1978), I, 179-354; and H. Inalcik, 'Ottoman Galata', *Première rencontre Internationale sur l'Empire ottoman et la Turquie moderne*, ed. E. Eldem, Istanbul: IFEA, 1991, 17-105.

56 Khurshid Ahmad, ed. *Studies in Islamic Economics* (Jeddah, 1980).

57 C. Geertz, *Islam Observed,* (Chicago: University of Chicago Press, 1968), 56-62.

specific information is partly due to lack of available sources.'[58] He seems not to be aware of the existence of the vast collections of the qāḍī court records from Islamic cities. It should be emphasized that Islamic social history and institutions cannot be understood without constant reference to the stipulations of the Sharī'a and the crucial role which the qāḍī and *muftī* played in the Islamic city. Now with the discovery and the use of the qāḍī court records the urban historian has at his disposal a most detailed primary source on Islamic social history, and particularly urban institutions and life. Ottoman court records, from the middle fifteenth down to the twentieth century, form an immense collection amounting to thousands of volumes —for Istanbul alone there exist 9,870 registers[59] —, scattered today in city archives from Tirana in Albania to Jerusalem. Without the 'simplistic, rigid' discipline of the orientalist (according to M. Bonine, 'From Uruk to Casablanca', p. 169), deciphering and properly interpreting this source is not possible for the student of the Islamic city.

Anthropologists and geographers will discover 'meaning' only after the necessary 'fieldwork' in the court records of Islamic cities has been done. Excellent studies, mostly ignored by the anthropologists and geographers, have already been published. Here it suffices to mention the works of R. Jennings, A. Marcus, and A. Cohen.[60]

Excursus II: The Central Asiatic *Ordug*

Using the latest archaeological findings, Emel Esin[61] showed that the nucleus of the Central Asiatic imperial city was a four-cornered fort or palace built on a sacred mountain. It was thought of as the centre of the cosmic order, a sacred city, symbolizing the four cardinal points under the polar star around which the universe revolves. Connected with the divine nature of imperial sovereignty, this symbolism determined not only the topography of the imperial city but also the basic institutions of the Turco-Mongol empires which arose in Euroasia in ancient times. Esin points out the evident connection with the Chinese notion of sovereignty and the imperial centre. For the later periods she also refers to the East Iranian, Sogdian, influence upon the Kök-Türk and Uyghur empires whose heritage was continued with the Turkish empires in the Islamic cultural area—the Karakhanids, the Seljukids and the Ottomans. In fact, when considered with all its cosmographical symbols, this particular notion of imperial power and its

---

58 M. Bonine, *Sacred Direction,* see note 54 above.

59 See H. Inalcik, 'The Rūznamče Registers...' *Turcica,* xx (1988), 252.

60 For the titles see *Türkologischer Anzeiger,* i-xii (1974-86).

61 "Ordug", *Tarih Araştırmaları Dergisi ,* (Ankara, 1972), vi/10-11.

cosmic imperial centre apparently originated first in the ancient centralist empires of Mesopotamia, and spread from there to the East and the West. At any rate, the Ottoman sultans continued the Turco-Mongol belief that the imperial power rested on a sacred spot on the planet and later, after the conquest of Constantinople, they combined this with the Roman-Western tradition.[62] The claim of possessing, by God's grace, the capital city of the Roman empire guided Mehmed the Conqueror in the creation and legitimation of his empire and his imperial authority as well as his plan of conquests.[63] In their letters to the European powers Mehmed II and his successors took pride in inserting the title of *Kaysar* (Caesar) into their titulature. Suleyman I challenged the Emperor Charles V, claiming that he was the sole heir to the Roman empire, and denied to him the use of the title of caesar or emperor.[64] Mehmed II's palaces, the first in the centre of Istanbul near the Great Bazaar, then the second on the hill of Saray-Burnu near the Aya Sofya mosque, were surrounded by high walls. The latter complex was called *kal'at al-sulṭāniyye.* The Sulṭānic Fortress with its central palace, kiosks, and gardens constituted a quasisacred city, totally separate from the city of Istanbul and believed to be the locus where God's grace or Good Fortune (*sa'āda* or *kut)* manifested itself. This nucleus was formally called *Dār al-Salṭana*, 'The Abode of the Imperial Power'. Considering all the features peculiar to it, the Conqueror's 'fort' evidently replicated the Central Asiatic *ordug*. The *shahristān* or *shahr*, the larger metropolis, grew around the nucleus *ordug,* with the settlement of the commoners—merchants, artisans and so on.[65] As a result of the ruler's arrangement through his *waqf,* the residential quarters had their own social and ethnic character. The quarters and houses of the élite surrounded the palace; the houses expressly constructed for the use of the *ulema* were next to the Fatih mosque complex.

---

62 See H. İnalcık, "Pādişāh" in *İslâm Ansikolopedisi,* ix, 491-95.

63 See H. İnalcık, "Mehmed II" in *İslâm Ansikolopedisi,* vii, 514-30.

64 See H. Inalcik, "The Origin of the Ottoman-Russian Rivalry and the Don-Volga Canal (1596)", *Annales de l'Université d'Ankara,* I (1957), 47. For an interesting manifestation of this claim in regalia see Gülru Necipoğlu, 'Suleyman the Magnificent and the Representation of power in the Context of Ottoman-Hapsburg-Papal Rivalry', *The Art Bulletin,* XXI/3 (New York, 1989), 421-6.

65 Esin, 'Ordug'.

3

Ottoman Galata, 1453-1553

Ottoman Galata, 1453-1553

The 'ahd-nāme of June 1, 1453

The story of how the "treaty" concluded between the Genoese of Pera and Mehmed II in 1453 was discovered is well known.[1] The use of defective French and Italian translations and of J. von Hammer's faulty copy of the Greek original gave rise to a great deal of controversy over the nature and the precise contents of the document until the British Museum acquired the original copy and made it public in 1898.[2] The original document, in Greek, was edited, first, by N. Jorga in 1914[3] and, later, by E. Dallegio d'Alessio whose transcription has been generally accepted.[4] An official translation of the original document into Italian which was made by the Genoese authorities in Pera on August 30, 1453 was widely used and reproduced.[5] The Turkish version, which was evidently a translation from the original in Greek, also exists either as an independent document or inserted in the official renewals of the capitulatory privileges.[6]

---

[1] See, E. Dallegio d'Alessio, "Traité entre les Génois de Galata et Mehmet II (1er Juin 1453), versions et commentaires", *Échos d'Orient,* XXXIX (1940), pp. 161-175; T. C. Skeat, "Two Byzantine Documents", *The British Museum Quarterly,* XVIII (1953), pp. 71-73; and recently Mahmut Şakiroğlu, "Fatih Sultan Mehmed'in Galatalılara verdiği Fermanın Türkçe Metinleri", *Tarih Araştırmaları Dergisi,* (1983), pp. 211-216.

[2] See, Skeat, note 1 above.

[3] N. Iorga, "Le privilège de Mohammet II pour la ville de Pera (1er Juin 1453)", *Bulletin de la Section de l'Académie Roumaine,* 2e année, no 1 (1914), pp. 11-32.

[4] E. Dallegio d'Alessio, "La texte grec du traité conclu par les Génois de Galata avec Mehmet II, le 1er Juin 1453", *Hellenika,* 9 (1939), pp. 115-124; for the original text, see Appendix n° 2.

[5] E. Belgrano, "Documenti riguardanti la colonia genevese di Pera", *Atti della Soc. lig. di Stor. Patria,* XIII (1877-1884), Genoa, 1886, pp. 226-228; E. D. d'Alessio, "Traité...", p. 162; for the Italian and French versions see M. A. Belin, *Histoire de la Latinité de Constantinople,* second edition, R. P. Arsène de Chatel, Paris, 1894.

[6] The Turkish text has been published by the following: I. İ. Hoci, "Galata'nın Osmanlılara Teslimi", *Tārīkh-i 'Osmānī Endjümeni Medjmū'ası,* XXV (1330 H.), pp. 52-53; he says he took it from "an old manuscript" without specifying the source. It is dated *awākhir-i Djumād'al-ūlā,* sene 857/1-10 June 1453; the names of the Genoese envoys are omitted; II. As an independent document, the Turkish text is reproduced in facsimile and translated into French by N. Beldiceanu, *Recherche sur la ville ottomane au XVe siècle,* Paris, 1973, pp. 153-154, facsimile, pp. 423-424; it is taken from a collection of state papers now preserved in *MS fonds turcs ancien* 130, Bibliothèque Nationale, Paris; it is dated *awākhir-i Djumād'al-ūlā,* sene 857/1-10 June 1453, and it contains the names of the

The following is a translation of the Turkish version of the document as found in a collection of state papers, MS Bibliothèque Nationale, Paris (see n° II in note 6, *infra* and Appendix 1).

> I, the Great Pādishāh and the Great Shehinshāh Meḥmed Khan, son of Sultan Murād, give my solemn oath unto God, creator of the earth and the heavens, and by the enlightened and pure soul of Mohammad, his messenger and by the seven *muṣḥaf* (the Qur'an) and by the 124 thousand prophets of God and by the souls of my grandfather and my father and by my own life and my sons' lives and by the sword I am wearing, that since, at present, the people of Galata and their noblemen have sent to my Sublime Porte in order to show their friendship, their envoys Babilan Paravazin and Markiz de Franko and the dragoman Nikoroz(o) Papudjo with the keys of the aforesaid fortress and to submit to me as my subjects *(ḳul),* I, in return, agree that they may follow their own customs and rites as were in force before, that I will not go against them and demolish their fortress. So I ordered [and agreed] that their money, provisions, properties, storehouses, vineyards, mills, ships and boats, in short, all their possessions as well as their wives, sons, and slaves, of both sexes, be left in their hands as before and that nothing be done contrary thereof nor to molest them; that they pursue their livelihood, as in other parts of my dominions, and travel by land and by sea in freedom without any hindrance or molestation by anyone and be exempt [from extraordinary impositions]; that I impose upon them the Islamic poll tax *kharādj* which they pay each year as other non-Muslims do, and in return I will give my attention [and protection] as I do to those in other parts of my dominions; that they keep their churches and perform their customary rites in them with the exception of ringing their church bells and rattle *(nāḳūs);* that I do not take away from them their present churches and

envoys; III. The original of Aḥmed I's renewal, made *awāsiṭ-i Muḥarrem* 1022/1-10 March 1610, preserved in the Genoa archives (see M. Şakiroğlu, *art, cit.,* p. 213, see Appendix 3) is reproduced in facsimile for the first time in *Storia maritima dell'Italia,* Milano, 1947, p. 653 and then by Şakiroğlu, *art. cit.,* pp. 223-224; Şakiroğlu published a copy from a register in the collection *Maliyeden Müdevver Defterler, Başvekâlet Arşivi* (now *Devlet Arşivleri, Osmanlı Arşivi),* Istanbul, no. 6004, p. 96; this particular register contains copies of the outgoing firmans between 1028-1030/1618-1620; Şakiroğlu transcribed and compared (p. 216) Aḥmed I's renewal with the text of the renewal by Murād IV; IV. The renewal by Murād IV dated *Rabīʿul-ūlā* 1033/10-20 January 1624 is reproduced by M. Şakiroğlu, *art. cit.,* facsimile text, pp. 220-221. We followed the transliteration system of *Encyclopaedia of Islam*, 2nd edition with the exception of (چ),ç.

turn them into mosques, but that they also do not attempt to build new churches; that the Genoese merchants come and go on land and by sea for trade, pay the customs dues as required under the established rules and be free from molestation by anyone. And I, also, ordered that their sons not be taken as janissaries; that no infidel be converted to Islam against his will; that they elect freely someone from among themselves as *ketkhudā,* steward, to look after their own affairs; that no *doghandjı* or *ḳul,* Sultan's men, will come and stay as guests in their houses; that the inhabitants of the fortress as well as the merchants be free from all kinds of forced labor. Let all take notice of this order and trust my imperial seal above. This document is written in the third part of the month of *Djumād' al-ūlā* in the Hidjra year of 857.

The date and the signature of the Greek document is discussed by E. d'Alessio.[7] The Greek text, he observes, gives the exact date as the first of June 1453 which is confirmed by the Arabic dating on the same document as *tahrīran fī awākhir Djumād' al-Awwal sene sab' wa ḥamsīn wa ṣamānamie* or the last part of the month *Djumādā* I, 857 which corresponds to the first ten days of the month of June 1453. The signature of Zaghanos on the bottom of the Greek text can be explained by the fact that Meḥmed II had appointed him to organize the last assault against Constantinople on the 27th of May and from the beginning of the siege he was entrusted to watch the Genoese of Pera. Upon the fall of Constantinople, the Sultan sent him to appease the terrified Genoese in Pera, and to prevent panic and the ruin of this mercantile center, which was so important for the reconstruction of his imperial capital. Upon the arrest of the grand vizir Çandarlı Khalīl on May 30, Zaghanos succeeded him in the grand vizirate.[8] In sum, all these circumstances allowed Zaghanos to assume chief responsibility for an orderly takeover of the Genoese city.

What is surprising is that no one has attempted to examine the document by comparing it with similar contemporary Ottoman documents.[9] E.

---

[7] E. Dallegio d'Alessio, "Traité...", pp. 165-167.

[8] See H. İnalcık, *Fâtih Devri Üzerinde Tetkikler ve Vesikalar,* Ankara 1954, pp. 127-133.

[9] For early Islamic *'ahd-nāmes* see H. A. R. Gibb, "The Fiscal Rescript of Umar II", *Arabica,* II, pp. 1-16; M. Hamidullah, *Muslim Conduct of State,* Lahore, revised fourth ed., 1961, pp. 75-156; for an Ottoman *'ahd-nāme* text in Greek before 1453, see the *'ahd-nāme* of Joannina dated 1430: C. Amantọs, "La reconnaissance par les Mahométans des droits politiques et religieux des Chrétiens et le décret de Sinan Pacha", *Epirotika Kronika* (1930), pp. 197-210; for an English translation of this *'ahd-nāme* see N. J. Pentazopoulos, *Church and Law,* Salonica, 1967, p. 21; the Joannina *'ahd-nāme* of 1430 is of particular interest for a comparison with that of Pera; for the *'ahd-nāmes* given by Meḥmed II after 1453, see V. Boškov, "Pitanje autentičnosti Fojničke *ahd-name*

d'Alessio suggests[10] that originally the document must have been drawn up in Turkish in the Ottoman chancery, at least in the form of a draft, and then put into the definitive Greek version. Suspecting that certain turcisms existed in the Greek text, Elizabeth Zachariadou[11] also shared this opinion. However, it is now a well established fact that Greek was used in Ottoman diplomatic correspondence with the Latin states during that period and that Greek scribes were employed in the Ottoman chancery.[12]

As for the authenticity of the Greek version, Paspati's arguments are found to be inadmissible by Lambros and E .d'Alessio.[13] Irrefutable indications of the originality of the Greek document are, first, the *tughra,* the Sultan's seal, which has been proven to be original when compared with the authentic firmans of the same Sultan.[14] The fact that the existing Turkish text is a direct translation from the Greek text can also be substantiated by such awkward grammatical forms as *rendjberlik edeler ghayrı memleketlerim gibi,* or *oḳuyalar ayinlerindje,* etc. The introductory sentence in the Turkish translation of the document[15] reads:

> The following is the *'ahd-nāme* of the *dhimmīs* of Galata; Meḥmed the Conqueror granted it when he conquered Istanbul. It is written in Greek and sealed by the Sultan's *tughra.*

By these words, the Ottoman chancery recognized that this was an *'ahd-nāme,* that the Genoese of Galata were given the status of Islamic *dhimmī*

Mehmeda II iz 1463 godine", *Godišnjaka,* XXVIII-XXX (1977-1979), pp. 87-104; examples of *'ahd-nāmes* given to cities in the sixteenth century are numerous; typical is the *'ahd-nāme* of Andivar (Antivari) given by Pertev Pasha in 1571, edited by M. Grignaschi, "Una raccolta inedita di 'Münşeât': il MS. Veliyüddin ef. 1970 della Biblioteca Beyazit Umumi di Istanbul e gli 'Ahdname' concessi dalla Sublime Porta a Chio *(Muharrem* 927h), a Firenze *(Muharrem* 934) e ad Antivari *(Ramadan* 983)", *Studi Preottomani e Ottomani,* Napoli, 1976, pp. 105-127, and V. Boškov, *"Ahd-nama* Murata II stanovnicima Bara iz 1575 godine", *Godišnjaka,* XXVIII-XXX (1977-1979), pp. 279-285; no comparative study has yet been made of the types of *'ahd-nāmes* given to communities and cities.

10 E. Dallegio d'Alessio "Traité...", p. 168.

11 Professor E. Zachariadou made this remark to me while we were discussing this text.

12 See A. Bombaci, "Nuovi firmani greci di Maometto II", *Byz. Zeitschrift,* 47 (1954).

13 E. Dallegio d'Alessio "Traité...", pp. 165-167.

14 For example, see F. Kraelitz, *Osmanische Urkunden in türkischer Sprache aus der zweiten Hälfte des 15. Jahrhunderts,* Wien 1921.

15 See the text in *MS fonds turc ancien* 130, Bibliothèque Nationale, Paris, ff. 78 a-b, pub. and translated into French by N. Beldiceanu, *Recherce sur la ville ottomane au XVe siècle,* Paris 1973, pp. 153-154; facsimile: p. 423.

subjects, and that the document bearing the Sultan's seal was written originally in Greek.

This Turkish text is the only one which is known thus far. As we described above (see note 6), the same Turkish text came to us, also as an insertion into the capitulations renewed by Ahmed I (1603-1617) and, later, by his successors (see Appendix 3). A critical comparison of the renewals with the earlier translated Turkish text leaves no doubt that the former is a copy of the latter. The main differences between the two Turkish texts are as follows:

MS Paris	The Capitulations of 1022 H.
Line 1: ben	Line 5: ben ki
Line 1: Murādım	Line 5: Murād Khānım
Line 2: Yeri göğü	Line 5: Yerleri
Line 2: resūlün	Line 6: resūl Moḥammed Muṣṭafā
Line 3: Muṣḥaf ḥaḳḳiyçün	Line 6: Muṣḥaf
Line 4: oghlanlarım	Line 7: oghlandjıḳlarım
Line 5: Babilan	Line 8: elçileri Babilan
Line 10: kharāb etmiyem buyurdum ki	Line 10: kharāb etmiyem
Line 17: oḳuyalar āyinlerindje	Line 14: ayinlerindje oḳuyalar
Line 20: etmeye ve buyurdum ki	Line 14: etmeye
Line 23: olalar shöyle bileler 'alāmet-i sherīfe i'timād ḳılalar taḥrīren	Line 18: olalar deyü

The differences obviously consist of only stylistic changes which the writer of the renewal deemed necessary to make in a capitulation. He omitted the formula *buyurdum ki* and the validation formula at the end, which were both unnecessary in the text of the renewal of a capitulation.

In western literature dealing with this document, it is generally admitted that it is a "treaty concluded between the Genoese of Galata and Mehmed II" or a capitulation.[16] In the Turkish text it is clearly called an *'ahd-nāme.* An *'ahd-nāme* is quite different from our understanding of a treaty as an agreement negotiated and agreed upon bilaterally between two sovereign states. In general an *'ahd-nāme* is not a treaty in the strictest sense; it is a unilateral pledge or privilege granted to a submitted or friendly group. It is an

---

[16] See for example E. Dallegio d'Alessio, "Traité...", p. 161; F. Babinger, *Mehmed the Conqueror,* p. 101: "the rights and liberties of the inhabitants of Galata were confirmed in a formal treaty (in *einem förmlichen... Vertrag)";* Şakiroğlu calls it a *ferman* or *'ahd-nāme.* All *'ahd-nāmes* are issued in the particular type of *nishān* or *berāt;* on types of *berāt,* see R. Anhegger and H. İnalcık, *Ḳānūnnāme-i Sulṭānī ber Mūceb-i 'Örf-i 'Osmānī,* Ankara, 1954, Giriş.

amān, the guarantee of life and property.[17] Such an act is related to the Qur'anic notion of reconciliation *(ta'līf al-ḳulūb)* which found expression in the dealings of the Ottoman sultans with various non-Muslim communities and was commonly called *istimālet.*[18] *İstimālet,* reconciliation, manifested itself in various ways according to circumstances, and was formulated in different types of documents. Documents granting a privilege are in general *'ahd-nāme*s, *berāt*s or *nishān*s. The *'ahd-nāme,* a document guaranteeing privileges under oath *('ahd)*, is legally different from the *berāt* granting specific privileges without *'ahd.* The latter category of documents comprises diplomas of the Sultan investing a person or a group with a certain status, ordering third parties to observe the privileges, immunities or delegated authority; thus it is formulated in the form of a *ḥukm (fermān),* order. With an *'ahd-nāme,* the Sultan is bound before God to abide by the pledge given and he cannot change or abolish the contents of the *'ahd* as long as the other party –a government, a nation or community– continue to abide by the conditions of the pledge, which involve primarily "sincere loyalty and friendship" *(ikhlāṣ ile inḳiyād ve dostluḳ).* In practice, the sincerity provision gave the Sultan the discretion to judge whether or not the other party was abiding by the conditions. The *'ahd-nāme* category included the capitulations -- *'ahd-nāme*s given to non-Muslim foreigners acting individually or as a group, or to a state, as well as the *'ahd-nāme*s granted to vassal states or cities enjoying full internal autonomy under their own government.

Our renewal documents are rendered solely to the subjects of Genoa as capitulations without distinguishing the first part concerning the Genoese who, in 1453, expressed their willingness to become the Sultan's subjects *(ḳul)* and, as such, were ready to pay the annual *djizya,* poll tax (see *infra).* In the original document, this group of Genoese and the Genoese citizens residing in Galata under the capitulatory privileges were not yet distinguished, so they were treated in the same *'ahd-nāme.* From 1453 onwards, the Genoese called the document *capituli,*[19] i.e., capitulations. In fact, Islamic *amān* or *'ahd* comprised both situations. But at the time of renewals the two groups should have been distinguished and only the second part of the *'ahd-nāme* of 1453 rendered to the non - subject, *ḥarbī*, Genoese. Apparently, like modern authors, the scribes also did not realize the two separate dealings with the Genoese considered *dhimmī* and *ḥarbī* in the

---

[17] See the literature given in note 9 above; also see *"Imtiyāzāt", EI²*, vol. III.

[18] On *istimālet* see H. Inalcik, "Ottoman Methods of Conquest", *The Ottoman Empire: Conquest, Organization and Economy,* London: Variorum, 1979, pp. 112-122.

[19] In the letter of Soderini, a Florentine envoy in Genova, dated August 30, 1453, cited by E. d'Alessio, "Traité...", p. 162, note 3.

original document. Or, they preserved the section concerning the first group, apparently in order to avoid the complications of adjusting the document to present conditions, and found no harm in leaving this part in the text.

What actually happened must be recalled here.[20] Upon the conquest of Constantinople, the Sultan's policy actually was aimed at bringing Pera under his direct rule without being obliged to use force. He wanted to avoid disrupting the normal life of the city, which he considered so vitally important for the reconstruction of his new capital and the economy of his empire in general.[21] For their part, the Genoese hoped to preserve their independence as established under the Byzantine Empire[22] and which had, in fact, been guaranteed by the agreement made with Meḥmed II in 1451, and renewed during the siege of Constantinople. But after the conquest of Constantinople, events would take a different turn for them. Mehmed II's candid account of the events in his letter of victory to the Sultan of Egypt[23] clearly illustrates the new situation. In this letter (see Appendix 4) Mehmed said:

> At the time of the siege [of Constantinople] the Genoese of this fortress [Pera] came into our presence and renewed in a strong fashion their oath and agreement with us. In return, we said that you will be [in peace] as before on condition that you not give aid to the enemy and abide by the agreement. They accepted our condition and obeyed the order. But when Constantinople was conquered we discovered among the dead and the captives men of Galata who had fought against us. So it became apparent that they acted ambivalently and violated their sworn agreement *(mīṣāḳ)*. We, therefore, decided to do the same with them as we did with the other [enemies]. Meantime they came in supplication and 'begging' and said 'if you don't have mercy on us we will be definitely losers'.[24] Whereupon we pardoned them, for God is the forgiver, and we favored them, and favor is from God the Mighty, the One, the Subduer. And we confirmed them in their dominion *(mulk)*, and dominion is from God the Mighty, the Omnipotent, and we have

[20] A principal source on the fall of Genoese Pera is edited and published by A.Pertusi, *La Caduta,* vol. II, p. 549: Pera and bibliography, pp. 492-512; also L.Sauli, *Dalla Colonia,* vol. I; E. Belgrano, *Documenti,* CXLVIII ff.

[21] See H. Inalcik, "Istanbul", *EI²*, p. 225; and "Mehmed II", *İA,* VII, pp. 519-520.

[22] For the character of Byzantine sovereignty over Galata, see E. Dallegio d'Alessio, "Galata et la souveraineté de Byzance", *Revue des Études Byzantines,* 1962, pp. 315-327.

[23] Ferīdūn, *Münshe'āt al-Salāṭīn*, I, 237. I am indebted to Professor Farouk Mustafa for helping me in the translation of the letter from Arabic.

[24] Qur'an: VII-23.

> levelled their fortress in such a way as no crookedness nor refuge can be seen therein. And we seized their land and water and we entered their names in the *djizya* register 'so that they would deliver *djizya* in humility'.[25]

It is clear that the Sultan sought to justify both the abrogation of his previous *mīsāḳ*, a religiously binding sworn agreement, and his decision to reduce the Genoese to *djizya* paying subjects no different from subject peoples in other parts of his domain.

In his famous letter to his brother, dated June 23, 1453,[26] the *Podestà* of Pera Angelo Giovanni Lomellino, confessed that he had been looking forward to an Ottoman defeat with keen anticipation and said:

I sent in defense of the city [of Istanbul] all the mercenaries from Chios and all those sent from Genoa as well as a good many citizens and burgesses from here (Galata). I always recognized that, if Constantinople were lost, this place would be lost.

Upon the fall of Constantinople, Lomellino tells us that the Genoese of Pera attempted to flee, and that the majority of them returned to their families; others were captured on the quay because the sea captains *(patroni)* were in such a terror that they did not wait.[27]

The *Podestà* continues "I immediately sent ambassadors to the Sultan with beautiful gifts saying 'Let us have peace, begging and submitting ourselves", and asked those Genoese who reached the ships to wait another day but they sailed at midnight while the *Podestà*'s ambassadors were still in the Sultan's camp. The *Podestà* wrote:

> When in the morning the Sultan received the news of the departure of the ships, he informed my ambassadors that he wanted *terra libera,* we could scarcely save ourselves and our personal property; for he said that we did everything possible to save Constantinople and that this was the reason why the Turks had not taken the place on the first day.

---

25 Qur'an: IX-29.

26 Pertusi, La Caduta I, p. 45. Upon the unexpected fall of Constantinople, the *Podestà* decided to surrender Galata and the inhabitants of Galata agreed to become the Sultan's subjects. This decision, in general, was criticized by the Genoese: see Lionardo of Chios in his letter of June 23, 1453 to the Pope: Pertusi, pp. 169-178. To justify his decision to surrender the place, the *Podestà* said, he wanted to save Galata from an inevitable sack. The *Podestà*'s visit to the Sultan's camp most probably occurred on the first of June, and the fifth the Sultan entered Galata.

27 Compare Nicolò Barbarò, "Giornale dell'assiedo di Costantinopoli", ed. Pertusi, *Caduta,* I, pp. 35-36.

Kenneth Setton translated *terra libera* as "an unconditional surrender".[28] In fact, the flight of the Genoese made the Sultan angry and led him to treat Galata as "free (abandoned) land". In Islamic law, the land deserted by its population under similar conditions is considered *fay'*, that is, a land belonging to the *bayt al-māl,* state treasury.[29] Our survey of Galata of 1455 leaves no doubt that Galata's land was treated accordingly and that plots and houses were subjected, as state properties, to *muḳāṭa'a,* or rent.[30] As was customary in Ottoman diplomatic practice, the grand vizir, then Zaghanos Pasha, appears to have played a major part in mollifying Galata and in reaching a new agreement with the Genoese. According to Doucas,[31] Zaghanos went in haste to Pera and in an effort to put a stop to the Genoese flight, gave them guarantees, "by the oath of the Sultan's life" and promised "conditions for an agreement better than those made with the Sultan and with the Emperor". Zaghanos added that their flight could only further arouse the anger of the Sultan. Except for those who had already run away, the rest of the Latins now were persuaded to remain in the town. The *Podestà* had the gates of the town shut and permitted no one to leave. The town was occupied by Zaghanos and his troops apparently on the 30th of May and as Critovoulos remarked,[32] "they did them (Perans) no harm". Abandoning all hope of restoring the town's previous status, and threatened with war conditions, the *Podestà* sent his envoys, "Babilan Paraveso and Markeso Drifankis"[33] to offer Pera's surrender and, as apparently suggested by Zaghanos, to submit by asking for peace and amnesty *(amān).* Thus, our document was issued upon the arrival of the second legation. Now the Sultan proceeded according to the prescriptions of the Islamic law concerning submitted populations.

The document is a typical *'ahd-nāme* granting *amān,* many examples of which are to be found in pre-Ottoman and Ottoman collections of state

---

[28] *The Papacy and the Levant,* Madison 1990. p. 134.

[29] See, F. Løkkegaard, *Islamic Taxation,* Copenhagen, 1950, Index: *fay'.*

[30] In Akkermn conquered in 1484, the houses and shops of the deported citizens and the bathhouse were confiscated for the fisc and rented to individuals under the *muḳāṭa'a* system (see the document published by N. Beldiceanu, *Ville,* ff. 238b-239, facsimile, pp. 410-412, dated August 23, 1484).

[31] Trans. H. J. Magoulias, p. 230.

[32] Trans. C. T. Riggs, p. 76.

[33] E.d'Alessio, "Traité", pp. 174-175; in Turkish translation: Babilan Paravazin and Markiz di Franko; Belgrano, *Documenti,* p. 227, identified them as *Babilano Pallavicino* and *Marchesio di Franchi;* in the Ottoman survey of 1455 their names occur as Paravazin and Markiz di Franko; being indigenous citizens they were registered as rich *dhimmīs* in the survey register (see *infra).*

papers.[34] Due to special conditions, this *'ahd-nāme* considered two separate groups in Pera: first, those permanent inhabitants who agreed to pay *kharādj/djizya* and became Ottoman non-Muslim subjects, thereby achieving special status as *dhimmīs* under the *dhimma* law of Islam; and secondly, *ḥarbī*, those "Frank" merchants who were subjects of Genoa and were residing in the city on a temporary basis for business purposes. The stipulations for the first group were made clear by the repeated phrase, *ghayrı memleketlerim gibi,* meaning "as is the case in other parts of my dominion". In return for submission and yearly individual payment of the *djizya,* poll tax, the Sultan enumerated the usual guarantees for the *dhimmīs,* that is, he pledged not to take military action against the city and its inhabitants, recognized their ownership rights of property, and promised security for their people, families, and slaves, free circulation in the Ottoman lands, and the free exercise of their religion in their churches. This first group included Greeks, Jews and Armenians of Galata as well as Genoese.

The second group is distinguished from the first by the term *Djeneviz bāzirgānları,* literally, Genoese merchants, for whom freedom of trade in the Ottoman territories was guaranteed on the condition that they pay customs dues as required by the regulations. Such non-Muslim foreigners were called *musta'min,* literally, those given *amān*, and were subject to the stipulations of capitulation. In the *Podestà*'s letter[35] this group is distinguished as *mercanti* from *abitanti.* In fact, the distinction between these two groups is seen in the Ottoman survey of Pera made in 1455, where each individual was to be marked *dhimmī,* payer of the poll tax, or *Frank* or *Djeneviz,* exempt from the poll tax *(bī-djizya).* The western writers did not notice or accept the basic distinction between subjects and foreigners, and this was to become a source of misunderstandings. Though many of the guarantees were shared by both groups, their legal status was absolutely distinct. For the privileges common to both, our document mentioned both groups side by side as *"ḳal'a-i mezbūre khalḳı ve bāzirgānları",* that is "the inhabitants and the merchants of the aforesaid fortress", as was the case in the exemption of both from all kinds of *angarias,* corvées. The exemption from the periodic levy of boys for the janissary corps was one often mentioned in similar documents given to various groups of the population in the Empire. The article "no *doghandjı* or *ḳul* shall come and stay as guests in their households" is also a common stipulation about exemption from the military's quartering of private

---

34 H. Inalcik, "Dār al-'Ahd", *EI*², II, p. 116.

35 Text ed. Pertusi, I, p. 47: "fece fare poi l'inventario di tutti i beni dei *mercanti* e degli abitanti del borgo che sono scappiva". Also Lomellino distinctly refers to "compagnie commerciali".

houses;[36] this has sometimes mistakenly been interpreted as "no Turk or Sultan's official will be allowed to settle in Pera", and the settlement of Turks in Pera was mistakenly interpreted as a breach of promise.

I believe the article "I will not go against them and demolish their fortress" which caused a great deal of debate simply means: "I promise not to declare war against them nor to expose them to the soldiery's looting". In actual fact, he ordered parts of the city's land walls to be demolished while leaving the sea walls[37] intact before he set out for Edirne on June 18, 1453.[38] Attack by a Crusaders' fleet, and the resistance of the Genoese of Galata, were always possibilities.

Before he left, the Sultan appointed Karadja, one of his *ḳuls,* as *subashı* or *voyvoda* over Galata. Mentioned in the survey of 1455, ḥe must have been the first *voyvoda* of Ottoman Galata.

Critique of L. Sauli / M.-A. Belin's Interpretation

According to Sauli, as summarized by M. Belin[39] , immediately after the conquest of Istanbul, Mehmed II sent Zaghanos Pasha to Galata to persuade the Genoese to stay in their homes and assure them of the renewal of the treaties formerly made between them and the Byzantine emperors, which guaranteed the autonomous existence of Pera under the Genoese administration. Then, the Conqueror accusing them of not having abided by the agreement not to aid the Greeks during the siege, changed his initial promise and said to them that from now on they should be content with his decision. The Genoese were now anxious to renew the capitulatory privileges that were previously granted. Therefore, the Genoese envoys presented the Sultan with the texts and asked for the renewal of the capitulations given by Orkhān and Murād I, as well as those given by Mehmed II himself, upon his accession to the Ottoman throne, dated 7 *Ṣafar* 855/March 11, 1451.

---

36 For such exemptions see P. Wittek, "Zu einigen...", *WZKM,* vol. 54, pp. 240-255; vol. 57, pp. 102-117.

37 The *Podestà* Lomellino wrote: "*fece abbattere i borghi e parte dei fossati della fortificazione, fece demolire La Torre di Santa Croce, mentre lasciò in piedi soltanto parte della cortina che si trova tra la zona merlata e parte dei barbacani, e ha intenzione di prendersi tutte le munizioni e tutte le armi degli abitanti del borgo*". For the repairs under Bāyezīd II see Evliyā Çelebi, *Seyāhatnāme,* I, pp. 428-429; Belin, *Latinité,* pp. 158-159; S. Eyice, *Galata and its Tower,* Istanbul, 1969, pp. 43-77.

38 In Doucas, p. 241, his departure date is given as June 18, 1453; for discussion of this date see Pertusi, *La Caduta,* I, p. 372, note 11.

39 *Latinité,* p. 155.

Belin believes[40] that the document given by the Sultan is nothing but the renewal of the Ottoman capitulations and the abolition of the autonomy of the Genoese of Pera. "On peut considérer cette capitulation de Mehemmed II, comme l'origine de la communauté dite des Latins", or *millet-i re'āyā-i Latin* as expressed on the seal of the chief of the chancery of the community. In other words, Sauli/Belin believe that the new Genoese status was not different in any way from that of the foreign communities living in the Ottoman Empire under the guarantees of the capitulations.

This interpretation is not correct because, as explained above, the document specifies those Genoese who chose to stay permanently in Pera, and thus became *dhimmī* subjects *(re'āyā)* of the Empire along with the payment of the *kharādj/djizya,* poll-tax while the Genoese merchants, clearly distinguished in the *'ahd-nāme* and the survey of 1455 as remaining the subjects of Genoa, could only enjoy the immunities contained in the capitulations. The failure to understand this essential point has always been the source of misinterpretations concerning this document.

True, the Genoese *re'āyā* had a new organization according to the stipulations of the *'ahd-nāme*, which, Belin himself stresses, had nothing to do with "a corps municipal, civil et religieux".[41] The activities of *la Magnifica Comunità di Pera,* as described by Belin,[42] reveal no political character. In fact, they were not even given the status of a *ṭā'ife* or *millet* - status which the Greeks and Armenians enjoyed. The Latin *re'āyā* of Galata now had a council of twelve which appointed officers exclusively to run the affairs of the churches in the community, including the churches of St Anne, St Benedict, St John, St Sebastian, St Anthony, and St George in Galata, and St Mary and St Nicolas in Istanbul.[43] The community met at the church of St Anne and was called the *confraternity of St Anne.* The officers were responsible in their religious administration to the Roman Catholic Church, specifically to the *Cardinale Protettore di Levante* and the Patriarchal Vicar of Constantinople. Since the Papacy never accepted a peace settlement with the Ottomans and was always the initiator and the force behind the Crusades against the Ottoman Empire, the Sultans, dating back to the fourteenth century, banned the Latin Church from its territory while they recognized and officially supported the Greek Orthodox and Armenian Churches. However, those Catholics living within the Empire were given a special *amān* in order that they could live in security and exercise their religion freely as a simple

---

40 *Ibid.,* pp. 159-161.

41 *Ibid.,* p. 167.

42 *Ibid.,* pp. 167-173.

43 This is based on the statement made in 1583, see Belin, *op.cit.,* pp. 168-169.

religious community *(djemā'at)*. In the official Ottoman records, the Latin community of Istanbul is referred to as *Latin Djemā'ati* and its head who was authorized to look after its affairs and represent it with the Ottoman government was called *vekīl,* agent (in the *'ahd-nāme, prôtogeros or ketkhudā;* in the *Podestà*'s letter, *capitano*).[44]

The following imperial order[45] dated January 9, 1907 makes clear the status of the Latins in Istanbul:

Since there is no officially recognized religious head *(re'īs)* or specific Church for the Latin subjects of the Ottoman Empire living in Istanbul, they used to go to the churches belonging to the foreign communities for their religious services, and their religious affairs were dealt with by the foreign priests. The settlement of their daily affairs *(maṣāliḥ-i 'ādiyye)* was entrusted to an agent *(vekīl)* who contacted the Ottoman authorities when need be... and they do not have an organization like the Greek and Armenian Patriarcates... but rather an agency *(Latin Vekāleti)* similar to a district community representative *(mukhtarlıḳ).*

In brief, modern authors, like the contemporary Greek and Latin sources, blame the Sultan for not keeping his promises and for violating his sworn pledges. Obviously, the Conqueror changed his attitude toward the Genoese of Pera as the situation changed, and both the threat of a western Crusade and the Sultan's concern of not causing the ruin of the city influenced the judgement of the Ottoman government. But it should be remembered that the surprise and disappointment of those who submitted might also have been due to the lack of knowledge on their part about the implications of submission in Islamic Law. On the other hand, it should not be forgotten that the feelings of the underprivileged majority of the population in Galata, including the Greeks, Armenians and Jews might not have been supportive of their Genoese masters who were now completely at the mercy of the Sultan. The social and economic conflict between the "natives" and the privileged Genoese who monopolized the lucrative overseas trade used to create constant disagreement and periodic explosions in the Genoese colonies in the Levant. Also it must be remembered that there was a deep-seated hatred among the Greeks towards the Genoese. During the two centuries long conflict, the Genoese captured all the east Aegean islands and the Black Sea trade from the Greeks; and they made the population of Constantinople dependent upon the Genoese for its wheat and fish supplies from the Northern Black Sea, and ultimately, Pera became an economically dominant

---

44 Pertusi, p. 49.

45 The Osmanlı Arşivi, Istanbul, *İrāde Dosyaları, Djemā'at-i Ghayr-i Müslime,* no. 62.

city in the face of Constantinople.[46] The prominent Greeks who ransomed themselves after the fall of Byzantium came to settle in Galata. Under Mehmed II, the Greek tax farmers of Galata, in collaboration with the Greeks of Istanbul and Trebizond, became the leading financiers of the Empire while the Greek converts assumed as vizirs the highest responsibility in the government.[47]

The Ottomans definitely took advantage of such a hatred and tension. As a matter of fact, with the Ottoman take over of the Genoese colonies in Pera (1453), Caffa (1475), and Kilia and Akkerman (1484), the "natives" soon replaced the Genoese in the trade between Asia Minor and the Northern Black Sea port cities; and along with the Turkish merchants and shipowners, the Armenians, Jews and Greeks acquired a dominant position in commerce with Lithuania, Poland and Muscovy. At Lwów (Lemberg), the emporium of oriental goods, Indian spices, Bursa silk fabrics and Aegean wines, the Armenian colony played a dominant role thanks to their connections with Pera and Bursa.[48] Even the *dhimmī* Genoese of Pera profited from the change since in their new status they benefited from Ottoman protection and a lower rate of customs duties -- 2 percent as against 4 percent. Using the Genoese documents of the Ottoman period, G. Pistarino came to the conclusion that the Genoese of Pera resumed their business activities under normal conditions under the Ottomans (see *infra).*

In the period after the Ottoman defeat at Vienna in 1683, when the Ottoman government began to seek the diplomatic support of western nations, particularly France, and gave new privileges under the capitulations, the Latin community strengthened its presence at Pera. Also, the Papacy's policy and the activities of the missions in Turkey which were strongly supported by France, were instrumental in the developments of the period. Despite the fact that Galata and Beyoğlu were considered by their lifestyle as part of *Frengistān,* or Europe, by the Ottomans themselves and that the Catholic nations with their embassies and churches achieved[49] a growing

---

46 A. Laiou, *Constantinople and the Latins,* Cambridge, Mass., 1972.

47 H. Inalcik,"Notes on N. Beldiceanu's Translation of the *Ḳānūnnāme* fonds turcs ancien 39, Bibliothèque Nationale, Paris", *Der Islam,* vol. 43/1-2 (1967), pp. 153-157.

48 M. Berindei, "L'Empire ottoman et la 'route moldave' avant la conquête de Chilia et Cetătea-albă (1484)", *Journal of Turkish Studies,* vol. X (1989), pp. 47-72, and the literature therein.

49 Evliyā Çelebi, I, p. 431, made the remark that there was no tomb of a Muslim saint *(ziyāretgāh)* in Galata. According to an early 19th century document (Topkapı P. Ar., D. 8803), on the waterfront of Galata from Meyyit İskelesi to the Tophane gate "those places where prohibited things took place", the inns *(han)* and cellars *(mağaza)* as well as rooms *(oda)* on the upper floors of the coffee houses, barber shops or groceries were

presence and influence in Galata, no change occurred in the status of the Latin *re'āyā* of Pera. The distorted interpretation of the 'ahdnāme of Mehmed II as a treaty guaranteeing the administrative, and even political autonomy of Pera/Galata has been to this date favored by some Levantines and those westerners who grew into a large community in Galata in the course of the nineteenth century.[50]

I The Ottoman Survey of 1455

While I was conducting research on the history of Istanbul under Ottoman rule, the late Professor Bekir Sıtkı Baykal of Ankara University kindly showed me, and allowed me to use, a photocopy of an Ottoman survey book of Istanbul and Galata. The document, he said, was in the Turkish archives, but is not catalogued. So I had to rely on his photocopy without seeing the original.[51] The survey, which was made two and a half years after the surrender of the city, is a unique document on the population, topography, and economic situation of the city during the first years of Ottoman rule (for sample pages see Appendix 5).

In the *'ahd-nāme (supra)* it was expressly stated:

I impose upon them (the submitted Genoese) Islamic *kharādj* which they pay each year as other non-Muslims [in my dominions] do.

It was Djübbe 'Alī Bey, then the governor of Bursa, who was entrusted with the task of conducting the survey of Istanbul and Galata in 1455. He chose his cousin, Ṭursun Beg, the famous historian of the reign of Mehmed

---

pulled down by the order of the Sultan. They numbered altogether 469 in Kalkan-Yeri, Çeşme-Meydanı, Yağ-Kapanı, Kürkçüler-Başı, Kara-Köy, Balık-Pazarı, Kurşunlu-Mahzen, Mumhane, Tophane-Kapısı, Kule-Kapısı and Sandık-Başı. An additional 108 rooms *(oda)* in Kasım-Paşa in the quarters of Lonca, Sel-Kuyusu and Yağhane were also pulled down. Galata imported 771 casks *(fuçı)* of wine annually (Topkapı P. Ar., D. 8979).

50 Louis Mitler, "The Genoese in Galata: 1453-1682", *IJMES,* 10 (1979), p. 74: "The merchants immediately surrendered the colony to the Turks and obtained a treaty granting all the rights and privileges formerly enjoyed under the Paleologi".

51 I am trying to discover the original to prepare an edition of this important document for publication. The non-Turkish names in the survey are transliterated here as they appear in the Turkish text. Since in rendering the names in Arabic letters the scribe did not always put vowels, it is not certain how we should transliterate some names. For example نقروز can be read Nikiroz, Nikeroz or Nikoroz. Also there are inconsistencies in the text for the same name. We find for example the forms اسكنوپلوق and اسكنه پلوق. I attempted to identify and render the original form only for a few well known names. It is likely that a Greek helped the Ottoman surveyor in the registration process, as some of the Italian names were apparently grecized. A more systematic effort will be made for the identification of names in the edition of the survey book.

the Conqueror, as scribe *(kātib)* of the survey.[52] In his history, Ṭursun Beg describes[53] the purpose and the general background of the registration.

After the conquest of Constantinople, Mehmed II declared that anyone, either of upper or lower class, who comes of his own free will and takes possession and resides in a house which has been abandoned by its former non-Muslim resident, will become the proprietor of that house. Thereupon, people rich and poor, flocked into the city and occupied houses and palaces. Thus, the population increased in the city. Later the Sultan issued another edict to the effect that all such houses shall be registered and each charged with a rent *(muḳāṭa'a)* suitable for its conditions. The explanation given for that was that in principle what was granted as freehold *(tamlīk)* was the building; the ground itself belonged to the *waḳf* (for the mosque of Ayasofya). The plot of the building could not be held without a rent.

The actual registration business, Ṭursun tells us,[54] was quite strenuous:

> Going from house to house and visiting each room of all low and high buildings in the city, the houses, gardens and vineyards were written down and a rent for each was determined. Because of this registration many houses changed hands. For instance, a person who was not able to pay the rent on the plot in his possession had to leave the house and get another one suitable for his means. When the register was completed and submitted to the Sultan it became apparent that approximately two thousand *fuçı,* or 100 million aḳça in annual revenue was realized. But immediately after, the Sultan, out of his favors, granted the rent to his *ḳul*s and subjects and ordered that certificates, adorned with his *tughra,* be given to them free from any charge of rent *(muḳāṭa'a).*

Ṭursun adds[55] that at an appropriate time, an intimate of the Sultan asked him why in the registration of Istanbul an unnecessary job had been done and why the Sultan had renounced his own promise. The Sultan replied that the real purpose of the registration and imposition of rent was not to collect new revenues but simply to make sure that a big house appropriated by a man of low income should pass to someone who would be able to do all the necessary repairs and prevent the building from falling into disrepair. Ṭursun

---

[52] See Inalcik, "Tursun Beg, Historian of Mehmed the Conqueror", *WZKM,* 69 (1977), pp. 55-71.

[53] Tursun Beg, *The History of Mehmed the Conqueror,* eds. H. Inalcik and R. Murphey, Chicago and Minneapolis, 1978, Text: ff. 53b-55b.

[54] *Ibid.,* f. 53b.

[55] *Ibid.,* ff. 54b-55b.

Beg does not give any details of the methods under which Galata was surveyed. But as is clear from the survey itself, the initial purpose was to impose a poll-tax on the non-Muslim *dhimmī* population and a rent on the buildings. These two impositions are separately shown under the terms of *djizya* and *muḳāṭa'a* or *idjār* or *udjra (üdjret)* in the survey book.[56]

Here is the introduction to the survey book (see Appendix 5):

This is a copy of the survey book of the population and the houses of the city of Galata to ascertain who is subject to *djizya* and who is not and who is wealthy and who is poor and which houses are *emīrīye,* i.e. state owned, subject to rent or without rent with their annual or monthly rents. [This survey is made] by the order of Sultan Meḥmed, son of Sultan Murād... in the first days of the month of *Muḥarrem* of the year 860 of Hidjra/11-21 December, 1455.

Unfortunately, parts of the document are missing, especially for the western quarters of Galata (for the parts dealing with Istanbul, see my article "Istanbul", *EI*², III, 238). The information we are going to give concerns only the central and eastern parts of Galata

---

[56] The detailed description (Donado da Lezze, pp. 72-80) of how the Ottomans registered the non-Muslim population following the surrender of Caffa in 1475 can give an idea of the case of Galata. The Genoese of Caffa surrendered the city upon an *'ahd-nāme* similar to that of Pera, guaranteeing the security of life and property on condition that all indigenous population had to pay an annual *kharādj.* Since they did not know how such pledges were actually applied in accordance with the *Sharī'a* and Ottoman laws, the Caffans believed they would continue to live in their city without change as before. But immediately after the conclusion of the agreement Aḥmed Pasha occupied the city, captured all those foreign soldiers who had fought against the Ottomans, and sold them as slaves. Then he ordered the registration of all the inhabitants of the city and Franks (Latins), with information on each one's financial condition and possessions, marital status, children, home country and duration of his stay in Caffa. This survey was necessary to apply Ottoman regulations designed for each different group. Distinguished from the native population, all of the Latins were subject to deportation as the ruling elite in the city. In Caffa, contrary to the exemption granted to the Perans, the Ottoman practice of *devshirme,* the levy of children for the Sultan's palace and the janissary corps, was applied and three thousand (?) children between 10 to 20 years of age and 450 selected ones were levied and taken to Istanbul. About 3,000 slaves who were found in the hands of Caffans were also taken away. Then, announcing the completion of the survey, the Ottoman commander asked the citizens to resume their everyday occupation without fear. But immediately after, the Latins learned, in great surprise, the new command of Aḥmed Pasha to the effect that they had to surrender half of their possessions to the Ottoman fisc and carry them aboard the ships to be taken to Istanbul. A contemporary Armenian source (see Cazacu, pp. 514-537) confirms the basic points in the story. According to this source, following the surrender of the fortress upon a sworn pledge of amnesty, the Ottomans registered people, collected arms and imposed "tribute" *(kharādj)* on the indigenous population, i.e., Greeks, Armenians and Jews. All of their possessions were recorded in the registers.

Quarters and Houses in the Survey of 1455

Most of the names of the quarters in the survey book (see Table 1) can be identified as names of persons living in the city at the time. The quarters, *contrade* under the Genoese administration, often bore the name of a Genoese family, and apparently the Ottoman surveying in 1455 followed the Genoese division of the *contrade.* Thus, the Genoese *contrade* of Draperiis, in our survey Drpoza, was named after the rich Peran family of Draperiis. The following persons gave their names to the quarters they lived in:

1. Zani Drapoza who lived in the quarter of Drapoza; a member of a wealthy family (see *infra),* he stayed on under Ottoman rule. Another member of the family, Djan Drapoza, sold a bath house in the quarter of Fabya to Ḥādjī Meḥmed of Ankara, while Pero Drapoza had two houses in the Jewish quarter.

2. Zani Dabdañ, after whose name the second quarter in the survey was called, was a poor man at the time of the survey.

3. Nikoroz Sikay, a man of average means, lived in the quarter named after him.

4. Nikoroz Bonazonda and his brother Zorzo lived in the quarter named Nikoroz Bonazita.

5. Anton di Garzan, a poor man, and his father Rafa di Garzan, lived in the quarter named Anton di Garzan.[57]

6. Kosta and Andrea Iskinaplok lived in the quarter of Kosta İskinaplok.

7. In the quarter of Gargondji lived a certain Gargondji.

8. In the quarter of Papa Yani lived a certain Papa Yani.

9. In the quarter of Zani di Pagani lived Zani, Zorzo, and Mekdad di Pagana. In a Genoese notarial document of 1459[58] we find a certain Valentino de Pagano in Chios, probably a relative of our Pagani.

10. Pero di Lankashko who evidently gave his name to the quarter of Pero di Lankashko (Langasco), belonged to a well known wealthy family in Pera and Chios. Zani, Luviz, and Andjelo di Lankashko had several houses in Pera and Chios. Zani and Luviz apparently left Pera while Pero di Langasco lived on in the quarter of Zani Dabdañ. A Benedetto de Langasco

---

[57] *Il Libro dei Conti di Giacomo Badoer,* ed. U. Dorini and T. Bertelè, Roma, 1956, contains the name of a certain Franceso di Garzoni, doing business in the Levant in 1439.

[58] Ph. P. Argenti, *The occupation of Chios by the Genoese and their administration of the island: 1346-1566,* I, Cambridge 1958, p. 459.

(Langascho) lived in Chios around 1460.[59] The Daryovas, Luviz and Operto, represented another wealthy family who lived in this quarter. Daryovas possessed properties in various quarters in Pera at the time of the survey.

11. In the quarter of Yorgi Argendjelu, a certain Yorgi Arganzele had a house, but he left Pera after the conquest.

12. The quarter of Ayodhkimo Manderino must have been named after Ayodhkimo Manderina, a wealthy man who, with his son Yani Manderina, became an Ottoman subject and stayed on.

13. Yani Vasilikov, a man recorded in the survey book as of average means, lived in the quarter of Yani Vasilikov.

Since many of the quarters bore the names of the persons who lived in Pera as Ottoman subjects at the time of the survey, we can speculate that the Ottoman surveyor named the quarters after the persons who seemed to him as representative of the quarter at that time. The other quarters bear the names of either the religious-ethnic groups, such as *Maḥalle-i Yahūdiyān* or *Asudar Ermeniyān,* or of the chief church in the quarter such as *Maḥalle-i Fabya,* after *the church* of San Fabyan (Plan I, Galata 1455).

Evidently, particular ethnic-religious groups were assembled in different sectors of the city. Italians were to be found in a majority in the quarters within the first Genoese enclosure in Sykai between Azeb-Kapu and Karaköy-Kapu on the slope toward the Galata Kulesi (the Tower of Christ) in the quarters of Zani Drapoza, Zani Dabdañ, Nikoroz Sikay (Sykai), Nikoroz Bonazita, Anton di Garzan, Zani di Pagani, İskinoplok (İskinaplok), Fabya, and Pero di Lankashko. The checkerboard arrangement of streets in this section as against the casual development of the street plan in other sections is noteworthy.[60] The main Latin churches –San Domenigo, San Francesco, Santa Anna, San Michele, Santa Maria and San Fabyan– were all in this sector. Near the market hall, nine adjacent shops, formerly in the hands of *Podestas,*, were made state property and were rented to Italians such as Karlo Konfroti (Confortus?), Domenico Lansavidjo, Zani di Milo, Martin Paravazin

---

59 *Ibid.;* a Iohannes de Langascho is referred to in the *cartularium* of 1377 of the Genoese customs, see John Day, *Les Douanes de Gênes, 1376-1377,* II, Paris, 1963, p. 814; the *Podestà* of Pera sent Bartolomeo di Langasco, a resident of Galata, with the envoys from Genoa to Bāyezīd I in September 1391 (Balard, I, p. 98). Evidently, the Langasco family was well known to the Ottomans by 1455. Earlier, we find Bartolomeo as a tax farmer of the customs revenues at Licostomo *(Ibid.,* pp. 146-147).

60 See Balarad, I, pp. 179-192; Evliyā Çelebi, I, p. 433, noticed this characteristic of the original Genoese city. He says that the part of Galata from the seashore to the tower is occupied by the Genoese buildings and the streets there are arranged "in checkerboard fashion" *(s̲h̲aṭrandj-vārī).*

and others. Five shops near the market hall were in the hands of Karadja, the *subashı, or,* governor of Galata in 1455. Also, the business quarter with the market hall, the *Ḳabbān-i Emīrīye* under the Ottomans, the two *Logia,* ancient and new, and several soap factories were located in this section, behind the *Londja (Logia)* gate, later known as *Eski-Yagh-Ḳapanı* gate with the main quay or landing place, *Iskele.*[61] It formed the main shopping area with 41 of the 58 shops in the section of Galata covered by our document.[62] The other shopping area was around San Michele church, already mentioned in 1296 as the cathedral church of the colony, was located in this initial trade center of the Genoese. After the conquest, the trade center behind the *Londja* gate evidently continued its function. Under the Ottomans, later on, the main commercial center of Galata, with the *Bedestān* and Rüstem Pasha caravanserai, was to develop here right behind the *Londja-Kapu.* In scenic views and plans of Istanbul this point is always shown crowded with big round ships. The street leading to the *Bash-Ḥiṣar* (Galata Tower) on the hill, later on called the *Perşenbe-Pazarı* street, was the major thoroughfare of the city with the city's main buildings on either side — the San Michele Church, *Logia* and *Palazzo del Comune.* It continued to be the main street of Galata under the Ottomans until the Karaköy bridge was built in 1845. However, the Karaköy - Pazarı too appears to have been an important business area already in the fifteenth and sixteenth centuries Ottoman surveys.[63]

Buildings and their Possessors

The buildings are categorized as *khāne* (houses), *dükkān* (shops), *burghāz-i emīrīye* (forts at the city walls), *kenīsā* (church), *zāviye* (convent), and *djumarākhāne* (house endowed for the poor). Houses were also classified as inhabited by people *(mutamakkin* or *sākin)* or uninhabited *(khālī),* or in ruins *(kharāb),* or *waḳf* (endowed to a church or synagogue). In the totals for the houses it is specified how many are *emīrīye,* state-owned, and how many are freehold property, and how many pay rent for the house or the plot belonging to the state *(muḳāṭa'a-i arḍ-i emīrī)* (see Table II). Then, under a separate heading, *ru'ūs* (adult people) are recorded as those who were subject to pay *djizya* and those exempted from it. Those living in the same house are

---

61 The old *logia (loggia)* was built in 1316 (Balard, I, p. 193).

62 In his picture of Galata, Maṭraḳdjı (see View III) showed these two business areas in two blocks of shops with men working in them, one behind the sea wall, the other near the *'Arab Djāmi'i* (San Domenigo). Another such block of shops is shown in his picture near Tophane-Kapı behind the sea wall. Pictures of such blocks of shops are used by the painter as a symbol of bazaar areas throughout his work; for earlier views and plans see Oberhummer, Tafel XXII.

63 Cf. Pistarino, p. 75: "the bazaar near the Santa Chiara".

referred to as *be-hem,* together. Woman are registered as *dhimmīya, adjūza* (old), *bīwa* (widow).

It should be kept in mind that the survey document has reached us in an incomplete form, covering only 25 quarters in the central part of the city (see Table I). In these 25 quarters, there were 908 houses with a population of 1108 individuals. The Conqueror had declared that those who returned within three months were to keep their properties, so that their houses were sealed and the properties registered in June 1453.[64] Our survey shows that there were indeed people who returned and recovered ownership of their houses. Those who did not return or were captured on the day of the conquest made up about eight percent of the total population recorded. The houses of all those captured or classified as non-returned became the property of the state, as did the houses whose proprietors left no heirs *(bayt al-māl).*

Those who stayed on, or whose wives did so, or who left the city later on with the permission of the Ottoman authorities, retained ownership of their houses. Thus, the great majority of the houses were left in the possession of their former owners. Among those who ran away or were captured, Italians made up about 60% and Greeks 35%. Only two Armenians were on this list, and apparently no Jews. It seems that in order to avoid confiscation, some Genoese left their wives or slaves behind on their properties while they themselves left the city.

In view of the fact that half the state-owned houses could not find a renter and many houses were unoccupied or fell in ruin, the situation must still have

---

64 The *Podestà* of Galata, Angelo Giovanni Lomellino and Doucas concur in observing that Sultan wanted the Genoese merchants and citizens of Galata *(mercanti e abitanti)* who had fled to come back and recover their possessions. Lomellino says" *fece fare poi l'inventario di tutti i beni dei mercanti e degli abitanti del borgo che sono scappivia, dicendo: 'Se torneranno, saranno loro restituti; se non torneranno, rimarranno di proprieta del signore'. Per questa ragione abbiamo ottenuto dal signore una lettera assieme ad un messaggero da inviare a Chio, per far presente a tutti mercanti ed abitanti del borgo fuggiti di qui che possono tornare e che ritornando rientreranno in possesso dei loro beni; e abbiamo avvisato tutti i mercanti che i veneziani hanno abbandonato qui tutti i loro magazzeni pieni di merci. Quanto agli abitanti del borgo che se n'erano andati con le loro famiglie... con i loro familiari, ho fatto loro sapere con lo stesso messagio che tutti i genovesi potevano* [riprendere] *navigare in questo zone* (ed. Pertusi, *La Caduta,* pp. 47 and 373 note 14). And Doucas says: "On the fifth day Mehmed visited Galata ordering a census taken of all the inhabitants and he found that many of the homes had been bolted because the Latins had fled in the ships. He ordered that the homes be opened and an inventory be taken of their belongings. He stipulated that should the owners return within a period of three months, they would be allowed to repossess their possessions but if they failed to return all would then be confiscated by the ruler. Afterwards, he commanded the entire army with the assistance of the outlying villages to demolish the walls of Galata. [...] the land walls were overthrown but the walls along the harbor were allowed to stand" (trans. H. J. Magoulias, pp. 240-241).

been quite unstable two and a half years after the Ottoman occupation. In the meantime, some of those who returned to become subjects of the Sultan by paying the *djizya* left the city again. The abandoned and unoccupied houses numbered about one tenth of the total. Thirty one houses were endowed to the churches or were made into shelters for the poor *(djumarā)*. The houses converted into state property were leased out to anyone ready to pay the rent. As a rule, the occupants at the moment of the survey were subjected to the rent estimated by the surveyor. Rents varied from 1 to 10 gold ducats. The houses left in the possession of their former owners were charged only a land tax, *muḳāṭa'a-i arḍ*. This tax or rent, estimated for each case individually by the surveyor varied between 1/2 to 7 gold pieces. Many houses once in the possession of Genoese were now rented to poor people or to Jews, Greeks, or Armenians by the treasury. This situation considerably altered the social and ethnic character of the Italian quarters after the Ottoman occupation. In the survey, *khāne*, residence, was entered as a single unit even though it sometimes included more than one house or even shops.[65] To most of the churches were annexed several houses in which priests or religious servants usually lived. Sixteen houses of this character are recorded in the survey. An interesting sample is the church and abbey of San Benito.[66] Located in the Armenian neighborhood, the church, *kenīsā*, had as its annex three houses occupied by Nikola, the Armenian priest, and two other Armenians. In the church itself there were eight monks, all free from *djizya*. But a big house near the church was the subject of a dispute between a certain Armenian Gülshā Khātūn and Franks.

Many buildings fell into ruin after the conquest as a result of being neglected or left unoccupied. Repairs in the state-owned houses were the responsibility of the treasury; but by a special agreement the lessee undertook repairs in return for a reduction in the original rent.

In the big houses, several families often lived together. An interesting example is the house of Festodjon, in the quarter of Zani Dabdañ, which housed several wealthy Genoese merchants. Festodjon, a wealthy man, agreed to pay the *djizya*, and thus became a subject of the Sultan, while his wife left the city. Later on he followed his wife. Also in the same house lived Karyaba (?) Saraviko, a wealthy *dhimmī*, Markiz di Franko, recorded as a wealthy *dhimmī*, evidently the same person who was sent by the *Podestà* to

---

65 We translated *khāne (hāne)* as house, not as family, because the shops and *khānes*, were added together. *Khāne* here must mean a residence, housing a nuclear or extended family. On the other hand, as observed in Galata, a large building housed several families.

66 See Belin, *La Latinité*, pp. 232-270; E. d'Alessio, "Recherches", *Échos d'Orient*, vol. XXIV, pp. 32-33; Schneider, *op.cit.*, pp. 22-23.

the Sultan in 1453; his brother Lujad, a wealthy *dhimmī;* three wealthy Genoese merchants — Akostin Larka, Djorma Masura, Djorma di Frank—, Yani Konori, of average means and free of *djizya;* and Zani Das, a wealthy merchant and an unmarried *dhimmī.* In the same quarter lived many other wealthy Italians such as Kristofa Paravazin probably a relative of Babilan Paravazin, the envoy sent to Meḥmed II in 1453, Luviz Darva, Anton Gara, Angelo di Lankasko, and Amperto Bavilana, who were all Ottoman subjects paying the poll tax. Also in the quarter were endowed houses in which monks lived together.

Population

Composed of four main groups, namely Genoese, Greeks, Armenians and Jews, the population of Galata prior to the Ottoman occupation was analogous to that of Caffa (see Table I and Plan of Galata, 1455). These two most important Genoese cities in the Levant were in close contact with each other, people shifting from one to the other.

Franks

In our survey book, the Genoese of Galata formed three groups under a different status according to Islamic Law. The first group was composed of those Genoese classified as non-Muslims from the *Dār al-Ḥarb,* the Abode of War, who lived in the Islamic territory under the capitulatory guarantees. These Genoese were not subject to *djizya* so long as their stay did not exceed one year.[67] They were entered into the survey book under the term *Djeneviz* (Genoese) *tādjiri,* or simply *Frenk,* or *Efrendjī* and no *djizya* was imposed upon them *(bī-djizya).* At the time of the survey, a group of them stayed together in the house of Festodjon in the quarter of Zani Dabdañ. Also in the quarter of Anton di Garzan, the Genoese merchant Duka Kanata (Caneto?) and the Venetian Manakka, both free from *djizya,* rented a house belonging to Anton Karantiya, although the house was later made state property. In the same quarter, the wealthy Genoese Anton di Rotori (Retori), Zano Bisuda and Anton Drizide, all free from *djizya,* rented for 200 akça (about 5 Venetian ducats) a year, a house and three shops that formerly belonged to Toma Miso who was living in Genoa at the time of the survey. The quarter of Zani di Pagani was another quarter chosen by the Genoese merchants to live in. In this quarter Leonardo Waldjo and Operto Penlo were both registered as wealthy Genoese free from *djizya* (see also Table II).

---

[67] See H. İnalcık, "Imtiyāzāt", *EI*[2], III, pp. 1179-1189.

The second group was composed of those who stayed on in Pera and, by paying the Islamic poll tax, *djizya,* became *dhimmī,* subjects of the Ottoman state. These constituted by far the greater part of the Genoese in Ottoman Galata. As *djizya*-payers they were classified into three categories, wealthy *(ghanī),* of average means *(avsaṭ),* and poor *(faḳīr),* since the rate of the poll tax differed for each category in Islamic Law.[68] There was only one example of a Genoese adopting Islam. Zenato Borselo, evidently a rich man who ran away on the day of the conquest and then returned, adopted Islam and disappeared again. His house with five shops in the quarter Zani di Pagani were confiscated. As noted earlier, these two groups, *muste'min*s under the capitulatory regime, and *dhimmīs,* non-Muslim subjects of the Islamic state, were distinguished in the firman issued at the time of surrender on June 1, 1453. In his letter of June 23, 1453 the *Podestà* Lomellino distinguished them as *mercanti* and *abitanti.* Evidently, *abitanti* were the Genoese who settled in Galata as indigenous inhabitants.

Captives, whether Italian, Greek or Armenian, made up the third group who were also treated according to the strict stipulations of Islamic Law. Those persons who were captured in their attempt to run away at the time of surrender were either freed upon payment of ransom or made *mukāteb,*[69] that is, set free under contract in order to make enough money to pay their ransom within a defined period of time. *Mukāteb*s were all free from *djizya.* The following are examples of the third group: Zani Messina, who was captured but paid his ransom and left for Italy; Yorgi Poskinos, who with his wife was made *mukāteb,* lived in a house belonging to the church Iplakhosa. Likewise, Praskoya registered his wife as *mukāteb* and lived in a house endowed to the monastery San Zani. The slave Theodoros Sankato lived with his wife in a house of which she retained proprietorship. Marya and his son, both *mukāteb,* lived in the house of Manul, a shoemaker in the quarter of Nikoroz Sikay. Zani Russo, captured the day of the surrender, still kept his slave status at the time of the survey. That he was allowed to stay in his house must

---

68 See "Djizya" *EI*²; the rate of the *djizya* was to be determined by the Imam/Sultan according to the rate stipulated by Islamic Law. For practical reasons, the Ottomans in general collected *djizya* at the rate of one gold piece per household since submitted Christian masses in the Balkans used to pay a similer hearth tax in the pre-Ottoman era. According to Benedetto Dei (Belgrano, p. 227, note 2) "Maometto II obbligò tutti gli abitanti di Pera a paghare ogni anno un duchato per ocha, cosi povero chome richo". Despite the fact that non-Muslims were specified as wealthy, of average means, and poor, Dei's testimony must be true. A Genoese source (Sauli, p. 172 cited by Mitler, p. 75) tells us that "Mehmed imposed a 2-5 percent capital tax upon the non-Muslims". This must refer to the rent *(muḳāṭa'a)* imposed on the houses.

69 For *mukātaba* in Islamic Law and Ottoman practice see İnalcık, "Servile Labor" in the Bibliography.

be due to an agreement with his master or to the Sultan's special order. *Mukātebs* and slaves permitted to live in Galata numbered fifteen persons, mostly Latins.

Greeks

In 1455, the Greek population was concentrated in the quarters around the first Genoese city, namely in those of Dhraperyo, Gargandji, Papa Yani, Pero di Lankashko, Varto Khristo, Kosta Lupadji, Ayodhkimo Manderino, and Yani Visilikov. And the main Greek churches, Kasteliutissa (Gennisis Theotokhu), Ayios Nikolas, and Papa Yani, were located in the eastern section of Galata towards the Tophane-Kapı between the Jewish and Armenian quarters (see Plan I). There was another concentration of Greeks in the quarter of Iskinoplok, to the north of the first Genoese city, around the former Byzantine church of Aya Yorgi. Located in the eastern part of the second sector and enclosed by the Genoese walls, the quarter encompassed the *palazzo del comune* and the San Pietro Church. But, in the western section of the main street near the Tower of Christ, Genoese seem to have been in the majority. Most of the Greeks living in the quarter were poor people, shoemakers or porters. I counted twelve porters out of 31 residents of the quarter. A large residence with a garden was comprised of eight houses belonging to Andon di Liko before the conquest, but subsequently it was converted into state property. Its occupants included five Greek porters and their relatives. In the same quarter lived Pero Spinora, a wealthy Italian who left for Europe before the conquest but whose wife stayed on and paid the *djizya* for him. The residence of the monk Francesco with two shops and two storehouses was turned into state property and rented by an Armenian. Zorzi and Luviz de Kanya and Luviz Daryo owned houses in the same quarter.

The Greek quarter where the wealthy Greeks lived was that of Varto Khristo. In the quarter, Kosta Istasno (Stasinos), Kosta Hovaru (Khovaras), Yorgi Hovaru, Kosta Melonlahti (Melanolokhti), Yorgi Proskoga, Mikhal Mazulu, Yani Hovaru, Yani Istimad, Manoli Darpatu, Mikhal Djimorti, Sutyani Lipodhyani, Ditrano Likofas were all recorded as wealthy *dhimmīs*. Greeks were engaged primarily in trades or crafts as shoemakers, bakers, tailors, weavers, porters, *boza* makers, or keepers of wine shops. Among the Greeks of Galata at least seven persons were identified as being of Caffan origin, including one bearing a Turkish name, Asil Beg.

Armenians

Armenians made up Galata's third largest population group after the Greeks and the Franks (Latins) in 1455. They lived in majority in the borough of

Lagirio to the east, annexed by the Genoese around 1330.[70] Clustering around San Benito and Aya Khorkhoro (St Gregor) churches, these quarters included Asudar Ermeniyān, Nurbeg-Kosta, Iskinoplok, Papa Yani, and the so-called quarter of Jews. Armenians who mingled with Greeks and Italians were also to be found in the quarters of Yorgi Argandjelu (six names), Dhraperyo and Gargandji (four names and two names respectively). That they were concentrated in the quarters farthest from the early Genoese nucleus of the city can be taken as an indication that they came late to settle around the city. In fact, the oldest Armenian church, Aya Khorkhoro or Surp Grigor Lussavoritsch, founded in 1436, was reported to have been built by Armenian settlers coming from Caffa in 1391.[71]

Our survey confirms the Caffan origin of the Armenians of Pera, at least for an important part of them. The majority of the Armenians in the quarter of Nurbeg Kosta and Iskinoplok bear such Turkish names as Shīrīn, Djevher Khātūn, Tādjī Khātūn, Sürme Khātūn and Melek Khātūn for women, and Orkhān, Murād, Tanrıvermish, Yūnus, Pul Beg, Eyne Beg, Shādī Beg, and Çolpan for men. The last two names indicate origins in the Kiptchak-Kuman region of the northern Black Sea. A customs book of Caffa dated 1478[72] contains similar Turkish names for Armenians. The individual who gave his name to the principal Armenian quarter of Nurbeg must also have been an Armenian from Caffa. In the quarter called *Maḥalle-i Yahūdiyān,* "Quarter of Jews", near the church of San Benito, Armenians were in the majority and Greeks were the second largest group, while only a few Jews —a wealthy Jewish physician by the name of Istvri (?) with his three sons along with a wealthy Jew and his two sons and another Jew — were to be found there at the time of the survey.

---

70 Balard, pp. 189-190; by the early years of the 15th century these eastern quarters were surrounded by the walls which completed the fortifications of Pera as a fortified city.

71 İncicyan, cited by Schneider, p. 26; the majority of the population in Caffa was Armenian in 1475. An exodus to the Crimea of Armenians from Eastern Anatolia occured during Timur's invasions in 1400 and 1402 (for the Armenian literature see M. Cazacu et K. Kévonian, "La chute de Caffa en 1475", *CMRS,* XVII (1976), p. 497; E. Schutz, "Armeno-Kiptschakische Ehe Kontrakte und Testamente", *Acta Orientalia* (Budapest), vol. XXIV (1971), pp. 265-300; Idem., "An Armeno-Kiptchak Document of 1640 from Lwów and its background in Armenia and the Diaspora", *Between the Danube and the Caucasus,* ed. G. Kara, Budapest, 1987, pp. 247-330; Berindei, *art. cit.*

72 H. İnalcık, *Sources and Studies on the Black Sea,* I. *The Customs Register of Caffa* (1487-1490), Cambridge, 1995.(1487-1490).

Jews

The Jews lived in large numbers in the quarters of Fabya and Samona. The synagogue *(kenīsā-i Yahūdiyān)* stood in the quarter of Samona near Karaköy, but there too, only a few Jews were to be found (six Jews as against seventy-one Greeks and six Franks). A Jew by the name of Samarya owned three houses there. The only Jewish quarter in the Byzantine capital since the eleventh century was located in this area until it was burnt down by the Crusaders in 1203. The quarter which can be properly called Jewish was that of Fabya, around the Church of San Fabyan, near the business center. In this quarter, there were 44 Jews as against 24 Franks, three Greeks and one Armenian. For the purpose of the poll tax, an unusually large number of Jews, exactly 18 in number, were designated as wealthy, including two physicians, Ilyās and Suleymān. Three of them –Mūsā, son of Ilyās, Mūsā, son of Aslan, and Ismāīl, son of Aslan– were designated as very rich. One of the wealthy Jews, Aslan, son of Sha'bān lived in Istanbul although he maintained a house in Pera. Since 29 out of 39 houses were listed as belonging to the Jews, Jews were evidently in the majority in this quarter even before the Ottoman occupation. There was also a house endowed to the Jewish religious men. The fact that Jewish names were rendered in Turkish forms and that a Jew even bore the typical Turkish name Arslan/Aslan may indicate that like the Armenians, they were immigrants from places under Kipchak-Tatar rule, Crimea or other Ottoman dominions. It appears that on the day of the surrender, the Jews remained while many of the Franks in the quarters in the port area abandoned their houses and fled.

Muslims

At the time of the survey, a few Muslims lived in Galata. They numbered twenty; five of them owning houses in different quarters, Karadja, *subashı* or governor of Galata lived in the quarter of Pero di Lankashko in a house owned before the surrender by Thodorkho Eflak. The *subashı* also held a lease on another house in the same quarter and on a shop in the quarter Yorgi Argandjelu. Most of the Muslim inhabitants had non-Muslim wives, either Armenian or Greek. A Muslim child named Muṣṭafā lived in his own house with his mother, a Christian woman named Theodora. Hādjī Meḥmed of Ankara had a bathhouse in the fashionable quarter of Fabya which he had bought from Djan Drapoza, a well-known Peran. Meḥmed was married to Shekire or Shikra, a Christian woman who owned a house in the quarter of Anton di Garzan. Muṣṭafā, another Muslim, rented a house to use as a *bashkhāne* or eating house. An Arab, by the name of 'Arab-oghlu Ḥādjī leased from the treasury a shop in the trade center of Galata. In the Varto Khristo quarter of rich Greeks, Süleymān Beg, most probably the Karıshtıran Süleymān Beg who was then the Governor of Istanbul, owned a complex of two bathhouses for men and women.

II Meḥmed II's *Waḳfiyye* of ca. 1472

The second important document on Galata is the Arabic *waḳfiyye* of Meḥmed II,[73] drawn up for his mosque and complex of buildings which was completed in Istanbul on *radjab* 875/December 1470. The *waḳfiyye* (no. I) records the state owned buildings in Galata the revenues of which were endowed to his mosque. This original *waḳfiyye* of Meḥmed II must have been written anywhere between 1470 and 1474. Maḥmūd Pasha (d. July 18, 1474) is referred to as living. I believe this text, published in facsimile by Osman Ergin, has a gap between pages 50 and 51; page 50 ends with بد قوست ، and the next page begins with يدى اوذو كه. The missing area is between the *Baluk -Pazarı* Gate and the quarter of Karaköy. In describing the endowed buildings, the *waḳfiyye* refers to the adjacent buildings belonging to individuals as their freehold properties. Thus, the document gives us information on not only the renters of the public buildings, but also of the other buildings and their possessors living in Galata at that time.

Our *waḳfiyye* refers to the survey of 1455 by Djübbe ʻAlī, which was used as the basis for the new survey. Each public building, whether a tower *(al-Burghāz al-Sulṭānī),* a shop *(khānūt),* a home *(bayt)*, or a room *(hudjra),* is described and delimited with the adjacent buildings in the quarter, and the name of its possessor-renter *(fī-yad* so and so) is given.

The document ends with a note (facsimile ed. p. 52) saying:

In sum, in Galata there are 286 buildings which were registered as public properties under rent as determined by Djübbe ʻAlī in his survey *(min al-amlāk wa'l-muḳāṭaʻāt Djübbe ʻAlī).*

Here the word *amlāk* refers to the buildings while *muḳāṭaʻa* refers to the rent as determined *(mawḍūʻ)* by Djübbe ʻAlī.

The following quarters are included in this waḳfiyye:

1. Hādjī Ḥamza Quarter (see facsimile, p. 45). This quarter was adjacent to that of Londja and the Köke Gate. It must have been named after either Ḥamza Beg b. ʻAbdullāh, the commander of the *Boghaz-Kesen*

---

[73] Published in facsimile by. O. N. Ergin, *Fatih İmareti Vakfiyesi,* Istanbul 1945, pp. 1-68; taken from the mausoleum of Meḥmed II, the original is now preserved in *Türk-İslam Eserleri Müzesi,* Istanbul, no. 667.

(Rumeli) *Ḥiṣār,* apparently a convert who had properties and was living there, or a grocer from Edirne by the name of Ḥādjī Ḥamza. There was a tower, *burghāz al-Sulṭānī,* in this quarter. A shop was rented to a certain blacksmith *(ḥaddād)* by the name of Meḥmed. Sunḳur Agha, evidently a member of the ruling elite held three state-owned shops. In the same quarter lived Hādjī of Ankara, Barlo (or Maryo) the Jew and, near the gate of Londja, 'Abdī, the sea captain, as well as other Muslims by the names of Karagöz, Turgut, Seyyidī Maḥmūd, Ḥādjī and Dervīsh Aḥmed. In the same quarter lived Angeloy, an Italian, Asbara (or Isbata), a soap manufacturer, amid the Greeks Yorgi Komninos who was a dyer and Dhijanoz. Near the gate, there was a Muslim convent *(zāviye)* and on the side of Londja there was an olive oil press. The *waḳfiyye* mentions a *sūḳ,* bazaar, in this quarter located near the tower while most of the shops are to be found around the Gate of Londja, Next to the quarter of Ḥādjī Ḥamza, there were forty one state owned rooms *(ḥudjra)* between the quarter of Usta Sinān and the Limon Gate, some of which were set up against the city walls.

2. The Londja Quarter (facs. 46-48), evidently named after the (old) *Logia (Londja)* referred to as "near the *İskele -Ḳapusı"* (later *Yagh -Kapanı).* The gate and *İskele,* landing, are clearly shown in the Matraḳdjı plan (1537) (see Plan III in Appendix). This quarter was connected with that of Ḥamza to the north and Karaköy to the east. *Baluk-Pazarı -Kapusı (Bāb al-Semek)* to the sea was also in this quarter.

Muslims with properties in this quarter included the cadi of Şili (Şile) by the name of Kemāl al-Dīn, Çakır Agha, the governor of Istanbul (see *infra)* and the sea captain İskender. Also, Ḳapıdjı 'Alī held in rent a tower, *al-burghāz al-sulṭānī,* on the upper part of the Londja Gate. Hādjī of Ankara and 'Abdī of Ankara were apparently merchants from this city. A certain Ḥādjī Ḳaraman possessed a state owned shop used as a *boza-khāne,* boza drinking house, which had the same social function as a coffee house before the introduction of coffee in the mid-sixteenth century. Muslim scribes and a designer *(naḳḳāsh)* named Yūsuf also lived in this prosperous quarter.

The non-Muslims living in this quarter included many Italians who were designated as *al-efrendj* or only by name. These were Andoni Foka, Duka, Luviz, Ambroz, Anton, Zorzo, Fransa (a woman), Bernardo Ovanis, Toma, Zani, Talashdari, Masturi Klano (a physician), Andrea Parvik, Karaby Bredano, Yakomi Djidji, Nikoroz Davya. Those Italians who were not specified as *al-efrendj* must have been Genoese Ottoman subjects *(dhimmī).*

In the Londja Quarter, which was the business center of the city, were also mentioned Greeks, Armenians, and Jews. The Greek community included Mikhal, a *boza* maker, Manul, Kolovyani Aleksi, another Mihal, a ship caulker Toma, Anamami, Preshkova, Yakomi, children of Khristo Parvavandi, Yorgi, a bow maker, Yorgi, a pulley maker, and Mihal, a barber. Greeks appear to have made up the majority of the inhabitants of this quarter. The name of an Armenian Uveys or Ovanis is also mentioned in the Londja Quarter. Evidently, this cosmopolitan business area was predominantly settled by wealthy Italians and Greeks in this time.

According to the *wakfiyye* in front of the Londja building there were eight state owned shops, evidently abandoned by the Genoese during the Ottoman takeover, and a prison; Çakır Agha's house was also in the same area. On its east side, there were five other state-owned shops reaching the *Baluk* gate *(Bāb al-Semek).* Three towers, *al-burhgāz al-sulṭānī*s, at the walls were rented to private persons ('Alī, Anerlo and Kolovyani, a Greek) apparently to be used as depots. This area appears to have functioned, as it had before the Ottomans, as the main port area where the Genoese merchants used to do business, but which they had partly deserted upon the fall of Constantinople. Other buildings to be noted in this quarter were oil-presses, the office of the public scales *(kapan)* and the *kilīsā al-Efrendjiyīn,* or the cathedral church of the Latins, evidently S. Michele.

3. The quarter of Esbihar (facs. 48-49). Esbihar Bortoyora lived in this quarter where Genoese were apparently in the majority. Duka Verdi, Mandona Thomay, Manderina (woman), Karlo, Andosh, Kapolonya Raziti, Padeshti di Shavati, Musina (woman), Ludj di Gadjan, Marya di Bakarto (woman), Ovanis, Zor Dabliko, Borto Daryo, Ludja Dhugaya, Luviz Boriz, Angelozi, Latkash, Dhomeniko di Kurina, Andoni, Andjele di Lankashko, Kora and Thoma; most of them registered as *al-efrendj,* that is subjects of the Republic of Genoa, lived in this quarter. Only the names of three Muslims, Yūsuf, a painter, İskender, a sea captain, and Muṣṭafā, a scribe, are mentioned. Only one Jew, İbrāhīm, is mentioned.

The quarters briefly referred to in the *wakfiyye* after the Londja are those of Dhano Bagano (Pagano), Zani Dabdañ and 'Azebler. These quarters must have been situated on the shore along with those of Londja and Eshibar. Further to the east, the quarter of Usta Sinān, apparently between the quarter of Ḥādjī Ḥamza and the *Limon* (port) Gate, formed part of the Karaköy complex.

4. The quarters in the district of Karaköy were that of Limon Kapı, situated outside the walls of Galata, and those of Andjele Pagamino, Yani Gonadova, Manul Kalafatdjı-Bashı, Laviz Laberda, Torodh, Shemseddīn Kürkdjü. According to the *wakfiyye* "the quarters comprised in the district of Karaköy *(Karye Sawdā)* contained altogether 199 public

properties under rent as investigated and written down by Djübbe 'Alī upon the Sultan's order.

The four quarters in the port area appear to have been the main commercial center of Galata. Under the Ottomans, the Genoese population and the Genoese properties which were converted to state properties were found concentrated in this area, in particular in the Londja *(Logia)* and Esbihar quarters.[74]

Our *waḳfiyye* also describes the presence of Muslims as residents or landlords in the same quarters. The Muslims who lived in this area included people from Anatolian cities such as Ankara and Karaman, who apparently were engaged in trade and had settled in the city. Ankara mohairs and cotton goods of Karaman were in great demand by the Italians. Also, apparently to secure extra income, members of the Ottoman ruling class are seen as renters of the state owned properties including storehouses, towers and houses in the economically recovering Galata. Among these were Çakır Agha, governor of Istanbul, cadis, *ḳapıdjı*s, secretaries and a painter-designer *(naḳḳāsh)*. Apparently some of these people were actually living in Galata itself, while the others seem to have been absentee landlords. In any event, during the period 1453-1472, the Italians, either *ḥarbī,* as foreigners, or *dhimmī,* constituted the majority of the population in the area.

III The second Waḳfiyye of Meḥmed II, ca. 1481

The second *waḳfiyye* which was written presumably toward the end of his reign, came down to us in a copy made on 2 *Dhūlḳa'da* 901/19 August 1496. It is a faithful copy of the original bearing the *tuhgra* of Bāyezīd II.[75] This second *waḳfiyye* (no. II) can be considered a document reflecting the situation in Galata toward the end of Meḥmed's reign. An important difference in the arrangement of the *waḳfiyye* II is the lack of names of the renters or possessors so that no information can be inferred about the population living in the quarters mentioned.

However, judging from the number and names of the quarters in the *waḳfiyye* II, it can be said that Galata experienced spectacular growth and was transformed into a strongly turkicized city in population during the last ten years of Meḥmed's Sultanate. It is apparent that the quarters changed in structure, were repopulated, divided into new quarters and renamed, and that completely new Muslim-Turkish quarters came into being. E. H. Ayverdi's

---

[74] Cf. Balard, pp. 192-194.

[75] See Bibliography: *waḳfiyye* II.

comparison,[76] however, cannot reflect the real transformation because the *wakfiyye* I is not complete. According to Ayverdi, only 5 quarter names from the *wakfiyye* I occur in the *wakfiyye* II and apparently 53 new quarters were added in the latter. Only two quarters kept their names from 1455 in the *wakfiyye* I, Zani Pagano and Vasiliko, and only one (Vasiliko) in the *wakfiyye* II.

In the *wakfiyye* II there were:

20 quarters with Turkish names
13 quarters with Italian names
8 quarters with Greek names
6 quarters with Armenian names
11 quarters with neutral names
Total: 58

The striking fact is that all of the Galata quarters as found in the mid-sixteenth century *(wakfiyye* III) appear to have been already in existence by the date of the *wakfiyye* II. Apparently, earlier quarters were divided into new ones when they became crowded mainly as a result of the arrival of new Muslim settlers. These new quarters came into being with Muslim names. The names were connected with a craft (ʻAbāyīci [felt maker] Ḥādjī İlyās, Bashdjı Akhī, Ḥamāmdjı Ḥādjī Mubārek, Kürkdjü Khızır, Süleymān Naḥḥās, Usta Sinān) or with a religious person (ʻAbdī Faḳīh), or with a military-administrative function (Ḳaptan İbrāhīm Pasha, Bali Re'īs, İsḳandil Ḳāsım Re'īs, Kemāl Re'īs, ʻAses Meḥmed, İskender Ketkhudā, Ḳapıdjı İlyās, Okdju Mūsā, Tañrıvermish Agha) or with a building (Djāmiʻ, Kalʻa-i Djedīde). Some of these names — İlyās, Tañrıvermish, Khızır can be traced back to the survey of 1455, while many of them occur as simple inhabitants in the quarters, otherwise named in the *wakfiyye* I. A quarter *(maḥalle)* in the Ottoman society was named after a prominent person in the neighborhood, either a craftsmen or religious man or an official. Usually this person agreed to build a *mesdjid,* small quarter mosque, or a fountain, etc. for the quarter[77] community. In Galata, the quarters of ʻAbdī Faḳīh Anḳaravī, Bereket-zāde, Oḳdju Mūsā, Hādjī Aʻver, Shehsüvār were named after the *mesdjid*s they had built.

In the period 1470-1481, many of the non-Muslim quarters too were renamed following the same pattern. Some took the name of a professional such as Ermeni Ekmekdji (baker), Ermeni Khodja (merchant) Ker, Ḳalafatdjılar re'īsi (head caulker) Deli Mikhal, Frenk Kuyumdju (Italian

---

[76] See E. H. Ayverdi, *İstanbul Mahalleleri,* in the Bibliography.
[77] See H. İnalcık, "İstanbul", *EI*², pp. 234-237.

Jeweller) Domeniko, Frenk Ḳapānī (Italian tax farmer of the public scales) Fikron, Meykhānedji (keeper of wine house) Manul. Some quarters were named after its economic function such as Urgandjılar (rope-makers for the navy, formerly İskinoplok), Londja *(Logia)* or Eski Londja.

IV The *Djābī* Register of 1489

Each *waḳfiyye* is coupled with a detailed survey used for the collection of revenues, the so-called *djibāyet* (collection), where each estate with its exact revenue as well as special conditions, exemptions, etc., were recorded. The *djibāyet* survey for the *waḳfiyye* I has not come down to us. But such a survey exists for the *waḳf*s of the Ayasofya mosque. It is dated *Shawwāl* 894/August 1489.[78]

We learn from this register that the status of some buildings was modified after Djübbe 'Alī's survey by order of the Sultan and was granted as freehold property mostly to soldiers and members of the ruling elite. Such properties were taken out of the new *waḳf* surveys. Our Ayasofya *djibāyet* book, however, records all buildings with their location and owner, thus providing a complete list. So, by 1489, 145 such houses in Istanbul and Galata were left out of the *waḳfiyye* and the rents cancelled because they had been granted as freehold property by the Sultan. In Galata, in the quarter of Ḥādjī Ḥamza, 27 houses were given as freehold property to Muslims or bought by non-Muslims by the years 861/1456-57 and 863/1458-59. For example, we learn that Çaḳır Agha, the governor of Istanbul, was granted a house in this quarter in *Sha'bān* 862/June 1458. Another house was granted to Ḥamza Beg, the Commander of the Boghaz-Kesen (Rumeli-Ḥiṣār) fortress, while the sons of the Greek Manul bought a house in the same quarter from the Ottoman fisc, which formerly used to pay 500 *akça* (about 11 gold pieces) a year as rent to the public treasury. In Galata, in the quarter of *Kumiyān* or *Kumiler,*[79] many Muslims from Gelibolu (Gallipoli) and Bursa came to settle and were granted houses as freehold properties. Also, the house of Pavlo was granted to a Muslim woman by the name of Dilshād; and the house of the Greek Angeline was granted to a shoemaker by the name of Dāvūd. A big house belonging to Pandelyo Koris was confirmed as his freehold property. Other Greeks, such as İstimad, the son of Nikefor, for instance, acquired the ownership rights to abandoned houses in the quarter of Kumiyān.

---

[78] See Bibliography: Djibāyet register of 894/1489.

[79] Kumi, from Latin *Comes,* was the officer in charge of the galley-slaves, see Tietze and Kahane, no. 789; the district *Kumiler* must have been the one where *Kumis* resided. In Ayverdi's plan the *Kumiler* district is shown to the North of the *Ḥādjī Ḥamza* and *Djāmi'* (Mosque) districts. The church of San Francesco was in the *Kumiler* district.

In the quarter of Londja, the *Efrendjiyīn,* i.e., foreign Italians, included Zorzo d'Ambligo, Zandjan, Ludj Sakiba, Lankoshko, and a glass seller Efrendj. The *dhimmī* Italians were Batashtiya, the dyer Bastiyan, Batishto, Atadja, the sons of Danyal, the broker Zani and Servago Luviz. Among the Greeks in the same quarter were the barber Yani, Nikola, Andronika, Andriya, Thodhora of Galata and Nikola of Galata. There were a few Muslims, namely 'Abdī Faḳīh of Ankara, Khodja Uveys and Ya'ḳūb, the son of 'Alī. The church Françeshḳo (San Francesco) (See *infra)* was mentioned in this quarter.

The next quarter was the Batishto quarter which was all Italian, while those of San Benito and Aghabi, near the gate of the fishermen *(Bāb al-Sammākīn),* were both Greek. The church of Sampero was in the quarter of Aghabi. The quarter of Pars had a mixed population of Greeks, Armenians and Muslims. The quarters of Limon and Vizal were predominantly Greek. Other quarters mentioned in our register were the quarter of Dimitri, the quarter of Panamenoz, the quarter of the church of Khristod (Khristot), the quarter of Leshkeri, the quarter of Ḳapudan Meḥmed Beg, the quarter of Santo Marya, the quarter of San Yanko, and the quarter of the Greek Mikhal, the head of the caulkers (we assume that ship caulkers were Greek). An interesting person in the quarter was Ḳaragöz Ḥayālī, evidently a performer of the Karagöz shadow theatre. The majority of the population in these quarters were Greek. In several of the 33 houses in the quarter of Kumiler, persons were exempted from the payment of rent to the fisc. We learn that the church of Santa Fabyan was in the quarter of Petro, which had a mixed population of Greeks, Italians (sons of Batishto) and Muslims (sons of Khodja Ḳāsım and the surgeon Ḥamza). Apparently, this quarter was still inhabited by wealthy merchants.

The next quarter was that of Limon (port)-Kapı in the district of Karaköy. The population of the quarter was almost completely Greek. A Muslim named 'Alī was the owner of a storehouse, while eight shops were rented by a Greek named Manul. A state-owned *boza*-house was also in this quarter. In the quarter of Tophane there were seven shops outside the city walls along the shore which are called *silāḥ-hāne.* This note indicates that a foundry existed here by the year 1489; and that, in addition, there were seven shops making or storing "weapons", *silāḥ* (muskets?). In the quarter of San Yanko or Niko which was inhabited by both Greeks and Armenians, there were 21 houses, all serving as rental property since pre-Ottoman times.

The imperial edict dated January 1493, copied in the same survey book, exempted from rent all of the soldiers on the Sultan's payroll *('alūfe)* who actually resided in the houses belonging to the fisc. It is a well known fact that, prior to the edict, the janissaries who were permitted to live in the houses which were abandoned by their non-Muslim owners were required to pay rent to the fisc.[80] Bāyezīd II (1481-1512) who felt insecure on the throne as long as Djem Sultan was alive, tried to please the soldiery by making such exemptions. It is of interest to point out that a number of salaried *ḳul*s and their relatives had lived in Galata since Meḥmed II's time and were among the first Muslim settlers in the city. The survey of 1489 informs us that originally there were 178 such houses in Istanbul and Galata. In 1489 there were 139 houses exempt from rent.

In brief, by 1489 we find that in Galata the Muslim population increased in the quarters of *Kumiler, Ḳapudan Meḥmed Beg, Bali Re'īs, Mesdjid-i Ḥādjī 'Abdī.* In the quarter of *Kumiler* or *Kumiyān* lived two Arabs, a public crier *(dellāl)* by the name of İskender, and persons connected with sea navigation including captains Muṣṭafā, Ḥamza and Ṣafā, as well as craftsmen such as a baker, a cook, a porter and a saddler. There, non-Muslims, mostly Greeks, also were to be found. *Kenīsā al-Munaḳḳasha,* the church of San Francesco which in 1697 was converted to a mosque (see Appendix 6), was situated in this quarter. In the quarters of Ḳapudan Meḥmed Beg and Bali Re'īs, near the 'Azeb Kapı on the western end of Galata, many sea captains, including Baraḳ Re'īs, Murād Re'īs, and Atmadja Re'īs had their own houses. These famous captains of the Ottoman navy were, at the same time, actively engaged in the commercial traffic between Galata and the Black Sea ports, in particular Caffa.[81] In other words, the *Tersāne* shipyard, though not yet replacing that of Gelibolu in importance, had already become a factor in the settlement of the Muslim population in the western quarters of the city.

V. Vavassore's Plan of ca. 1490

Vavassore's original view of Istanbul and Galata (Plan II) belongs to this period. It is dated around 1490 and has come to us through several copies made during the sixteenth century.[82] In this plan, before the *İskele* (later*Yagh-Ḳapanı)* and the *Limon* or *Baluḳ-Pazarı* gates there are two boats indicating that they were centers of traffic. There is no trace of the Rüstem Pasha *bedestanı* and *hanı* in this plan; instead, there is a building with a dome which could be the church of San Michele. This port area is separated by a large street (Tersane street) from the block in the heart of the city where the towers of San Francesco and San Domenico at either end of the *Forum Platea* are visible.

---

[80] İnalcık, "The Policy", pp. 231-249.

[81] See İnalcık, *Sources and Studies on the Ottoman Black Sea,* 113-116.

[82] Mordtmann, *Ancien Plan,* p. 2, believes the original plan goes back to Meḥmed II's time, cf. Oberhummer, *Konstantinopel,* pp. 21-22; Schneider and Nomidis, p. 48.

At the west side of the sea walls, the *Porta di San Antonio* is identified as *'Azeb-Ḳapı* or *'Azebler Ḳapısı.*[83] Inside this gate, as well as behind the Porta S. Chiara (Karaköy), there are large open spaces. Another large open space lay in the north-western part of the city, towards the land walls. All of these squares were later shown as densely filled with blocks of buildings in the views of the city from the late sixteenth century (see the views in the copies of Pīrī Re'īs' *Kitāb-i Baḥriyye*:[84] Plan IV).

The latter open space, comprising the area from Galata Kulesi down to the Arab Camii (the triangle between Oḳcu Musa and Galata Kulesi streets today), was later occupied by the Turks and the Moriscos. According to the map based on the *waḳfiyyes*, including the sixteenth century ones,[85] this area comprised the quarters of Oḳcu Musa, Şehsüvar, 'Ases Meḥmed, Arta-Bilmez and Ḳal'a-i Djedīde. Next to this district, the quarters to the west were all Muslim — Silāḥī Meḥmed, Ḳapıdjı İlyās, Tañrıvermish, Melek Khātūn, Ḳaptan İbrāhīm Pasha, Bashdjı 'Alī, Kemāl Re'īs, Bali Re'īs and Ḥādjī A'ver. In other words, the garrison and military stores placed in the Galata Kulesi on the one hand, and the naval installations on the western side on the other, were from the outset the centers of Muslim settlement which appear to have been mostly of military personnel. One of the earliest quarters in this part of the city was *'Azebler* (marines), which gave its name to the *'Azeb* Gate. Our *waḳfiyyes* and surveys do not include the west side of the city, apparently because already under the Genoese, this western area of the fortress was sparsely inhabited. Vavassore's view of 1490 attests to this fact.

The Ottoman colonization of the cities which were peacefully occupied through an agreement followed the same pattern of settlement in other regions, namely that the first settlers usually consisted of military and administrative personnel.

As Vavassore's plan shows, the Ottoman *Tersāne* in Galata did not have its impressive rows of arcades for galley construction and shelter at this time. Selīm I (1512-1520) started to expand the *Tersāne* by constructing a number of arcades to strengthen the navy. However, the Matraḳdjı plan of 1537 (Plan III in the Appendix) still shows only a few arcades on the 'Azeb-Ḳapı side of Ḳāsım Pasha bay which was used for the shelter and repair of galleys already under Meḥmed II, as confirmed by the existence of the 'Azebs, the caulkers (ḳalafatdjı) and the sea captains in the western quarters of Galata at that time.

---

[83] Schneider and Nomidis, p. 15.

[84] See in Oberhummer, *op.cit.*

[85] See Ayverdi, *İstanbul Mahalleleri.*

VI. The Survey of 1519

The *djibāyet* register of the Ayasofya mosque *waḳfs* written in *Muḥarrem* 926/December 1519 contains a detailed chapter on Galata (see Bibliography and sample pages in Appendix No. 7). In general, rents in this survey were determined in accordance with the original *waḳf* deed and the previous register of revenues. At the time of the new survey, rents, when put at auction, went up substantially, sometimes doubled. The striking fact emerging from this register is that by 1519, Galata had fully developed Muslim quarters (see Appendix No. 9: Population), economic activities intensified, and more members of the Ottoman elite invested money in renting or purchasing real properties in Galata for their *waḳfs*. Many old Genoese buildings were now made part of the *waḳfs* founded by pashas and aghas. The state-owned properties were acquired by them either through the grants made by the Sultan, or simply rented from the fisc to be exploited in the economically thriving city.

Apparently, the surveyor began with the description of the Muslim quarters, each-having its own *mesdjid,* mosque. The main Muslim quarter was that of *Djāmi'* near the *Iskele* and the old Genoese *logia* (in Turkish *londja)* at the busy port area where we find many warehouses *(makhzen).* Other Muslim quarters were Kör Ḥādjī (Ḥādjī A'ver), Hüsām Beg, Oḳdju Mūsā, Bereket-zāde and the newly established Sulṭān Bāyezīd Djāmi'i quarter near the Tophane gate. In the Muslim quarters, however, we find also houses belonging to the non-Muslims, mostly Greek *dhimmīs.* The general trend is that such houses were passing into the possession of Muslims as time went by. Many sea captains resided in the quarters of Kör Ḥādjī (near the *'Azebler* gate), Hüsām Beg and Oḳdju Mūsā. Already by this date, there lived in Galata many Arabs — Ḥādjī 'Alī from the Maghreb, Meḥmed son of 'Abd al-Wahhāb, 'Abdullāh, a mosque servant, and others. They lived mostly in the quarter of Djāmi'. An Arab sea captain, *re'īs,* by the name of 'Alī was from Alexandria in Egypt. Another Arab sea captain called Manṣūr lived in the quarter of Hüsām Beg. Among the Arabs living in Galata, we find also a looking-glass maker or seller *(mir'ātī).*

A great number of Muslim men of Galata were registered as sons of 'Abdullāh which refers, in most cases, to being a convert. Likewise, many of the wives of Muslims were daughters of 'Abdullāh. In the new Muslim quarter of Sulṭān Bāyezīd Djāmi'i, a public bathhouse was built as part of the Ḳāsım Pasha *waḳfs*. Additionally, in the same quarter lived many Greeks engaged in small trades.

By 1519, the following men endowed properties for their *waḳf* in Galata: Ṭopdju Bashı, Kürkdjü Bashı Shemseddīn, Çaḳır Agha, Mawlānā Yārḥiṣārī,

'Alī Pasha, Dizdār-oghlu Meḥmed, Ḥüseyn Agha, Muftī 'Alī Djemālī, Kātib Ferhād Beg, Yoldju-oghlu 'Ömer, and Emīn Khayreddīn.

In the heart of Galata, in the quarter of San "Françeshḳa" (San Francesco) lived wealthy Italians and Greeks, including the famous tax farmer Yani Palologoz (Palaeologos) who owned several houses in Galata. Italians, however, constituted the majority of the inhabitants in this quarter as well as in those of Aya Yorgi, and the church of San Bashtiyan (San Bastiano). Among the Latins, we find a Catalan by the name of Pero. Greeks appear to have been in majority in the quarters of Karaköy, the church of Panaya (Panagia), the church of Kastelyut (Kasteliutissa), Aya Yorgi (this particular church was situated near the Tophane gate), and the church of Khristod (the church of *Likosta,* apparently *Ekosieletsa,* was in the same quarter). Greeks were also to be found in the predominantly Latin quarters and there were instances in which Greeks replaced Italians in the possession of the houses and stores. Some Greeks were immigrants from the Aegean — for instance Yani from Euboea (Agriboz). Most of the Greeks were engaged in trades and crafts as shopkeepers, coppersmiths, builders, silk weavers, basket makers or barbers. Many were fishermen. The main Armenian quarter was that of the church of the Armenians. In the quarter of the church of San Benito, Armenians, Greeks, Muslims and Italians lived together.

The general impression we have from this survey is that Galata had recovered economically and, next to the rapidly growing Ottoman Istanbul, became a thriving city. Reference to the construction of new storehouses in the port area and rising prices in real estate can be interpreted as signs of growing trade and business activity in parallel to population increase. Galata's indigenous industries appear to have been flourishing, particularly in soap manufacturing and dyeing, mostly practiced by the Latins. Zani and his sons were known as watch-makers. There were many Greek coppersmiths in Galata. The city was apparently a center of fur trade probably because of its connection by sea with Caffa which was visited by Muscovite merchants since the 1490's, if not earlier. Several Muslim fur merchants, Ḳāsım, Khızır and İskender, mentioned in our register of 1519, had residence in Galata. And one of the earliest Muslim quarters was named after the Kürkdjü-Bashı Shemseddīn.

Our register yields important topographical data, too. In 1519, many houses in Galata, particularly in the new Muslim quarters, were situated in gardens.

Economic Conditions, 1453-1500

The impression that we get from the 1455 survey is that the first years after the conquest were difficult for Galata. Many of the wealthy Genoese had left the city on the day of the conquest and they preferred to live in Chios. But the number of fugitives does not justify our speaking of a real exodus of the Latins from the city, as is often asserted. The majority of the Genoese chose to stay on as Ottoman *dhimmī* subjects. Among them were wealthy families such as the Gara, Langasco, Francesco, and Daryova. Also, we learn from the register that the rich Jews, Armenians and Greeks whose numbers exceeded the Genoese also remained in Pera. The houses of those who left were confiscated. Their new tenants were mostly poor, aged people, and many of the buildings remained unoccupied and went to ruin. In the business district, out of 33 shops, 15 remained in the hands of their original owners, while 18 were confiscated. Fifteen of those remaining found renters. Some of the soap workshops remained idle. In fact, all evidence points to a picture of a decaying city.

The Sultan was having difficulty repopulating Istanbul since the deportees from Rumelia and Anatolia were returning home.[86] Thus, with the depopulated city on the other side, Galata's own chances for recovery seemed to be slim.

Actually, Pera's decline had started from the middle of the fourteenth century. Professor Roberto Lopez observes[87] that in the fifteenth century, Pera's commercial activity was reduced to one seventh of what it had been in the previous century. On the other hand the rise of Bursa as an emporium for the caravan trade of Iran and Syria and the revival of the traffic in luxury goods, especially, silk and spices, which now operated in the reverse direction, from Bursa to the northern countries, became a new source of prosperity for the Genoese and partly compensated for the decrease in the benefits of the inner Asian trade.[88] In the words of Heers[89]

En fait c'est la proximité de Brousse qui, à cette époque, explique la fortune de Pera. On vient de toutes parts se ravitailler à Brousse en produits de luxe et l'on passe par Pera, évitant soigneusement, semble-t-il, un séjour à Constantinople. Au point de vue économique, Pera dépend davantage de l'Empire turc que de Constantinople.

---

86 H. İnalcık, "Istanbul", *EI²*, p. 225.

87 Discussed by R. Lopez, "Market Expansion"; Idem, *Storia,* p. 405.

88 Heers, *Gênes,* Index: Pera; also İnalcık, "Bursa and the Commerce of the Levant", pp. 131-147.

89 Heers, *op. cit.,* p. 382.

One could find quite convincing data for this statement in *Il Libro dei Conti* of Giacomo Badoer, of the period 1436-1440, where Iranian and Caucasian silk and European cloth appear to be the subject of a lively exchange.[90]

In point of fact, Galata's ill-fortune in the first years of the Ottoman occupation was only of short duration. After the Ottoman occupation, Pera's dependence on the Bursa market increased and trade expanded appreciably as the cadi records of Bursa for the last two decades of the fifteenth century and the correspondence of J. Maringhi,[91] a Florentine agent residing in Galata at the turn of the century, fully demonstrate. Now, Ottoman subjects, Turks, Greeks, Armenians and Jews, began to supplant the Genoese in this inter-regional trade, especially after the fall of the Genoese ports in the Crimea as the trade of the Black Sea became vitally important for the growing capital of the Ottoman Empire. Also, under Meḥmed the Conqueror, the Florentines were favored at the expense of the other Italian nations in Pera (see *infra).* The Florentines and the Genoese now specialized in the trade of Iranian silk which was to a large extent bartered for European cloth on the Bursa market. Maringhi noted in 1501[92] that every year several silk caravans arrived in Bursa from Iran, and his letters reflect the impatience with which the Italian merchants awaited the arrival of the caravans, their rush to buy the goods and the fierce competition that ensued. The rewards were substantial, for in Italy each *fardello* –about 150 kg– yielded a profit of seventy to eighty ducats. The price of silk rose constantly. An average caravan brought about two hundred *fardelli* of silk. The value of the customs receipts from silk in Bursa was 40,000 gold ducats in 1487, 33,000 in 1507 and 43,000 in 1512.[93] It should also be remembered that the second half of the fifteenth century was marked by considerable expansion of the silk industry in Genoa.

VII. Genoese Notarial Documents of Galata, 1453-1490

An important source on the Genoese in Galata after the surrender in 1453 is the collection of notarial documents covering the period 1453-1490.[94] Analyzed by Geo Pistarino, the documents not only provide us with

---

[90] Eds. U. Dorini and T. Bertelè, in *Il Nuovo Ramusio III,* Venice, 1956.

[91] See İnalcık, "Bursa and the Commerce of the Levant", *JESHO*, 3 (1960), 131-167, and "Bursa", *Belleten,* vol. XXIV (1960), pp. 45-102; G. R. B. Richards, *Florentine Merchants in the Age of the Medici,* Cambridge (Mass.), 1932.

[92] Richards, *Florentine Merchants,* Index: *setta, seta, silk.*

[93] See H. İnalcık, *"Ḥarīr", EI²,* III, 213.

[94] A. Roccatagliata, *Notai Genovesi in Oltremare. Atti rogati a Pera e Mitilene, 1: Pera, 1408-1490,* Collanca Storica di fonti et studi, ed. G. Pistarino, 34, I, Genoa, 1982.

information on the legal aspects of Genoese life, which completely adhered to the practices and procedures of the Genoese period, but they also shed light on the social and economic conditions, trade and navigation and life in Ottoman Pera in general in that period. "A persistent", Pistarino notes,[95] "Genoese presence and activity in Pera" is confirmed by the documents for the period.

For Pistarino the "charter", i.e. *'ahd-nāme,* is a document guaranteeing "local self-government and the right of the Latins of Pera to elect a *protogerus".* He admits that the Latins of Pera being subject to the *kharādj* became "non-Muslim subjects of the Porte" and that once "the Porte's sovereignty" was established it was no more "the Genoese city it used to be", an entity separate from Constantinople. Considering the fact that the Genoese administrative framework and institutions with a community head (but now only a *protogerus* instead of a *podestà)* and the Council of Pera, the Genoese *cives* and *burgenses Pere* continued to be called as such and the relations with Genoa and the Genoese colonies in the Levant took their normal course, giving the impression that nothing had happened.[96] However, one must not forget that Galata was now under an Ottoman cadi and a *voyvoda,* representing all civil and political authority in the name of the Sultan. The kind of communal autonomy established under an *'ahd-nāme* should not be exaggerated (see *supra).* Pistarino also underlines the fact[97] that "the names of important Genoese families and noblemen were prominent in Turkish Galata". As the Genoese documents as well as the Ottoman survey attest, after the surrender in 1453, a great number of Genoese stayed on in Galata under the status of *dhimmī* or *ḥarbī/musta'min* while others who had left the city to take refuge in the Genoese Chios or elsewhere came back to stay either temporarily or permanently. On the other hand, there came in Pera Latins from other cities or areas. The Ottoman survey of 1455 distinguished these as *Sakızlu* (from Chios), *Drabizonlu* (from Trebizond), *Djeneviz* (the Genoese citizen) or *Venetik* (Venetian).

In the wake of the Ottoman conquest of Caffa, in 1475, the Latins of Caffa were deported *en masse* to Istanbul to give rise to the *Kefeli* district, near Edirne Kapı. We are told[98] that most of these deportees, subjects to the *sürgün* regulation,[99] paying a tax *(avaria),* managed to move to Pera and

---

95 Pistarino, "The Genoese in Pera" (see Bibliography).

96 Pistarino, *op. cit.,* p. 82.

97 *Ibid.,* p. 69.

98 *Ibid.,* p. 76.

99 On *sürgün* see H. Inalcik "Ottoman Methods of Conquest", *Studia Islamica,* vol. II (1954), pp. 122-129.

formed another group of the Peran Latins, distinguished as *Kefeli* or *burgenses Caffe.* The *Kefeli*s of Pera, organized as a separate *djemā'at* appear to have had their own *protogerus (prôtogeros).*

The well known names of the Genoese residents of Galata occur both in the Ottoman survey and the notary documents of Galata. Françeshḳo referred to as *'āmil,* the tax farmer, in our survey of 1455, is Francesco de Draperiis or Draperio, a resident of Galata who, in the capacity of tax farmer of the Ottoman alum mines since the reign of Murad II (1421-1444, 1446-1451), was a well known figure among the Ottomans.[100] In the summer of 1455, Francesco was aboard the Ottoman fleet under admiral Ḥamza to claim a debt of 40,000 gold ducats which the Genoese of Chios (Sakız) owed to him for alum. Since the sum was ultimately to be delivered to the Sultan's treasury, Meḥmed II had taken the matter into his own hands.[101] The Langascos, another wealthy Genoese family in Galata is also mentioned in both the Ottoman survey of 1455 and the notary documents. On August 17, 1453, Angelo di Langasco (Andjelo di Lanḳashḳo in our survey) assumed a mandate of Lorenzo Gattilusio.[102] Anton Gara, of the embassy which concluded the capitulations with Meḥmed II in Edirne in March 1451, appears in the survey of 1455 as a wealthy Genoese registered as a native of Galata, a *dhimmī.*[103] Anton di Lashtrego mentioned in the Ottoman survey as a poor *dhimmī,* is found in the notary records under the name of Antonio de Lastrego, a blacksmith.[104]

As the Genoese notarial documents demonstrate,[105] the Genoese of Pera under Ottoman sovereignty carried on their communal affairs and civil cases among themselves under their own laws and *protogerus/ketkhudā* as guaranteed in the Conqueror's *'ahd-nāme.* No doubt the Genoese of Pera at the same time had recourse to the cadi of Galata for their legal cases, particularly when one party was a Muslim. In 1475, a textile merchant, Francesco Fieschi, brought his complaint against Spinola, another Genoese, before the cadi of Galata. The court records of Bursa from the 1470's show[106] that Latins from Galata frequently employed the Bursa court even

---

100 See Babinger *op. cit.,* p. 130.

101 Doucas, *op. cit.,* pp. 246-249; Babinger, *op. cit.,* pp. 130-132.

102 Pistarino, p. 68.

103 Antonio Gara was active in the Genoa-Constantinople (Pera) trade arround 1438 (see Giacomo Badoer, pp. 388, 389).

104 Pistarino, p. 69.

105 For example, see Pistarino, pp. 78-79.

106 See İnalcık, "Bursa", *Belleten,* XXIV (1960) pp. 45-102.

for legal matters between themselves because sometimes this could ensure better security.

Under the Ottomans, the first problem for the Peran Genoese was a rebellion of the slaves against their Genoese masters. That was expected because among these slaves there were Muslim Turkish-Tatar slaves (Gingibei, the Circassian Acmet and others).

In general, Pistarino concludes,[107] life for the Genoese of Pera returned to normality and business resumed its normal course. Pera maintained close relations with the Genoese colonies of Caffa (Ottoman after 1475) and of Chios. Ships from Italy or Genoese colonies visited Pera regularly and maintained trade with the Black Sea. Thus, Pera continued its role as a "bridgehead" for Caffa and Chios which Sultan considered among his own dominions since they agreed to pay tribute starting from 1455. All this is to be expected if we remember that most of the Peran Genoese became the subjects of the Sultan as *dhimmīs* (the *burgenses Pere* in the Genoese documents) and were encouraged to carry on their economic activities as before. Now, as the Genoese notary records show, the Genoese ships continued to bring caviar and pickled sturgeon from the Black Sea to Galata which were so important for feeding the expanding imperial city of Istanbul. Also, those *ḥarbī,* foreign Genoese keeping their Genoese citizenship (the *cives Ianue),* were also protected and encouraged under the capitulatory guarantees.

Florentines in Galata

By the years 1463-1500, the Florentine colony of Pera had become very influential and prosperous thanks to Meḥmed II's deliberate policy. While the Venetians and the Genoese challenged the plans of Meḥmed II to expand his rule over Morea, Albania, Bosnia and the Black Sea, he showed special favor toward the Florentines, the rivals of the Venetians, in order to lessen dependency on the former in the vital trade relations of his empire with the West. The Ottomans were also well aware that fine woolen cloth, the principal export item from the West, was originally made or finished by the *arte della lana* of Florence, and imported to the Ottoman markets through Venice.[108] Despite Venice's attempts to disrupt the Florentine Levantine trade, principally based on the exchange of Iranian silk for woolen cloth at

---

107 Pistarino, pp. 66-67, 82.

108 Heyd, II, 296; H. Hoshino, "Il commercio Fiorentino nell' Impero ottomano: costi e profiti negli anni 1484-1488", *Contributi del Convegno di Studi "Aspetti della vita economica medievale",* Firenze-Pisa-Prato, 1984, pp. 45-57.

Bursa, the trade levels experienced a spectacular growth in this period.[109] Benedetto Dei, a Florentine agent settled in Galata whose chronicle[110] is one of our best sources on Florentine activities in the Ottoman Empire, became the most trusted advisor to the Sultan in the years 1460-1472. In fact, Meḥmed II's interest in encouraging Florence in the Levantine trade dated back to the days of the conquest of Constantinople. Already by 1455, Florence was grateful to the Sultan for the favors he was extending to the Florentines in his territories. What is indicative of the growth of Florentine trade after 1454 is that the number of Florentine ships visiting Istanbul increased from one to a convoy of three ships in 1461.

Considering the huge benefits they obtained, Florentines gladly paid the annual expense of 5,000 gold pieces to maintain their agents in Galata. In 1461, the Sultan found a pretext to expel the Venetians[111] from their houses and settled Florentines instead (apparently these were state-owned houses in Pera which were rented to foreigners). The following year when Meḥmed conquered Mytilene, three Florentine ships, then anchored at the Golden Horn, joined in the victory celebration to please the Sultan. Again in 1463, on the occasion of the Sultan's victory in Bosnia, the Florentines of Pera decorated their houses and streets and the Sultan himself honored them by visiting and dining at the mansion of the banker Carlo Martelli. Finally, the Consul Mainardo Ubaldini, head of the Florentine colony of Pera, and the Florentine agents and merchants of Pera were actively involved in Meḥmed II's decision to declare war against Venice in 1463.[112]

While at war with the Sultan, the Republic of Venice dispatched a special ambassador to Florence asking that ships not be sent to Istanbul during that particular year.[113] The reaction of the *Signora* is of interest. A great amount of cloth, they said, was already prepared for the Ottoman market, and the ships to be sent may actually protect the large number of Florentines residing there. In fact, political and economic circumstances created a natural alliance between the Sultan and Florence against Venice. The pressure which Venice and the Pope placed on Florence was countered by Meḥmed II who, as a

---

[109] See G. R. B. Richards (see Bibliography), Index: *Panni;* H. Hashino and M. F. Mazzaoui, "Ottoman Markets for Florentine Woolen Cloth in the Late Fifteenth Century", *International Journal of Turkish Studies,* III-2 (1985-1986), 17-31.

[110] See F. Babinger, "Mehmed II. der Eroberer und Italien", *Byzantion,* 21 (1951), p. 151 ff. and its Italian version with additions and corrections: *Rivista Storica Italiana,* LXIV-4.

[111] The Ottoman survey of 1455 attests a few Venetians residing in Galata by that time.

[112] Heyd, *op. cit,* pp. 339-340; Babinger, *ibid.*

[113] Heyd. *ibid.*

skillful diplomat, demonstrated an unusual friendship toward the Florentines in Galata.

When, in 1467, under pressure from public opinion in Italy, Florence decided to evacuate the city and all the heads of the commercial houses set sail with their wealth for home on Anconitan ships, the Venetians intercepted them and looted everything. Florentine traffic with Galata was halted until 1472. Although Florentines were now able to continue traffic with Galata via the Genoese, in 1467 and 1469, the outbreak of a terrible plague in the Ottoman territories, including Istanbul and Pera, caused another setback to Florentine trade in the Levant. The epidemic began in mid-summer of 1467 and, according to Critovoulos,[114] an eyewitness, there were more than six hundred deaths a day in the Ottoman capital. "Some fled and never returned... the city was emptied of its inhabitants, both citizens and foreigners". Despite these setbacks, in 1469, Mainardo Ubaldini, the Florentine Consul in Pera, calculated that there were fifty Florentine commercial agents still active in Turkey. They were located in Edirne, Istanbul, Gallipoli and Pera. A Florentine source tells us[115] that there was always a flow of new arrivals attracted by the prospects for trade in Turkey.

The first formal *'ahd-nāme* was granted to the Florentines by Meḥmed II, the text of which has not been discovered.[116] Without such an instrument the Florentine colony could not have remained in Galata.

Despite the restitution of peace with Venice in 1479, Bāyezīd II (1481-1512) was no less concerned with encouraging friendship with the Florentines and their continued presence in his capital; perhaps all the more so because of Djem Sultan, the pretender to the Ottoman throne who had been in Europe since 1482.[117] In 1483, through his ambassador to Florence, the new Sultan promised to purchase, annually and exempt from tax, five thousand *pastav* (one *pastav* was about 50 *arshın* or 34 m) of woolen cloth for the Palace.[118] In 1507, Florentine merchants in Galata numbered sixty or seventy whose annual turnover reached five to six hundred thousand gold ducats.[119]

---

[114] Trans. Riggs, p. 220; Heyd, II, p. 341.

[115] Documents cited by Heyd, II, p. 341.

[116] There was, however, a reference to it in the instructions to the Florentine ambassador to the Porte in 1488 (Heyd, II, p. 342).

[117] H. İnalcık, "A Case Study in Renaissance Diplomacy: The Agreement Between Innocent VII and Bayezid II on Djem Sultan", *Journal of Turkish Studies,* 3 (1979-1980), pp. 209-230.

[118] Heyd, *op. cit.,* II, p. 342.

[119] *Ibid.,* p. 344.

The *'ahd-nāmes* (capitulations) granted by Bāyezīd II and Selīm I to the Florentines were renewed by Süleyman I in October 1527[120] (see the Turkish text, Appendix No. 8). It contained the following provisions:

1 The Seigneurs of Florence shall send a *Baylos* to my Porte in order to supervise the affairs of their subjects;
2 The rate of customs dues shall be the same as that paid by the Venetians;[121]
3 If a subject of Florence is in debt (to the Ottoman subjects) the payment of the debt shall be required from the debtor alone and no other subjects of Florence shall be held responsible for it;
4 When a subject of Florence dies in the Ottoman territory his personal property shall be taken by whomever the deceased appointed in his will. If there is no will, it will be taken by the *Baylos* and the Ottoman agent in charge of confiscating such property *(beytülmaldjı)* shall not interfere;
5 The subjects of Florence are to go and conduct business anywhere in the Ottoman territories, and no one shall prevent or hinder them in their visits. Their ships will be free to sail to the Black Sea for trade, buying and selling, and they will pay no extra taxes once they paid the established dues;
6 Their disputes and legal cases among themselves shall be heard and decided by their own *Baylos;*
7 Those ships and subjects (or other nationalities which arrive in the Ottoman territories under the flag of Florence) are free to come and trade once they have paid the established dues;
8 If their ships run aground, their salvaged property shall be delivered to their owners and (if the local people have them) the cadis and *subashıs* from that area shall help the owners to recover their property;
9 Every time a Florentine ship arrives, the merchants shall visit the Sultan's palace with substantial gifts;
10 If extraordinary taxes *('awāriḍ)* are levied in a region where the Florentine merchants are present, no such taxes shall be demanded from them;

---

120 In a collection of state papers *(munsha'āt)* preserved in the Veliyüddin Efendi Library, Beyazit Genel Library, Istanbul, MS 1970; for the facsimile copy see Appendix, No. 8; also see M. Grignaschi, "Una raccolta inedita di 'Münşeât'", *Studi Preottomani e Ottomani,* Napoli, 1976, pp. 111-116, Text: pp. 119-122.

121 In 1482 the rate of customs duty for non-Muslim foreigners *(ḥarbī)* was 4 percent, see H. İnalcık, "Notes on N. Beldiceanu's Translation", *Der Islam,* vol. 43 (1967), p. 153.

11 The Sultan is told that when the Florentines have a legal dispute with members of other non-Muslim communities, the plaintiffs used to reject the Florentine witnesses (in Ottoman courts) and create difficulties by insisting on witnesses from among the local non-Muslims. If this is the case, it is ordered that if they have a dispute with a non-Muslim and need witnesses, these witnesses may be from any of the non-Muslim communities after they are legally proven to be acceptable by the cadi. Such witnesses shall be accepted and the cadi will give his decision which will be final and will not be disputed, because according to Islamic Law all non-Muslims are considered part of a single community;

12 The Florentine merchants do not have to pay the brokerage dues *(resm-i simsār)*[122] a second time in Istanbul for the raw silk they buy in Bursa. If they transfer their silk loads by land to Istanbul, the tax-farmers in charge of collecting the brokerage dues *(simsār 'āmilleri)* in Istanbul are ordered not to demand or bother the Florentine merchants in such cases;

13 When Florentine merchants arrive in the Ottoman territories and need to employ non-Muslims to serve and assist them, they may hire such persons with permission, but such (Ottoman subjects) shall not be taken with them to Italy;

14 When a merchant of their nation, being a resident of Galata and having legal disputes with a non-Muslim, appears with him for trial at the court of Istanbul and the case is decided here in Istanbul in accordance with the stipulations of Islamic Law, the decision shall be accepted as final since there is no conflict of jurisdiction in such cases according to the *Sharī'a;* and when a Florentine merchant has a legal case with someone in Istanbul it will be heard and the final decision will be given in the imperial council for which no further hearing shall be demanded; if the imperial council is not held in Istanbul (because of the campaign) then, the case shall be heard and decided by the cadi of Istanbul;

15 (In a legal case) if the Baylos becomes guarantor[123] for Florentine merchants, Ottoman authorities shall not detain or annoy him; no Florentine merchant shall leave the country unless he pays all his debts to individuals and to the customs house;

16 If the Florentine merchants arrive in Avlona (Vlorë) and board a boat to pass to Italy and Venetians, Genoese or other infidels intercept the boat and seize their goods, the Ottoman authorities shall demand all the

---

122 For *resm-i simsār* see R. Anhegger and H. İnalcık, *K̲ānūnnāme-i Sulṭānī Ber Mūceb-i 'Örf-i 'Os̲mānī,* Ankara 1956, pp. 42-43.

123 *Boyun olmak* means "to become a guarantor or surety", see *Tarama Sözlüğü,* I, Ankara, 1963, p. 652.

captured goods from them when the infidel attackers are found in the Ottoman territories;

17 Sometimes Ottoman authorities take Florentine merchants[124] [who were not found in the houses they had resided in] into custody and injure them even after they have liquidated their debts with the customs agent and have received a document for that. In such situations, the case shall be examined in court and action will be taken according to whatever decision is given; no one shall be injured in contravention with the law;

18 If the merchants bring slave women with them from their own country to use for their own purposes, no one shall hinder their departure back home; but it is required that such women be registered in the cadi's court book upon their arrival, so that they may be examined at the time of departure for an exit permit;

19 If goods and personal possessions of the merchants are stolen from the places they stayed or camped, in town or in the countryside, the case shall be investigated in accordance with the stipulations of the law and properties returned to the owner;

20 Since it is reported that the hired carriers of the Florentine merchants may dispute with or even hinder them, saying that their animals have to be grazed in the countryside, and so they force them to stay in a pasture land in the open country and that as a result sometimes harm occurs to the merchants, the Sultan ordered that the hired carriers shall depend on and follow the merchants and wherever the latter wanted to stay, the carriers would stay also. If the carriers object to the merchants and a loss then occurs, the carriers shall have to make up for the loss in accordance with a court decision.

This document is the decisive proof that Bāyezīd II and Selīm I granted *'ahd-nāmes* to the Florentine *Signora* guaranteeing the establishment of a Florentine community in Galata under a *Baylos* on the same basis as the Venetians.[125] The reason that Meḥmed II's *'ahd-nāme* is not mentioned in this renewal may be that the Florentines were given a community status with a Baylos at the head, like the Venetians, for the first time under Bāyezīd II.

A comparison with the capitulations granted to Venice in 1482[126] shows that the Florentines were granted the same guarantees for freedom of trade

---

[124] Here a phrase must have been skipped over by the copist.

[125] Heyd, II, p. 342-345, doubts the appointment of a Florentine *baylos*.

[126] Turkish texts of the *'ahd-nāme* of 1482 and that of 1540 are published by T. Gökbilgin, in *Belleten* V-VII (1968-1971) and I (1965), pp. 121-128.

and travel, and had security for the persons and properties of the merchants and the rates of the customs dues were the same.

Already by the time of the negotiations of the formal capitulation in 1488, guarantees concerning the *Baylos'* jurisdiction over the Florentines in civil and criminal matters, free choice of the witnesses, etc. were stressed.

In the instructions to the Florentine envoy at that time, complaints were voiced about the difficulties caused by the local Ottoman authorities at Avlona when the Florentines took the sea route of Lecce-Avlona, as well as the reimposition of the same dues twice or three times on the way from Avlona to Edirne (Adrianople).

The Florentine merchants took the sea route from Ancona or Ragusa to Istanbul usually on Anconitan or Ragusan ships. But in order to avoid corsairs or Venetians, they preferred the overland routes of Ancona - Ragusa - Sarajevo - Novi Bazar - Edirne - Pera, or Lecce (in Apulia) - Avlona - Edirne - Pera. These overland routes, also used by Ragusans and Muslim merchants, became the main trade routes crossing he Balkan peninsula from the Adriatic to Edirne, and contributed to the prosperity of the towns along the route and of the city of Pera. Finally, provision no. 20 tells us what difficulties and hazards the Florentine merchants were exposed to while crossing the Balkans overland.

The Ottoman government was seriously concerned about security along the route to Edirne. In 1500, when some silk bales were stolen in a village in Bosnia, the Sultan ordered an investigation and sent a chaush from Istanbul.[127] The security of the merchants' passage from Avlona to the Italian coasts was also of vital importance for the Florentine merchants, so a special provision (No. 16) guaranteed the security of their property against piracy committed by the Venetians and the Genoese at sea. By implication, the same guarantee was applicable to the corsary acts of the Ottoman privateers *(levends)* at Avlona. The Florentines felt it necessary to enter into the *'ahd-nāme* special provisions concerning double taxation (No. 12), hiring native non-Muslims as aides (No. 13), and the validity of the documents issued in different zones of jurisdiction (No. 14 and 15), because the local authorities often annoyed them in such situations. It was indeed a special favor on the part of the Ottoman government to agree to add such specific provisions in the *'ahd-nāme.*

[127] Richards, *Florentine Merchants,* pp. 121-122, 163.

Arab Immigration to Galata

Among the first Muslim settlers in Galata we find Arabs, as confirmed in the first survey in 1455 (*supra).* In the pre-Ottoman period, Arabs, particularly Syrians, participated in the Genoese North-South trade between Pera, Syria and, Egypt and, using the so-called Moldavian Route via Akkerman, they went as far as Lwów (Lemberg).[128] It is likely that some Arab merchants had already settled in Galata under the Genoese and had stayed on during the Ottoman period. Our register of 1455 contains an 'Arab-oghlu Ḥādjī.

In subsequent surveys there were even more Arabs who had settled in Galata near the church of San Domenico because the Galata port was the terminus for most of the ships coming from the Mediterranean. Thus, a tradition seems to have been established that Arabs could find in this part of the city their compatriots and a place to come and settle. The fact that Meḥmed II converted to a mosque the church of San Domenico (later called *'Arab Djāmi'i)* which was apparently abandoned by the Genoese who had left the city *en masse* on May 29, 1453, also attracted Muslims to settle in that area. Later on when Khayr al-Dīn Pasha became the grand admiral of the Ottoman navy (1533) with the Ḳāsım-Pasha district as his seat, the city became a place for Arab seamen from the Maghreb to come and settle.

Folk traditions emerged,[129] or perhaps were promulgated by the Ottoman authorities, to legitimate the settlement of Muslims and the conversion of the church of San Domenico into a mosque. In any event, as a result of the Genoese flight, this area, which contained large houses, was an ideal place to colonize.

According to these folk traditions[130] the Umayyad Caliph 'Umar b. 'Abd al-'Azīz built two forts, the *Ḳal'a al-Ḳahr* to the north of Galata and another one on the shore where the *Kurshunlu Makhzen* stood. Obviously these two forts must be the Tower of Christ (Galata Kulesi) on the hill and the Castle of Galata (Castrum Galathe) on the shore. The same traditions also claim that the church of St Paul and St Dominic, known under the Ottomans as *'Arab Djāmi'i,* as originally built as a mosque by Maslama, the son of Caliph 'Abd al-Malik during his blockade of Constantinople in the years 672-79. The legitimation effort is evident in this Ottoman-Islamic tradition. According to Islamic tradition, a place where Muslims once prayed is considered Muslim

---

128 See Berindei, *art. cit.*, p. 57.

129 See Evliyā Çelebi, *op. cit.,* p. 428.

130 For these traditions cf. Hasluck, II, pp. 717-735; M. Canard, "Les éxpeditions des Arabes contre Constantinople dans l'histoire et dans le légende", *Journal Asiatique,* CCVII (1926), pp. 61-121.

territory forever. Churches were converted into mosques in Istanbul on the other side of the Haliç (Golden Horn) on the assumption that the district was settled by Muslims who were in need of a mosque. Obviously, because of this early Arab settlement, the so-called Moriscos –Arab refugees from Andalusia– also choose to come and settle in the same district of Galata, and thus, reinforced its Arab character.

Distorted from the Arabic *mudadjdjan* (Spanish *mudejar),* meaning "permitted to stay on the land", the Ottoman words *mubtadjal* or *mudadjdjal* designated the Muslims of Spain who immigrated to the Ottoman territories in north Africa and Turkey during the sixteenth century. The persecution which the Muslim population under the Spanish inquisition suffered was indeed a tragic experience.[131] They were compelled to choose between abjuration of their religion or slavery, or expulsion from the country.[132] The attempts of the Andalusian Muslims to attract the attention of the Ottoman Sultan to their plight had started already by 1477 when a delegation visited Meḥmed the Conqueror and solicited his aid and protection. After the Spanish invasion of Granada in 1492, the Algerians, fearing the same fate for themselves, sent the venerated scholar Seyyid Abū al-ʿAbbās to Istanbul in 1519 and requested the Conqueror of Egypt Selim I to aid and protect them. In particular, they asked him to permit Khayr al-Dīn, the leader of the sea *ghāzī*s in Algeria, to remain with them.[133] In a letter written in the name of the cadi, men of religion, merchants and the population of Algeria, they expressed a desire to become the Ottoman Sultan's "dependents" *(khidmetkār* or *khademe).* Selim I, who was believed to have prepared a large-scale naval expedition in the Mediterranean and to have built shipyards in Galata (Ḳāsım Pasha), died the following year.

The successful counterattack of the Ottomans against the Spanish attempts to continue the *Reconquista* in the Maghreb in the period 1520-1570 resulted in growing suspicion and persecution by the Spaniards of the Andalusian Arabs and a stiffening resistance of the Moriscos. In the year 1529, Khayr al-Dīn evacuated 70,000 Moriscos from Spain in six expeditions. In a letter to Sultan Süleymān dated November 29, 1541,[134] the

---

131 Braudel, II, pp. 787-795; A. Hess, *Forgotten Frontier. A History of Ibero-African Frontier,* Chicago, 1978.

132 On Moriscos in Spain see, *Religion, Identité et Sources Documentaires sur les Morisques Andalous,* ed. A. Temimi, Tunis, 1984; A. Temimi, *Le gouvernement ottoman et le problème morisque,* Zaghouan, 1989.

133 A. Temimi, "Lettre de la population algéroise au Sultan Selim Ier en 1519", *Revue d'Histoire Maghrébine,* vol. V (1976). pp. 95-101.

134 A. Temimi, "Une lettre des Moriscos de Grenade au Sultan Suleiman al-Kanunī en 1541", *Revue d'Histoire Maghrébine,* III (1975), pp. 98-106.

Moriscos, numbering they said 364,000 in Andalusia, offered their submission to him and implored him to continue his support of Khayr al-Dīn Pasha. The migration took on the character of an exodus after the dramatic confrontation between the Ottoman and Spanish Empires at Lepanto in 1571. Morisco uprisings in Spain in the years 1569-1570 and in 1589 resulted in deportations, confiscations and a systematic policy of christianizing. Finally, in 1599, the Spanish Council of State reached a decision to expel the Morisco population and confiscate their properties. The operation started in 1609 and affected 300,000 people.[135] A new mass migration into Ottoman territories including Galata occured in 1609-1610. The immigrants, called *Grenatini* by the Christians of Galata, arrived under the protection of the Ottoman Sultan, who sent letters to the King of France and to the Venetian Doge asking them not to hinder their free passage.

For the Arab settlement in Galata during the period 1570-1610, there exist quite detailed accounts. In 1594 the Venetian *bailo* M. Zane reported that *di Spagna concorrono ogni giorne Mori in Constantinople, che si nominano Mondesari, come se uscissero solamente di Granata, ma in effetto tutta La Spagna n'e contaminata, e subito giunti Levano il tolpante.*[136] Hasluck suggests that the Morisco refugees, who were naturally hostile to the Christians, may have heightened anti-Christian feelings among the Turks during that period; and their settlement in the heart of Galata "may have been made to appear as a political necessity at a time when the Turks were concerned about Christian plots".[137] Knolles[138] reports that, in 1612, the Moriscos of Galata drove out the Jews and destroyed their synagogues. Belin[139] and Hasluck[140] believe that the church of Saint Paul and Saint Dominic *('Arab Djāmi'i)* must have been taken over to serve as a mosque for Moriscos at this time.

By 1623, the *Comunità* worried that the Andalusian Arabs were still threatening to take over the Catholic churches to convert them into mosques. As a result of increasing anti-Catholic feelings, many churches were indeed converted into mosques in Istanbul itself during this period. Towards the

---

135 See Braudel, II, pp. 780-802.

136 Cited by Hasluck, p. 724, note 3.

137 Letter to Henri III dated March 1579 cited by Belin, *La Latinité,* p. 217, note 1.

138 Cited by Hasluck, p. 726.

139 *La Latinité,* p. 217; but we know through the *wakfiyye* of Mehmed II that the church was converted into a mosque under Meḥmed II (see Appendix No. 6).

140 Hasluck, *op. cit.,* p. 724.

mid-seventeenth century Evliyā[141] recognizes the large Arab settlement in Galata:

The people of Galata, consist of several separate groups: seamen, merchants, artisans, carpenters, and caulkers. Most of the (Muslim) population wear clothes in the fashion of Algerians and a great number of them are from Arab lands. Also there are very rich sea captains.

In the district of *Bash-Ḥiṣār* (Galata Kulesi) and in the second *Ḥiṣār* down to the *Arab Djāmi'i* (San Domenico) there is no Christian resident. The Muslim inhabitants of these quarters hold the imperial edict of Meḥmed the Conqueror, and thus they allow no Christian to settle among themselves. The reason is that at this time most of the inhabitants in these quarters consist of those afflicted Muslims of the so-called *Mubtedjel* community who immigrated under Sultan Ahmed I. They take great care of these quarters.

Evliyā[142] adds that these Arabs introduced an exotic taste of their own into the city with their popular *Mubtedjel sherbeti,* a sweet soft drink, and colorful spiced *halva.*

Of the Arabs of Galata, 'Arab Aḥmed Pasha,[143] an Ottoman admiral during the invasion of Cyprus in 1570, distinguished himself first as a money changer, and then a seaman in Galata.[144] Another Arab, by the name of 'Arab Ḳayyūm, gave his name to a busy street in the port area. Finally we find an Arab of Galata occupying the post of the cadiship of the city. The extensive court records of Galata, covering a long period from the middle of the sixteenth down to the twentieth century, currently preserved in the archives of the Istanbul *Müftülük,* contain details on the activities of the Galata Arabs (see Bibliography: Primary Sources: C).

---

141 *Seyāhatnāme,* I, p. 434.

142 *Ibid.,* pp. 433, 434.

143 The first English ambassador to the Porte, William Harborne, chose to live in Rapamat (Arab Aḥmed) Pasha's house, at the Fındıklı shore (S. Skilliter, *William Harborne and Trade with Turkey, 1578-1582,* London, 1977, pp. 32, 112).

144 *Muṣṭafā 'Ālī's Counsel for Sultans of 1581,* ed., trans., notes by A. Tietze, Wien, 1979, Index; 'Ālī despises him for his mundane origin and early profession of money-changer.

BIBLIOGRAPHY

I. Primary Sources

A. Wakfiyyes

Wakfiyye I: The oldest *wakfiyye* of the Fâtih mosque is a copy in Arabic now preserved in the *Türk-İslâm Eserleri* Museum, Istanbul, cod. 667; originally found in the mausoleum of Mehmed II, the roll pasted to a green satin is 38.85 m. long and 0.28 m. wide with missing parts. The portions bearing the *tughra* at the top and the date at the end are missing; O. N. Ergin, p. 13, dates it as 1472 or 1473. It is an officially certified copy of the missing original. This *wakfiyye* is published in facsimile by O. N. Ergin, *Fatih İmareti Vakfı,* Istanbul, 1945; but the facsimile in this publication has been reduced so much that it makes reading difficult. The portion of this *wakfiyye* belonging to a second copy is preserved in the *Başvekâlet (Osmanlı)* Archives, Istanbul, *Fatih devri vesikaları,* No. 108.

Wakfiyye II: The second surviving *wakfiyye* of the Fâtih mosque, an officially certified copy is preserved in the Topkapı Palace Museum: Saray 16/1141. It is published in facsimile by Tahsin Öz (in collaboration with Paul Wittek) with an introduction under the title "Zwei Stiftungsurkunden des Sultans Mehmed II. Fatih", *Istanbuler Mitteilungen,* Heft 4, 1935. It is a copy dated 8 *Dhu'lka'da* 901/July 19, 1496 bearing Bāyezīd II's *tughra.* It is a faithful copy of the original as attested by the remark "This is copied from the original copy with no additions or omissions". The fact that the copier made no changes at all in the original is confirmed by the phrase which mentioned Mehmed II as living. The only? change is the omission of the date of the original, evidently because this is a copy revalidated by the new Sultan so that we find only the revalidation date.

Wakfiyye III: A third version of the *wakfiyye* of Mehmed II for his mosque is in Turkish and was made in the second half of the sixteenth century. It is published in facsimile: *Fatih Mehmet II Vakfiyeleri,* Ankara 1938, pp. 13-198, in modern Turkish, pp. 199-284. This *wakfiyye* III is in essence a translation into Turkish of the Arabic *wakfiyye* II. The section on Galata is to be found on pages 167-228 in the facsimile publication. A comparison of *wakfiyyes* II and III reveals, however, some slight omissions (cf. *wakfiyye* II p. 45, and *wakfiyye* III, p. 167).

B. Djibāyet Registers

I. The detailed *djibāyet* register of the Ayasofya *waḳfs* in the cities of Istanbul, Galata and Üsküdar by Yūsuf b. Khalīl in *Shawwāl* 894/August-July 1489. This inspection and detailed survey is made on the basis of the survey by ābilī (Küpeli)-zāde Muḥyī al-Dīn Meḥmed and Fanārī-zāde 'Alā'al-Dīn 'Alī, *kaḍī'asker* of Anadolu sometime between 867/1462 and 872/1468, the period of the *kaḍīi'askership* of Kābilī-zāde (see *Shaḳā'iḳ,* p. 215). This latter register or registers have not yet been discovered.

II. The second *djibāyet* register concerns the *waḳfs* of the Ayasofya mosque in Istanbul, Galata and Üsküdar. This register is preserved in the archival collection of Muallim Cevdet, currently making part of the Istanbul *Belediye* Library, n 0.64. The survey was made under the supervision of the well known scholar Meḥmed son of 'Alī al-Fanārī. The survey, written in Arabic, bears the completion date of *Muḥarrem* 926/December 1519. It is a big volume of 223 folios; the section on Galata goes from fol. 159 to the end. This is the most detailed description of the buildings in Galata with valuable supplementary information on the city's topography, inhabitants and social and economic life.

C. The cadi records of Galata in the Archives of the Istanbul Müftülüğü

The archives of the *Istanbul Müftülüğü* contain the Galata court documents. This particular series, the *Galata Mahkemesi Şeriyye Sicilleri,* comprises 1040 registers covering the period 943/1536-1343/1924. This is the most important collection of documents on the history of Galata. In the same archives other collections dealing specifically with Galata include: documents and accounting registers for the religious endowments in Galata (No. 198), court documents and copies of the imperial decrees on Galata (no. 218, 229, 235). In the *ma'rūḍ* collection in the same archives, which contains the cases submitted or reported to the Porte for a government decision or Sultanic order, there are a great number of documents concerning the city and people of Galata (Examples from this series can be seen in Appendix No. 10).

The earliest register of court documents *(sidjillāt)* is a register of 388 pages (first pages missing) containing court documents *(hudjadj)* of all sorts of cases concerning civil law, the property lists of the deceased *(mukhallafāt)* as well as public accountings *(muhāsabāt)* and other public affairs documents. These records have all the characteristics of the registers of court records of the Empire. But its special interest is due to the fact that a great number of records deal with the navy — sea captains, crews, caulkers, and makers of naval equipment. A number of documents have to do with Hayreddin Barbaros and his men. Also, these registers provide details on the foreign embassies and people connected with them. They complement the *Ecnebī Defterleri* preserved at the *Başvekâlet* archives which comprise the imperial orders concerning the official correspondence of the embassies with the Sublime Porte. On the other hand, the Galata court records could be considered as the most important collection of documents on Ottoman maritime commerce and its legal aspects such as the commenda *(muḍāraba)* contracts and cases, ship ownership in shares, captains and shipowners, as well as shipments of commodities both imported and exported, and on those people engaged in commercial dealings. Another interesting series of documents in the Galata registers deals with the interrelations between Muslims and non-Muslims, *dhimmī* Greeks, Italians, Armenians and Jews as well as foreign non-Muslims who comprised half of Galata's population. Also, not infrequently, non-Muslims used the cadi's court for dealings among themselves including civil matters such as marriage and the division of inheritance. Thus, the Ottoman society of Galata was unique to the Ottoman Empire in that people of different ethnic, social, religious and cultural backgrounds formed a viable urban society.

Page 1

The following summaries of the documents from the Galata cadi *sidjill*s (see Appendix 10) give an idea as to the significance of the court records for the history of the city. The cadi under whom the register was kept was Mawlānā Meḥmed Ḥamīd, son of Neylī Aḥmed (p. 1 no. 1), also known as Neylī-zāde.

Page 2

Doc. 1. Concerning the release of the baker 'Alī from the Boghaz-Kesen prison. He had made and sold bread to the public in violation of the regulations in force. His incarceration, which was a *ta'zīr* punishment, ended upon the Sultan's order when a surety was given by the deputy of the bakers of Galata and two master bakers. Their petition is reported *(ma'rūḍ)* to the grand vizir, dated 6 *Radjab* 1175/January 31, 1762.

Doc. 2. Report to the grand vizir concerning the recording in the cadi register of the election of a trustee *(kethkudā, mu'tamad)* by the merchants holding the monopoly on buying (and selling) imported crystal wares (from Europe), dated 11 *Radjab* 1175/February 5, 1762.

Doc. 3. Report of the release from prison of another baker.

Doc. 4. Report concerning wheat purchased at Isakcı (Isaccea on the Danube) three years previously. Of the 69,064 kile purchased 5,996 kile are missing.

Page 3

Doc. 1. Copy of the Sultan's order to the voyvoda of Galata, dated beginning of *Muḥarrem* 1127 (January 1715), concerning the 4,000 *medre* of wine permitted to be purchased without tax for the domestic use of the Genoese merchants and their employees.

Page 4

Doc. 1. Order of the grand vizir for the illumination of the city of Galata to celebrate the recent success of the imperial army (over the Venetians). Dated 14 *Dhilḥidjdja* 1127 (December 11, 1715).

Page 5

Doc. 1. List of the distribution of the eight *iskemle* in the districts of Galata: Balık Pazarı, Karaköy, Yahudiler Çarşısı, the new grocery *(djedīd baḳḳāl)* shop in the Karaköy district, shop of the Jews of Hasköy behind the public bathhouse, shop of the used-cloth dealer Muṣṭafā in the Abadjılar bazaar in Karaköy, shop of Sha'bān across the Çartak, the shop adjacent to the coffee house *(ḳahvekhāne),* the shop of al-Ḥādj Ḳāsım in Tophane square. In addition there were five *iskemle* at the Ḳurşunlu Makhzen. Signed by the cadi Aḥmed.

Page 6

Record, registered by the cadi, of a transaction which took place in the house of the associates of the French *(Fransız)* merchant Anan (?), residing in the district of Bereket-zāde. The transaction was concluded in the presence of the cadi's agent Mawlānā Muṣṭafā, the dragoman *(tercümān)* Forent (?), the *musta'min* (foreigners under the capitulations) merchants, and 'Alī Agha, residing in the neighborhood of Sultan-Aḥmed. 'Alī Agha stated that the foreign merchants owed him 1,300 groush on he account of the 600 ells *(dhirā')* of variegated French woolen cloth *(elvān Fransız çukası)* which he purchased from them. Arrangement was made for the payment to be made through the agents of the indebted. Dated 5 *Rabī I* 1128/February 28, 1716.

D. Collections of Documents and Narrative Sources

A. Roccatagliata: A. Roccatagliata, *Notai genovesi in Oltramare, Atti rogati a Pera e Mitilene,* 1: *Pera 1408-1490,* Collana storica di fonti et studi,, ed. G. Pistarino, 34, 1, Genoa, 1981.

Belgrano, Documenti: L. T. Belgrano, *Documenti riguardanti la Colonia Genovesse di Pera,* Atti della Società Ligura di Storia Patria, XIII, Genoa, 1886.

Donado da Lezze: Donado da Lezze, *Historia Turchesca,* ed. I. Ursu, Bucharest, 1910.

Ducas: Doucas, *Historia Turco-Byzantina,* trans. Harry J. Magoulias: *Decline and Fall of Byzantium to the Ottoman Turks,* Detroit, 1975.

Evliyā Çelebi: *Evliyā Çelebi Seyāhatnāmesi,* ed. A. Cevdet, Istanbul, 1314/1896.

Ferīdūn: Ferīdūn Beg, *Munshe'āt al-Salāṭīn,* I, Istanbul, 1274/1857.

Giacomo Badoer: Giacomo Badoer, *Il Libro dei Conti di Giacomo Badoer,* eds. U. Dorini and Tommaso Bertelè, Venice, 1956.

Maṭraḳdjı: Nasūhü's-Silāḥī (Maṭraḳcı), *Beyān-i Menāzil-i Sefer-i 'Iraḳeyn-i Sulṭān Süleymān Ḫan,* Ankara, 1976, Plan of Galata, facsimile text: fol. 9a.

Pertusi, *La Caduta:* Agostino Pertusi, *La Caduta di Costantinopoli,* vol. I: *Le Testimonianze dei Contemporanei* vol. II: *L'eco nel mondo,* Verona, 1976.

Tursun Beg, *The History of Mehmed the Conqueror,* eds. H. İnalcık and R. Murphey, Minneapolis and Chicago, 1978.

II. Modern Works

Ayverdi, *İstanbul Mahalleleri*: Ekrem Hakkı Ayverdi, *Fatih Devri Sonlarında İstanbul Mahalleleri, Şehrin İskânı ve Nüfusu,* Ankara, 1958.

Babinger, *Mehmed the Conqueror*: Franz Babinger, *Mehmed the Conqueror and His Time,* trans. R. Manheim, ed. W. C Hickman, Princeton, 1978.

Babinger, "Drei Stadtansichten": Franz Babinger, "Drei Stadtansichten von Konstantinopel, Galata (Pera) und Skutar aus dem Ende des 16. Jahrhunderts", *Österreichische Akademie der Wissenschaften, Denkschriften*: 77. Band, Wien, 1959.

Balard: Michel Balard, *La Romanie génoise,* 2 vols. Genova, 1978.

Beldiceanu, *Ville:* Nicoăra Beldiceanu, *Recherche sur la ville ottomane au XVe* siècle, Paris, 1973.

Berindei: M. Berindei, "L'Empire ottoman et la 'route moldave' avant la conquête de Chilia et Cetătea-albă (1484)", *Journal of Turkish Studies,* vol. 10 (1986), pp. 47-72.

Braudel: Fernand Braudel, *The Mediterranean and the Mediterranean World in the Age of Philip II,* 2 vols., trans. S. Reynolds, New York, 1972.

CMRS: *Cahiers du Monde Russe et Soviétique*, Paris.

Hasluck: F. W. Hasluck, *Christianity and Islam under the Sultans,* reprint, New York, 1973.

Heers, Gênes: J. Heers, *Gênes au XVe siècle, activité économique et problèmes sociaux,* Paris, 1961.

Heyd: Wilhelm Heyd, *Histoire du Commerce du Levant,* ed. F. Raynaud, 2 vols., Leipzig, 1936.

İnalcık, "Bursa": H. İnalcık, "Bursa: XV. Asır Sanayi ve Ticaret Tarihine Dair Vesikalar", *Belleten,* vol. XXIV (1960), pp. 45-102.

Inalcik, "Bursa and the Commerce of the Levant": H. İnalcık, "Bursa and the Commerce of the Levant", *Journal of the Economic and Social History of the Orient",* vol. 3 (1960), pp. 131-147.

Inalcik, "Servile Labor": H. Inalcik, "Servile Labor in the Ottoman Empire", *Mutual Effects Between the Islamic and Judeo-Christian World,* eds. A. Archer, T. Halasi-Kun and B. K. Király, New York, 1979.

Inalcik, "The Policy": H. Inalcik, "The Policy of Mehmed II toward the Greek Population of Istanbul and the Byzantine Buildings of the City", *Dumbarton Oaks Papers,* vol. 23-24 (1969-1970), pp. 231-249.

Lopez, "Market Expansion": R. S. Lopez, "Market Expansion: The Case of Genoa", *Journal of Economic History,* vol. 24 (1964), pp. 445-464.

Lopez and Miskimin: R. S. Lopez and H. A. Miskimin, "The Economic Depression of the Renaissance", *Economic History Review,* 2nd series, vol. XIV (1962), pp. 408-426; vol. XVI (1964), pp. 525-527.

Lopez, *Storia:* R. S. Lopez, *Storia delle colonie genovesi nel Mediterraneo,* Bologna, 1938.

Cazacu: Matei Cazacu and Kéram Kévonian, "La chute de Caffa en 1475 à la lumière de nouveaux documents", *CMRS,* XVII-4 (1976), pp. 495-538.

Pistarino, "The Genoese in Pera": Geo Pistarino, "The Genoese in Pera-Turkish Galata", *Mediterranean Historical Review,* I (1980), pp. 63-85.

Richards: G. R. B. Richards, *Florentine Merchants in the Age of the Medici,* Cambridge, Mass., 1932.

L. Sauli, *Dalla Colonia dei Genovesi::a Galata,* 2 vols. Torino, 1831.

Schneider: A. M. Schneider and M. Nomidis, *Galata,* Istanbul, 1944.

Tietze and Kahane: A. Tietze and H. and R. Kahane, *The Lingua Franca in the Levant,* reprint: Istanbul, 1988.

Wittek, "Zu einigen": Paul Wittek, "Zu einigen frühosmanischen Urkunden", *Wiener Zeitschrift für die Kunde des Morgenlandes,* vol. 53, pp. 300-313; vol. 54, pp. 240-256; vol. 55, pp. 122-141; vol. 56, pp. 267-284; vol. 57, pp. 102-117.

APPENDICES

1. Turkish version of the *'ahd-nāme* of 1453, granted to the Genoese of Galata.
2. The original Greek text of the *'ahd-nāme* of 1453.
3. The 1610 renewal of the *'ahd-nāme* of 1453.
4. Section concerning the *'ahd-nāme* of 1453 in Meḥmed the Conqueror's letter to the Sultan of Egypt.
5. Sample pages from the Survey of 1455.
6. Churches, 1455.
7. The *Djibāyet* Register of the Ayasofya Mosque of 1519, sample Pages.
8. The Capitulations granted to the Florentines, the renewal text of 1527.
9. Population of Galata: Documents, I-VII.
10. Sample pages from the Court Records of Galata.
11. Views and Plans of Galata.
12. Tables I and II.

1.

Turkish version of the *'ahd-nāme* of 1453, granted to the Genoese of Galata.

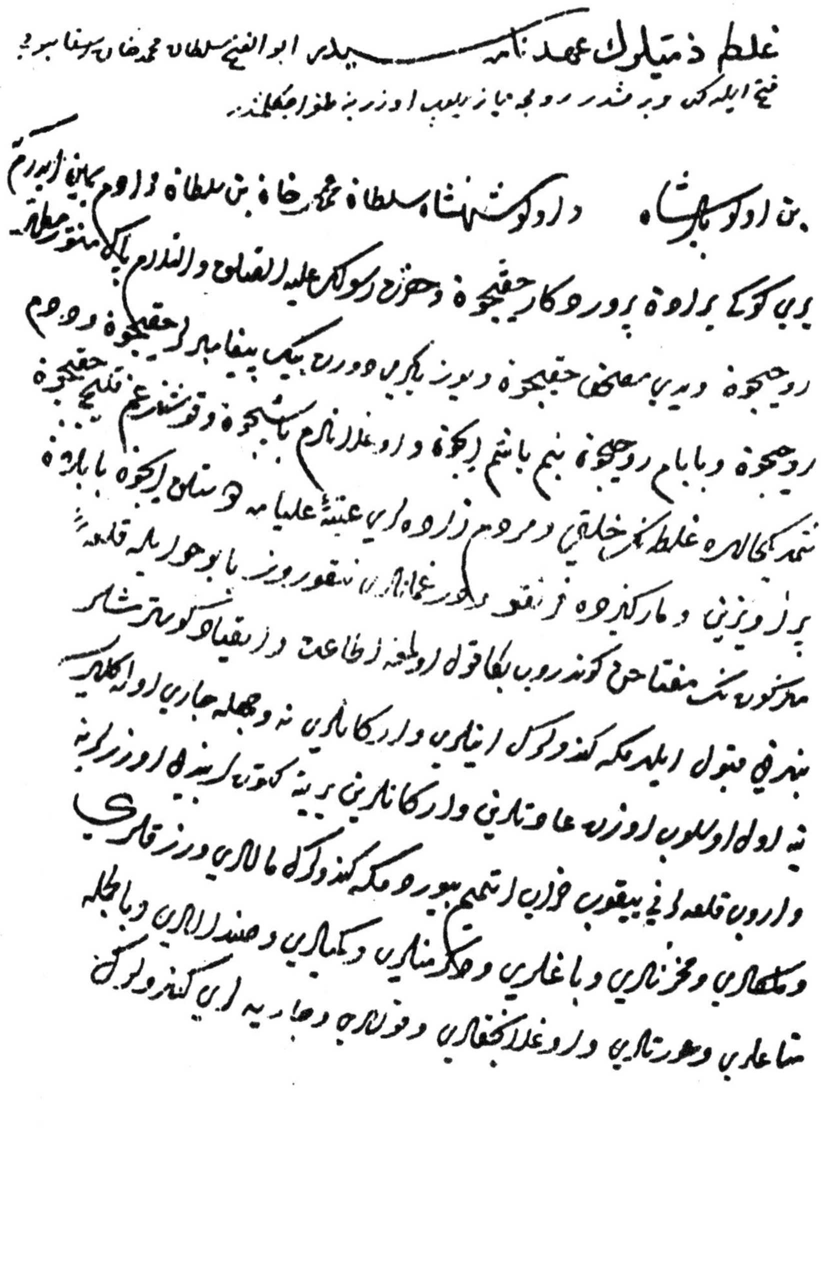

دالارنده مقرر اوله متعارض اولمیم واوکشنده دریم انلر دخی زنجیرکش

اولمیه‌لر غیری مملکتلرم کبی دریادن و قورودن سفر ایدرکسنه مانع و مزاحم

اولمیه معاف ومسلم اوله‌لر انلر دخی اوزرلرنه شرعی خراج وضع ایدرم سال بسال

ادا ایدلر غیریلر کبی و بنده دخی بونلرکه اوزرلرنه نظر ایتمیم و دیوارلرنی بوزمیوب

قوریم غیری مملکتلرم کبی و کلیسالری الارنده اوله اونی آیینلرنجه اما چان

وناقوس چالمیه‌لر و کلیسالرین آلوب مسجد ایتمیم بونلر دخی یکی کلیسا یاپمیه‌لر

و جنویز بازرکانلری دریادن و قورودن زنجیرلو ایدوب کلوب کیده‌لر

کمرکلرین عادت اوزرنه ویره‌لر انلره کمسنه تعرض ایتمیه و بیوردم که یکیچری ایلکه اوغلان

المیم و بر کافر رضاسی اولمدین مسلمان ایتمیه‌لر دکنده ارلرین کمی اختیار

ایدرلرسه مصلحتلرکچون کتمه‌ز نصب ایدلر و بیوردم که اولرنه طوغانجی و قول قونمیه

و قلعهٔ مذکوره خلقی و بازرکانلری انکاریده معاف ومسلم اوله‌لر شویله بیله‌لر

علامت شریفه اعتماد قیله‌لر تحریراً فی اوایل جمادی الاول

سنه سبع وخمسین وثمانمایه .

2.
The original Greek text of the *'ahd-nāme* of 1453*

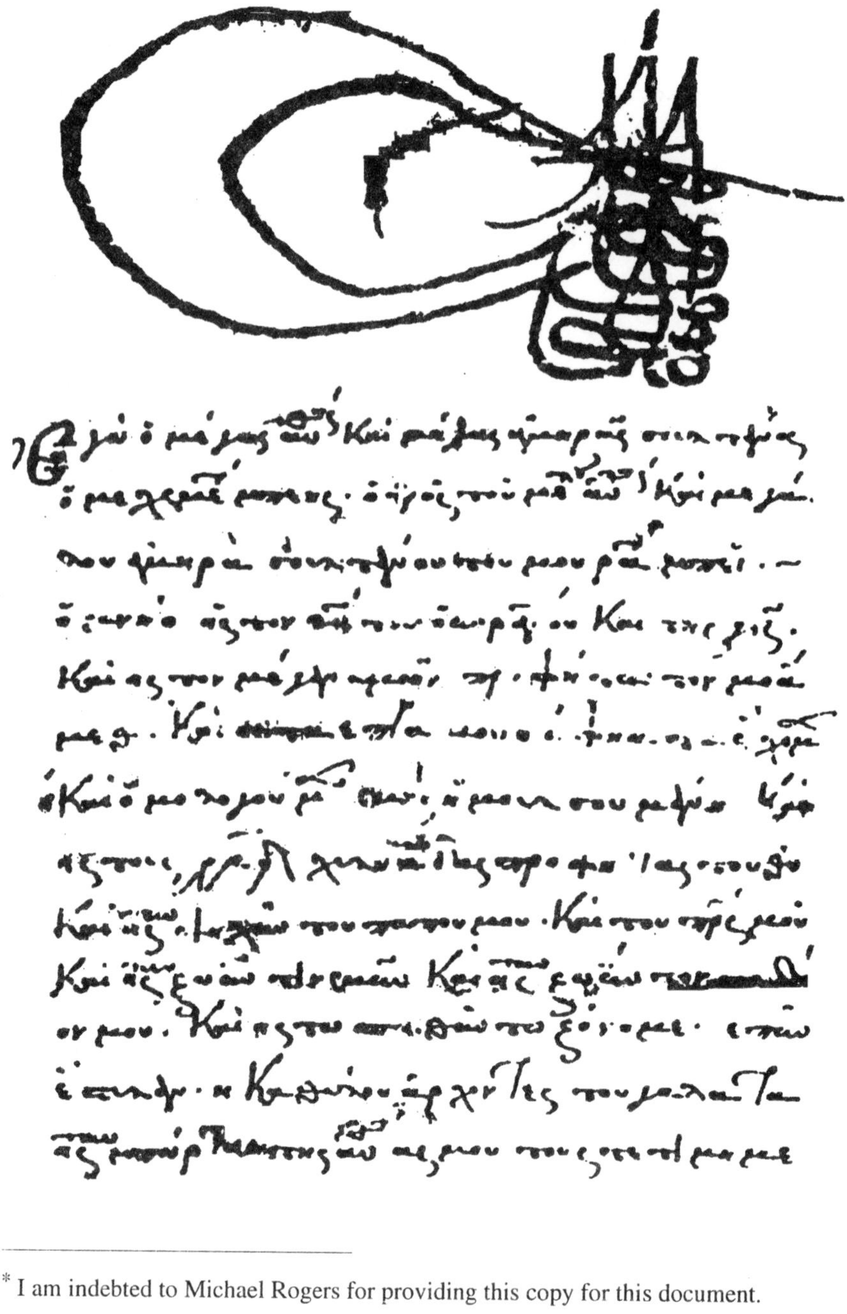

* I am indebted to Michael Rogers for providing this copy for this document.

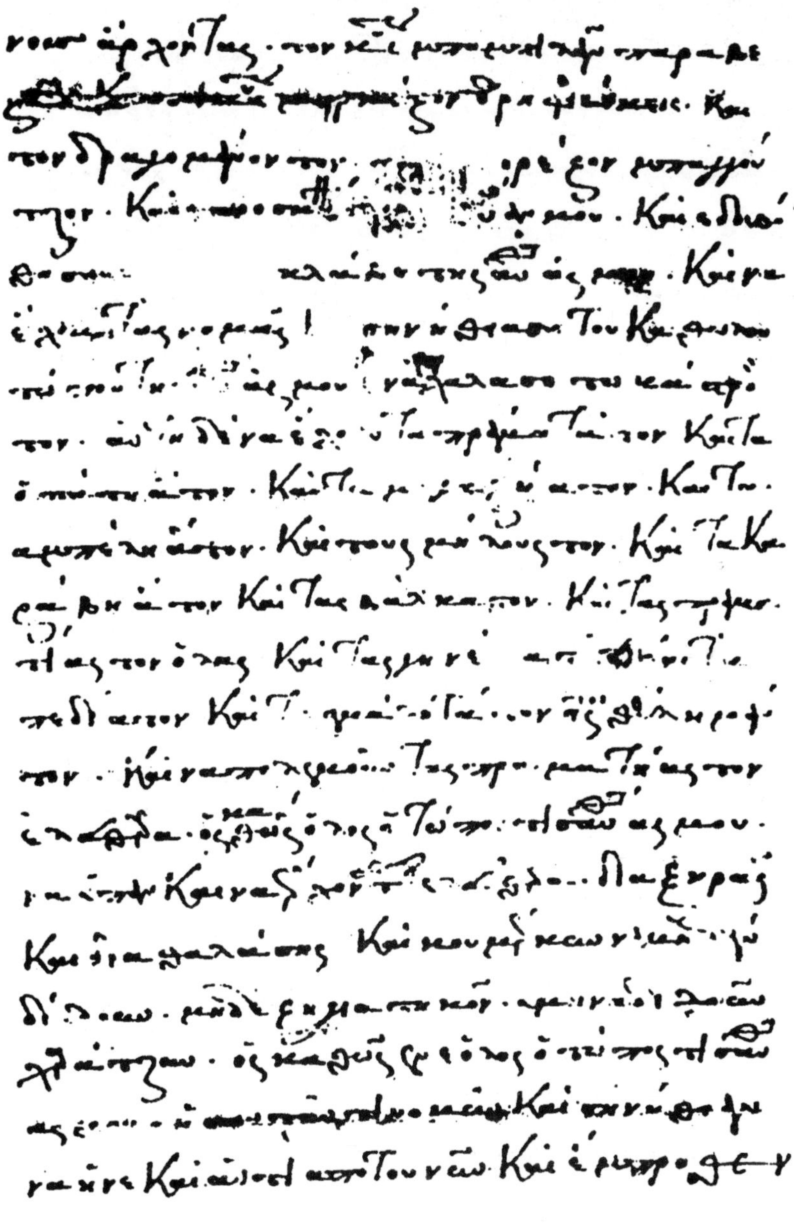

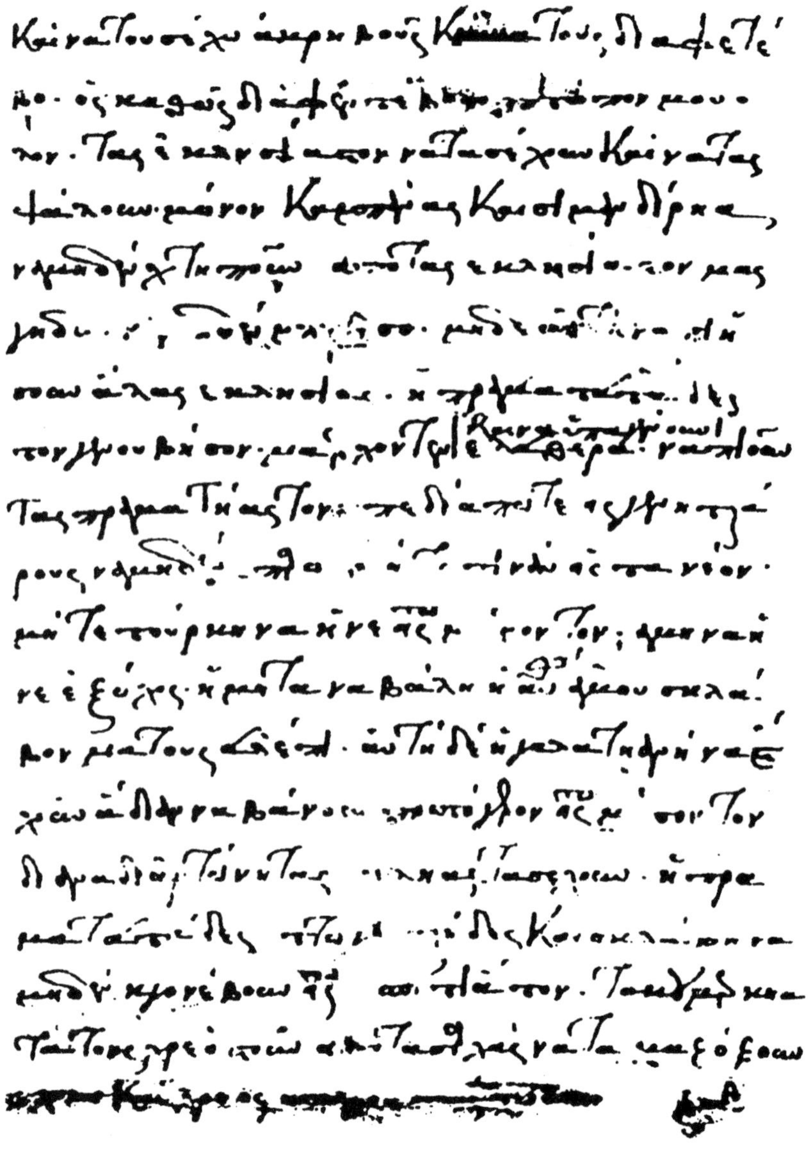

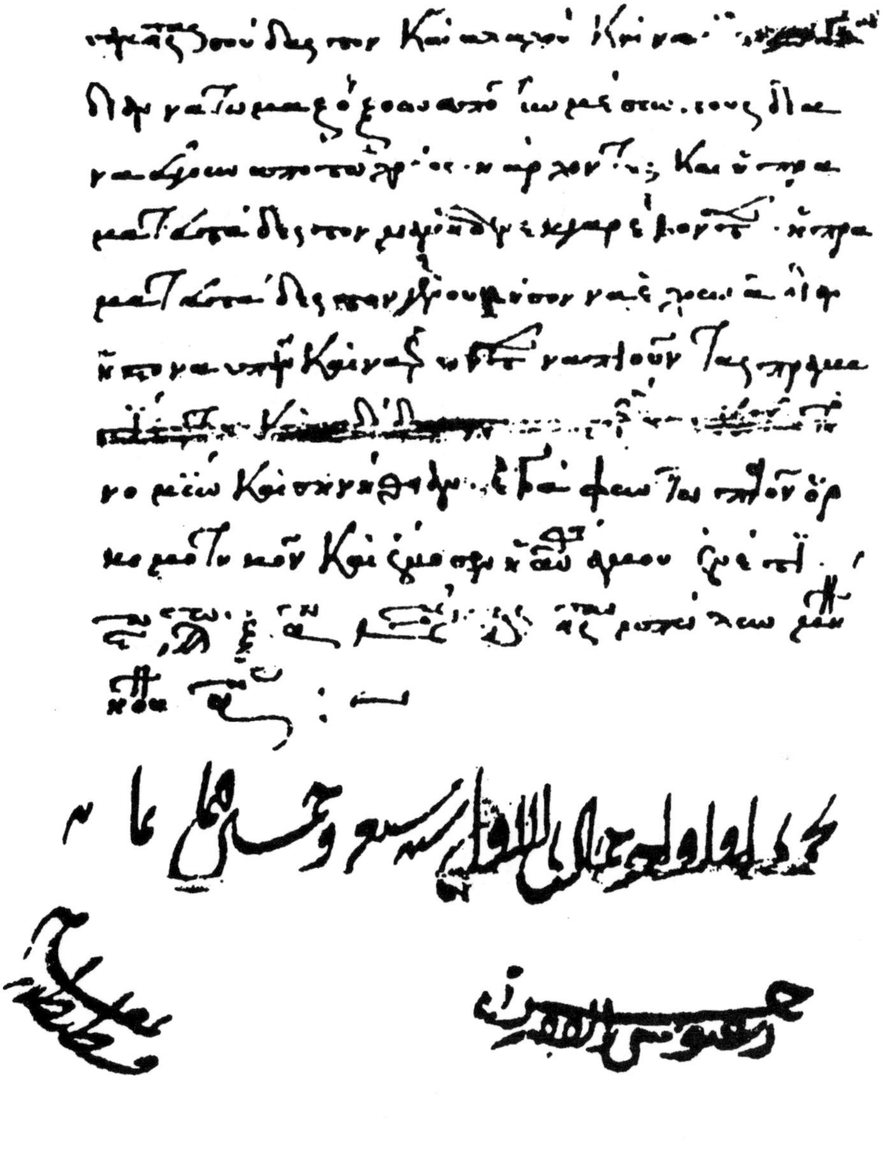

3.

The 1610 renewal of the *'ahd-nāme* of 1453.

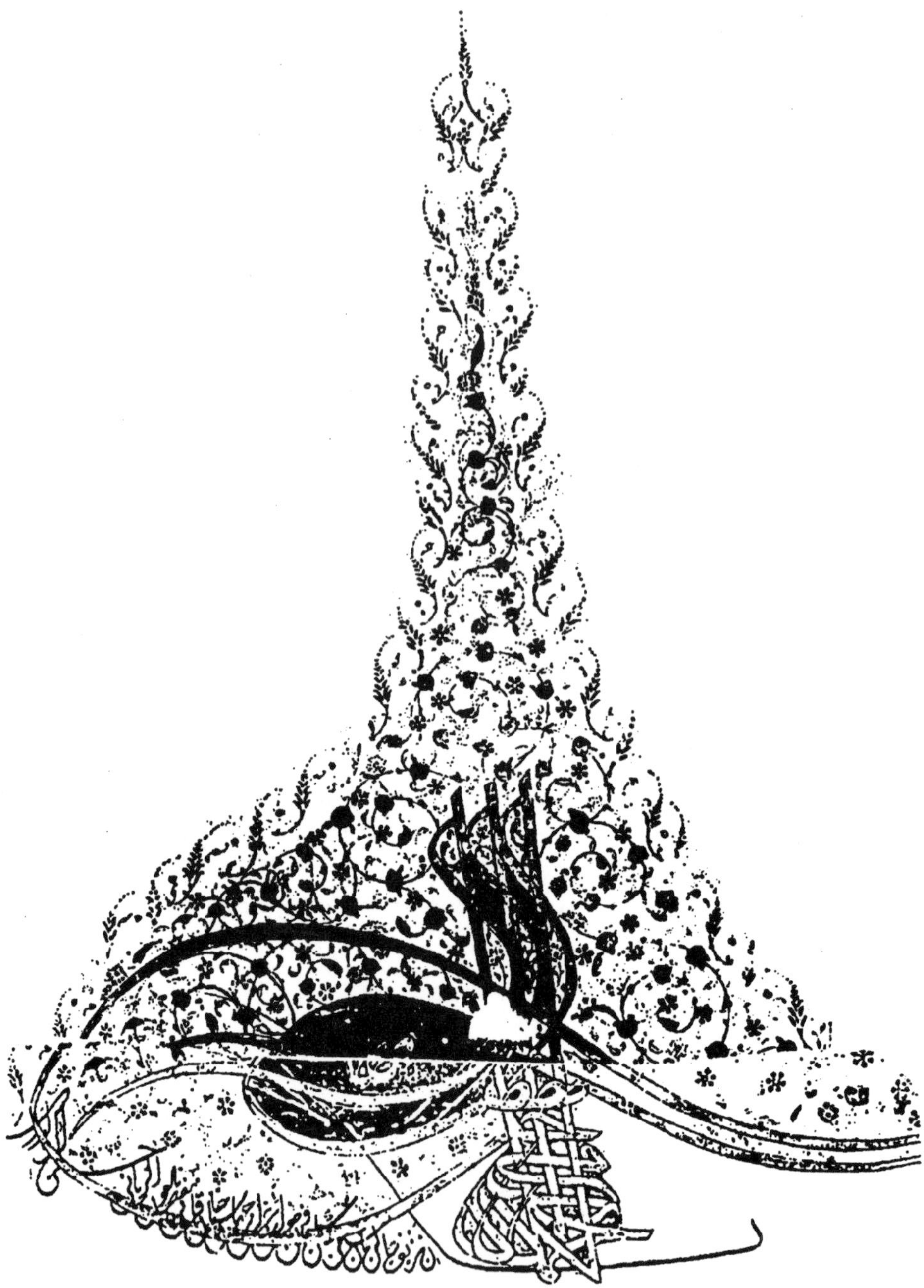

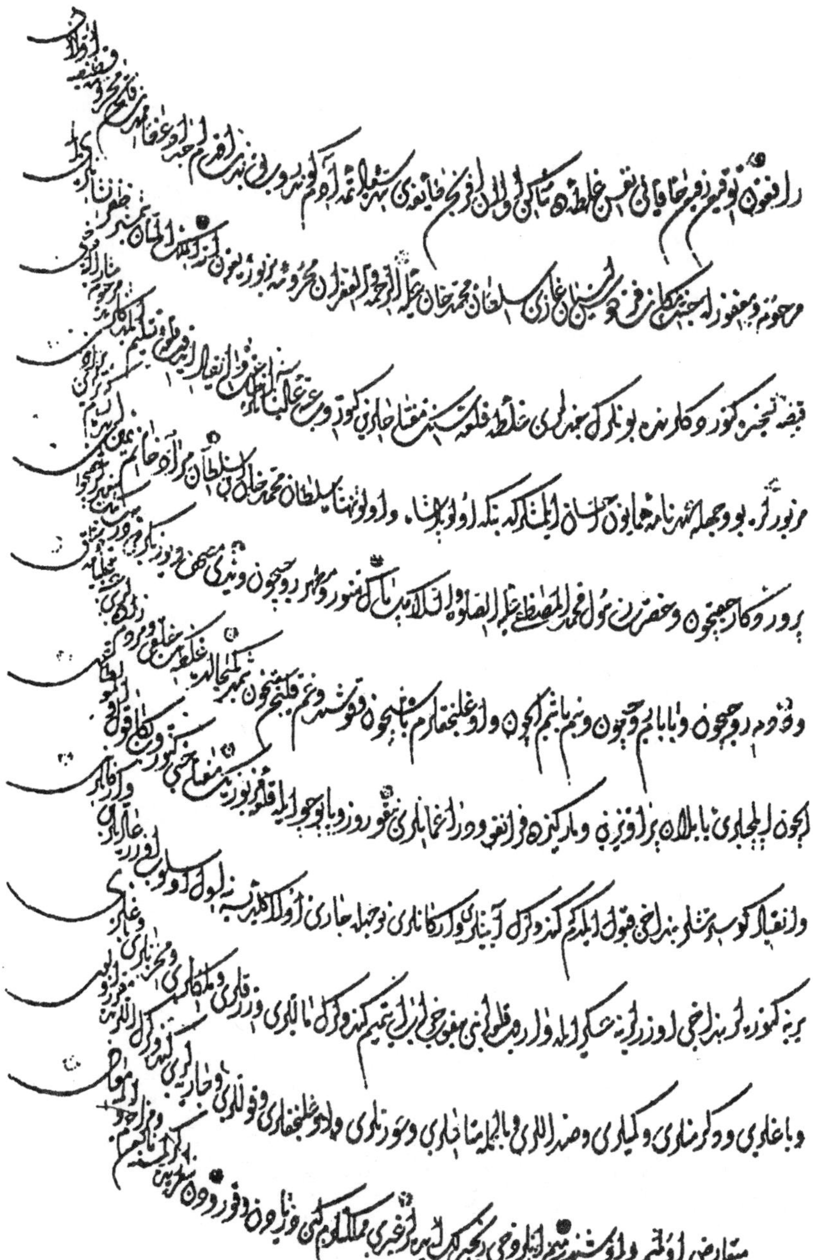

4.
Section concerning the *'ahd-nāme* of 1453 in Meḥmed the Conqueror's letter to the Sultan of Egypt*

«... فلما حاصرنا قسطنطنية جاءنا اهل تلك القلعة وشدوا بنا ميثاقهم وجددوا معنا وفاقهم وقلنا لهم كونوا كما كنتم واثبتوا على ما أنتم عليه بشرط ان لاتعينو بها فقبلوا شرطنا واطاعوا امرنا فلما وقع ما وقع على قسطنطنية وجد بين القتلى والاسرى من اهل غلطه وهم قد حاربونا وبدأ انهم نقضوا ميثاقهم واظهروا نفاقهم فاردنا ان نفعل بهم مافعلنا بالاخرى فبينما هم جاؤا مبتهلين ومتضرعين وقالوا ان **لم ترحمنا لنكونن من الخاسرين** فعفونا عنهم أنه هو العفو الغفار ومننا عليهم المنة لله العزيز الواحد القهار وقررنا على ملكهم الملك له العزيز الجبار ولكن جعلنا حصنهم صعيدا جرزا بحيث لا نرى فيها عوجا ولا امنا وملكنا ارضهم وماءهم و كتبنا في جريدة الجزى اسماءهم **حتى يعطوا الجزية عن يد وهم صاغرون**...».

* Source: Feridūn, *Munsha āt al-Salāṭīn,* I, İstanbul, 1274, p. 237.

5.
Sample pages from the Survey of 1455.

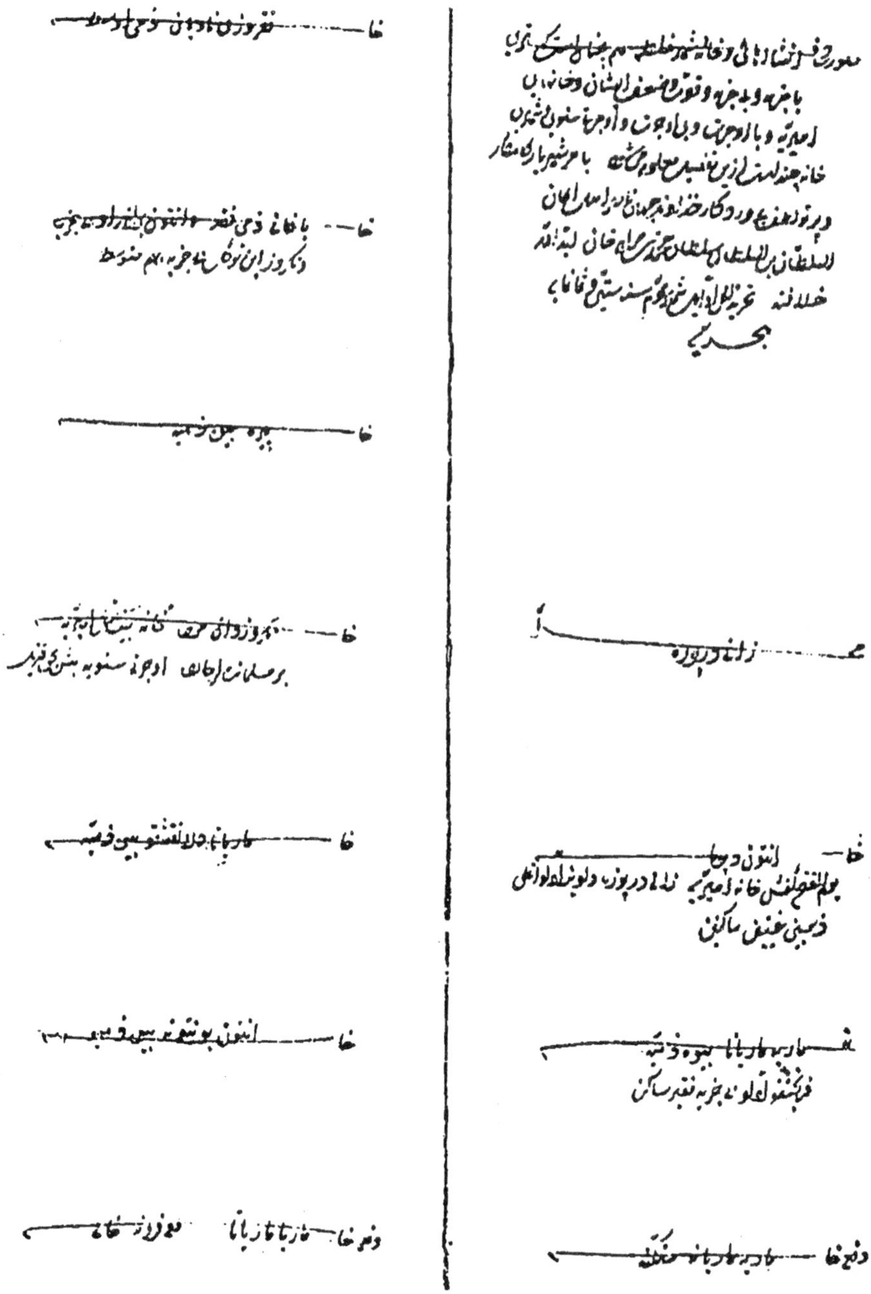

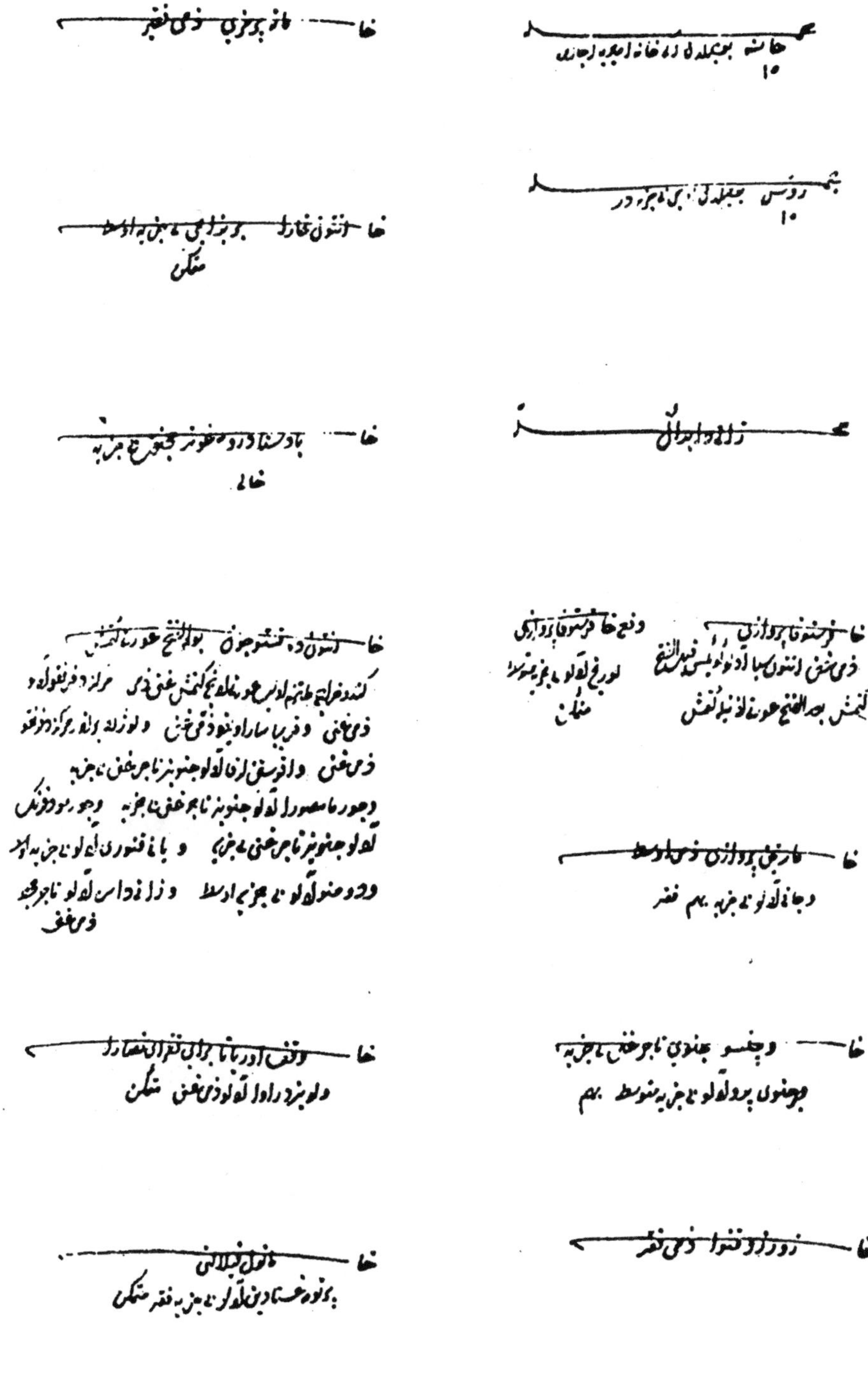

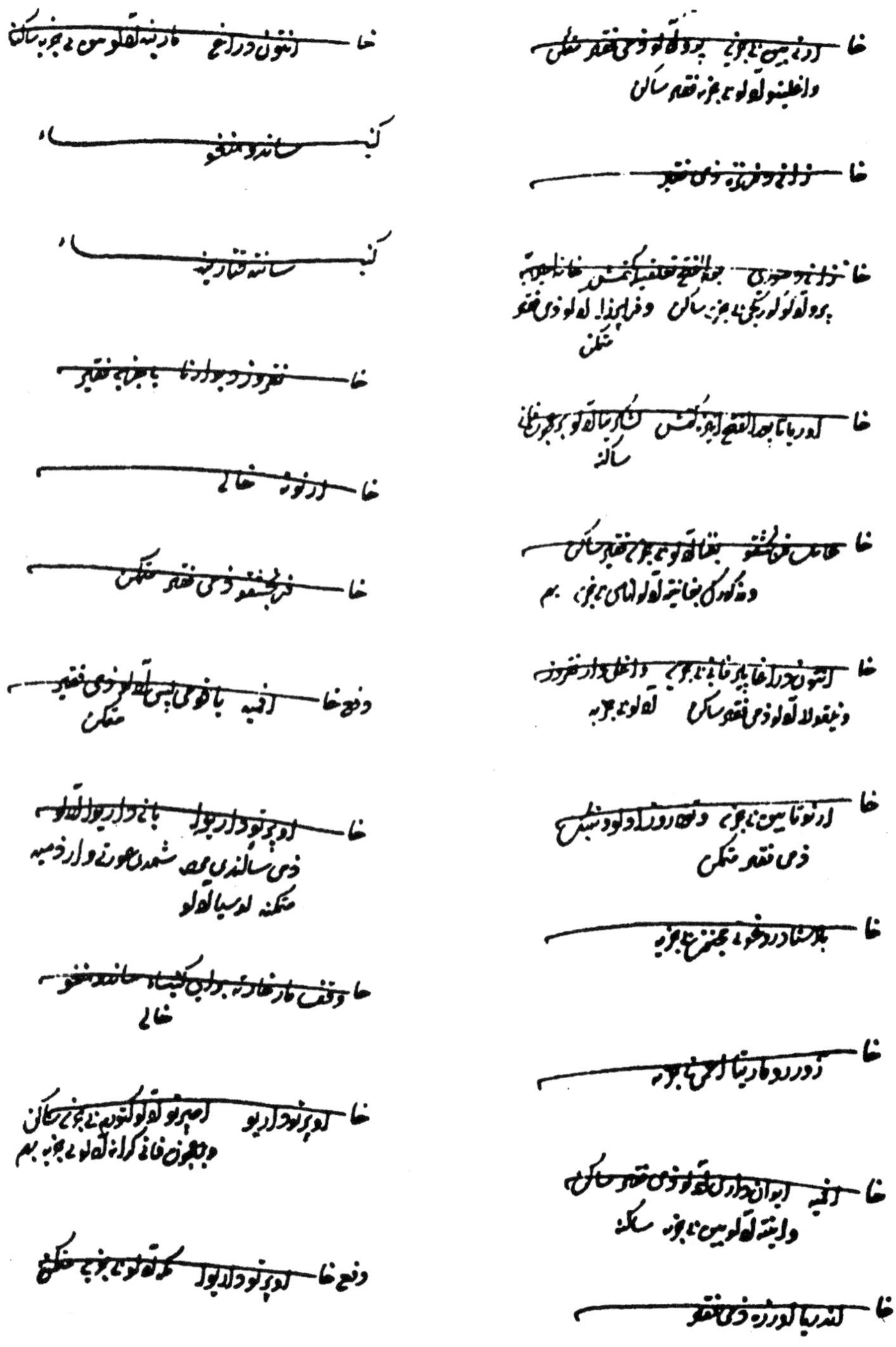

6.
Churches, 1455

For the topography of Galata and the localization of the quarters, it is essential to determine the exact sites of the churches from the pre-Ottoman period (see Table I and Map).

Meḥmed the Conqueror converted the church of St Paul and St Dominic (San Domenigo) into a mosque after the surrender of Galata. *Waḳfiyye* III states:

"[one of the buildings Meḥmed the Conqueror converted into a mosque] is the church in the al-Ḥādj Ḥamza quarter near the *İskele-Ḳapusı,* which was known as *Mesa Domenko* among the Genoese. The western and northern sides of it overlook the public road, the southern side overlooks a private lane and the eastern side overlooks the property of Khwādja Muḥyī al-Dīn Ibn Khwādja Shams al-Dīn, also known as Djenderedji-oghlu, the garden known as *Derskhāne* (Lecture Room) and the *Munaḳḳash Kenīse."*

The Mesa Domenko church is identified as the Dominican church called S. Paolo e S. Domenico in the center of the city. Later, this mosque was known as *'Arab Djāmi'i* because the Moriscos, Arab refugees from Spain, came and settled around it during the sixteenth century (see *supra).*

Al-Kenīsā al-Munaḳḳasha, the "Decorated Church", is identified as the Franciscan church of San Francesco[143] in the quarter of Djāmi'. However, the Arabic register of Ayasofya dated 1519 states:

المخزن السلطاني المعروف بالكنيسة المنقشة المتصل بالجامع

In the Turkish *waḳfiyye* III this passage is translated as follows:

كنيسهٔ سلطانيه ديدكلری منقش كنيسه

Obviously the word *makhzen* was changed to *kenīse.* In fact, the mosque is another building adjacent *(muttaṣıl)* to the *kenīsa al-munaḳḳasha* also known as *al-Makhzen al-Sulṭānī.* In other words, this abandoned church

---

143 Schneider, *op. cit.,* pp. 23-24.

must have been converted into a storehouse belonging to the fisc. In the *Djāmi'* quarter there was indeed a church converted to a *makhzen.*

اخزن السلطاني الذي كان كنيسة النصارى سابقا

Al-Kenīsa al-efrandjiyīn, the church of the Genoese, in the quarter of *Londja* is evidently San Michele, the cathedral of the Genoese colony of Pera.[144] It was torn down sometime in the years 1544 to 1550 and on its site the caravenserai of Rüstem Pasha was erected. It was situated on the southern end of the Genoese *Piazza.* Therefore, our *Londja* quarter must be situated between the *Piazza* or quarter of *Kumiler (Djami')* and the gate of *İskele* or *Yagh-Ḳapanı.* The Ottoman *waḳfiyye* III refers to an old *Londja* near the *İskele-Ḳapısı,* and the New-Londja *(Yeni-Londja)* was near the church of San Francesco. The New-Londja is evidently the *Palazzo del Comune* which under the Ottomans was known as *Han Franchini* on the Voyvoda Caddesi. For other churches see Table I.

---

144 *Ibid.*, p. 283.

7.
The Djibayet Register of the Ayasofya Mosque dated 1519. Sample pages.

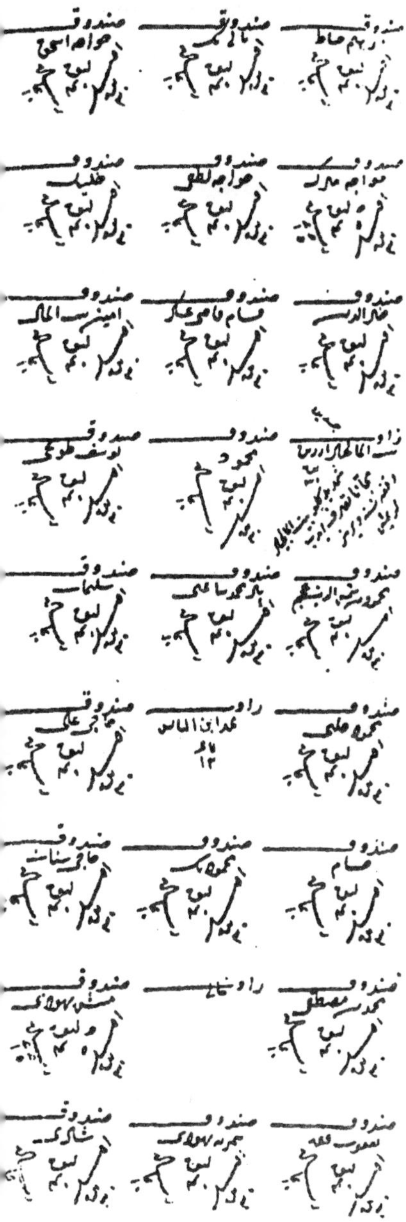

8.

The Capitulations granted to the Florentines, the renewed text of 1527.

بیوروم سلطان سلیمان ده دولتلو فلورین بکلرینه
عهدنامه‌لری تجدید بدی [illegible]
بن که سلطان السلاطین برهان الخواقین تاج بخش خسروان
روی زمین ظل الله فی الارضین اق دکزک و قره دکزک

و روم ایلینک و اناطولینک و روم و قرمان ولایتلرینک
و ولایت ذو القدریه نک و دیار بکرک و آذربایجانک
و شامک و حلبک و مصرک و قدس شریفک و مدینه
منوره نک و مکه مکرمه نک و جده نک و سایر ولایتلرینک
و یمنک و دخی بابا اکرام و اجداد عظامم انار الله تعالی
براهینهم قوت قاهره لری ایله فتح ایتدکلری نیجه مملکتلرک و جناب
جلالتمآبم دخی تیغ آتشبار و شمشیر ظفر نگارم ایله فتح
ایلدوکم نیجه دیارلرک و نیجه مملکتلرک سلطانی و پادشاهی
سلطان سلیمان شاه [illegible] فلورین بکلری کوندردکی
[illegible]
و عتبه علیه [illegible] ایلجیلکه کوندروب
جدم سلطان بایزید شاه و بابام سلطان سلیم خان
[illegible] عهدنامه [illegible] تجدید عهد
اولنمه‌سین طلب [illegible]
[illegible]
[illegible]
[illegible] و اگر [illegible]
برکسنه [illegible] طلب اولنه
[illegible]
طلب اولنمیه و برکسنه فوت [illegible]
ایدرسه اول [illegible]

9.

Population of Galata

— I —

Population of Istanbul and Galata in 1478

Source : Topkapı Palace Archives, N.D. 9524 *

محاسبة خانهاء مسلمانان ونصرانيان ويهوديان وارمنيان وغيرهم بمعرفة مولانا محي الدين قاضئ استانبول ومحمود زعيم استانبول تحريراً في اوايل ذي الحجة سنة اثنى وثمانين وثمانمائة [١]

در نفس استانبول

خانهاء مسلمانان استانبول	٨٩٥١
خانهاء نصرانيان استانبول	٣١٥١
خانهاء يهوديان استانبول	١٦٤٧
خانهاء كفه لولر	٢٦٧
خانهاء ارمنيان استانبول	٣٧٢
خانهاء قرمانيان با شكل ارمنى	٣٨٤
خانهاء چنكنهٔ استانبول	٣١

جمعاً خانها ودكاكين در استانبول	١٨٤٧٠
خانهاء مسلمانان وغيرهم در استانبول	١٤٨٠٣
دكاكين مسلمانان وغيرهم در استانبول	٣٦٦٧

در نفس غلطه

خانهاء مسلمانان غلطه	٥٣٥
خانهاء نصرانيان غلطه	٥٩٢
خانهاء افرنجيان غلطه	٣٣٢
خانهاء ارمنيان غلطه	٦٢

* This document has been published by S. Ünver, in the *Vatan* newspaper (July 4, 1948) and by R. M. Meriç in *İstanbul Enstitüsü Dergisi*, III (1957), pp. 133-135.

جمعا خانها ودكاكين نفس غلطه المذكور	١٧٨١
خانهاء مسلمانان وغيرهم در غلطه	١٥٢١
دكاكين مسلمانان وغيرهم در غلطه	٢٦٠
الجملتان خانها ودكاكين در استانبول وغلطه	٢١٢٥١
خانهاء استانبول وغلطه	١٦٣٢٤
دكاكين استانبول وغلطه	٣٩٢٧

Translation

The account of the households of Muslims, Greeks, Jews, Armenians and others, written by the cadi of Istanbul Mawlānā Muḥyī al-Dīn and the governor of Istanbul Maḥmūd on the first ten days of the month *Dhū'l-ḥidjdja* in the year of 882/6-16 March, 1478.

In the City of Istanbul	
Households of Muslims	8,951
Households of Greeks	3,151
Households of Jews	1,647
Households of Caffans	267
Households of Armenians	372
Households of Karamāniān of Armenian appearance	384
Households of Gypsies	31
Total	14,803
Shops of Muslims and others	3667
Total	18,470
In Galata	
Households of Muslims	535
Households of Greeks	592
Households of Europeans (*Efrendjiyān*)	332
Households of Armenians	62
Total	1,521
Shops of Muslims and others	260
Total	1781
Grand Total of Households (*khāne*) in İstanbul and Galata	16,324
Grand Total of Shops in Istanbul and Galata	3927
Grand Total	20,251 *

* In the text: 21,251

In order to make his capital city the metropolis of a world empire, Meḥmed the Conqueror considered the re-population of Istanbul to be a first priority and took a series of measures. This list of the population of Istanbul and Galata from 1478, just before he set out on a long campaign to the distant Albania against the Venetians, must have been prepared to inform the Sultan of the results of his long efforts. Since Muslims and shops were included in the survey together with the non-Muslims, the purpose seems to be not for taxation, but just for information.

— II —

The Non-Muslim Population of Istanbul and Galata, 894/begins 5 December 1488

Source : *Belediye* Library, Istanbul, M. Cevdet Collection, n° 091, edited by Ö. L. Barkan, "894 (1488/1489) Yılı Cizyesinin Tahsilâtına ait Muhasebe Bilançoları", *Belgeler*, vol. I-1 (1964), p. 39.

	Khāne	Widow	Djizya (in *akça*)
From the non-Muslims of Istanbul together with the Armenians, *Efrendjiyān* (Latin Catholics) of Caffa including the newly found liable for tax without deducting the dead.	4773	630	267,120
From the Jews of Istanbul including the newly found liable for tax without deducting the dead.	2027	464	125,721
From non-Muslims of the city of Galata including the European Latin Catholics and Armenians, including the newly found liable for tax without deducting the dead.	726	87	40,857

Grand Total of the non-Muslims of Istanbul and Galata and the total amount of their *djizya* in the year 894; *khāne* and Widows : 8667 ; *Djizya* : 433,698.

— III —

The Non-Muslim Population of Galata, 947/1540

Source : The *Başvekâlet* (*Osmanlı*) Archives, Istanbul, *Tapu Defterleri*, n° 210.

گبران غلطه

جماعت افرنجیان

	خانه	جزیه
عن جماعت سانتو ماریه	۳	٤۳۲
عن جماعت قدماء غلطه	۲۰	۱۰٥٦
عن جماعت الکسندرو دماوجه زرکو (؟)	٤٦	۳۱٦۸

جماعت رومیان غلطه

محلهٔ انتونموچله	۸	۳۸٤
محلهٔ ماغوله	۱۳	٦۲٤
محلهٔ نیقولا لوز	۱۷	۸۱٦
محلهٔ میرچو	۳	٤۳۲
محلهٔ یانی قوندراتی	۱۳	٦۲٤
محلهٔ یورکی غولیارمو	۳۲	۱٥۳٦
محلهٔ یورکی غوزجیله	۱٥	۷۲۰
محلهٔ اغریبوزلیان غلطه	۱۷	۸۱٦
محلهٔ قره کوی	۷	۳۳٦

جماعت ارمنیان غلطه

خانه ۳۲ جزیه ۱٥۳٦

جماعت بالقجیان غلطه

خانه ۳٤ جزیه ۱۲۲٤

یکون افرنجیان ورومیان وارمنیان غلطه

خانه ۲٦۱ جزیه ۱۳۷۰٤

.. ..

جمعاً گبران رومیان وارمنیان ویهودیان استانبول وافرنجیان ورومیان غلطه

خانه ۰۳۰۷۷ جزیه ۲۰۰۲٥۲

Translation

Non-Muslims of Galata

A. The community of Latin Catholics	Households	*Djizya* (in *akça*)
1. From the Community of Santo Marya سانتوماریه	3	432
2. From the community of ancient Catholic (*Frendj*) inhabitants of Galata	21	1,056
3. From the community of Alexandro de Mavca Zerko (?)	46	3,168
Total	70	4,656
B. The Community of Greeks	**Households**	**Djizya (in *akça*)**
1. Quarter of Anton Modjila انتوغموجله	8	384
2. Quarter of Magula ماغوله	13	624
3. Quarter of Nikola Luviz نیقولا لوز	17	816
4. Quarter of Mirço میرچو	3	432
5. Quarter of Yani Kondurati قوندراتی	13	624
6. Quarter of Yorgi Gulyarmo یو ی غولیارمو	32	1,536
7. Quarter of Yorgi Guzdjile یورکی غوزجیله	15	720
8. Quarter of the Euboeans اغریبوزلیان	17	816
9. Quarter of Karaköy	7	336
Total	125	6,288
C. The community of Armenians	32	1,536
D. The fishermen of Galata	34	1,224
Total of the Latin Catholics, Greeks and Armenians of Galata	261	13,704
Grand Total of non-Muslim Greeks, Armenians, Jews of Istanbul and of Latin Catholics and Greeks of Galata	3,077	200,252

— IV —

The Non-Muslim Population of Galata, 952/1545

Source : *Tapu Defter* n° 240 and n° 210, ***Başvekâlet*** Archives, Istanbul, pp. 89-96.

جزيه	خانه	جماعت افرنجيان در غلطه
٥٤٤	٨	جماعت سانتوماريه
١٢٩٦	١٣	محلهٔ قدماء غلطه
٣٧٨٩	٥٣	جماعت الكسندرو دماوجه
٥٦٢٩	٧٤	
		جماعت روميان غلطه
١٢٥٦	١٩	محلهٔ كليساء قاستيلوت
٦٨٦	١٢	محلهٔ كليساء الاغوسته (؟)
٤٢٤	٨	محلهٔ كليساء ايوياني
٩٨٦	١٦	محلهٔ كليساء ايونيقولا
٦٠٣	١٠	محلهٔ كليساء خرثوبى (؟)
٦٤١	١٢	محلهٔ كليساء ايا يوركى
٤٥٩٦	٧٧	

جزيه	خانه	
٣٠٠٨	٣٠	جماعت ارمنيان غلطه
٧٨٧	١٤	محلهٔ كليساء خرستوس
١٢٢٣	٢١	محلهٔ كليساء خرستوس ديكر
٥٩٠	٩	محلهٔ كليساء ايو ديمترى
٨٣٠	١٥	محلهٔ كليساء پنايه (؟)
٦٥٤٨	٨٩	
١٣٤٤	٢٨	جماعت بالقجيان غلطة
١٠٥٠	٢٠	جماعت كه عن بالقجيان افراز شدند

يكون افرنجيان وارمنيان وروميان خانه ٢٩٣ جزيه ١٨٠٣٧ جمعاً يهوديان وارمنيان وروميان
استانبول وافرنجيان وروميان وارمنيان غلطه

جزيه	خانه
٢٤٤٥٠٢	٤١٠٢

Translation

	Households	Djizya
A. Community of Europeans (*Efrendjiyān*) in Galata		
1. Community of Santo Marya سانتوماريه	8	544
2. Quarter (*mahalle*) of the ancient Catholic (*Frendj*) inhabitants of Galata	13	1,296
3. Community of Alexandro de Mavdja (or di Barca)	53	3,789
Total	74	5,629
B. Community of the Greeks (*Rumiyān*) of Galata		
1. Quarter of the Church of Kastiliutissa قاستليوت	19	1,256
2. Quarter of the Church of Alaghosta ؟ الاغوسته	12	686
3. Quarter of the Church of Ayo Yani ايو ايوياني	8	424
4. Quarter of the Church of Ayo Nikola نيقولا	16	986
5. Quarter of the Church of Khrisopi ؟ خرثوپى	10	603
6. Quarter of the Church of Aya Yorgi ايو يوركى	12	641
Total	77	4,596
C. Community of Armenians of Galata	30	3,008
1. Quarter of the Church of Khristos خرستوس	14	787
2. Quarter of the Church of Khristos خرستوس	21	1,223
3. Quarter of the Church of Ayo Dimitri ايو ديمترى	9	590
4. Quarter of the Church of Panaya ؟ پنايه	15	830
Total	89	6,438
Community of the fishermen of Galata	28	1,344
Community separated from the fishermen	20	1,050
Total of the Europeans, Armenians and Greeks (of Galata)	288	18,037
Grand Total of the Jews, Armenians and Greeks of Istanbul together with the Europeans, Greeks and Armenians of Galata	4,102	244,502

According to this survey there were 74 Latin Catholic, 77 Greek Orthodox and 89 Armenian households or family chiefs paying the poll-tax in Galata in 952/1545. In addition, those non-Muslim fishermen, mostly Greeks, who enjoyed a special tax status were registered in two separate groups numbering 48 households. The grand total amounts to only 288 (293 in the register). The Ottoman survey of 952/1545 shows that, of the Genoese families who were registered in 1453 as Ottoman subjects, only 13 families survived in Galata living in a distinct quarter.

It is also interesting to note that according to the register, there appears to have been no Jews in Galata between 1478 and 1545, while they formed quite a large community in Istanbul itself. 1,647 households in 1478 and 1,491 households by 1545. This situation must be connected with an earlier deportation. Among the Jews of Istanbul, 19 households are referred to as being from Galata, while in the survey of 1455 there was quite a sizeable Jewish community. In fact, in order to restore the prosperity of the port area of Istanbul, formerly occupied by the Venetians, Meḥmed II ordered the deportation of the Jews of Rumeli, and their settlement there when the settlement of the Muslim-Turkish population proved to be a failure following the conquest.

However, in the mid-seventeenth century, Evliyā Çelebi (I, 431-432) mentions one Jewish quarter and two synagogues in Galata adding that here Jews were fearful of the Christians so that gate-keepers at the inner walls of the city were always on guard.

Recapitulation of Galata's Population, 1478-1545

	Households				Latin		
	Muslims	Greeks	Armenians	Jews	Catholics	Fishermen	Total
882/1478	535	592	62	—	332	—	1,521
894/1488-1489	—	—	—	—	—	—	813
947/1540	—	125	32	—	70	34	261
952/1545	—	77	89	—	74	48	288

In the table, the striking fact is the constant decline in the non-Muslim population subject to *djizya* in Galata to almost half the previous number within a period of ten years between 1478 and 1488, and then to one third of the population of 1488 in about half a century. This may be due to flight, to conversion, deportation, change of status or simply to a transfer of tax accounts to another register. It should be kept in mind that our figures are taken from *vaḳf* registers. Flight from the poll-tax was frequent ; those who immigrated were entered into the tax registers every few years under the name *nev-yāftegān*, "newly found". What is noteworthy is that in the registers, the decrease appears to have occurred equally with all the communities. The most dramatic fall, from 592 to 77 families, was found with the Greeks despite the fact that a constant immigration of Greeks, particularly from the Aegean islands, was referred to in other sources[1]. The only community which showed an increase in population was that of Armenians which following a fifty percent drop almost tripled between 1540 and 1545.

As for the Latin Catholic community, the number given in the Ottoman registers of the "ancient" Latin Catholic community was 21 in

1 Since in the second half of the sixteenth century immigration into Galata from the Aegean islands caused depopulation, Joseph Nasi, who had the monopoly of Aegean wine exports, asked the government to curb the migration (A. Galanté cited by D. d'Alessio, "La Communauté", p. 311).

1540, but was 13 in 1545. According to the western sources, by the early 17th century, there survived only seventeen families from the group of Genoese from the time of the conquest. In his estimates of the Latin Catholic population in Galata in 1581, Pietro Cedulini[2] obviously exaggerates :

— V —

The Latin Catholic Population of Galata according to the estimates of Pietro Cedulini, 1581

Free subjects of the Sultan	500
Manumitted from Slavery	500
Slaves of various origins	2,000
Foreigners (temporary, mostly from Spain, Sicily and Venice)	500 to 600
Embassies	100
Total	3,600

In the early seventeenth century, the Catholics from Caffa, 700 in number according to an estimate[3], deserted their quarter in Istanbul and came to settle in Galata where embassies of the Catholic nations offered a more favorable environment. In fact, their quarter in Istanbul was surrounded over time by a more dense Muslim population and caused their desertion. Their churches of St. Nicholas and St. Mary were converted into mosques, Kefeli Mesdjid at Salma-Tomruk and Kemankeş Mustafa Pasha mosque respectively.

In 1606, the *Comunità* itself wrote to the Catholic authorities that the Latin population numbered no more than fifty houses (Belin, p. 180).

Latin Population of Galata according to the Report of P. Tarillon, March 11, 1714
(Source : Belin, *La Latinité*. pp. 180-181)

	Persons
Those from the Genoese period	300 to 400
Embassies and their merchants	3,000
Galley slaves at the *bagno*.	4,000 to 5,000

Catholics of Galata in 1765 according to the archives of the Church of St. Mary
(Source : Belin, *La Latinité*, p. 280)

Catholics having their own house	60
Catholics	134
Servants, all foreign	67
Total	261

2 E. d'Alessio, "La communauté", p. 312.
3 *Ibid.*

In this figure, Perans numbered 73, Germans 17, French 33, Italians 13, Jerosolimitans 4, Ragusans 4, Islanders 50. In 1802, there were 685 Catholics altogether.

According to the Venetian Bailo B. Moro *, Muslims constituted the majority of the population of Galata in 1590. According to Evliyā Çelebi (I, 431) there were 18 Muslim, 70 Greek, 3 *Frenk*, 2 Armenian, and 1 Jewish quarter in the city. The figures he gives on population of 200,000 non-Muslims and 60,000 Muslims are obviously a gross exaggeration. What is interesting is that he claims a non-Muslim majority. Muslims, he notes, occupied the areas all around the Bash-Ḥiṣar, i.e. *Galata Kulesi*, and the way down to the *ᶜArab Camiᶜi* in the second inner fortress. They do not permit, he says, any non-Muslims to settle in their quarters since they claim Meḥmed II gave them an imperial order to this effect.

— VI —

The definite figures on the population of Galata are available only through the census of 1927.

Population of Beyoğlu (Greater Galata), census of 1927

Muslims	145,140	49.80%
Greeks	63,284	21.72%
Armenians	23,517	8.07%
Jews	32,277	11.08%
Catholics	19,793	6.79%
Christians	6,059	2.08%
Other	1,336	0.46%
Total	291,406	

— VII —

The Number of Houses in Greater Istanbul

(Source : Mayer, *Byzantion, Constantinople, Istanbul*, taken from **Annuaire Statistique de la ville d'Istanbul**, vol. II (1931-1932).

Istanbul	51,442	38%
Galata	41,088	30%
Üsküdar	10,967	8.1%
Kadıköy	10,344	7.6%

56.13 percent of the houses were built of wood and 38.6 percent of stone.

* *"Galata prima abitato da Cristiani...è occupato al presente per la maggior parte da Turchi, tanto dentro, quanto all'intorno"*. (Sauli, II, 163, cited by Belin, *La Latinité...*, p. 158).

10. Sample pages from the Court Records of Galata

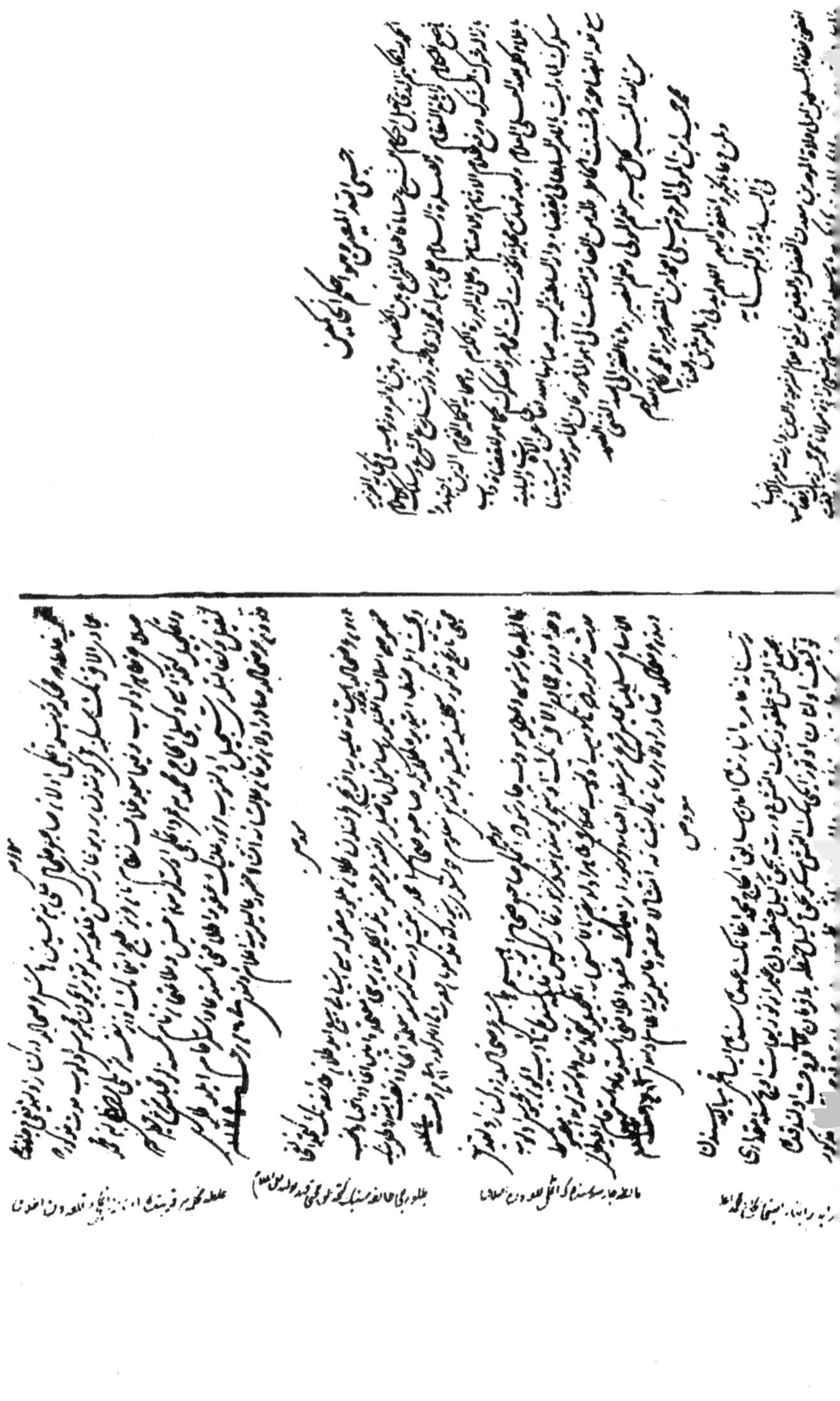

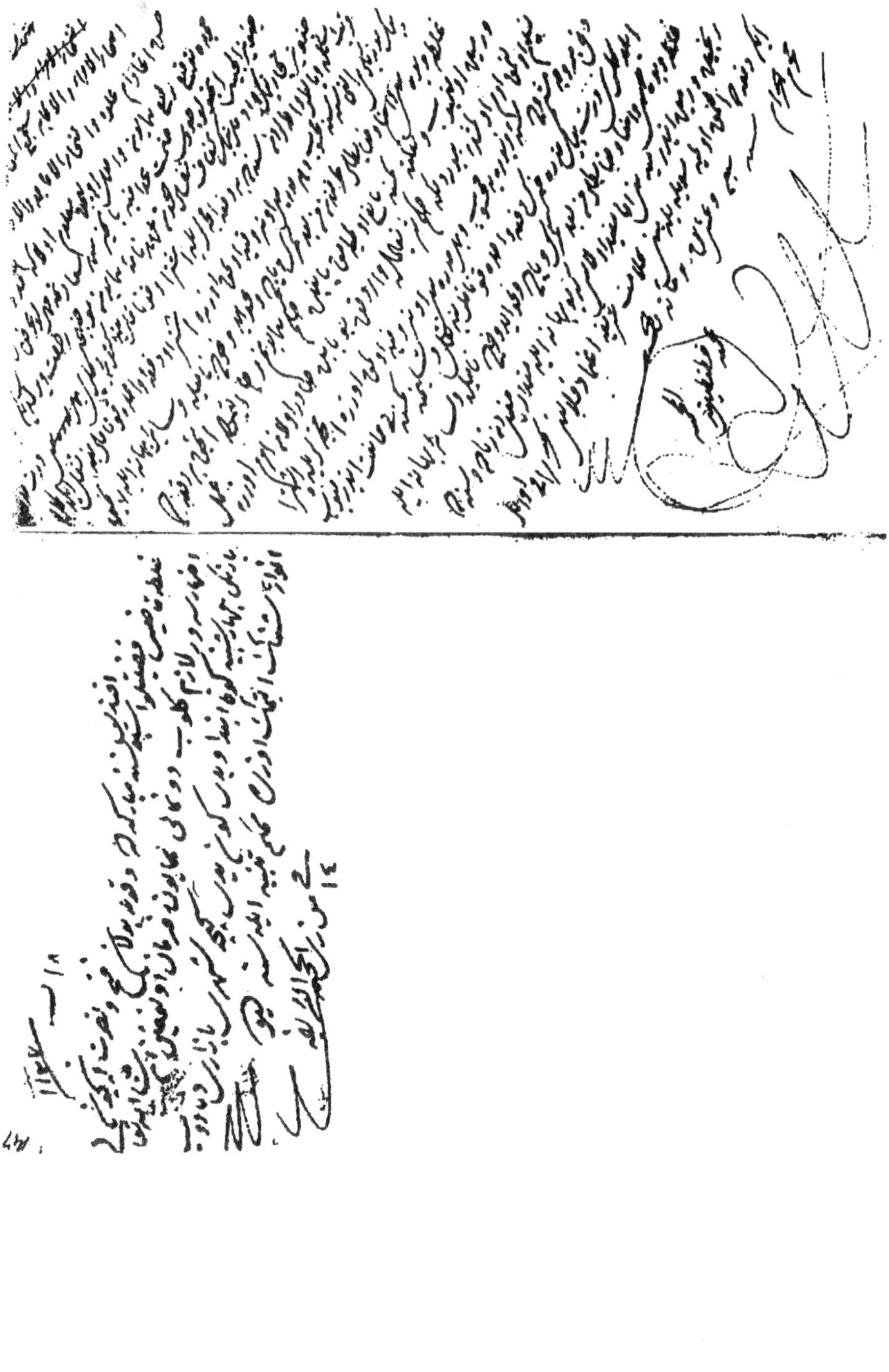

Views
and Plans of Galata

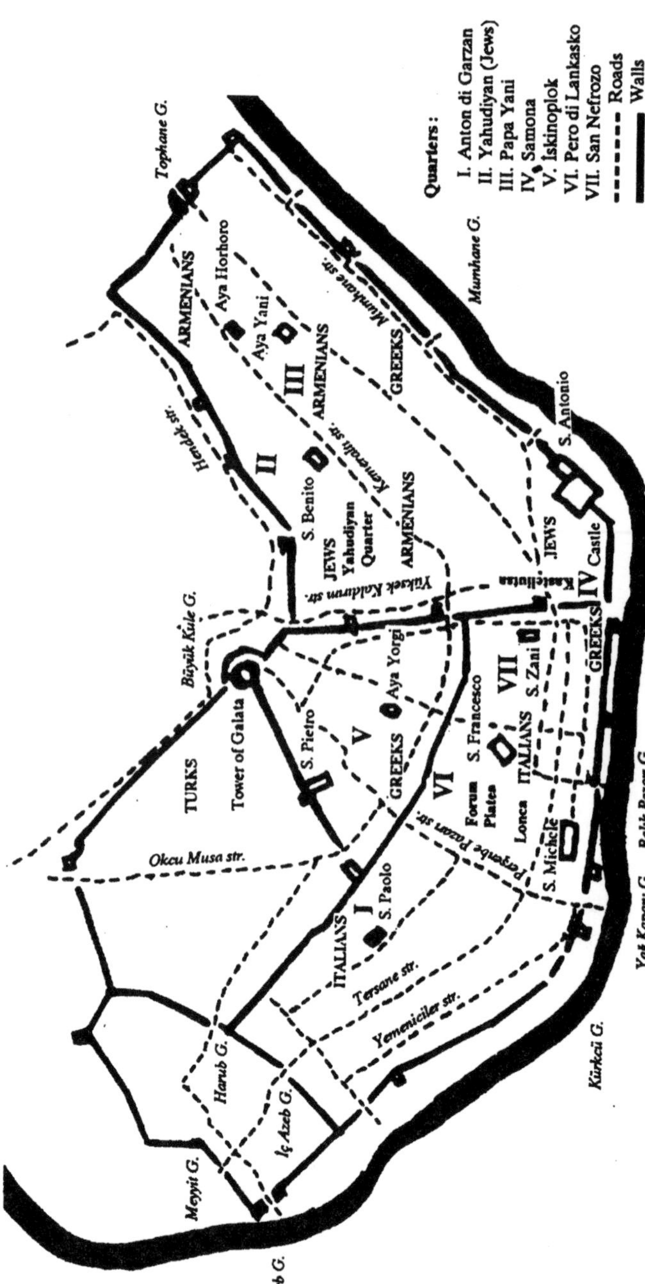

PLAN I

Galata in 1455, according to the Survey of 1455.

PLAN II

Vavassore's view of Galata, ca. 1490.

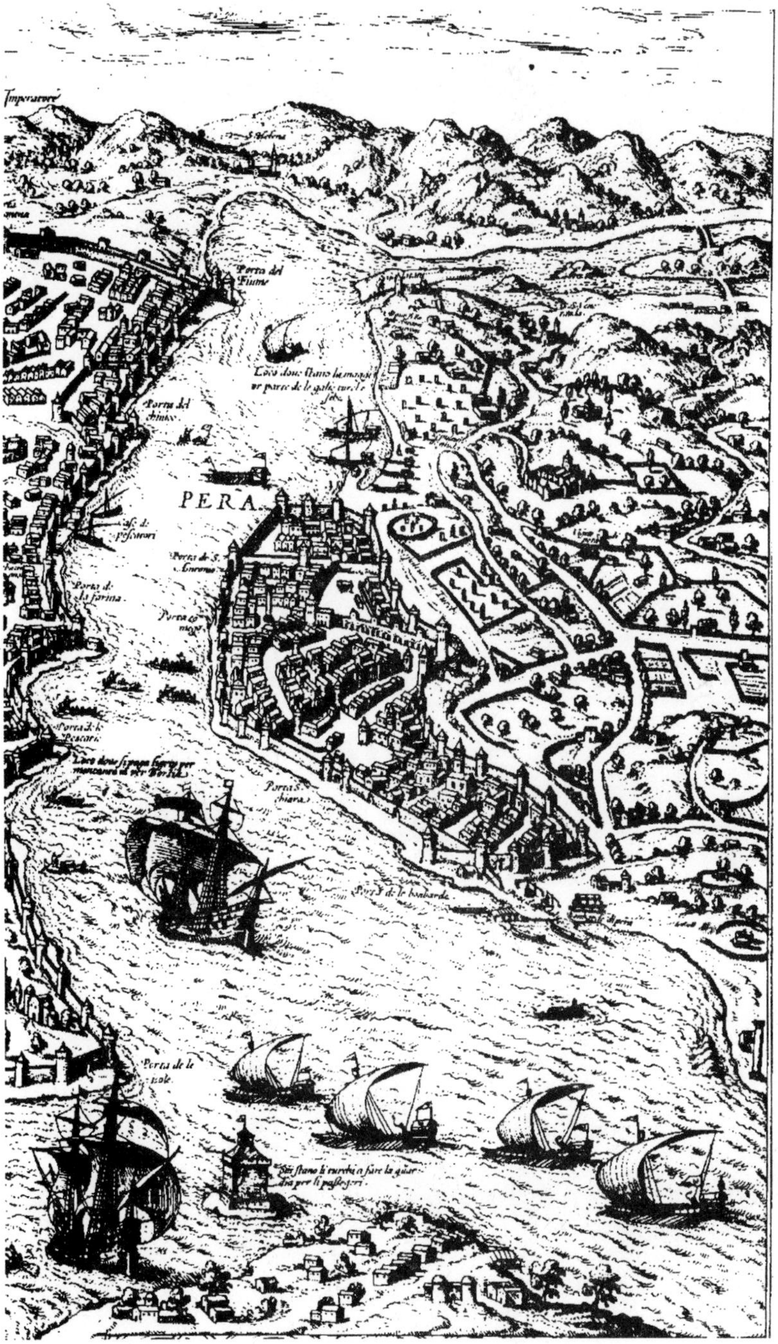

PLAN III

Galata in Maṭraḳdjı, 1537

PLAN IV
Galata in the seventeenth century

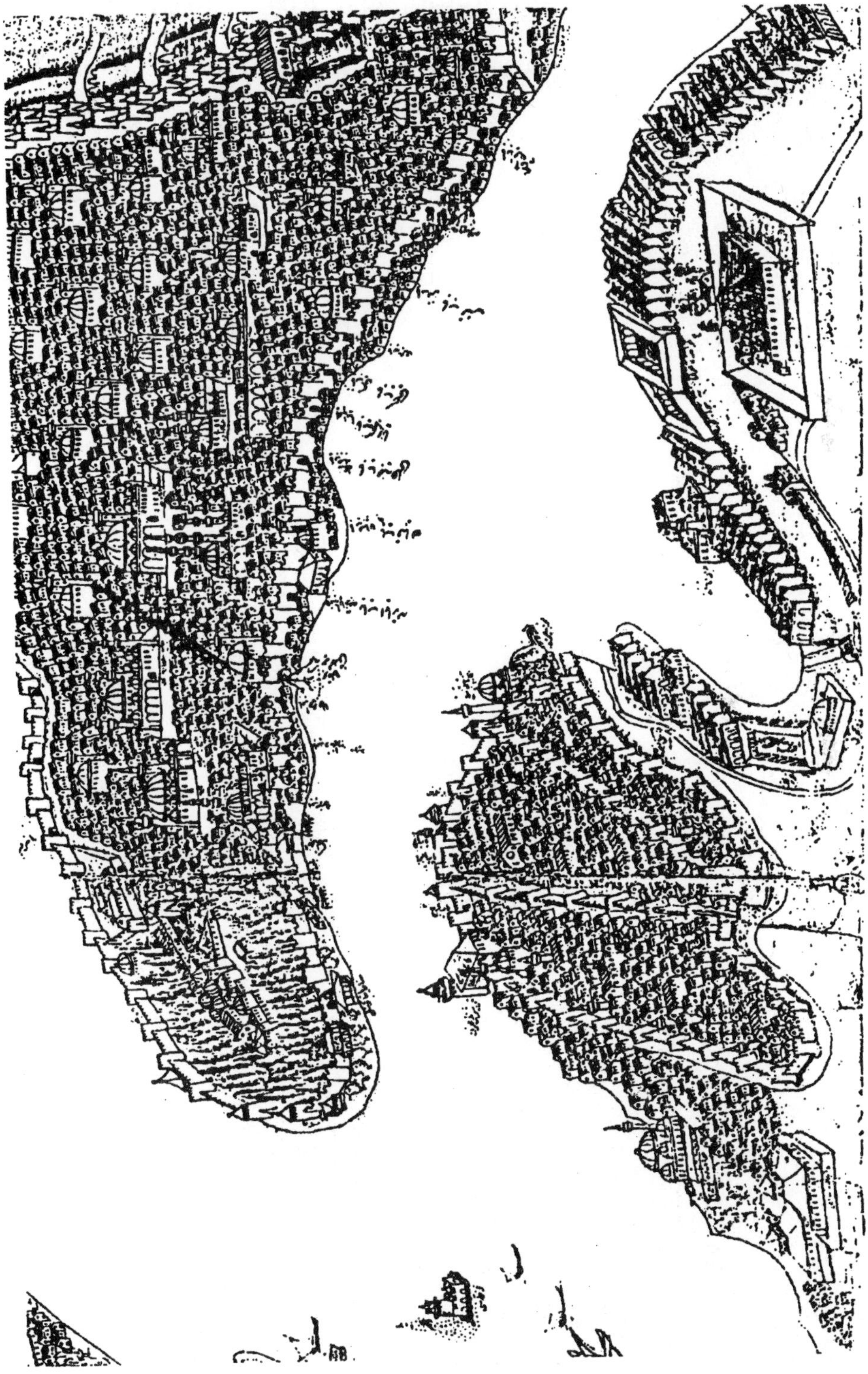

PLAN V

Galata's plan of 1934 (*İstanbul Şehir Rehberi*, 1934)

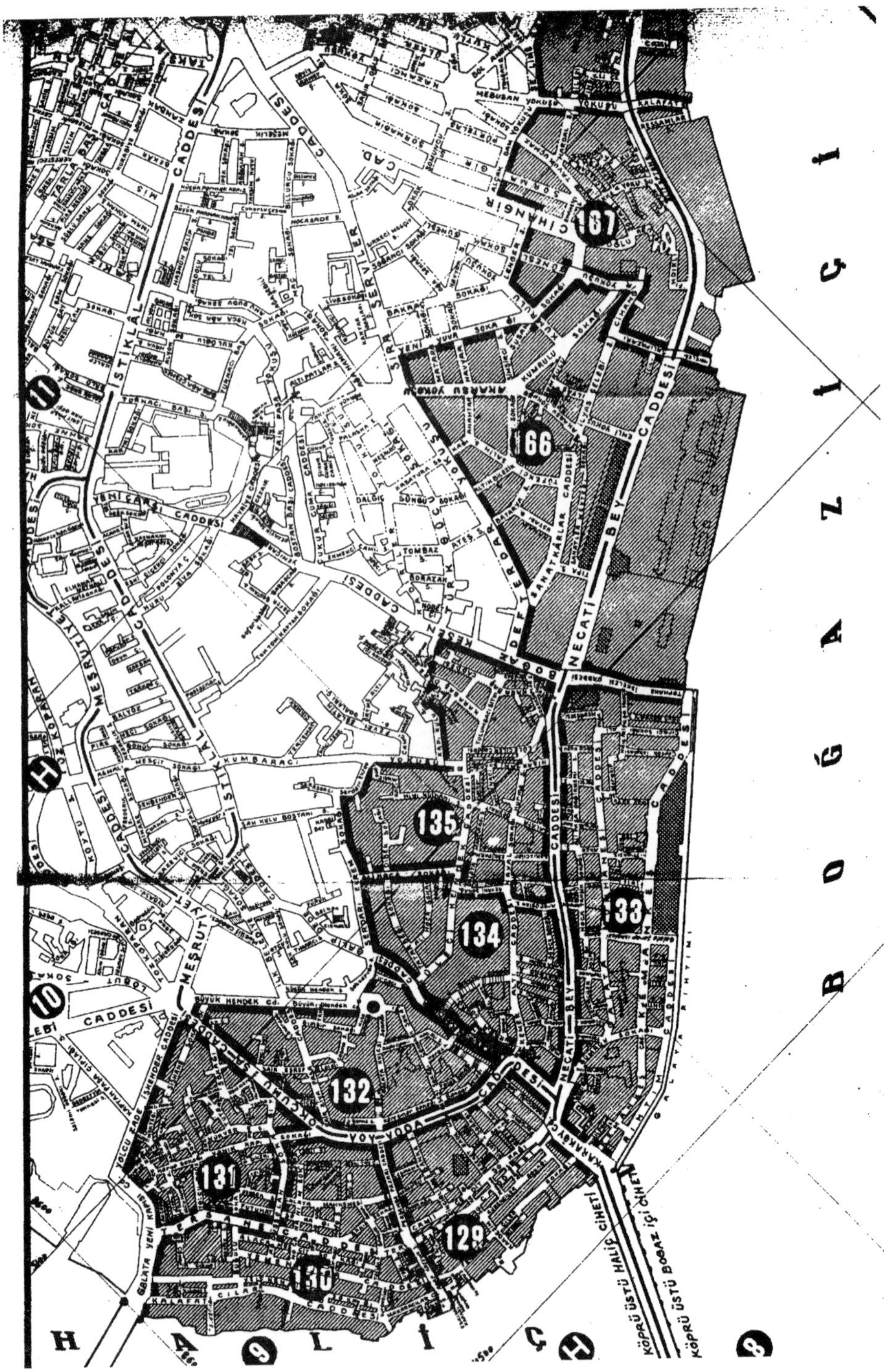

TABLE I
Quarters and Churches of Galata, Survey of 1455

Quarter (Mahalle)	Churches mentioned in the survey	
1. Zani Drapoza		
2. Zani Dabdañ	1. Endowment for the Church of San Tanthon	
3. Nikoroz Sikay	1. Endowment for the Church of Santo Firija (or Foruza)	
4. Nikoroz Bonazita		
5. Anton di Garzan	1. San Domenigo 2. Santa Katarina	San Paolo e San Domenico, later Arab Camii Mosque, built 1225-1230; Latin church of Santa Catarina (Schneider, p. 23)
6. Jews	1. Aya Khorkhoro 2. San Benita	St Gregory Armenian Church-Surp Lussavorich, built 1436; San Benito, Latin monastery founded 1420, Armenian in 1455.
7. Nurbeg Kosta İskinoplok	—	
8. Dhraperyo	1. Vahani or Vuhani	At the time of the survey a *kaligruya* called Françeshḳo Katarina lived in it
9. Gargandji	1. Iplakhosam	
10. Papa Yani	1. Papa Yani 2. Aya Yani	1. Greek church of Ioannis o Prodromos, exists today (Schneider, p. 21)
11. Asudar Armenians	—	
12. Quarter?	—	
13. Zani di Pagani	—	
14. Business Quarter	—	
15. Samona	1. Synagogue, 2. Ayani, 3. Arkhi Istokhoras, 4. Santa Andoni	1. Saynagogue at Karaköy, Perçemli Sokak (Schneider, p. 34), It was not in use at the time of the survey; 4. Latin church of San Antonio, mentioned in 1390, near the Castle of Galata.
16. Iskinoplok	1. Aya Yorgi	Greek church, later a Latin church (Schneider, p. 22, no. 1)
17. Fabya	1. Home for Jewish Rabbis, 2. San Fabyan	

18. Pero di Lankashko	1. San Françeshko, 2. Santa Anna; monastery San Zani	1. San Francesco, Latin church, 2. Latin church near San Francesco (Schneider, p. 22)
19. Yorgi Argandjelu		
20. Yorgi Mavroyani	1. Aya Yorgi	Greek church
21. Varto Khristo	1. Khristos	Greek church Khristos (Schneider, p. 20)
22. Kosto Lupadji	—	
23. Ayodh Kimo Manderino	—	
24. Yani Vasilikoz	1. Ayos Nikolos	Greek church of Ayios Nikolaos (Schneider, p. 21)
25. San Neferzo	1. Istavrano,	Greek church of Kasteliutissa situated near the Castle of Galata
	2. Kasteliutsa,	Latin church of Santa Maria between San Francesco and the sea (Schneider, pp. 24-25)
	3. Sanda Marya, Monastery San Zani	Latin hospice, later used as a church, mentioned in 1370 at Karaköy (Schneider, p. 24)
Totals	23 churches, 1 synagogue, 2 monasteries	

4

Greeks in Ottoman Economy and Finances, 1453-1500

Greeks in Ottoman Economy and Finances, 1453-1500

The Ottoman Empire succeeded the Byzantine Empire in Anatolia and the Balkans. In the Turkish archives today Ottoman land and population surveys *(mufaṣṣal* and *idjmāl taḥrīr defteri)* of these areas go back to the middle of the fifteenth century and contain a considerable amount of information not only on taxation and demography but also on the religious, economic and social conditions of the Greek population in the countryside and towns.[1] Since the Ottomans, as a rule, maintained preconquest conditions, in particular in the areas acquired by agreement,[2] their surveys can be used as a basis of comparison with the data provided by the Byzantine *praktika.* It has been suggested that there is, in fact, a parallelism between peasant status as classified in the *praktika* and in the Ottoman *taḥrīrs,* and that feudal taxes and labor services from Byzantine times survived under the Ottomans.[3] In addition to the *taḥrīr* registers the Ottoman customs registers, public account-books and law court records, covering five centuries, provide innumberable data on the role Greeks played in interregional and international trade, handicrafts, tax farming, sea transportation and other economic activities in the Ottoman Empire. From the 15th century on, Greeks were particularly active in transportation as ship captains or ship owners in the exchange of goods between Istanbul, and Aegean and Black Sea ports.[4]

---

1 For example, see Evangelia Balta, *L'Eubée à la fin du XVe siècle, économie et population, Les registres de l'anné 1474,* Athens: Society of Euboean Studies Pub., 1989.

2 See H. Inalcik, "Ottoman Methods of Conquest", *Studia Islamica,* II (Paris 1954), 104-129; reprint: *The Ottoman Empire: Conquest, Organization and Economy,* London: Variorum Reprints, 1978, no. 1.

3 On praktika see G. Ostrogorsky, *Pour l'histoire de la féodalité byzantine,* Brussels 1954; N. Svoronos, "Recherche sur la cadastre byzantine et la fiscalité au XI et XII siècles: La cadastre de Thebes, *"Bulletin de Correspondance Hellenique,* 1959; for the continuity, see H. Inalcik, "The Problem of Relationship Between Byzantine and Ottoman Taxation", *Akten des XI. Internationalen Byzantinisten-Kongresses,* 1958, Munich 1960.

4 See H. Inalcik, *Sources and Sudies on the Ottoman Black Sea,* Cambridge, Mass. 1955; also see, H. Inalcik, "The Question of the Closing of the Black Sea under the Ottomans", *Symposium on the Black Sea, Birmingham, March 18-20,* 1978, publ. *Arkheion Pontu,* 35 (Athens 1979), 74-110.

Any researcher of the Greeks in the Ottoman empire should keep in mind that all non-Muslim minorities were treated according to Islamic Law as *dhimmī* subjects of the Islamic state. Non-Muslim minorities enjoyed the same rights as Muslims under the protection of the state as far as their economic activities and property rights were concerned. *Dhimma* meant this guarantee and obligation on the part of the Islamic state.[5] For the interests of their empire the Ottomans applied the Islamic prescriptions in a particularly liberal way in favor of their *dhimmī* subjects.

Besides the guarantees of Islamic Law the protection of commerce and the merchants was a long tradition with the Turco-Mongol states in general. As the only group besides the ruling class accumulating cash capital, the merchants had various functions in this pre-industrial society.[6] "Look with favor on the merchants in the land", says an Ottoman wisdom book of the 15th century,[7] "always care for them; let no one harass them; let no one order them about; for through their trading the land becomes prosperous, and by their wares cheapness abounds in the world; through them, the excellent fame of the Sultan is carried to surrounding lands and by them wealth within the land is increased".

In the Ottoman Empire, merchants' activity was not confined to trade, but at the same time, with the accumulated cash in their possession, they also acted as money-changers, bankers and tax-farmers. Many of them combined these various activities.

In this paper, using unpublished material from the Ottoman archives, focus will be put on the Greek tax-farmers in the period 1453-1500.

In order to evaluate changs in the conditions of the Greek mercantile class under the Ottomans one must first examine pre-Ottoman conditions in the fourteenth and fifteenth centuries.

The prominent feature of Greek mercantile activity in the fourteenth century, A. Laïou asserts,[8] was its dependence on the Latins, in particular on the Genoese, who monopolized the grand commerce on the export from and import into the Aegean and the Black Sea, including that of slaves and

---

5 See "Dhimma" *Encyclopaedia of Islam,* 2d edition (hereafter *EI*[2]).

6 H. Inalcik, "Capital Formation in the Ottoman Empire", *The Journal of Economic History,* XIX-1 (1969), 97-140.

7 *Ibid.,* 102.

8 Angeliki E. Laïou-Thomadakis, "The Greek Merchant of the Palaeologan Period: A Collective Portrait", *Praktika,* 57 (1982), 113.

oriental goods. In the pre-Ottoman period, "the Byzantines", Laïou notes,[9] "rarely gained access to the Italian markets". That the Geneose systematically prevented the indigenous traders, Jews, Armenians, Tatars and Greeks, by using force when necessary,[10] from participating in international commerce was a fact confirmed by contemporary documents. Greeks were even prohibited bringing such vital provisions as grain from the northern Black Sea ports on which Constantinople's provisioning was dependent.

The evidence available indicates that during the period Greek traders were mostly engaged in retail trade by funneling goods imported by Italians to the local market and their business involved in general small investments.[11]

However, sporadic references show that there were Greek merchants engaged in distant trade with quite a sizeable capital.[12] Big capital accumulated in the hands of Greek "businessmen" of aristocratic origin, a fact attested to in the Christian and Ottoman sources (infra), came, at least partly, from long distance trade. Laïou's discovery of a relatively high proportion of merchants or "businessmen" belonging to the Byzantine aristocray[13] in the fourteenth century is confirmed through the Ottoman documentation for the subsequent period. Laïou believes that the Byzantine aristocracy, deprived their income from land as a result of the Ottoman conquests, by necessity turned to trade.[14] The evidence from later Ottoman sources show that these aristocrats with huge cash capital in their possession were mostly involved in tax farms. However, the original source of their wealth might have been interregional or international trade as Laïou suggests.[15]

In the period 1353-1402, Laïou calculated,[16] 20 percent of the Greek merchants referred to in the sources belonged to the aristocratic families. It is of particular interest to find the agents of the Palaeologan dynasty engaged in grain trade between Caffa and Genoa. Later, under the Ottomans, members of the Palaeologan family will be seen undertaking big tax-farms. That wealthy members of the high Byzantine aristocracy had established close

---

[9] *Ibid.;* cf. M. Balard, *La Romanie Génoise,* II, Geneva 1978. also see Nevra Necipoğlu, "Byzantines and Italians in Fifteenth-Century Constantinople: Commercial Cooperation and Conflict," *New Perspectives on Turkey,* Spring 1995, 129-143.

[10] Laïou-Thomadakis, *op.cit.* 102.

[11] *Ibid.,* 100-111.

[12] *Ibid.,* 102; for example, Cabasilas, a Greek merchant trafficking with Egypt around 1349 *(Ibid.,* 108-109).

[13] *Ibid.,* 108, 110-111.

[14] *Ibid.,* 105.

[15] *Ibid.,* 108-109.

[16] *Ibid.,* 108.

connections with the Genoese[17] is confirmed by the Ottoman survey of 1455. Wealthy Greek aristocrats had residences in Pera prior to the Ottoman occupation of the city in 1453 (*infra*).

Special mention should be made of Nicholas Notaras, father of Lucas Notaras, who made "a fortune in the Genoese public debt".[18]

In their business activities the family closely cooperated with the Latins, including the Venetians. Giacomo Badoer's account book,[19] covering the years 1436-1440, show that Greek merchants were quite active in Constntinople in the trade of imported goods including cloth and spices as retailers. Peran Greeks must have also been in close economic relations with the Ottomans as early as the mid-fourteenth century. It must not be a coincidence that the Byzantine Emperor and the Ottoman Sultan had simultaneously signed commercial treaties with the Genoese in 1352, following the Byzantines abandoning the Venetian alliance and making a rapproachment with the Ottoman-Genoese coalition.[20] In the following period Perans, obviously Greeks among them, receiving oriental goods, in particular spices and silk from Bursa, kept close relations with the Ottomans.[21] After the surrender of Pera in 1453 the Greek capitalist aristocrats of the city became Ottoman *dhimmī* subjects, cooperating closely with the Ottoman government (*infra*).

The continuing characteristics of the Greek enterprise are specified by a Greek source dated 1453,[22] telling us that Greeks made big money through tax-farms and sea transportation under the Ottomans as before under the Byzantines.

Sea transportation was indeed a prominent sector of the Greek economy in the thirteenth and fourteenth centuries. This was true in the ports under the Byzantines as well as in those conquered by the Ottomans in the Black Sea and Aegean although beyond these two areas Italian shipping was always

---

17 *Ibid.*, 108-110.

18 N. Oikonomides, *Hommes d'affaires grecs et latins en Constantinople (XIII e-XV e siècles)*, Montreal 1979, 68, 122; cf. Laïou-Thomadakis, *ibid.*, 109.

19 *Il libro dei Conti di Giacomo Badoer, (Constantinopoli, 1436-1440)*, eds, U. Dorini and T. Bartelè, Venice 1956, examined by Laïou-Thomodakis, *ibid.*, 109-111.

20 See H. Inalcik, "The Ottoman Turks and the Crusades, 1329-1522" *A History of the Crusades,* VI: General Ed. K. Setton, ed. of the vol.: H. Hazard and N. P. Zacour, Madison 1989.

21 See H. Inalcik, "Ottoman Galata", *Galata,* Edhem Eldem, ed., Istanbul (1990), 56-57.

22 Laïou-Thomodakis, *ibid.*, 111, note 30; the source in question is Nicholas Isidoros correspondance. Also see N.Necipoğlu, "Ottoman Merchants in Constantinople during the First Half of the Fifteenth Century, "*Byzantine and Modern Greek Studies*, 16 (1992), 158-169.

dominant. A total reversal of the situation came with the fall of Genoese Pera.[23]

Before 1453 the only people capable of competing in long distance trade with the Italian for predominance in the overseas traffic were the Ragusans. Perhaps an exceptional case was a wealthy Greek shipowner of Constantinople who lost his four ships with a capital totaling thirty thousand gold ducats. He was evidently trading in cooperation with the Venetians and Jews.[24]

Interestingly, the most important ports in which Greeks were present, namely Constantinople and Pera, both conquered in 1453, Caffa, conquered in 1475 and Chilia, conquered in 1484, were the same under the Ottomans as under the Byzantines and the Genoese. Thessaloniki, which the Ottomans occupied in 1430, was another important Greek center of business. However, the arithmetic book composed in Thessaloniki in which Greek bankers and traders were mentioned should be dated to the end, rather than the beginning of the fifteenth century.[25]

For the fourteenth century Laïou, using Genoese archival materials, asserts that "the Greeks formed a large proportion of the artisans and small shopkeepers of the Geneose colonies of Pera, Caffa and Chios".[26] Ottoman documents of the second half of the fifteenth century fully support this conclusion for Pera, Caffa, Akkerman (Moncastro) and Chilia (*infra*).[27] One of the principal changes, however, was that under the Ottomans Greek sailors began to carry European and oriental goods imported into Istanbul and Galata to the Black Sea ports in addition to their pre-Ottoman traditional traffic in foodstuffs.

It should be remembered that in 1453 almost the entire population of the Byzantine capital had been captured as prisoners of war and their properties taken as booty. But Galata (Pera) on the other side of the Golden Horn had surrendered under an *'ahdnāme* and consequently the population was spared

---

23 See H. Inalcik, "Ottoman Galata"; N. Oikonemides, *Hommes Affaires Grees et Latines à Constantinople (XIII-XVe siècles),* Montreal-Paris 1979; K.P. Matschke, "Byzantinische Politiker and byzantinische Kaufleute im Ringen und die Beteiligun am Schwarzmeerhandel in der Mitte des 14. Jh.," *Mitteilungen des Bulgarischen Forschungs institutes in Österreich* 2, 75-95.

24 F. Thiriet, *Régestes des déliberations du Senat de Venise concernant La Romanie,* III, document no. 3009.

25 See H. Inalcik, "Introduction to Ottoman Metrology", *Turcica,* XV (1983), 325; Laïou-Thomadakis, 110 note 29, agrees with H. Hunger and K. Vogel that the book was composed in the early fifteenth century.

26 Laïou-Thomadakis, *op. cit.,* 115.

27 See H. Inalcik, *Sources and Studies,* I, 1995.

a similer fate.[28] Mehmed the Conqueror was most concerned about keeping Galata intact as a commercial center of his new capital, Istanbul, and took measures to give assurances and guarantees to have them stay on. Prior to the siege of Constantinople some Greeks appear to have taken refuge in Galata. The Ottoman tax and population survey of 1455 [29] shows that Pera could properly be called a Greek city at the time of surrender as far as its population was concerned. Its Greek character became accentuated at the occupation as a result of the Genoese flight from the city. Among those who fled Italians made up about 60 percent and Greeks 35 percent. At the time of the occupation the Sultan, however, declared that those who returned within three months were to recover their properties. Their houses were then sealed and the properties registered. Our survey of 1455 shows that there were indeed people who returned.

According to the Ottoman survey of 1455, the Greek population within Galata was concentrated in the quarters around the Genoese district at the port area. The majority of the Greeks were poor people, shoemakers, porters or small traders or craftsmen. But in the district of Varto Khristo lived a group of wealthy Greeks. Twenty two years later in the survey of 1477 the population of Galata broken down by religion was as follows: Of total population of 1521 households, Greeks were still in the majority with 592 households; *Efrenc* or Latin households numbered 332, Armenian 62 and Muslim 535, already approaching the Greeks. Thus, in addition to the forced or voluntary settlement of Greeks in Istanbul itself,[30] Galata remained the center of Greek business with Greek bankers, shipowners and merchants. In 1455 the Greek community of Galata included members of the Greek "aristocratic" families, who were to play a key role in Ottoman finances in the following period.

In the period immediately after the conquest of Constantinople we find many Greeks particularly active in tax-farming.

Members of the old Byzantine aristocracy, the Palaeologi, Cantacuzeni, Chalcocondyli and Rhali were prominent tax-farmers under Mehmed the conqueror and his successors. During the 15th and 16th centuries the customs zone of western Anatolian ports with Istanbul as its center made up the principal customs zone of the empire and it often came under the control of Greek tax-farmers who, with huge amounts of capital in their possession, were competing with Muslim Turks and Jews for this lucrative undertaking.

---

28 See H. Inalcik, "Galata".

29 *Ibid.*

30 H. Inalcik, "The Policy of Mehmed II Toward the Greek Population of Istanbul and the Byzantine Buildings of the City", *Dumbarton Oaks Papers*, 23/24 (1969-1970).

Here is a list of the Ottoman treasury accounts demostrating how the customs of Istanbul changed hands during the period of October 1476 to December 1477.[31] (see Facsimile 1).

1 Ya'kūb, new Muslim, Palologoz of Kassandros, Lefteri son of Galyanos of Trebizond, Andriya son of Halkokondil and Manul Palologoz offered in company an increase of 1,500,000 akça for three years, on Djumāda II 25, 881. The estimated revenue was 9.5 million akça on this date.

2 Khodja Satı, Çirish Ilyās, Shahin, freed slave of Yūsuf Simsar (chief broker) and Khodja Bahā'al-Dīn offered an increase of 2 million on Dh'ul-hidjdja 23, 881.

3 Palologoz of Istanbul, Palologoz of Kassandros, Lefteri son of Galyanos of Trebizond and Andriya son of Halkokondil offered an additional increase of 833,334 on the condition that the *muḳāṭa'a* should be farmed out to them for a period of four years. This bid was on the 28th of Muḥarrem, 882.

4 Seydī Küçük of Edirne, Altana Jew and Nikoroz Efrendjī (an Italian?) offered an additional increase of one million on Djumāda I 23, 882.

5 The group of Palologoz, Lefteri and Andriya made a new bid on Djumada II 20, 882 and then the group of Seydī, Altans and Nikoroz offered 20 million 200,000 akça altogether for four years on Radjab 4, 882.

The Istanbul customs zone included the important ports of Istanbul, Galata, Gallipoli, the two Phoceas, Varna and Mudanya, controlling western Anatolian and Black Sea trade with Europe. The spectacular increase from 9.5 million akça to about 20 million akça or about four hundred thousand gold ducats offered by the competing bidders for the customs attest to the rapid expansion of this trade as well as the financial potential of the tax farmers involved.

Actually, of the various functions merchant-capitalists fulfilled in Ottoman society their services to the public finances as tax-farmers (*'āmil* or *mültezim*) were of vital importance. Since the state depended on cash revenues flowing regularly into its coffers to pay for a turbulent standing army and for its military campaigns, most of the taxes directly under the central treasury's control were farmed out to tax-farmers. As a rule it was the

[31] See H. Inalcik, "Notes on N. Beldiceanu's Translation of the Ḳānūnnāme, fonds turc ancien 39, Bibliothèque Nationale, Paris", *Der Islam,* vol. 43/1-2 (1957), 139-157. and Inalcik, *Sources and Studies*, 157-8.

merchant-capitalists who had sufficient amounts of ready money to undertake tax-farms and to provide cash to the public treasury at 3 or 6 month intervals, called *ḳist.*

Personal or factional connections as well as secret dealings appear to have played an important part in undertaking big tax-farms. Apparently, Greeks or converts with influence at the Sultan's court favored the Greek bidders. Complaints against favoritism for the Greek or Jewish tax farmers during the Conqueror's reign is voiced in the contemporary sources. Perhaps it is not just a coincidence that members of Plaeologan family obtained the tax-farm of Istanbul customs zone in the 1470's exactly when two pashas, Khāṣṣ Murād and Mesīḥ of the same family were the most influential people with the Sultan.[32]

It is a commonplace that Mehmed the Conqueror showed special favor to Greeks in his efforts to repopulate and revive the economic life of his new capital.[33] Aside from the pro-Latin Greeks who left for Italy, many Greeks cooperated and were favored by the Sultan in important positions as soldiers, councilors and finance experts. Also there is documentary evidence about the Sultan's interest in bringing back the Greeks who had migrated to Italy.

Besides the Palaeologi and Cantacuzeni there were other Greek archonts who were involved in Ottoman finances, in some cases probably continuing their positions from pre-Ottoman times. Prior to the Ottoman period, for instance, Theodore Rhali (Theodorus Rhali de Constantinopli) was involved in the customs revenues of Istanbul under the Byzantine government. In 1455 we find him in Crete.[34] But other members of the Rhali family stayed on in Istanbul after the conquest.

During the same period another Byzantine aristocratic family was active in Serbia farming out the rich silver and gold mines in that province. In 1474 Yani Cantacuzenus, his brother Yorgi, Nichola Dandjovil and Lika farmed out in partnership the silver and gold mines in the province of Vuk, or upper Serbia, for a total sum of 14 million akça (or about 290,000 Venetian gold ducats) for six years. In the previous year the contractors were Yani Cantacuzenus of Novobrdo, Yorgi Ivrana and Thoma Cantacuzenus both of

---

32 See F. Babinger, "Eine Verfügung des Palaeologen Chāṣṣ Murād-Paşa von Mitte Regeb 876 h. Dez.-Jan. 1471/2", *Documenta Islmica Inedita,* Berlin: Akademie Verlag, 1952, 197-210; "Mesīḥ Pa͟s͟ha" (H. Inalcik), *EI*², VI.

33 "Istanbul" (H. I . lcik), *EI*², IV.

34 N. Iorga, *Notes et extraits pour servir à l'histoire des croisades au XVe siècle*, IV, 106, note 34.

Serres, and Palaeologus of Istanbul acting as partners.[35] Later in 1476, they were replaced by a new group of partners: Yani and Yorgi Cantacuzenus, Vuk and Knez Yuvan and Andriya. In 1477 all of them were executed because they failed to pay sums under the contract. On the other hand, the mines of Kratovo in the province of Küstendil were farmed out by Yani Palaeologus of Istanbul in partnership with Istipa Blasica, Istepan Lesh, and Dimitri son of Konstantin in 1473 for a total sum of 1,600,000 akça. According to the survey of 1455 this Yani Palaeologus lived in Galata where he owned big residences.

In competition with Muslim or Jewish tax farmers, the Greek businessmen were also active as the contractors of the important monopolies of salt production and distribution in the Balkans or the Aegean or Black Sea coasts in this period. These monopolies were, as a rule, farmed out with the revenues of the fisheries in the neighborhood. Demetrius Palaeologus, the last despot of the Morea, was also involved in this business. According to the Ottoman register of tax-farms[36] "Kir Demetrius Tekfur" possessed the poll-tax and other state revenues of Aenos on the basis of *timar*. But from July 11, 1469 onwards, a partnership of three Jewish tax farmers, Eleazar son of Yakub of Salonika, Avraham son of Eleazar of Nicopolis and Musa son of Ismail of Vidin took over the job. The total sum of the revenues from it was estimated at 555,000 akça for three years. Six years later, Yuvan Dhapovik and Knez Yuvan of Novobrdo, evidently Slavs, attempted to outbid Yorgi Ivrana and Thoma Cantacuzenus without success. The reason for their failure was that the central administration had not approved the documents submitted by the latter. Greek tax farmers continued to be involved in salt production in the empire in the following century. In 1590, the government-appointed agent for the import of salt into Istanbul was a Greek by the same of Mikhayil, son of Komnen. The salt imported in one year amounted to 41,274 *kile,* or about 105 tons, transported by the ships of Sava, Istefan, Hüseyin, Abdurrahman and Nika.

In 1610 the government agent responsible for the import of salt into Istanbul and the agent in the Crimean Khanate for salt export were both Greeks by the names of Mikhal and Dimitri. Under their control the total import amounted to 50,000 *kile* or about 129 tons with a value estimated at

---

35 *Mukāṭa'āt* Register, mentioned in note 31, above; on this branch of Cantacuzenus family in Serbia see Iorga, *Byzance après Byaznce, Continuation de la vie byzantine,* Bucharest 1971, 36; D. M. Nicol, "The Byzantine Family of Cantacuzenus", *Dumbarton Oaks Papers,* XI.

36 T. Gökbilgin, *XV-XVI. Asırlarda ve Edirne ve Paşa Livâsı: Vakıflar-Mülkler-Mukataalar,* İstanbul 1952, Index.

one million akça. Again, this salt was transported for the most part on ships owned by the Greeks Yorgi, Sava and Djanali.

In the Ottoman merchant marine Greeks occupied a prominent place. In the customs registers of Caffa, Akkerman and Chilia[37] Greeks made up a high percentage of the sea captains and shipowners around 1,500. According to the customs register of Caffa dated 1487-1490 there were 21 Greek shipowners or captains all active in the traffic between Caffa, Istanbul, Galata, Sinop, Samsun, Inebolu and Trebizond as against 41 Muslims and 4 Italians. The Greek captains Paskal Rayis, Todoros, Pandazi and Yani of Inebolu were traficking between these Black Sea ports, carrying goods belonging to Muslim, Jewish and Armenian merchants. In contrast to the prominent place of the Greeks in maritime transportation there were in this period only a few Greek merchants trafficking in the Black Sea ports and most of them were engaged in the wine trade or other natural products. Many of the Greek captains, however, shipped merchandise belonging to themselves for which they paid customs dues. These goods consisted mostly of wine of Trebizond and of the Crimea, caviar and fish of Azak (Azov) and other natural products of the Black Sea region. That Greek captains were involved in the trade of bulky goods such as salt, wheat, flour, fruits, fish and lumber was apparently due to the high percentage of transportation costs in the prices of such goods. Already in the 15th century Greek captains must have accumulated fortunes through the transportation and trade of such provisions for the rapidly growing Istanbul market. Compared to the situation of the Palaeologan period during which the Black Sea traffic was basically dependent on the Latins, the Greek merchant marine under the Ottomans must have recorded a considerable expansion. Ottoman archives yield ample evidence of this development for the 15th and 16th centuries. During this period Galata-Pera became the principal emporium of olive oil, wine, fish and caviar under the control of the Greeks. Yeniköy on the Bosporous was the headquarters of the wealthy Greek shipowners and captains.

Replacing the Italians in transportation by sea Greeks were also active in the overseas trade in the eastern Mediterreanean during the same period. In a customs register dated 1560, for example, we find Greek sea captains active in the traffic between Antalya on the one hand the Syrian and Egyptian ports on the other. It should, however, be noted that Muslim captains and shipowners were in a majority in this traffic as they were in the Black Sea in the same period.

---

[37] See note 31 above.

Also, compared to the situation around 1453, the number of Greek captains, of vessels, and of wealthy merchants showed an increase in Venice in the sixteenth and seventeenth centuries as the archives of the Greek colony of the city attest.[38] Under Ottoman protection, Jews, Muslim Turks, Slavs and Greeks from the Ottoman lands formed flourishing merchant communities in Ancona and Venice by the mid sixteenth century.[39] The members of the Ottoman elite invested big capital in this overseas trade. For example, a letter from Suleyman I to the Venetian Doge in 1561 tells us that the *ḳapı-agha,* the chief officer of the Seraglio, had made a *commenda* contract with two Greek captains to go to Venice and do business for him.[40] The agha had entrusted to them two thousand gold pieces and his ship for this commercial venture. This particular case became the subject of correspondance because the Greek captains had cheated the kapı-agha. Greeks also played an outstanding part in Russian trade, in furs in particular, as the Sultan's private merchants, *khāṣṣa tādjir* during the period.[41]

---

38 Geanakoplos, *Byzantium and Venice,* 55, note 7.

39 See T. Stoianovich, "The Conquering Balkan Orthodox Merchant," *The Journal of Economic History,* XX (1960), 234-313; P. Earle, "The Commercial Development of Ancona, 1479-1551", *Economic History Review,* XII (1969).

40 T. Gökbilgin, "Venedik Devlet Arşivindeki Vesikalar Külliyatından Kanunî Sultan Süleyman Devri Belgeleri", *Belgeler,* V. 2 (1964), 161.

41 A. Bennigsen and C. L.-Quelquejay, "Les marchands de la cour ottomane et le commerce des fourrures moscovites dans la seconde moitié au XVIe siècle", *Cahiers du Monde Russe et Soviétique,* XI-3 (1970), 363-390.

5

“Arab” Camel Drivers in Western Anatolia in the fifteenth century

"Arab" Camel Drivers in Western Anatolia in the fifteenth century

In the chapter describing the settlement of the lands conquered by Süleyman Pasha on the European side of the Dardanelles in 1352 'Āşıḳ Pasha-zāde says:[1] "Süleyman Pasha sent word to his father (Sultan Orkhan) saying 'o fortunate one, with your miraculous care now Rumili has been conquered by us. The infidels here became extremely weak. So, let it be known that we need here many men of Muslim faith to make secure and proserous the lands and fortresses which have been conquered. These places need [to be protected], so, in order to place garrisons in the fortresses you should send us in particular fighters for Islam (ghāzī yoldaş). Orkhan Ghāzi agreed and sent over *those dark skinned Arab nomad families (Kara göçer Arab-evleri)* who had previously migrated over to Karesi-ili. These Arabs stayed for some time in the environs of Gelibolu. Süleyman pasha then continued his onslaught and reached the coasts of Tekvur-Daghı, on the way he took the above-mentioned fortresses by either convincing them to surrender or by conquering by force and pillaging them. He finally made the fortress of *Odkükelek* his headquarters on the frontier and advanced against Hayrabolu. In the meantime new settlers arrived day after day from Karesi-ili. As soon as they settled they busied themselves with the Holy War against the infidels. In sum, the fighters of Islam found support; wherever they went the infidels could not successfully resist them".

This is 'Āşıḳ Pasha-zāde's story of the first conquests of the Ottomans in Europe. The story, I first thought, was the product of 'Āşıḳ Pasha-zāde's imagination who wanted the Arabs, the people of the Prophet, to have had a part in this great deed of Islam. However, I then discovered, in the *vaḳfiyya* of Orkhan dated 762/1361 for the endowment established for Süleyman Pasha at Bolayır,[2] who had died there two or three years earlier, a village called *Arablu* near Eriklice (Greek: Herakleia).

---

[1] *Tevārīkh-i 'Āl-i 'Oṣmān*, ed. Çiftçioğlu N. Atsız, İstanbul 1947, chapter 41, p. 124.

[2] I. Beldiceanu-Steinherr, *Recherches sur les actes des règnes des Sultans Osman, Orhan et Murad I*, Munich 1867, 145-148, see below note 56.

"Arab Camel Driver" in the Çanakkale Peninsula

If 'Āşıḳ Pasha-zāde was right we should find "Arab nomads" on the Asiatic side of the Dardanels in early Ottoman history. Actually, in a regulation of Mehmed II (1451-1481)[3] four groups of "Arab" camel drivers , namely those of Karaburun, Edremid, Ayazmend and those of Kızılca-Dağ are mentioned in the sancak of Karesi in the service of transporting of the salt extracted at the Kızılca-Tuzla. Karaburun and Kızılca-Dağ (apparently Tuzla-Tepe on modern maps) are situated on the tip of the Çanakkale peninsula, Edremid on the bay of that name and Ayazmend (today Altınova) on the Aegean coast south of Ayvalık. The regulation refers to these "Arabs" as being in the service from "earlier times" ("evā'ilden"). Byzantine remains were found on top of Tuzla-Tepe and the old mosque in the village Tuzla displays some Byzantine features.[4] Moreover, since salt was produced from these famous salt-pans from antiquity it is sensible to suppose that production continued under the Turcoman principality of Karesi before the Ottoman occupation under Orkhan (1324-1362).

In a later document in the fiscal survey of 1528 "the immigrant Arab camel drivers"[5] in the transport service of the Kızılca-Tuzla were classified as follows:

A group (djemā'at) of 44 men in the Behram area
A group (djemā'at) of 27 men in Andavazlu village in the area of Ezine
A group (djemā'at) of 15 men again in the area of Ezine
A group (djemā'at) of 21 men in the area of Karaburun

Today, the village of *Araplar,* obviously a settlement of "Arabs" of Karaburun in the document, is to be found on the Ekmek (Etmek) -Yemez-Baba headland[6] (Strabo's *Altar of the Twelve Gods* is situated in the area). The name of *Araplar* was recently changed by the government to *Koca-Köy*

---

[3] *Ḳānūnāme-i Sulṭānī ber Müceb-i 'Örf-i 'Oṣmanī,* eds. R. Anhegger and H. Inalcik, Ankara: Turkish Historial Society, 1936, 30-31, cf. N. Beldiceanu, *Actes de Mehmed II et Bayezid II du MS. Fonds turc ancien 39,* I, Paris and The Hague: Mouton, 1960, 94 (corrections).

[4] See J. M. Cook, *The Troad,* Oxford: The Clarendon Press, 1973, 19, 222-223.

[5] L. Güçer, "XV-XVII. Asırlarda Osmanlı İmparatorluğunda Tuz İnhisarı ve Tuzlaların İşletme Nizami", *İstanbul Üniversitesi İktisat Fakültesi Mecmuası,* vol. 23, (1962-1963), 121.

[6] See Piri Reis, *Kitab-ı Bahriye,* eds. F. Kurdoğlu and H. Alpagot, İstanbul: Turkish Historical Society, 1935, 140.

but local people still call it *Araplar.* J. Cook[7] describes it as follows: "To the west of the great loop in the middle, southwest of the Ballu-Dag, the maps from Lechevalier to Philippson mark a village of *Araplar* whose name just survives in local memory. Napier marked it (without a name at point W) on his map as a *Turkish village* with a few remains and a fountain. Raoul-Rochette in 1838 noted a dilapidated Turkish cemetary and spoke of the village as deserted, but argued that it was the site of Scamandria".

Araplar is situated on the road from Behram to the small port of Baba-Kale. Pīrī Re'īs (writing in 1521)[8] found Baba-Burnu unsuitable for ships to anchor but four "miles" to the north there was a small harbor called Ak-Liman where small ships could find shelter against northerly winds. In the nineteenth century "the harbor at Baba", J. Cook[9] notes, "seems to have been a terminal where steamers called and where merchandise was unloaded to be transported by camel".

In 1904 Bacon saw camel drivers carrying valonia to the Behram-Iskele (Assos) to the east. On their return home they took a couple of blocks from the ruins of Assos. J. Cook discovered one such stone in *Araplar.*[10]

To the north in the area of Ezine *Arapaşireti* (Arab-Tribe) village is mentioned in the Turkish census of 1940 with a population of 410 inhabitants. It is evidently the same as *Araplar* shown in the maps on the Menderes River north of Ezine. While travelling in the area in 1975 I found about 10 kilometers from Edremit a village also named *Araplar* (The name was recently changed to Yol-Ören by government edict). Concerning the origin of the name *Araplar,* the only theory suggested by the villagers was that the place is very hot "like Arabia" and that was why it is called *Araplar.* The composition of the village population appears to have changed over time. Now there are a few immigrant families from Bosnia who still speak Serbo-Croatian, and many villagers apparently came from outside to rent and work in the village. I was told that once there was an old mosque which does not exist any more. I could not find any clue about the earlier inhabitants of the place or concerning the name *Araplar.*[11]

---

[7] *Op. cit.,* 237.

[8] Piri Reis, *ibid.*

[9] *Ibid.,* 227.

[10] Cook, *op. cit.,* 391.

[11] The principal cultivation in the village is presently cotton for market. Villagers do own land. It belongs to a few landowners living in the nearby towns. Villagers rented the arable land for 3,000-5,000 Turkish lira per *dönüm* usually for a period of four years. Some of them were sharecroppers. When cotton prices fell they switched to the cultivation of wheat or horticulture.

In the register of the pious endowments of Bergama dated 1455[12] Kızılca-Tuzla, Dere-Köyü and Baba-Deresi altogether made an endowment unit farmed out to a tax-farmer for 20,600 akça a year (or about 515 gold ducats).

Dere-Köyü, on the Tuzla River (ancient Satnioeis) was the central settlement *(nefs)* for the salt-works at Kızılca-Tuzla at the foot of Kızılca-Dağ. The population in the three settlements numbered 273 persons 115 of which were *çift* and 158 *benlak.*[13] The village population, all Muslim, consisted of 26 households with *çiftlik* (ba-çift) and 78 households with a piece of land less than half a *çiftlik* or no land *(benlak).* Out of the revenue of Kızılca-Tuzla, fifteen akça a day was endowed to the mosque built by Murad I (1362-1389) for which the local cadi was appointed a trustee (mütevellī). Apparently it was a prosperous village, the population of which included a jeweller and a dyer and two converts - Karaca son of Mikhal and Muhammed son of Vasil.

The population of Baba-Deresi, situated north of Tuzla, was made up of "tuzcu", workers at salt-works under government regulation. They were all Muslims at the time of the registration, including the freed man Şahin. Nine persons were appointed *headmen* or *supervisors* (re'īs) over the workers. In their possesion they had 606 salt-pans *(gölek)* altogether. They were responsible for supervising the production and delivering the product at the price set by the Porte. Except for a payment of 15 akça per day for the local mosque, the rest of the revenue from the salt-works and two villages was made an endowment by Bayezid I (1389-1402) to the tomb of the Prophet at Medina.

In the survey dated 1566[14] workers at the Kızılca-Tuzla numbered 343. In 1532 there were 14 headmen and 720 *gölek.* The post of *re'īs* or headman appears to have been hereditary.[15]

Salt was produced at the salt-pans in the plain at the Tuzla village. The waters from the hot and cold springs by the village of Tuzla flowed into small pools where water was left to be evaporated in the summer heat.[16] Another more primitive method described to me by the *muhtar* or elder of Behram Nuri Koç was that of placing sieves against the water running from

---

[12] Belediye Library, İstanbul, Cevdet Kitapları, no. O. 117, 136-138.

[13] For *çift* and *benlak (bennak)* see my, "Osmanlılar'da Raiyyet Rüsûmu", *Belleten,* XXIII (1959).

[14] *Hüdāvendigār Evḳāf Defteri,* Tapu ve Kadastro Genel Müdürlüğü, Ankara, no. 570; Güçer, *op. cit.,* 102.

[15] Güçer, *op. cit.,* 104.

[16] Cook, *op. cit.,* 224.

the springs; salt then accumulated in the sieves. The account books of the fifteenth century demonstrate that spring salt of Kızılca-Tuzla was appreciated for its high quality and consumed at the Sultan's palace as the account books of the fifteenth century show. Villagers at Behram today find its taste a little bitter.

A government agent *(emīn)* or a farmer of public revenues was responsible for the supervision of all activities and transactions connected with the production and marketing of the government controlled salt works.[17] In order to maintain the public revenue from the salt works the agent or farmer was responsible of marketing and maintaining the production at a certain level. All this was contingent upon the transport and distribution of this heavy good at a certain cost. Therefore, it became necessary to establish a monopoly on the production and the sale of salt within delimited areas, and to organize the task of transportion. The whole system depended on how the salt would be carried to distant places, and at what cost. From this situation originated the organization of camel drivers under government regulation in western Anatolia. Since the agent was concerned with keeping the transport costs at the lowest possible level disputes often arose over the transport rates between him and the camel drivers.[18]

Conversly, the camel drivers tried to escape this labor service or raise the rates of hire when they found more favorable condition at large. During Sinan Pasha's governorship of Anatolia (1481-1482 and 1486-1489) the Sultan issued strict regulations under severe penalties to keep camel drivers in the service.[19]

In 1522 the government's revenue from Kızılca-Tuzla salt-work amounted to 383,983 akça or about 6,400 gold ducats.[20] In the nineteenth century the annual production was estimated in various sources to be between 500 and 3,000 tons.[21] The latter figure corresponds to at least twelve thousand camel loads. Camels were used in the salt transport as late as the twentieth century. A photograph taken by Leaf in 1911 "shows the pans under water; and a great pile of the collected salt with two trains of camels waiting to take their loads".[22] Also, as late as the nineteenth century,

[17] Güçer, *ibid.*

[18] For examples see Güçer, *op. cit.,* 120-122.

[19] See Anhegger and Inalcik, *op. cit.,* 31; Beldiceanu, *Actes,* 95.

[20] Güçer, *op. cit.,* 130.

[21] Cook, *op. cit.,* 224.

[22] *Ibid.*

camels remained major means of the transporting native products (chiefly valonia) from the back country down to the Baba or Behram harbors.[23]

During my one day visit to Behram in the summer of 1975 the *muhtar* of Behram Nuri Koç informed me that in the village *Araplar* as well as in *Behram,* camels were employed until recently in the transport of crops, straw or wood. Now, he said, trucks superseded the use of the camel in transportation of heavy goods. In the past, the inhabitants of *Araplar* used their camels to transport a great amount of pottery made in Çanakkale to Anatolian towns as far as Adana.

Since the mine was state property and was farmed out to a tax farmer, salt produced at Kızılca-Tuzla was to be distributed in a monopoly area *(örü)* comprising the districts *(kadılık)* of Edremid, Kemer, Ivrindi, Balıkesir, Kepsud, Bigadiç, Mihaliç, Kirmasti and Lapseki in the province of Karesi, Every one in this larg area without exception had to buy exclusively the salt of Kızılca-Tuzla, at the government fixed price. Enforced by law in all major salt producing areas, the monopoly system was designed to maintain production and protect the interests of the treasury. Even when the population did not need salt each district was compelled to buy its annual share of salt . Every time the tax farmer complained against the people's reluctance and excuses not to purchase the salt the Porte sent strict orders to the local cadis to aid the tax farmer in enforcing the regulation. According to a fifteenth century decree issued to enforce the monopoly,[24] a special state agent *(yasakdjı)* was sent to the province with the authority to seize salt from any other source and punish its carrier, unofficial owner and buyer. Also, those local authorities who failed to cooperate with the agent to uncover non-monopoly salt were threatened with capital punishment.

The abovementioned document from apparently the last years of Mehmed II's reign (1451-1481) tells us that[25] "the Arabs living in the areas of Karaburun, Edremid, Ayazmend and Kızılca-Dağ since earlier times had loaded and transported on their camels the salt produced in the [Kızılca-Tuzla] region". The decree orders them to continue in this servic.

The following description of the Arab camel drivers of the area north of Tuzla is found in the register of Biga dated 1517.[26]

"The following groups of *'Arabān* take on their camels the salt produced at the Behram-Tuzla to the places ordered (in the regulation) and in return for

---

[23] Cook, 10, 227.

[24] Anhegger and Inalcik, *op. cit.,* 30-31; Beldiceanu, *ibid.*

[25] Anhegger and Inalcik, *op. cit.,*31

[26] *Biga mufaṣṣal defteri,* Başvekâlet Archives, Istanbul, Tapu Defteri dated Muharrem 923.

this service they were given diplomas of tax exemption by the past Sultans. Thus, they are exempted from all kinds of extraordinary impositions taken either by custom or by government edict. It is ordered that they carry the salt [of Bahram] to the usual places and that no extraordinary taxes be imposed. The imperial decrees order that. Now our Sultan Selim Khan, too, confirmed it by his diploma:

> The group of *Yatak Arabs:* 27 persons
> The group of *Andavazlu Arabs:* 15 person
> [Arabs] in the villages of Kınık, Alemshalu and Kara-Turakhan
> The Arabs of Karaburun live in the *kadılık* of Tuzla: they transport salt from the salt works of Behram.

The same document informs us that in the area near the sea passage at Gelibolu there were "camels belonging to the state" *(khaṣṣa develer)* that were used for transport.

Behram and its Nāhiyet

Behram was the administrative center of this complex and was responsible for with the organization of salt production and distribution.

According to the *vakf* surveys[27] covering the second half of the fifteenth century and the first two decades of the sixteenth century, Behram (originally from the Greek name *Machramion*)[28] was a village in the district *(nāhiyet)* of Bergama and comprised various groups of population with different status.

Originally the arable land of the village was divided into *çiftlik units* in possession of 32 Greek peasants. These Greeks were assigned as *nöbetdji,* guardians in the fortress of Bergama. Then, apparently under Mehmed II the number of guardians dropped to eleven who possessed eleven *çiftliks* in Berham while nine *çiftliks* (together with the peasant families) were made part of the timar of *Sipahi* Hamza. One *çiftlik* was possessed by the warden of the guardians by the name of Manul, a Greek. The remaining five *çiftliks* went back to the treasury as *mevḳūf.* Finally, we are told that around 1500 none of these Greek guardians were left in their places.

We know that native Greeks were assigned similar duties in return for exemption from certain taxes in Mytilene and other islands in the northern

---

27 *Hüdāvendigār Evḳāf Defteri,* Tapu ve Kadastro G. M., Ankara, no. 111.

28 See Paul Wittek, *Das Fürstentum Mentesche,* Istanbul, 1934, 21.

Aegean under Mehmed the Conqueror.[29] Those who were living in Behram were assigned to make oars (for the navy) under Mehmed II (1451-1481). This obligation was abolished, and then re-imposed, in 1522.

Above the village of Behram *(Karye-i Behram)* there stands on top of the hill the castle of Behram *(Behram-Kale),* a Byzantine castle used by the ottomans. Because of its economic and strategic position this area must have had an unusual significance for the Ottomans during the period before Mytilene came under the Ottoman rule (1462).[30] The main reason for the conquest of Mytilene by Mehmed II was that it gave refuge to the Christian (Catalan) pirates who tried to attack and ruin the opposite Turkish coastal areas.[31]

---

[29] H. W. Lowry, "A Corpus of Extant Kanunnames for the Island of Limnos...", *The Journal of Ottoman Studies,* I, (1980), 52, 58.

[30] Mention should be made of the construction of mosques and bridges in Behram, the village Kemâller (near Ezine) and other places in the area under Murad I (1362-1389); for the complex of the mosque, bath-house and mosque built by Aslihan Bey son of Kemâl Bey see E. H. Ayverdi, "I. Murad Devrinde Asilhan Bey Mimari Manzumesi", *Vakıflar Dergisi,* III.

[31] See Critovoulos, *History of Mehmed the Conqueror,* Princeton 1954, 180-185.

Table I

The district of Behram consisted of the following villages in 1522 and 1940

The survey of 1522	In the 1940 census and modern maps
—	Araplar (in the district of Ezine)
Arab-Köy	Araplar (Koca-Köy)
Büyük-Çepni	B. and K. Çipne (in Edremit) or B. and K. Çetme
Küçük-Çepni	
—	Çetmi-aşireti (in Ezine)
Hünkârlar also known as Kutlu	Kutlu-oba? (in the district of Bayramiç)
Ayvacık (or Ivecik)	Ayvacık
Dögendi?	—
Kozlu	Kozlu (in Ayvacık)
Çukur-Köy (abandoned)	—
Hızır-Şeyh (abandoned)	—
Ozer	—
Göksek	—
Kuyumcu also known as Menteşe	Menteşe
Ada-Tepe	Ada-Tepe (in Küçük-Kuyu)
Çanak	—
Koru	—
Borgos	Bergaz (in Gülpınar)
Paşa-Yigit	Yigitler (in Bayramiç) or Paşa-Köy (in Ayvacık)
Nusrat-Köy	Nusratlı (Musuratlı) (in Küçük-Kuyu)
Eşeklü-Köy	Eşeklü (Saidiye, Merkepli)
Eymirler	—
Şahi-Köy	—
Timurciler	Demirci (in Ayvacık)
Burunlu	—
Saruhanlu-Davud	—
Balaban-Lala	Balabanlı
Viranlu	Viranlı (in Bayramiç)
Kalfal	Kulfal (in Ayvacık)
Kapucı-Köy	—
Kalabaklu	Kalabaklı (in Erenköy)
Purun	—
Yeniler	—
Tura-Beg	—
Kızıl-Ya'kub	Kızıl-Köy (in Bayramiç) or Kızıl-Tepe (in Ezine) or Kızıl-Yar (in Ayvacık)
Güvendik	Güveniç (in Bayramiç)

Akpınar	Akçapınar (in Erenköy)
Akça-in	İn-Tepe? (in Erenköy)
Ali-Fakih	—
Üç-Kilise	—
Çoraklu	—
Sed-Obası	—
Ovacık	—
Bayramça	—
Mihlu	Mihlu
Çölmek	—
Behram	Behram-Köy (in Ayvacık)

Djemā'at-i Yürükān-i Behram (nomad, i.e. Yürük group of Behram).

"Arab Camel Drivers " in Western Anatolia

In the region south of Karesi "the migrant Arab camel drivers" are to be found in four groups in Saruhan, İzmir, Ayasolug (Hagios-Theologos, Ephesus) and Teke. The fiscal surveys and *ḳānūnnāme* (regulation) of Aydın[32] sandjak make clear that a group of "'Arabān-i boghurdjiyān", 82 men in record, lived "in the kadılık of İzmir". The second group, 58 men, came from the sandjak of Sarukhan (capital city: Magnisa > Manisa) and joined that of Izmir in the sixteenth century. In his book on the Yürüks of Sarukhan, İbrahim Gökçen[33] included a document dated 1611 concerning people from a nomadic group called "Arapemmiler". I am inclined to read it rather as *'Arab-boghurcılar.* The shift of the Arab camel drivers to the Izmir area might be connected with the fact that Izmir was on the way to becoming the major outlet of the western Anatolian products to Istanbul and later on to Europe.[34]

---

[32] Başvekâlet Archives, İstanbul, Tapu Defteri no. 537 dated Radjab 983/October 1575.

[33] *Saruhan'da Yürükler ve Türkmenler,* İstanbul 1946, 98.

[34] Some Anatolian products shipped from the Port of İzmir
Source: Necmi Ülker, *The Rise of the Port of Izmir,* Ph. D. Dissertation, Univ. of Michigan, Ann Arbor, 101, 104, 121.

Goods	*Quantity*	*Exported*
Cotton (1705)	353,222 quintals	to France
Opium (1701)	6/14 French lbs.	from Karahisar to France
Mohair yarn (1701)	279,835 French lbs.	from Ankara to France
Goat wool of Ankara (mohair) (1701)	302,785 English lbs.	To England

In addition to these items, İzmir exported great quantities of such bulky good as wheat, valonia (palamut), hides, figs, currants, madder (kökboya), and carpets which were all the

In 1628 mention was still made in Sarukhan of the "boghurcıyān" (camel drivers) who sent complaints to the Sultan against the exactions of the local military authorities.[35] Later in the middle of the eighteenth century a certain Araboghlu Hādji Mehmed, voyvoda of Bergama, who organized a militia known as *Arab-oghulları* played an important role in the power struggle between *a'yans* in western Anatolia. His hired men, *levends*, were accused of all kinds of violent acts, and the government finally declared him an outlaw.[36] We do not know whether he or his men had any connection with the "Arabs" of western Anatolia. The Ayasolug (Ephesus) group of *boghurdjı* Arabs must actually be one of the earliest camel driver groups since Ayasolug had become the most important commercial center between the Italians and Turcomans during the fourteenth century before the Ottomans came. From the fourteenth century on, cotton exported to Italy in great quantities from western Anatolia was carried to the port of Ayasolug. In the mid-fifteenth century the value of the annual export of cotton to Italy was estimated at over half a million gold ducats.[37] Cotton bales were usually transported on camel back from Çukur-Abad/Cilicia, and Magnisa.[38]

In the sandjak of Menteşe too, salt produced at the Peçin salt-works was taken by camel drivers into towns in the interior. Production was quite considerable in this region: In 1503 for example, the government drew 513,500 akça as revenue.[39]

Further south, in the sandjak of Teke another group of 'Arabān-i ghurbetān" (immigrant Arabs) is mentioned in a register dated 1671. Their total tax revenue was assessed in the amount of 133,333 akça.[40]

On the basis of documentary evidence, emphasis must be put on the importance of camel transport for the İzmir-Aydın area as late as the middle

---

products of western Anatolia brought to Izmir mostly on camel back. Pack animals in the caravans from Persia were mostly camels because the camel caravan could carry twice or three times more weight than the horse caravan.

35 Ç. Uluçay, *17. Asırda Saruhan'da Eşkiyalık ve Halk Hareketleri,* İstanbul 1944, 120, 171.

36 Ç. Uluçay, *18 ve 19. Yüzyıllarda Saruhan'da Eşkiyalık ve Halk Hareketleri,* Istanbul 1955, documents nos. 208-214; G. Veinstein, "'Ayān de la région d'Izmir et le commerce du Levant", *Revu de l'Occident Musulman et de la Méditerranée,* XX (1975), 144-46.

37 Heers, *Gênes au XVe siècle,* Paris 1961, 393.

38 Ö. L. Barkan, *XV inci ve XVI. Asırlarda Osmanlı İmparatorluğunda Ziraî Ekonominin Hukukî ve Malî Esasları,* İstanbul 1943, 205.

39 Güçer, *op. cit.,* 130.

40 Başvekâlet Archives, Nişan Defteri, 13.

of the nineteenth century.[41] Until the time Aydın-İzmir railroad was opened to the traffic in 1861, all bulky and heavy goods such as cotton, hides, figs, raisins, cereals and oilseeds were transported on camel back from inland to the port of İzmir. In 1856, rates per *kile* (25.6 kg) of grain were 5 ghroush for Magnisa-Izmir, 14 g. Aydın-İzmir, 25 g. Uşak-İzmir and 45 g. Konya-İzmir. It was estimated that this camel transport was five times more expensive than transport over good roads.[42]

As seen earlier in the Karesi province, the Arab camel drivers of Izmir and Ayasolug areas were also performing transport services with their camels *(boghur hizmeti)* for the state principally carrying salt to the various parts of the province, in addition to provisions as wheat, cotton, and dried fruits to the port of İzmir for the provisioning of the Sultan's crowded palace and the city of Istanbul. Prior to the spectacular expansion in its trade with Europe in the seventeenth century, Izmir appears to have steadily developed thanks to its growing trade with Istanbul, the Balkans and the Black Sea areas in the fifteenth and sixteenth centuries. It should not be overlooked that the largest salt works under government control at Menemen was in the İzmir region (public revenue in 983/1575 was 540.885 akça).[43]

The rather harsh conditions imposed on the camel drivers by the government during the second half of the fifteenth century (see supra: camel drivers of Kızılca-Tuzla) were relaxed under Süleyman I (1520-1566). The salt of Menemen, for instance, used to be taken by camel drivers to the interior (Adala and Demirci) at unreasonably low nates of transport. Later, the Porte intervened in favor of the camel drivers to settle disputes over the rates of transport fees.[44]

---

[41] Charles Issawi, *Economic History of Turkey, 1800-1914,* Chicago: The University of Chicago Press, 1980, 181.

[42] Orhan Kurmuş, *Emperyalizmin Türkiye'ye Girişi,* İstanbul: Bilim Yayınları, 1974, 46-47; The number of camels fell steadily as roads and modern means of transport spread in Turkey during the last decades. They are concentrated in southern an western Turkey as in earlier periords.

Date	*Camel population of Turkey, 1948-1968*
1948	108,852
1955	72,034
1965	45,900
1968	42,000

[43] Güçer, *op. cit.,* 130.

[44] *Ibid.,* 122; while the transport fee for one camel load from Menemen to Demirci was normally 45 akça the government agent at the salt-works had reduced it to 15.

An interesting note tells us that Bayezid the Thunderbolt (1389-1402) brought ten thousand camels from his campaign in the Antalya (Pamphylia) area in 1399.[45] No detail is given about to where so many camels were transferred. They were apparently needed for the transport of army baggage and provisions during the long campaigns carried out in areas as distant as the Danube and Eastern Anatolia. It is sensible to suggest that these camels might have been moved, at least partly, to western Anatolia conquered by Bayezid I in 1389-1390 which has the same climate as the Antalya plain. Karaman land conquered in 1397, might also have become a new home for these camel drivers. In fact, in the subsequent periods we find there were Turcoman camel breeders in the region. But it appears that these Arab camel drivers in western Anatolia migrated there earlier, probably in the first half of the fourteenth century.

Thus, nomadic "Arabs" with their camels, usually referred to in the fiscal surveys as *"boghurdjı 'Arablar"* that is, "camel *(boghur)* driver Arabs" or "urubetān-i ghurbetān",[46] that is "immigrant Arabs", were to be found not only in the area of the eastern coasts of the Dardanelles but also down to the bay of Antalya. The government granted them the special status of performing transport service with their camels in return for which they were exempted from the extraordinary levies and services *('avāriḍ-i divāniyye)*. A change in the status of the *boghurdjı* Arabs in the regulation of Aydın sandjak dated 1528 is recorded as follows.[47]

"The boghurdjı Arabs in the areas of Ayasolug (Ephesus) and Izmir (Smyrna) used to perform service with their camels in earlier times. Then, this service was abolished, and by law, eighty akça was taken instead. At the present, it is still done in the same way".

It was a common Ottoman practice to exempt a group of the reaya from extraordinary impositions whenever they were required to provide services to the state in mining, agriculture, transport or security matters. Whenever such services were no longer required the government subjected them to a fixed

---

[45] Johann Schiltberger, who was in the retinue of Bayezid I writes in his memoirs (*Reisebuch*, ed. V. Langmental, Tübingen 1885, 21, quoted by Barbara Flemming, *Landschaftsgeschichte von Pamphylien, Psidien und Lykien im Spätmittlalter*, Wisbaden 1964, 106) as follows: "und to der chönig Weyasit die state (Adalia) und das landt gewan, do schenckt im das landt zehen thausent chamel-tier; und besetzett er die stat und das land und die Chamel fürt er in sein landt".

[46] The Word 'urūba signifies "être d'origine arabe", (J. B. Belot, *Vocabulaire Arab-Français,* Beyrouth 1929, 483); the survey agents, sophisticated chancery secretaries or ulema, were often responsible for such unusual terms; boghur or bughur stands for a male camel in Turkish.

[47] Ö. L. Barkan, *op. cit.*, 12 (there bogurcu arabalar or *wagons* driven by camels).

amount of money in lieu of the abolished services. In the Ottoman tax system the personal tax, which every person of reaya status had to pay, was rendered either in public service or in cash.[48] The legal status of the camel drivers in public service should be viewed in light of these provisions.[49]

In 1636 the tax revenue from the "ʿArabān-i ghurbetān" in Aydın amounted to 133,333 akça. If the tax rate was still eighty akça per household at this date this gives 1666 households. These "ʿArabs" called *ghurbetān* (immigrants) might be those who immigrated there after 1516. Again in the sandjak of Aydın another group called "ʿArabān-i Boghurcıyān-i Halebī" ("camel driver Arabs from Aleppo") is mentioned in the same treasury register of 1636.[50] This group must number 416 households on the same basis of computation. What is of particular interest for us in the record is the reference to their place of origin *Haleb* (Aleppo). This is the only positive clue we can find about the Arab ethnic origin of such groups in western Anatolia.

The circumstances which might have attracted "Arab camel drivers" to western Anatolia can be summarized as follows: in general, the transport of heavy and bulky goods such as grain, salt, and cotton from production centers to towns was economically feasible only by camel transport. The use of other available means of transport -horse or mule, which were twice as expensive as camel- made the trade of these goods almost prohibitive despite the fact that these goods were of vital importance for provisioning the towns, and for providing raw materials for the town handicrafts.[51]

---

[48] See my "Osmanlılar'da Raiyyet Rüsûmu", 594.

[49] In 1596, boghurdjı ʿArabs were still counted among those reʿāyā groups who enjoyed certain privileges for performing public services: Ç. Uluçay, *XVII asırda...*, 171.

[50] I am indebted for this information to Rhoads Murphey who is preparing this register of *muḳāṭaʿāt* for publication.

[51] In the twelfth century Egypt the standard camel load was about 500 pounds. Richard W. Bulliet, *The Camel and the Wheel,* Cambridge, Mass., 1972, 176-215, accepts 430 pounds avoirdupoids as the standard camel load, while a limite of more than 500 pounds is argued by others. On the basis of Diocletian's edict issued in 301 A. D., he concludes that the cost of camel transport was 20% lower in price than a wagonload drawn by two oxen. He believes that this is "the clue to the entire transformation of the transport economy of the Middle East". At any rate the western Anatolian case discussed here supports R. W. Bulliet's basic hypothesis. Under particular circumstances camel transport had great advantages over other means of transport. Bulliet summarizes these advantages from the observation of Major Leonard, an expert on the Camel subject was, first, most economical since it cost less and carried twice as much as the horse. In particular, the camel did not need the construction of roads it was necessary for cart or wagon transportation. The camel is faster and is able to cover more ground daily, and will make many journeys in a year and in their respective lifetimes; it has greater tenacity and endurance, abstinence from food and water. Ottomans employed one man for

Salt production and distribution under government control apparently played the most important role in the widespread use of camels from the early Turcoman conquest of western Anatolia. Being a necessity for the population and an important source of revenue for the treasury, the production and distribution of salt was regulated by the government over large areas. It was within this system that Arab camel drivers must have been organized and controlled by the government as a group under a special status. Also, the growing need for heavy transport which resulted from the expansion of trade at the ports of Ayasolug and Izmir with Europe and Istanbul in such bulky goods as wheat, cotton, hides and dried fruits must have been another important factor attracting camel driver Arabs to western Anatolia. Arab tribesmen had long been specialized in caravan transport in the Middle East, and we know from the examples of the later nomad migrations from northern Syria into western Anatolia that the shift was not very difficult.

"Araplu" Turcomans

The question is raised as to whether or not we are justified in considering all the groups bearing the name *'Arab* (or Arap) in Anatolia as ethnic Arabs.[52] The word *'Arab,* it was argued, is used not only for ethnic Arabs but also for any dark-skinned people including those of gypsy and negroe in Turkey. It is true that the quarters referred to as "Arap mahallesi" in many Anatolian towns

---

six camels (an individual camel was called *mehār* and a train of six camel *ḳaṭar*). Since its purchase price was high, the Ottoman administration avoided this expense by organizing Arab and Turcoman camel breeders into the government service, or by using a hiring system. In the Ottoman Empire, especially after the annexation of Syria in 1516, there was apparently a sufficient number of camels to meet general transport needs. Apparently, Suleyman I's first great campaign against Hungary in 1520 was facilitated by the use of camels (thirty thousand camels were assembled from Asiatic provinces for the army transport under Ferhad Pasha). In 1555 Dernschwam was impressed by the sight of about one thousand camels carring the tents and baggage of the Sultan in Anatolia. On his way to Amasya he also saw camels carrying merchandise to Ankara. A description cannot be given here of the vast and elaborate organization of the transport of the baggage and provisions for the Sultan's palace and army during the campaigns where the camel was always the cheif means of transport of heavy goods. On the other hand the camel was the most important animal for Yürüks who not only employ them in the transport business and make money, but also they use them in carrying their bagage between their summer and winter pasturelands. Considering the importance of their camels they do not slaughter them for food and call them "the major capital" *(ulu-māl):* Kemal Güngör, *Cenubî Anadolu Yörüklerinin Etno-Antropolojik Tetkiki,* Ankara 1941); also see S. Faroqhi, "Camels, Wagons and the Ottoman State in the Sixteenth and Seventeenth Centuries", *Interl. Journ. of Middle East Studies,* vol. 14 (1982), 523-539.

52 I am indebted to Professor Adnan Erzi and Yaşar Yücel for drawing my attention to this point.

included, in the nondistant past, Turkish speaking gypsies or dark-skinned people. It is possible, however, to distinguish as ethnic Arabs those groups who speak Arabic or who keep some linguistic evidence in their language. As far as we know no such linguistic study has been undertaken of Anatolian camel drivers. Besides Arabs there were, in fact, groups of gypsies and Turcomans who were engaged in camel transport activities in Asia Minor. As attested by archival documents, during the early seventeenth century, Turcomans of Akça-Koyunlu, for example, were breeding a great number of camels. The number of camels in the possession of each registered man varied in average between 30 and 80; there were some owning as many as 800.[53]

On the other hand, *Yürüks* (Turcomans) called *'Arablu* (Araplu) should not be confused with groups who were specifically called *'Arab. 'Arablu* does not actually signify an ethnic Arab, but people connected with the Arabs or Arabia. The *'Arablu Yürüks* made up quite a large group scattered in western Anatolia and eastern Balkans. Today in Turkey, *Araplar* and *Araplı* survive as village names in widely spread areas.

Table II

Araplı	Araplar
Denizli (Acıpayam and Buldan), Mersin, Malatya (Adıyaman), Manisa (Alaşehir, Akhisar), Maraş, Seyhan (Karaisalı), Zonguldak (Devrek), Aydın (Bozdoğan), Sivas (Zara), Balıkesir (Edremid)	Afyon (Egret), Aydın, Elazığ (Çan), Giresun (Keşap), Kastamonu (Kuzyaka), Seyhan (Karaisali), Sinop (Gerze), Yozgat (Musabeyli), Maraş (Camuzlu)

Source: *Türkiye'de Meskûn Yerler Kılavuzu,* I, Ankara 1946.

This list does not include either quarters in towns with the name *Arab,* or compound toponyms derived from the word *Arab* such as *Arapoğlu, Arapzāde, Arapören, Arapözü.* Also, we are not concerned here with the Arabic speaking minorities in southern Asia Minor in the provinces of Hatay, Seyhan, Gaziantep, Urfa, Mardin and Diyarbakır.

It appears that toponyms directly referring to Arabs are to be found concentrated in western Anatolia, whereas those referring to *Araplı* are more scattered.

In historical sources we find an *Araplu* ('Arablu) tribe settled in the eighteenth century in Ilıca, Musacalu and Mendoharya in the province of

---

53 In a document dated 1014/1605: Başvekâlet Archives, *Maliyeden Müdevver Defterler,* no. 6022.

Saruhan. A separate group under an *Araplı Battal Bey* is also mentioned in this province.[54] In Rumili, *Araplı* (ʻAraplu) Yürük groups are referred to in Hādji-Oğlu-Pazardjık (Dobrudja), Rusikasrı (southern Bulgaria) and Silistre in the sixteenth century.[55]

As mentioned above earlier records mention *Araplu Yürüks* in the Tekirdağı province on the European side of the Dardanelles.

The vakf deed of Orkhan (1324-1362) dated 762/1361 mentions an *Araplu* (ʻArablu) village situated near Eriklice (Byzantine Herakleia)[56] on the Marmara coast which was one of the early Ottoman conquests in Thrace between 1353 and 1358. Twenty six Christian and five Muslim households lived in the village according to the survey of *Musellems* made in 1519.

Dr. Tekin, who is himself from the *Araplu Yürüks* in origin, informed me that the *Araplu Yürüks* are presently settled in about forty villages around Atranos. Tribal tradition tells us that they moved north in this area from the Gediz valley to escape heavy taxation, and disputes with the local landowners. According to the tradition, they were formerly "in the service of the Arabs" in the Syrian desert before they migrated in the areas of Gediz and Domaniç. They were pastoralists breeding sheep and goats. Also, Dr.Şinasi Tekin says that his father remembers the time of the pastoralist life of the tribe and that they also had herds of horses (yılkı).

There was an *Araplu Yürük* (Turcoman) tribe which appears to have spread in western Anatolia and eastern Balkans during the early Ottoman conquests along with other Turcoman groups such as *Saruhanlu* and *Yuva (Yiva)* under Orkhan and Murad I. Ottoman conquests in Rumili seem to have attracted many nomadic groups from western Anatolia towards the Dardanelles and the Balkans. Therefore, ʻĀşıḳ Pasha-zāde's "Arab göçer-evleri" might have been either these *Araplu* (ʻArablu) Turcomans or a group belonging to be the Arab camel drivers, "Arabs" settled on the Asiatic side of the Dardanelles and in western Anatolia. In fact, the salt works at Seydi-Kavağı in Thrace came under Ottoman control in the period before Süleyman Pasha's death (1357 or 1358).[57]

---

54 Uluçay, *18. ve 19. Yüzyıllar'da,* 83.

55 Tayyib Gökbilgin, *Rumeli'de Yürükler, Tatarlar ve Evlâd-i Fâtihân,* İstanbul, 1957, 110, 139, 143.

56 See above note 2; the earliest copy available of this document appears to have been arranged under Mehamed II (1451-1481), this copy is preserved today at the *Türk Islâm Eserleri Müzesi,* Istanbul, no. 2197. A later copy of it published in facsimile by T. Gökbilgin, *Edirne ve Paşa Livâsı,* supplement: 218-220. I have not seen Hikmet Çevik, *Tekirdağ Yürükleri,* İstanbul 1971.

57 Also we find an *'Arab Hadjı-köy* (village) in the Maritsa valley (Gökbilgin, *ibid.*). A certain Eymir-Khan (a typical Turcoman name) son of *'Arab Hadjı* is referred to as

With its rich pasturelands the Çanakkale peninsula from Edremit to the Dardanelles, and the Kazdağı massif in particular, became an attractive region for pastoralist nomads when a general westward move began at the turn of the fourteenth century. Byzantine historian Pachymeres (d. 1310) tells us how around 1300 the population of Assos (Behram) emigrated and took refuge in Mytilene under the pressure of the invading Turcomans.[58] Later on the area continued to attract Turcoman nomads from various origins who, over time, settled in the villages or *oba*s in the area. In the survey of 1522 (Tapu Kadastro Genel Müdürlügü, Eski Kayıtlar, no. 111) the villages Menteşe, Eymirler, Saruhanlu, Büyük-Çepni and Küçük-Çepni in the *nāhiyet* (district) of Behram can be mentioned as examples of the Turcoman settlements. According to the same survey, the *Yürük*s of Behram *(djemā'at-i Yürükān-i Behram)* paid 3564 akça in sheep tax and personal *(bennak)* tax during the same period (one akça for two sheep). Apparently, Turcoman *Yürük*s from the Saruhan area (the Gediz River valley) migrated into the Çanakkale peninsula and the Marmara basin as far as Koca-eli before the sixteeth century.[59] The Yürük groups of Kubaşlar, for example, or Saruhanlu were found in the *nāhiyet* of Kızılca-Tuzla as well as in the Saruhan province.[60] In the Marmara area, *Kubaşlar* had their summer pastureland in the *kadılık* of Manyas, and their taxes were included as those of the Behram Yürüks in the endowment of Medina.[61] Their move in this area from Saruhan apparently dated back to the establishment of the pious foundation by Bayezid I (1389-1402), or even to an earlier date. In later periods Kızılkeçili settlements were found in the area (two villages bore the name).

In the Ottoman fiscal surveys, mostly of the sixteenth century, Faruk Sümer[62] found Turcoman groups of the Çepni (in the nāhiyet of Behram), Afşar (in the Ayazmend and Kepsut areas), Karkın (in Ezine), Eymir (Eymür) (in the Behram and Edremid areas), Kınık, Bügdüz and Igdır (in the Çan area). Apparently, Yürük camel drivers existed among the Yürüks of

---

founder of a small pious endowment in the Filibe area dating back to Murad I's time (1362-1389). Apparently *'Arab-Hadjı* and his son were more than ordinary people.

[58] P. Wittek, *ibid.*, but as seen above many Greek peasant families survived in Behram after the Turcoman conquest.

[59] Saruhanlu village near Yalova: Başvekâlet Archives, *Defter-i Mufaṣṣal-i Kocaeli,* no. 49, dated 1034, p. 20; I have not seen Kemal Özer, *Balıkesirde Yürük ve Çepni Türkleri,* Bursa 1948; and Kâmil Su, *Balıkesir Civarında Yürük ve Türkmenler,* Istanbul, 1938.

[60] İ. Gökçen, *op. cit.*, 97.

[61] *Hüdāvendigār Evḳāf Defteri,* (see note 14, above), 5 b.

[62] *Oğuzlar (Türkmenler)-Tarihleri-Teşkilâtı-Destanları* Ankara 1967, 424, 428, 434, 438, 443, 445, 447.

Karaca-Dağ in the sandjak of Karesi. The government tried to keep them as a separate group from the ordinary peasant population.[63] Part of the settlements in the area reflected a rather transitory phase in the process from nomadic to the sedentary life as they were not called *karye* or *köy* ,but simply *oba* which means a nomadic clan or its pastureland.[64]

Within *oba* population settled in *bölük*s, a term also used for the small tribal groups.

It appears that most of the Turcoman nomads arrived in the Çanakkale peninsula from Aydın and Saruhan. At the same time, however, according to the early Ottoman surveys nomadic groups from eastern Anatolia were also encountered in the region; for example, there were the *Çepni*s who must have migrated from eastern Asia Minor, and also a group of Abī-Sāfī Kurds who arrived in Geyve in 1487, and then, were transferred into the Balkans and dispersed.[65] Thus, mobile elements, Turcomans, Kurds and Arabs, could migrate to western Asia Minor from Eastern Anatolia or the Syrian desert without great difficulty, especially when there were economic attractions on this side.[66]

---

63 See Barkan, *Kanunlar,* 22, dated 1576.

64 For *oba* (in Mongol *obak)* in other Central Asiatic groups see: L. Krader, *Social Organization of the Mongol-Turkish Pastoral Nomads.* The Hague 1963, 323; for a recent bibliography on the Yürük see Ingvar Svanberg, *A bibliography of the Turkish-Speaking Tribal Yürüks,* Upsala: Etnologiska Institutionen, 1982.

65 Başvekâlet Archives, *Hüdāvendigār Defteri,* no. 3 dated 892/1487, p. 676.

66 Even today on the mountainous areas of Gümüşlük (Bodrum) the transportation by camel is still a profitable business because of small profit margin makes impractical the use of modern means of transportation for bulky goods.

6

The Question of the closing of The Black Sea under The Ottomans

The Question of the closing of The Black Sea under The Ottomans

A. The Black Sea

Obviously the question of the Black Sea cannot be studied independently of that of the Straits.[1]

Historically, that state which controlled the Straits has consequently always striven to establish control over the Black Sea. And in fact, those states ruling over the mainland on both sides of the Straits, first the Byzantines and then the Ottomans, did achieve this. Conversely, those states which were dominant on the Black Sea, and those which were a naval power in the Mediterranean, have endeavored to extend their control over the Straits, as did Venice, Genoa, Russia and England. Furthermore, as the Straits constitute a passage way between the Mediterranean and the Black Sea, one can posit that the two lands and two seas connected by the Straits make up a kind of "historical region", or "geopolitical unit" as it is sometimes called. Certainly that is how Mehmed the Conqueror viewed his empire when he styled himself "the Sultan of the two lands and the Khakan of the two seas". The course of events, as it had in the Byzantine past, led him to create his empire out of this territory, which area was to remain the core area of the Ottoman Empire for four centuries.[2]

Again, specific geographic conditions determined that, from antiquity on, the Southern and Northern coasts of the Black Sea should form a closely knit economic unit. The Northern Black Sea, with its immediate hinterland in Moldavia, the Crimea, the Dasht (the steppe area between Kuban and Akkerman) and Circassia, sparsely inhabited and producing in surplus great

---

1 On the question of the Straits in the Middle Ages see G. I. Bratianu, *La Mer Noire des origines à la conquête ottomane,* Munich 1969, Livre IV: L'enjeu des Détroits, pp. 253-328; N. Iorga (Jorga), *La politique vénitienne dans les eaux de la Mer Noire,* Bulletin Historique, Academia Romana, Sectiunea istorica 2 (1914) pp. 289-334; Freddy Thiriet, *La Romanie vénitienne au moyen âge,* Paris 1959, III. partie: *La conquête ottomane et ses effets au XV siècle,* pp. 353-439.

2 For the role of the geographical factor in the formation of Mehmed II's empire see H. Inalcık, "Mehmed II", *İslâm Ansiklopedisi,* vol. VII, pp. 506-531.

quantities of grain, meat, fish and other animal products on the one hand, and of the Southern Black Sea, extending into Asia Minor and the Aegean, with exports of Mediterranean products such as wine, olive oil, fruits, cotton and rice as well as certain manufactured goods, on the other, constituted two integral parts of a regional economy. This regional trade was of basic importance, keeping the whole area economically healthy even at times when the international trade between Central Asia and the Mediterranean countries or the Arab lands and those of the North might slacken. The analysis of the customs registers of the 1480's in the following will, I hope, sufficiently illustrate this point.

It should be stressed that Istanbul played a key role in the formation of this highly developed regional economy; while the city depended heavily for its provisions in wheat, meat and salt on the Northern Black Sea, this area in turn was dependent not only on the stimulus of the Istanbul market to maintain its export production level but also on the import from that great transit center of many of its basic commodities: silk and cotton cloths of Asia Minor, fine woolens of Europe, arms, minerals, paper, spices, drugs, sugar and all kinds of manufactured goods. Istanbul imported by sea from the North its bulky necessities at the lowest prices possible, while the North realized high profits for its foodstuffs in the crowded capital of the Empire. Istanbul's spectacular growth under the Ottomans from a population of 30 to 50 thousand in the 1450's to over 300,000 in the first half of the sixteenth century[3] was made possible, obviously, by an increase in the supply of essential commodities, most of which came from the Northern Black Sea area. The growing demand of the imperial capital for foodstuffs and raw materials brought about an extension of animal husbandry and wheat cultivation in the steppes of the Crimean peninsula, and even in the Dasht among the Nogays. It is interesting to note that in response to the growing wheat demand from Istanbul, the Crimeans exploited slave labor on a large scale to put the steppe area in the Crimea under cultivation. It is reported that the slave population of Cossack origin in the Crimea thus employed numbered four hundred thousand and that there were six thousand agricultural estates as against one thousand six hundred villages.[4] Slave raids into Russia, Poland and Circassia were for the Crimeans a regular business venture, through which they supplied the Crimea and the slave markets of

---

[3] For Istanbul's population see H. İnalcık, "Istanbul", *Encyclopaedia of Islam*, second edition (thereafter *EI²*), vol. IV, pp. 238-244.

[4] Evliyâ Çelebi, *Seyâhatnâme*, vol. VII, (İstanbul 1928), p. 601. Evliyâ's figures are usually grossly exaggerated. In 1783, under the Russian occupation there were 1411 villages in the Crimean peninsula (Russian census).

Istanbul, and Bursa and other Anatolian cities. Novoselskij has calculated from Russian archival sources that in the period 1607-1645 alone, the Crimeans took 126,840 slaves.[5] In brief, already in the fifteenth century, the Black Sea area was totally integrated into the Ottoman imperial economy, of which Istanbul had been made the center. It was the policy of focusing on Istanbul which entailed the prohibition of the export of certain goods from the Black Sea area on foreign merchant ships. Mehmed the Conqueror, in building up his empire around the city of the Caesars, concerned himself above everything else with its repopulation and with the promotion of its trades and industries;[6] just as he transferred urban populations, artisans and merchants in particular, from conquered cities, among them Amastris (1460), Trebizond (1461), and Caffa (1475), so also from the very beginning he took measures to ensure the provisioning of the city with foodstuffs and raw materials. Logically, he was led to control the export of these goods beyond the Straits by the Italians. Whenever a shortage or a famine occurred the export of necessities was prohibited. The things the export of which were prohibited included grain, cotton, leather, beeswax, lard, slaves as well as other items considered strategic.[7] To enforce the prohibition, inspection of foreign vessels was made mandatory at the castles on the Bosporus and sometimes at the Dardanelles.[8] As will be discussed later on this did not mean a total prohibition of trade and closing of the Black Sea, although the unusual growth of Istanbul population in the second half of the sixteenth century and frequent shortages and famines did compel the government to take increasingly stringent measures against foreign trade on the Black Sea.

As a result of the restrictions on navigation Istanbul became the principal market for goods of the Black Sea area. The Ottoman Sultans, as the Byzantine Emperors before them did, consciously pursued the policy of making their capital the main market for foreign traders.

---

[5] On the slave trade in the Ottoman empire see H. İnalcık, "Servile Labor in the Ottoman Empire", *The Mutual Effects of the Islamic and the Judeo-Christian Worlds: The East European Pattern*, New York 1978; A. A. Novoselskij, *Struggle of the Muscovite State Against Tatars in the Seventeenth Century*, Moscov, 1948, pp. 416-436 (in Russian).

[6] See H. İnalcık. "Istanbul", pp. 224-238; also H. İnalcık, "The Policy of Mehmed II Toward the Greek Population of Istanbul and the Byzantine Buildings of the City", *Dumbarton Oaks Papers*, pp. 23-24, (1960-1970), pp.231-249.

[7] Here is an example of such an export prohibition from 1560's (A collection of documents, Veliyyüddin Library, Istanbul, no. 1970, p. 1b): "The following are the goods the export of which are prohibited: grain, gunpowder, horses, cotton, cotton thread, lead, beeswax, leather, tallow". The following are added later on: raw leather, morocco leather, sheepskin, sulphur and pitch. For goods prohibited under Mehmed II see *Ḳānūnnāme-i Sulṭānī*... ed. R. Anhegger and H. İnalcık, Ankara 1956, 59.

[8] See p. 422 below.

B. The Ottoman Expansion and the closing of The Black Sea

It was the declared policy of the Ottomans from start not to allow any Latin sovereignty to survive in the Balkans or in Anatolia. Appropriating for themselves the heritage of Byzantium, they considered all the territories and fortresses in Latin hands to be under a form of usurpation. Even when they agreed later to a Latin presence in the form of foreign trading communities, the territorial rights of the Latins were never respected.[9] In 1387, Venice failed totally in negociations with Murad I to get a piece of land at Scutari, facing Pera, on which to set up a commercial center with capitulatory guarantees.[10] There is no single case of the Ottomans granting such a territorial concession to a foreign nation.

It should be added that at least down to 1354, and despite the efforts at the Union of the Churches, the Orthodox world felt the same threat of a crusade that the Ottomans were to feel later.[11] Latin economic exploitation, coupled with naval supremacy and political dominance, was the reality for the peoples of the area, making a prolonged struggle inevitable, and bringing into the picture the frontier Turks, first as mercenaries and the most efficient military force to be found and then as allies, under able leaders such as Umur, Orkhan and Süleyman, who cooperated with the anti-Latin Byzantines.[12]

In brief, the Ottomans, in their efforts at reviving the centralized empire of the Caesars, consciously and systematically followed an anti-Latin policy, and skilfully exploited the anti-Latin feelings of the Orthodox masses, who saw in the Genoese and the Venetians the source of all their material miseries. The Greek populace in Byzantium, suffering from famine under the Palaeologi, was wont to accuse, and not without justification, the Latin merchants of speculation in grain and of the diversion from Istanbul of the

[9] See H. İnalcık, "Imtiyāzāt", *EI*[2], IV, pp. 1180-84. The so-called "treaty" of 1453 with the Genoese of Pera was simply an amnesty document (*amân-nâme*), granted by the Sultan within the framework of the Islamic Law which did not recognize any territorial rights.

[10] See W. Heyd, *Histoire du commerce du Levant*, I, ed. F. Raynaud, Paris 1936, p. 259-60; cf. N. Iorga, *La politique vénitienne dans les eaux de la Mer Noire,* p. 309-18; F. Thiriet, *Régestes des déliberations du senat de Venise concernant la romanie,* I, Paris and The Hague, 1958, p. 165, no. 678.

[11] For the change of policy between Byzantium and the West see Angeliki E. Laiou, *Constantinople and the Latins,* Cambridge, Mass., 1972, pp. 308-329; cf. Oscar Halecki, *Un empereur de Byzance à Rome,* reprint: London 1972, pp. 9-30.

[12] For the details see "The Ottomans and the Crusades", in *The Crusades,* ed. K. Setton, vol. VI, eds. H. V. Hazard and N. P. Zacour, Madison 1989.

wheat produced on the northern Black Sea coasts, in Thrace and the Marmara basin.[13]

The process by which the Ottomans achieved annexation of the Karesi principality in the 1340's, which gave them possession of the east coast of the Dardanelles and the south western coast of the Marmara Sea opposite Thrace, has not yet satisfactorily been clarified. It appears that the ghâzîs in Karesi-ili, whose livelihood depended on raids to the other side of the Dardanelles, saw that the continued success of their raids was dependent on the support of a strong state like the Ottomans'. By 1348 they had no choice, since the navies of Umur Ghâzî, and Sarukhan-oghlu were effectively neutralized by the Holy League, and the ghâzîs of Western Anatolia were now turning their eyes toward the Ottomans for leadership in the ghazâ.

Immediately after the incorporation of the northern part of the Karesi principality the area was organized for ghazâ as an Ottoman frontier sandjak, with Biga (Pegai) as its center, under the leadership of Süleyman Pasha. The new sandjak had important sea bases at Lapseki (Lampsacus), Aydıncık (near Cyzicus) and Kemer (Keramides?), which in Byzantine times had sheltered corsairs preying on the merchant ships travelling between the Bosporus and the Dardanelles. It was from Kemer in 1352 that the main Ottoman forces were to embark for their decisive conquest of the isthmus of the Gallipoli peninsula.

The struggle for the control of the Eastern Aegean and the Straits, which broke out between Genoa on the one hand and Venice, Aragon and Byzantium on the other in 1348 (especially the Genoese reconquest of Chios from the Byzantines and their construction of new fortifications at Pera) was principally responsible for creating the circumstances which made the Ottoman settlement on European soil possible.

The details of the first Ottoman-Genoese cooperation on the Straits, which was to maintain its strategic importance for a century, are worth recapitulating here. The negociations with the Genoese ambassadors, two Peran citizens, Filippo Delomede and Bonifazio Sauli, sent by the admiral of the Genoese fleet, ended with a formal treaty of alliance between Sultan Orkhan and the Genoese. The Genoese promised to pay tribute, which, in the eyes of the Ottomans, put Pera under Ottoman protection. During the war, in

---

[13] The extremely important question of grain trade in the Levant has drawn closer attention since the publication of G. I. Bratianu, *Études byzantines d'histoire économique et sociale,* Paris 1938, pp. 129-81; see A. Laiou, *Constantinople and the Latins,* pp. 62-63, 73, 123-24, 182-83, 194, 310-11; A. Laiou-Thomadakis, *Peasant Society in the Late Byzantine Empire,* Princeton 1977; Anthony Bryer, "The Latins in the Euxine", *XV. Congrès Internl. d'Études Byzantines, Rapports, I. Histoire*, Athens 1976, p. 6-9.

fact, the Ottomans supplied the Genoese with one thousand archers, who were stationed at Pera and on the Genoese ships. These forces defended Pera in the summer of 1351, when the city was besieged by joint Venetian-Byzantine forces. Orkhan himself, with his army, met Doria on the southern shores of the Bosporus at Chalcedon. Following the crucial battle of the Bosporus (February 1352) between the Genoese armada and the allied fleet of Venice and Aragon, the Genoese cited with praise the aid given to them by Orkhan. John VI Cantacuzenus, surrounded in his capital by Ottoman and Genoese forces after the battle, had to submit to a treaty of peace with the Genoese on May 6, 1352. The treaty forbade that Greek territories or seamen be used by the Venetians against the Genoese, and recognized new additions to the territorial limits of the Genoese possessions at Pera.[14]

The Genoese-Ottoman alliance, which was to last up until the Ottoman occupation of Pera in 1453, was to become of great importance for both sides. For the Ottomans the safe crossing of the Straits was a factor of vital importance in their ability to maintain an empire on two continents. It should be emphasized that it was not a coincidence that the Ottomans developed their foothold on European soil shortly after the battle of the Bosporus in 1352. Already in 1351 the Genoese had occupied Heraklea (Eregli), on the European coast, forty miles to the north of Tzympe, which was to be the first Ottoman bridgehead on European soil. As for the Genoese they secured Ottoman protection for Pera against the Byzantines and the Venetians, as well as commercial privileges in the expanding Ottoman territories. The close ties between Pera and Bursa, the Ottoman capital, were to enhance the prosperity of both cities.

During the course of the struggle for the control of the Straits, the question of Tenedos soon came to the forefront. The Venetians persuaded John V Palaeologus to relinquish the island in return for their support against John VI Cantacuzenus (October 1352). While the Venetians were eventually disappointed in their efforts to seize Tenedos,[15] the Ottomans managed, following an earthquake on March 2, 1354, to occupy Gallipoli and surrounding fortresses. The success not only gave the Ottomans a strong position from which to establish themselves in Thrace, but also from which to control sea traffic between the Mediterranean and the Black Sea. The occupation of Gallipoli made Europe conscious of the Ottoman peril for the first time, and its recovery now became one of the main objectives of the crusades.

---

[14] On all these now see my chapter in *The Crusades,* VI.

[15] F. Thiriet, "Venise et l'occupation de Ténédos au XIV siècle," *Mélanges d'Archéologie et d'Histoire*, 65, (1953) p. 219-45.

Gallipoli was captured from the Ottomans in 1366 by a Western crusader, Count Amadeo VI of Savoy. Until its re-conquest was achieved ten years later, the Ottoman presence in the Balkans was under constant threat.[16] During Murad I's reign (1362-1389) Gallipoli was turned into a naval base, but, even then, it continued to be threatened by the Venetians until full Ottoman control was established over the Dardanelles in 1452. The Venetian fleet first appeared before the Ottoman Gallipoli in 1388.[17]

Bayezid I (1389-1402), in his determination to secure mastery of the Straits, constructed an inner harbor at Gallipoli to accomodate his fleet, and a castle on the Bosporus, Anadolu-Hisarı. Nevertheless, Ottoman naval forces were not strong enough to prevent Marshal Boucicaut from sailing past Gallipoli on his way to bring relief to Constontinople in 1399. At any rate, the Venetian Senate passed decisions to seize Gallipoli at various dates: in 1402, during the war of 1423-1430, and in 1444. In 1416 the Venetians under Pietro Loredano destroyed the Ottoman fleet in front of Gallipoli, and in 1429 Silvestro Mocenigo launched an attack on the inner harbor in an attempt once again to destroy the Ottoman fleet. To protect its merchant ships in the Dardanelles, Venice was forced, from the 1400's on, to mount arbalestriers on them, and to send warships to the Dardanelles, and sometimes as far as Istanbul. Tenedos was used by the Venetians during this period as base from which to monitor navigation through the Straits.[18]

The years 1431-1451 are considered the best years of the Venetian trade in Constantinople, with the Venetians obtaining there alum, copper, beeswax, hides and lumber from the Black Sea area. The Ottomans followed a peaceful policy towards Venice during this time except in the period 1444-1446.[19] In those years Venice joined the Crusaders' navy in attempting to cut off Ottoman communications on the Straits, and hoped to occupy Gallipoli and Salonica, and even Scutari on the Asiatic side of the Bosporus.[20] In the fall of 1444, when the collapse of the Ottoman power was thought imminent, an event of historic significance took place on the Bosporus: Murad II crossed the Strait under the protection of artillery placed on the spot where later

---

[16] See I. Beldiceanu-Steinherr, "La conquête d'Adrianople par les Turcs", *Travaux et Mémoires d'histoire et civilisation byzantines* I (1965) pp. 439-61; cf. my chapter in *The Crusades,* VI.

[17] H. İnalcık, "Gelibolu", *EI*^{2}, pp. 983-84; Iorga, *La politique vénitienne,* p. 14-15.

[18] *Ibid.*

[19] F. Thiriet, *La Romanie vénitienne au moyen age,* Paris 1959, p. 427.

[20] Thiriet, *Les régestes,* nos. 2651, 2668.

mehmed II would build his Boghaz-Kesen castle. One of the Byzantine ships trying to hinder the Sultan's passage was sunk by gunfire.[21]

After the Ottoman victory at Varna Constantinople was doomed. Mehmed II realized that now he had the weapon not only to demolish the walls of Constantinople but also to cut off the Straits to navigation. In 1452, under the protection of his navy he built on the opposite side of Akça-Hisar (Anadolu-Hisarı)a castle "so that" as Critovoulos put it[22] "he might control as much of the shore as possible for the sake of the stone hurling machines... They were not all in a straight line, but pointed in various directions at the deep water and guarded both approaches... and in this way he united the two continents and placed the crossing under his own control".

At the same time two castles were built on both sides of the Dardanelles and huge guns were placed to cut off the passage of ships coming from the Mediterranean.[23] After the conquest of Constantinople when in 1462 war seemed imminent againts Venice, the Conqueror extended and reinforced these two castle to make his capital city invulnerable.

As soon as the Boghaz-Kesen Hisarı was completed (August 31, 1452) on the Bosporus, Mehmed II declared his absolute sovereignty over the Straits, asking all ships to lower their sails at the castles of the Bosporus, pay dues and obtain a permit to proceed on their way, That these were not just empty words became apparent when the ship of the Venetian Antonio Erizzo, carrying a cargo of grain for Constantinople, was sunk by gunshot from the castle (November 25, 1452) upon his refusal to obey.[24]

Ottoman customs regulations of the Conqueror's time[25] required that customs dues for the whole cargo of a ship be paid at the rate of 5 per cent or 4 per cent ad valorem by foreigners and Ottoman subjects respectively at one of the ports of Istanbul, Gallipoli or Mudanya. Export of grain, beeswax, sulphur, cotton and silk was prohibited except from Istanbul. Ships sailing without stopping at Istanbul or Mudanya paid no dues there except in the case

---

[21] See H. Inalcık, *Fâtih Devri Üzerinde Tetkikler ve Vesikalar,* Ankara 1954, pp. 71-2.

[22] *History of Mehmed the Conqueror*, trans. Charles T. Riggs, Princeton 1954, pp. 20-21; V. Parry, "Boghaz-ici", *EI*[2], I, pp. 1251-52; E. H. Ayverdi. *Osmanlı Mimarisinde Fatih Devri,* IV (Istanbul 1974) pp.626-62, 617-24.

[23] For the guns placed there see Charles Efoulkes, "The'Dardanelles' Gun at the Tower", *The Antiquaries Journal* X (1930) 217-27.

[24] Nicoló Barbaro, *Diary of the Siege of Constantinople*, trans. J. R. Jones, New York 1969, p. 10.

[25] *Kānûnname-i Sultānî ber Muceb 'Örf-i Osmānî*, eds.R. Anhegger and H. İnalcık, Ankara 1954, nos. 33, 34, 35, 36, 43, 53, 55. On various rates of customs dues see H. İnalcık, "Notes on N. Beldiceanu's Translation of the Ḳānûnname," *Der Islam,* 43, (1967) pp. 152-53.

of non-Muslim foreigners. All ships paid customs dues at Gallipoli if they had not done so at Istanbul or Mudanya. Severe punishments were prescribed against smugglers. All ships were examined and given sailing permits at the castles of the Bosporus and Gallipoli. It was customary for each ship to give presents to local authorities.

By special stipulations put in the capitulations the Porte exempted foreign ships from a second examination at the Dardanalles.[26] Compared with the free trade and passage imposed by the Latins during the Byzantine period, all these restrictions meant, of course, a drastic change in the situation. And, in addition to export restrictions and various taxes, there were exactions by the local authorities. Such conditions must have caused further shrinkage in the international Black Sea trade under the Ottomans.

The story of how after 1453 the whole Black Sea area came under Ottoman sovereignty is well known.[27] What we are going to deal with in the following is the Black Sea trade and navigation in the last decades of the fifteenth century in the light of the Ottoman documents.

C. Characteristics of The Black Sea trade before The Ottomans

G. I. Bratianu[28] put emphasis on the fact that the Black Sea entered into the orbit of the international trade between East and West, and became one of the commercial centers of the medieval world during that period in the 13th century when the great Mongol Empire established itself in Asia and Eastern Europe. It was also asserted that this trade was based on luxury goods, satisfying the conspicuous consumption needs of a ruling class with immense accumulated wealth, and that it was a basic contribution to the expansion of commercial capitalism centered in Italy. Also, it was argued[29] that its survival depended on the maintenance of the caravan routes terminating at the principal transit ports of Azov, Caffa, Soldaja and Trebizond on the Black Sea. This new development in the Black Sea trade should not lead us to ignore regional

---

[26] See the Venetian capitulations of 1482, 1513, 1517 and 1521, published by M. Tayyib Gökbilgin, in *Belgeler*, no. 9-12 (Ankara, Turkish Historical Society, 1968-1971), pp. 39-54 and the document dated 1530, pp. 103-104.

[27] The main collection of documents for this period is Amadeo P. Vigna, *Codice diplomatico delle colonie Tauro-Liguri durante la Signoria dell' ufficio di San Giorgio* (1453-1475), 3 vols. Atti della Società Ligure di Storia Patria, 1868-1879; W. Heyd, op. cit., II, pp. 360-407; F. Babinger, *Mehmed the Conqueror and his Time,* ed. W. C. Hickman, trans. R. Manheim, Princeton, 1978.

[28] *La Mer Noire,* p. 230.

[29] See R. H. Bautier, "Les relations économiques des occidentaux avec les pays d'Orient au moyen age, points de vue et documents", *Sociétés et compagnies de commerce en Orient et dans l'Océan Indien*, ed. M. Mollat, Paris 1970, pp. 263-331.

trade, based on the exchange of food stuffs, raw materials and slaves from the North, with the locally produced textiles and other Mediterranean products of the South, the significance of which had not diminished in the least from ancient times.[30] By the time the Ottomans came onto the scene, the Black Sea's significant role in international trade was already a thing of the past.[31]

Golden Horde, Tatars and The Black Sea trade

In discussing the Black Sea trade, emphasis should be placed on the changing conditions of the vast market of the Golden Horde Empire and the Tatar world in Eastern Europe in the 13th through 15th centuries. Saray, its capital on the Volga, became, at the height of the Golden Horde Empire, not only a great consumption market for luxury goods,[32] but also an emporium of "the great commerce" between Europe and the Orient, the Crimea (Caffa and Azak) and Khwarezm (Urgendj) being the transit centers of this lively transcontinental traffic.[33] Also it is now a commonplace that the North-South international trade between Egypt and the Golden Horde passing through Anatolia became livelier than ever during this period, due in particular to the exchange of the luxury goods of the Middle East for the slaves and furs of the North.[34]

One cannot ignore or simply dismiss as myth the observations on the cities and economic conditions of the Golden Horde Empire made by travellers, which archaeological findings corroborate. In this connection, one

---

[30] R. H. Bautier, *ibid,* and. M. Berindei and Gilles Veinstein, "La Tana-Azak, de la présence italienne à l'emprise ottomane", *Turcica*, VIII/2, (1976), 110-201.

[31] R. Lopez, "Market Expansion: The Case of Genoa", *Journal of Economic History* 24 (1964), pp.451-53, showes a dramatic decline in the trade of Pera in the fifteenth century.

[32] *The Travels of Ibn Baṭṭuṭa,* trans. H. A. R. Gibb, vol. II, Cambridge 1962, pp. 479, 515-17; B. Spuler, *Die Goldene Horde,* 1223-1502, Leipzig 1943, p. 424-52; A. J. Yakubovskiy and B. D. Grekov, *Le Horde d'Or,* trans. F. Thuret, Paris 1939, chapter VII. For the Crimea in particular see A. L. Jacobson. *The Crimea in the Middle Ages,* Moscow-Leningrad 1964 (in Russian).

[33] Yakubovskiy, *Ibid.*, emphasizes the importance of the trade between Khwarezm and the Crimea; W. Hinz, *Ein orientalisches Handelsunternehmen im 15. Jahrhundert,* Die Welt des Orients IV (1949) pp. 313-40, describes in detail, according to *Shamso's-Siy q,* how a certain Khwâdje Shams al-Dîn of Shiraz made a business trip between his native town and Saray via Herat, Urgendj, in 1438-1440. He had a capital of 30,000 dînâr or 19,500 Goldmark, and trading in luxury goods, realizing a profit of 430 percent.

[34] See Mas Latrie, Des relations politiques et commerciales de l'Asie Mineure avec l'île de Chypre, Bibl. Ecole des Chartes, 2 series, vol. I-II, p. 302-30, 483-521; Osman Turan, *Türkiye Selçukluları Hakkında Resmî Vesikalar*, Ankara, 1958; *Idem. Selçuklular Tarihi ve Türk-İslâm Medeniyeti*, Ankara 1965, p. 246-85.

also commonly finds mention of the collapse of central power in the Golden Horde and the outbreak of the long struggle among the various branches of Djodji's descendants. What I should like to emphasize is the resurgence of tribal warfare on the steppes, resulting in the weakening of the population and economic well-being of the core area around Saray. Many tribes migrated, some to the steppes east of Astrakhan and others to the Crimea. The latter area, one of the most economically developed areas of the Golden Horde land, became a center of attraction for many tribes under princes descending from Tokhtamish, thus giving rise to a new political formation in the Northern Black Sea region.[35]

Timur's intervention in the internal struggles of the Golden Horde in the last decades of the fourteenth century not only contributed to the fall of Azak (Azov), Saray and Astrakhan as international trade centers, but, perhaps more importantly, by destroying the rising power of Tokhtamish, further accelerated the process of the dissolution and polarization of the tribal confederations in the Eurasian steppes. The Tatars of the Crimea and of the *Dasht* now under the Gireys, a branch of the Tokhtamish family, were now to separate themselves from the rest of the Golden Horde, and become increasingly integrated into the economic and political system of the Black Sea, which was to entail eventually their complete fusion with the Ottoman Empire.

The analysis in this paper of the Caffa customs register of 1487 shows clearly, I belive, how the whole area, with its large Turkish-Tatar population, was integrated into the economy of the Black Sea region, an economic system encompassing not only the southern coasts of the Black Sea, Istanbul and Bursa, but also Asia Minor and the Aegean.

Islamization and the growing cultural and political ties with the South, which go back to the early thirteenth century, greatly contributed to the consolidation of the Black Sea economic system. Due to the common cultural background and ways of life within Islam, the Crimean Tatars and the *Dasht* Nogays imported innumberable "articles of culture", manufactured in Anatolian towns, including such luxury articles as swords, caftans of costly brocades and mohair, and even fine European woolens for the upper class of the steppe aristocracy.

Apparently, in the second half of the fifteenth century, the caravan route from the Middle Volga basin to Azak and the Crimea had not yet been cut off.

---

[35] For the disintegration of the Golden Horde see Yakubovskiy, enlarged third edition, Moscow, 1950; and Z. V. Togan, *Bugünkü Türkistan*, Cairo 1929-1939, pp. 90-120. On Timur's impact see A. P. Novosel'tsev, "On the Historical evaluation of Tamerlane", *Soviet Studies in History* XII/3 (1973-1974) pp.37-70.

The Ottoman customs registers of the period mention goods of Tatar origincompletely, among them *bulgarî*, a kind of fine morocco of the Kazan area, furs, and Tatar bows. In the first half of the sixteenth century, the Crimean Gireys, supported by the Ottomans, were able temporarily to extend their rule to the Kazan and Astrakhan areas, and tried to protect the caravan route between the Volga and the Crimea from the Nogays.[36] The Great Nogays seem to have been alienated from the Black Sea trade region from the 1520's on, when Muscovy began to supply their needs in arms, textiles, precious northern furs, minerals and, in times of famine, grain, in exchange for Nogay horses. The caravan routes from Kazan and Astrakhan to the Crimea then became the targets of the Nogays and the Muscovites.

When Ivan IV invaded Kazan and Astrakhan in 1552 and 1556 respectively, the Khans of Khwarezm and Turkestan complained of the cut-off of the trade and pilgrimage route between their lands and the Crimea, and urged the Ottoman Sultan to take action against the Tsar.[37]

Regional trade and international trade

F. Thiriet[38] concluded taht the Venetian Black Sea trade was in decline long before the Ottoman conquest of Constantinople. He suggested that because of growing local insecurity Venetians migrated from Azak (La Tana) and other Black Sea ports including Trebizond, to Constantinople, in the first half of the fifteenth century, and that the movement grew in momentum in the period 1431-1451, leading to an expansion of commercial activities in the Byzantine capital in this period.[39] In other words, Constantinople became the center of the Venetian Black Sea trade, rivaling Pera on the other side of the Golden Horn. From our standpoint what is to be noted is that during this period the bulk of the Venetian trade consisted of grain, honey, fish, hides and slaves imported from La Tana, and silk from Trebizond. The establishment of a

---

[36] See A. Bennigsen and C. Lemercier-Quelquejay, "La Grande Horde Nogay et le problème des communications entre l'empire Ottoman et l'Asie centrale en 1552 A- 1556", *Turcica,* VIII/2, (1976), pp. 203-36; A. Bennigsen and G. Veinstein, "Le commerce de l'empire ottoman avec la Grande Horde Nogay, 1475-1552," paper submitted to the *I. Intern. Congress on the Social and Economic History of Turkey*, Ankara 1977; Remmâl Khodja, *Vâki'ât-i Sahib Giray Khan,* MS, Bibl. Nationale, Paris, suppl. turc no. 61.

[37] See H. Inalcık, "The Origins of the Ottoman-Russian Rivalry and the Don-Volga Canal", *Annales del'Université d'Ankara,* I (1947) 47-110; W. E. D. Allen, *Problems of Turkish Power in the Sixteenth Century,* London 1963.

[38] *La Romanie,* pp. 427-28.

[39] Thiriet, *ibid.,* estimated the annual volume of trade in Constantinople in this period at 100-150,000 gold ducats. As a result of the Ottoman conquest and pillage of the city Venetian losses were estimated 200,000 ducats, see S. Runciman, *The Fall of Constantinople,* Cambridge 1965, p. 162.

Venetian factory at Akkerman (Maurocastro) in 1435, and the creation of a Venetian consulate in Caffa in june 1444, seem not to have promoted appreciably, Thiriet observed,[40] Venetian trade in the Black Sea.

On Azak we now have M. Berindei and G. Veinstein's study,[41] based mainly on Ottoman documents. Agreeing with R. H. Bautier's suggestions for earlier periods, they have argued that the trade of the Italian maritime states at Azak or in the Crimea relied essentially, from the beginning, not on the "great trade" of spices and silk coming over the Asiatic transcontinental route—the so-called "Mongol Route"—but on regional trade. Even if in the fifteenth century the Italians found spices, pearls, gold and "Russian" furs at Azak, the profits realized, Berindei and Veinstein have argued, were quite modest and they have questioned if Azak was ever a major emporium of "the great commerce" in luxury goods.

While the spice trade was of quite a modest size in Azak, the greater part of Venetian silk imports from the Levant came from the Black Sea ports of Azak and Trebizond, the first being an outlet for Chinese silk, the second for Iranian.[42] Before Bursa became the emporium of Iranian silk for the Italian silk industries, Trebizond seems to have been the most important outlet of Iranian silk in the Levant,[43] brought by caravans from Tabriz, the great center of raw silk and silk cloths, as well as of spices. Because of its high quality, large production for export, and existence of relatively convenient transport facilities, Iranian silk from the Caucasus and the Caspian provinces appear to have dominated the silk market in the Black Sea area at all times, but

---

40 *La Romanie,* p. 428. For the appointment of F. Duodo as the first vice-consul at Akkerman in March 1436, see N. Iorga, *Notes et extraits pour servir à l'histoire des croisades,* vol. I, Paris 1899, p. 581; cf. N. Beldiceanu, "La conquête des cités marchandes de Kilia et de Cetatea Alba par Bayezid II", *Südost-Forschungen,* XXIII (1964) pp. 36-115.

41 "La Tana-Azak, de la présence italienne à l'emprise ottomane (fin XIIIe siècle-milieu XVIe siècle)", *Turcica,* XVII/2 (1976) 110-201.

42 For the export of Chinese silks to the Golden Horde via Khwarezm around 1438 see Hinz, *art. cit.,* pp. 331, 338; according to Bautier, pp. 291-92, Chinese silk had ceased to arrive in the Levant ports already before the middle of the thirteenth century, and then Northern Iran alone supplied the growing import needs of the Italian silk industries. In Tana-Azak was to be found Iranian silk, also, which arrived there via Caspian Sea-Astrakhan, see Bautier, p. 287. We know that Genoese adventurers used this route in the fifteenth century. The silk bought by the Venetians at Vosporo and Azak in 1399 was apparently from Iran, not from Georgia as suggested by Berindei-Veinstein, *La Tana-Azak,* p. 126.

43 For the route Tabriz-Trebizond see Bautier, pp. 282-86. Venetians obtained the right to settle at Trebizond in 1319, see Berindei- Veinstein, p. 118.

definitely after 1336.[44] Prices at Azak seem to be subject to fluctuations: In 1361 a one fourth increase in silk prices is noted there, but towards the end of the century the price at Azak went down to its previous level.[45]

D. The Rise of Bursa and change of trade route in the Region

The system of trade routes through Asia Minor which had developed under the Ilkhanids collapsed in the 1340's as the main thoroughfare of East-West trade, with Constantinople-Pera via Caffa and Trebizond, on the one hand, and with the great Mediterranean port of Ayas via Sivas in Central Anatolia, on the other.[46]

It is the collapse of Mongol power first in inner Asia, and then in Iran in the first half of the fourteenth century, that must be stressed as having permanent repercussions for the Levant trade in the Black Sea area and Asia Minor. However, for Asia Minor as a whole, the ensuing changes seem not to have been as radical as sometimes assumed, since the valuable silk production of the Caspian provinces of Iran, that area's main object of international trade in medieval times, continued to be brought into Turkey by caravan. The difference was that in the course of the second half of the fourteenth century, the Iranian silk caravans began mostly to make their destination the capital of the Ottoman state, Bursa. Following this new route Iran's silk caravans came overland the entire way to Bursa, travelling from Tabriz via Erzerum-Erzincan-Tokat-Amasya-Ankara-Bolu or Eskişehir to Bursa.[47] Trebizond, Caffa and Constantinople suffered from this diversion of the silk trade, but Pera, by sending its agents to Bursa, continued to receive Iranian silk there.[48]

The rise of Bursa as an international silk market and important center of silk industries, which has generally been overlooked by economic historians, must be considered as one of the major factors in the decline of the silk trade and industry in the Black Sea area. Caffa silk cloths, mentioned as famous

---

44 For Byzantine times see R. Lopez, "Silk Industry in the Byzantine Empire", *Speculum,* XX (1945) pp. 1-42; for the periods of competition for Chinese silk Bautier, p. 291.

45 See Thiriet, *Les Régestes,* nos. 375 and 955.

46 Z. V. Togan, "Mogollar Devrinde Anadolu'nun İktisadî Vaziyeti", *Türk Hukuk ve İktisat Tarihi Mecmuası,* I, (1943); Bautier, *art. cit.* pp. 280-86; H. Inalcık, "Bursa, and the Commerce of the Levant", *Journal of Economic and Social History of the Orient,* III/2, (1900) p. 133.

47 H. İnalcık, "Bursa", *Belleten,* XXIV, (1960), pp. 45-54.

48 *Ibid.*

towards the end of the fourteenth century,[49] must have been a thing of the past at the end of the 15th century as witnessed in our customs register.

The switch-over in trade routes, which had apparently taken place already under Bayezid I (1389-1402), was an outcome of Ottoman imperial policy, which sought to secure control of the main centers on the route to Tabriz, such as Ankara (1354), Osmancık and Amasya (1392).

Strict state control meant that silk loads could be sent safely along this route without danger of diversion to other areas, or of being opened and subjected to dues until they arrived at the Bursa market.[50] The sea route from Trebizond to Istanbul, on the other hand, involved various hazards: in particalar ship wrecks and seizure by corsairs were not infrequent occurences. Apparently the higher cost of land transportation were offset by the high value of the loads and the large profit margins. During these centuries the majority of the silk merchants in the caravans were Azeri-Iranians who must have felt themselves more comfortable in the Ottoman capital than in a Chirstian city. At any rate, since the local silk industry consumed a large part of the imports and since Italian and Jewish purchasers, mostly from Pera, were waiting eagerly to buy the rest,[51] Bursa became an attractive and busy market for silk, a second Tabriz in many ways, in the fifteenth century. It appears that Pera greatly benefited from the expansion of so close a market in silk, thereby offsetting its declining trade in the Black Sea.

Ottoman documents prove[52] that Istanbul received silk via Trebizond as late as the second half of the fifteenth century. This must, however, have been quite a limited amount. In the customs register of Caffa dated 1487 silk is mentioned as arriving in Caffa not from Trebizond but from Bursa.

---

49 J. Schiltberger, *Travels and Bondage,* ed. J. B. Telfer, London 1879, p. 34. Caffa brocade (Kefe Kemhâsı) is still mentioned in the Ottoman documents of 1475, see *Kānūnnāme*, ed. R. Anhegger and H. İnalcık, p. 49, for the date see, *Der Islam,* 43 (1967) pp. 152-54.

50 H. İnalcık, "Bursa", p. 52.

51 G. R. B. Richards, *Florentine Merchants in the Age of Medici,* Cambridge, Mass., 1932, p. 110.

52 See *Kānūnnāme*, ed. R. Anhegger and H. İnalcık, p. 43, 52a; *Sources and Studies on the Ottoman Black Sea,* I. The *Customs Register of Caffa, 1487-1490,* Cambridge, Mass. 1995.

E. Black Sea trade during The Ottoman Period

This essay on Ottoman trade and navigation on the Black Sea during the period 1487-1505 is based on the following customs registers and regulations:

1 The customs register of Kefe (Caffa) 1487-1490, from the Başvekâlet Archives, Istanbul, Kâmil Kepeci tasnifi, Kefe-Avlonya Mukataaları, no. 5280 Mükerrer. It contains only the arrears of the customs dues, apparently drawn up upon an order given by the Ottoman Imperial Treasury in 1490. 52 a.

2 A volume from the Başvekâlet Archives, İstanbul, Maliyeden Müdevver Defterler, no. 6, containing the following fiscal registers:

I. A rûznâmçe, day-book, for the produce of the saltworks of Ahyuli for the years 1491-1493.

II. Rûznâmçe, day-book, for the fisheries of Kilia for the year 1504.

III. A register of the customs dues for Akkerman for the years 1505-1506.

IV. A register of the customs dues and other dues for Kilia for the years 1486-1490 and 1504-1506.

3 The survey book of the population and revenues of the sandjak and city of Kefe for the year 1542, from the Başvekâlet Archives, Istanbul, Tapu Defterleri, no. 214. Regulations on customs dues and tolls are to be found in the introductory part. These have been translated into French by M. Berindei and G. Veinstein (Réglement de Süleyman I er concernant le Livā' de Kefe, in *Cahiers du Monde Russe et Soviétique,* XVI-I [1975], 57-104).

Important descriptions of the Black Sea countries in the seventeenth and eighteenth centuries are to be found in *Evliyâ Çelebi Seyâhatnâmesi,* vol. 7 (Istanbul 1928), 486-604, and Claude C. Peyssonel's accounts based on personal experience:*Traité sur la Commerce de la Mer Noire,* Paris 1787, and *Observations Historiques et Géographiques sur les Peuples Barbares qui ont Habité les Bord du Danube et du Pont-Euxin,* Paris 1765.

A list of Shipowners in the register 1487-1490 of customs dues arrears,

Ship Owner	*Itinerary*
Haraccı-oghlu	apparently Trabzon-Sinop-Kefe
Veled-i Salman, Merchant	Istanbul-Inebolu-Kefe
Hasan of Inebolu	Istanbul-Inebolu-Kefe
Mahmûd Atcı	Kerpe-Kefe
Cici-oghlu, Merchant	Istanbul-Inebolu-Sinop-Kefe
Yusuf of Izmir	—
Bali Rayis (re'is), Captain	Istanbul-Inebolu-Kefe
Resûl of Samsun	Samsun-Kefe
Mihal	Azak-Kefe
Hoca Seyyidî	Istanbul-Inebolu-Kefe
Kara Tayyib	Samsun-Kefe
Zorzi	Istanbul-Inebolu-Kefe
Çepni Ali Rayis, Captain	apparently Samsun-Sinop-Kefe
Knoto	—
Gündüz Rayis, Captain	Samsun or Sinop-Kefe
Turak Rayis of Izmit.	Captain and Merchant apparently Istanbul-Inebolu-Sinop-Kefe
Lorenc, Italian	Azak-Kefe
Kara-Tulum	Istanbul-Kefe
Yusuf Fakîh	Istanbul-Kefe
Buri Şâtir	Istanbul-Inebolu-Sinop-Kefe
Sinân Beg	Kerpe-Inebolu-Kefe
Nikiroz	Samsun-Kefe
Yani of Inebolu	Istanbul-Inebolu-Kefe
Eyne Hoca	Inebolu-Kefe
Bostan Rayis	—
Karaca-Oghlu	—
Kara-Oghlan	Istanbul-Kefe
Pandazi	apparently Istanbul-Inebolu-Kefe
Hasan of Inebolu	Istanbul-Inebolu-Kefe
Mesîh Paşa	Istanbul-Sinop-Kefe
Salman of Taşköprü, Merchant	Inebolu-Kefe
Mubarek, Merchant	Trabzon-Kefe
Hacı Rayis of Gerze, Captain Balıklagu	Sinop-Kefe and other Crimean ports, of and Taman
Ahmed Çelebi, Merchant	Istanbul-Sinop-Kefe
Veled-i Karak	—
Küreleş-oghlu	apparently Istanbul- Inebolu-Kefe
Vasil	Sinop-Kefe
Praskova	—

Ali Rayis of Samsun	Samsun-Kefe
Paskal Rayis, Captain	Inebolu-Kefe
Afendul	Sugdak-Kefe
Istrepan	—
Sava	Özen-Kefe, Hurzuf-Kefe
Todoros	Istanbul-Kefe
Manul	Uskut-Kefe
Kapucu Sinân	Crimean ports-Kefe
Yani Altuncı	—
Yorgi Kileci	Hurzuf-Kefe
Kaliyoros	Crimean ports-Kefe
Sava Manul	Crimean ports-Kefe
Todoros Afendike	Crimean ports-Kefe
Baştiya Drad	Crimean ports-Kefe
Halil	Kopa-Kefe
Kılaguz	—
Gerge, Italian	apparently Galata-Kefe
Todor	Sugdak-Kefe
Emirze	—
Murâd	—

Shipowners, as far as we can identify, can be classified as sea-captains, state officials and merchants. Nine Muslim *rayis* are specified in the register as shipowners: Bali, Çepni Ali, Gündüz, Turak, Hacı of Gerze, Ali of Samsun, Resûl of Samsun, Bostan and Dâvûd. Hâmid Rayis, Hayreddin Rayis and Salih Rayis are mentioned only in their capacities as guarantors.

The title *rayis* (from Arabic *ra'īs*) designates a sea captain, private or official. Apparently many sea captains were engaged in trade since they are registered as owning customs dues for wares for which no other owner is shown. In times of war private captains were ordered by the Sultan to join the navy with their ships, or to engage in corsary activities or ghazā' against the ships of unfriendly nations. Of course, following the establishment of Ottoman control over the Straits in 1452, the Turkish sea captains of the Black Sea coasts no longer had occasion for such naval activities in this area. On our list Çepni Ali Rayis, obviously of the Çepni Türkmens (Turcoman) of the Eastern Black Sea coast, must have been one of these local captains, now engaged in transportation and trade. Hacı of Gerze, Hasan of Inebolu, Resûl of Samsun, Salman of Taşköprü, and Salman of Sinop must all have been shipowners of the same region. Seamanship would seem to have been a hereditary profession, for obvious reasons (Ali Rayis was the son of Resûl of Samsun and Veled-i Salman was evidently the son of Salman of Taşköprü).

Turak Rayis of Izmit and Hâmid Rayis, on the other hand, seem to have been captains in active service in the Ottoman navy at the time. It was Ottoman practice at all times to permit, sometimes even encourage, members of the Ottoman military class to engage in long distance caravan and overseas trade and transport. On our list Mesîh Pasha and Sinân Pasha, both grand-admiral under Bâyezid II appear to have employed their privately owned ships in the profitable Black Sea trade.

The majority of the Muslim ship owners, two thirds of the total, were evidently not professional seamen or officials but rather merchants or businessmen, "resident" in the big commercial centers of the empire. From this group we can cite Hoca Seyyidî, Yusuf Fakîh Mubarek Ahmet Çelebi. In Ottoman society, moreover, not only resident merchants but also ordinary citizens possessing of some wealth were engaged in what was called *mud raba* (*commenda*) trade ventures and transport.[53] There is no way to distinguish the persons in our list belonging to this group.

The non-Muslim shipowners, 25 in number, make up 41 percent of the total shipowners in our list. Three of them, Zorzi, Lorenc and Gerge are designated as *efrenc,* which in general means European, but in this case Italian. Baştiya Drad and possibly also Knoto and Karak can be included in this group. Zorzi was active on the Istanbul-Kefe line, and Lorenc between Azak and Kefe. The rest of the non-Muslim shipowners are Greeks and evidently sea captains, although this is specified only in the case of Paskal Rayis, who was active between Samsun and Caffa. The majority of the Greek shipowners (Afendul, Istrepan, Manul son of Praskova, Sava, Yani Kaliyoros, Sava Manul and Todoros Afendike) were engaged in the regional traffic in fish, fish oil, caviar, salt, and especially wine, between Kefe on the one hand, and the Crimean ports of Sugdak, Hurzuf, Ozan (Özen) and Azak on the other. Other ships beloging to Greeks (Mihal, Pandazi, Vasil, Paskal, Praskova, Sava, Todoros) were active between Kefe and Inebolu, or Kefe, Samsun and Trabzon.

Shipowners

	Muslims		Non-Muslims	
	Sea Captains	Others	Greeks	Efrenc (Italians)
	9	32	21	4
Total		41		25

53 See H. Inalcik, "Capital Formation in the Ottoman Empire", *Journal of Economic History,* XXIX, (1969) 101, 137.

As to itineraries, they can be established even when they are not specified in the registers, according to the origin of the merchant and his goods. The most active lines across the Black Sea were apparently Istanbul-Inebolu-Kefe, Sinop-Kefe and Samsun-Kefe, while traffic between Trabzon (Trebizond) and Kefe seems less significant in this period.

It appears that merchants from Western Anatolia and Bursa embarked at Istanbul, which was the main transit center between Kefe end Mediterranean ports. Under the Ottomans as before, ships from Istanbul called, on their way to Kefe, at Inebolu and Sinop, taking on merchants from as far away in the hinterland as Ankara, Sivrihisar, Beyşehri, and Konya.

The great volume of trade between the Crimea and the Kastamoni-Sinop-Amasya area kept direct lines between Kefe and the ports of Inebolu, Sinop and Samsun quite active as they had been in pre-Ottoman times. The Samsun-Kefe line seems to have been particularly active as an outlet for the economically well developed area of the hinterland containing the towns of Merzifon, Amasya and Karahisar. Sinop appears to have been a rallying point between Eastern and Western portions of the Black Sea. Ships from Trebizond apparently stopped at Sinop to take aboard merchants from Tosya, Merzifon, and Amasya. Sea communication between the Circassian port of Kopa (Copa) and Kefe seems to have been active as it had been under the Genoese. Kerpe, a small port near the mouth of Sakarya, had a direct sea link with Kefe. Kerpe was an outlet for wood and lumber from the surrounding forest area, and a transit port for the slave traffic between Kefe and Anatolia. Sea traffic between Kefe and the other Crimean ports of Hurzuf, Ozan (Özen), Taman, Sugdak and Uskut as well as with Azak appears to have been quite busy.

What we can assert is that certain individual captains were particularly active along certain trade routes: Bali Rayis, Cici-oghlu, Yusuf Fakîh, Yani, Hasan of Inebolu, Ahmed Çelebi, Küreleş-oghlu, Todoros, Pandazi and the ship of Mesîh Pasha on the Istanbul-Inebolu-Kefe route; Hacı Rayis between Sinop and Kefe; Eyne Hoca between Inebolu and Kefe; Kara Tayyib, Nikiroz and Ali Rayis between Samsun and Kefe; and Haraccı-oghlu between Trebizond and Kefe. The ships of Bali Rayis, Hasan, Mesîh Pasha, and Hacı Rayis apparently made more than one journey during the year 892 A. H. (the year starting 28 Jan. 1486), and that of Bali Rayis appears to have been particularly active during this period. At least 13 merchants and their merchandise were carried on Bali Rayis' ship, 10 on that of Pandazi, and 7 on that of Mesîh Pasha that year.

Since the register includes only those merchants in debt to the treasury it is not possible to get an exact idea of the number of the merchants on board and the size of the ships. However, judging from the number of merchants and the amount of goods in our register, the ships belonging to Sinân Beg, Yani, Pandazi and Bali Rayis would appear to have been particularly large.

Special shipments known as *irsâliye* were made from Kefe to Istanbul under the responsibility of an agent known as the *irsâlât' âmili*. The shipment included slaves, flour, wheat and clarified butter, sent by members of the military class, and customs dues had to be paid on them. The *irsâlât'â'âmili* was an agent in charge of forwarding goods beloging to the Sultan and the members of the military class.

As to the merchants the register shows a total of 212 people engaged in some way in trade. Of these, the professional merchants, as far as can be identified, numbered 182; the rest include shipowners, military persons engaged in mercantile activity, and persons such as tax-farmers (*'âmil*) or their employees, brokers, and slaves (*ghulâm*) or freed slaves (*'atîk*), acting as traders on behalf of their masters.

Fourteen shipowners acted at the same time as traders, bringing goods on their own account: Veled-i Salman, Yusuf of Izmir, Cici-oghlu, Bostan Rayis, Karaca-oghlu, Ahmed Çelebi, Rayis Hayreddin, Sava, Yani Altuncı, Yorgi Kileci, Istrepan, Sava, Manul, Todoros, Afendike and Yorgi.

As for the military persons, these were mostly simple *'azebs*, fortress guardians, or their commanders (*agha, kethudâ, dizdâr, ser-oda*), stationed in the fortresses of the Crimea (Kefe, Taman, Mangup, Sugdak and Azak). Among the military group can also be included a chief-waiter (*çasnîgîr-bashı*) and the chief gate-keeper (*ser-bevvâbîn*) of Mesîh Pasha, both of whom were engaged in trade. Most of them are entered in the register as paying a slave tax on slaves to be sent to Istanbul, obviously for sale. However, some of them were engaged professionally in trade activities, such as the *kethudâ* of the garrison of Azak who exported caviar, and that of Taman who shipped out wheat, and Ali, guard at the fortress of Caffa, and Sinân, commander of the garrison at Sugdak, who imported various kinds of textiles and foodstuffs. Some of this trade was apparently in goods needed by local garrisons.

In some cases the port of departure of the merchant or ship is specified by the scribe.

The following is a list of such ships with the merchandise aboard

Port of Departure	Ship Owner	Merchants Aboard	Merchandise Aboard
Azak	Mihal	Todoros, Anton *Efrenc*	Caviar
Azak	Lorence *Efrenc*	Owner, Nikola, Murâd of Sinop	Fish, ustensils, textiles
Hurzuf	Yorgi	Hoca Dravdik, Hudaverdi, Danişmend	Wine, Hardware, Mats, Raisins
Hurzuf	Yorgi	Owner	Wine
Hurzuf	Sava	Owner	Fish oil
Inebolu	Eyne Hoca	Hacı Safa of Amasya, Ibrahim of Kastamoni, Hacı Ali of Tire, Hoca Ali of Merzifon	Mohair, Cotton Goods, Leather
Istanbul	Veled-i Salman	Owner	*Kirbas* (Sea below), Rice
Istanbul	Hasan	Murâd of Istanbul	Kidney Beans
Istanbul	Bali Rayis	Mustafa of Kastamoni	Mohair
Istanbul	Yani	Mehmed of Istanbul, Seyyidî of Konya, Yakub of Amasya, Hasan of Istanbul	Leather, Silk and Cotton Textiles, Spices, Hardware
Istanbul	Kara-Oghlan	Seyyidî of Istanbul	Silk and cotton goods, Cotton
Istanbul	Mesîh Pasha	Hamza of Istanbul, Mahmud of Sinop, Hüseyin of Sinop, Hüseyin of Küre	Silk and Cotton Goods, Cotton, Rice, Copper Hardware
Istanbul	Bali Rayis	Ahmed of Karahisar, Seyyid Ali of Denizli, Hacı Mehmed of Ankara, Hacı Veli of Uşak, Hacı Baba of Karaman, Yusuf of Sinop, Cuki of Istanbul	Cotton Goods, Leather, Furs, Shoes, Copper, Rice
Istanbul	Ahmed Çelebi	Owner, Gâyib Tatar, Mehmed of Tire, Mehmed of Kefe, Hacı Ali of Bursa, Arslan and Tuta (Jews)	Rice, Leather, Mohair, Nails, Soap, Hardware, Silkens, Iron, European woolen cloth
Kerpe	Mahmûd Atcı	his agent Halil	Wood and lumber
Samsun	Nikiroz	Ahmed of Amasya	Silk, Silken Textiles
Sugdak	Afendul	Nikola	Wine
Sugdak	Todor	Owner, Ayas	Wine
Trabzon	Mubârek	Owner	Alum, Hazel-nuts, Hemp, Pots

The following table breaks down the professional merchant by religion and origin:

Total no. of merchants	Muslim		Non-Muslis				
	Ott. subject	Foreigners	Orth. Greek	Armenian	Jew	*Efrenc* (Italian)	Others
182	130	5 (Hacı Ali the Persian, Hoca Cemal from Shemâkî, Mehmed of Maghreb, Murâd and Tevekkül of Georgia)	23	2 (Isfador, Toros)	8	11	Baba-Çesare Papo Petrac

The striking fact about this table is the overwhelming majority of the Ottoman-subject Muslim Turks, about two thirds of the total number. Ottoman subject non-Muslims make up about 18 per cent of the total. Among these must be included some *efrenc* of Galata. Since the *efrenc* from Chios and Moldavia came from tribute-paying lands one can justifiably wonder whether there were really any foreign traders (i. e. directly from the D r al-Harb, Abode of War) in the Black Sea at this time. The customs registers of Kilia and Akkerman do not provide any more of a clear cut answer to this question.

a. Muslims

Though few in number, foreign Muslim merchants were to be found in Caffa. Caucasians were in a majority in this group. Only one Iranian is recorded, though we know that Iranian merchants, mostly from Azerbeidjan, and travelling with the silk caravans, were to be found in great numbers in Bursa and Istanbul during the fifteenth and sixteenth centuries. Another Muslim foreigner, Mehmed of Maghreb, traded in goods originating in the Ottoman lands.

Those Muslim merchants from Ottoman territories whose birthplace or origin were specified in our register (such as *Istanbulî* or *Amâsî* or *'an Amasya*) can be classified according to their origins as follows:

Birthplace or Origin	Number of Merchants
Sinop	9
Istanbul	8
Konya and Karaman	6
Bursa	5
Trabzon	4
Ankara	4
Merzifon	4
Amasya	4
Kastamoni	4
Kefe	4
Küre	3
Bolu	3
Kayseri	3
Zile	3
Niğde	2
Gördos (Gördes)	2
Tire	2
Taşköprü	2
Bayburd	1
Beyşehri	1
Sivrihisar	1
Gümüş	1
Canik	1
Karahisar	1
Tokat	1
Toñuzlu (Denizli)	1
Uşak	1
Bor	1
Milan	1
Tosya	1
Samsun	1

The above list covers about half the merchants, showing their place of origin, which was apparently in most cases also the center of their commercial activities. In some cases they seem to have chosen to settle in such important commercial centers as Istanbul, Sinop, Amasya, Inebolu and Kastamoni. According to this list, 42 per cent of the Muslim merchants originated from the towns and cities of the Anatolian Black Sea coast. Those from Istanbul and from Bursa, Ankara and Kayseri, commercial and industrial centers in the south, on the other hand, also made up quite a high percentage (29 per cent). Bursa and Istanbul were the transit centers for goods brought by the merchants of western Anatolia, the Aegean area and Europe. Some merchants from western Anatolia as far as Denizli (20 per cent) and from Central Anatolia (10 per cent), appear, however, to have travelled as far as Kefe. This picture of the Turkish merchants trading in Caffa presumably reflects the general pattern in this period. The native Muslim Caffans, interestingly enough, occupy a very modest place in the overseas trade of the city, numbering only four. The Muslim Tatar merchants, on the other hand, acting mostly on behalf of the Crimean Khan or the military, appear to have been among the wealthiest of the merchants.

b. Greeks

The Greek merchants, who make up the second largest group in our register, were mostly from the South Crimean ports, Hurzuf, Ozan, Uskut, Sugdak, or from Azak (Todoros, Nikola), or from the Southern Black Sea coast ports, Trebizond (Konstandin, Dimitri, Manul), Samsun (Kiryakoz), Kerpe (Karli), and Bartın (Aleksi). Those from the Crimean ports were mostly captains engaged in the wine trade and those from Azak in the fish and caviar trade. The Greek merchants from Trebizond imported into Caffa wine, arak and hazel-nuts, while other Greek captains or merchants also brought local products: Kiryakoz of Samsun ropes, Karli from Kerpe coarse textiles of flax, Aleksi from Bartın wheat, millet and rice. Luka, who imported silk and silk cloth, and Vasil, who imported rice and large amounts of alum, must also have been from the Southern Black Sea coast, while Yorgi, who imported soap, was probably from Galata.

c. Jews and Armenians

The Jews make up two groups: those who exported horse or cow hides from the Crimea (Yusuf, Avram, Tamarin, Ilyado and Ilyadon; perhaps these last two are the same), and those who imported costly silk or European woolen cloth (Arslan Yahudi, Hoca Bikeş, Tuta, and Netil), obviously via Istanbul. Those of the latter group appear to be rich merchants. Arslan Yahudi, or Khodja Arslan, was a former tax-farmer (*'âmil*), and his title, Khodja, denotes the status of a large scale merchant usually with a place of business in the *bezzâzistân* (bedestan).

Of the two Armenians in our register, Isfador of Kefe was a wealthy merchant engaged in the trade in silk cloths, while Toros imported large amount of henna. Apparently, after the conquest of Caffa, Ottoman-Turkish merchants replaced partly the Jews, and especially the Armenians in the important and growing commerce in imported fine textiles (Khodja Dravdik was probably also an Armenian).

d. Efrenc, Italians

The Franks, or *Efrenc,* which for the Black Sea area means the Italians, were active as captains and ship-owners, as well as merchants, in the period after 1475 when the Ottomans established complete control over the Black Sea. In the register we count four merchant ships belonging to the Italians (Zorzi, Lorenc, Baştiya Drad, Gerge) and eleven Italian merchants. The Italian merchants were involved either in regional trade, such as bringing to Caffa caviar and fish from Azak (Anton, Lorenc, Cakomi), or in importing costly European clothes (Cakomo son of Filip, Markete and Bortema Balestrin) or soap (Zani Beliekseri), or in exporting regional products such as fox skins (Zani) or leather (Zorzi) or beeswax (Karagöz Efrenc). This last mentioned, bearing a Turkish name, was a guard at the fortress of Caffa, who was probably taken into Ottoman service as a mercenary after the conquest. Yet another Italian merchant, Zorzi, traded in goods typical of the Southeastern Black Sea coasts such as hemp of Fasha, arak and vinegar.

Among the non-Muslims is to be found a certain Aksina or Eksina, a merchant from Kara-Bogdan (Moldavia), who engaged in the silk trade. Petraç who brought logs and lemon juice in containers to Caffa, might also have been from the the Balkans. Ön-Yarun, who came from Taman with a cargo of hemp and caviar, must have been a Circassian. The nationalities of Papo, son of Aylo, and Baba (or Papa) Çesara, who brought lumber from Hurzuf, we have been unable to identify.

Merchant Cargoes classified according to value (in akcha)

below 2,000	2,000-5,000	5,000-10,000	above 10,000
20 %	23 %	21 %	36 %

Thus, those merchants with merchandise which valued above 5,000 *akcha* (111 gold ducats) constituted about half the total number. Those with merchandise valued below 2,000 (44 gold ducats) were only one fifth. This shows that the merchants engaged in the Caffa trade were mostly business men of some importance. The highest figures belong to the following merchants (see 391).

It becomes clear that a great majority of the big merchants were engaged in textile made of cotton, flax, or hemp for common use. Luxury textiles, such as silk cloth, fine woolen cloth of European origin, and mohair (*sof*) from Asia Minor, are of next most importance, On the other hand, the export of sheep skins, hides and especially Crimean salt, was also a big business. The wealthiest merchants appear to be those doing business with or for the Crimean ruling class (Şaban, Cat Cat Hacı Ahmed, Hacı Tanrıvermiş). These merchants imported for the ruling class luxury textiles (silk, fine woolens or cottons) and for the army arms and other materials—swords, iron and tents. Thus, Şaban imported iron, and exported, apparently, sheep skins for the Crimean Khan; Emir Hasan was guarantor for the dues to be paid on cereals imported from Bartın by Aleksi, and on *kirbas* and caftans imported by Ali of Zile. Cat Cat Hacı Ahmed, a noteworthy figure in our register, exported salt, which was a monopoly of the Crimean Khanate.

The local wine trade, mostly in the hands of Greek captains, also appears to have been an important business.

Professional merchants specialized mainly in textiles, foodstuffs and slaves. Since it was considered good in medieval trade practice to invest in various types of wares, we sometimes find textile merchants trading also in spices, henna, dyes, sugar, hashish, soap, swords, combs, leather and hardware. Likewise, we find that the slave merchant Hacı Veys was engaged at the same time in the textile trade. Provincial merchants were specialized mostly in the export of local products. Merchants from Bursa and Amasya imported into Caffa mostly silk stuffs, those from Ankara mohair and rice, those from the Kastamoni area copper and rice, those from western Anatolia carpets and cotton goods, and those from north-east Anatolia alum, hemp, hazel-nuts and wine while those from Istanbul carried wares of various origins, including European cloth, ready-made clothes, hardware and tin. Merchants of the Crimean riviera traded in wine; those of Azak in fish, caviar and slaves. Cotton and leather goods were brought in by the textile dealers from all over Asia Minor, some dealers specializing exclusively in leather goods. The Italians, and some Jewish and Muslim merchants from Istanbul, specialized in imported woolen cloths.

Since our register gives data only on those merchants who owed arrears to the customs no estimate can be made of the total number of merchants or volume of freight at the port of Caffa for the period in question.

Cargoes valued above 19,000 *Akcha*

Marchant's name	Total value of merchandise taxed	Principal Goods	
Şaban	55,000	silk cloths, sheep skins and iron	for Mengli Giray Khan
Yusuf of Bursa	22,800	*kirbas,* carpets, and coverlets	
Mustafa of Istanbul	19,500	*kirbas*	
Seyyid Ali of Denizli	29,600	*kirbas*	
Kutlu Beg	19,200	hemp textiles, hides	
Ahmed, slave of Bursavî	32,950	*kirbas*	
Ömer of Uşak	18,900	*kirbas* (its vulue 13,000)	
Hacı Tanrıvermiş of Merzifon	43,000	*kirbas* (its value 36,000)	
Cat Gat Hacı Ahmed		189 *sapo* of salt	one *sapo* =410.56 kgr.
Veled-i Salman of Sinop	20,000	all *kirbas*	
Ishak of Kayseri	30,000	all *kirbas*	
Sadullah of Nigde	20,150	*kirbas* (its value 18,600)	
Hacı Hamza	22,000	all *kirbas*	
Sinân, son of Sarrâf of Sinop	60,900	*kirbas* (40,000) mohair and silk cloth	
Ahmed of Istanbul	30.800	*kirbas* (11,000) felt (7,000), fox skin (6,000)	
Musa	19,000	indigo and *halva*	
Gaybî	20,000	coarse wollens	He left for Copa in Circassia
Yahya of Konya	20,000	indigo and fine woolen cloth	
Hoca Nimyan	19,100	silk cloth and silk	
Agent of Mengli Giray Khan	—	225 *sapo* of salt	paid 2,500 akcha customs dues

Conclusion

1 The Ottomans attempted to establish their control on the Dardanelles from the moment they settled on both sides of the strait in 1352. The capture and fortification of Gallipoli (1354), with the construction of a naval arsenal and base there, was the first step in this direction. The Ottomans became particularly threatening on the Straits between 1393 and 1430. But since they did not have a navy powerful enough to control the sea the Straits remained free until with the guns placed at the castles they built on the Bosporus and the Dardanelles in the period 1452-1455. Then, were able to cut off passage.

2 The Ottoman motives in controlling navigation on the Straits and Black Sea were: a. To establish a complete safeguard on the passage between Anatolia and Rumelia and to protect their capital against a surprise attack b. To secure the provisioning of Istanbul, c. To put an end, in favor of the indigenous populations, to the economic and political dominance of the Italian maritime states, which exploited and diverted the wealth of the region as alien colonial powers.

3 The Ottoman state was concerned with maintaining the commercial and fiscal benefits of the Black Sea international trade so long as the above objectives were not impaired. However, in the area of the international trade too, native or tribute-paying nations were given preferential treatment.

4 To protect and expand the economic resources of the countries surrounding the Black Sea the Ottoman Empire established its control over them by steps, first as suzerain state in the period 1453-1475, and then through direct rule over the main transit centers such as Amastris (1460), Trebizond and Sinope (1461) on the southern coasts of the sea; Caffa, Sugdak, Balıklava, Gözleve, Kersh and Azak (1475) in the Crimea; Copa and Anapa (1479) in Cirsassia, and Akkerman and Kilia (1484) in Moldavia. The Black Sea became an Ottoman lake when Southern Bessarabia or *Budjak* was annexed to the Ottoman Empire in 1538.[54] Thus, the Black Sea countries were integrated into a regonal economy much more completely by the Ottoman Empire than they had been by the Italian maritime states. This development in turn entailed a more stringent and jealous control of the area by the Ottoman government. While the Black Sea's place in international trade shrunk in the new period, the growing demand of an expanding empire and the giant city of Istanbul for foodstuffs and raw materials as well as for

54 H. Inalcik, "Budjak", *EI*^{2}, I, pp. 1286-87.

slaves resulted in the economic expansion and specialization of the individual Black Sea countries. The extension of estate agriculture and animal husbandry in the Crimea, the *Dasht*, Moldavia and Dobrudja, and the increase in slave raids by the Crimeans should be recalled. From the end of the sixteenth centrury while Western industrialized economies, especially the English, French and Dutch, tried to get access to the Black Sea's abundant and low-priced foodstuffs, rising prices in the Ottoman market made the Ottoman gorvernment more than ever reluctant to open the Black Sea to international trade.

5 The closing of the Black Sea to international trade was a gradual process. Restrictions were imposed only when new conditions demanded it. Prohibition of the export of an individual commodity by a particular nation was initiated at a particular time, and maintained or extended according to contitions. As a strict state policy "the closing of the Black Sea to any foreign vessel" must be considered as something of a later date. While Maurice Aymard,[55] on the evidence of an Ottoman document, suggested 1551 as the final date for the wheat exports from the Black Sea, English merchants still had permission to trade at Caffa and Azak in their capitulations of 1675,[56] Venice had capitulatory guarantees to trade with Caffa and Trebizond until 1540, when the special reference to these Black Sea ports in the capitulations was omitted.[57] However, the Ottoman regulations dated 1542 contained stipulations about grain export by European ships from Caffa, and in 1549 the Sultan warned the cadi of Istanbul not to interfere with the Venetian merchants who were buying caviar, fish and other provisions in the Black Sea.[58] The Venetian wine trade with the northern countries via the Black Sea continued until about 1592,[59] although Joseph Nasi tried to make a monopoly of it under a special charter from Sultan Selim II (1566-1574). A fiscal record made in 1560[60] reads: "Most of the fish caught at the fisheries of Kilia had been sold to the Christian foreigners who brought wine from Europe (*Frengistan*) in their ships. This wine was not sold here at Kilia, but after the customs dues were taken, it was exported to Poland and Muscovy where it was exchanged with native products. These in turn were subject to

---

55 Maurice Aymard, *Venise, Raguse et le commerce du blé,* Paris 1966, p. 46.

56 G. Noradounghian, *Recueil d'actes internationaux de l'empire ottoman,* I, Istanbul 1878, pp. 167-68.

57 See H. Inalcik, "Imtiyāzāt", *EI*^{2}, IV, p. 1183.

58 C. Villain-Gandossi, "Contribution à l'étude des relations diplomatiques et commerciales entre Venise et la Porte ottomane au XVIe siècle", *Südost-Forschungen,* XXVI, (1967), p. 40.

59 H. Inalcik, "Capital Formation in the Ottoman Empire", pp. 122-23.

60 *The Başvekâlet* Archives, İstanbul, Maliye'den Müdevver Defter no. 255.

customs dues here at Kilia in transit, and thus the Ottoman treasury obtained substantial revenue from it. Since the wine ships have ceased to come to this port the fish cannot be sold, and consequently the Sultan's treasury is to lose annually three hundred thousand *akcha* (5,000 gold ducats)". However, the Venetian documentation tells us that by 1592 Venetians imported into Poland alone seven or eight galleon loads of wine from Crete via the Black Sea.[61]

Strict measures against European navigation on the Black Sea seem to have been introduced about the time that the Cossacks started their devastating raids against the Ottoman coasts in the last decade of the sixteenth century.[62]

---

[61] E. Albéri, *Relazione degli ambasciatori Veneti al senato,* series 3, vol. II, p. 412 cited by T. Stoianovich, "The Conquering Balkan Merchant", *Journal of Economic History,* XX, (1960).

[62] N. Jorga, *Geschichte des Osmanischen Reiches,* vol. III, Gotha 1910, pp. 290-91; C. M. Kortopeter, *Ottoman Imperialism during the Reformation, Europe and the Caucasus,* New York 1972, Index: Cossacks.